The Ring of the Nibelung

Richard Wagner

The Ring of the Nibelung

German text with

English translation

by

Andrew Porter

W · W · NORTON & COMPANY

New York · London

W. W. Norton & Company, Inc., 500 Fifth Avenue, New York, N.Y. 10110
W. W. Norton & Company Ltd., 37 Great Russell Street, London WC1B 3NU

This edition first published in 1977 by arrangement with Faber Music Ltd.

Library of Congress Cataloging in Publication Data
Wagner, Richard, 1813-1883.
The ring of the Nibelung.
1. Operas—Librettos. I. Porter, Andrew, 1928-
II. Title.
ML50.W14R32 1977 782.1'2 77-24107

7 8 9 0

ISBN 0-393-00867-3

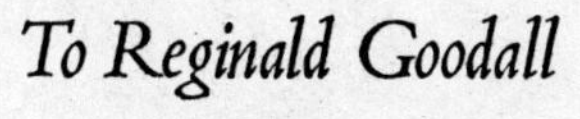

To Reginald Goodall

Contents

Introduction

ANDREW PORTER

This translation of *The Ring* was made for singing, acting, and hearing, not for reading. It is neither a straight, literal crib to the sense of the German such as, in our day, Peggie Cochrane, William Mann, and Lionel Salter[1] (see Notes & References at the end of this essay) have ably provided nor an attempt to render Wagner's verse into English verse such as an English translator-poet uncumbered by the need to frame his lines to fit Wagner's music might make. With unfeigned diffidence I offer to the eyes of a reader, rather than to the ears of a listener, a version that has been shaped by the rhythms, inflexions, weights, lengths, and sounds of Wagner's score. To someone who remarks 'This phrase doesn't translate the German at all precisely' or asks 'Why this rude inversion?' I can reply 'No literal translation would fit the musical phrase' and 'The harmony required those words in that order'. But to prove it a score is needed. This translation is incomplete until it meets the music. But people have asked to see it. It is over a century since the first rhythmic translation of a *Ring* opera—Alfred Forman's *The Walkyrie*, which appeared in 1873—was printed.[2] It found many successors. And there is perhaps something to be said for as well as against English versions that attempt to convey the sense of Wagner's lines while moving in the measure of his verse.

The translator who chooses his own metre has an easier task. In blank verse (varied by 'lyrics' for the Rhinemaidens, the forging Siegfried, the Woodbird, the awakened Brünnhilde, and the Norns), Oliver Huckel[3] endeavoured 'to transfuse into English the very spirit of Wagner's lofty thought'. In his preface he declared that

> The usual English librettos of The Ring are totally inadequate and confusing as translations of Wagner's text. They are made to suit the musical requirements rather than to present the thought in literary form. It is often a perplexing task rather than a pleasure to read them. Tenfold more involved and obscure than Browning, they have none of his redeeming grace of thought or speech.

Dr Huckel was the author of *Through England with Tennyson*, of *Mental Medicine*, and of *Spiritual Surgery* (*Some Pointed Analogies between Body and Soul*). The concerns evinced in the latter titles gave him a clear grasp of the moral and psychological parables of *The Ring*, and Tennyson was his poetic model. Two brief excerpts will show the flavour. From Act I of *The Valkyrie*:

But Siegmund shook himself, and springing up
From the rude bearskin, spake with new-found strength:
'My wounds? Speak not of them—they are no more;
Again I feel my strength in every limb.
Yea, had my shield and spear been strong as now

This strong right arm, ne'er had I fled my foes;
But spear and shield were shattered, foes pressed sore . . .'

And, from the final scene of the cycle:

Upon her steed, impetuous she leaped,
And for the last time sounding forth the cry:
'Hoyotoho!'—her dear old Valkyr call—
She bounded headlong in the flaming pyre.

Huckel's *Ring*, published in New York, appeared between 1907 and 1911. In England, Reginald Rankin, B.A., of the Inner Temple, Barrister-at-law, had already produced a version in blank verse (1899),[4] and Randall Fynes another (two volumes, 1899 and 1901),[5] interspersed, like Huckel's, with a few lyrics. Fynes declared it 'astonishing . . . that the attempt seems never to have been made before'; earlier versions are either fettered to the original metre or else mere paraphrases 'in most cases . . . told in the language of the nursery'. He himself uses the language of Tennyson, and adopts the conceit of an epic tale told on successive nights by a medieval bard. In passages like

And then there came,
Borne on the night, a faint and distant cry,
As from beyond the limit of the World,
Like a chill wind that blows in a waste land,
Moaning, and crying, 'The great Gods are dead!'

the specific allusions (in this case to *The Passing of Arthur*) are, in the manner of T. S. Eliot's *The Waste Land*, identified.

Early paraphrases 'in the language of the nursery' I have not examined. In 1903, E. F. Benson produced *The Valkyries*, a rendering in flummery prose.[6] Two prose versions of the thirties are hardly worth examination. C. L. LeMassena's[7] begins: '"Time for our morning dip," exclaims Woglinda'. Gertrude Henderson's[8] mingles baby-talk with fancy words: 'Clump, clump. The black heads of the Giants lifted above the shag of the mountain side. Clump, clump they came, until they stood in the presence of the Aesir'. John Updike's more recent version[9] is a bedtime tale for children clearly and quickly told. It takes ingenious advantage of Wagner's 'recapitulations', jumping from the end of *Das Rheingold* to the Mime-Wanderer riddle scene; the action of *Die Walküre* is related in those questions and answers and by the Wanderer's informing Siegfried, at the foot of the mountain, that he has 'fired' Brünnhilde—a nice word-play—for insubordination. *Götterdämmerung* gets only three sentences: Siegfried and Brünnhilde 'did not live happily ever after. No human beings do. In time they died, and in dying returned the Ring to the mermaids of the Rhine.' These versions are all abundantly illustrated. So—famously, by Arthur Rackham—is Margaret Armour's,[10] which is in verse that has a syllabic equivalence, more or less, to the original but does not lend itself to singing.

What of the singing versions? When Alfred Forman sent his first (privately printed) translation of *The Walkyrie* to the Master, in 1873, he said: 'I trust that the day is not distant when an edition of the music with English words will become necessary. . . . I have compared the whole with the music, and I think a very few alterations of the words would fit them to appear with the score.' But when the first German/English vocal scores of *The Ring* appeared, from Schott, in the early 1880s, the translation was that of H. and F. Corder.[11] F. was the composer and conductor Frederick Corder, and H. his wife Henrietta Louisa, *née* Walford.

Forman's first aim had been to keep the alliteration. It led him to lines like:

on the steadfast pair of thy eyes,—
that so oft were stars of my storm,
when hope was fierce
in my heart like fire,
when world's-delightwards
my will was lifted
from dread wildering darkness,—
for latest healing
here I must lean
in last farewell
of lingering lips!

(Dr. Huckel's comments quoted above are plainly not unfair.) The Corders also strove to preserve the *Stabreim*—but less rigorously, and with happier results:

these effulgent, glorious eyes,
whose flash my gloom oft dispell'd
when hopeless cravings
my heart discouraged,
or when my wishes
toward wordly pleasure
from wild warfare were turning:—
their lustrous gaze
lights on me now,
as my lips imprint
this last farewell!

The Corders' *Valkyrie* was sung six times at Covent Garden in 1895, with a largely American cast. The following season the opera was done there in French!

Wagner himself is said to have disliked the Corders' translation. At the end of the century, Schott published new bilingual vocal scores, with English words by Frederick Jameson,[12] and the Jameson version has remained in the Schott and, in America, G. Schirmer editions ever since. It was heard in 1908 when Hans Richter gave Covent Garden its first complete English *Ring*, and as late as 1948, in a *Valkyrie* there with Kirsten Flagstad and Hans Hotter; and it has often been performed elsewhere. Jameson's version sings well and sounds well:

those gleaming, radiant eyes
that oft in storms on me shone,
when hopeless yearning
my heart had wasted,
when world's delights
all my wishes wakened,
through wild, wildering sadness:
once more to-day,
lured by their light,
my lips shall give them
love's farewell!

When all Wagner's music entered the public domain, in 1914, Breitkopf & Härtel undertook a new, complete edition, and for the Breitkopf vocal scores Ernest Newman made a new English translation,[13] along lines similar to Jameson's:

those unclouded glorious eyes,
that oft have lighted my gloom,
when hopeless longing
my heart had wasted,
when wordly pleasures
I wished to win me,
by fear fettered and maddened—
their gleam once more
gladdens me now,
as my lips meet thine
in love's last kiss.

The first *Ring* in America, built up at the Metropolitan Opera between 1885 and 1888, was assembled in 1889. In New York, F. Rullman, the main provider of librettos, had already published some bilingual texts, with line-for-line but non-metrical translations by John P. Jackson, back in 1877 (when *Die Walküre* had its American première, at the New York Academy of Music). Rullman replaced at least *Siegfried* with the Corder version in the 1880s,[14] and brought out Charles Henry Meltzer's translations of *Das Rheingold* and *Die Walküre* in 1904. Another, uncredited—and discreditable—translation appeared in the vocal scores edited by Henry T. Finck and published by the John Church Co., of Cincinnati, in 1903. But the earlier American *Ring* translations, often reprinted,[15] and usually unattributed, form a tangled and unprofitable study. The information about them above is scrappy—but there are better ways of spending time than ploughing through and comparing the numerous 'theatre libretti' scattered in many libraries throughout America. The first significant and independent singing version produced in America is Stewart Robb's, of 1960.[16]

Robb set out 'to translate *The Ring* into clear, understandable modern English, avoiding obscurities of expression and archaic words . . . yet preserving the rhythms of the original German where possible, and even some of the alliterative effects. . . . Here', he concludes, 'is a new English version of *Der Ring des Nibelungen* which can be enjoyed by the general reader as well as sung on the opera stage. . . . Withal, it does not sound like a translation, but as though already written in English.' (Or written in American, an English reader may remark, as he comes across 'slowpoke', ''fraid-cat', a Mime who has 'fixed' soup for Siegfried, and—for Waltraute's 'Bist du von Sinnen?'—'Have you gone crazy?'.) I admire Robb's work but find it mixty-maxty: his vocabulary ranges from the colloquialisms quoted, through 'Frolic, good fellows' and 'He blows a rollicking horn', to 'wish-maid', 'lot-chooser', and 'hest'. Wagner's tone varies widely, but Robb's more widely still. Fricka's measured 'Die Walküre wend auch von ihm!' becomes 'Just keep Brunnhild out of his way'; but in the previous act of *The Valkyrie*, when Sieglinde pushes the hair back from Siegmund's forehead, her diction is surprisingly formal:

How wide and open
gleams your brow.
Your temple displays
all the interlaced veins.

I tremble and my captive
holds me entranced.
A wonder takes my attention:
Before this time we met
my eyes had seen your face!

Some of the differences between Robb's modern version and mine can be more readily shown by quotation than defined. My Fricka says 'The Valkyrie leaves him to die!', and my Sieglinde:

Your noble brow
is broad and clear;
its delicate veins
with my fingers I trace!
I tremble with the rapture
of my delight!
A marvel stirs in my memory:
although you came but today,
I've seen your face before!

And in doing so she lifts two lines ('I tremble with the rapture/of my delight!') directly from Jameson. Robb's Sieglinde is closer to the Corders', who sang 'I tremble with emotion/resting entranced!'. (The German is 'Mir zagt es vor der Wonne/die mich entzückt!'.) In fact, one soon discovers that all *Ring* translators—after the pioneering Forman—have leant on the work of their predecessors. This is reasonable and right; in any case, the ways of translating a short sentence in tempo are not limitless. Compare: 'Who art thou, stalwart stripling, that hath struck my heart?' (Corders); 'Who art thou, valiant stripling, that hast pierced my breast?' (Jameson); again, 'Who art thou, valiant stripling, that hast pierced my breast?' (Newman); 'Who are you, valiant stripling, that have pierced my heart?' (Robb); and "Who are you, youthful hero, who have pierced my breast?' (Porter, who didn't care for 'stripling', especially since its first syllable must be sustained). My indebtedness to the Corders, Jameson, Newman, and Robb is great, and gratefully owned. I worked in full knowledge of their translations. When I was stuck, I turned to see what they had done. They suggested useful words, turns of phrase, syntactical short-cuts out of the thicket, and sometimes—not often, though I have chosen to quote an example above—whole lines that I could steal for my own purposes. I hope the next translator of *The Ring* finds my version similarly useful.

When the Sadler's Wells (now English National) Opera invited me to prepare a new English text for *The Ring*, I looked first at these earlier singing versions to see whether there was really room for a new translation—and decided that perhaps there was. I thought it might be possible to try for something a little more fluent and direct, a little easier to understand, than Jameson or Newman had been, and also—this is where my version differs most from its predecessors—a translation more closely bound to the details of the music, more accurately reflecting and not contradicting the melodic and harmonic 'articulations' of its phrases. I did the Annunciation of Death scene, in Act II of *The Valkyrie*, as a test piece; Sadler's Wells approved, and I went ahead. The large inducement was that the musical interpretation, the production, and the translation would be created together, by a team of British artists new to *The Ring*, inspired by

Reginald Goodall, whom I revered as the greatest of living Wagnerian interpreters. The rehearsals were long, and at every stage the conductor, the producers, the musical coaches, and the singers themselves made suggestions that helped to provide a more comprehensible, singable, dramatic, and 'musical' text.

Opera translations intended for singing have a limited life. Whether the translator of, say, an eighteenth-century opera chooses to employ a neutral and 'timeless' or a mock-eighteenth-century idiom, his work is likely to bear the stamp of the time it was made. It is easy to date to a decade or so a photograph of a soprano dressed, wigged, and painted as Mozart's Countess Almaviva or Richard Strauss's Feldmarschallin. Similarly, in the 1970s one can distinguish between 'eighteenth-century English' written in the 1850s, the 1890s, and the 1930s. After perhaps a century, a translation made at the time of an opera's composition, possibly under its composer's eye, may acquire a certain 'period authenticity' and warrant revival—though this is not the case with, for example, the standard Italian translations of Verdi's *Les Vêpres siciliennes* and *Don Carlos*. In the former, fiery sentiments such as Giovanni da Procida's cry of 'la liberté!' were quenched, to avoid clashes with Italian censorship, and in both, Verdi, too permissive with his translators, allowed fine dramatic and fine musical points to be blunted. In any event, French-into-Italian is hard. Masculine endings are feminized; *fort* becomes *forte* and *Elisabeth, Elisabetta.* Once upon a time, poetic usage permitted the dropping of final syllables; *destin cruel* could move south as *destin crudel* rather than *destino crudele.* But now, as Gian Carlo Menotti has remarked, a modern Italian librettist is more or less committed to feminine phrase endings except when his characters visit the *città* to drink a *caffé.*

Italian-into-French is somewhat easier. French-into-English raises constant problems of how to treat not-quite-mute *-e.* Italian-into-English often results in phrase after phrase ending with an accusative pronoun: *Soccorso!* becomes *Oh help me!*, and *Son tradita!, He betrayed me!* Moreover, all English translators, from whatever language, tend to keep on hand a box filled with *thens* and *nows* into which they can dip to fill out their lines. Since Italians take four syllables to bid one another goodnight, Sparafucile, Preziosilla and the rest usually say *Well, goodnight then!*

Germans characters on the English lyric stage usually say *So, goodnight.* The difficulties of German-into-English are rather different, and in the case of *Ring*-into-English they are compounded by Wagner's *Stabreim* or alliteration, his hard syntax, and his archaic vocabulary. For many of the recurrent key words there are syllabic equivalents. *Blut* is *blood, Schwert* is *sword*, and *Tod* is *death. Liebe* and *Auge* give more trouble; on a few occasions the singers of my *Ring*-in-English are asked to slur two notes to *love* and *eye*, and Fafner the *Wurm* was not easily transformed into a *dragon.* But syllabic equivalents are not sonic equivalents: the long, dark vowels of a sustained *Blut* or *Tod* are ill-represented by *blood* and *death.* A German Siegmund can cry *Schwert* with a bright, forward ring that a mere *sword* is powerless to provide. Although *vengeance* is a word that can be said vehemently, *Rache* is more powerfully a swift double explosion. If all British and American singers, conductors, producers, and designers of *The Ring* and all their audiences commanded, not just German, but specifically Wagner's strange German as a second language—if, using the original words, the singers could express themselves fully and be sure of being understood, in detail, by those who heard them—there would be no call to translate *The Ring* into English. As one of its translators, I am dismayed when I compare, say, Wagner's:

Wie liebliche Luft
wieder uns weht,
wonnig Gefühl
die Sinne erfüllt!
Traurig ging es uns allen,
getrennt für immer von ihr,
die leidlos ewiger Jugend
jubelnde Lust uns verleiht

—Froh's 'arietta' in the last scene of *Das Rheingold*—with my:

How sweetly the air
charms us again;
joy and contentment
steal through my heart!
Life indeed would be wretched
if we were parted from her;
she brings us youth eternal,
fills us with joy and delight.

But there were compensations. When I heard Rita Hunter fill even so stilted a phrase as 'You who this love in my heart inspired' with tender, swelling emotion, Ava June utter Sieglinde's long solo that begins 'My husband's kinsmen', Norman Bailey 'think aloud' in Wotan's monologue, and Alberto Remedios relate Siegfried's young adventures, to audiences that followed what was said, I could believe there had been some gains as well as the inevitable and enormous losses.

All translation is a matter of weighing gains and losses. *The Ring*—despite what some German critics of Wagner's verse may feel—is not one of the works of which it can be said, as it was of James Fenimore Cooper's novels, that they have been 'often translated, never without improvement'. In the lyric theatre, the gains are in verbal and dramatic communicativeness. (Has there ever been a great composer who did not prefer his works to be performed in the language of the country?) The losses are of that other 'sense' conveyed by the sound and the untranslatable subtleties of the original words. And the translator's task is to make such losses as light as possible. I began work on *The Ring* without theories, almost instinctively—holding the sound of a German phrase in my ears and the literal sense of it in my mind, and rejecting version after version until I hit on English words that seemed to fit. Much later—when *The Valkyrie* was almost finished—I realized that I had been guided by six different, linked, and for the most part mutually unachievable intentions.

(1) To provide a translation that is close to the original and at the same time makes audible sense at first hearing, without needing to be 'worked out' by a puzzled listener. Towards the close of *The Rhinegold*, Fricka, hearing the name Walhall for the first time, asks what it means. The Corders' Wotan replied: 'What might 'gainst our fears my mind may have found, if proved a success, soon shall explain that name.' And Forman's: 'What, in might over fear, my manfulness found, shall matchlessly live and lead the meaning to light'. Both are fair representations of some tortuous German. But I felt that unless the meaning could be led to light a little more directly than that, the speech might as well be left in German. So, natural words in a natural order.

(2) To keep important words—such as *Liebe, Leid, Ring, Rhein*—and especially the proper names exactly where Wagner placed them. Their sounds and rhythms often have

a motivic significance; they coincide with particular harmonies. In my first draft, instead of that stilted phrase of Brünnhilde's quoted above, I had the more direct 'You who inspired me to feel this love'. Reginald Goodall pointed out that the chord on the fourth syllable was inseparable from *Liebe*; hence, 'You who this love in my heart inspired,' which reads less well but makes far better musical sense. For the same reason, Brünnhilde's 'One thing I did know, that you still loved the Wälsung', a little earlier, was changed to '. . . that the Wälsung you loved'.

(3) To keep, wherever possible, the *Stabreim*, as an essential part of the patterning in the score's structure.

(4) To echo the sound of the German—the ring of bright, forward vowels, the full shadows casts by dark ones, the attack of hammer-stroke consonants, the hiss and splutter of certain sibilant sequences. (Wagner's invented language is richer in long vowels and percussive consonants than even modern German; it would be easier to translate its sounds into Old English or into Northumbrian dialect.) Sound sometimes took precedence of literal sense. For Alberich's 'Zertrümmert! Zerknickt!' (literally 'Destroyed! Crushed!'), Jameson has 'Defeated! Destroyed!'. I made him 'Defeated! and tricked!'.

(5) To reflect the differing tones, ranging from the elevated and rhetorical (notably Wotan's harangues in Act III of *Die Walküre*), through Froh's—and Fasolt's—lyricism in *Das Rheingold*, to Loge's airy wit and Siegfried's boisterous sallies; to let such jokes as Siegfried and the Wanderer make be heard as such. The gods, Desmond Shawe-Taylor told me early on, shouldn't talk like the people next door. I hope mine do not—but I know he thinks that they have shed some of their dignity together with the second person singular. That form offered to the old translators a syllabic flexibility—*thou dost* or *doest, didest* or *didst*—denied to a modern translator who has decided, rightly or wrongly, against its use. He, on the other hand, is likely to gain new alternatives by resorting to contractions (*I have, I've*) more freely than they did. Wagner made liberal use of such contractions and elisions ('dir werf' ich's zu'; 'Ist's der, den du Gunther'n gab'st'), often introducing them when he came to set his written words to music. In English, I confess, similar forms sometimes strike too modern and colloquial a note, but I've used them when disruption of the musical rhythm (dividing, say, a minim on *I've* into two crotchets for *I have*) would be more disturbing still. They can look worse than they sound. When 'Do you think . . .?' is said quickly it becomes two syllables, 'D'you think', pronounced *dew think*. Although the ear notices nothing amiss, an eye seeing it thus written would be distressed. And so for that eye's sake I have once or twice in this printed text spelt out in full what in performance is meant to be elided. However, the frequent omission of the final -*e* of Brünnhilde, Gutrune, etc., is not a misprint but Wagner's practice; and Nibelung and Niblung are his alternatives.

(6) Most important of all—sometimes I felt that, like Brünnhilde, *im Auge das eine ich hielt* and ignored all other imperatives—to find words that fit the music closely. Take the last two lines of that passage from Wotan's farewell quoted above in Forman's, the Corders', Jameson's, and Newman's versions. The German is 'mit dem Lebewohles/letztem Kuss'; -*woh*- is a B suspended over an F major chord, and -*les* is its resolution on to A; then there is a semiquaver rest, a small break, before *letztem Kuss*. Only Jameson's lines fit the music. Forman's give us, in effect, 'farewellov/lingering lips'; the Corders' 'imprint-this/last farewell'; and Newman's 'thine-in/love's last kiss'. Robb has 'brief and final/farewell kiss', which fits well enough—but is Wotan's kiss really 'brief'?

(My version—to save any curious reader from paging on—is 'loving,/last farewell'.) Or take the opening words of Brünnhilde's immolation scene, 'Starke Scheite/schichtet mir dort'. One old translation, 'Mighty faggots', will plainly not do today. But for other reasons Jameson's 'mighty logs I' (*log's eye*) and Robb's 'Let great logs be' (*Great Logsby*, inflected like the *Great Gatsby*) must be deemed unfitting. Even though the soprano may draw no breath between the lines, the declamation is wrong. Insufficient care about such points of declamation, I believe, has done much to give opera-in-English its reputation of 'sounding awful'. Earlier *Ring* translations contain things like Sieglinde's 'And his packper/Sue in mighty force', Siegmund's 'What has ensnared/Me now well I know', Wotan's 'A lu—ckier manwill/Joy in thy stars' (*lu-* sustained, *man will* given the inflexion of *mandrill*), and Brünnhilde's:

The world's most glorious hear,
Roe-bears, o woo,
Man thy shell, tering womb!

There are some things like that in my version but, I hope, not many. I can think of no English phrase that correctly 'articulates' the awakening Brünnhilde's 'Heil dir, Sonne!' except 'Hi there, sunshine!'—and that won't do. (So each Brünnhilde, with her conductor, has chosen, from a list of variously unsatisfactory compromises provided, the version she finds least unmusical.) Most of the revisions undertaken after hearing the translation in performances have been directed towards obtaining a better musical fit.

A seventh requirement is conspicuously absent from those above: any attempt to reflect what Martin Cooper has called 'the cloudy, archaic literary style that was an organic part of Wagner's mystique.'[17] Deliberately so. For I felt that anyone who wanted to listen to *The Ring* not-quite-understanding what is said could well listen to it, unspoiled, in the original cloudy German; what would be the point of devising yet another translation 'tenfold more involved and obscure than Browning'? So this is not a text acceptable to those who believe, with Mr Cooper, that the listener's attention should be 'lulled rather than alerted by the words', that 'only the suspension of the intellectual processes will make him accept the time-scale which Wagner imposes'. It is a belief that I understand but do not fully share. From my first encounter with *The Ring*, I wanted to know exactly what all those characters were saying.

In any case, a translator cannot do everything. A glance at the following pages will reveal how very, very seldom even my 'six points' could all be met. Phrase by phrase, it was a matter of deciding which of them, in that particular place, should be deemed paramount, of discovering which were achievable at all, and then of settling for the least unsatisfactory, most singable English. Often but not always the *Stabreim* was the first thing to go; intelligible and otherwise accurate words were usually preferred to fancier alternatives that happened to begin with the right letters. So, not 'Notung! Notung! needfullest sword!' or 'Needful! Needful! Notable sword!' (Corders). And, for other reasons, not 'Notung! Notung! conquering sword!' (Jameson) or 'Needful! Needful! conquering sword!' (Robb's amalgam of Corders and Jameson). I chose this example (I have 'Notung! Notung! sword of my need!') because it brings up another recurrent 'crux'—the proper names, which in *The Ring* always mean something. The Valkyries' function—choosing those slain in battle—is defined by their name. In *The Ring*, I would be a doorkeeper. Valkyrie has been an English word since the eighteenth century, and so I used it. But so has Valhalla, the hall of those slain in battle; musical reasons, however, predicate the two syllables of Wagner's *Walhall.* I could have spelt it with a *V*—but that could lead to Votan, Vellgunde, and Valtrauta. (Lord Acton, who told Mr. Gladstone that 'neither Pitt nor Peel lives in my Walhalla', provides some precedent for keeping the *W* even in English.) On the whole I have left the names and the puns that are made upon them untranslated. Siegmund and Sieglinde could hardly be Victor and gentle Vicky. My 'Wehwalt der Wölfing' is not 'Woeful the Wolf-cub'. And if, at the Coliseum, Hunding (as in Robb) were to call out 'Woe-King! Woe-King!' in Act II of *The Valkyrie*, a British audience's reaction might be: 'Next stop, Basingstoke'. But sometimes I tried to gloss: 'I'm Wehwalt, named for my sorrow'; 'Siegfried, victorious and free' for 'Siegfried erfreu sich des Siegs!', when Brünnhilde tells Sieglinde the name of her son-to-be. (*Free* may not be in the German, but it does point towards *den Freien* whom Wotan has longed for, and it also keeps Wagner's vowel.) About orthography I have been inconsistent. 'Hoyotoho!' gives a reasonable approximation to the sounds wanted, but things like the Rhinemaidens' 'Wallala weiala' defeated me—*viala* is sonically ambiguous, and any attempts to show that the *i* is long began to suggest Viyella—so I left them in German spelling. As in most prints of the German libretto since Breitkopf's, I have omitted the unsounded *h* in *Not(h), Not(h)ung*, etc., and many of the apostrophes indicating Wagner's elided *e*'s. *Rhinegold* (like rhinestone) is so well established in English usage as one word that to transform it into *Rhine Gold*, as some advised, seemed to me pedantic.

The Ring is on the first level a rousing and splendid old tale of gods and dwarfs and men, of giants and dragons, loves and hates, murder, magic, and mysteries, unfolded amid vast and picturesque scenery. Beyond that, it is about (among other things) man's conquest of the natural world for his own uses (the first action recorded is Wotan's tearing a branch from the World Ashtree); about man's dominion over men (well-intentioned oligarchy and capitalist tyranny are both condemned); and about man's understanding of himself (the forces influencing his action, at the start located in gods, are finally discovered to lie within himself). By intention, Wagner patterned his drama on Attic tragedy but chose as his symbolic matter the ancestral myths of the North. To mankind's collective unconsciousness he gave form; that is easily said, but for that matter it can easily—if not briefly—be demonstrated. Instinct, inspiration, the composer's comprehensive grasp of what men before him had thought, dreamed, and done, and his powerful controlling mind directed the creation of *The Ring* over more than a quarter-century. In words, music, and vivid theatrical imagery combined it took shape.

Each of the clauses above has been the subject of many books; I mention here these large matters in summary form only to make the point, that believing *all* these things about *The Ring* to be true, I have not endeavoured to translate it with special reference to any one of them. This is not a particular 'interpretation'. Such interpretations—usually they are the work of ambitious producers, who have determined to disassemble the components of the *Gesamtkunstwerk*—can cast exciting new light on aspects of the work. They can be maddening. And, however brilliant, they are achieved only by diminishing the force and richness of the whole.

For five years, scores of *The Ring* accompanied me wherever I went—*wo ich mich fand, wohin ich zog.* Some lines now always recall places: the Kent garden where a tricky line of Sieglinde's was suddenly solved; a journey from Coimbra to Lisbon during which the Fricka-Wotan argument of *The Valkyrie* fell into place; the Glasgow hotel bedroom where all day long I worked at translating, leaving at night to hear—in German—Scottish Opera's *Ring*; and, above all, William Weaver's farmhouse in the Tuscan hills, where much of the work was done. My debts are great, and of many kinds: as I have said, to several previous translators; to Kirsten Flagstad, Astrid Varnay, Hans Hotter, Ludwig Weber, Wilhelm Furtwängler, Hans Knappertsbusch, Rudolf Kempe, and all those who taught me how *The Ring* could sound; to Reginald Goodall, Glen Byam Shaw and John Blatchley, John Barker, Edmund Tracey, Leonard Hancock, and all the singers who worked on the Sadler's Wells production, *in langer Zeiten Lauf*, refining my phrases and bringing them to life; to George London, who, while producing this English *Ring* in several American cities, made helpful new suggestions; to critical colleagues—especially David Cairns, Bernard Levin, Max Loppert, Peter Stadlen, and David Hamilton—who encouraged me; and to Claire Brook, without whose help I could never have got the thing into print at all.

The Valkyrie was first performed by the Sadler's Wells Opera (now English National Opera), at the London Coliseum, on 29 January 1970; *Twilight of the Gods* on 29 January 1971; *The Rhinegold* on 1 March 1972; and *Siegfried* on 8 February 1973. The full cycle was first given in July and August 1973. As I write, three of the operas have been recorded, by the English National Opera, for EMI, and the recording of *Twilight of the Gods* is imminent.

NEW YORK, JUNE 1976

Notes and References

1 Peggie Cochrane's translation appeared with the Decca recordings conducted by Georg Solti. William Mann's was published (in short lines) by the Friends of Covent Garden, in 1964, and later (with Wagner's lineation) to accompany the EMI recording conducted by Furtwängler. Lionel Salter's translations of *Das Rheingold, Siegfried*, and *Götterdämmerung* accompanied the Deutsche Grammophon recordings conducted by Karajan (for *Die Walküre*, the Mann version was used).

2 Alfred Forman: *The Walkyrie* (privately printed, London, 1873); *The Nibelung's Ring, English words to Richard Wagner's Ring des Nibelungen, in the alliterative verse of the original* (London: Schott, 1877).

3 Oliver Huckel: *The Rhine-Gold, A Dramatic Poem by Richard Wagner freely translated into poetic narrative form* (New York: Thomas Y. Crowell, 1907); followed by *The Valkyrie* (1909), *Siegfried* (1910), and *The Dusk of the Gods* (1911)—and by all Wagner's other dramas, from *Rienzi* to *Parsifal.*

4 Reginald Rankin: *Wagner's Nibelungen Ring done into English verse* (London: Longmans, Green, 1899, 2 vols.).

5 Randall Fynes: *The Ring of the Nibelung, An English version* (London: Smith, Elder, 1899–1901, 2 vols.; 1913, one-volume edition).

6 E. F. Benson: *The Valkyries, A Romance* (London: T. Fisher Unwin, 1903).

7 C. L. LeMassena: *The Ring of the Nibelung* (New York: Grossman-Roth, 1930).

[8] Gertrude Henderson: *The Ring of the Nibelung* (New York: Alfred A. Knopf, 1932).

[9] John Updike: *The Ring* (New York: Alfred A. Knopf, 1964).

[10] Margaret Armour: *The Ring of the Niblung . . . translated into English* (London: Wm. Heinemann, 1911, 2 vols.).

[11] The only firmly dated Corder vocal score I have seen is a *Götterdämmerung* of 1881. The plate number of the German/English *Rheingold* is 23504, of *Die Walküre* 23188; 1882 is the date usually assigned to the vocal scores and the bilingual libretti.

[12] Frederick Jameson: *The Nibelung's Ring, English words to Richard Wagner's Ring des Nibelungen, An accurate translation* (London: Schott, 1896). This was followed at the turn of the century by individual bilingual libretti and by vocal scores from both Schott and G. Schirmer. The Jameson version also appears in the Schott and Eulenburg miniature scores.

[13] Newman's translations of *The Rhinegold* and *The Valkyrie* had already been published in London, in 1912, as Nos. 4 and 5 of Breitkopf & Härtel's Textbooks. The vocal scores are in the Hofmeister catalogue for the years 1914–18.

[14] The Corder translations were also reprinted by C. F. Tretbar, of New York, in 1893, and by Oliver Ditson, of Boston, in 1904.

[15] For example, as late as 1938 *The Authentic Librettos of the Wagner Operas* (New York: Crown Publishers) gathers in facsimile four different 'theatre libretti' (*Siegfried* with cuts and all) in different type-faces—basically the Corders' text, mingled with some Meltzer prefatory material.

[16] Stewart Robb: *The Ring of the Nibelung* (New York: Dutton, 1960); English only; useful introductory essays by Edward Downes and by the translator. Published as individual, bilingual libretti by G. Schirmer. (I have not seen Walter Ducloux's unpublished singing translation of *Das Rheingold*.)

[17] Martin Cooper: 'Wagner without the wizardry', *Daily Telegraph*, 18 August 1973.

The Rhinegold

Preliminary Evening to the Festival Play

The Ring of the Nibelung

Dramatis Personae

Gods

WOTAN	*Bass-baritone*
DONNER	*Baritone*
FROH	*Tenor*
LOGE	*Tenor*

Giants

FASOLT	*Bass-baritone*
FAFNER	*Bass*

Nibelungs

ALBERICH	*Bass-baritone*
MIME	*Tenor*

Goddesses

FRICKA	*Mezzo-soprano*
FREIA	*Soprano*
ERDA	*Contralto*

Rhinemaidens

WOGLINDE	*Soprano*
WELLGUNDE	*Soprano*
FLOSSHILDE	*Contralto*

Nibelungs

Scene One

Erste Szene

Auf dem Grund des Rheines

Grünliche Dämmerung, nach oben zu lichter, nach unten zu dunkler. Die Höhe ist von wogendem Gewässer erfüllt, das rastlos von rechts nach links zu strömt. Nach der Tiefe zu lösen sich die Fluten in einen immer feineren feuchten Nebel auf, so daß der Raum der Manneshöhe vom Boden auf gänzlich frei vom Wasser zu sein scheint, welches wie in Wolkenzügen über den nächtlichen Grund dahinfließt. Überall ragen schroffe Felsenriffe aus der Tiefe auf und grenzen den Raum der Bühne ab; der ganze Boden ist in ein wildes Zackengewirr zerspalten, so daß er nirgends vollkommen eben ist und nach allen Seiten hin in dichtester Finsternis tiefere Schluchten annehmen läßt. Das Orchester beginnt bei noch geschlossenem Vorhange.
Der Vorhang wird aufgezogen. Volles Wogen der Wassertiefe. Um ein Riff in der Mitte der Bühne,

Scene One

On the Bed of the Rhine

Greenish twilight, brighter towards the top, darker below. The upper part of the stage is filled with swirling waters that flow restlessly from right to left. Towards the bottom, the waters resolve into an increasingly fine damp mist, so that a space a man's height from the ground seems to be completely free of the water, which courses like a train of clouds over the dusky bed. Craggy points of rock rise everywhere from the depths and mark the confines of the stage. The whole river bed is broken up into a craggy confusion, so that nowhere is it completely flat, and on all sides, in the dense darkness, there seem to be deeper gorges. The orchestra begins while the curtain is still closed.

When the curtain rises, the watery depths are in full flood. In the centre of the stage, around a rock

welches mit seiner schlanken Spitze bis in die dichtere, heller dämmernde Wasserflut hinaufragt, kreist in anmutig schwimmender Bewegung eine der Rheintöchter.

WOGLINDE
Weia! Waga!
Woge, du Welle!
Walle zur Wiege!
Wagalaweia!
Wallala weiala weia!

WELLGUNDES STIMME
(von oben)
Woglinde, wachst du allein?

WOGLINDE
Mit Wellgunde wär' ich zu zwei.

WELLGUNDE
(taucht aus der Flut zum Riff herab.)
Laß sehn, wie du wachst.
(Sie sucht Woglinde zu erhaschen.)

WOGLINDE
(entweicht ihr schwimmend.)
Sicher vor dir.
(Sie necken sich und suchen sich spielend zu fangen.)

FLOSSHILDES STIMME
(von oben)
Heiala weia!
Wildes Geschwister!

WELLGUNDE
Floßhilde, schwimm!
Woglinde flieht:
hilf mir die Fliehende fangen!

FLOSSHILDE
(taucht herab und fährt zwischen die Spielenden.)
Des Goldes Schlaf
hütet ihr schlecht;
besser bewacht
des Schlummernden Bett,
sonst büßt ihr beide das Spiel!
(Mit muntrem Gekreisch fahren die beiden

whose slender point reaches up into the brighter area of densely swirling water, one of the Rhine-maidens is circling with a graceful swimming motion.

WOGLINDE
Weia! Waga!
Wandering waters,
lulling our cradle!
Wagalaweia!
Wallala, weiala weia!

WELLGUNDE'S VOICE
(from above)
Woglinde, watching alone?

WOGLINDE
Till Wellgunde joins me below.

WELLGUNDE
(dives down from the waters to the rock.)
Let's see how you watch!
(She tries to catch Woglinde.)

WOGLINDE
(swims away from her.)
Safe from your grasp!
(They tease and playfully try to catch one another.)

FLOSSHILDE'S VOICE
(from above)
Heiala weia!
Careful, my sisters!

WELLGUNDE
Flosshilde, swim!
Woglinde flies:
hurry and help me to catch her!

FLOSSHILDE
(dives down and comes between them in their play.)
The sleeping gold
calls for your care!
Back to your task
of guarding its bed,
or else you'll pay for your games!
(With merry cries the other two separate;

auseinander: Floßhilde sucht bald die eine, bald die andere zu erhaschen; sie entschlüpfen ihr und vereinigen sich endlich, um gemeinschaftlich auf Floßhilde Jagd zu machen; so schnellen sie gleich Fischen von Riff zu Riff, scherzend und lachend.
Aus einer finsteren Schlucht ist währenddem Alberich, an einem Riffe klimmend, dem Abgrunde entstiegen. Er hält, noch vom Dunkel umgeben, an und schaut dem Spiele der Wassermädchen mit steigendem Wohlgefallen zu.)

Flosshilde tries to catch first one, then the other; they elude her, and then join again in pursuit of her; thus they dart like fish from rock to rock, playing and laughing.
Meanwhile Alberich, clambering up a rock, has emerged from a dark chasm at the bottom. He pauses, still surrounded by darkness, and with increasing pleasure watches the water-maidens at play.)

ALBERICH
Hehe! Ihr Nicker!
Wie seid ihr niedlich,
neidliches Volk!
Aus Nibelheims Nacht
naht' ich mich gern,
neigtet ihr euch zu mir.
(Die Mädchen halten, als sie Alberichs Stimme hören, mit ihrem Spiele ein.)

ALBERICH
He, he! you nixies!
What a delightful,
delicate sight
From Nibelheim's night
I would draw near
if I thought you'd be kind.
(At the sound of Alberich's voice, the maidens stop playing.)

WOGLINDE
Hei! wer ist dort?

WOGLINDE
Hi, who is there?

FLOSSHILDE
Es dämmert und ruft.

FLOSSHILDE
A voice in the dark.

WELLGUNDE
Lugt, wer uns belauscht!
(Sie tauchen tiefer herab und erkennen den Nibelung.)

WELLGUNDE
Look who is below!
(They dive down deeper and perceive the Nibelung.)

WOGLINDE und WELLGUNDE
Pfui! der Garstige!

WOGLINDE and WELLGUNDE
Pfui! He's horrible!

FLOSSHILDE
(schnell auftauchend)
Hütet das Gold!
Vater warnte
vor solchem Feind.
(Die beiden andern folgen ihr, und alle drei versammeln sich schnell um das mittlere Riff.)

FLOSSHILDE
(swiftly darting upwards)
Be on your guard!
Father warned us
about such a foe.
(The others follow her, and all three swiftly gather round the central rock.)

ALBERICH
Ihr, da oben!

ALBERICH
You, above there!

DIE DREI
Was willst du dort unten?

ALL THREE
What want you, below there?

ALBERICH
Stör ich eu'r Spiel,
wenn staunend ich still hier steh?
Tauchtet ihr nieder,
mit euch tollte
und neckte der Niblung sich gern!

WOGLINDE
Mit uns will er spielen?

WELLGUNDE
Ist ihm das Spott?

ALBERICH
Wie scheint im Schimmer
ihr hell und schön!
Wie gern umschlänge
der Schlanken eine mein Arm,
schlüpfte hold sie herab!

FLOSSHILDE
Nun lach ich der Furcht:
der Feind ist verliebt.

WELLGUNDE
Der lüsterne Kauz!

WOGLINDE
Laßt ihn uns kennen!
(Sie läßt sich auf die Spitze des Riffes hinab, an dessen Fuße Alberich angelangt ist.)

ALBERICH
Die neigt sich herab.

WOGLINDE
Nun nahe dich mir!

ALBERICH
(klettert mit koboldartiger Behendigkeit, doch wiederholt aufgehalten, der Spitze des Riffes zu.)
Garstig glatter
glitschriger Glimmer!
Wie gleit ich aus!
Mit Händen und Füßen
nicht fasse noch halt ich
das schlecke Geschlüpfer!

ALBERICH
Only to stand
admiring your charming games;
then if you're friendly
you'll dive down
to the bottom, so I can join in!

WOGLINDE
He wants us to join him?

WELLGUNDE
He must be mad!

ALBERICH
You shine and gleam
in the watery gloom!
How I would love
to enfold such maids in my arms:
please come join me below!

FLOSSHILDE
I laugh at my fears;
the dwarf is in love!

WELLGUNDE
The languishing dwarf!

WOGLINDE
Teach him a lesson!
(She sinks to the top of the rock the foot of which Alberich has reached.)

ALBERICH
She sinks to the rock!

WOGLINDE
Come closer to me!

ALBERICH
(clambers with gnome-like agility towards the top of the rock, but keeps falling back.)
Slimy, slippery,
slithery smoothness!
The slope's too steep!
My hands and my feet
cannot get any grip
on the slippery surface!

Feuchtes Naß
füllt mir die Nase:
verfluchtes Niesen!
(Er ist in Woglindes Nähe angelangt.)

WOGLINDE
(lachend)
Prustend naht
meines Freiers Pracht!

ALBERICH
Mein Friedel sei,
du fräuliches Kind!
(Er sucht sie zu umfassen.)

WOGLINDE
(sich ihm entwindend)
Willst du mich frein,
so freie mich hier!
(Sie taucht auf einem andern Riff auf.)

ALBERICH
(kratzt sich den Kopf.)
O weh; du entweichst?
Komm doch wieder!
Schwer ward mir,
was so leicht du erschwingst.

WOGLINDE
(schwingt sich auf ein drittes Riff in größerer Tiefe.)
Steig nur zu Grund:
da greifst du mich sicher!

ALBERICH
(klettert hastig hinab.)
Wohl besser da unten!

WOGLINDE
(schnellt sich rasch aufwärts nach einem hohen Seitenriffe.)
Nun aber nach oben!

WELLGUNDE und FLOSSHILDE
Hahahahaha!

ALBERICH
Wie fang ich im Sprung

And the water
tickles my nostrils:
oh, curse this sneezing!
(He has got close to Woglinde.)

WOGLINDE
(laughing)
Sneezing tells me
my lover is near!

ALBERICH
You're mine at last,
you beautiful child!
(He tries to embrace her.)

WOGLINDE
(eluding him)
If I am yours,
then follow me here!
(She dives to another rock.)

ALBERICH
(scratches his head.)
Alas! you escape?
Ah, come nearer!
You can swim,
but I stumble and slide.

WOGLINDE
(swims off to a third rock, further down.)
Would you prefer
this rock at the bottom?

ALBERICH
(clambers down hastily.)
It's certainly safer!

WOGLINDE
(darts upwards to a high rock at the side.)
And now to a high one!

WELLGUNDE and FLOSSHILDE
Hahahahaha!

ALBERICH
Oh, how can I catch

den spröden Fisch?
Warte, du Falsche!
(Er will ihr eilig nachklettern.)

WELLGUNDE
(hat sich auf ein tieferes Riff auf der andern Seite gesenkt.)
Heia! Du Holder!
Hörst du mich nicht?

ALBERICH
(sich umwendend)
Rufst du nach mir?

WELLGUNDE
Ich rate dir wohl:
zu mir wende dich,
Woglinde meide!

ALBERICH
(klettert hastig über den Bodengrund zu Wellgunde.)
Viel schöner bist du
als jene Scheue,
die minder gleißend
und gar zu glatt.
Nur tiefer tauche,
willst du mir taugen!

WELLGUNDE
(noch etwas mehr zu ihm sich herabsenkend)
Bin nun ich dir nah?

ALBERICH
Noch nicht genug!
Die schlanken Arme
schlinge um mich,
daß ich den Nacken
dir neckend betaste,
mit schmeichelnder Brunst
an die schwellende Brust mich dir [schmiege!

WELLGUNDE
Bist du verliebt
und lüstern nach Minne,
laß sehn, du Schöner,
wie bist du zu schaun?
Pfui, du haariger,

this flighty fish?
Wait for me, false one!
(He scrambles up after her.)

WELLGUNDE
(has sunk to a deeper rock on the other side.)
Heia! fair lover,
turn you this way.

ALBERICH
(turning towards her)
Calling to me?

WELLGUNDE
And hear this advice:
Why chase Woglinde?
Wellgunde calls you!

ALBERICH
(hastily clambering over the bottom towards Wellgunde.)
And you are fairer still
than your sister,
who gleams less brightly,
who's far too sleek.
Now come towards me
so I can clasp you!

WELLGUNDE
(descending a shade closer still towards him)
Well, now am I near?

ALBERICH
Not near enough!
Those lovely arms
come twine round my neck,
so I can touch you
and play with your tresses,
and fondle your breasts
in my passionate, burning embraces!

WELLGUNDE
So you're in love
and longing to hold me;
let's see, my beauty,
just what you are like?
Pfui! You hairy old

höckriger Geck!
Schwarzes, schwieliges
Schwefelgezwerg!
Such dir ein Friedel,
dem du gefällst!

hideous imp!
Scaly, spotted
and sulphurous dwarf!
Look for a sweetheart
black as yourself!

ALBERICH
(sucht sie mit Gewalt zu halten.)
Gefall ich dir nicht,
dich faß ich doch fest!

ALBERICH
(trying to hold her by force)
What though I am black—
you're tight in my grasp!

WELLGUNDE
(schnell zum mittleren Riffe auftauchend)
Nur fest, sonst fließ ich dir fort!

WELLGUNDE
(swiftly diving away to the central rock)
So tight, I slip from your hands!

WOGLINDE und FLOSSHILDE
Hahahahaha!

WOGLINDE and FLOSSHILDE
Hahahahaha!

ALBERICH
Falsches Kind!
Kalter, grätiger Fisch!
Schein ich nicht schön dir,
niedlich und neckisch,
glatt und glau—
hei! so buhle mit Aalen,
ist dir eklig mein Balg!

ALBERICH
Faithless thing!
Bony, cold-blooded fish!
So I'm not handsome,
pretty and playful,
slim and sleek—
Eh! Make love with an eel, then,
if he's more to your taste!

FLOSSHILDE
Was zankst du, Alp?
Schon so verzagt?
Du freitest um zwei!
Frügst du die dritte,
süßen Trost
schüfe die Traute dir!

FLOSSHILDE
Stop grumbling, dwarf.
So soon dismayed?
With two you have failed!
Try now the third one.
Seek her love;
she may console your grief!

ALBERICH
Holder Sang
singt zu mir her.
Wie gut, daß ihr
eine nicht seid!
Von vielen gefall ich wohl einer:
bei einer kieste mich keine!
Soll ich dir glauben,
so gleite herab!

ALBERICH
Lovely sounds
ravish my ears!
What luck to find
three of them here;
for one of the three may accept me
while one alone would reject me!
Show I can trust you,
and glide to my arms!

FLOSSHILDE
(taucht zu Alberich hinab.)
Wie törig seid ihr,

FLOSSHILDE
(dives down to Alberich.)
Oh foolish sisters,

dumme Schwestern,
dünkt euch dieser nicht schön?

ALBERICH
(ihr nahend)
Für dumm und häßlich
darf ich sie halten,
seit ich dich Holdeste seh.

FLOSSHILDE
(schmeichelnd)
O singe fort
so süß und fein:
wie hehr verführt es mein Ohr!

ALBERICH
(zutraulich sie berührend)
Mir zagt, zuckt
und zehrt sich das Herz,
lacht mir so zierliches Lob.

FLOSSHILDE
(ihn sanft abwehrend)
Wie deine Anmut
mein Aug erfreut,
deines Lächelns Milde
den Mut mir labt!
(Sie zieht ihn zärtlich an sich.)
Seligster Mann!

ALBERICH
Süßeste Maid!

FLOSSHILDE
Wärst du mir hold!

ALBERICH
Hielt' ich dich immer!

FLOSSHILDE
(ihn ganz in ihren Armen haltend)
Deinen stechenden Blick,
deinen struppigen Bart,
o säh' ich ihn, faßt' ich ihn stets!
Deines stachligen Haares
strammes Gelock,
umflöss' es Floßhilde ewig!

blind to beauty,
can't you see that he's fair?

ALBERICH
(approaching her)
And I declare them
stupid and ugly,
now that the loveliest is mine!

FLOSSHILDE
(cajolingly)
Oh sing your song
so soft and sweet:
your voice bewitches my ear!

ALBERICH
(caressing her fondly)
My heart bounds
and flutters and burns,
hearing this praise from your lips.

FLOSSHILDE
(gently restraining him)
Oh how your beauty
delights my eyes,
and your smile so tender
inspires my soul!
(She draws him tenderly towards her.)
Dearest of men!

ALBERICH
Sweetest of maids!

FLOSSHILDE
Now you are mine!

ALBERICH
Faithful for ever.

FLOSSHILDE
(holding him close in her arms)
Oh the sting of your glance,
and the prick of your beard—
Oh how they have captured my heart!
And the locks of your hair,
so shaggy and sharp,
must float round Flosshilde ever!

Deine Krötengestalt,
deiner Stimme Gekrächz,
o dürft ich staunend und stumm
sie nur hören und sehn!

WOGLINDE und WELLGUNDE
Hahahahahaha!

ALBERICH
(erschreckt aus Floßhildes Armen auffahrend)
Lacht ihr Bösen mich aus?

FLOSSHILDE
(sich plötzlich ihm entreißend)
Wie billig am Ende vom Lied.
(Sie taucht mit den Schwestern schnell auf.)

WOGLINDE und WELLGUNDE
Hahahahahaha!

ALBERICH
(mit kreischender Stimme)
Wehe! ach wehe!
O Schmerz! O Schmerz!
Die dritte, so traut,
betrog sie mich auch?
Ihr schmählich schlaues,
lüderlich schlechtes Gelichter!
Nährt ihr nur Trug,
ihr treuloses Nickergezücht?

DIE DREI RHEINTÖCHTER
Wallala! Lalaleia! Leialalei!
Heia! Heia! Haha!
Schäme dich, Albe!
Schilt nicht dort unten!
Höre, was wir dich heißen!
Warum, du Banger,
bandest du nicht
das Mädchen, das du minnst?
Treu sind wir
und ohne Trug
dem Freier, der uns fängt.
Greife nur zu
und grause dich nicht!
In der Flut entfliehn wir nicht leicht.

And your shape like a toad,
and the croak of your voice—
oh, how they ravish my soul:
I want nothing but these!

WOGLINDE and WELLGUNDE
Hahahahahaha!

ALBERICH
(starting from Flosshilde's embrace in alarm)
Are they daring to laugh?

FLOSSHILDE
(suddenly darting away from him)
And laughter's the end of my song!
(She dives quickly upward with her sisters.)

WOGLINDE and WELLGUNDE
Hahahahahaha!

ALBERICH
(screeching)
Sorrow! oh sorrow!
Oh, shame! Oh, shame!
The third one, so dear,
betrays me as well.
You shameless, slippery
underhand, infamous wretches!
Shifty and sly,
you treacherous watery tribe!

THE THREE RHINEMAIDENS
Wallala! Lalaleia! Leialalei!
Heia! Heia! Haha!
Shame on you, Alberich!
Stop your complaining!
Wait, and hear what we tell you!
You foolish Niblung,
you should have held us
tightly while you could.
You'll find
that we can be true
and faithful, once we are caught!
Back to the chase
and grab without fear!
In the waves it's hard to escape.

Wallala! Lalaleia! Leialala!
Heia! Heia! Hahei!
(Sie schwimmen auseinander, hierher und dorthin, bald tiefer, bald höher, um Alberich zur Jagd auf sie zu reizen.)

ALBERICH
Wie in den Gliedern
brünstige Glut
mir brennt und glüht!
Wut und Minne
wild und mächtig
wühlt mir den Mut auf!
Wie ihr auch lacht und lügt,
lüstern lechz ich nach euch,
und eine muß mir erliegen!
(Er macht sich mit verzweifelter Anstrengung zur Jagd auf: mit grauenhafter Behendigkeit erklimmt er Riff für Riff, springt von einem zum andern, such bald dieses, bald jenes der Mädchen zu erhaschen, die mit lustigem Gekreisch stets ihm entweichen; er strauchelt, stürzt in den Abgrund hinab, klettert dann hastig wieder in die Höhe zu neuer Jagd. Sie neigen sich etwas herab. Fast erreicht er sie, stürzt abermals zurück und versucht es nochmals. Er hält endlich vor Wut schäumend atemlos an und streckt die geballte Faust nach den Mädchen hinauf.)

ALBERICH
(kaum seiner mächtig)
Fing' eine diese Faust!...
(Er verbleibt in sprachloser Wut, den Blick aufwärts gerichtet, wo er dann plötzlich von folgendem Schauspiele angezogen und gefesselt wird. Durch die Flut ist von oben her ein immer lichterer Schein gedrungen, der sich an einer hohen Stelle des mittelsten Riffes allmählich zu einem blendend hell strahlenden Goldglanze entzündet; ein zauberisch goldenes Licht bricht von hier durch das Wasser.)

WOGLINDE
Lugt, Schwestern!
Die Weckerin lacht in den Grund.

WELLGUNDE
Durch den grünen Schwall
den wonnigen Schläfer sie grüßt.

Wallala! Lalaleia! Leialalei!
Heia! Heia! Hahei!
(They swim apart, hither and thither, now deeper, now higher, inciting Alberich to pursue them.)

ALBERICH
Passionate fevers,
fervid desires,
have set me on fire!
Rage and longing,
wild and frantic,
drive me to madness!
Though you may laugh and lie,
yearning conquers my heart
and I'll not rest till I've caught you!
(He sets out in pursuit with desperate exertions; with terrible agility he clambers from rock to rock, leaps from one to another, tries to catch first one, then another of the maidens, who always elude him with merry cries. He stumbles, tumbles down to the bottom, then climbs quickly up to the heights again for a further chase. They lower themselves a little. He almost reaches them but again tumbles down, and tries once more. At last he stops, foaming with rage and breathless, and shakes his clenched fists up at the maidens.)

ALBERICH
(almost out of control)
One, I swear, shall be mine...
(He remains speechless with rage, looking upwards, and then is suddenly attracted and spellbound by the following spectacle. Through the waters an increasingly bright light makes its way from above, gradually kindling, on a high point of the central rock, to a dazzling, brightly-beaming gleam of gold; a magical golden light streams through the waters from this point.)

WOGLINDE
Look, sisters!
The sunlight is greeting the gold.

WELLGUNDE
Through the watery gloom
she calls to the sleeper to wake.

FLOSSHILDE
Jetzt küßt sie sein Auge,
daß er es öffne.

WELLGUNDE
Schaut, es lächelt
in lichtem Schein.

WOGLINDE
Durch die Fluten hin
fleißt sein strahlender Stern.

DIE DREI
(zusammen das Riff anmutig umschwimmend)
Heiajaheia!
Heiajaheia!
Wallalallalala leiajahei!
Rheingold!
Rheingold!
Leuchtende Lust,
wie lachst du so hell und hehr!
Glühender Glanz
entgleißet dir weihlich im Wag!
Heiajahei!
Heiajaheia!
Wache, Freund,
wache froh!
Wonnige Spiele
spenden wir dir:
flimmert der Fluß,
flammet die Flut,
umfließen wir tauchend,
tanzend und singend,
im seligen Bade dein Bett.
Rheingold!
Rheingold!
Heiajaheia!
Wallalaleia heiajahei!
(Mit immer ausgelassenerer Lust umschwimmen die Mädchen das Riff. Die ganze Flut flimmert in hellem Goldglanze.)

ALBERICH
(dessen Augen, mächtig vom Glanze angezogen, starr an dem Golde haften.)
Was ist's, ihr Glatten,
das dort so glänzt und gleißt?

FLOSSHILDE
She kisses his eyelids,
tells them to open.

WELLGUNDE
See him smile now
with gentle light.

WOGLINDE
Through the floods afar
shines his glittering beam.

ALL THREE
(swimming together gracefully around the rock)
Heiajaheia!
Heiajaheia!
Wallalallalala leiajahei!
Rhinegold!
Rhinegold!
Radiant joy!
We laugh in your joyful shine!
Glorious beams
that glitter and gleam in the waves!
Heiajahei!
Heiajaheia!
Waken friend!
Wake in joy!
Wonderful games
we'll play in your praise:
flash in the foam,
flame in the flood,
and floating around you,
dancing and singing,
in joy we will dive to your bed!
Rhinegold!
Rhinegold!
Heiajaheia!
Wallalaleia heiajahei!
(With increasingly exuberant joy, the maidens swim round the rock. All the waters are a-glitter with the golden radiance.)

ALBERICH
(whose eyes are powerfully attracted to the gleam, stares fixedly at the gold.)
What's that, you nymphs,
up there, that shines and gleams?

DIE DREI MÄDCHEN
Wo bist du Rauher denn heim,
daß vom Rheingold nie du gehört?

WELLGUNDE
Nichts weiß der Alp
von des Goldes Auge,
das wechselnd wacht und schläft?

WOGLINDE
Von der Wassertiefe
wonnigem Stern,
der hehr die Wogen durchhellt?

DIE DREI MÄDCHEN
Sieh, wie selig
im Glanze wir gleiten!
Willst du Banger
in ihm dich baden,
so schwimm und schwelge mit uns!
Wallalalala leialalei!
Wallalalala leiajahei!

ALBERICH
Eurem Taucherspiele
nur taugte das Gold?
Mir gält' es dann wenig!

WOGLINDE
Des Goldes Schmuck
schmähte er nicht,
wüßte er all seine Wunder!

WELLGUNDE
Der Welt Erbe
gewänne zu eigen,
wer aus dem Rheingold
schüfe den Ring,
der maßlose Macht ihm verlieh'.

FLOSSHILDE
Der Vater sagt' es,
und uns befahl er,
klug zu hüten
den klaren Hort,
daß kein Falscher der Flut ihn entführe:
drum schweigt, ihr schwatzendes Heer!

THE THREE RHINEMAIDENS
Ignorant dwarf, where have you lived?
Of the Rhinegold have you not heard?

WELLGUNDE
The dwarf's not heard
of the golden radiance
which sleeps and wakes in turn?

WOGLINDE
In the watery deeps
this wonderful star
shines forth and brightens the waves.

ALL THREE
Ah, how gladly
we glide in its radiance!
Come to join us
and bathe in brightness,
come sport and swim in the shine!
Wallalalala leialalei!
Wallalalala leiajahei!

ALBERICH
Is that all it's good for,
to shine at your games?
Why, then it is worthless!

WOGLINDE
This golden charm
you would revere,
oh, if you knew of its marvels!

WELLGUNDE
The world's wealth can
be won by a man who,
seizing the Rhinegold,
fashions a ring:
that ring makes him lord of the world.

FLOSSHILDE
Our father told us,
but then he warned us
we should guard it
and keep it safe,
lest some false one should wickedly steal it:
be quiet, you chattering fools!

WELLGUNDE
Du klügste Schwester,
verklagst du uns wohl?
Weißt du denn nicht,
wem nur allein
das Gold zu schmieden vergönnt?

WOGLINDE
Nur wer der Minne
Macht versagt,
nur wer der Liebe
Lust verjagt,
nur der erzielt sich den Zauber,
zum Reif zu zwingen das Gold.

WELLGUNDE
Wohl sicher sind wir
und sorgenfrei:
denn was nur lebt, will lieben;
meiden will keiner die Minne.

WOGLINDE
Am wenigsten er,
der lüsterne Alp:
vor Liebesgier
möcht er vergehn!

FLOSSHILDE
Nicht fürcht ich den,
wie ich ihn erfand:
seiner Minne Brunst
brannte fast mich.

WELLGUNDE
Ein Schwefelbrand
in der Wogen Schwall:
vor Zorn der Liebe
zischt er laut.

DIE DREI MÄDCHEN
Wallala! Wallaleialala!
Lieblichster Albe,
lachst du nicht auch?
In des Goldes Schein
wie leuchtest du schön!
O komm, Lieblicher, lache mit uns!
Heiajaheia! Heiajaheia!

WELLGUNDE
My prudent sister,
no need to be cross!
Surely you know
all that's required
of him who would master the gold?

WOGLINDE
He must pronounce
a curse on love,
he must renounce
all joys of love,
before he masters the magic,
a ring to forge from the gold.

WELLGUNDE
And that's a thing
that will never be:
all men who live must love;
no one could ever renounce it.

WOGLINDE
And least of all he,
that lecherous dwarf,
all hot desire,
panting with lust!

FLOSSHILDE
Well, I confess
we've nothing to fear.
I was nearly scorched
when he came near.

WELLGUNDE
A sulphur-brand
in the swirling waves,
inflamed with longing,
sizzling loud!

ALL THREE
Wallala! Wallaleialala!
Loveliest Niblung,
share in our joy.
In the golden radiance,
how handsome you seem!
Oh come, lovely one, laugh and be glad!
Heiajaheia! Heiajaheia!

Wallalalala leiajahei!
(Sie schwimmen lachend im Glanze auf und ab.)

ALBERICH
(die Augen starr auf das Gold gerichtet, hat dem Geplauder der Schwestern wohl gelauscht.)
Der Welt Erbe
gewänn' ich zu eigen durch dich?
Erzwäng' ich nicht Liebe,
doch listig erzwäng' ich mir Lust?
(furchtbar laut)
Spottet nur zu!
Der Niblung naht eurem Spiel!
(Wütend springt er nach dem mittleren Riff hinüber und klettert in grausiger Hast nach dessen Spitze hinauf. Die Mädchen fahren kreischend auseinander und tauchen nach verschiedenen Seiten hin auf.)

DIE DREI RHEINTÖCHTER
Heia! Heia! Heiajahei!
Rettet euch!
Es raset der Alp!
In den Wassern sprüht's,
wohin er springt:
die Minne macht ihn verrückt!
(Sie lachen im tollsten Übermut.)

ALBERICH
(gelangt mit einem letzten Satze zur Spitze des Riffes.)
Bangt euch noch nicht?
So buhlt nun im Finstern,
feuchtes Gezücht!
(Er streckt die Hand nach dem Golde aus.)
Das Licht lösch ich euch aus;
entreiße dem Riff das Gold,
schmiede den rächenden Ring;
denn hör es die Flut:
so verfluch ich die Liebe!
(Er reißt mit furchtbarer Gewalt das Gold aus dem Riffe und stürzt damit hastig in die Tiefe, wo er schnell verschwindet. Dichte Nacht bricht plötzlich überall herein. Die Mädchen tauchen nach dem Räuber in die Tiefe nach.)

FLOSSHILDE
Haltet den Räuber!

Wallalala leiajahei!
(They swim up and down in the glow, laughing.)

ALBERICH
(his eyes fixed on the gold, has listened attentively to the sisters' chatter.)
The world's wealth
can be mine if I utter the curse?
Though love be denied me,
yet cunning can bring me delight?
(terribly loud)
Laugh if you will!
the Niblung's near to your toy!
(Furiously, he leaps across to the central rock and clambers up towards its summit in dreadful haste. The maidens separate with screams and swim upward in various directions.)

THE THREE RHINEMAIDENS
Heia! Heia! Heiajahei!
Save yourselves!
the dwarf has gone mad;
and the water swirls
where he has leapt.
His love has cost him his wits!
(They laugh with the wildest bravado.)

ALBERICH
(reaches the summit of the rock with one last bound.)
Still not afraid?
Then laugh in the darkness,
nymphs of the waves!
(He reaches out his hand towards the gold.)
Your light yields to my hand:
I'll seize from the rock your gold,
forge that magical ring.
Now hear me, you floods:
Love, I curse you for ever!
(With terrible force, he tears the gold from the rock and hastily plunges down with it into the depths, where he quickly disappears. Thick darkness suddenly descends on everything. The maidens rapidly dive down after the robber into the depths.)

FLOSSHILDE
Capture the robber!

WELLGUNDE
Rettet das Gold!

WOGLINDE und WELLGUNDE
Hilfe! Hilfe!

DIE DREI MÄDCHEN
Weh! Weh!
(Die Flut fällt mit ihnen nach der Tiefe hinab, aus dem untersten Grunde hört man Alberichs gellendes Hohngelächter. In dichtester Finsternis verschwinden die Riffe; die ganze Bühne ist von der Höhe bis zur Tiefe von schwarzem Wassergewoge erfüllt, das eine Zeitlang immer noch abwärts zu sinken scheint.)

WELLGUNDE
Rescue the gold!

WOGLINDE and WELLGUNDE
Help us!

ALL THREE
Woe! Woe!
(The waters sink down with them into the depths. From the lowest depth, Alberich's harsh, mocking laughter is heard. The rocks disappear in the thick darkness; the whole stage is filled from top to bottom with black billowing water, which for some time seems to be continually sinking.)

Zweite Szene

Allmählich sind die Wogen in Gewölke übergegangen, welches, als eine immer heller dämmernde Beleuchtung dahinter tritt, zu feinerem Nebel sich abklärt. Als der Nebel in zarten Wölkchen gänzlich sich in der Höhe verliert, wird im Tagesgrauen eine

Freie Gegend auf Bergeshöhen

sichtbar. Der hervorbrechende Tag beleuchtet mit wachsendem Glanze eine Burg mit blinkenden Zinnen, die auf einem Felsgipfel im Hintergrunde steht; zwischen diesem burggekrönten Felsgipfel und dem Vordergrunde der Szene ist ein tiefes Tal, durch welches der Rhein fließt, anzunehmen. Zur Seite auf blumigem Grunde liegt Wotan, neben ihm Fricka, beide schlafend. Die Burg ist ganz sichtbar geworden.

FRICKA
(erwacht; ihr Blick fällt auf die Burg; sie staunt und erschrickt.)
Wotan, Gemahl! Erwache!

Scene Two

The waves are gradually transformed into clouds, which, as an increasingly brighter dawn light passes behind them, resolve into fine mist. When the mist has completely vanished aloft in gentle little clouds, in the dawning light an

Open Space on a Mountain Height

becomes visible. The daybreak illuminates with increasing brightness a castle with gleaming battlements, which stands on a rocky summit in the background. Between this and the foreground of the stage a deep valley is to be imagined, through which the Rhine flows. Wotan and, beside him, Fricka, both asleep, are lying on a flowery bank at one side. The castle has become completely visible.

FRICKA
(wakes; her eyes fall on the castle; she starts in alarm.)
Wotan, my lord! awaken!

WOTAN
(im Traume leise)
Der Wonne seligen Saal
bewachen mir Tür und Tor:
Mannes Ehre,
ewige Macht
ragen zu endlosem Ruhm!

FRICKA
(rüttelt ihn.)
Auf, aus der Träume,
wonnigem Trug!
Erwache, Mann, und erwäge!

WOTAN
(erwacht und erhebt sich ein wenig, sein Auge wird sogleich vom Anblick der Burg gefesselt.)
Vollendet das ewige Werk:
auf Berges Gipfel
die Götterburg,
prächtig prahlt
der prangende Bau!
Wie im Traum ich ihn trug,
wie mein Wille ihn wies,
stark und schön
steht er zur Schau;
hehrer, herrlicher Bau!

FRICKA
Nur Wonne schafft dir,
was mich erschreckt?
Dich freut die Burg,
mir bangt es um Freia.
Achtloser, laß dich erinnern
des ausbedungenen Lohns!
Die Burg ist fertig,
verfallen das Pfand:
vergaßest du, was du vergabst?

WOTAN
Wohl dünkt mich's, was sie bedangen,
die dort die Burg mir gebaut;
durch Vertrag zähmt' ich
ihr trotzig Gezücht,
daß sie die hehre
Halle mir schüfen;

WOTAN
(gently, still dreaming)
The sacred hall of the gods
is guarded by gate and door:
manhood's honour,
unending power,
rise now to endless renown!

FRICKA
(shakes him.)
Up from your dreams
of flattering deceit!
My husband, wake and consider!

WOTAN
(wakes and raises himself a little; his eyes are at once attracted by the sight of the castle.)
Completed, the eternal work!
On mountain summits
the gods will rule!
Proudly rise
those glittering walls
which in dreams I designed,
which my will brought to life.
Strong and lordly
see it shine;
holy, glorious abode!

FRICKA
Though it delights you,
I am afraid!
You have your hall,
but I think of Freia!
Can I believe you have forgotten
the price you still have to pay?
The work is finished,
the giants must be paid;
remember it, all that you owe!

WOTAN
I've not forgotten the bargain,
the giants shall have their reward;
for that proud race
was subdued by my spear;
graved on its shaft
the terms for the castle.

die steht nun—Dank den Starken:
um den Sold sorge dich nicht.

It stands now; thank the workers,
and forget what it will cost.

FRICKA
O lachend frevelnder Leichtsinn!
Liebelosester Frohmut!
Wußt' ich um euren Vertrag,
dem Truge hätt' ich gewehrt;
  doch mutig entferntet
  ihr Männer die Frauen,
um taub und ruhig vor uns
allein mit den Riesen zu tagen.
  So ohne Scham
  verschenktet ihr Frechen
Freia, mein holdes Geschwister,
froh des Schächergewerbs.
  Was ist euch Harten
  doch heilig und wert,
giert ihr Männer nach Macht!

FRICKA
What carefree, frivolous lightness!
Loveless, coldhearted folly!
If I had known of your deal,
I might have stopped it in time;
  but slyly you men
  did your talking in secret,
and kept us women away;
alone you discussed with the giants.
  Then to your shame
  you promised to give them
Freia, my beautiful sister;
oh, how pleased you were then!
  Nothing is sacred,
  you harden your hearts,
when you men lust for might!

WOTAN
(ruhig)
  Gleiche Gier
  war Fricka wohl fremd,
also selbst um den Bau sie mich bat?

WOTAN
(calmly)
  And is Fricka
  free from reproach?
Remember, you begged for the hall!

FRICKA
Um des Gatten Treue besorgt,
muß traurig ich wohl sinnen,
wie an mich er zu fesseln,
zieht's in die Ferne ihn fort:
  herrliche Wohnung,
  wonniger Hausrat
  sollten dich binden
  zu säumender Rast.
Doch du bei dem Wohnbau sannst
auf Wehr und Wall allein:
  Herrschaft und Macht
  soll er dir mehren;
nur rastlosern Sturm zu erregen,
erstand dir die ragende Burg.

FRICKA
For I wished you faithful and true;
my thoughts were for my husband,
how to keep him beside me
when he was tempted to roam:
  safe in our castle,
  calm and contented,
  there I might keep you
  in peaceful repose.
But you, when you planned it,
thought of war and arms alone:
  glory and might
  all that you cared for;
you built it for storm and adventure—
constructed a fort, not a home.

WOTAN
(lächelnd)
  Wolltest du Frau
  in der Feste mich fangen,
mir Gotte mußt du schon gönnen,

WOTAN
(smiling)
  Wife, though you wish me
  confined in the castle,
some freedom still you must grant me;

daß, in der Burg
gefangen, ich mir
von außen gewinne die Welt.
Wandel und Wechsel
liebt, wer lebt:
das Spiel drum kann ich nicht sparen.

FRICKA
Liebeloser,
leidigster Mann!
Um der Macht und Herrschaft
müßigen Tand
verspielst du in lästerndem Spott
Liebe und Weibes Wert?

WOTAN
(ernst)
Um dich zum Weib zu gewinnen,
mein eines Auge
setzt' ich werbend daran:
wie törig tadelst du jetzt!
Ehr ich die Frauen
doch mehr, als dich freut!
Und Freia, die gute,
geb ich nicht auf:
nie sann dies ernstlich mein Sinn.

FRICKA
(mit ängstlicher Spannung in die Szene blickend)
So schirme sie jetzt;
in schutzloser Angst
läuft sie nach Hilfe dort her!

FREIA
(tritt wie in hastiger Flucht auf.)
Hilf mir, Schwester!
Schütze mich, Schwäher!
Vom Felsen drüben
drohte mir Fasolt,
mich Holde käm' er zu holen.

WOTAN
Laß ihn drohn!
Sahst du nicht Loge?

FRICKA
Daß am liebsten du immer

though I may stay
beside you, yet
from our home I must rule all the world;
wandering and change
inspire my heart;
that sport I cannot relinquish!

FRICKA
Cruel, heartless,
unloving man!
for the vain delights of
ruling the world,
you'd carelessly gamble away
love and woman's worth?

WOTAN
(serious)
Recall the days when I wooed you,
when I for Fricka
paid the price of an eye.
Your scolding is wide of the mark!
I worship women
much more than you'd like;
and Freia, the fair one,
I shall not yield;
such thoughts were far from my mind.

FRICKA
(with anxious tension, looking off-stage)
Then shelter her now;
defenceless, afraid,
see how she runs here for help!

FREIA
(enters in hasty flight.)
Help me, sister!
shelter me, brother!
On yonder mountain
Fasolt is threatening,
and now he's coming to take me.

WOTAN
Let him come!
Saw you not Loge?

FRICKA
In that infamous rogue

dem Listigen traust!
Viel Schlimmes schuf er uns schon,
doch stets bestrickt er dich wieder.

WOTAN
Wo freier Mut frommt,
allein frag ich nach keinem;
doch des Feindes Neid
zum Nutz sich fügen,
lehrt nur Schlauheit und List,
wie Loge verschlagen sie übt.
Der zum Vertrage mir riet,
versprach mir Freia zu lösen:
auf ihn verlaß ich mich nun.

FRICKA
Und er läßt dich allein!
Dort schreiten rasch
die Riesen heran:
wo harrt dein schlauer Gehilf?

FREIA
Wo harren meine Brüder,
daß Hilfe sie brächten,
da mein Schwäher die Schwache
Zu Hilfe, Donner! [verschenkt?
Hieher, hieher!
Rette Freia, mein Froh!

FRICKA
Die im bösen Bund dich verrieten,
sie alle bergen sich nun.
(Fasolt und Fafner, beide in riesiger Gestalt, mit starken Pfählen bewaffnet, treten auf.)

FASOLT
Sanft schloß
Schlaf dein Aug:
wir beide bauten
Schlummers bar die Burg.
Mächt'ger Müh
müde nie,
stauten starke
Stein' wir auf;
steiler Turm,
Tür und Tor
deckt und schließt

do you still put your trust?
Much harm he's done to the gods,
yet time and again you still use him.

WOTAN
Where simple truth serves,
I need no one to help me;
but to use the hate
of foes to serve me—
that needs guile and deceit;
then Loge's the one for the deed.
He said he'd think of a plan
to keep our Freia in safety;
so I rely on him now.

FRICKA
And he leaves you alone!
Here come the giants
seeking their pay,
while Loge loiters afar!

FREIA
Come here to me, my brothers,
Oh help me and save me,
now that Wotan abandons the weak!
Oh help me, Donner!
Hear me, help me!
Rescue Freia, my Froh!

FRICKA
The disgraceful men who betrayed you
have all abandoned you now!
(Fasolt and Fafner enter, both of gigantic stature, and armed with stout clubs.)

FASOLT
Soft sleep
closed your eyes,
while we were working
hard to build your hall.
Working hard,
day and night,
heavy stones
we heaped up high,
lofty towers,
gates and doors,
guard and keep

im schlanken Schloß den Saal.
(auf die Burg deutend)
Dort steht's,
was wir stemmten;
schimmernd hell
bescheint's der Tag:
zieh nun ein,
uns zahl den Lohn!

WOTAN
Nennt, Leute, den Lohn:
was dünkt euch zu bedingen?

FASOLT
Bedungen ist's,
was tauglich uns dünkt:
gemahnt es dich so matt?
Freia, die holde,
Holda, die freie—
vertragen ist's—
sie tragen wir heim.

WOTAN
(schnell)
Seid ihr bei Trost
mit eurem Vertrag?
Denkt auf andren Dank:
Freia ist mir nicht feil.

FASOLT
(steht, in höchster Bestürzung, einen Augenblick sprachlos.)
Was sagst du? Ha,
sinnst du Verrat?
Verrat am Vertrag?
Die dein Speer birgt,
sind sie dir Spiel,
des beratnen Bundes Runen?

FAFNER
(höhnisch)
Getreuster Bruder!
Merkst du Tropf nun Betrug?

FASOLT
Lichtsohn du,
leicht gefügter,

your castle walls secure.
(pointing to the castle)
There stands
what you ordered,
shining bright
in morning light.
There's your home;
we want our wage!

WOTAN
You've earned your reward;
what wages are you asking?

FASOLT
The price was fixed,
our bargain was made;
have you so soon forgot?
Freia, the fair one,
Holda, the free one—
your hall is built
and Freia is ours.

WOTAN
(quickly)
Plainly your work
has blinded your wits.
Ask some other wage:
Freia cannot be sold.

FASOLT
(utterly amazed, is for a moment speechless.)
What's this now? Ha!
Breaking your bond?
Betraying your word?
On your spear shaft,
read what is graved;
would you dare to break your bargain?

FAFNER
(scornfully)
My trusting brother,
now do you see his deceit?

FASOLT
God of light,
light of spirit!

hör und hüte dich:
Verträgen halte Treu!
  Was du bist,
bist du nur durch Verträge:
  bedungen ist,
wohl bedacht deine Macht.
  Bist weiser du,
  als witzig wir sind,
  bandest uns Freie
  zum Frieden du:
all deinem Wissen fluch ich,
fliehe weit deinen Frieden,
  weißt du nicht offen,
  ehrlich und frei
Verträgen zu wahren die Treu!
  Ein dummer Riese
  rät dir das:
du, Weiser, wiss' es von ihm!

WOTAN
Wie schlau für Ernst du achtest,
was wir zum Scherz nur beschlossen!
  Die liebliche Göttin,
  licht und leicht,
was taugt euch Tölpeln ihr Reiz?

FASOLT
  Höhnst du uns?
  Ha, wie unrecht!
Die ihr durch Schönheit herrscht,
schimmernd hehres Geschlecht,
  wie törig strebt ihr
  nach Türmen von Stein,
setzt um Burg und Saal
Weibes Wonne zum Pfand!
Wir Plumpen plagen uns
schwitzend mit schwieliger Hand,
  ein Weib zu gewinnen,
  das wonnig und mild
bei uns Armen wohne:
und verkehrt nennst du den Kauf?

FAFNER
Schweig dein faules Schwatzen,
Gewinn werben wir nicht:
  Freias Haft
  hilft wenig;

hear a giant's advice,
and learn to keep your word!
  What you are,
you became by your bargains;
  you base your power
on the bonds there defined.
  Since you are wise,
  we giants were bound;
  freely we promised
  to keep the peace;
yet I shall curse your wisdom;
war, not peace, will reward you
  if you don't fairly,
  frankly uphold
the terms of the bargain you swore!
  This simple giant
  speaks his mind:
you wise one, learn now from him.

WOTAN
How sly to take in earnest
what as a joke we decided!
  The beautiful goddess,
  fair and bright,
what use can she be to you?

FASOLT
  How unjust!
  Wotan mocks us!
You who through beauty reign,
glittering, glorious race,
  like fools you yearned
  for your towers of stone;
pledged as pay for your hall
woman's beauty and grace.
We dull ones toil away,
sweat with our work-hardened hands;
  we longed for a woman,
  so charming and fair,
to grace our poor dwelling—
and you say all was a joke?

FAFNER
Stop your foolish chatter;
the girl's not what we want.
  Freia's charms
  mean nothing,

doch viel gilt's,
den Göttern sie zu entführen.
Goldne Äpfel
wachsen in ihrem Garten;
sie allein
weiß die Äpfel zu pflegen!
Der Frucht Genuß
frommt ihren Sippen
zu ewig nie
alternder Jugend;
siech und bleich
doch sinkt ihre Blüte,
alt und schwach
schwinden sie hin,
müssen Freia sie missen.
Ihrer Mitte drum sei sie entführt!

WOTAN
(für sich)
Loge säumt zu lang!

FASOLT
Schlicht gib nun Bescheid!

WOTAN
Sinnt auf andern Sold!

FASOLT
Kein andrer: Freia allein!

FAFNER
Du da, folge uns!
(Sie dringen auf Freia zu. Donner und Froh kommen eilig.)

FREIA
(fliehend)
Helft, helft vor den Harten!

FROH
(Freia in seine Arme fassend)
Zu mir, Freia!
Meide sie, Frecher!
Froh schützt die Schöne.

DONNER
(sich vor die beiden Riesen stellend)
Fasolt und Fafner,

but we gain
as soon as the gods have lost her.
Golden apples
ripen within her garden,
she alone
knows how they are tended;
that golden fruit
given to her kinsmen
each day renews
youth everlasting:
pale and grey
they'll lose all their beauty,
wan and weak
they will grow old,
when that fruit is denied them.
And that's why we'll take her away!

WOTAN
(aside)
Loge lingers long!

FASOLT
Well, what shall it be?

WOTAN
Ask some other wage!

FASOLT
No other: Freia alone!

FAFNER
You there! Come with us!
(They make towards Freia. Donner and Froh rush in.)

FREIA
(fleeing)
Help! Help from these hard ones!

FROH
(clasping Freia in his arms)
To me, Freia!
Back from her, giant!
Froh shields the fair one!

DONNER
(planting himself before the two giants)
Fasolt and Fafner,

fühltet ihr schon
meines Hammers harten Schlag?

FAFNER
Was soll das Drohn?

FASOLT
Was dringst du her?
Kampf kiesten wir nicht,
verlangen nur unsern Lohn.

DONNER
Schon oft zahlt' ich
Riesen den Zoll;
kommt her! Des Lohnes Last
wäg ich mit gutem Gewicht!
(Er schwingt den Hammer.)

WOTAN
(seinen Speer zwischen den Streitenden ausstreckend)
Halt, du Wilder!
Nichts durch Gewalt!
Verträge schützt
meines Speeres Schaft:
spar deines Hammers Heft!

FREIA
Wehe! Wehe!
Wotan verläßt mich!

FRICKA
Begreif ich dich noch,
grausamer Mann?

WOTAN
(wendet sich ab und sieht Loge kommen.)
Endlich Loge!
Eiltest du so,
den du geschlossen,
den schlimmen Handel zu schlichten?

LOGE
(ist im Hintergrunde aus dem Tale heraufgestiegen.)
Wie? Welchen Handel
hätt' ich geschlossen?
Wohl was mit den Riesen

know you the weight
of my hammer's heavy blow?

FAFNER
What is this threat?

FASOLT
What brings you here?
We've not come to fight,
but all we want is our pay.

DONNER
And I know
how giants should be paid.
Come here, receive your wage,
weighed with a generous hand.
(He swings his hammer.)

WOTAN
(stretching out his spear between the disputants)
Back, you wild one!
Force will not serve!
This bond is graved
on my spear's strong shaft:
spare them your hammer's blow!

FREIA
Help me! Help me!
Wotan forsakes me!

FRICKA
Is this your resolve,
merciless man?

WOTAN
(turns round and sees Loge approaching.)
There is Loge!
Where have you been,
you who assured me
that I'd escape from this contract?

LOGE
(has climbed up from the valley at the back.)
What? How am I
concerned in a contract?
Do you mean that agreement

dort im Rate du dangst?
   In Tiefen und Höhen
   treibt mich mein Hang;
   Haus und Herd
   behagt mir nicht:
   Donner und Froh,
die denken an Dach und Fach!
   Wollen sie frein,
ein Haus muß sie erfreun.
   Ein stolzer Saal,
   ein starkes Schloß,
danach stand Wotans Wunsch.
   Haus und Hof,
   Saal und Schloß,
   die selige Burg,
sie steht nun fest gebaut;
   das Prachtgemäuer
   prüft' ich selbst;
   ob alles fest,
   forscht' ich genau:
   Fasolt und Fafner
   fand ich bewährt;
kein Stein wankt im Gestemm.
   Nicht müßig war ich,
   wie mancher hier:
der lügt, wer lässig mich schilt!

WOTAN
   Arglistig
   weichst du mir aus:
   mich zu betrügen
hüte in Treuen dich wohl!
   Von allen Göttern
   dein einz'ger Freund,
   nahm ich dich auf
in der übel trauenden Troß.
Nun red und rate klug!
Da einst die Bauer der Burg
zum Dank Freia bedangen,
   du weißt, nicht anders
   willigt' ich ein,
als weil auf Pflicht du gelobtest,
zu lösen das hehre Pfand.

LOGE
   Mit höchster Sorge
   drauf zu sinnen,

you have made with these giants?
   I roam through the whole wide
   world as I please:
   I'm not held
   by house or home.
   Donner and Froh
are dreaming of household joys!
   If they would wed,
a house first they must own.
   And castle walls,
   and lofty halls,
they were what Wotan craved.
   Lofty halls,
   castle walls,
   a home for the gods—
it stands there, strongly built.
   I inspected all
   the place myself;
   it's firmly made,
   safe and secure:
   Fasolt and Fafner,
   excellent work!
No stone stirs on its bed.
   So I was not lazy,
   like others here;
he lies, who says that I was!

WOTAN
   Don't try
   to escape from the point!
   If you betray me,
if you have tricked me, beware!
   Recall that I
   am your only friend,
   I took your part
when the other gods were unkind.
So speak, I need your help!
When first those giants made terms
and asked Freia as payment,
   you know I only
   gave my consent
because you promised you would find
something else they would rather have.

LOGE
   I merely promised
   I'd consider

wie es zu lösen,
das—hab ich gelobt.
Doch daß ich fände,
was nie sich fügt,
was nie gelingt,
wie ließ' sich das wohl geloben?

how we might save her—
and that's all I said.
But to discover
what can't be found,
what never was—
who'd ever make such a promise?

FRICKA
(zu Wotan)
Sieh, welch trugvollem
Schelm du getraut!

FRICKA
(to Wotan)
That's the knave
whom you thought you could trust!

FROH
Loge heißt du,
doch nenn ich dich Lüge!

FROH
Loge, hear me,
your name should be Liar!

DONNER
Verfluchte Lohe,
dich lösch ich aus!

DONNER
Accursed Loge,
I'll quench your flame!

LOGE
Ihre Schmach zu decken
schmähen mich Dumme.
(Donner holt auf Loge aus.)

LOGE
To conceal his blunders
every fool blames me!
(Donner threatens Loge.)

WOTAN
(tritt dazwischen.)
In Frieden laßt mir den Freund!
Nicht kennt ihr Loges Kunst:
reicher wiegt
seines Rates Wert,
zahlt er zögernd ihn aus.

WOTAN
(intervening)
Now cease reviling my friend!
You know not Loge's ways:
his advice
is worth all the more,
when we wait on his words.

FAFNER
Nicht gezögert!
Rasch gezahlt!

FAFNER
Wait no longer!
Pay our wage!

FASOLT
Lang währt's mit dem Lohn.

FASOLT
Come, no more delay!

WOTAN
(wendet sich hart zu Loge, drängend.)
Jetzt hör, Störrischer!
Halte Stich!
Wo schweiftest du hin und her?

WOTAN
(turning sharply to Loge, urgently)
Speak out, stubborn one!
Keep your word!
And tell me now where you've been.

LOGE
Immer ist Undank

LOGE
Never one word

Loges Lohn!
Um dich nur besorgt,
sah ich mich um,
durchstöbert' im Sturm
alle Winkel der Welt,
Ersatz für Freia zu suchen,
wie er den Riesen wohl recht.
Umsonst sucht' ich
und sehe nun wohl,
in der Welten Ring
nichts ist so reich,
als Ersatz zu muten dem Mann
für Weibes Wonne und Wert.
(Alle geraten in Erstaunen und verschiedenartige Betroffenheit.)
So weit Leben und Weben,
in Wasser, Erd und Luft,
viel frug ich,
forschte bei allen,
wo Kraft nur sich rührt
und Keime sich regen:
was wohl dem Manne
mächtiger dünk'
als Weibes Wonne und Wert?
Doch so weit Leben und Weben,
verlacht nur ward
meine fragende List:
in Wasser, Erd und Luft
lassen will nichts
von Lieb und Weib.
Nur einen sah ich,
der sagte der Liebe ab:
um rotes Gold
entriet er des Weibes Gunst.
Des Rheines klare Kinder
klagten mir ihre Not:
der Nibelung,
Nacht-Alberich,
buhlte vergebens
um der Badenden Gunst;
das Rheingold da
raubte sich rächend der Dieb:
das dünkt ihm nun
das teuerste Gut,
hehrer als Weibes Huld.
Um den gleißenden Tand,
der Tiefe entwandt,

of praise or thanks!
For your sake alone,
hoping to help,
I restlessly roamed
to the ends of the earth,
to find a ransom for Freia,
one that the giants would like more.
I sought vainly,
but one thing I learnt:
in this whole wide world
nothing at all
is of greater worth to a man
than woman's beauty and love!
(All express astonishment and diverse forms of bewilderment.)
I asked every one living,
in water, earth, and sky,
one question;
sought for the answer
from all whom I met;
I asked them this question:
What in this world
means more to you
than woman's beauty and love?
But wherever life was stirring
they laughed at me
when they heard what I asked.
In water, earth, and sky,
none would forego
the joys of love.
But one I found then
who scorned the delights of love,
who valued gold
more dearly than woman's grace.
The fair and shining Rhinemaids
came to me with their tale:
the Nibelung dwarf,
Alberich,
begged for their favours,
but he begged them in vain;
the Rhinegold
he tore in revenge from their rock;
and now he holds it
dearer than love,
greater than woman's grace.
For their glittering toy,
thus torn from the deep,

erklang mir der Töchter Klage:
 an dich, Wotan,
 wenden sie sich,
daß zu Recht du zögest den Räuber,
 das Gold dem Wasser
 wiedergebest
und ewig es bliebe ihr Eigen.
 Dir's zu melden
 gelobt' ich den Mädchen:
nun löste Loge sein Wort.

WOTAN
 Törig bist du,
 wenn nicht gar tückisch!
Mich selbst siehst du in Not:
wie hülf ich andern zum Heil?

FASOLT
(der aufmerksam zugehört, zu Fafner)
Nicht gönn ich das Gold dem Alben,
viel Not schon schuf uns der Niblung,
doch schlau entschlüpfte unserm
Zwange immer der Zwerg.

FAFNER
 Neue Neidtat
 sinnt uns der Niblung,
gibt das Gold ihm Macht.
 Du da, Loge!
 Sag ohne Lug:
was Großes gilt denn das Gold,
daß es dem Niblung genügt?

LOGE
 Ein Tand ist's
 in des Wassers Tiefe,
lachenden Kindern zur Lust:
 doch, ward es zum runden
 Reife geschmiedet,
hilft es zur höchsten Macht,
gewinnt dem Manne die Welt.

WOTAN
(sinnend)
 Von des Rheines Gold
 hört' ich raunen:
 Beute-Runen

the maidens are sadly mourning:
 They turn, Wotan,
 sadly to you,
for they hope that you will avenge them;
 the gold—they pray
 that you'll restore it,
to shine in the waters for ever.
 So I promised
 I'd tell you the story;
and that's what Loge has done.

WOTAN
 Are you mad,
 or simply malicious?
You know I am in need;
how can I help some one else?

FASOLT
(who has been listening attentively, to Fafner)
That gold I begrudge to Alberich;
we've suffered much from the Niblung,
and yet that crafty dwarf
has always slipped through our hands.

FAFNER
 We shall suffer
 more in the future,
now he's gained the gold.
 You there, Loge!
 tell me the truth;
what glory lies in the gold,
that the Niblung holds so dear?

LOGE
 A toy, while
 it was in the waters,
lighting the Rhinemaidens' games;
 but when as a shining
 ring it is fashioned,
helped by its magic power,
its owner conquers the world.

WOTAN
(reflectively)
 I have heard men tell
 of the Rhinegold:
 charms of riches

berge sein roter Glanz,
  Macht und Schätze
schüf' ohne Maß ein Reif.

FRICKA
(leise zu Loge)
  Taugte wohl
  des goldnen Tandes
  gleißend Geschmeid
auch Frauen zu schönem Schmuck?

LOGE
  Des Gatten Treu
  ertrotzte die Frau,
  trüge sie hold
  den hellen Schmuck,
den schimmernd Zwerge schmieden,
rührig im Zwange des Reifs.

FRICKA
(schmeichelnd zu Wotan)
  Gewänne mein Gatte
  sich wohl das Gold?

WOTAN
(wie in einem Zustande wachsender Bezauberung)
  Des Reifes zu walten,
rätlich will es mich dünken.
  Doch wie, Loge,
  lernt' ich die Kunst?
Wie schüf' ich mir das Geschmeid?

LOGE
  Ein Runenzauber
zwingt das Gold zum Reif.
  Keiner kennt ihn;
doch einer übt ihn leicht,
der sel'ger Lieb entsagt.
(Wotan wendet sich unmutig ab.)
  Das sparst du wohl;
  zu spät auch kämst du:
Alberich zauderte nicht;
  zaglos gewann er
  des Zaubers Macht:
geraten ist ihm der Ring.

DONNER
(zu Wotan)
  Zwang uns allen

lurk in that golden gleam;
  mighty powers
are his who can forge that ring.

FRICKA
(softly to Loge)
  Could a woman use
  the golden ring
  for herself,
and wear it to charm her lord?

LOGE
  No husband dare
  be false to his wife
  when she commands
  that glittering wealth
that busy dwarfs are forging,
ruled by the power of the ring.

FRICKA
(cajolingly, to Wotan)
  Oh, how can my husband
  win us the gold?

WOTAN
(as if in a state of increasing enchantment)
  And I should possess it!
Soon this ring should be Wotan's.
  But say, Loge,
  what is the art
by which the gold can be forged?

LOGE
  A magic spell
can change the gold to a ring.
  No one knows it,
but he who would use the spell
must curse the joys of love.
(Wotan turns away in ill-humour.)
  Could you do that?
  Too late, in any case,
Alberich did not delay;
  he cursed and mastered
  the magic spell;
and he is lord of the ring!

DONNER
(to Wotan)
  We shall all

schüfe der Zwerg,
würd' ihm der Reif nicht entrissen.

WOTAN
Den Ring muß ich haben!

FROH
Leicht erringt
ohne Liebesfluch er sich jetzt.

LOGE
Spottleicht,
ohne Kunst wie im Kinderspiel!

WOTAN
(grell)
So rate, wie?

LOGE
Durch Raub!
Was ein Dieb stahl,
das stiehlst du dem Dieb:
ward leichter ein Eigen erlangt?
Doch mit arger Wehr
wahrt sich Alberich;
klug und fein
mußt du verfahren,
ziehst du den Räuber zu Recht,
um des Rheines Töchtern
den roten Tand,
das Gold, wiederzugeben;
denn darum flehen sie dich.

WOTAN
Des Rheines Töchter?
Was taugt mir der Rat?

FRICKA
Von dem Wassergezücht
mag ich nichts wissen:
schon manchen Mann
—mir zum Leid—
verlockten sie buhlend im Bad.
(Wotan steht stumm mit sich kämpfend; die übrigen Götter heften in schweigender Spannung die Blicke auf ihn. Währenddem hat Fafner beiseite mit Fasolt beraten.)

be slaves to the dwarf
unless the ring can be captured.

WOTAN
The ring—I must have it!

FROH
Easily done,
now that love you need not renounce.

LOGE
Child's play!
at a stroke you can make it yours!

WOTAN
(harshly)
Then tell me, how?

LOGE
By theft!
What a thief stole,
you steal from the thief;
you seize it and make it your own!
But you'll need your wits
fighting Alberich;
he'll defend
what he has stolen,
so be skilful, swift and shrewd
if you'd please the Rhinemaids,
and then restore
their gold, back to the waters.
They yearn and cry for their gold.

WOTAN
To please the Rhinemaids?
That's not what I plan!

FRICKA
Leave that watery brood
weeping and wailing;
to my distress,
many a man
they've lured by their charms to the Rhine.
(Wotan is struggling silently with himself. The other gods, tense and silent, look fixedly at him. Meanwhile, to one side, Fafner has quietly been conferring with Fasolt.)

FAFNER
(zu Fasolt)
Glaub mir, mehr als Freia
frommt das gleißende Gold:
auch ew'ge Jugend erjagt,
wer durch Goldes Zauber sie zwingt.
(Fasolts Gebärde deutet an, daß er sich wider Willen überredet fühlt. Fafner tritt mit Fasolt wieder an Wotan heran.)
Hör, Wotan,
der Harrenden Wort!
Freia bleib' euch in Frieden;
leichtren Lohn
fand ich zur Lösung:
uns rauhen Riesen genügt
des Niblungen rotes Gold.

WOTAN
Seid ihr bei Sinn?
Was nicht ich besitze,
soll ich euch Schamlosen schenken?

FAFNER
Schwer baute
dort sich die Burg:
leicht wird's dir
mit list'ger Gewalt,
was im Neidspiel nie uns gelang,
den Niblungen fest zu fahn.

WOTAN
Für euch müht' ich
mich um den Alben?
Für euch fing ich den Feind?
Unverschämt
und überbegehrlich
macht euch Dumme mein Dank!

FASOLT
(ergreift plötzlich Freia und führt sie mit Fafner zur Seite.)
Hieher, Maid!
In unsre Macht!
Als Pfand folgst du uns jetzt,
bis wir Lösung empfahn.

FREIA
(wehklagend)
Wehe! Wehe! Weh!

FAFNER
(to Fasolt)
Trust me, more than Freia
we can gain from the gold:
eternal youth can be ours,
when we lay our hands on that gold.
(Fasolt's demeanour suggests that he has been persuaded against his will. Fafner, with Fasolt, returns to Wotan again.)
Hear, Wotan,
I'll speak my last word!
We will leave you with Freia;
we will take less
for our payment:
for us rude giants, enough
is Nibelheim's shining gold.

WOTAN
Have you gone mad?
For how can I give you
what is not mine, as your payment?

FAFNER
Hard labour
built you those walls;
your cunning
can lightly achieve
what has proved too hard for our
to capture the Niblung foe. [strength,

WOTAN
For you must I
deal with the Niblung?
for you, capture the foe?
Unashamed, you dare
to propose it,
stupid, insolent pair!

FASOLT
(suddenly seizes Freia and, with Fafner, pulls her to one side.)
Come here, maid!
You're in our power!
We'll hold you as a hostage
till all has been paid!

FREIA
(crying out in dismay)
Save me! Save me! Woe!

(Alle Götter sind in höchster Bestürzung.)

FAFNER
Fort von hier
sei sie entführt!
Bis Abend, achtet's wohl,
pflegen wir sie als Pfand:
wir kehren wieder;
doch kommen wir,
und bereit liegt nicht als Lösung
das Rheingold licht und rot—

FASOLT
Zu End ist die Frist dann,
Freia verfallen:
für immer folge sie uns!

FREIA
(schreiend)
Schwester! Brüder!
Rettet! Helft!
(Sie wird von den hastig enteilenden Riesen fortgetragen.)

FROH
Auf, ihnen nach!

DONNER
Breche denn alles!
(Sie blicken Wotan fragend an.)

FREIA
(aus weiter Ferne)
Rettet! Helft!

LOGE
(den Riesen nachsehend)
Über Stock und Stein zu Tal
stapfen sie hin;
durch des Rheines Wasserfurt
waten die Riesen:
fröhlich nicht
hängt Freia
den Rauhen über dem Rücken!
Heia! hei!
Wie taumeln die Tölpel dahin!

(All the gods are dismayed.)

FAFNER
We shall take
Freia with us!
Till evening, mark me well,
she remains in our hands;
then we'll return
but when we come,
if we don't find what we have asked for,
the Rhinegold heaped on high—

FASOLT
—our truce then is over;
Freia is forfeit;
forever she stays with us!

FREIA
(screaming)
Sister! Brothers!
Save me! Help!
(She is dragged away by the hastily departing giants.)

FROH
On, to her aid!

DONNER
Everything's ended!
(They look inquiringly at Wotan.)

FREIA
(from the distance)
Save me! Help!

LOGE
(gazing after the giants)
Over rock and stone they stride,
down to the vale;
through the Rhine they forge ahead,
waddling and wading.
Sad at heart
hangs Freia,
while borne on the backs of those ruffians!
Heia! hei!
They stumble and stride on their way!

Durch das Tal talpen sie schon:
wohl an Riesenheims Mark
erst halten sie Rast!
(Er wendet sich zu den Göttern.)
Was sinnt nun Wotan so wild?
Den seligen Göttern wie geht's?
(Ein fahler Nebel erfüllt mit wachsender Dichtheit die Bühne; in ihm erhalten die Götter ein zunehmend bleiches und ältliches Aussehen: alle stehen bang und erwartungsvoll auf Wotan blickend, der sinnend die Augen an den Boden heftet.)
Trügt mich ein Nebel?
Neckt mich ein Traum?
Wie bang und bleich
verblüht ihr so bald!
Euch erlischt der Wangen Licht;
der Blick eures Auges verblitzt!
Frisch, mein Froh,
noch ist's ja früh!
Deiner Hand, Donner,
entsinkt ja der Hammer!
Was ist's mit Fricka?
Freut sie sich wenig
ob Wotans grämlichem Grau,
das schier zum Greisen ihn schafft?

FRICKA
Wehe! Wehe!
Was ist geschehn?

DONNER
Mir sinkt die Hand.

FROH
Mir stockt das Herz.

LOGE
Jetzt fand ich's: hört, was euch fehlt!
Von Freias Frucht
genosset ihr heute noch nicht:
die goldnen Äpfel
in ihrem Garten,
sie machten euch tüchtig und jung,
aßt ihr sie jeden Tag.
Des Gartens Pflegerin
ist nun verpfändet;
an den Ästen darbt

Now they're through, climbing the slope.
They'll not rest till they've reached
rough Riesenheim's bounds.
(He turns to the gods.)
Why is Wotan brooding and sad?
Alas, what's troubling the gods?
(A pale mist, growing denser, fills the scene: it gives the gods an increasingly wan and aged appearance: fearful, they all stand gazing expectantly at Wotan, who is lost in thought, his eyes fixed on the ground.)

Mists, do you deceive me?
Is this a dream?
How grey you've grown,
so weary and weak!
From your cheeks the bloom dies out;
the flash from your eyes fades away!
Come, my Froh!
Day is still young!
From your hand, Donner,
you're dropping the hammer!
What's wrong with Fricka?
Can she be mourning
that Wotan, gloomy and grey,
should seem so suddenly old?

FRICKA
Sorrow! Sorrow!
What can it mean?

DONNER
My hand is weak!

FROH
My heart is still!

LOGE
I see now! Hear what is wrong!
Of Freia's fruit
you've not yet eaten today.
The golden apples
that grow in her garden,
they kept you so vigorous and young,
eating them every day.
But she who tended them
now is a hostage;
on the branches droops

und dorrt das Obst:
bald fällt faul es herab.
Mich kümmert's minder;
an mir ja kargte
Freia von je
knausernd die köstliche Frucht:
denn halb so echt nur
bin ich wie, Selige, ihr!
Doch ihr setztet alles
auf das jüngende Obst:
das wußten die Riesen wohl;
auf euer Leben
legten sie's an:
nun sorgt, wie ihr das wahrt!
Ohne die Äpfel,
alt und grau,
greis und grämlich,
welkend zum Spott aller Welt,
erstirbt der Götter Stamm.

FRICKA
Wotan, Gemahl,
unsel'ger Mann!
Sieh, wie dein Leichtsinn
lachend uns allen
Schimpf und Schmach erschuf!

WOTAN
(mit plötzlichem Entschluß auffahrend)
Auf, Loge,
hinab mit mir!
Nach Nibelheim fahren wir nieder:
gewinnen will ich das Gold.

LOGE
Die Rheintöchter
riefen dich an:
so dürfen Erhörung sie hoffen?

WOTAN
Schweige, Schwätzer!
Freia, die gute,
Freia gilt es zu lösen.

LOGE
Wie du befiehlst,
führ ich dich schnell

and dies the fruit;
it rots, falls to the ground.
To me it's nothing;
because to Loge
Freia was mean;
I never tasted her fruit:
so I'm not god-like,
I'm not so glorious as you!
But you staked your future
on that youth-giving fruit;
the giants knew that all too well;
and at your lives
this blow has been aimed;
so think how to escape!
Lacking the apples,
old and grey,
worn and weary,
withered and scorned by the world,
the gods grow old and die.

FRICKA
Wotan, my lord!
Unhappy man!
See how your selfish
folly has brought us
sore disgrace and shame!

WOTAN
(starts up with sudden resolve.)
Come, Loge,
descend with me!
To Nibelheim we'll go together:
and there I'll win me the gold.

LOGE
The Rhinemaidens
called for your help:
so will you return them their treasure?

WOTAN
Stop your chatter!
Freia, the fair one,
Freia has to be rescued!

LOGE
As you command,
down we shall go.

steil hinab:
steigen wir denn durch den Rhein?

WOTAN
Nicht durch den Rhein!

LOGE
So schwingen wir uns
durch die Schwefelkluft?
Dort schlüpfe mit mir hinein!
(Er geht voran und verschwindet seitwärts in einer Kluft, aus der sogleich ein schwefliger Dampf hervorquillt.)

WOTAN
Ihr andern harrt
bis Abend hier:
verlorner Jugend
erjag ich erlösendes Gold!
(Er steigt Loge nach in die Kluft hinab: der aus ihr dringende Schwefeldampf verbreitet sich über die ganze Bühne und erfüllt diese schnell mit dickem Gewölk. Bereits sind die Zurückbleibenden unsichtbar.)

DONNER
Fahre wohl, Wotan!

FROH
Glück auf! Glück auf!

FRICKA
O kehre bald
zur bangenden Frau!
(Der Schwefeldampf verdüstert sich bis zu ganz schwarzem Gewölk, welches von unten nach oben steigt; dann verwandelt sich dieses in festes, finstres Steingeklüft, das sich immer aufwärts bewegt, so daß es den Anschein hat, als sänke die Szene immer tiefer in die Erde hinab. Wachsendes Geräusch wie von Schmiedenden wird überallher vernommen.)

Choose your way:
shall we descend through the Rhine?

WOTAN
Not through the Rhine!

LOGE
Then follow my steps
through this smoky cleft:
and slip down there after me!
(He goes ahead and disappears sideways into a crevice, from which at once a sulphurous vapour rises.)

WOTAN
You others wait
till evening falls:
the youth we're losing
I'll buy back again with the gold!
(He descends through the crevice after Loge. The sulphurous steam emerging from it spreads across the entire stage and rapidly fills it with thick clouds. The remaining gods are already invisible.)

DONNER
Fare you well, Wotan!

FROH
Good luck! Good luck!

FRICKA
And soon return
to your sorrowing wife!
(The sulphurous vapour darkens into completely black cloud, which ascends from below to above. This is then transformed into a solid, dark rocky crevice, moving continually upwards so as to give the impression that the stage is sinking deeper into the earth. An increasing clamour, as of forging, is heard on all sides.)

Dritte Szene

Von verschiedenen Seiten her dämmert aus der Ferne dunkelroter Schein auf: eine unabsehbar weit sich dahinziehende

Unterirdische Kluft

wird erkennbar, die nach allen Seiten hin in enge Schachte auszumünden scheint.

Alberich zerrt den kreischenden Mime an den Ohren aus einer Seitenschlucht herbei.

ALBERICH
Hehe! hehe!
Hieher! hieher!
Tückischer Zwerg!
Tapfer gezwickt
sollst du mir sein,
schaffst du nicht fertig,

Scene Three

A dark red glow shines from various quarters in the distance.

A Subterranean Cavern

stretching further than the eye can reach, becomes visible. It seems to open on every side into narrow shafts.
Alberich tugs Mime, who is screeching, by the ear out of a shaft at the side.

ALBERICH
Hehe! hehe!
Come here! Come here!
Treacherous imp!
You will be pinched,
painfully pricked
if it's not ready,

wie ich's bestellt,
zur Stund das feine Geschmeid!

MIME
(heulend)
Ohe! Ohe!
Au! Au!
Laß mich nur los!
Fertig ist's,
wie du befahlst;
mit Fleiß und Schweiß
ist es gefügt:
nimm nur die Nägel vom Ohr!

ALBERICH
(loslassend)
Was zögerst du dann
und zeigst es nicht?

MIME
Ich Armer zagte,
daß noch was fehle.

ALBERICH
Was wär' noch nicht fertig?

MIME
(verlegen)
Hier . . . und da.

ALBERICH
Was hier und da?
Her das Geschmeid!
(Er will ihm wieder an das Ohr fahren; vor Schreck läßt Mime ein metallenes Gewirke, das er krampfhaft in den Händen hielt, sich entfallen. Alberich hebt es hastig auf und prüft es genau.)
Schau, du Schelm!
Alles geschmiedet
und fertig gefügt,
wie ich's befahl!
So wollte der Tropf
schlau mich betrügen,
für sich behalten
das hehre Geschmeid,
das meine List
ihn zu schmieden gelehrt?
Kenn ich dich dummen Dieb?

flawlessly forged,
that helm I told you to make!

MIME
(howling)
Ohe! Ohe!
Ow! Ow!
Leave me alone!
All's been done,
just as you asked;
I toiled away,
finished the work.
Only stop twisting my ear!

ALBERICH
(letting him go)
Then why did you wait?
I want it now!

MIME
I wasn't certain
of every detail.

ALBERICH
And what is not finished?

MIME
(embarrassed)
Here—and there—

ALBERICH
What 'here' and 'there'?
Give me the thing!
(He makes for Mime's ear again. Mime in his terror lets fall a piece of metalwork that he was clutching tightly in his hands. Alberich rapidly picks it up and examines it closely.)
Ha, you rogue!
Everything's perfect
and carefully forged,
just as I asked!
But maybe the fool
thought he could trick me,
and keep this wonderful
work for himself—
work which my cunning
had taught him to forge!
Villain do I read your mind?

(Er setzt das Gewirk als »Tarnhelm« auf den Kopf.)

Dem Haupt fügt sich der Helm:
ob sich der Zauber auch zeigt?
»Nacht und Nebel,
niemand gleich!«

(Seine Gestalt verschwindet; statt ihrer gewahrt man eine Nebelsäule.)

Siehst du mich, Bruder?

MIME
(blickt sich verwundert um.)
Wo bist du? Ich sehe dich nicht.

ALBERICH
(unsichtbar)
So fühle mich doch,
du fauler Schuft!
Nimm das für dein Diebesgelüst!

MIME
(schreit und windet sich unter empfangenen Geißelhieben, deren Fall man vernimmt, ohne die Geißel selbst zu sehen).
Ohe! Ohe!
Au! Au! Au!

ALBERICH
(lachend, unsichtbar)
Hahahahahaha!
Hab Dank, du Dummer!
Dein Werk bewährt sich gut.
Hoho! hoho!
Niblungen all,
neigt euch nun Alberich!
Überall weilt er nun,
euch zu bewachen;
Ruh und Rast
ist euch zerronnen;
ihm müßt ihr schaffen,
wo nicht ihr ihn schaut;
wo nicht ihr ihn gewahrt,
seid seiner gewärtig:
untertan seid ihr ihm immer!
Hoho! hoho!
Hört ihn, er naht:
der Niblungen Herr!

(Die Nebelsäule verschwindet dem Hintergrunde

(He puts the metalwork on his head, as a 'Tarnhelm'.)

The helm fits on my head:
now will the spell do its work?
'Night and darkness,
fade from sight!'

(His form disappears. In its place is seen a a column of vapour.)

Where am I, brother?

MIME
(looks around in astonishment.)
Where are you? You've gone from my [sight.

ALBERICH
(invisible)
Then feel me instead,
you lazy rogue!
I'll teach you to steal from me!

MIME
(screams, and writhes under the blows of a scourge, whose strokes can be heard though it is invisible.)
Ohe! Ohe!
Ow! Ow! Ow!

ALBERICH
(laughing, invisible)
Hahahahahaha!
I thank you, brother!
Your work was true and good.
Hoho! hoho!
Niblungs below,
bow down to Alberich!
I shall be watching
to see that you're working;
day and night
you must be toiling,
sweating to serve
your invisible lord,
who can watch you unseen
and spy on his subjects!
You are my slaves now for ever!
Hoho! hoho!
Hear me, I'm near—
the Niblungs' great lord!

(The column of vapour disappears towards the

zu: man hört in immer weiterer Ferne Alberichs Toben und Zanken; Geheul und Geschrei antwortet ihm, das sich endlich in immer weiterer Ferne unhörbar verliert. Mime ist vor Schmerz zusammengesunken. Wotan und Loge lassen sich aus einer Schlucht von oben herab.)

back. Alberich's raging and scolding are heard receding into the distance. Screams and cries answer him, from further and further away, until at last they are inaudible. Mime has cowered down with pain. Wotan and Loge descend through a crevice.)

LOGE
Nibelheim hier:
durch bleiche Nebel
wie blitzen dort feurige Funken!

LOGE
Nibelheim here!
The murky darkness
is broken by fiery flashes!

MIME
Au! Au! Au!

MIME
Ow! Ow! Ow!

WOTAN
Hier stöhnt es laut:
was liegt im Gestein?

WOTAN
But what's that groan?
Who lies at our feet?

LOGE
(neigt sich zu Mime.)
Was Wunder wimmerst du hier?

LOGE
(bends over Mime.)
What have we whimpering here?

MIME
Ohe! Ohe!
Au! Au!

MIME
Ohe! Ohe!
Ow! Ow!

LOGE
Hei, Mime! Muntrer Zwerg!
Was zwickt und zwackt dich denn so?

LOGE
Hi, Mime! cheerful dwarf!
And what's the trouble with you?

MIME
Laß mich in Frieden!

MIME
Leave me in quiet!

LOGE
Das will ich freilich,
und mehr noch, hör:
helfen will ich dir, Mime!
(Er stellt ihn mühsam aufrecht.)

LOGE
That I'll do gladly.
Not just that, but—
help I'll offer you, Mime!
(With difficulty, he sets him on his feet.)

MIME
Wer hälfe mir?
Gehorchen muß ich
dem leiblichen Bruder,
der mich in Bande gelegt.

MIME
What help for me!
I must obey
the commands of my brother,
for he has made me his slave.

LOGE
Dich, Mime, zu binden,
was gab ihm die Macht?

LOGE
But, Mime, what gave him
the power to command?

MIME

Mit arger List
schuf sich Alberich
aus Rheines Gold
einen gelben Reif:
seinem starken Zauber
zittern wir staunend;
mit ihm zwingt er uns alle,
der Niblungen nächt'ges Heer.
Sorglose Schmiede,
schufen wir sonst wohl
Schmuck unsern Weibern,
wonnig Geschmeid,
niedlichen Niblungentand,
wir lachten lustig der Müh.
Nun zwingt uns der Schlimme,
in Klüfte zu schlüpfen,
für ihn allein
uns immer zu mühn.
Durch des Ringes Gold
errät seine Gier,
wo neuer Schimmer
in Schachten sich birgt:
da müssen wir spähen,
spüren und graben,
die Beute schmelzen
und schmieden den Guß,
ohne Ruh und Rast
dem Herrn zu häufen den Hort.

MIME

The Rhine's bright gold,
seized by Alberich,
was shaped and forged
to a shining ring:
at its magic spell
the Nibelungs tremble;
that ring makes him our master;
we Niblungs are now his slaves.
Once we were carefree,
worked at our anvils,
forged for our women,
trinkets and jewels,
delicate Nibelung toys;
we merrily hammered away.
But now he compels us
to creep through the mineshafts,
for him alone
we sweat and we slave.
And the golden ring
has magical power
to show where treasure
lies hid in the rocks;
and then we must mine it,
forge and refine it
and smelt the ore down
to pure, shining gold;
so by day and night
we serve the greed of our lord.

LOGE

Dich Trägen soeben
traf wohl sein Zorn?

LOGE

And you were so idle
that you were whipped?

MIME

Mich Ärmsten, ach,
mich zwang er zum ärgsten:
ein Helmgeschmeid
hieß er mich schweißen;
genau befahl er,
wie es zu fügen.
Wohl merkt' ich klug,
welch mächt'ge Kraft
zu eigen dem Werk
das aus Erz ich wob:
für mich drum hüten
wollt' ich den Helm,

MIME

Poor Mime, ah,
my fate was the hardest!
A magic helm
I had to make him;
he gave me detailed,
careful instructions.
And so I guessed
some wondrous spell
must lie in the work
that I forged so well;
I thought I'd keep
one thing for myself,

durch seinen Zauber
Alberichs Zwang mich entziehn—
vielleicht, ja vielleicht
den Lästigen selbst überlisten,
in meine Gewalt ihn zu werfen,
den Ring ihm zu entreißen,
daß, wie ich Knecht jetzt dem Kühnen,
mir Freien er selber dann frön'!

LOGE
Warum, du Kluger,
glückte dir's nicht?

MIME
Ach, der das Werk ich wirkte,
den Zauber, der ihm entzuckt,
den Zauber erriet ich nicht recht!
Der das Werk mir riet
und mir's entriß,
der lehrte mich nun
—doch leider zu spät!—
welche List läg' in dem Helm:
meinem Blick entschwand er,
doch Schwielen dem Blinden
schlug unschaubar sein Arm.
Das schuf ich mir Dummen
schön zu Dank!
(Er streicht sich den Rücken. Wotan und Loge lachen.)

LOGE
(zu Wotan)
Gesteh, nicht leicht
gelingt der Fang.

WOTAN
Doch erliegt der Feind,
hilft deine List.

MIME
(von dem Lachen der Götter betroffen, betrachtet diese aufmerksamer.)
Mit eurem Gefrage,
wer seid denn ihr Fremde?

LOGE
Freunde dir;

and use the spell
to free me from Alberich's power;
perhaps, yes, perhaps
the tyrant himself could be conquered;
by using the helm I might catch him.
That ring—could I but seize it,
then, though I'm forced now to serve him,
when free, I could make him my slave!

LOGE
Your plan was clever;
why did it fail?

MIME
Ah! when the helm was finished,
the magic that makes it work,
that magic I could not guess right:
then he seized the helm
and spoke the charm;
he showed me—alas,
I learnt it too late—
mighty spells lay in that helm.
From my sight he vanished;
and out of the darkness
dealt invisible blows.
And that's all the thanks
my work has won!
(He rubs his back. Wotan and Loge laugh.)

LOGE
(to Wotan)
Admit, your task
may well be hard.

WOTAN
We'll succeed at last,
thanks to your wits.

MIME
(perplexed by the gods' laughter, observes them more closely.)
But why all these questions?
Who are you, you strangers?

LOGE
Friends to you;

von ihrer Not
befrein wir der Niblungen Volk.

MIME
(schrickt zusammen, da er Alberich sich wieder nahen hört.)
Nehmt euch in acht!
Alberich naht.

WOTAN
Sein harren wir hier.
(Er setzt sich ruhig auf einen Stein; Loge lehnt ihm zur Seite. Alberich, der den Tarnhelm vom Haupte genommen und an den Gürtel gehängt hat, treibt mit geschwungener Geißel aus der unteren, tiefer gelegenen Schlucht aufwärts eine Schar Nibelungen vor sich her: diese sind mit goldenem und silbernem Geschmeide beladen, das sie, unter Alberichs steter Nötigung, all auf einen Haufen speichern und so zu einem Horte häufen.)

ALBERICH
Hieher! Dorthin!
Hehe! Hoho!
Träges Heer,
dort zu Hauf
schichtet den Hort!
Du da, hinauf!
Willst du voran?
Schmähliches Volk,
ab das Geschmeide!
Soll ich euch helfen?
Alles hieher!
(Er gewahrt plötzlich Wotan und Loge.)
He, wer ist dort?
Wer drang hier ein?
Mime! Zu mir,
schäbiger Schuft!
Schwatztest du gar
mit dem schweifenden Paar?
Fort, du Fauler!
Willst du gleich schmieden und schaffen?
(Er treibt Mime mit Geißelhieben unter den Haufen der Nibelungen hinein.)
He, an die Arbeit!
Alle von hinnen!
Hurtig hinab!
Aus den neuen Schachten

we can set free
the suffering Nibelung folk.

MIME
(shrinks back in terror as he hears Alberich approaching.)
Better take care;
Alberich's near.

WOTAN
We'll wait for him here.
(He seats himself calmly on a stone. Loge leans at his side. Alberich, brandishing a whip, enters, driving a team of Nibelungs in front of him out of a cavern lying farther below. He has removed the Tarnhelm from his head and hung it from his belt. The Nibelungs are laden with golden and silver work, which, under Alberich's constant supervision, they pile up in a heap.)

ALBERICH
Hither! Thither!
Hehe! Hoho!
Lazy herd!
Pile the gold,
there in a heap!
You there, get up!
On with your work!
Indolent dogs!
Stack up the treasure!
Want me to help you?
There in a heap!
(He is suddenly aware of Wotan and Loge.)
Hey, who is there?
Who's broken in?
Mime, come here!
Pestilent imp,
chattering away
with that scoundrely pair!
Off, you idler!
Back to your welding and whining!
(He drives Mime with blows of his whip into the crowd of Nibelungs.)
Hey! to your labour!
Back to the forges!
Back to the mines!
From the new-dug shafts

schafft mir das Gold!
Euch grüßt die Geißel,
grabt ihr nicht rasch!
Daß keiner mir müßig,
bürge mir Mime,
sonst birgt er sich schwer
meiner Geißel Schwunge:
daß ich überall weile,
wo keiner mich wähnt,
das weiß er, dünkt mich, genau!
Zögert ihr noch?
Zaudert wohl gar?
(Er zieht seinen Ring vom Finger, küßt ihn und streckt ihn drohend aus.)
Zittre und zage,
gezähmtes Heer:
rasch gehorcht
des Ringes Herrn!
(Unter Geheul und Gekreisch stieben die Nibelungen, unter ihnen Mime, auseinander und schlüpfen in die Schächte hinab. Alberich betrachtet lange und mißtrauisch Wotan und Loge).
Was wollt ihr hier?

WOTAN
Von Nibelheims nächt'gem Land
vernahmen wir neue Mär:
mächt'ge Wunder
wirke hier Alberich:
daran uns zu weiden,
trieb uns Gäste die Gier.

ALBERICH
Nach Nibelheim
führt euch der Neid:
so kühne Gäste,
glaubt, kenn ich gut.

LOGE
Kennst du mich gut,
kindischer Alp?
Nun sag: wer bin ich,
daß du so bellst?
Im kalten Loch,
da kauernd du lagst,
wer gab dir Licht
und wärmende Lohe,

go fetch me more gold!
And if you're lazy
you shall be whipped.
Let no one be idle;
Mime will watch you
or else he will find
that my whip rewards him.
I'll be everywhere, spying
where no one expects;
ask Mime; he can explain!
Off to your work!
Lingering still?
(He draws the ring from his finger, kisses it, and holds it out threateningly.)
Tremble in terror,
you wretched slaves:
and obey
the ring's great lord!
(With howling and shrieking the Nibelungs, Mime among them, scatter and scuttle away into the shafts. Alberich gives a long, suspicious look at Wotan and Loge.)
What brought you here?

WOTAN
Of Nibelheim's dusky land
we've heard a most marvellous tale:
mighty wonders
worked here by Alberich;
and, eager to see them,
we arrive as your guests.

ALBERICH
Attracted by
Nibelheim's gold:
I know
the sort of guests that you are!

LOGE
Well, if you know,
impudent dwarf,
then say, who am I!
Why do you bark?
In chilly caves
you shivered and froze;
who gave you light
and who lit your fires then?

wenn Loge nie dir gelacht?
Was hülf' dir dein Schmieden,
heizt' ich die Schmiede dir nicht?
Dir bin ich Vetter
und war dir Freund:
nicht fein drum dünkt mich dein Dank!

ALBERICH
Den Lichtalben
lacht jetzt Loge,
der list'ge Schelm:
bist du Falscher ihr Freund,
wie mir Freund du einst warst,
haha! mich freut's!
Von ihnen fürcht ich dann nichts.

LOGE
So denk ich, kannst du mir traun.

ALBERICH
Deiner Untreu trau ich,
nicht deiner Treu!
(eine herausfordernde Stellung annehmend)
Doch getrost trotz ich euch allen.

LOGE
Hohen Mut
verleiht deine Macht:
grimmig groß
wuchs dir die Kraft.

ALBERICH
Siehst du den Hort,
den mein Heer
dort mir gehäuft?

LOGE
So neidlichen sah ich noch nie.

ALBERICH
Das ist für heut,
ein kärglich Häufchen:
kühn und mächtig
soll er künftig sich mehren.

WOTAN
Zu was doch frommt dir der Hort,
da freudlos Nibelheim

Was Loge not once your friend?
What use are your forges
till they are heated by me?
I am your kinsman
and once was kind:
for that you owe me your thanks!

ALBERICH
The gods have
befriended Loge,
that crafty rogue:
are you, schemer, their friend,
as my friend once you were?
Haha! I laugh!
In that case, what need I fear?

LOGE
And so, instead, you can trust.

ALBERICH
I can trust your untruth,
never your truth!
(assuming a defiant attitude)
Yet today I can defy you!

LOGE
Have you grown
so daring and bold?
Have you gained
such mighty power?

ALBERICH
See all the gold
that my slaves
heaped over there?

LOGE
I've never seen so much before.

ALBERICH
That's just today's—
the merest trifle.
In the future
it will tower far more grandly.

WOTAN
But what's the use of your wealth?
In joyless Nibelheim,

und nichts für Schätze hier feil?

ALBERICH
Schätze zu schaffen
und Schätze zu bergen,
nützt mir Nibelheims Nacht;
doch mit dem Hort,
in der Höhle gehäuft,
denk ich dann Wunder zu wirken:
die ganze Welt
gewinn ich mit ihm mir zu eigen.

WOTAN
Wie beginnst du, Gütiger, das?

ALBERICH
Die in linder Lüfte Wehn
da oben ihr lebt,
lacht und liebt;
mit goldner Faust
euch Göttliche fang ich mir alle!
Wie ich der Liebe abgesagt,
alles, was lebt,
soll ihr entsagen!
Mit Golde gekirrt,
nach Gold nur sollt ihr noch gieren.
Auf wonnigen Höhn
in seligem Weben
wiegt ihr euch;
den Schwarzalben
verachtet ihr ewigen Schwelger!
Habt Acht! Habt Acht!
Denn dient ihr Männer
erst meiner Macht,
eure schmucken Frau'n—
die mein Frein verschmäht—
sie zwingt zur Lust sich der Zwerg,
lacht Liebe ihm nicht.
Hahahaha!
Habt ihr's gehört?
Habt Acht!
Habt Acht vor dem nächtlichen Heer,
entsteigt des Niblungen Hort
aus stummer Tiefe zu Tag!

WOTAN
(auffahrend)
Vergeh, frevelnder Gauch!

with gold there's nothing to buy!

ALBERICH
Gold can be mined here,
and gold can be stored here,
deep in Nibelheim's caves.
Then with my wealth
from the darkness I'll rise,
rise and be master of all things;
the whole wide world
I'll buy for myself with the treasure!

WOTAN
My good Niblung, how would you start?

ALBERICH
In the clouds, you great ones
far above us may live,
laugh, and love.
My golden grasp
will seize on you gods and destroy you!
Once I renounced all joys of love.
All those who live,
all shall renounce them!
Enchanted by gold,
your greed for gold shall enslave you!
On glorious heights
you gods live in gladness,
lulled by ease,
despising those
who work below, sure you are eternal!
Beware! Beware!
For first your men
shall yield to my might,
then your lovely women,
who despise me and jeer,
shall grant to Alberich's force
what love could not win!
Hahahaha!
You have been warned!
Beware!
Beware of my armies of night!
Beware the day when the Niblung's gold
shall vanquish the world!

WOTAN
(vehemently)
No more, impious wretch!

ALBERICH
Was sagt der?

LOGE
(ist dazwischengetreten; zu Wotan)
Sei doch bei Sinnen!
(zu Alberich)
Wen doch faßte nicht Wunder,
erfährt er Alberichs Werk?
Gelingt deiner herrlichen List,
was mit dem Hort du heischest,
den Mächtigsten muß ich dich rühmen:
denn Mond und Stern'
und die strahlende Sonne,
sie auch dürfen nicht anders,
dienen müssen sie dir.
Doch wichtig acht ich vor allem,
daß des Hortes Häufer,
der Niblungen Heer,
neidlos dir geneigt.
Einen Reif rührtest du kühn,
dem zagte zitternd dein Volk:
doch wenn im Schlaf
ein Dieb dich beschlich',
den Ring schlau dir entriss',
wie wahrtest du, Weiser, dich dann?

ALBERICH
Der Listigste dünkt sich Loge;
andre denkt er
immer sich dumm:
daß sein ich bedürfte
zu Rat und Dienst
um harten Dank,
das hörte der Dieb jetzt gern!
Den hehlenden Helm
ersann ich mir selbst;
der sorglichste Schmied,
Mime, mußt' ihn mir schmieden:
schnell mich zu wandeln
nach meinem Wunsch,
die Gestalt mir zu tauschen,
taugt mir der Helm.
Niemand sieht mich,
wenn er mich sucht;
doch überall bin ich,
geborgen dem Blick.

ALBERICH
What says he?

LOGE
(stepping between them; to Wotan)
Try to be patient!
(to Alberich)
All must stand in amazement,
beholding Alberich's work!
If only your craft can achieve
all that you plan with your treasure,
then all would acclaim you as master;
the moon and stars,
and the sun in his splendour,
how could they not obey you,
serve you, bow to your will?
But, most of all, it's important
that your army of workers,
your Nibelung slaves,
never should rebel!
By your ring you can command;
your people trembled in fear.
But, while you sleep,
a thief might approach;
the ring he'd steal from your hand:
so guard yourself, wise one, from that!

ALBERICH
So no one is wise like Loge?
He can see where
others are blind?
You give me a warning
and hope I'll beg
for your advice.
Well, I do not need your help!
This magical helm,
invented by me,
was skilfully forged.
Mime made it to guard me.
It can transform me;
I can assume
any shape that I wish for,
through this helm.
None can see me,
search as he will;
invisible master
and all-seeing lord!

So ohne Sorge
bin ich selbst sicher vor dir,
du fromm sorgender Freund!

So I'm protected;
even from you I am safe,
my kind, provident friend!

LOGE
Vieles sah ich,
Seltsames fand ich:
doch solches Wunder
gewahrt' ich nie.
Dem Werk ohnegleichen
kann ich nicht glauben;
wäre dies eine möglich,
deine Macht währte dann ewig.

LOGE
Many marvels
I have encountered,
but such a marvel
is new to me.
This work without equal—
I don't believe it!
If you could work this wonder,
then your power would be everlasting!

ALBERICH
Meinst du, ich lüg
und prahle wie Loge?

ALBERICH
I do not lie
or boast like Loge!

LOGE
Bis ich's geprüft,
bezweifl' ich, Zwerg, dein Wort.

LOGE
Show me a proof,
and then I'll believe your boast.

ALBERICH
Vor Klugheit bläht sich
zum Platzen der Blöde!
Nun plage dich Neid!
Bestimm, in welcher Gestalt
soll ich jach vor dir stehn?

ALBERICH
You're puffed up with prudence
and pride till you're bursting!
Well, envy me now!
Command, and tell me what shape
you would like me to be!

LOGE
In welcher du willst:
nur mach vor Staunen mich stumm!

LOGE
Oh, choose for yourself,
but make me dumb with surprise!

ALBERICH
(hat den Helm aufgesetzt.)
»Riesen-Wurm
winde sich ringelnd!«
(Sogleich verschwindet er: eine ungeheure Riesenschlange windet sich statt seiner am Boden; sie bäumt sich und streckt den aufgesperrten Rachen nach Wotan und Loge hin.)

ALBERICH
(has put on the Tarnhelm.)
'Dragon dread,
curling and coiling!'
(He disappears instantly. In his place an enormous dragon writhes on the ground; it rises up and snaps with open jaws at Wotan and Loge.)

LOGE
(stellt sich von Furcht ergriffen.)
Ohe! Ohe!

LOGE
(pretends to be seized with terror.)
Ohe! Ohe!

Schreckliche Schlange,
verschlinge mich nicht!
Schone Logen das Leben!

Terrible dragon,
have mercy on me!
Spare my life, do not eat me!

WOTAN
Hahaha! Gut, Alberich!
Gut, du Arger!
Wie wuchs so rasch
zum riesigen Wurme der Zwerg!
(Die Schlange verschwindet; statt ihrer erscheint sogleich Alberich wieder in seiner wirklichen Gestalt.)

WOTAN
Hahaha! Good, Alberich!
Good, you rascal!
Your change from dwarf
to dragon was skilful and swift!
(The dragon disappears. In its place, Alberich reappears in his own form.)

ALBERICH
Hehe! Ihr Klugen,
glaubt ihr mir nun?

ALBERICH
Hehe! You doubters!
Now do you believe?

LOGE
Mein Zittern mag dir's bezeugen.
Zur großen Schlange
schufst du dich schnell:
weil ich's gewahrt,
willig glaub ich dem Wunder.
Doch, wie du wuchsest,
kannst du auch winzig
und klein dich schaffen?
Das Klügste schien' mir das,
Gefahren schlau zu entfliehn:
das aber dünkt mich zu schwer!

LOGE
My trembling proves it too clearly!
A giant dragon
rose in your place;
now that I've seen,
how can I not believe you?
You can grow larger—
can you be tiny?
a tiny creature?
the safest way I know
to hide yourself from your foes.
That, maybe, that would be hard?

ALBERICH
Zu schwer dir,
weil du zu dumm!
Wie klein soll ich sein?

ALBERICH
Too hard for you,
ignorant fool!
How small shall I be?

LOGE
Daß die feinste Klinze dich fasse,
wo bang die Kröte sich birgt.

LOGE
So the smallest crack could conceal you,
where a frightened toad could be hid.

ALBERICH
Pah! nichts leichter!
Luge du her!
(Er setzt den Tarnhelm wieder auf.)
»Krumm und grau
krieche Kröte!«
(Er verschwindet; die Götter gewahren im Gestein eine Kröte auf sich zukriechen.)

ALBERICH
Pah! That's easy!
Look at me now!
(He puts on the Tarnhelm again.)
'Tiny toad,
creeping and crawling!'—
(He disappears; the gods perceive a toad on the rocks, creeping towards them.)

LOGE
(zu Wotan)
Dort die Kröte,
greife sie rasch!
(Wotan setzt seinen Fuß auf die Kröte, Loge fährt ihr nach dem Kopfe und hält den Tarnhelm in der Hand.)

ALBERICH
(wird plötzlich in seiner wirklichen Gestalt sichtbar, wie er sich unter Wotans Fuße windet).
Ohe! Verflucht!
Ich bin gefangen!

LOGE
Halt ihn fest,
bis ich ihn band.
(Er hat ein Bastseil hervorgeholt und bindet Alberich damit Hände und Beine; den Geknebelten, der sich wütend zu wehren sucht, fassen dann beide und schleppen ihn mit sich nach der Kluft, aus der sie herabkamen.)
Schnell hinauf:
dort ist er unser.
(Sie verschwinden, aufwärts steigend.)

LOGE
(to Wotan)
There, the toad!
Capture it quick!
(Wotan puts his foot on the toad. Loge catches it by the head and seizes the Tarnhelm in his hand.)

ALBERICH
(suddenly becomes visible in his own form, writhing under Wotan's foot.)
Ohe! Ohe!
Now they have caught me!

LOGE
Hold him tight,
till he is bound.
(He has brought out a rope, and with it he binds Alberich hand and foot; then both seize the prisoner, who is violently trying to escape, and drag him to the shaft by which they entered.)

Now swiftly up!
He is our prisoner!
(They disappear, climbing upwards.)

Vierte Szene

Die Szene verwandelt sich, nur in umgekehrter Weise, wie zuvor; die Verwandlung führt wieder an den Schmieden vorüber. Fortdauernde Verwandlung nach oben. Schließlich erscheint wieder die

Freie Gegend auf Bergeshöhen

wie in der zweiten Szene; nur ist sie jetzt noch in fahle Nebel verhüllt, wie vor der zweiten Verwandlung nach Freias Abführung. Wotan und Loge, den gebundenen Alberich mit sich führend, steigen aus der Kluft herauf.

LOGE

Da, Vetter,
sitze du fest!
Luge, Liebster,
dort liegt die Welt,
die du Lungrer gewinnen dir willst:
welch Stellchen, sag,

Scene Four

The scene changes as before, but in the opposite direction. The transformation again leads past the forging. There is continual upward motion. Finally, there reappears the

Open Space on a Mountain Height

as in the second scene; but now it is still veiled in thin mist, as at the end of Scene 2, after Freia's abduction. Wotan and Loge, bringing Alberich, bound, with them, come up out of the crevice.

LOGE

There, Alberich,
sit on your throne!
Look around you,
there lies the world
that you thought you would rule as your
What spot for me [own.

bestimmst du drin mir zum Stall?
(Er schlägt ihm tanzend Schnippchen.)

ALBERICH
Schändlicher Schächer!
Du Schalk! Du Schelm!
Löse den Bast,
binde mich los,
den Frevel sonst büßest du Frecher!

WOTAN
Gefangen bist du,
fest mir gefesselt,
wie du die Welt,
was lebt und webt,
in deiner Gewalt schon wähntest,
in Banden liegst du vor mir.
Du Banger kannst es nicht leugnen!
Zu ledigen dich
bedarf's nun der Lösung.

ALBERICH
Oh, ich Tropf,
ich träumender Tor!
Wie dumm traut' ich
dem diebischen Trug!
Furchtbare Rache
räche den Fehl!

LOGE
Soll Rache dir frommen,
vor allem rate dich frei:
dem gebundnen Manne
büßt kein Freier den Frevel.
Drum, sinnst du auf Rache,
rasch ohne Säumen
sorg um die Lösung zunächst!

ALBERICH
So heischt, was ihr begehrt!

WOTAN
Den Hort und dein helles Gold.

ALBERICH
Gieriges Gaunergezücht!
(für sich)

has been reserved in your realm?
(He dances round him, snapping his fingers.)

ALBERICH
Infamous schemer!
You knave! You thief!
Loosen my bonds,
let me go free
or else for your crime you will suffer!

WOTAN
You're now my captive,
bound in my fetters—
you who declared
you'd bind the world,
and lay it in chains before you;
my captive, bound at my feet.
I have you now at my mercy!
So if you'd be free,
then pay for your freedom.

ALBERICH
I was blind
and lost in my dreams!
A fool, caught by
that cowardly trick!
I shall have vengeance,
cruel and keen!

LOGE
Well, dream of your vengeance,
but first, set yourself free:
when a man's a captive,
no one cares if he curses.
Still planning your vengeance?
Better think quickly,
think of the ransom we need!

ALBERICH
Then say what you demand.

WOTAN
The gold, all your shining gold.

ALBERICH
Greedy and criminal pair!
(aside)

Doch behalt ich mir nur den Ring,
des Hortes entrat ich dann leicht:
  denn von neuem gewonnen
  und wonnig genährt
ist er bald durch des Ringes Gebot.
  Eine Witzigung wär's,
  die weise mich macht:
zu teuer nicht zahl ich die Zucht,
laß für die Lehre ich den Tand.

WOTAN
  Erlegst du hen Hort?

ALBERICH
  Löst mir die Hand,
  so ruf ich ihn her.
(Loge löst ihm die Schlinge an der rechten Hand. Alberich berührt den Ring mit den Lippen und murmelt heimlich einen Befehl.)
  Wohlan, die Niblungen
  rief ich mir nah:
  dem Herrn gehorchend
  hör ich den Hort
aus der Tiefe sie führen zu Tag.
Nun löst mich vom lästigen Band!

WOTAN
Nicht eh'r, bis alles gezahlt.
(Die Nibelungen steigen aus der Kluft herauf, mit den Geschmeiden des Hortes beladen. Während des Folgenden schichten sie den Hort auf.)

ALBERICH
  O schändliche Schmach,
  daß die scheuen Knechte
geknebelt selbst mich erschaun!
(zu den Nibelungen)
  Dorthin geführt,
  wie ich's befehl!
  All zu Hauf
  schichtet den Hort!
  Helf ich euch Lahmen?
  Hieher nicht gelugt!
  Rasch da, rasch!
  Dann rührt euch von hinnen:
  daß ihr mir schafft!
  Fort in die Schachten!
Weh euch, find ich euch faul!

But so long as I keep the ring,
the rest can be given away;
  I can quickly replace it
  again and again
by commanding the powerful ring.
  Now a lesson I've learnt,
  and wiser I'll be;
the warning is cheap at the price,
though it has cost me so much gold.

WOTAN
  You'll give me the gold?

ALBERICH
  Loosen my hand;
  I'll summon it here.
(Loge unties the rope from his right hand. Alberich puts the ring to his lips and secretly murmurs a command.)
  And now the Niblungs
  will come to my call,
  for their lord commands them;
  up from the depths
of the darkness they'll bring you the gold;
so now set me free from my bonds!

WOTAN
Not yet, till all has been paid.
(The Nibelungs ascend from the crevice, laden with the treasures of the hoard. During what follows, they pile up the treasure.)

ALBERICH
  O shameful disgrace!
  that my shrinking servants
should see me bound like a slave!
(to the Nibelungs)
  Put it down there,
  as I command!
  In a heap
  pile up the gold!
  Want me to help you?
  No, don't look at me!
  Hurry! quick!
  Then back to your labour!
  Off to the mines!
  Off to the forges!
Idlers, back to your work!

Auf den Fersen folg ich euch nach.
(Er küßt seinen Ring und streckt ihn gebieterisch aus. Wie von einem Schlage getroffen, drängen sich die Nibelungen scheu und ängstlich der Kluft zu, in die sie schnell hinabschlüpfen.)
Gezahlt hab ich:
nun laßt mich ziehn!
Und das Helmgeschmeid,
das Loge dort hält,
das gebt mir nun gütlich zurück!

For your lord comes hard on your heels!
(He kisses his ring and stretches it out commandingly. As if struck by a blow, the Nibelungs hurry in fear and trembling to the crevice and quickly scuttle down it.)
The gold lies there;
now let me go:
and the Tarnhelm there,
which Loge still holds,
now kindly return it to me!

LOGE
(den Tarnhelm zum Horte werfend)
Zur Buße gehört auch die Beute.

LOGE
(throwing the Tarnhelm on to the hoard)
The Tarnhelm is part of the ransom.

ALBERICH
Verfluchter Dieb!
Doch nur Geduld!
Der den alten mir schuf,
schafft einen andern:
noch halt ich die Macht,
der Mime gehorcht.
Schlimm zwar ist's,
dem schlauen Feind
zu lassen die listige Wehr!
Nun denn! Alberich
ließ euch alles:
jetzt löst, ihr Bösen, das Band!

ALBERICH
Accursed thief!
Yet, wait a while!
He who forged me the first
can make me another.
I still hold the power
that Mime obeys.
Yet it's sad
that crafty foes
should capture my cunning defence!
Well then! Alberich's
paid his ransom;
untie, you tyrants, my bonds!

LOGE
(zu Wotan)
Bist du befriedigt?
Bind ich ihn frei?

LOGE
(to Wotan)
Are you contented?
Can he go free?

WOTAN
Ein goldner Ring
ragt dir am Finger:
hörst du, Alp?
Der, acht ich, gehört mit zum Hort.

WOTAN
A golden ring
shines on your finger:
well, my dwarf,
that also is part of the price.

ALBERICH
(entsetzt)
Der Ring?

ALBERICH
(appalled)
The ring?

WOTAN
Zu deiner Lösung
mußt du ihn lassen.

WOTAN
To win your freedom
you'll have to yield it.

ALBERICH
(bebend)
Das Leben—doch nicht den Ring!

WOTAN
(heftiger)
Den Reif verlang ich:
mit dem Leben mach, was du willst!

ALBERICH
Lös ich mir Leib und Leben,
den Ring auch muß ich mir lösen:
Hand und Haupt,
Aug und Ohr,
sind nicht mehr mein Eigen
als hier dieser rote Ring!

WOTAN
Dein Eigen nennst du den Ring?
Rasest du, schamloser Albe?
Nüchtern sag,
wem entnahmst du das Gold,
daraus du den schimmernden schufst?
War's dein Eigen,
was du Arger
der Wassertiefe entwandt?
Bei des Rheines Töchtern
hole dir Rat,
ob ihr Gold sie
zu eigen dir gaben,
das du zum Ring dir geraubt.

ALBERICH
Schmähliche Tücke,
schändlicher Trug!
Wirfst du Schächer
die Schuld mir vor,
die dir so wonnig erwünscht?
Wie gern raubtest
du selbst dem Rheine das Gold,
war nur so leicht
die List, es zu schmieden, erlangt?
Wie glückt' es nun
dir Gleißner zum Heil,
daß der Niblung ich
aus schmählicher Not,
in des Zornes Zwange,

ALBERICH
(trembling)
My life, but not the ring!

WOTAN
(more violently)
The ring surrender:
with your life, do what you will!

ALBERICH
But if my life is spared me,
the ring must stay on my finger:
hand and head,
eye and ear
are not mine more truly
than mine this golden ring!

WOTAN
What right have you to the ring?
Insolent, impudent Niblung?
Tell me now,
where did you get the gold
from which you created the ring!
Did you own it,
when you grasped it,
the Rhinemaids' radiant toy?
Let those Rhinemaids answer:
will they declare
that they gave you
their gold as a present;
or did you seize it by theft?

ALBERICH
Infamous schemer!
Shameful deceit!
Thief, you blame me
for doing that crime
which you were burning to do!
Though you lusted
to steal the gold for yourself,
you couldn't pay
the price that alone would suffice.
It serves you well,
you smooth, sneering rogue,
that the Niblung, I,
in shameful distress,
in a frenzied outburst,

den schrecklichen Zauber gewann,
des Werk nun lustig dir lacht?
Des Unseligsten,
Angstversehrten
fluchfertige,
furchtbare Tat,
zu fürstlichem Tand
soll sie fröhlich dir taugen,
zur Freude dir frommen mein Fluch?
Hüte dich,
herrischer Gott!
Frevelte ich,
so frevelt' ich frei an mir:
doch an allem, was war,
ist und wird,
frevelst, Ewiger, du,
entreißest du frech mir den Ring!

WOTAN
Her den Ring!
Kein Recht an ihm
schwörst du schwatzend dir zu.
(Er ergreift Alberich und entzieht seinem Finger mit heftiger Gewalt den Ring.)

ALBERICH
(gräßlich aufschreiend)
Ha! Zertrümmert! Zerknickt!
Der Traurigen traurigster Knecht!

WOTAN
(den Ring betrachtend)
Nun halt ich, was mich erhebt,
der Mächtigen mächtigsten Herrn!
(Er steckt den Ring an.)

LOGE
Ist er gelöst?

WOTAN
Bind ihn los!

LOGE
(löst Alberich vollends die Bande.)
Schlüpfe denn heim!
Keine Schlinge hält dich:
frei fahre dahin!

did win for myself, by a curse,
this gold that smiles on you now!
And my sacrifice,
all I suffered,
my criminal,
curse-laden deed—
have they merely served
to procure you a plaything?
Will you win the world by my curse?
Guard yourself,
proud, cruel god!
If I have sinned,
I sinned but against myself:
but against all that was,
is, and shall be,
you are planning a crime
by laying your hand on the ring!

WOTAN
Yield the ring!
No chatter can prove
your right to the ring!
(He seizes Alberich and violently tears the ring from his finger.)

ALBERICH
(with a terrible cry)
Ha! Defeated! And tricked!
Of wretches, the wretchedest slave!

WOTAN
(contemplating the ring)
It shines there, lifts me on high,
of mighty ones, mightiest of all!
(He puts on the ring.)

LOGE
Can he be freed?

WOTAN
Set him free!

LOGE
(frees Alberich from his bonds.)
Slip away home!
Not a fetter holds you:
free, Alberich, free!

ALBERICH
(sich erhebend)
Bin ich nun frei?
Wirklich frei?
So grüß' euch denn
meiner Freiheit erster Gruß!
Wie durch Fluch er mir geriet,
verflucht sei dieser Ring!
Gab sein Gold
mir Macht ohne Maß,
nun zeug' sein Zauber
Tod dem, der ihn trägt!
Kein Froher soll
seiner sich freun;
keinem Glücklichen lache
sein lichter Glanz!
Wer ihn besitzt,
den sehre die Sorge,
und wer ihn nicht hat,
den nage der Neid!
Jeder giere
nach seinem Gut,
doch keiner genieße
mit Nutzen sein!
Ohne Wucher hüt' ihn sein Herr,
doch den Würger zieh' er ihm zu!
Dem Tode verfallen,
feßle den Feigen die Furcht;
solang er lebt,
sterb' er lechzend dahin,
des Ringes Herr
als des Ringes Knecht:
bis in meiner Hand
den geraubten wieder ich halte!
So segnet
in höchster Not
der Nibelung seinen Ring!
Behalt ihn nun,
hüte ihn wohl,
meinem Fluch fliehest du nicht!
(Er verschwindet schnell in der Kluft. Der dichte Nebelduft des Vordergrundes klärt sich allmählich auf.)

LOGE
Lauschtest du
seinem Liebesgruß?

ALBERICH
(raising himself)
Am I now free?
truly free?
I greet you then
in my freedom: mark my words!
Since a curse gained it for me,
my curse lies on this ring!
Though its gold
brought riches to me,
let now it bring
but death, death to its lord!
Its wealth shall yield
pleasure to none;
let no fortunate owner
enjoy its gleam.
Care shall consume
the man who commands it,
and mortal envy
consume those who don't—
striving vainly
to win that prize.
But he who obtains it
shall find no joy!
It will bring no gain to its lord;
only death is brought by its gleam!
To death he is fated,
doomed by the curse on the ring:
and while he lives,
fears will fill all his days.
Who owns the ring
to the ring is a slave,
till the gold returns
to this hand from which you have torn it!
In anguish
and sore distress,
the Nibelung blesses the ring!
You hold it now;
guard it with care!
From my curse you can't escape!
(He disappears quickly into the crevice. The thick mists in the foreground gradually clear.)

LOGE
Did you hear
Alberich's loving song?

WOTAN
(in den Anblick des Ringes an seiner Hand versunken)
Gönn ihm die geifernde Lust!
(Es wird immer heller.)

LOGE
(nach rechts in die Szene blickend)
Fasolt und Fafner
nahen von fern;
Freia führen sie her.
(Aus dem sich immer mehr zerteilenden Nebel erscheinen Donner, Froh und Fricka und eilen dem Vordergrunde zu.)

FROH
Sie kehrten zurück.

DONNER
Willkommen, Bruder!

FRICKA
(besorgt zu Wotan)
Bringst du gute Kunde?

LOGE
(auf den Hort deutend)
Mit List und Gewalt
gelang des Werk:
dort liegt, was Freia löst.

DONNER
Aus der Riesen Haft
naht dort die Holde.

FROH
Wie liebliche Luft
wieder uns weht,
wonnig Gefühl
die Sinne erfüllt!
Traurig ging es uns allen,
getrennt für immer von ihr,
die leidlos ewiger Jugend
jubelnde Lust uns verleiht.
(Der Vordergrund ist wieder hell geworden; das Aussehen der Götter gewinnt wieder die erste Frische: über dem Hintergrunde haftet jedoch noch

WOTAN
(lost in contemplation of the ring on his finger)
Let him give way to his wrath!
(It continues to get lighter.)

LOGE
(looking offstage to the right)
Fasolt and Fafner,
coming this way!
Freia soon shall be freed.
(Through the mists, as they continue to disperse, Donner, Froh, and Fricka appear and hasten towards the foreground.)

FROH
So you have returned!

DONNER
Be welcome, brother!

FRICKA
(to Wotan, anxiously)
Have you gained the ransom?

LOGE
(points to the treasure.)
By cunning and force
the deed was done:
behold, there's Freia's price.

DONNER
From the giants' power
soon we can free her.

FROH
How sweetly the air
charms us again;
joy and contentment
steal through my heart!
Life indeed would be wretched
if we were parted from her;
she brings us youth eternal,
fills us with joy and delight.
(The foreground is now completely clear again. The appearances of the gods have regained their former freshness. The veil of mist still hovers over

der Nebelschleier, so daß die Burg unsichtbar bleibt. Fasolt und Fafner treten auf, Freia zwischen sich führend.)

FRICKA
(eilt freudig auf die Schwester zu, um sie zu umarmen.)
Lieblichste Schwester,
süßeste Lust!
Bist du mir wieder gewonnen?

FASOLT
(ihr wehrend)
Halt! Nicht sie berührt!
Noch gehört sie uns.
Auf Riesenheims
ragender Mark
rasteten wir:
mit treuem Mut
des Vertrages Pfand
pflegten wir.
So sehr mich's reut,
zurück doch bring ich's,
erlegt uns Brüdern
die Lösung ihr.

WOTAN
Bereit liegt die Lösung:
des Goldes Maß
sei nun gütlich gemessen.

FASOLT
Das Weib zu missen,
wisse, gemutet mich weh:
soll aus dem Sinn sie mir schwinden,
des Geschmeides Hort
häufet denn so,
daß meinem Blick
die Blühende ganz er verdeck'!

WOTAN
So stellt das Maß
nach Freias Gestalt.
(Freia wird von den beiden Riesen in die Mitte gestellt. Darauf stoßen sie ihre Pfähle zu Freias beiden Seiten so in den Boden, daß sie gleiche Höhe und Breite mit ihrer Gestalt messen.)

the background, however, so that the castle remains invisible. Fasolt and Fafner enter, bringing Freia between them.)

FRICKA
(hastens joyfully to her sister, to embrace her.)
Loveliest sister!
sweetest delight!
now once again I can greet you.

FASOLT
(restraining her)
Wait! Don't touch her yet!
Freia still is ours.
On Riesenheim's
far rocky heights,
there we did rest;
we guarded her
and we kept our word
faithfully.
Though sore at heart,
I now return her;
so keep your bargain
and pay our wage.

WOTAN
Behold, there's the ransom:
the golden heap
will reward you most generously.

FASOLT
To lose the woman
sorely distresses my heart.
If I am forced to forget her,
you must pile the gold,
heap up the hoard,
till you conceal
her beauty and charms from my sight.

WOTAN
Then heap the gold
till Freia is hid.
(The two giants place Freia in the middle. Then they thrust their staves in the ground on each side of Freia, so as to measure her height and breadth.)

FAFNER
Gepflanzt sind die Pfähle
nach Pfandes Maß:
gehäuft nun füll es der Hort.

FAFNER
We've planted our poles here
to frame her form;
now heap your gold to her height!

WOTAN
Eilt mit dem Werk:
widerlich ist mir's!

WOTAN
On with the work:
oh, this is shameful!

LOGE
Hilf mir, Froh!

LOGE
Help me, Froh!

FROH
Freias Schmach
eil ich zu enden.
(Loge und Froh häufen hastig zwischen den Pfählen die Geschmeide.)

FROH
Freia's shame
soon shall be ended.
(Loge and Froh quickly pile up the treasure between the staves.)

FAFNER
Nicht so leicht
und locker gefügt!
(Er drückt mit roher Kraft die Geschmeide dicht zusammen.)
Fest und dicht
füll er das Maß!
(Er beugt sich, um nach Lücken zu spähen.)
Hier lug ich noch durch:
verstopft mir die Lücken!

FAFNER
Far too loose
you're piling the gold.
(Roughly, he presses the treasure together tightly.)
Firm and hard,
pack it tight!
(He stoops down to look for crevices.)
Look, here is a chink:
and stop up this crevice!

LOGE
Zurück, du Grober!

LOGE
Stand back, you ruffian!—

FAFNER
Hierher!

FAFNER
Look here!

LOGE
Greif mir nichts an!

LOGE
Off with your hands!

FAFNER
Hierher! Die Klinze verklemmt!

FAFNER
And here! this crack must be closed!

WOTAN
(unmutig sich abwendend)
Tief in der Brust
brennt mir die Schmach.

WOTAN
(turning away in dejection)
Deep in my breast
burns the disgrace!

FRICKA
(den Blick auf Freia geheftet.)
Sieh, wie in Scham

FRICKA
(her eyes fixed on Freia)
See where she stands;

schmählich die Edle steht:
um Erlösung fleht
stumm der leidende Blick.
Böser Mann!
Der Minnigen botest du das!

FAFNER
Noch mehr! Noch mehr hierher!

DONNER
Kaum halt ich mich:
schäumende Wut
weckt mir der schamlose Wicht!
Hieher, du Hund!
Willst du messen,
so miß dich selber mit mir!

FAFNER
Ruhig, Donner!
Rolle, wo's taugt:
hier nützt dein Rasseln dir nichts!

DONNER
(holt aus.)
Nicht dich Schmählichen zu [zerschmettern?

WOTAN
Friede doch!
Schon dünkt mich Freia verdeckt.

LOGE
Der Hort ging auf.

FAFNER
(mißt den Hort genau mit dem Blick und späht nach Lücken.)
Noch schimmert mir Holdas Haar:
dort das Gewirk
wirf auf den Hort!

LOGE
Wie, auch den Helm?

FAFNER
Hurtig her mit ihm!

how can she bear this shame?
And the glorious maid
pleads in silence for help.
Heartless man!
For you she endures this disgrace!

FAFNER
Still more! Heap on some more!

DONNER
I'll stand no more;
furious rage
rouses my heart to revenge!
Come here, you cur!
If you'd measure,
then try your measure with me!

FAFNER
Patience, Donner!
roar where it helps:
but here you thunder in vain!

DONNER
(preparing to strike)
Not in vain, since it can crush you!

WOTAN
Patience, friend!
I think that Freia is hid!

LOGE
The gold runs out.

FAFNER
(measures the gold closely with his eye, looking for crevices.)
But still I can see her hair!
You have some gold—
add it to the pile.

LOGE
What? not the helm?

FAFNER
Quickly, give it us.

WOTAN
Laß ihn denn fahren!

LOGE
(wirft den Tarnhelm auf den Hort.)
So sind wir denn fertig.
Seid ihr zufrieden?

FASOLT
Freia, die schöne,
schau ich nicht mehr:
so ist sie gelöst?
Muß ich sie lassen?
(Er tritt nahe hinzu und späht durch den Hort.)
Weh! Noch blitzt
ihr Blick zu mir her;
des Auges Stern
strahlt mich noch an:
durch eine Spalte
muß ich's erspähn!
Seh ich dies wonnige Auge,
von dem Weibe laß ich nicht ab.

FAFNER
He! Euch rat ich,
verstopft mir die Ritze!

LOGE
Nimmersatte!
Seht ihr denn nicht,
ganz schwand uns der Hort?

FAFNER
Mitnichten, Freund!
An Wotans Finger
glänzt von Gold noch ein Ring,
den gebt, die Ritze zu füllen!

WOTAN
Wie! Diesen Ring?

LOGE
Laßt euch raten!
Den Rheintöchtern
gehört dies Gold:
ihnen gibt Wotan es wieder.

WOTAN
Give them the Tarnhelm!

LOGE
(throws the Tarnhelm on the pile.)
At last we have finished!
Are you contented?

FASOLT
Freia, the fair one,
see I no more:
The ranson is paid?
Fasolt must lose her?
(He goes up close and peers through the pile.)
Ah! Her glance
still pierces my heart;
her eyes like stars
shine on me still,
for through this crack
I look on their light.
I cannot turn from this maiden,
while her eyes inspire me with love.

FAFNER
Hey! I charge you,
now stop up this crevice!

LOGE
Never contented!
Surely you see
our gold's at an end?

FAFNER
Not wholly, friend!
On Wotan's finger
gleams the gold of a ring:
and that will fill up this crevice!

WOTAN
What? Give my ring?

LOGE
Just a moment!
The Rhinemaidens
must have that gold,
and to them Wotan will give it.

WOTAN
Was schwatzest du da?
Was schwer ich mir erbeutet,
ohne Bangen wahr ich's für mich.

LOGE
Schlimm dann steht's
um mein Versprechen,
das ich den Klagenden gab.

WOTAN
Dein Versprechen bindet mich nicht:
als Beute bleibt mir der Reif.

FAFNER
Doch hier zur Lösung
mußt du ihn legen.

WOTAN
Fordert frech, was ihr wollt:
alles gewähr ich,
um alle Welt
doch nicht fahren laß ich den Ring!

FASOLT
(zieht wütend Freia hinter dem Horte hervor.)
Aus dann ist's,
beim Alten bleibt's:
nun folgt uns Freia für immer!

FREIA
Hilfe! Hilfe!

FRICKA
Harter Gott,
gib ihnen nach!

FROH
Spare das Gold nicht!

DONNER
Spende den Ring doch!
(Fafner hält den fortdrängenden Fasolt noch auf; alle stehen bestürzt.)

WOTAN
Laßt mich in Ruh!
Den Reif geb ich nicht.

WOTAN
What chatter is this?
This prize that I have won me,
without fear I'll keep for myself!

LOGE
But then how will I
keep the promise
I gave those sorrowful maids!

WOTAN
What you promised is nothing to me:
I took the ring for myself.

FAFNER
And now you'll yield it,
paying the ransom.

WOTAN
Freely ask what you want;
all I shall grant you;
but for the world
I will not surrender the ring!

FASOLT
(angrily pulling Freia out from behind the pile)
Keep your gold,
and keep your ring;
and we'll keep Freia for ever!

FREIA
Help me! Help me!

FRICKA
Cruel god!
Do what they ask!

FROH
Pay them the ransom!

DONNER
Give them the ring too!
(Fafner restrains Fasolt, who is making off. All stand perplexed.)

WOTAN
Leave me in peace!
The ring stays with me!

(Wotan wendet sich zürnend zur Seite. Die Bühne hat sich von neuem verfinstert; aus der Felskluft zur Seite bricht ein bläulicher Schein hervor: in ihm wird plötzlich Erda sichtbar, die bis zu halber Leibeshöhe aus der Tiefe aufsteigt; sie ist von edler Gestalt, weithin von schwarzem Haar umwallt.)

(Wotan turns angrily away. The stage has again become dark. A bluish light breaks from the rocky cleft at the side, and in it Erda suddenly appears, rising from below to half her height. Her noble features are ringed by a mass of black hair.)

ERDA
(die Hand mahnend gegen Wotan ausstreckend)
Weiche, Wotan, weiche!
Flieh des Ringes Fluch!
Rettungslos
dunklem Verderben
weiht dich sein Gewinn.

ERDA
(stretching out her hand to Wotan in warning)
Yield it, Wotan, yield it!
Yield the accursed ring!
Wretchedness,
doom and disaster
lie there in the ring.

WOTAN
Wer bist du, mahnendes Weib?

WOTAN
Who brings this warning of doom?

ERDA
Wie alles war, weiß ich;
wie alles wird,
wie alles sein wird,
seh ich auch:
der ew'gen Welt
Ur-Wala,
Erda mahnt deinen Mut.
Drei der Töchter,
ur-erschaffne,
gebar mein Schoß:
was ich sehe,
sagen dir nächtlich die Nornen.
Doch höchste Gefahr
führt mich heut
selbst zu dir her:
Höre! Höre! Höre!
Alles, was ist, endet.
Ein düstrer Tag
dämmert den Göttern:
dir rat ich, meide den Ring!
(Sie versinkt langsam bis an die Brust, während der bläuliche Schein zu dunkeln beginnt.)

ERDA
All of the past, know I.
All things that are,
all things that shall be—
all I know:
the endless world's
all-wise one,
Erda, bids you beware.
My three daughters,
born in Erda's
primeval womb,
shape my visions,
tell you each night of the future.
Today I myself,
drawn by dread,
come to advise.
Hear me! Hear me! Hear me!
All things that are, perish!
An evil day
dawns for the immortals:
I warn you, yield up the ring!
(Erda sinks slowly to breast level, as the bluish glow begins to fade.)

WOTAN
Geheimnis-hehr
hallt mir dein Wort:
weile, daß mehr ich wisse!

WOTAN
Mysterious doom
sounds in your words:
stay here, and warn me further!

ERDA
(im Versinken)
Ich warnte dich—
du weißt genug:
sinn in Sorg und Furcht!
(Sie verschwindet gänzlich.)

WOTAN
Soll ich sorgen und fürchten—
dich muß ich fassen,
alles erfahren!
(Er will der Verschwindenden in die Kluft nach, um sie zu halten. Froh und Fricka werfen sich ihm entgegen und halten ihn zurück.)

FRICKA
Was willst du, Wütender?

FROH
Halt ein, Wotan!
Scheue die Edle,
achte ihr Wort!
(Wotan starrt sinnend vor sich hin.)

DONNER
(sich entschlossen zu den Riesen wendend)
Hört, ihr Riesen!
Zurück und harret:
das Gold wird euch gegeben.

FREIA
Darf ich es hoffen?
Dünkt euch Holda
wirklich der Lösung wert?
(Alle blicken gespannt auf Wotan; dieser nach tiefem Sinnen zu sich kommend, erfaßt seinen Speer und schwenkt ihn wie zum Zeichen eines mutigen Entschlusses.)

WOTAN
Zu mir, Freia!
Du bist befreit.
Wiedergekauft
kehr uns die Jugend zurück!
Ihr Riesen, nehmt euren Ring!
(Er wirft den Ring auf den Hort. Die Riesen lassen Freia los; sie eilt freudig auf die Götter zu, die sie abwechselnd längere Zeit in höchster

ERDA
(disappearing)
You heard my words;
you know enough:
brood in dread and fear!
(She disappears completely.)

WOTAN
But if dread will torment me,
then I must hold you;
all you must tell me!
(He tries to follow and stop her as she disappears into the crevice. Froh and Fricka throw themselves in his way and hold him back.)

FRICKA
Be careful, calm yourself!

FROH
Be wise, Wotan!
Erda is holy;
do as she says!
(Wotan gazes thoughtfully before him.)

DONNER
(turning decisively to the giants)
Hear, you giants!
Come back, be patient!
The gold, Wotan will give you.

FREIA
Ah, dare I hope it?
Is your Freia
worth such a great reward?
(All look eagerly at Wotan. After thinking deeply, he rouses himself, seizes his spear and brandishes it as the sign of a bold decision.)

WOTAN
To me, Freia!
You shall be freed.
Bought with the gold,
bring us our youth once again!
You giants, there is your ring!
(He throws the ring on the pile. The giants release Freia. She hurries happily over to the gods, who spend some time embracing her in turn with

Freude liebkosen. Fafner breitet sogleich einen ungeheuren Sack aus und macht sich über den Hort her, um ihn da hineinzuschichten.)

FASOLT
(dem Bruder sich entgegenwerfend)
Halt, du Gieriger!
Gönne mir auch was!
Redliche Teilung
taugt uns beiden.

FAFNER
Mehr an der Maid als am Gold
lag dir verliebtem Geck:
mit Müh zum Tausch
vermocht' ich dich Toren.
Ohne zu teilen,
hättest du Freia gefreit:
teil ich den Hort,
billig behalt ich
die größte Hälfte für mich.

FASOLT
Schändlicher du!
Mir diesen Schimpf?
Euch ruf ich zu Richtern:
teilet nach Recht
uns redlich den Hort!
(Wotan wendet sich verächtlich ab.)

LOGE
(zu Fasolt)
Den Hort laß ihn raffen:
halte du nur auf den Ring!

FASOLT
(stürzt sich auf Fafner, der immerzu eingesackt hat.)
Zurück, du Frecher!
Mein ist der Ring;
mir blieb er für Freias Blick.
(Er greift hastig nach dem Reif. Sie ringen.)

FAFNER
Fort mit der Faust!
Der Ring ist mein!
(Fasolt entreißt Fafner den Ring.)

the utmost delight. Meanwhile Fafner has spread out an enormous sack, and prepares to stow the hoard in it, to take it away.)

FASOLT
(intercepting his brother)
Stop, you greedy one!
What about my share?
Fairly and squarely
we'll divide it.

FAFNER
You'd set your heart on the maid.
What do you care for the gold?
You hoped for love
and I wanted riches;
if you had won her,
would you have shared her with me?
Since it's the gold,
trust me to seize
on the greater part for myself!

FASOLT
Shame on you, thief!
mocking me so!
You gods be the judges:
how should this gold
be shared into two?
(Wotan turns contemptuously away.)

LOGE
(to Fasolt)
Let him keep the treasure;
all that you need is the ring!

FASOLT
(hurls himself upon Fafner, who has been busily packing away.)
Stand back, you robber!
Mine is the ring;
I won it for Freia's glance!
(He snatches hastily at the ring. They struggle.)

FAFNER
Off with your hands!
the ring is mine!
(Fasolt wrests the ring from Fafner.)

FASOLT
Ich halt ihn, mir gehört er!

FAFNER
(mit einem Pfahle nach Fasolt ausholend)
Halt ihn fest, daß er nicht fall'!
(Er streckt Fasolt mit einem Streiche zu Boden, dem Sterbenden entreißt er dann hastig den Ring.)
Nun blinzle nach Freias Blick:
an den Reif rührst du nicht mehr!
(Er steckt den Ring in den Sack und rafft dann gemächlich vollends den Hort ein. Alle Götter stehen entsetzt. Langes, feierliches Schweigen.)

WOTAN
Furchtbar nun
erfind ich des Fluches Kraft!

LOGE
Was gleicht, Wotan,
wohl deinem Glücke?
Viel erwarb dir
des Ringes Gewinn;
daß er nun dir genommen,
nützt dir noch mehr:
deine Feinde—sieh,
fällen sich selbst
um das Gold, das du vergabst.

WOTAN
(tief erschüttert)
Wie doch Bangen mich bindet!
Sorg und Furcht
fesseln den Sinn;
wie sie zu enden,
lehre mich Erda:
zu ihr muß ich hinab!

FRICKA
(schmeichelnd sich an ihn schmiegend)
Wo weilst du, Wotan?
Winkt dir nicht hold
die hehre Burg,
die des Gebieters
gastlich bergend nun harrt?

WOTAN
(düster)
Mit bösem Zoll

FASOLT
I have it, I shall keep it!

FAFNER
(striking out with his staff)
Hold it fast, else it may fall!
(He fells Fasolt with a single blow and then wrenches the ring from the dying giant.)
Now dream of your Freia's glance!
For the ring you'll see no more!
(He puts the ring in the sack, and then calmly finishes packing the treasure. All the gods are appalled. A long, solemn silence.)

WOTAN
Fearful power
lies hid in that fatal curse!

LOGE
Your luck, Wotan,
what could surpass it?
Much you gained from
the ring and the gold,
but that now you have lost them,
that's better still:
for your enemies, see,
murder each other
for the gold that you let go.

WOTAN
(profoundly agitated)
Dark forebodings oppress me!
Fear and dread
seize on my soul.
Erda can teach me
how I can end them:
to her, I must descend!

FRICKA
(caressing him, cajolingly)
What keeps you, Wotan?
See where our home
awaits you there,
shining and glorious,
glad to welcome its lord.

WOTAN
(gloomily)
An evil wage

zahlt' ich den Bau!

DONNER
(auf den Hintergrund deutend, der noch in Nebel gehüllt ist)
Schwüles Gedünst
schwebt in der Luft;
lästig ist mir
der trübe Druck:
das bleiche Gewölk
samml' ich zu blitzendem Wetter;
das fegt den Himmel mir hell.
(Er besteigt einen hohen Felsstein am Talabhange und schwingt dort seinen Hammer; Nebel ziehen sich um ihn zusammen.)
Heda! Heda! Hedo!
Zu mir, du Gedüft!
Ihr Dünste, zu mir!
Donner, der Herr,
ruft euch zu Heer.
Auf des Hammers Schwung
schwebet herbei:
dunstig Gedämpf,
schwebend Gedüft!
Donner, der Herr, ruft euch zu Heer!
Heda! Heda! Hedo!
(Er verschwindet völlig in einer immer finsterer sich ballenden Gewitterwolke. Man hört Donners Hammerschlag schwer auf den Felsstein fallen: ein starker Blitz entfährt der Wolke; ein heftiger Donnerschlag folgt. Froh ist mit dem Gewölk verschwunden.)

DONNER
(unsichtbar)
Bruder, hieher!
Weise der Brücke den Weg!
(Plötzlich verzieht sich die Wolke; Donner und Froh werden sichtbar: von ihren Füßen aus zieht sich, mit blendendem Leuchten, eine Regenbogenbrücke über das Tal hinüber bis zur Burg, die jetzt, von der Abendsonne beschienen, im hellsten Glanze erstrahlt. Fafner, der neben der Leiche seines Bruders endlich den ganzen Hort eingerafft, hat, den ungeheuren Sack auf dem Rücken, während Donners Gewitterzauber die Bühne verlassen.)

FROH
(der der Brücke mit der ausgestreckten Hand den

paid for the work!

DONNER
(pointing to the background, which is still wreathed in mist)
Sweltering mists
hang in the air;
I'm oppressed
by their gloomy weight.
I'll gather the clouds,
summon the lightning and thunder
to sweep the mist from the sky!
(He climbs onto a high rock by the precipice and there swings his hammer. Mists gather around him.)
Heda! Heda! Hedo!
Now come to my call!
You vapours, to me!
Donner, your lord,
summons you here!
As my hammer swings,
sweep from the sky!
Vapours and cloud!
Wandering fog!
Donner, your lord, summons you here!
Heda! Heda! Hedo!
(Donner vanishes completely behind a thundercloud which grows ever thicker and blacker. His hammer-blow is heard striking hard on the rock. A large flash of lightning shoots from the cloud, followed by a violent clap of thunder. Froh has vanished with him into the cloud.)

DONNER
(invisible)
Brother, to me!
Show them the bridge to the hall.
(Suddenly the clouds lift. Donner and Froh are visible. From their feet a rainbow bridge of blinding radiance stretches across the valley back to the castle, which now glows in the rays of the evening sun. Fafner has at last collected up all the treasure lying near his brother's corpse, put the enormous sack on his back, and left the stage during Donner's conjuration of the storm.)

FROH
(to the gods, indicating with outstretched hand the

Weg über das Tal angewiesen, zu den Göttern)
Zur Burg führt die Brücke,
leicht, doch fest eurem Fuß:
beschreitet kühn
ihren schrecklosen Pfad!
(Wotan und die andern Götter sind sprachlos in den prächtigen Anblick verloren.)

WOTAN
Abendlich strahlt
der Sonne Auge;
in prächt'ger Glut
prangt glänzend die Burg.
In des Morgens Scheine
mutig erschimmernd,
lag sie herrenlos
hehr verlockend vor mir.
Von Morgen bis Abend
in Müh und Angst
nicht wonnig ward sie gewonnen!
Es naht die Nacht:
vor ihrem Neid
biete sie Bergung nun.
(wie von einem großen Gedanken ergriffen, sehr entschlossen)
So grüß ich die Burg,
sicher vor Bang und Graun—
(Er wendet sich feierlich zu Fricka.)
Folge mir, Frau:
in Walhall wohne mit mir!

FRICKA
Was deutet der Name?
Nie, dünkt mich, hört' ich ihn nennen.

WOTAN
Was, mächtig der Furcht,
mein Mut mir erfand,
wenn siegend es lebt,
leg es den Sinn dir dar!
(Er faßt Fricka an der Hand und schreitet mit ihr langsam der Brücke zu; Froh, Freia und Donner folgen.)

LOGE
(im Vordergrunde verharrend und den Göttern nachblickend)
Ihrem Ende eilen sie zu,

bridge as the way across the valley)
The bridge leads you homeward,
light, yet firm to your feet:
so boldly tread
on that shining path!
(Wotan and the other gods are lost in speechless astonishment at the glorious sight.)

WOTAN
Evening rays flood
the sky with splendour;
those glorious beams
shine there on my hall.
In the morning radiance
bravely it glistened,
standing masterless,
proud, awaiting its lord.
From morning till evening,
in fear and dread,
I worked dark deeds till I'd gained it!
The night is near:
from all its ills
we have our refuge now.
(very resolutely, as if seized by a grand thought)
So greet I the hall,
safe from all fear and dread.
(He turns solemnly to Fricka.)
Follow me, wife:
in Walhall, reign there with me!

FRICKA
What name did you call it?
No name that I've ever heard of.

WOTAN
When all that I've dreamed
and planned comes to pass,
when victory is mine,
you'll understand that name!
(He takes Fricka by the hand and with her strides slowly towards the bridge. Froh, Freia and Donner follow.)

LOGE
(remaining in the foreground and looking back at the gods)
They are hastening on to their end,

die so stark im Bestehen sich wähnen.
Fast schäm ich mich,
mit ihnen zu schaffen;
zur leckenden Lohe
mich wieder zu wandeln,
spür ich lockende Lust.
Sie aufzuzehren,
die einst mich gezähmt,
statt mit den Blinden
blöd zu vergehn,
und wären es göttlichste Götter!
Nicht dumm dünkte mich das!
Bedenken will ich's:
wer weiß, was ich tu!
(Er geht, um sich den Göttern in nachlässiger Haltung anzuschließen. Aus der Tiefe hört man den Gesang der Rheintöchter heraufschallen.)

DIE DREI RHEINTÖCHTER
(in der Tiefe des Tales, unsichtbar)
Rheingold! Rheingold!
Reines Gold!
Wie lauter und hell
leuchtest hold du uns!
Um dich, du klares,
wir nun klagen!
Gebt uns das Gold!
O gebt uns das reine zurück!

WOTAN
(im Begriff, den Fuß auf die Brücke zu setzen, hält an und wendet sich um.)
Welch Klagen klingt zu mir her?

LOGE
(späht in das Tal hinab.)
Des Rheines Kinder
beklagen des Goldes Raub.

WOTAN
Verwünschte Nicker!
Wehre ihrem Geneck!

LOGE
(in das Tal hinabrufend)
Ihr da im Wasser,
was weint ihr herauf?
Hört, was Wotan euch wünscht.

though they think they are great in their [grandeur.
Ashamed I'd be
to share in their dealings;
I feel a temptation
to turn and destroy them;
change to flickering fire,
and burn those great ones
who thought I was tamed,
rather than blindly
sink with the blind,
although they're so gracious and god-like!
I think that might be best!
I must consider:
who knows what I'll do?
(He goes nonchalantly to join the gods. The singing of the Rhinemaidens is heard rising up from below.)

THE THREE RHINEMAIDENS
(from the depths of the valley invisible)
Rhinegold! Rhinegold!
Shining gold!
how brightly and clear
glittered your beams on us!
For your true radiance
we are mourning;
give us the gold!
Oh give us its glory again.

WOTAN
(in the act of setting foot on the bridge, pauses and turns round.)
What cries arise from the deep?

LOGE
(looking down into the valley)
The mournful Rhinemaidens
cry for their stolen gold.

WOTAN
Accursed nixies!
Stop their tiresome lament!

LOGE
(calling down into the valley)
You in the water,
stop wailing to us.
Hear what Wotan decrees.

Glänzt nicht mehr
euch Mädchen das Gold,
in der Götter neuem Glanze
sonnt euch selig fortan!
(Die Götter lachen und beschreiten dann die Brücke.)

Never more
will you see your gold;
let the gods' new golden splendour
shine upon you instead!
(The gods laugh and stride on to the bridge.)

DIE RHEINTÖCHTER
(aus der Tiefe)
Rheingold! Rheingold!
Reines Gold!
O leuchtete noch
in der Tiefe dein lautrer Tand!
Traulich und treu
ist's nur in der Tiefe:
falsch und feig
ist, was dort oben sich freut!
(Während die Götter auf der Brücke der Burg zuschreiten, fällt der Vorhang.)

THE RHINEMAIDENS
(from below)
Rhinegold! Rhinegold!
Shining gold!
Return to the deep,
let us bathe in your light again!
Goodness and truth
dwell but in the waters:
false and base
all those who dwell up above!
(While the gods are crossing the bridge to the castle, the curtain falls.)

The Valkyrie

First Day of the Festival Play

The Ring of the Nibelung

Dramatis Personae

SIEGMUND	*Tenor*
HUNDING	*Bass*
WOTAN	*Bass-baritone*
SIEGLINDE	*Soprano*
BRÜNNHILDE	*Soprano*
FRICKA	*Soprano*
VALKYRIES	*Sopranos and Contraltos*

GERHILDE
ORTLINDE
WALTRAUTE
SCHWERTLEITE
HELMWIGE
SIEGRUNE
GRIMGERDE
ROSSWEISSE

Erster Aufzug

Das Innere eines Wohnraumes

In der Mitte steht der Stamm einer mächtigen Esche, dessen stark erhabene Wurzeln sich weithin in den Erdboden verlieren; von seinem Wipfel ist der Baum durch ein gezimmertes Dach geschieden, welches so durchschnitten ist, daß der Stamm und die nach allen Seiten hin sich ausstreckenden Äste durch genau entsprechende Öffnungen hindurchgehen; von dem belaubten Wipfel wird angenommen, daß er sich über dieses Dach ausbreite. Um den Eschenstamm, als Mittelpunkt, ist nun ein Saal gezimmert; die Wände sind aus roh behauenem Holzwerk, hier und da mit geflochtenen und gewebten Decken behangen. Rechts im Vordergrunde steht der Herd, dessen Rauchfang seitwärts zum Dache hinausführt: hinter dem Herde befindet sich ein innerer Raum, gleich einem Vorratsspeicher, zu dem man auf einigen hölzernen Stufen hinaufsteigt: davor hängt, halb

Act One

Inside a Dwelling

In the middle stands a mighty ash-tree, whose prominent roots spread wide and lose themselves in the ground. The summit of the tree is cut off by a jointed roof, so pierced that the trunk and the boughs branching out on every side pass through it, through openings made exactly to fit. We assume that the top of the tree spreads out above the roof. Around the trunk of the ash, as central point, a room has been constructed. The walls are of rudely hewn wood, here and there hung with plaited and woven rugs. In the foreground, right, is a hearth, whose chimney goes up sideways to the roof; behind the hearth is an inner room, like a storeroom, reached by a few wooden steps. In front of it, half-drawn, is a plaited hanging. In the background, an entrance-door with a simple wooden latch. Left, the door to an inner chamber, similarly reached by steps. Further forward, on the same side, a table with a

zurückgeschlagen, eine geflochtene Decke. Im Hintergrunde eine Eingangstür mit schlichtem Holzriegel. Links die Tür zu einem inneren Gemache, zu dem gleichfalls Stufen hinaufführen; weiter vornen auf derselben Seite ein Tisch mit einer breiten, an der Wand angezimmerten Bank dahinter und hölzernen Schemeln davor.

broad bench fastened to the wall behind it and wooden stools in front of it.

Ein kurzes Orchestervorspiel von heftiger, stürmischer Bewegung leitet ein. Als der Vorhang aufgeht, öffnet Siegmund von außen hastig die Eingangstür und tritt ein: es ist gegen Abend, starkes Gewitter, im Begriff, sich zu legen. Siegmund hält einen Augenblick den Riegel in der Hand und überblickt den Wohnraum: er scheint von übermäßiger Anstrengung erschöpft; sein Gewand und Aussehen zeigen, daß er sich auf der Flucht befinde. Da er niemand gewahrt, schließt er die Tür hinter sich, schreitet auf den Herd zu und wirft sich dort ermattet auf eine Decke von Bärenfell.

A short orchestral prelude of violent, stormy character introduces the scene. When the curtain rises, Siegmund, from without, hastily opens the main door and enters. It is towards evening; a fierce thunderstorm is just about to die down. For a moment, Siegmund keeps his hand on the latch and looks around the room; he seems to be exhausted by tremendous exertions; his raiment and general appearance proclaim him a fugitive. Seeing no one, he closes the door behind him, walks to the hearth, and throws himself down there, exhausted, on a bearskin rug.

Erste Szene

SIEGMUND
Wes Herd dies auch sei,
hier muß ich rasten.
(Er sinkt zurück und bleibt einige Zeit regungslos ausgestreckt. Sieglinde tritt aus der Tür des inneren Gemaches. Sie glaubte ihren Mann heimgekehrt: ihre ernste Miene zeigt sich dann verwundert, als sie einen Fremden am Herde ausgestreckt sieht.)

SIEGLINDE
(noch im Hintergrunde)
Ein fremder Mann?
Ihn muß ich fragen.
(Sie tritt ruhig einige Schritte näher.)
Wer kam ins Haus
und liegt dort am Herd?
(Da Siegmund sich nicht regt, tritt sie noch etwas näher und betrachtet ihn.)
Müde liegt er
von Weges Mühn:
schwanden die Sinne ihm?
Wäre er siech?
(Sie neigt sich zu ihm herab und lauscht.)
Noch schwillt ihm der Atem;
das Auge nur schloß er.

Scene One

SIEGMUND
The storm drove me here;
here I must shelter.
(He sinks back and remains for a while stretched out, motionless. Sieglinde enters from the door of the inner room, thinking that her husband has returned. Her grave look changes to one of surprise when she sees a stranger on the hearth.)

SIEGLINDE
(still at the back)
A stranger here?
Where has he come from?
(Quietly, she comes a few steps closer.)
Who sought this house,
and lies by the fire?
(As Siegmund does not move, she comes a little closer and looks at him.)
He's exhausted
and makes no move.
Can he have fainted there,
or is he dead?
(She bends over him and listens.)
Ah no, he is breathing;
it seems that he's sleeping.

Mutig dünkt mich der Mann,
sank er müd auch hin.

SIEGMUND
(fährt jäh mit dem Haupt in die Höhe.)
Ein Quell! Ein Quell!

SIEGLINDE
Erquickung schaff ich.
(Sie nimmt schnell ein Trinkhorn, geht damit aus dem Hause, kommt zurück und reicht das gefüllte Trinkhorn Siegmund.)
Labung biet ich
dem lechzenden Gaumen:
Wasser, wie du gewollt!

SIEGMUND
(trinkt und reicht ihr das Horn zurück. Als er ihr mit dem Haupte Dank zuwinkt, haftet sein Blick mit steigender Teilnahme an ihren Mienen.)
Kühlende Labung
gab mir der Quell,
des Müden Last
machte er leicht;
erfrischt ist der Mut,
das Aug' erfreut
des Sehens selige Lust.
Wer ist's, der so mir es labt?

SIEGLINDE
Dies Haus und dies Weib
sind Hundings Eigen;
gastlich gönn' er dir Rast:
harre, bis heim er kehrt!

SIEGMUND
Waffenlos bin ich:
dem wunden Gast
wird dein Gatte nicht wehren.

SIEGLINDE
(mit besorgter Hast)
Die Wunden weise mir schnell!

SIEGMUND
(springt lebhaft vom Lager zum Sitz auf.)
Gering sind sie,
der Rede nicht wert;

Valiant, strong is the man,
though he's weary now.

SIEGMUND
(suddenly raises his head.)
A drink! a drink!

SIEGLINDE
I'll bring some water.
(She quickly takes a drinking-horn and goes out of the house with it. Returning with it filled, she offers it to Siegmund.)
Cool your lips with this drink
that I've brought you!
Water—will you not drink?

SIEGMUND
(drinks and hands her back the horn. As he signals his thanks with his head, his glance fastens on her features with growing interest.)
Cool and refreshing—
now I am well;
my load of care
suddenly light;
my spirits revive;
my eyes enjoy
a blessed, glorious sight.
And who has brought me to life?

SIEGLINDE
This house and this wife
belong to Hunding.
He will welcome his guest:
wait here till he returns.

SIEGMUND
Weaponless am I:
a wounded guest
cannot trouble your husband.

SIEGLINDE
(with anxious haste)
Oh quickly show me the wounds!

SIEGMUND
(shakes himself and sits up quickly.)
A scratch merely,
unworthy your care;

noch fügen des Leibes
Glieder sich fest.
Hätten halb so stark wie mein Arm
Schild und Speer mir gehalten,
nimmer floh ich dem Feind;
doch zerschellten mir Speer und Schild.
Der Feinde Meute
hetzte mich müd,
Gewitterbrunst
brach meinen Leib;
doch schneller, als ich der Meute,
schwand die Müdigkeit mir;
sank auf die Lider mir Nacht,
die Sonne lacht mir nun neu.

no bone in my body
broken at all.
Had my shield and spear been as strong,
half as strong as my body,
I would never have fled;
but they shattered my spear and shield.
And so I fled
the enemys' rage;
a thunderstorm
broke overhead.
Yet, swifter than I was fleeing,
all my faintness has fled.
Darkness had covered my eyes—
the sunlight smiles on me now.

SIEGLINDE
(geht nach dem Speicher, füllt ein Horn mit Met und reicht es Siegmund mit freundlicher Bewegtheit.)
Des seimigen Metes
süßen Trank
mögst du mir nicht verschmähn.

SIEGLINDE
(goes to the storeroom, fills a horn with mead, and offers it to Siegmund with friendly eagerness.)
I bring you a drink
of honeyed mead;
say that you'll not refuse.

SIEGMUND
Schmecktest du mir ihn zu?
(Sieglinde nippt am Horne und reicht es ihm wieder. Siegmund tut einen langen Zug, indem er den Blick mit wachsender Wärme auf sie heftet. Er setzt so das Horn ab und läßt es langsam sinken, während der Ausdruck seiner Miene in starke Ergriffenheit übergeht. Er seufzt tief auf und senkt den Blick düster zu Boden. Mit bebender Stimme:)
Einen Unseligen labtest du:
Unheil wende
der Wunsch von dir!
(Er bricht schnell auf, um fortzugehen.)
Gerastet hab ich
und süß geruht:
weiter wend ich den Schritt.
(Er geht nach hinten.)

SIEGMUND
Will not you taste it first?
(Sieglinde sips from the horn and gives it back to him. Siegmund takes a long draught, while his gaze rests on her with growing warmth. Still gazing, he takes the horn from his lips and lets it sink slowly, while the expression on his face tells of strong emotion. He sighs deeply, and gloomily lowers his gaze to the ground. With trembling voice:)
Evil fortune's never far from me:
may I keep it
away from you!
(He starts up to go.)
I rested sweetly;
I feel refreshed.
I must go on my way.
(He moves towards the back.)

SIEGLINDE
(lebhaft sich umwendend)
Wer verfolgt dich, daß du schon fliehst?

SIEGLINDE
(turning round quickly)
Who pursues you? Why must you flee?

SIEGMUND
(von ihrem Rufe gefesselt, langsam und düster)
Mißwende folgt mir,

SIEGMUND
(arrested by her cry; slowly and sadly)
Ill fate pursues me,

wohin ich fliehe;
Mißwende naht mir,
wo ich mich zeige.
Dir, Frau, doch bleibe sie fern!
Fort wend ich Fuß und Blick.
(Er schreitet schnell bis zur Tür und hebt den Riegel.)

follows my footsteps;
ill fate advances—
soon it will reach me.
This ill fate you must not share!
So I must leave your house.
(He strides swiftly to the door and lifts the latch.)

SIEGLINDE
(in heftigem Selbstvergessen ihm nachrufend)
So bleibe hier!
Nicht bringst du Unheil dahin,
wo Unheil im Hause wohnt!

SIEGLINDE
(calling to him with impetuous self-forgetfulness)
No, do not leave!
You bring no ill fate to me,
for ill fate has long been here!

SIEGMUND
(bleibt tief erschüttert stehen und forscht in Sieglindes Mienen; diese schlägt verschämt und traurig die Augen nieder. Langes Schweigen. Siegmund kehrt zurück.)
Wehwalt hieß ich mich selbst:
Hunding will ich erwarten.
(Er lehnt sich an den Herd; sein Blick haftet mit ruhiger und entschlossener Teilnahme an Sieglinde: diese hebt langsam das Auge wieder zu ihm auf. Beide blicken sich in langem Schweigen mit dem Ausdruck tiefster Ergriffenheit in die Augen.)

SIEGMUND
(deeply moved, remains where he is; he gazes intently at Sieglinde, who lowers her eyes in embarrassment and sadness. A long silence. Siegmund returns into the room.)
Wehwalt, that is my name.
Hunding—I will await him.
(He leans against the hearth; his eyes fix themselves with calm and steady sympathy on Sieglinde. Slowly, she raises her eyes again to his. They gaze into one another's eyes, during a long silence, with an expression of the deepest emotion.)

Zweite Szene

Sieglinde fährt plötzlich auf, lauscht und hört Hunding, der sein Roß außen zum Stall führt. Sie geht hastig zur Tür und öffnet; Hunding, gewaffnet mit Schild und Speer, tritt ein und hält unter der Tür, als er Siegmund gewahrt. Hunding wendet sich mit einem ernst fragenden Blick an Sieglinde.

Scene Two

Suddenly Sieglinde starts, listens, and hears Hunding, who is leading his horse to the stable outside. She goes quickly to the door and opens it. Hunding, armed with shield and spear, enters, and pauses at the threshold on perceiving Siegmund. He turns to Sieglinde with a glance of stern inquiry.

SIEGLINDE
(dem Blicke Hundings entgegnend)
Müd am Herd

SIEGLINDE
(in answer to Hunding's look)
There he lay,

fand ich den Mann:
Not führt' ihn ins Haus.

feeble and faint;
need drove him in here.

HUNDING
Du labtest ihn?

HUNDING
You cared for him?

SIEGLINDE
Den Gaumen letzt' ich ihm,
gastlich sorgt' ich sein!

SIEGLINDE
I said you'd welcome him;
greeted him as guest.

SIEGMUND
(der ruhig und fest Hunding beobachtet)
Dach und Trank
dank ich ihr:
willst du dein Weib drum schelten?

SIEGMUND
(watching Hunding calmly and firmly)
Rest and drink,
both she brought:
Why should you then reproach her?

HUNDING
Heilig ist mein Herd:
heilig sei dir mein Haus!
(Er legt seine Waffen ab und übergibt sie Sieglinde. Zu Sieglinde:)
Rüst uns Männern das Mahl!
(Sieglinde hängt die Waffen an Ästen des Eschenstammes auf, dann holt sie Speise und Trank aus dem Speicher und rüstet auf dem Tische das Nachtmahl. Unwillkürlich heftet sie wieder den Blick auf Siegmund. Hunding mißt scharf und verwundert Siegmunds Züge, die er mit denen seiner Frau vergleicht; für sich:)
Wie gleicht er dem Weibe!
Der gleißende Wurm
glänzt auch ihm aus dem Auge.
(Er birgt sein Befremden und wendet sich wie unbefangen zu Siegmund.)
Weit her, traun,
kamst du des Wegs;
ein Roß nicht ritt,
der Rast hier fand:
welch schlimme Pfade
schufen dir Pein?

HUNDING
Sacred is my hearth;
sacred keep you my house.
(He hands his weapons to Sieglinde, and says to her:)
Go, make ready our meal!
(Sieglinde hangs the weapons on the branches of the ash-tree, fetches food and drink from the storeroom, and prepares the table for supper. Involuntarily she turns her eyes again to Siegmund. Hunding looks keenly and with astonishment at Siegmund's features, comparing them with his wife's; aside:)
He looks like my wife there!
A glittering snake
seems to shine in their glances.
(He hides his surprise and turns, as if unconcerned, to Siegmund.)
You have strayed
far from your path;
you rode no horse
to reach my house.
What painful journey
brought you to me?

SIEGMUND
Durch Wald und Wiese,
Heide und Hain,
jagte mich Sturm
und starke Not:
nicht kenn ich den Weg, den ich kam.
Wohin ich irrte,

SIEGMUND
Through field and forest,
meadow and marsh,
driven by storm
and starkest need—
I know not the way that I took;
nor can I tell you

weiß ich noch minder:
Kunde gewänn' ich des gern.

HUNDING
(am Tische und Siegmund den Sitz bietend)
Des Dach dich deckt,
des Haus dich hegt,
Hunding heißt der Wirt;
wendest von hier du
nach West den Schritt,
in Höfen reich
hausen dort Sippen,
die Hundings Ehre behüten.
Gönnt mir Ehre mein Gast,
wird sein Name nun mir genannt.
(Siegmund, der sich am Tisch niedergesetzt, blickt nachdenklich vor sich hin. Sieglinde, die sich neben Hunding, Siegmund gegenüber, gesetzt, heftet ihr Auge mit auffallender Teilnahme und Spannung auf diesen. Hunding, der beide beobachtet:)
Trägst du Sorge,
mir zu vertraun,
der Frau hier gib doch Kunde:
sieh, wie gierig sie dich frägt!

SIEGLINDE
(unbefangen und teilnahmsvoll)
Gast, wer du bist,
wüßt' ich gern.

SIEGMUND
(blickt auf, sieht ihr in das Auge und beginnt ernst.)
Friedmund darf ich nicht heißen;
Frohwalt möcht' ich wohl sein:
doch Wehwalt muß ich mich nennen.
Wolfe, der war mein Vater;
zu zwei kam ich zur Welt,
eine Zwillingsschwester und ich.
Früh schwanden mir
Mutter und Maid;
die mich gebar
und die mit mir sie barg,
kaum hab ich je sie gekannt.
Wehrlich und stark war Wolfe;
der Feinde wuchsen ihm viel.
Zum Jagen zog
mit dem Jungen der Alte:
von Hetze und Harst

where I have wandered.
May I now learn it from you?

HUNDING
(at the table, motioning to Siegmund to sit)
This house is mine,
this land is mine;
Hunding is your host.
Turn to the west
when you leave my house,
and there my kin
dwell in rich homesteads,
where Hunding's honour is guarded.
You may honour me too:
will my guest not tell me his name?
(Siegmund, who has sat down at the table, gazes thoughtfully in front of him. Sieglinde has placed herself next to Hunding, opposite Siegmund, on whom she fastens her eyes with evident sympathy and intentness. Hunding, observing them both:)
Though you fear
to trust it to me,
my wife here longs to hear it.
See, how eagerly she asks!

SIEGLINDE
(unembarrassed and eager)
Guest, I would know
who you are.

SIEGMUND
(looks up, gazes into her eyes, and begins gravely.)
Friedmund no one could call me;
Frohwalt—would that I were!
I'm Wehwalt, named for my sorrow.
Wolfe, he was my father;
his two children were twins—
my unhappy sister and I.
Both mother and sister
were lost—
my mother killed
and my sister borne off—
taken while I was a boy.
Valiant and strong was Wolfe;
his foes were many and fierce.
And hunters bold
were the boy and his father.
Once, weary and worn,

einst kehrten sie heim:
da lag das Wolfsnest leer.
Zu Schutt gebrannt
der prangende Saal,
zum Stumpf der Eiche
blühender Stamm;
erschlagen der Mutter
mutiger Leib,
verschwunden in Gluten
der Schwester Spur.
Uns schuf die herbe Not
der Neidinge harte Schar.
Geächtet floh
der Alte mit mir;
lange Jahre
lebte der Junge
mit Wolfe im wilden Wald:
Manche Jagd
ward auf sie gemacht;
doch mutig wehrte
das Wolfspaar sich.
(zu Hunding gewandt)
Ein Wölfing kündet dir das,
den als »Wölfing« mancher wohl kennt.

HUNDING
Wunder und wilde Märe
kündest du, kühner Gast,
Wehwalt, der Wölfing!
Mich dünkt, von dem wehrlichen Paar
vernahm ich dunkle Sage,
kannt' ich auch Wolfe
und Wölfing nicht.

SIEGLINDE
Doch weiter künde, Fremder:
wo weilt dein Vater jetzt?

SIEGMUND
Ein starkes Jagen auf uns
stellten die Neidinge an:
Der Jäger viele
fielen den Wölfen,
in Flucht durch den Wald
trieb sie das Wild:
wie Spreu zerstob uns der Feind.
Doch ward ich vom Vater versprengt;

we came from the chase,
and found our home laid waste.
A heap of ash
was all that was left;
a stump where once
an oak tree had stood;
the corpse of my mother
lay at my feet;
all trace of my sister
was lost in smoke.
This cruel blow was dealt
by ruffians who sought revenge.
As outlaws then
we took to the woods;
there I lived
with Wolfe my father;
in hunting I spent my youth.
Many a raid
was made on us both,
but we had learnt
to defend our lives.
(turning to Hunding)
A Wölfing tells you this tale,
and as 'Wölfing' often I'm known.

HUNDING
Wonderful, wild adventures
came to our daring guest,
Wehwalt the Wölfing!
I think that I've heard of the pair,
I've heard unholy stories
spoken of Wolfe
and Wölfing too.

SIEGLINDE
But tell us more, O stranger:
where is your father now?

SIEGMUND
The ruffians raided again,
fell on my father and me;
and many hunters
fell in the battle;
they fled through the wood,
chased by us both;
like chaff we scattered the foe.
They parted my father from me;

seine Spur verlor ich,
je länger ich forschte:
eines Wolfes Fell nur
traf ich im Forst;
leer lag das vor mir,
den Vater fand ich nicht.
Aus dem Wald trieb es mich fort;
mich drängt' es zu Männern und Frauen.
Wieviel ich traf,
wo ich sie fand,
ob ich um Freund',
um Frauen warb,
immer doch war ich geächtet:
Unheil lag auf mir.
Was Rechtes je ich riet,
andern dünkte es arg,
was schlimm immer mir schien,
andere gaben ihm Gunst,
In Fehde fiel ich, wo ich mich fand,
Zorn traf mich, wohin ich zog;
gehrt' ich nach Wonne,
weckt' ich nur Weh:
drum mußt' ich mich Wehwalt nennen;
des Wehes waltet' ich nur.
(Er sieht zu Sieglinde auf und gewahrt ihren teilnehmenden Blick.)

in the fight I lost him.
A long while I sought him.
Though I found the wolf-skin
that he had worn,
no more could I find;
my father was not there.
Then I lost my love for the woods;
I mingled with warriors and women.
But all in vain,
often I tried
to find a friend,
to woo a maid—
everywhere I was rejected.
Ill fate lay on me.
For what I thought was right,
others reckoned was wrong,
and what seemed to me bad,
others held to be good.
And so it was wherever I went,
outlawed by all whom I met;
striving for gladness,
found only woe!
And so I was Wehwalt always;
Yes, Wehwalt!—sad was my fate.
(He turns his eyes to Sieglinde and observes her sympathetic glance.)

HUNDING
Die so leidig Los dir beschied,
nicht liebte dich die Norn':
froh nicht grüßt dich der Mann,
dem fremd als Gast du nahst.

HUNDING
So the Norn who dealt you this fate,
she felt no love for you:
No one greets you with joy
when you arrive as guest.

SIEGLINDE
Feige nur fürchten den,
der waffenlos einsam fährt!
Künde noch, Gast,
wie du im Kampf
zuletzt die Waffe verlorst!

SIEGLINDE
Manly hearts do not fear
a weaponless lonely man!
Tell us more, guest;
tell of the fight
in which your weapons were lost.

SIEGMUND
(immer lebhafter)
Ein trauriges Kind
rief mich zum Trutz:
vermählen wollte
der Magen Sippe
dem Mann ohne Minne die Maid.

SIEGMUND
(with increasing excitement)
A girl in distress
called for my aid;
her kinsmen wanted
to force the maiden
to marry a husband she feared.

Wider den Zwang
zog ich zum Schutz,
der Dränger Troß
traf ich im Kampf:
dem Sieger sank der Feind.
Erschlagen lagen die Brüder:
die Leichen umschlang da die Maid,
den Grimm verjagt' ihr der Gram.
Mit wilder Tränen Flut
betroff sie weinend die Wal:
um des Mordes der eignen Brüder
klagte die unsel'ge Braut.

Der Erschlagnen Sippen
stürmten daher;
übermächtig
ächzten nach Rache sie;
rings um die Stätte
ragten mir Feinde.
Doch von der Wal
wich nicht die Maid;
mit Schild und Speer
schirmt' ich sie lang,
bis Speer und Schild
im Harst mir zerhaun.
Wund und waffenlos stand ich—
sterben sah ich die Maid:
mich hetzte das wütende Heer—
auf den Leichen lag sie tot.
(mit einem Blicke voll schmerzlichen Feuers auf Sieglinde)
Nun weißt du, fragende Frau,
warum ich Friedmund—nicht heiße!
(Er steht auf und schreitet auf den Herd zu. Sieglinde blickt erbleichend und tief erschüttert zu Boden.)

HUNDING
(erhebt sich.)
Ich weiß ein wildes Geschlecht,
nicht heilig ist ihm,
was andern hehr:
verhaßt ist es allen und mir.
Zur Rache ward ich gerufen,
Sühne zu nehmen
für Sippenblut:
zu spät kam ich
und kehre nun heim,

Hearing her cry,
I came to her help.
Her cruel kin
met me in fight;
they fell before my spear.
I'd killed her fierce, cruel brothers.
The maid threw her arms round the dead;
her rage had turned into grief.
With wildly streaming eyes
she bathed the dead with her tears,
as she mourned for the death of those
who'd wronged her—that ill-fated bride.

Then her brothers' kinsmen
rushed to the fight;
vowing vengeance,
angrily fell on me,
raging around me,
eager to kill me.
Meanwhile the maid
stayed by the dead;
my shield and spear
sheltered her life,
till spear and shield
were hacked from my hand.
I was weaponless, wounded;
she was killed while I watched:
I fled from the furious host;
on the bodies she lay dead.
(turning to Sieglinde with a look filled with sorrowful fervour)
You asked me, now you must know
why I'm not Friedmund—but Wehwalt!
(He stands up and walks to the hearth. Sieglinde, pale and deeply stirred, lowers her eyes.)

HUNDING
(rises.)
I know a quarrelsome race;
they do not respect
what we revere;
they are hated by all men—and me.
I heard a summons to vengeance:
Death to the stranger
who killed our kin!
Too late came I,
but now that I'm home,

des flücht'gen Frevlers Spur
im eignen Haus zu erspähn.
(Er geht herab.)
Mein Haus hütet,
Wölfing, dich heut;
für die Nacht nahm ich dich auf;
mit starker Waffe
doch wehre dich morgen;
zum Kampfe kies ich den Tag:
für Tote zahlst du mir Zoll.
(Sieglinde schreitet mit besorgter Gebärde zwischen die beiden Männer vor. Hunding, barsch:)
Fort aus dem Saal!
Säume hier nicht!
Den Nachttrunk rüste mir drin
und harre mein zur Ruh'.
(Sieglinde steht eine Weile unentschieden und sinnend. Sie wendet sich langsam und zögernden Schrittes nach dem Speicher. Dort hält sie wieder an und bleibt, in Sinnen verloren, mit halb abgewandtem Gesicht stehen. Mit ruhigem Entschluß öffnet sie den Schrein, füllt ein Trinkhorn und schüttet aus einer Büchse Würze hinein. Dann wendet sie das Auge auf Siegmund, um seinem Blicke zu begegnen, den dieser fortwahrend auf sie heftet. Sie gewahrt Hundings Spähen und wendet sich sogleich zum Schlafgemach. Auf den Stufen kehrt sie sich noch einmal um, heftet das Auge sehnsuchtsvoll auf Siegmund und deutet mit dem Blicke andauernd und mit sprechender Bestimmtheit auf eine Stelle am Eschenstamme. Hunding fährt auf und treibt sie mit einer heftigen Gebärde zum Fortgehen an. Mit einem letzten Blick auf Siegmund geht sie in das Schlafgemach und schließt hinter sich die Tür. Hunding nimmt seine Waffen vom Stamme herab.)
Mit Waffen wahrt sich der Mann.
(im Abgehen sich zu Siegmund wendend)
Dich, Wölfing, treffe ich morgen;
mein Wort hörtest du—
hüte dich wohl!
(Er geht mit den Waffen in das Gemach; man hört ihn von innen Riegel schließen.)

I find that stranger here;
he sought my house for his rest.
(He advances.)
My house guards you,
Wölfing, today;
for the night you are my guest.
But find some weapons
to serve you tomorrow;
I choose the day for our fight:
You'll pay me blood for their blood.
(With anxious gestures Sieglinde steps between the two men. Hunding, harshly:)
Go from the room!
Why are you here!
Prepare my drink for the night,
and wait for me in there.
(Sieglinde stands awhile undecided and thoughtful. Then she turns slowly and with hesitating steps towards the storeroom. There she again pauses and remains standing, lost in thought, with her face half turned away. With quiet resolve she opens the cupboard, fills a drinking horn, and shakes some spices into it from a container. Then she turns her eyes on Siegmund so as to meet his gaze, which he keeps unceasingly fixed on her. She perceives that Hunding is watching, and goes at once towards the bedchamber. On the steps she turns once more, looks yearningly at Siegmund, and indicates with her eyes, persistently and with eloquent earnestness, a particular spot in the ash-tree's trunk. Hunding starts, and drives her with a violent gesture from the room. With a last look at Siegmund, she goes into the bedchamber, and closes the door behind her. Hunding takes down his weapons from the tree-trunk.)
With weapons man should be armed.
(to Siegmund, as he goes)
You, Wölfing, meet me tomorrow,
and then—fight with me!
Guard yourself well!
(He goes into the chamber; the closing of the bolt is heard from within.)

Dritte Szene

Siegmund allein. Es ist vollständig Nacht geworden; der Saal ist nur noch von einem schwachen Feuer im Herd erhellt. Siegmund läßt sich, nah beim Feuer, auf dem Lager nieder und brütet in großer innerer Aufregung eine Zeitlang vor sich hin.

SIEGMUND
Ein Schwert verhieß mir der Vater,
ich fänd' es in höchster Not.
Waffenlos fiel ich
in Feindes Haus;
seiner Rache Pfand,
raste ich hier.
Ein Weib sah ich,
wonnig und hehr:
entzückend Bangen
zehrt mein Herz.
Zu der mich nun Sehnsucht zieht,
die mit süßem Zauber mich sehrt,
im Zwange hält sie der Mann,
der mich Wehrlosen höhnt!
Wälse! Wälse!
Wo ist dein Schwert?
Das starke Schwert,
das im Sturm ich schwänge,
bricht mir hervor aus der Brust,
was wütend das Herz noch hegt?
(Das Feuer bricht zusammen; es fällt aus der aufsprühenden Glut plötzlich ein greller Schein auf die Stelle des Eschenstammes, welche Sieglindes Blick bezeichnet hatte und an der man jetzt deutlich einen Schwertgriff haften sieht.)
Was gleißt dort hell
im Glimmerschein?
Welch ein Strahl bricht
aus der Esche Stamm?
Des Blinden Auge
leuchtet ein Blitz:
lustig lacht da der Blick.
Wie der Schein so hehr
das Herz mir sengt!
Ist es der Blick
der blühenden Frau,
den dort haftend
sie hinter sich ließ,

Scene Three

Siegmund is alone. It has become quite dark. The room is lit only by a feeble fire on the hearth. Siegmund sinks down on the couch near the fire and broods silently for a while, in great agitation.

SIEGMUND
A sword was pledged by my father,
to serve in my hour of need.
I am unarmed
in my enemy's house;
as a hostage here
helpless I wait.
But she's here too,
lovely and fair:
a new emotion
fills my heart.
This woman who holds me bound,
whose enchantment tears at my heart,
as slave she's held by a man
who mocks his weaponless foe.
Wälse! Wälse!
Where is your sword?
The shining sword
that alone can save me,
when there should break from my breast
that fury my heart still hides?
(The fire collapses, and a bright glow springs up, striking the place on the ash-trunk indicated by Sieglinde's look, where now a sword-hilt is clearly seen.)

What's glinting there
to light the gloom?
On the ash-tree
there's a starry gleam.
My eyes are blinded,
dazzled with light;
lightnings flash from the tree.
How the shining gleam
inspires my heart!
Is it the glance
that shone from her eyes,
did she leave it
to linger behind,

als aus dem Saal sie schied?
(Von hier an verglimmt das Herdfeuer allmählich.)
Nächtiges Dunkel
deckte mein Aug';
ihres Blickes Strahl
streifte mich da:
Wärme gewann ich und Tag.
Selig schien mir
der Sonne Licht;
den Scheitel umgliß mir
ihr wonniger Glanz,
bis hinter Bergen sie sank.
(ein neuer schwacher Aufschein des Feuers)
Noch einmal, da sie schied,
traf mich abends ihr Schein;
selbst der alten Esche Stamm
erglänzte in goldner Glut:
da bleicht die Blüte,
das Licht verlischt;
nächtiges Dunkel
deckt mir das Auge:
tief in des Busens Berge
glimmt nur noch lichtlose Glut.
(Das Feuer ist gänzlich verloschen: volle Nacht. Das Seitengemach öffnet sich leise: Sieglinde, in weißem Gewande, tritt heraus und schreitet leise, doch rasch, auf den Herd zu.)

SIEGLINDE
Schläfst du, Gast?

SIEGMUND
(freudig überrascht aufspringend)
Wer schleicht daher?

SIEGLINDE
Ich bin's: höre mich an!
In tiefem Schlaf liegt Hunding;
ich würzt' ihm betäubenden Trank:
Nütze die Nacht dir zum Heil!

SIEGMUND
(hitzig unterbrechend)
Heil macht mich dein Nah'n!

SIEGLINDE
Eine Waffe laß mich dir weisen:

when she was sent away?
(From now on, the fire on the hearth gradually sinks.)
Shadows of darkness
covered my eyes;
but her radiant glance
fell on me then,
warming and lighting my heart.
Glorious rays
of the golden sun,
with gladdening splendour
encircled my head,
till in the mountains it sank.
(a new faint gleam from the fire)
Yet once more, as it went,
evening radiance did shine;
and the ancient ash-tree's trunk
was bathed in a golden glow;
that light is fading;
the gleam has gone;
shadows of darkness
gather around me:
deep in my breast there lingers on
that last smouldering glow.
(The fire has burnt out; complete darkness. The door at the side opens softly. Sieglinde, in a white garment, comes out and advances lightly but quickly towards the hearth.)

SIEGLINDE
Are you awake?

SIEGMUND
(springing up in joyful surprise)
Who steals this way?

SIEGLINDE
I do. Listen to me!
In heavy sleep lies Hunding;
I gave him a drug in his drink.
Now, in the night, you are safe!

SIEGMUND
(interrupting her passionately)
Safe when you are near!

SIEGLINDE
There's a sword for him who can win it;

O wenn du sie gewännst!
Den hehrsten Helden
dürft' ich dich heißen:
dem Stärksten allein
ward sie bestimmt.
O merke wohl, was ich dir melde!
Der Männer Sippe
saß hier im Saal,
von Hunding zur Hochzeit geladen.
Er freite ein Weib,
das ungefragt
Schächer ihm schenkten zur Frau.
Traurig saß ich,
während sie tranken;
ein Fremder trat da herein:
ein Greis in grauem Gewand;
tief hing ihm der Hut,
der deckt' ihm der Augen eines;
doch des andren Strahl,
Angst schuf er allen,
traf die Männer
sein mächt'ges Dräu'n:
Mir allein
weckte das Auge
süß sehnenden Harm,
Tränen und Trost zugleich.
Auf mich blickt' er
und blitzte auf jene,
als ein Schwert in Händen er schwang;
das stieß er nun
in der Esche Stamm,
bis zum Heft haftet' es drin:
dem sollte der Stahl geziemen,
der aus dem Stamm es zög'.
Der Männer alle,
so kühn sie sich mühten,
die Wehr sich keiner gewann;
Gäste kamen
und Gäste gingen,
die stärksten zogen am Stahl—
keinen Zoll entwich er dem Stamm:
dort haftet schweigend das Schwert.
Da wußt' ich, wer der war,
der mich Gramvolle gegrüßt;
ich weiß auch,
wem allein
im Stamm das Schwert er bestimmt.

and when that sword is won,
then I can call you
noblest of heroes:
the strongest alone
masters the sword.
So listen well, mark what I tell you!
My husband's kinsmen
sat in this room,
they'd come here to witness his wedding.
He married a wife
against her will;
robbers had made her their prize.
Sad, I sat here
while they were drinking;
a stranger entered this house:
an old man dressed all in grey;
his hat hung so low
that one of his eyes was hidden;
but the other's flash
filled them with terror:
none could counter
that threatening gaze.
I alone
felt in those glances
sweet, yearning regret—
sorrow and solace in one.
On me smiling,
he glared at the others;
in his hand he carried a sword;
then drove it deep
in the ash-tree's trunk;
to the hilt buried it there.
But one man alone could win it,
he who could draw it forth.
The guests were warriors;
they rose to the challenge;
but none could master the sword.
Many tried it
but all were baffled;
the strongest seized it in vain—
none could move the blade from its place.
That sword is still in the tree.
I knew then who he was,
come to greet me in my grief;
I know too
who alone
can draw the sword from the tree.

O fänd' ich ihn heut
und hier, den Freund;
käm' er aus Fremden
zur ärmsten Frau:
Was je ich gelitten
in grimmigem Leid,
was je mich geschmerzt
in Schande und Schmach—
süßeste Rache
sühnte dann alles!
Erjagt hätt' ich,
was je ich verlor,
was je ich beweint,
wär' mir gewonnen,
fänd' ich den heiligen Freund,
umfing' den Helden mein Arm!

And oh, have I found
today that friend,
come from the distance
to end my grief?
Then all I have suffered
in pain and distress,
yes, all I have suffered
in sorrow and shame,
all is forgotten,
all is atoned for!
Regained all things
I thought I had lost;
my fondest desires
gain their fulfilment,
if I have found that friend,
and hold that hero to me!

SIEGMUND
(mit Glut Sieglinde umfassend)
Dich, selige Frau,
hält nun der Freund,
dem Waffe und Weib bestimmt!
Heiß in der Brust
brennt mir der Eid,
der mich dir Edlen vermählt.
Was je ich ersehnt,
ersah ich in dir;
in dir fand ich,
was je mir gefehlt!
Littest du Schmach,
und schmerzte mich Leid;
war ich geächtet,
und warst du entehrt:
freudige Rache
ruft nun den Frohen!
Auf lach ich
in heiliger Lust—
halt ich die Hehre umfangen,
fühl ich dein schlagendes Herz!
(Die große Tür springt auf.)

SIEGMUND
(embracing Sieglinde with ardour)
Yes, loveliest bride,
I am that friend;
both weapon and wife I claim!
Fierce in my breast
blazes the vow
that binds me ever to you.
For all that I've sought
I see now in you;
in you, all things
I longed for are found.
Though you were shamed,
though sad was my life,
though I was outlawed,
and you were disgraced,
joyful vengeance
calls us to gladness!
I laugh now
in fullest delight,
as I embrace your glory,
feel your beating heart!
(The large door flies open.)

SIEGLINDE
(fährt erschrocken zusammen und reißt sich los.)
Ha, wer ging? Wer kam herein?
(Die Tür bleibt weit geöffnet: außen herrliche Frühlingsnacht; der Vollmond leuchtet herein und wirft sein helles Licht auf das Paar, das so sich plötzlich in voller Deutlichkeit wahrnehmen kann.)

SIEGLINDE
(starts in alarm, and tears herself away.)
Ah, who went? or who has come?
(The door remains open; outside, a glorious spring night; the full moon shines in, throwing its bright light on the pair, so that suddenly they can fully and clearly see each other.)

SIEGMUND
(in leiser Entzückung)
Keiner ging,
doch einer kam:
siehe, der Lenz
lacht in den Saal!
(Siegmund zieht Sieglinde mit sanfter Gewalt zu sich auf das Lager, so daß sie neben ihm zu sitzen kommt. Wachsende Helligkeit des Mondscheines.)
Winterstürme wichen
dem Wonnemond,
in mildem Lichte
leuchtet der Lenz;
auf linden Lüften
leicht und lieblich,
Wunder webend
er sich wiegt:
durch Wald und Auen
weht sein Atem,
weit geöffnet
lacht sein Aug'.
Aus sel'ger Vöglein Sange
süß er tönt,
holde Düfte
haucht er aus:
seinem warmen Blut entblühen
wonnige Blumen,
Keim und Sproß
entspringt seiner Kraft.
Mit zarter Waffen Zier
bezwingt er die Welt;
Winter und Sturm wichen
der starken Wehr:
Wohl mußte den tapfern Streichen
die strenge Türe auch weichen,
die trotzig und starr
uns—trennte von ihm.
Zu seiner Schwester
schwang er sich her;
die Liebe lockte den Lenz:
in unsrem Busen
barg sie sich tief;
nun lacht sie selig dem Licht.
Die bräutliche Schwester
befreite der Bruder;
zertrümmert liegt,
was sie je getrennt;

SIEGMUND
(in gentle ecstasy)
No one went—
but one has come:
see him, the Spring
smiles on our love!
(Siegmund draws Sieglinde to him on the couch with tender vehemence, so that she sits beside him. Increasing brilliance of the moonlight.)
Winter storms have vanished
at Spring's command;
in gentle radiance
sparkles the Spring,
on balmy breezes,
light and lovely,
working wonders
on his way;
on wood and meadow
softly breathing;
wide and smiling
are his eyes.
The songs of happy birds
reflect his voice;
sweet the fragrance
of his breath;
from his ardent blood the flowers
are joyfully blooming;
buds and blooms
have sprung at his call.
He waves his wand of magic
over the world;
winter and storm yield
to his strong command:
as soon as his word was spoken
the doors that barred him were broken,
for how could they keep us
parted from him?
To clasp his sister
here he has flown;
for Love called to the Spring;
and Love lay hidden
deep in our hearts;
but now she laughs to the light.
The bride and sister
is freed by her brother;
the barriers fall
that held them apart;

jauchzend grüßt sich
das junge Paar:
vereint sind Liebe und Lenz!

joyful greeting
as now they meet:
united are Love and Spring!

SIEGLINDE
Du bist der Lenz,
nach dem ich verlangte
in frostigen Winters Frist.
Dich grüßte mein Herz
mit heiligem Grau'n,
als dein Blick zuerst mir erblühte.
Fremdes nur sah ich von je,
freundlos war mir das Nahe;
als hätt' ich nie es gekannt,
war, was immer mir kam.
Doch dich kannt' ich
deutlich und klar:
als mein Auge dich sah,
warst du mein Eigen;
was im Busen ich barg,
was ich bin,
hell wie der Tag
taucht' es mir auf,
wie tönender Schall
schlug's an mein Ohr,
als in frostig öder Fremde
zuerst ich den Freund ersah.
(Sie hängt sich entzückt an seinen Hals und blickt ihm nahe ins Gesicht.)

SIEGLINDE
You are the Spring,
that Spring I have yearned for
in frost and in winter's ice.
My heart felt the spell,
grew warm when you came;
when my eyes beheld you, I knew you.
Everything used to be strange,
friendless all that was round me;
like far off things and unknown,
all that ever drew near.
But you came
and all was clear:
for I knew you were mine
when I beheld you.
What I hid in my heart,
all I am,
bright as the day,
all was revealed;
the sound of this truth
rang in my ear,
when in winter's frosty desert
my eyes first beheld my friend.
(She throws her arms around his neck, enraptured, and gazes closely into his face.)

SIEGMUND
(mit Hingerissenheit)
O süßeste Wonne!
Seligstes Weib!

SIEGMUND
(carried away)
Oh sweetest enchantment,
woman most blessed!

SIEGLINDE
(dicht an seinen Augen)
O laß in Nähe
zu dir mich neigen,
daß hell ich schaue
den hehren Schein,
der dir aus Aug'
und Antlitz bricht
und so süß die Sinne mir zwingt.

SIEGLINDE
(close to his eyes)
Oh hold me near you,
and clasp me to you,
to see more clearly
that holy light
that shines from eyes,
from countenance,
and so sweetly steals to my heart.

SIEGMUND
Im Lenzesmond

SIEGMUND
The Spring's fair moon

leuchtest du hell;
hehr umwebt dich
das Wellenhaar:
Was mich berückt,
errat ich nun leicht—
denn wonnig weidet mein Blick.

shines on you here,
crowns with glory
your lovely hair.
Ah, now I know
what captured my heart;
my glances feast in delight.

SIEGLINDE
(schlägt ihm die Locken von der Stirn zurück und betrachtet ihn staunend.)
Wie dir die Stirn
so offen steht,
der Adern Geäst
in den Schläfen sich schlingt!
Mir zagt es vor der Wonne,
die mich entzückt!
Ein Wunder will mich gemahnen:
den heut zuerst ich erschaut,
mein Auge sah dich schon!

SIEGLINDE
(pushes the locks back from his brow, and gazes at him in astonishment.)
Your noble brow
is broad and clear;
its delicate veins
with my fingers I trace!
I tremble with the rapture
of my delight!
A marvel stirs in my memory:
although you came but today,
I've seen your face before!

SIEGMUND
Ein Minnetraum
gemahnt auch mich:
in heißem Sehnen
sah ich dich schon!

SIEGMUND
I know your dream,
I feel it too:
in ardent yearning
you were my dream!

SIEGLINDE
Im Bach erblickt' ich
mein eigen Bild—
und jetzt gewahr ich es wieder:
wie einst dem Teich es enttaucht,
bietest mein Bild mir nun du!

SIEGLINDE
The stream has shown
my reflected face—
and now I find it before me;
in you I see it again,
just as it shone from the stream!

SIEGMUND
Du bist das Bild,
das ich in mir barg.

SIEGMUND
Yours is the face
that I knew in my heart.

SIEGLINDE
(den Blick schnell abwendend)
O still! Laß mich
der Stimme lauschen:
mich dünkt, ihren Klang
hört' ich als Kind—
Doch nein, ich hörte sie neulich,
(aufgeregt)
als meiner Stimme Schall
mir widerhallte der Wald.

SIEGLINDE
(quickly turning her eyes away from him)
Be still! Again
that voice is sounding,
the voice that I heard
once as a child—
But no! I know when I heard it:
(excitedly)
when through the woods I called,
and echo called in reply.

SIEGMUND
O lieblichste Laute,
denen ich lausche!

SIEGLINDE
(ihm wieder in die Augen spähend)
Deines Auges Glut
erglänzte mir schon:
So blickte der Greis
grüßend auf mich,
als der Traurigen Trost er gab.
An dem Blick
erkannt' ihn sein Kind—
schon wollt' ich beim Namen ihn [nennen!
(Sie hält inne und fährt dann leise fort.)
Wehwalt heißt du fürwahr?

SIEGMUND
Nicht heiß ich so,
seit du mich liebst:
nun walt ich der hehrsten Wonnen!

SIEGLINDE
Und Friedmund darfst du
froh dich nicht nennen?

SIEGMUND
Nenne mich du,
wie du liebst, daß ich heiße:
den Namen nehm ich von dir!

SIEGLINDE
Doch nanntest du Wolfe den Vater?

SIEGMUND
Ein Wolf war er feigen Füchsen!
Doch dem so stolz
strahlte das Auge,
wie, Herrliche, hehr dir es strahlt,
der war: Wälse genannt.

SIEGLINDE
(außer sich)
War Wälse dein Vater
und bist du ein Wälsung,
stieß er für dich
sein Schwert in den Stamm—

SIEGMUND
Oh loveliest music,
voice that I longed for!

SIEGLINDE
(again gazing into his eyes)
And your gleaming glance,
I've seen it before:
the stranger in grey
gazed on me thus
when he came to console my grief.
By that glance
his child knew him well—
I knew by what name I should call him!

(She pauses a moment and then continues softly.)
Wehwalt, is that what you're called?

SIEGMUND
No more that name,
now you are mine:
my sorrow has turned to gladness!

SIEGLINDE
And Friedmund was no name
for a sufferer.

SIEGMUND
Name me yourself;
by what name can you love me?
My name, I'll take it from you!

SIEGLINDE
You told me that Wolf was your father.

SIEGMUND
A Wolf when he hunted foxes!
But when his eye
shone on me proudly,
as your eyes shine on me now,
why then—Wälse his name.

SIEGLINDE
(beside herself)
Was Wälse your father,
and are you a Wälsung?
Then it is yours,
that sword in the tree!

so laß mich dich heißen, wie ich dich liebe: Siegmund— so nenn ich dich!	So now let me name you as I have loved you: Siegmund— that is your name!
SIEGMUND *(springt auf, eilt auf den Stamm zu, und faßt den Schwertgriff.)*	SIEGMUND *(leaps up, hurries to the trunk, and grasps the sword hilt.)*
Siegmund heiß ich und Siegmund bin ich! Bezeug' es dies Schwert, das zaglos ich halte! Wälse verhieß mir, in höchster Not fänd' ich es einst: ich faß es nun! Heiligster Minne höchste Not, sehnender Liebe sehrende Not brennt mir hell in der Brust, drängt zu Tat und Tod: Notung! Notung! So nenn ich dich, Schwert. Notung! Notung! Neidlicher Stahl! Zeig deiner Schärfe schneidenden Zahn: heraus aus der Scheide zu mir!	Siegmund call me, and Siegmund am I! The proof is the sword, my hand soon shall hold it! Promised by Wälse in hour of need, now it is found; I grasp it now! Holiest love in highest need, yearning desire in longing and need, burning bright in my breast, drives to deeds and death. Notung! Notung! so name I the sword! Notung! Notung! Bright, shining steel. Show me your sharpness, glorious blade! Come forth from the scabbard to me!
(Er zieht mit einem gewaltigen Zuck das Schwert aus dem Stamme und zeigt es der von Staunen und Entzücken erfaßten Sieglinde.)	*(With a powerful effort, Siegmund draws the sword from the tree, and shows it to the astonished and enraptured Sieglinde.)*
Siegmund, den Wälsung, siehst du, Weib! Als Brautgabe bringt er dies Schwert: so freit er sich die seligste Frau; dem Feindeshaus entführt er dich so. Fern von hier folge mir nun, fort in des Lenzes lachendes Haus: dort schützt dich Notung, das Schwert, wenn Siegmund dir liebend erlag!	Siegmund, the Wälsung, here you see! As bride-gift he brings you this sword; he claims with it his loveliest bride; and from this house he leads her away. Far from here, follow me now, forth to the laughing land of bright Spring. Your guard is Notung, the sword, should Siegmund die, conquered by love!
(Er hat sie umfaßt, um sie mit sich fortzuziehen.)	*(He has embraced her, to draw her away with him.)*

SIEGLINDE
(reißt sich in höchster Trunkenheit von ihm los und stellt sich ihm gegenüber.)
Bist du Siegmund,
den ich hier sehe—
Sieglinde bin ich,
die dich ersehnt:
Die eigne Schwester
gewannst du zu eins mit dem Schwert!

SIEGMUND
Braut und Schwester
bist du dem Bruder—
so blühe denn, Wälsungenblut!
(Er zieht sie mit wütender Glut an sich, sie sinkt mit einem Schrei an seine Brust. Der Vorhang fällt schnell.)

SIEGLINDE
(in highest excitement tears herself away, and stands before him.)
Is this Siegmund,
standing before me?
Sieglinde am I;
I longed for you.
Your own dear sister
and bride you have won with the sword!

SIEGMUND
Bride and sister
be to your brother;
the blood of these Wälsungs is blessed!
(He draws her to him with passionate fervour; with a cry, she falls on his breast. The curtain falls quickly.)

Zweiter Aufzug

Wildes Felsengebirge

Im Hintergrunde zieht sich von unten her eine Schlucht herauf, die auf ein erhöhtes Felsjoch mündet; von diesem senkt sich der Boden dem Vordergrund zu wieder abwärts.

Act Two

A Wild, Craggy Place

In the background, a gorge slopes up from below to a high ridge of rocks, from which the ground again sinks to the front.

Erste Szene

Wotan, kriegerisch gewaffnet, mit dem Speer; vor ihm Brünnhilde, als Walküre, ebenfalls in voller Waffenrüstung

WOTAN
Nun zäume dein Roß,
reisige Maid!
Bald entbrennt
brünstiger Streit:
Brünnhilde stürme zum Kampf,
dem Wälsung kiese sie Sieg!

Scene One

Wotan, armed for battle, carrying his spear; before him Brünnhilde, as a Valkyrie, likewise fully armed

WOTAN
Go bridle your horse,
warrior maid!
Seize your shield;
battle is near.
Brünnhilde's off to the fight,
the Wälsung is victor today!

Hunding wähle sich,
wem er gehört;
nach Walhall taugt er mir nicht.
Drum rüstig und rasch
reite zur Wal!

Hunding falls to him;
leave him to lie;
for Walhall he is not fit.
So hasten away,
ride to the field!

BRÜNNHILDE
(jauchzend von Fels zu Fels die Höhe rechts hinaufspringend)
Hojotoho! Hojotoho!
Heiaha! Heiaha!
Hojotoho! Heiaha!
(Sie hält auf einer hohen Felsspitze an, blickt in die hintere Schlucht hinab und ruft zu Wotan zurück.)
Dir rat ich, Vater,
rüste dich selbst;
harten Sturm
sollst du bestehn.
Fricka naht, deine Frau,
im Wagen mit dem Widdergespann.
Hei, wie die goldne
Geißel sie schwingt!
Die armen Tiere
ächzen vor Angst;
wild rasseln die Räder;
zornig fährt sie zum Zank!
In solchem Strauße
streit ich nicht gern,
lieb ich auch mutiger
Männer Schlacht.
Drum sieh, wie den Sturm du bestehst:
ich Lustige laß dich im Stich!
Hojotoho! Hojotoho!
Heiaha! Heiaha!
Heiahaha!
(Brünnhilde verschwindet hinter der Gebirgshöhe zur Seite. In einem mit zwei Widdern bespannten Wagen langt Fricka aus der Schlucht auf dem Felsjoche an: dort hält sie rasch an und steigt aus. Sie schreitet heftig in den Vordergrund auf Wotan zu.)

BRÜNNHILDE
(shouting as she leaps from rock to rock up to the heights on the right)
Hoyotoho! Hoyotoho!
Hiaha! Hiaha!
Hoyotoho! Hiaha!
(On a high peak she stops, looks into the gorge at the back, and calls back to Wotan.)

I warn you, father,
look to yourself;
brave the storm
blowing your way
Fricka's coming—your wife;
she's drawn along by two of her rams.
Hi! How she swings
her glittering whip!
The wretched beasts
are sweating with fear;
wheels rattle and rumble,
whirl her on to the fray.
A woman's battle
is not to my taste,
rather the clangour
of martial arms.
Be sure that you weather the storm;
I'm happy to leave it to you!
Hoyotoho! Hoyotoho!
Hiaha! Hiaha!
Hiahaha!
(Brünnhilde disappears behind the mountain height at the side. Fricka, in a chariot drawn by two rams, comes up from the gorge to the top of the rocky ridge, where she stops suddenly and alights. She strides impetuously towards Wotan in the foreground.)

WOTAN
(Fricka auf sich zuschreiten sehend, für sich)
Der alte Sturm,
die alte Müh'!
Doch stand muß ich hier halten!

WOTAN
(seeing Fricka approaching; aside)
The usual storm,
the usual strife!
But here I must be steadfast!

FRICKA
(je näher sie kommt, mäßigt sie den Schritt und stellt sich mit Würde vor Wotan hin.)
Wo in den Bergen du dich birgst,
der Gattin Blick zu entgehn,
einsam hier
such ich dich auf,
daß Hilfe du mir verhießest.

WOTAN
Was Fricka kümmert,
künde sie frei.

FRICKA
Ich vernahm Hundings Not,
um Rache rief er mich an:
der Ehe Hüterin
hörte ihn,
verhieß streng
zu strafen die Tat
des frech frevelnden Paars,
das kühn den Gatten gekränkt.

WOTAN
Was so Schlimmes
schuf das Paar,
das liebend einte der Lenz?
Der Minne Zauber
entzückte sie:
wer büßt mir der Minne Macht?

FRICKA
Wie törìcht und taub du dich stellst,
als wüßtest fürwahr du nicht,
daß um der Ehe
heiligen Eid,
den hart gekränkten, ich klage!

WOTAN
Unheilig
acht ich den Eid,
der Unliebende eint;
und mir wahrlich
mute nicht zu,
daß mit Zwang ich halte,
was dir nicht haftet:
denn wo kühn Kräfte sich regen,

FRICKA
(as she approaches, moderates her pace and places herself with dignity before Wotan.)
In the mountains where you hide,
to shun the sight of your wife,
here I have
found you at last,
to claim the help that you owe me.

WOTAN
Let Fricka's troubles
freely be told.

FRICKA
I have heard Hunding's cry:
Revenge the wrong they have done!
As wedlock's guardian
I answered him.
I swore
I would punish the deed
this pair dared to commit,
who wronged a husband and me.

WOTAN
But what evil
have they done?
The Spring enticed them to love.
The power of love
overcame them both;
and who can resist that power?

FRICKA
Pretend that you don't understand!
And yet you know all too well
that I have come
to avenge marriage vows,
the holy vows they have broken!

WOTAN
Unholy
call I the vows
that bind unloving hearts;
and do you
expect me to act,
to exert my power
where yours is helpless?
For where bold spirits are moving,

da rat ich offen zum Krieg.

FRICKA
Achtest du rühmlich
der Ehe Bruch,
so prahle nun weiter
und preis es heilig,
daß Blutschande entblüht
dem Bund eines Zwillingspaars!
Mir schaudert das Herz,
es schwindelt mein Hirn:
bräutlich umfing
die Schwester der Bruder!
Wann ward es erlebt,
daß leiblich Geschwister sich liebten?

WOTAN
Heut—hast du's erlebt!
Erfahre so,
was von selbst sich fügt,
sei zuvor auch noch nie es geschehn.
Daß jene sich lieben,
leuchtet dir hell;
drum höre redlichen Rat:
Soll süße Lust
deinen Segen dir lohnen,
so segne, lachend der Liebe,
Siegmunds und Sieglindes Bund!

FRICKA
(in höchste Entrüstung ausbrechend)
So ist es denn aus
mit den ewigen Göttern,
seit du die wilden
Wälsungen zeugtest?
Heraus sagt' ich's;
traf ich den Sinn?
Nichts gilt dir der Hehren
heilige Sippe;
hin wirfst du alles,
was einst du geachtet;
zerreißest die Bande,
die selbst du gebunden,
lösest lachend
des Himmels Haft:
daß nach Lust und Laune nur walte
dies frevelnde Zwillingspaar,

I stir them ever to strife.

FRICKA
If you encourage
adulterous love,
then proudly go further
and praise as holy
the incest there has been,
the love of a pair of twins!
My senses are shocked,
my mind is amazed—
bridal embrace
of sister and brother!
When came it to pass
that brother and sister were lovers?

WOTAN
Now it's come to pass!
And learn from this
that a thing may happen
although it's not happened before.
They love one another,
as you must know;
so hear my words of advice:
Since Fricka is famed
for her blessing on lovers,
bestow on them your blessing,
on Siegmund's and Sieglinde's love!

FRICKA
(breaking out in deep indignation)
So this is the end
of the gods and their glory,
now you have fathered
Wölfing the Wälsung?
I speak frankly;
am I not right?
The race of the gods
by you is forgotten!
You cast aside
what you once held in honour;
you break every bond
that you tied to unite us;
loosen, laughing,
your hold on heaven!
that the lustful lovers may flourish,
this sinful incestuous pair,

deiner Untreue zuchtlose Frucht!
Oh, was klag ich
um Ehe und Eid,
da zuerst du selbst sie versehrt.
Die treue Gattin
trogest du stets;
wo eine Tiefe,
wo eine Höhe,
dahin lugte
lüstern dein Blick,
wie des Wechsels Lust du gewännst
und höhnend kränktest mein Herz.
Trauernden Sinnes
mußt' ich's ertragen,
zogst du zur Schlacht
mit den schlimmen Mädchen,
die wilder Minne
Bund dir gebar:
denn dein Weib noch scheutest du so,
daß der Walküren Schar
und Brünnhilde selbst,
deines Wunsches Braut,
in Gehorsam der Herrin du gabst.
Doch jetzt, da dir neue
Namen gefielen,
als »Wälse« wölfisch
im Walde du schweiftest;
jetzt, da zu niedrigster
Schmach du dich neigtest,
gemeiner Menschen
ein Paar zu erzeugen:
jetzt dem Wurfe der Wölfin
wirfst du zu Füßen dein Weib!
So führ es denn aus!
Fülle das Maß!
Die Betrogne laß auch zertreten!

WOTAN
(ruhig)
Nichts lerntest du,
wollt' ich dich lehren,
was nie du erkennen kannst,
eh' nicht ertagte die Tat.
Stets Gewohntes
nur magst du verstehn:
doch was noch nie sich traf,
danach trachtet mein Sinn.

who were born as the fruit of your shame!
Oh, why mourn
over virtue and vows,
when they first were broken by you!
Your faithful wife
you've always betrayed;
down in the caverns,
high on the mountains,
your glance searched
and lusted for love,
where your raving fancy might lead you.
Your scorn has broken my heart.
Sad in my spirit,
I had to see you
leading to battle
those barbarous maidens
your lawless love
had brought into being;
but you still respected your wife,
for the Valkyrie brood,
and Brünnhild herself
whom you love so well—
they were bound in obedience to me.
But now a new name
has taken your fancy,
and 'Wälse' prowls
like a wolf through the woodland;
now you have stooped
to the depth of dishonour,
a common woman
has borne you her children:
now to whelps of a she-wolf
you would abandon your wife!
Go on with your work!
Fill now my cup!
You betrayed me; let me be trampled!

WOTAN
(quietly)
You never learn
what I would teach you,
to try to conceive a deed
before that deed comes to pass.
Your concern
is for things that have been;
but what is still to come—
to that turn all my thoughts.

Eines höre!
Not tut ein Held,
der, ledig göttlichen Schutzes,
sich löse vom Göttergesetz.
So nur taugt er
zu wirken die Tat,
die, wie not sie den Göttern,
dem Gott doch zu wirken verwehrt.

FRICKA
Mit tiefem Sinne
willst du mich täuschen:
was Hehres sollten
Helden je wirken,
das ihren Göttern wäre verwehrt,
deren Gunst in ihnen nur wirkt?

WOTAN
Ihres eignen Mutes
achtest du nicht?

FRICKA
Wer hauchte Menschen ihn ein?
Wer hellte den Blöden den Blick?
In deinem Schutz
scheinen sie stark,
durch deinen Stachel
streben sie auf:
du reizest sie einzig,
die so mir Ew'gen du rühmst.
Mit neuer List
willst du mich belügen,
durch neue Ränke
mir jetzt entrinnen;
doch diesen Wälsung
gewinnst du dir nicht:
in ihm treff ich nur dich,
denn durch dich trotzt er allein.

WOTAN
(ergriffen)
In wildem Leiden
erwuchs er sich selbst:
mein Schutz schirmte ihn nie.

FRICKA
So schütz auch heut ihn nicht!

Hear this one thing!
We need a man
who lives without our protection,
who is free from the rule of the gods.
He alone
can accomplish the deed,
which, although it will save us,
the gods are forbidden to do.

FRICKA
With crafty reasoning
you would deceive me.
What marvel can be worked
by these mortals?
What is this deed which gods cannot do?
And who gives the mortals their power?

WOTAN
Do you rate their own
achievement so low?

FRICKA
Who breathed the soul into men?
Who kindled the light in their eyes?
When you are near,
then they are strong;
when you inspire them,
then they can strive.
You fill them with daring,
then sing their praises to me.
With new deceits
you are trying to trick me;
with new excuses
you would escape me;
but for this Wälsung
you plead all in vain:
in him I find only you;
what he does, he does through you.

WOTAN
(with emotion)
In wildest sorrow
he grew by himself;
and I gave him no help.

FRICKA
Then do not help him now!

Nimm ihm das Schwert,
das du ihm geschenkt!

Take back the sword
you placed in his hand.

WOTAN
Das Schwert?

WOTAN
The sword?

FRICKA
Ja, das Schwert,
das zauberstark
zuckende Schwert,
das du Gott dem Sohne gabst.

FRICKA
Yes, the sword,
the magical,
glittering sword,
that the god has given his son!

WOTAN
(heftig)
Siegmund gewann es sich
(mit unterdrücktem Beben)
selbst in der Not.
(Wotan drückt in seiner ganzen Haltung von hier an einen immer wachsenden unheimlichen, tiefen Unmut aus.)

WOTAN
(violently)
Siegmund has won it himself
(with a suppressed shudder)
in his need.
(From this point, Wotan's whole demeanour expresses an ever-increasing uneasy, profound dejection.)

FRICKA
(eifrig fortfahrend)
Du schufst ihm die Not
wie das neidliche Schwert.
Willst du mich täuschen,
die Tag und Nacht
auf den Fersen dir folgt?
Für ihn stießest du
das Schwert in den Stamm,
du verhießest ihm
die hehre Wehr:
willst du es leugnen,
daß nur deine List
ihn lockte, wo er es fänd'?
(Wotan fährt mit einer grimmigen Gebärde auf. Fricka immer sicherer, da sie den Eindruck gewahrt, den sie auf Wotan hervorgebracht hat.)
Mit Unfreien
streitet kein Edler,
den Frevler straft nur der Freie.
Wider deine Kraft
führt' ich wohl Krieg:
doch Siegmund verfiel mir als Knecht!
(neue heftige Gebärde Wotans, dann Versinken in das Gefühl seiner Ohnmacht)
Der dir als Herren
hörig und eigen,

FRICKA
(continuing eagerly)
You sent him the need,
as you sent him the sword.
Can you deceive me,
when day and night
I have watched every step?
For him you prepared
that sword in the tree,
and you promised him
it would be found.
Can you deny it,
that your hand alone
has led him where it was found?
(Wotan makes a wrathful gesture. Fricka becomes ever more confident, as she sees the impression she has made on Wotan.)
With bondsmen
the gods do not battle;
rebellious slaves must be punished.
As an equal
I argue with you;
but Siegmund I claim as my slave.
(Wotan makes another vehement gesture, and then is overcome by the sense of his powerlessness.)
For soul and body,
he is your servant,

gehorchen soll ihm
dein ewig Gemahl?
Soll mich in Schmach
der Niedrigste schmähen,
dem Frechen zum Sporn,
dem Freien zum Spott?
Das kann mein Gatte nicht wollen,
die Göttin entweiht er nicht so!

and now must I
be subjected to him?
Am I his slave,
to smile when he scorns me?
despised by the world,
and mocked by the free?
And can my husband allow me,
his goddess, to suffer this shame?

WOTAN
(finster)
Was verlangst du?

WOTAN
(gloomy)
What must I do?

FRICKA
Laß von dem Wälsung!

FRICKA
Abandon the Wälsung!

WOTAN
(mit gedämpfter Stimme)
Er geh seines Wegs.

WOTAN
(with muffled voice)
He goes his own way.

FRICKA
Doch du schütze ihn nicht,
wenn zur Schlacht ihn der Rächer ruft!

FRICKA
And you'll give him no help
when he's called to defend his life?

WOTAN
Ich schütze ihn nicht.

WOTAN
I'll give him no help.

FRICKA
Sieh mir ins Auge,
sinne nicht Trug:
die Walküre wend auch von ihm!

FRICKA
Do not deceive me;
look in my eyes;
the Valkyrie leaves him to die!

WOTAN
Die Walküre walte frei.

WOTAN
The Valkyrie is free to choose.

FRICKA
Nicht doch; deinen Willen
vollbringt sie allein:
verbiete ihr Siegmunds Sieg!

FRICKA
Not so; your commandment
is all she obeys:
command her that Siegmund dies!

WOTAN
(in heftigen inneren Kampf ausbrechend)
Ich kann ihn nicht fällen:
er fand mein Schwert!

WOTAN
(breaking out after a violent inner struggle)
I cannot destroy him;
he found my sword!

FRICKA
Entzieh dem den Zauber,
zerknick es dem Knecht!
Schutzlos schau' ihn der Feind!

FRICKA
Destroy all its magic,
command it to break!
Siegmund falls in the fight!

BRÜNNHILDE
(noch unsichtbar von der Höhe her)
Heiaha! Heiaha! Hojotoho!

FRICKA
Dort kommt deine kühne Maid;
jauchzend jagt sie daher.

BRÜNNHILDE
Heiaha! Heiaha!
Heiohotojo! Hotojoha!

WOTAN
(dumpf für sich)
Ich rief sie für Siegmund zu Roß!
(Brünnhilde erscheint mit ihrem Roß auf dem Felsenpfade rechts. Als sie Fricka gewahrt, bricht sie schnell ab und geleitet ihr Roß still und langsam während des Folgenden den Felsweg herab; dort birgt sie es dann in einer Höhle.)

FRICKA
Deiner ew'gen Gattin
heilige Ehre
beschirme heut ihr Schild!
Von Menschen verlacht,
verlustig der Macht,
gingen wir Götter zugrund:
würde heut nicht hehr
und herrlich mein Recht
gerächt von der mutigen Maid.
Der Wälsung fällt meiner Ehre!
Empfah ich von Wotan den Eid?

WOTAN
(in furchtbarem Unmut und innerem Grimm auf einen Felsensitz sich werfend)
Nimm den Eid!
(Fricka schreitet dem Hintergrunde zu: dort begegnet sie Brünnhilde und hält einen Augenblick vor ihr an.)

FRICKA
(zu Brünnhilde)
Heervater harret dein:
laß ihn dir künden,
wie das Los er gekiest!
(Sie besteigt den Wagen und fährt schnell davon.)

BRÜNNHILDE
(still invisible, calling from the heights)
Hiaha! Hiaha! Hoyotoho!

FRICKA
And here is your valiant maid,
joyfully coming this way.

BRÜNNHILDE
Hiaha! Hiaha!
Hiohotoyo! Hotoyoha!

WOTAN
(dejected, to himself)
To fight now for Siegmund she rides.
(Brünnhilde appears, with her horse, on the rocky path to the right. On seeing Fricka, she breaks off suddenly and, during the following, she slowly, silently leads her horse down the mountain path, and then stables it in a cave.)

FRICKA
And her shield today
must shelter the honour
of your immortal wife!
For men in their scorn
would laugh at our might,
jeer at the glorious gods,
if today your warlike daughter
should not revenge
all the wrongs of your wife!
The Wälsung dies for my honour!
Will Wotan now give me his oath?

WOTAN
(throwing himself on to a rocky seat in terrible dejection and inner anger)
Take my oath!
(Fricka strides towards the back: there she meets Brünnhilde and stops for a moment before her.)

FRICKA
(to Brünnhilde)
Wotan is waiting there:
let him instruct you
how the lot must be cast.
(She mounts her chariot and drives quickly away.)

Zweite Szene

Brünnhilde tritt mit besorgter Miene verwundert vor Wotan, der, auf dem Felssitz zurückgelehnt, das Haupt auf die Hand gestützt, in finsteres Brüten versunken ist.

BRÜNNHILDE
Schlimm, fürcht ich,
schloß der Streit,
lachte Fricka dem Lose.
Vater, was soll
dein Kind erfahren?
Trübe scheinst du und traurig!

WOTAN
(läßt den Arm machtlos sinken und den Kopf in den Nacken fallen.)
In eigner Fessel
fing ich mich,
ich Unfreiester aller!

BRÜNNHILDE
So sah ich dich nie!
Was nagt dir das Herz?

WOTAN
(Von hier an steigert sich Wotans Ausdruck und Gebärde bis zum furchtbarsten Ausbruch.)
O heilige Schmach!
O schmählicher Harm!
Götternot!
Götternot!
Endloser Grimm!
Ewiger Gram!
Der Traurigste bin ich von allen!

BRÜNNHILDE
(wirft erschrocken Schild, Speer und Helm von sich und läßt sich mit besorgter Zutraulichkeit zu Wotans Füßen nieder.)
Vater! Vater!
Sage, was ist dir?
Wie erschreckst du mit Sorge dein Kind?
Vertraue mir!
Ich bin dir treu:

Scene Two

Brünnhilde advances with astonished and anxious mien to Wotan, who, leaning back on the rocky seat, his head propped on his hand, is sunk in gloomy brooding.

BRÜNNHILDE
Fricka
has won the fight;
since she smiles at the outcome.
Father, what news
have you to tell me?
Why this sadness and sorrow?

WOTAN
(drops his arm helplessly and lets his head sink on his breast.)
I forged the fetters;
now I'm bound.
I, least free of all living!

BRÜNNHILDE
What troubles you so;
what new grief is this?

WOTAN
(whose expression and gestures grow in intensity from this point, until they culminate in a fearful outburst)
Oh infinite shame!
Oh shameful distress!
Gods' despair!
Gods' despair!
Endless remorse!
Grief evermore!
The saddest of beings is Wotan!

BRÜNNHILDE
(terrified, throws shield, spear and helmet from her and sinks at Wotan's feet in anxious solicitude.)
Father! Father!
Tell me, what is it?
For your daughter is filled with dismay!
Oh trust in me!
you know I'm true!

sieh, Brünnhilde bittet!
(Sie legt traulich und ängstlich Haupt und Hände ihm auf Knie und Schoß.)

WOTAN
(blickt ihr lange ins Auge; dann streichelt er ihr mit unwillkürlicher Zärtlichkeit die Locken. Wie aus tiefen Sinnen zu sich kommend, beginnt er leise:)
Laß ich's verlauten,
lös ich dann nicht
meines Willens haltenden Haft?

BRÜNNHILDE
(ihm ebenso erwidernd)
Zu Wotans Willen sprichst du,
sagst du mir, was du willst;
wer bin ich,
wär' ich dein Wille nicht?

WOTAN
(sehr leise)
Was deinem in Worten ich künde,
unausgesprochen
bleib es denn ewig:
mit mir nur rat ich,
red ich zu dir.
(Mit noch gedämpfterer, schauerlicher Stimme, während er Brünnhilde unverwandt in das Auge blickt.)
Als junger Liebe
Lust mir verblich,
verlangte nach Macht mein Mut:
von jäher Wünsche
Wüten gejagt,
gewann ich mir die Welt.
Unwissend trugvoll,
Untreue übt' ich,
band durch Verträge,
was Unheil barg:
listig verlockte mich Loge,
der schweifend nun verschwand.
Von der Liebe doch
mocht' ich nicht lassen,
in der Macht verlangt' ich nach Minne.
Den Nacht gebar,
der bange Nibelung,
Alberich, brach ihren Bund;

See, Brünnhilde begs you.
(She lays her head and hands with loving concern on his knees and lap.)

WOTAN
(looks long in her eyes; then he strokes her hair with involuntary tenderness. As if coming to himself out of deep brooding, he begins softly:)
If I should tell you,
might I not lose
the controlling power of my will?

BRÜNNHILDE
(answers him equally softly)
To Wotan's will you're speaking;
you can say what you will;
what am I,
if not your will alone?

WOTAN
(very softly)
These thoughts that I never have uttered,
though I may think them,
still they're unspoken.
I think aloud, then,
speaking to you.
(in a still more muted, fearful voice, while he gazes steadily into Brünnhilde's eyes)
When youth's delightful
pleasures had waned,
I longed in my heart for power;
and driven
by impetuous desires,
I won myself the world;
yet all unwitting,
I acted wrongly;
trusted in treaties
where evil lay,
craftily counselled by Loge,
who lured me on—then left.
Yet the longing
for love would not leave me;
in my power I felt its enchantment.
That child of night,
the cringing Nibelung,
Alberich, broke from its bonds;

er fluchte der Liebe
und gewann durch den Fluch
des Rheines glänzendes Gold
und mit ihm maßlose Macht.
Den Ring, den er schuf,
entriß ich ihm listig;
doch nicht dem Rhein
gab ich ihn zurück:
mit ihm bezahlt' ich
Walhalls Zinnen,
der Burg, die Riesen mir bauten,
aus der ich der Welt nun gebot.
Die alles weiß,
was einstens war,
Erda, die weihlich
weiseste Wala,
riet mir ab von dem Ring,
warnte vor ewigem Ende.
Von dem Ende wollt' ich
mehr noch wissen;
doch schweigend entschwand mir das [Weib.
Da verlor ich den leichten Mut,
zu wissen begehrt' es den Gott:
in den Schoß der Welt
schwang ich mich hinab,
mit Liebeszauber
zwang ich die Wala,
stört' ihres Wissens Stolz,
daß sie Rede nun mir stand.
Kunde empfing ich von ihr;
von mir doch barg sie ein Pfand:
der Welt weisestes Weib
gebar mir, Brünnhilde, dich.
Mit acht Schwestern
zog ich dich auf;
durch euch Walküren
wollt' ich wenden,
was mir die Wala
zu fürchten schuf:
ein schmähliches Ende der Ew'gen.
Daß stark zum Streit
uns fände der Feind,
hieß ich euch Helden mir schaffen:
die herrisch wir sonst
in Gesetzen hielten,
die Männer, denen
den Mut wir gewehrt,

by cursing at love
he was able to gain
the Rhinemaids' glistering gold,
and with that gold, all his power.
The ring that he made,
I cunningly stole it;
but to the Rhine
it was not returned.
I used the gold
to pay for Walhall,
the hall the giants had built me,
the hall where I rule all the world.
For one who knows
all things that were,
Erda, the wisest,
holiest Wala,
warned me away from the ring,
told of eternal disaster.
When I asked her to say more,
she vanished;
in silence she sank from my sight.
Then I lost all my joy in life;
my only desire was to learn.
So I made my way
down into the depths;
by love's enchantment
I conquered the Wala,
humbled her silent pride,
till she told me all she knew.
Wisdom I won from her words;
the Wala demanded a pledge;
the wise Erda conceived
a daughter—Brünnhilde, you.
With eight sisters
you were brought up
as bold Valkyries,
who would avert
the doom that the Wala
had made me fear—
the shameful defeat of the immortals.
Our foes would find us
ready for fight;
you would assemble my army:
the men whom we held
by our laws in bondage,
the mortals, whom we
had curbed in their pride,

die durch trüber Verträge
trügende Bande
zu blindem Gehorsam
wir uns gebunden—
die solltet zu Sturm
und Streit ihr nun stacheln,
ihre Kraft reizen
zu rauhem Krieg,
daß kühner Kämpfer Scharen
ich sammle in Walhalls Saal!

BRÜNNHILDE
Deinen Saal füllten wir weidlich:
viele schon führt' ich dir zu.
Was macht dir nun Sorge,
da nie wir gesäumt?

WOTAN
Ein andres ist's:
achte es wohl,
wes mich die Wala gewarnt!
Durch Alberichs Heer
droht uns das Ende:
mit neidischem Grimm
grollt mir der Niblung:
doch scheu ich nun nicht
seine nächtigen Scharen,
meine Helden schüfen mir Sieg.
Nur wenn je den Ring
zurück er gewänne,
dann wäre Walhall verloren:
Der der Liebe fluchte,
er allein
nützte neidisch
des Ringes Runen
zu aller Edlen
endloser Schmach;
der Helden Mut
entwendet' er mir;
die Kühnen selber
zwäng' er zum Kampf;
mit ihrer Kraft
bekriegte er mich.
Sorgend sann ich nun selbst,
den Ring dem Feind zu entreißen.
Der Riesen einer,
denen ich einst

whom by treacherous treaties,
shameful agreements,
we'd bound in obedience
blindly to serve us;
and yours was the task
to stir them to battle,
and arouse brave men
to ruthless war,
till valiant hosts of heroes
had gathered in Walhall's hall!

BRÜNNHILDE
And that hall is guarded securely:
many a hero I brought.
So why are you troubled,
for we never failed?

WOTAN
There's more to tell;
mark what I say;
hear what the Wala foretold!
For Alberich's host
threatens our downfall;
an envious rage
burns in the Niblung.
Yet I have no fear
of his dusky battalions,
while my heroes keep me secure.
But if once the ring
returns to the Niblung,
he conquers Walhall for ever;
by his curse on love,
he alone
can employ
the ring's enchantment
to bring eternal
shame on the gods;
my heroes' hearts
he'd win for himself;
he'd make my army
bend to his will,
and with that force
give battle to me.
So I pondered a way
to keep the ring from the Niblung.
The giant Fafner,
one of the pair

mit verfluchtem Gold
den Fleiß vergalt:
Fafner hütet den Hort,
um den er den Bruder gefällt.
Ihm müßt' ich den Reif entringen,
den selbst als Zoll ich ihm zahlte.
Doch mit dem ich vertrug,
ihn darf ich nicht treffen;
machtlos vor ihm
erläge mein Mut:
Das sind die Bande,
die mich binden:
der durch Verträge ich Herr,
den Verträgen bin ich nun Knecht.
Nur einer könnte,
was ich nicht darf:
ein Held, dem helfend
nie ich mich neigte;
der fremd dem Gotte,
frei seiner Gunst,
unbewußt,
ohne Geheiß,
aus eigner Not,
mit der eignen Wehr
schüfe die Tat,
die ich scheuen muß,
die nie mein Rat ihm riet,
wünscht sie auch einzig mein Wunsch!
Der, entgegen dem Gott,
für mich föchte,
den freundlichen Feind,
wie fände ich ihn?
Wie schüf' ich den Freien,
den nie ich schirmte,
der in eignem Trotze
der Trauteste mir?
Wie macht' ich den andren,
der nicht mehr ich,
und aus sich wirkte,
was ich nur will?
O göttliche Not!
Gräßliche Schmach!
Zum Ekel find ich
ewig nur mich
in allem, was ich erwirke!
Das andre, das ich ersehne,
das andre erseh ich nie:

for whose work I paid
the fatal gold—
Fafner broods on the gold
he murdered his brother to gain.
From him must the ring be taken,
that ring he won as his wages.
Yet the bond that I made
forbids me to harm him;
if I should try
my power would fail.
These are the fetters
which have bound me;
since by my treaties I rule,
by those treaties I am enslaved.
Yet one can accomplish
what I may not:—
a man, a hero
I've never shielded,
whom I've not prompted,
foe to the gods,
free of soul,
fearless and bold,
who acts alone,
by his own design—
that man can do
what the god must shun;
though never urged by me,
he can achieve my desire!
One at war with all gods,
he can save us!
This friendliest foe,
oh how can I find?
Oh where is this free one,
whom I've not shielded,
who in brave defiance
is dearest to me?
How can I create one,
who, not through me,
but on his own
can achieve my will?
Oh godly distress!
Sorrowful shame!
With loathing
I can find but myself
in all my hand has created!
This free one whom I have longed for,
this free one can never be found;

denn selbst muß der Freie sich schaffen;
Knechte erknet ich mir nur!

BRÜNNHILDE
Doch der Wälsung, Siegmund,
wirkt er nicht selbst?

WOTAN
Wild durchschweift' ich
mit ihm die Wälder;
gegen der Götter Rat
reizte kühn ich ihn auf:
gegen der Götter Rache
schützt ihn nun einzig das Schwert,
(gedehnt und bitter)
das eines Gottes
Gunst ihm beschied.
Wie wollt' ich listig
selbst mich belügen?
So leicht ja entfrug mir
Fricka den Trug:
zu tiefster Scham
durchschaute sie mich!
Ihrem Willen muß ich gewähren.

BRÜNNHILDE
So nimmst du von Siegmund den Sieg?

WOTAN
Ich berührte Alberichs Ring,
gierig hielt ich das Gold!
Der Fluch, den ich floh,
nicht flieht er nun mich:
Was ich liebe, muß ich verlassen,
morden, wen je ich minne,
trügend verraten
wer mir traut!
(Wotans Gebärde geht aus dem Ausdruck des furchtbarsten Schmerzes zu dem der Verzweiflung über.)
Fahre denn hin,
herrische Pracht,
göttlichen Prunkes
prahlende Schmach!
Zusammenbreche,
was ich gebaut!
Auf geb ich mein Werk;

for I have no power to make him;
my hand can only make slaves!

BRÜNNHILDE
But the Wälsung, Siegmund,
is he not free?

WOTAN
Wild and free
was our life together;
I taught him to hate the gods,
urged his heart to rebel.
Now when the gods would kill him,
all that he has is a sword;
(emphatic and bitter)
and yet that sword
was given by a god.
How could I hope
to win by deception?
The lie was revealed
when Fricka appeared:
I stood ashamed;
I had no reply!
So to her I had to surrender.

BRÜNNHILDE
Then Siegmund must fall in his fight?

WOTAN
I set hands on Alberich's ring,
grasped in greed at the gold.
The curse that I fled
has fastened on me.
Though I love him, I must forsake him;
murder the son I love so;
basely betray him,
when he trusts!
(Wotan's demeanour changes from the expression of the most terrible suffering to that of despair.)
Fade from my sight,
honour and fame,
glorious godhead's
glittering shame!
And fall in ruins,
all I have raised!
I leave all my work;

nur eines will ich noch:
  das Ende,
  das Ende!
(Er hält sinnend ein.)
  Und für das Ende
  sorgt Alberich!
  Jetzt versteh ich
  den stummen Sinn
des wilden Wortes der Wala:
»Wenn der Liebe finstrer Feind
zürnend zeugt einen Sohn,
  der Sel'gen Ende
  säumt dann nicht!«
  Vom Niblung jüngst
  vernahm ich die Mär,
daß ein Weib der Zwerg bewältigt,
des Gunst Gold ihm erzwang:
  Des Hasses Frucht
  hegt eine Frau,
  des Neides Kraft
  kreißt ihr im Schoß:
  das Wunder gelang
  dem Liebelosen;
doch der in Lieb' ich freite,
den Freien erlang ich mir nicht.
(mit bitterem Grimm sich aufrichtend)
  So nimm meinen Segen,
  Niblungen-Sohn!
  Was tief mich ekelt,
  dir geb ich's zum Erbe,
der Gottheit nichtigen Glanz:
zernage ihn gierig dein Neid!

BRÜNNHILDE
(erschrocken)
  O sag, künde,
  was soll nun dein Kind?

WOTAN
(bitter)
Fromm streite für Fricka;
hüte ihr Eh' und Eid!
(trocken)
  Was sie erkor,
  das kiese auch ich:
was frommte mir eigner Wille?
Einen Freien kann ich nicht wollen:

but one thing I desire:
  the ending,
  that ending!
(He pauses in thought.)
  And to that ending
  works Alberich!
  Now I grasp
  all the secret sense
that filled the words of the Wala:
'When the dusky foe of love
gains in hatred a son,
  the gods may know
  their doom is near.'
  From Nibelheim
  the tidings have come
that the dwarf has forced a woman;
his gold bought her embrace;
  and she will bear
  Alberich's son;
  the seed of spite
  stirs in her womb;
  this wonder befell
  the loveless Niblung;
while I, who loved so truly,
my free son I never could win.
(rising up in bitter wrath)
  I give you my blessing,
  Nibelung son!
  Let all that irks me
  be yours to inherit;
in Walhall's glorious halls
achieve your unhallowed desires!

BRÜNNHILDE
(alarmed)
  Oh speak, father,
  and tell me my task.

WOTAN
(bitterly)
Fight boldly for Fricka,
guardian of wedlock's vow!
(drily)
  The choice she made,
  that choice must be mine:
my own desires are but useless.
Since that free one I cannot fashion,

für Frickas Knechte kämpfe nun du!	be Fricka's champion, fight for her slave!
BRÜNNHILDE Weh! Nimm reuig zurück das Wort! Du liebst Siegmund; dir zulieb, ich weiß es, schütz ich den Wälsung.	BRÜNNHILDE No, have mercy, take back your word! You love Siegmund; let your love command me: Fight for the Wälsung.
WOTAN Fällen sollst du Siegmund, für Hunding erfechten den Sieg! Hüte dich wohl und halte dich stark, all deiner Kühnheit entbiete im Kampf: ein Siegschwert schwingt Siegmund; schwerlich fällt er dir feig!	WOTAN You must conquer Siegmund, and Hunding must win in the fight! Guard yourself well, be stern and strong; bring all your boldness and force to the fight: a strong sword has Siegmund; he'll not easily yield!
BRÜNNHILDE Den du zu lieben stets mich gelehrt, der in hehrer Tugend dem Herzen dir teuer— gegen ihn zwingt mich nimmer dein zwiespältig Wort!	BRÜNNHILDE Him you have always taught me to love; for his noble courage and valour you love him; if you ask me to kill him, then I shall refuse!
WOTAN Ha, Freche du! Frevelst du mir? Wer bist du, als meines Willens blind wählende Kür? Da mit dir ich tagte, sank ich so tief, daß zum Schimpf der eignen Geschöpfe ich ward? Kennst du, Kind, meinen Zorn? Verzage dein Mut, wenn je zermalmend auf dich stürzte sein Strahl! In meinem Busen berg ich den Grimm, der in Grau'n und Wust wirft eine Welt, die einst zur Lust mir gelacht:	WOTAN Rebellious child! Do as I say! What are you but the obedient, blind slave of my will? When I told my sorrows, sank I so low, that I'm scorned, defied by the child whom I raised? Daughter, know you my wrath? Your soul would be crushed if you confronted that fierce, furious rage! Within my bosom anger is hid, that could lay to waste all of a world— that world I once used to love:

Wehe dem, den er trifft!
Trauer schüf' ihm sein Trotz!
Drum rat ich dir,
reize mich nicht!
Besorge, was ich befahl:
Siegmund falle!
Dies sei der Walküre Werk!
(Er stürmt fort und verschwindet schnell links im Gebirge.)

woe to him whom it strikes!
He would pay for his pride!
I warn you, then,
rouse not my rage!
But swiftly do my command.
Siegmund's fated!
That is the Valkyrie's work!
(He storms away, and quickly disappears among the crags to the left.)

BRÜNNHILDE
(steht lange erschrocken und betäubt.)
So sah ich Siegvater nie,
erzürnt' ihn sonst wohl auch ein Zank!
(Sie neigt sich betrübt und nimmt ihre Waffen auf, mit denen sie sich wieder rüstet.)
Schwer wiegt mir
der Waffen Wucht.
Wenn nach Lust ich focht,
wie waren sie leicht!
Zu böser Schlacht
schleich ich heut so bang.
(Sie sinnt vor sich hin und seufzt dann auf.)
Weh, mein Wälsung!
Im höchsten Leid
muß dich treulos die Treue verlassen!
(Sie wendet sich langsam dem Hintergrunde zu.)

BRÜNNHILDE
(stands for a long time, shocked and stunned.)
So I obey his command;
such rage I've never seen before.
(She stoops down sadly, and takes up her weapons, with which she arms herself again.)
Shield, spear
seem to weigh me down!
In a joyful fight
I found they were light!
This hateful task
fills my heart with fear.
(She gazes thoughtfully before her, and sighs.)
Woe, my Wälsung!
In deepest sorrow
this true one must falsely betray you!
(She turns slowly towards the back.)

Dritte Szene

Auf dem Bergjoche angelangt, gewahrt Brünnhilde, in die Schlucht hinabblickend, Siegmund und Sieglinde; sie betrachtet die Nahenden einen Augenblick und wendet sich dann in die Höhle zu ihrem Roß, so daß sie dem Zuschauer gänzlich verschwindet. Siegmund und Sieglinde erscheinen auf dem Bergjoche. Sieglinde schreitet hastig voraus; Siegmund sucht sie aufzuhalten.

SIEGMUND
Raste nur hier;
gönne dir Ruh!

Scene Three

Arrived at the rocky pass, Brünnhilde, looking into the gorge, perceives Siegmund and Sieglinde; she watches their approach for a moment and then goes into the cave to her horse, disappearing from the audience. Siegmund and Sieglinde appear on the pass. Sieglinde comes hastily forwards; Siegmund tries to restrain her.

SIEGMUND
Rest for a while;
stay by my side!

SIEGLINDE
Weiter! Weiter!

SIEGMUND
(umfaßt sie mit sanfter Gewalt.)
Nicht weiter nun!
(Er schließt sie fest an sich.)
Verweile, süßestes Weib!
Aus Wonne-Entzücken
zucktest du auf,
mit jäher Hast
jagtest du fort:
kaum folgt' ich der wilden Flucht;
durch Wald und Flur,
über Fels und Stein,
sprachlos, schweigend
sprangst du dahin,
kein Ruf hielt dich zur Rast!
Ruhe nun aus:
rede zu mir!
Ende des Schweigens Angst!
Sieh, dein Bruder
hält seine Braut:
Siegmund ist dir Gesell!
(Er hat sie unvermerkt nach dem Steinsitze geleitet.)

SIEGLINDE
(blickt Siegmund mit wachsendem Entzücken in die Augen; dann umschlingt sie leidenschaftlich seinen Hals und verweilt so; dann fährt sie mit jähem Schreck auf.)
Hinweg! Hinweg!
Flieh die Entweihte!
Unheilig
umfängt dich ihr Arm;
entehrt, geschändet
schwand dieser Leib:
flieh die Leiche,
lasse sie los!
Der Wind mag sie verwehn,
die ehrlos dem Edlen sich gab!
Da er sie liebend umfing,
da seligste Lust sie fand,
da ganz sie minnte der Mann,
der ganz ihre Minne geweckt:
vor der süßesten Wonne
heiligster Weihe,

SIEGLINDE
Further! Further!

SIEGMUND
(embraces her with gentle force.)
No further now!
(He clasps her firmly to him.)
Oh trust me, sweet, loving bride!
In bliss I embraced you,
then you escaped;
with frenzied haste
fled from my arms,
so fast I could scarce pursue;
through wood and field,
over rock and stone,
speechless, silent,
flying ahead,
I called you all in vain!
Now you must rest:
speak but a word,
ending this silent dread!
See, your brother
shelters his bride:
Siegmund guards you from harm!
(Without her noticing, he has drawn her to the rock seat.)

SIEGLINDE
(gazes with growing rapture into Siegmund's eyes, then throws her arms passionately round his neck and so remains. Then she starts up in sudden terror.)
Away! Away!
Fly from the cursed one!
Unholy
this form that you clasp;
disgraced, dishonoured,
dead in my heart.
Cast me from you,
fling me aside!
Let winds waft me away,
for I have defiled your embrace!
When in your loving embrace,
such blissful delight I found,
you gave me all of your heart,
and all my love was awaked.
In that holy enchantment,
sweetest rapture,

die ganz ihr Sinn
und Seele durchdrang,
Grauen und Schauder
ob gräßlichster Schande
mußte mit Schreck
die Schmähliche fassen,
die je dem Manne gehorcht,
der ohne Minne sie hielt!
Laß die Verfluchte,
laß sie dich fliehn!
Verworfen bin ich,
der Würde bar!
Dir reinstem Manne
muß ich entrinnen,
dir Herrlichem darf ich
nimmer gehören.
Schande bring ich dem Bruder,
Schmach dem freienden Freund!

when all my soul
and senses were won,
loathing and horror
for shameful dishonour
struck with dismay
this traitorous woman,
whom Hunding owned as a wife,
who loveless lay in his arms!
Fly from the cursed one,
far let her flee!
Dishonoured am I,
bereft of grace:
the purest hero
I must abandon,
for how can this guilty wife
dare to love him?
Shame I'd bring to my brother,
Shame to him whom I love!

SIEGMUND
Was je Schande dir schuf,
das büßt nun des Frevlers Blut!
Drum fliehe nicht weiter;
harre des Feindes;
hier soll er mir fallen:
Wenn Notung ihm
das Herz zernagt,
Rache dann hast du erreicht!

SIEGMUND
But this shame you have felt,
this shame shall be paid by blood!
So flee you no further;
Hunding shall find us;
here I shall defeat him:
with Notung
I shall pierce his heart;
vengeance then you will have won!

SIEGLINDE
(schrickt auf und lauscht.)
Horch, die Hörner!
Hörst du den Ruf?
Ringsher tönt
wütend Getös';
aus Wald und Gau
gellt es herauf.
Hunding erwachte
aus hartem Schlaf!
Sippen und Hunde
ruft er zusammen;
mutig gehetzt
heult die Meute,
wild bellt sie zum Himmel
um der Ehe gebrochenen Eid!
(Sie starrt wie wahnsinnig vor sich hin.)
Wo bist du, Siegmund?

SIEGLINDE
(starts up and listens.)
Hark! The horn call!
Do you not hear?
All around,
cries of revenge,
from wood and dale,
ring in my ears.
Hunding has wakened
from heavy sleep!
Hunters, I hear them;
all have assembled:
hard on the trail,
dogs are howling;
they lead the avengers;
they will kill us for breaking a vow!
(As if mad, she stares before her.)
Where are you, Siegmund?

Seh ich dich noch,
brünstig geliebter,
leuchtender Bruder?
Deines Auges Stern
laß noch einmal mir strahlen:
wehre dem Kuß
des verworfnen Weibes nicht!
(Sie hat sich ihm schluchzend an die Brust geworfen, dann schreckt sie ängstlich wieder auf.)
Horch, o horch!
Das ist Hundings Horn!
Seine Meute naht
mit mächt'ger Wehr:
Kein Schwert frommt
vor der Hunde Schwall:
wirf es fort, Siegmund!
Siegmund, wo bist du?
Ha dort! Ich sehe dich!
Schrecklich Gesicht!
Rüden fletschen
die Zähne nach Fleisch;
sie achten nicht
deines edlen Blicks;
bei den Füßen packt dich
das feste Gebiß—
du fällst—
in Stücken zerstaucht das Schwert.—
Die Esche stürzt—
es bricht der Stamm!
Bruder, mein Bruder!
Siegmund—ha!—
(Sie sinkt ohnmächtig in Siegmunds Arme.)

Are you still here?
bravest of lovers,
true, tender brother!
With your glorious eyes
for the last time behold me:
do not refuse
this accursed woman's kiss!
(She throws herself sobbing on his breast, then starts up again in terror.)
Hear! Again!
That is Hunding's horn!
And the huntsmen
come to take your life;
no sword helps you
against the hounds;
let it go, Siegmund!
Siegmund, where are you?
Ah there! I see you now!
Fearful the sight!
Dogs have fastened
their teeth in your flesh;
they take no heed
of your noble glance;
all around you leaping
to tear at your throat—
you fall—
in splinters the shining sword!
The ash is down—
that tree destroyed!
Brother! My brother!
Siegmund—ah!—
(She sinks senseless into Siegmund's arms.)

SIEGMUND
Schwester! Geliebte!
(Er lauscht ihrem Atem und überzeugt sich, daß sie noch lebe. Er läßt sie an sich herabgleiten, so daß sie, als er sich selbst zum Sitze niederläßt, mit ihrem Haupt auf seinem Schoß zu ruhen kommt. In dieser Stellung verbleiben beide bis zum Schlusse des folgenden Auftrittes. Langes Schweigen, währenddessen Siegmund mit zärtlicher Sorge über Sieglinde sich hinneigt und mit einem langen Kusse ihr die Stirn küßt.)

SIEGMUND
Sister! Beloved!
(He listens to her breathing and makes sure that she is still alive. He lets her slide downwards so that, as he himself sinks into a sitting posture, her head rests on his lap. In this position they both remain until the end of the following scene. A long silence, during which Siegmund bends over Sieglinde with tender care, and presses a long kiss on her brow.)

Vierte Szene

Brünnhilde, ihr Roß am Zaume geleitend, tritt aus der Höhle und schreitet langsam und feierlich nach vorne. Sie hält an und betrachtet Siegmund von fern. Sie schreitet wieder langsam vor. Sie hält in größerer Nähe an. Sie trägt Schild und Speer in der einen Hand, lehnt sich mit der andern an den Hals des Rosses und betrachtet so mit ernster Miene Siegmund.

BRÜNNHILDE
Siegmund,
sieh auf mich!
Ich bin's,
der bald du folgst.

SIEGMUND
(richtet den Blick zu ihr auf.)
Wer bist du, sag,
die so schön und ernst mir erscheint?

BRÜNNHILDE
Nur Todgeweihten
taugt mein Anblick;
wer mich erschaut,
der scheidet vom Lebenslicht.
Auf der Walstatt allein
erschein ich Edlen:
wer mich gewahrt,
zur Wal kor ich ihn mir!

SIEGMUND
(blickt ihr lange forschend und fest in das Auge, senkt dann sinnend das Haupt und wendet sich endlich mit feierlichem Ernste wieder zu ihr.)
Der dir nun folgt,
wohin führst du den Helden?

BRÜNNHILDE
Zu Walvater,
der dich gewählt,
führ ich dich:
nach Walhall folgst du mir.

SIEGMUND
In Walhalls Saal
Walvater find ich allein?

Scene Four

Brünnhilde, leading her horse by the bridle, comes out of the cave and advances slowly and solemnly forwards. She pauses and observes Siegmund from a distance. She again slowly advances. She stops, somewhat nearer. She carries her shield and spear in one hand, resting the other on her horse's neck, and thus she gravely regards Siegmund.

BRÜNNHILDE
Siegmund!
Look on me!
I come
to call you hence.

SIEGMUND
(raises his eyes to her.)
Who are you, say,
who so stern and beauteous appear?

BRÜNNHILDE
Those doomed to death
alone can see me;
who meets my gaze
must turn from the light of life.
I appear in the fight
to death-doomed heroes:
those whom I choose
have no choice but to die!

SIEGMUND
(looks long, firmly, and searchingly into her eyes, then bows his head in thought, and at length turns resolutely to her again.)
And if I come,
tell me, where will you lead me?

BRÜNNHILDE
To Wotan
who marks you for his.
He commands:
to Walhall come with me.

SIEGMUND
To Walhall's hall?
Does Wotan rule there alone?

BRÜNNHILDE
Gefallner Helden
hehre Schar
umfängt dich hold
mit hochheiligem Gruß.

SIEGMUND
Fänd' ich in Walhall
Wälse, den eignen Vater?

BRÜNNHILDE
Den Vater findet
der Wälsung dort.

SIEGMUND
Grüßt mich in Walhall
froh eine Frau?

BRÜNNHILDE
Wunschmädchen
walten dort hehr:
Wotans Tochter
reicht dir traulich den Trank!

SIEGMUND
Hehr bist du,
und heilig gewahr ich
das Wotanskind:
doch eines sag mir, du Ew'ge!
Begleitet den Bruder
die bräutliche Schwester?
Umfängt Siegmund
Sieglinde dort?

BRÜNNHILDE
Erdenluft
muß sie noch atmen:
Sieglinde sieht
Siegmund dort nicht!

SIEGMUND
(neigt sich sanft über Sieglinde, küßt sie leise auf die Stirn und wendet sich ruhig wieder zu Brünnhilde.)
So grüße mir Walhall,
grüße mir Wotan,
grüße mir Wälse

BRÜNNHILDE
The fallen heroes
dwell there too;
they'll welcome you
and greet you to their band.

SIEGMUND
And shall I find there
Wälse, my noble father?

BRÜNNHILDE
Your father waits there
to greet his son!

SIEGMUND
Are there in Walhall,
maidens as well?

BRÜNNHILDE
Fair maidens
wait on you there.
Wotan's daughter,
she will bring you the cup!

SIEGMUND
Fair goddess
with awe I salute you
as Wotan's child;
but one thing tell me, immortal!
This brother is blessed
by his bride and his sister.
You call Siegmund—
Sieglinde too?

BRÜNNHILDE
Here on earth
you have to leave her:
Sieglinde sees
Siegmund no more.

SIEGMUND
(bends softly over Sieglinde, kisses her gently on the brow, and again turns calmly to Brünnhilde.)
Then greet for me Walhall,
greet for me Wotan,
greet for me Wälse

und alle Helden,
grüß auch die holden
Wunschesmädchen:
zu ihnen folg ich dir nicht.

and all the heroes;
greet all those fair
and lovely maidens.
To Walhall I will not go!

BRÜNNHILDE
Du sahest der Walküre
sehrenden Blick:
mit ihr mußt du nun ziehn!

BRÜNNHILDE
You gazed on the Valkyrie's
searing glance,
and now you have no choice.

SIEGMUND
Wo Sieglinde lebt
in Lust und Leid,
da will Siegmund auch säumen.
Noch machte dein Blick
nicht mich erbleichen:
vom Bleiben zwingt er mich nie!

SIEGMUND
Where Sieglinde lives
in joy or pain:
there must Siegmund live with her:
I've gazed on your glance;
I do not fear you:
you cannot force me to go!

BRÜNNHILDE
Solang du lebst,
zwäng' dich wohl nichts:
doch zwingt dich Toren der Tod:
ihn dir zu künden,
kam ich her.

BRÜNNHILDE
I cannot force,
not while you live;
but death can force you to go!
I come to warn you
death is near.

SIEGMUND
Wo wäre der Held,
dem heut ich fiel'?

SIEGMUND
And who is the man
who'll take my life?

BRÜNNHILDE
Hunding fällt dich im Streit.

BRÜNNHILDE
Hunding kills you today.

SIEGMUND
Mit stärkrem drohe
als Hundings Streichen!
Lauerst du hier
lüstern auf Wal,
jenen kiese zum Fang:
ich denk ihn zu fällen im Kampf!

SIEGMUND
Do you think I'm threatened
by Hunding's anger?
If you lurk here,
lusting for blood,
choose that man as your prey:
I know he will fall in the fight!

BRÜNNHILDE
(den Kopf schüttelnd)
Dir, Wälsung,
höre mich wohl:
dir ward das Los gekiest.

BRÜNNHILDE
(shaking her head)
You, Wälsung,
hear what I say:
You have been marked for death.

SIEGMUND
Kennst du dies Schwert?

SIEGMUND
I have a sword!

Der mir es schuf,
beschied mir Sieg:
deinem Drohen trotz ich mit ihm!

BRÜNNHILDE
(mit stark erhobener Stimme)
Der dir es schuf,
beschied dir jetzt Tod:
seine Tugend nimmt er dem Schwert!

SIEGMUND
(heftig)
Schweig und schrecke
die Schlummernde nicht!
(Er beugt sich mit hervorbrechendem Schmerze zärtlich über Sieglinde.)
Weh! Weh!
Süßestes Weib,
du traurigste aller Getreuen!
Gegen dich wütet
in Waffen die Welt:
und ich, dem du einzig vertraut,
für den du ihr einzig getrotzt,
mit meinem Schutz
nicht soll ich dich schirmen,
die Kühne verraten im Kampf?
Ha, Schande ihm,
der das Schwert mir schuf,
beschied er mir Schimpf für Sieg!
Muß ich denn fallen,
nicht fahr ich nach Walhall:
Hella halte mich fest!
(Er neigt sich tief zu Sieglinde.)

BRÜNNHILDE
(erschüttert)
So wenig achtest du
ewige Wonne?
(zögernd und zurückhaltend)
Alles wär' dir
das arme Weib,
das müd und harmvoll
matt von dem Schoße dir hängt?
Nichts sonst hieltest du hehr?

SIEGMUND
(bitter zu ihr aufblickend)
So jung und schön

My father's gift
will guard me well:
I defy your threats with the sword!

BRÜNNHILDE
(with solemn emphasis)
Gift of the god
who ordered your death;
and he takes his spell from the sword!

SIEGMUND
(vehemently)
Still! You'll waken
my sister from sleep!
(He bends tenderly, in an outburst of grief, over Sieglinde.)
Woe! Woe!
Sister and bride,
you saddest of all trusting women!
Though the world rises
against you in arms,
yet I, whom alone you could trust,
yes, I, who have brought you this pain,
am not allowed
to shield you from danger,
but told I must fall in the fight!
Then shame on him
who bestowed the sword,
the sword that will bring my shame!
Yet though I die here,
I'll not go to Walhall:
hell may hold me instead!
(He bends low over Sieglinde.)

BRÜNNHILDE
(shocked)
So you would sacrifice
joy everlasting?
(slowly and hesitatingly)
Is she all
in the world to you,
that maid who lies there
limp and afraid in your arms?
You'd leave Walhall for her?

SIEGMUND
(looking up at her bitterly)
So young and fair

erschimmerst du mir:
doch wie kalt und hart
erkennt dich mein Herz.
Kannst du nur höhnen,
so hebe dich fort,
du arge, fühllose Maid!
Doch mußt du dich weiden
an meinem Weh,
mein Leiden letze dich denn;
meine Not labe
dein neidvolles Herz:
nur von Walhalls spröden Wonnen
sprich du wahrlich mir nicht!

you seem to my eyes;
but how cold and hard
I know in my heart!
You came to mock me;
now leave me alone,
you heartless, cold, cruel maid!
But if it delights you
to watch my woe,
you're free to feed on my pain;
may my grief gladden
your envious heart;
but of Walhall's loveless pleasures
you need tell me no more!

BRÜNNHILDE
Ich sehe die Not,
die das Herz dir zernagt,
ich fühle des Helden
heiligen Harm—
Siegmund, befiehl mir dein Weib:
mein Schutz umfange sie fest!

BRÜNNHILDE
I see the distress
and grief in your heart,
I feel all your suffering,
share in your pain!
Siegmund, I'll care for your wife;
I'll shield her safely from harm.

SIEGMUND
Kein andrer als ich
soll die Reine lebend berühren:
Verfiel ich dem Tod,
die Betäubte töt ich zuvor!

SIEGMUND
So long as she lives
I'll allow no other to touch her:
if I have to die,
I will kill her first while she sleeps.

BRÜNNHILDE
(in wachsender Ergriffenheit)
Wälsung! Rasender!
Hör meinen Rat:
befiehl mir dein Weib
um des Pfandes willen,
das wonnig von dir es empfing.

BRÜNNHILDE
(with increasing emotion)
Wälsung! Madman!
Hear my advice!
I'll care for your wife;
I will shield her safely;
a son shall be born from your love.

SIEGMUND
(sein Schwert ziehend)
Dies Schwert,
das dem Treuen ein Trugvoller schuf;
dies Schwert,
das feig vor dem Feind mich verrät:
frommt es nich gegen den Feind,
so fromm es denn wider den Freund!
(Er zückt das Schwert auf Sieglinde.)
Zwei Leben
lachen dir hier:

SIEGMUND
(drawing his sword)
This sword,
which a traitor bestowed on the true;
this sword
that fails me when faced with a fight:
since it must fail on my foe,
I'll use it instead on a friend!
(He aims the sword at Sieglinde.)
Two lives
now lie in your power;

nimm sie, Notung,
neidischer Stahl!
Nimm sie mit einem Streich!

BRÜNNHILDE
(im heftigsten Sturme des Mitgefühls)
Halt ein, Wälsung!
Höre mein Wort!
Sieglinde lebe—
und Siegmund lebe mit ihr!
Beschlossen ist's;
das Schlachtlos wend ich:
dir, Siegmund,
schaff ich Segen und Sieg!
(Man hört aus dem fernen Hintergrunde Hornrufe erschallen.)
Hörst du den Ruf?
Nun rüste dich, Held!
Traue dem Schwert
und schwing es getrost:
treu hält dir die Wehr,
wie die Walküre treu dich schützt!
Leb wohl, Siegmund,
seligster Held!
Auf der Walstatt seh ich dich wieder!
(Sie stürmt fort und verschwindet mit dem Rosse rechts in einer Seitenschlucht. Siegmund blickt ihr freudig und erhoben nach. Die Bühne hat sich allmählich verfinstert; schwere Gewitterwolken senken sich auf den Hintergrund herab und hüllen die Gebirgswände, die Schlucht und das erhöhte Bergjoch nach und nach gänzlich ein.)

take them, Notung,
glittering blade!
Two with a single stroke!

BRÜNNHILDE
(in a passionate outburst of sympathy)
Oh stay, Wälsung!
Hear what I say!
Sieglinde lives then—
and Siegmund lives by her side!
The choice is mine;
and fate is altered;
you, Siegmund,
take my blessing, and win!
(Horn-calls resound in the far distance.)
Hark to the call!
Prepare for your fight!
Trust in the sword
and strike at his heart.
Your sword shall be true,
and the Valkyrie is true as well!
Farewell, Siegmund,
hero I love!
I will meet you there in the battle!
(She rushes away, and disappears with her horse into a ravine on the right. Siegmund looks after her with joy and exultation. The stage has gradually darkened; heavy stormclouds sink down in the background, gradually veiling the cliffs, ravine and rocky pass completely from view.)

Fünfte Szene

SIEGMUND
(über Sieglinde geneigt, dem Atem lauschend)
Zauberfest
bezähmt ein Schlaf
der Holden Schmerz und Harm.
Da die Walküre zu mir trat,

Scene Five

SIEGMUND
(bending over Sieglinde, listening to her breathing)
Charms of sleep
are sent to soothe
my sister's grief and pain.
Did the Valkyrie cast this spell

schuf sie ihr den wonnigen Trost?
Sollte die grimmige Wal
nicht schrecken ein gramvolles Weib?
  Leblos scheint sie,
  die dennoch lebt:
  der Traurigen kost
  ein lächelnder Traum.
  So schlummre nun fort,
  bis die Schlacht gekämpft
  und Friede dich erfreu'!
(Er legt sie sanft auf den Steinsitz und küßt ihr zum Abschied die Stirn. Siegmund vernimmt Hundings Hornruf und bricht entschlossen auf.)
  Der dort mich ruft,
  rüste sich nun;
  was ihm gebührt,
  biet ich ihm:
Notung zahl' ihm den Zoll!
(Er zieht das Schwert, eilt dem Hintergrunde zu und verschwindet, auf dem Joche angekommen, sogleich in finsterem Gewittergewölk, aus welchem alsbald Wetterleuchten aufblitzt.)

and lull my beloved to sleep,
so that no sound of our fight
should frighten this suffering maid?
  Lifeless seems she,
  though still alive;
  her sorrow is eased;
  she smiles in her sleep.
  So peacefully sleep
  till the fight is fought;
  then wake when I have won!
(He lays her gently on the rocky seat and kisses her forehead in farewell. He hears Hunding's horn-call, and starts up resolutely.)
  I hear your call;
  guard yourself well;
  all you deserve
  comes to you.
Notung pays all my debt!
(He draws his sword, hastens to the background and, on reaching the pass, disappears in the dark stormcloud, from which a flash of lightning immediately breaks.)

SIEGLINDE
(beginnt sich träumend unruhiger zu bewegen.)
Kehrte der Vater nur heim!
Mit dem Knaben noch weilt er im Forst.
  Mutter, Mutter!
  Mir bangt der Mut:
  Nicht freund und friedlich
  scheinen die Fremden!
  Schwarze Dämpfe—
  schwüles Gedünst—
  feurige Lohe
  leckt schon nach uns—
  es brennt das Haus—
  zu Hilfe, Bruder!
  Siegmund! Siegmund!
(Sie springt auf. Starker Blitz und Donner.)
  Siegmund! Ha!
(Sie starrt in Angst um sich her: fast die ganze Bühne ist in schwarze Gewitterwolken gehüllt, fortwährender Blitz und Donner. Der Hornruf Hundings ertönt in der Nähe.)

SIEGLINDE
(begins to move restlessly in her dreams.)
Why doesn't father return?
With the boy he is still in the woods.
  Mother! Mother!
  I feel afraid;
  they seem unfriendly—
  who are the strangers?
  Smoky darkness—
  smouldering fires—
  now they are flaring,
  flaming around—
  they burn the house—
  Oh help me, brother!
  Siegmund! Siegmund!
(She leaps up. Violent thunder and lightning.)
  Siegmund! Ah!
(She stares about her in terror; nearly the whole stage is covered with black thunderclouds, the lightning and thunder continue. Hunding's horn-call sounds near.)

HUNDINGS STIMME
(im Hintergrunde vom Bergjoche her)
  Wehwalt! Wehwalt!

HUNDING'S VOICE
(in the background, from the pass)
  Wehwalt! Wehwalt!

Steh mir zum Streit,
sollen dich Hunde nicht halten!

Stand there and fight,
else with my hounds I will hunt you.

SIEGMUNDS STIMME
(von weiter hinten her aus der Schlucht)
Wo birgst du dich,
daß ich vorbei dir schoß?
Steh, daß ich dich stelle!

SIEGMUND'S VOICE
(from farther off in the ravine)
Then show yourself;
I've come in search of you!
Stand and let me face you!

SIEGLINDE
(in furchtbarer Aufregung lauschend)
Hunding! Siegmund!
Könnt' ich sie sehen!

SIEGLINDE
(listening in fearful agitation)
Hunding! Siegmund!
Could I but see them!

HUNDING
Hieher, du frevelnder Freier!
Fricka fälle dich hier!

HUNDING
Come here, you treacherous lover!
Fricka claims you as prize.

SIEGMUND
(nun ebenfalls vom Joche her)
Noch wähnst du mich waffenlos,
feiger Wicht?
Drohst du mit Frauen,
so ficht nun selber,
sonst läßt dich Fricka im Stich!
Denn sieh: deines Hauses
heimischem Stamm
entzog ich zaglos das Schwert;
seine Schneide schmecke jetzt du!
(Ein Blitz erhellt für einen Augenblick das Bergjoch, auf welchem jetzt Hunding und Siegmund kämpfend gewahrt werden.)

SIEGMUND
(now likewise from the pass)
Do you think that I'm weaponless,
boasting fool?
Don't call on Fricka,
but fight your own fight;
no help from Fricka today!
For see, in your house
I drew from the tree
the strongest, sharpest of swords,
and its sharpness strikes at your life!
(A flash of lightning illumines the pass for a moment, and Hunding and Siegmund are seen fighting there.)

SIEGLINDE
(mit höchster Kraft)
Haltet ein, ihr Männer!
Mordet erst mich!
(Sie stürzt auf das Bergjoch zu: ein von rechts her über den Kämpfern ausbrechender heller Schein blendet sie aber plötzlich so heftig, daß sie, wie erblindet, zur Seite schwankt. In dem Lichtglanze erscheint Brünnhilde über Siegmund schwebend und diesen mit dem Schilde deckend.)

SIEGLINDE
(with her utmost force)
Stop the fight, you madmen!
Murder me first!
(She rushes towards the pass, but suddenly, from above the combatants, on the right, a flash breaks forth so vividly that she staggers aside as if blinded. In the blaze of light Brünnhilde appears, hovering over Siegmund and protecting him with her shield.)

BRÜNNHILDE
Triff ihn, Siegmund!
Traue dem Schwert!
(Als Siegmund soeben zu einem tödlichen Streiche

BRÜNNHILDE
Strike him, Siegmund!
Trust in the sword!
(Just as Siegmund aims a deadly blow at Hunding,

auf Hunding ausholt, bricht von links her ein glühend rötlicher Schein durch das Gewölk aus, in welchem Wotan erscheint, über Hunding stehend und seinen Speer Siegmund quer entgegenhaltend.)

WOTAN
Zurück vor dem Speer!
In Stücken das Schwert!
(Brünnhilde weicht erschrocken vor Wotan mit dem Schilde zurück: Siegmunds Schwert zerspringt an dem vorgehaltenen Speere. Dem Unbewehrten stößt Hunding seinen Speer in die Brust. Siegmund stürzt tot zu Boden. Sieglinde, die seinen Todesseufzer gehört, sinkt mit einem Schrei wie leblos zusammen. Mit Siegmunds Fall ist zugleich von beiden Seiten der glänzende Schein verschwunden; dichte Finsternis ruht im Gewölk bis nach vorn: in ihm wird Brünnhilde undeutlich sichtbar, wie sie in jäher Hast sich Sieglinden zuwendet.)

BRÜNNHILDE
Zu Roß, daß ich dich rette!
(Sie hebt Sieglinde schnell zu sich auf ihr der Seitenschlucht nahe stehendes Roß und verschwindet sogleich mit ihr. Alsbald zerteilt sich das Gewölk in der Mitte, so daß man deutlich Hunding gewahrt, der soeben seinen Speer dem gefallenen S egmund aus der Brust zieht. Wotan, von Gewölk umgeben, steht dahinter auf einem Felsen, an seinen Speer gelehnt und schmerzlich auf Siegmunds Leiche blickend.)

WOTAN
(zu Hunding)
Geh hin, Knecht!
Knie vor Fricka:
meld ihr, daß Wotans Speer
gerächt, was Spott ihr schuf.
Geh! Geh!
(Vor seinem verächtlichen Handwink sinkt Hunding tot zu Boden. Wotan, plötzlich in furchtbarer Wut auffahrend:)
Doch Brünnhilde!
Weh der Verbrecherin!
Furchtbar sei
die Freche gestraft,
erreicht mein Roß ihre Flucht!
(Er verschwindet mit Blitz und Donner. Der Vorhang fällt schnell.)

a glowing red light breaks from the left through the clouds, in which Wotan appears, standing over Hunding, holding his spear diagonally out at Siegmund.)

WOTAN
Away from the spear!
I shatter the sword!
(Brünnhilde, with her spear, recoils in terror before Wotan. Siegmund's sword shatters on the outstretched spear. Hunding plunges his spear into the unarmed man's breast. Siegmund falls dead to the ground: Sieglinde, who has heard his death-sigh, falls with a cry, as if lifeless, to the ground. As Siegmund falls, the glowing lights on either side disappear at once; a cloud of thick darkness rolls forward; in it, Brünnhilde is indistinctly seen, as she turns in haste to Sieglinde.)

BRÜNNHILDE
To horse! Come, let me save you!
(She lifts Sieglinde quickly on to her horse, which is standing near the side gorge, and immediately disappears with her. At this moment the clouds part in the middle, so that Hunding, who had just drawn his spear from the fallen Siegmund's breast, is clearly seen. Wotan, surrounded by clouds, stands on a rock behind him, leaning on his spear and gazing sorrowfully at Siegmund's corpse.)

WOTAN
(to Hunding)
Go hence, slave!
Kneel before Fricka:
tell her that Wotan's spear
avenged her cause of shame.
Go! Go!
(At the contemptuous wave of his hand, Hunding falls dead to the ground. Wotan, suddenly breaking out in terrible rage:)
But Brünnhilde!
Where is the guilty one?
Fearful is the fate
I'll pronounce
when she is caught in her flight!
(He disappears in thunder and lightning. The curtain falls rapidly.)

Dritter Aufzug

Auf dem Gipfel eines Felsenberges

Rechts begrenzt ein Tannenwald die Szene. Links der Eingang einer Felshöhle, die einen natürlichen Saal bildet: darüber steigt der Fels zu seiner höchsten Spitze auf. Nach hinten ist die Aussicht gänzlich frei; höhere und niedere Felssteine bilden den Rand vor dem Abhange, der—wie anzunehmen ist—nach dem Hintergrunde zu steil hinabführt. Einzelne Wolkenzüge jagen, wie vom Sturm getrieben, am Felsensaume vorbei. Gerhilde, Ortlinde, Waltraute und Schwertleite haben sich auf der Felsspitze, an und über der Höhle, gelagert, sie sind in voller Waffenrüstung.

Act Three

On the Summit of a Rocky Mountain

On the right, a pinewood bounds the stage. On the left, the entrance to a cave which looks like a natural room; above it, the rock rises to its highest point. At the back the view is entirely open; rocks of various heights border a precipice, which, it is to be assumed, falls steeply to the background. Occasional cloudbanks fly past the mountain peak, as if driven by storm. Gerhilde, Ortlinde, Waltraute and Schwertleite have assembled on the peak, by and above the cave: they are in full armour.

Erste Szene

GERHILDE

(zuhöchst gelagert und dem Hintergrunde zurufend, wo ein starkes Gewölk herzieht)

Hojotoho! Hojotoho!
Heiaha! Heiaha!

Scene One

GERHILDE

(on the highest point, calling towards the background, where a thick cloud is passing)

Hoyotoho! Hoyotoho!
Hiaha! Hiaha!

Helmwige! Hier! Hierher mit dem Roß!	Helmwige! Here! Come here with your horse!
HELMWIGES STIMME *(im Hintergrunde)* Hojotoho! Hojotoho! Heiaha! *(In dem Gewölk bricht Blitzesglanz aus; eine Walküre zu Roß wird in ihm sichtbar: über ihrem Sattel hängt ein erschlagener Krieger. Die Erscheinung zieht, immer näher, am Felsensaume von links nach rechts vorbei.)*	HELMWIGE'S VOICE *(in the background)* Hoyotoho! Hoyotoho! Hiaha! *(A flash of lightning breaks through the cloud; in its light, a Valkyrie on horseback becomes visible; on her saddle hangs a slain warrior. The apparition comes closer, moving from left to right past the rocky ridge.)*
GERHILDE, WALTRAUTE, SCHWERTLEITE *(der Ankommenden entgegenrufend)* Heiaha! Heiaha! *(Die Wolke mit der Erscheinung ist rechts hinter dem Tann verschwunden.)*	GERHILDE, WALTRAUTE, SCHWERTLEITE *(calling to the newcomer)* Hiaha! Hiaha! *(The cloud with the apparition has disappeared to the right, behind the wood.)*
ORTLINDE *(in den Tann hineinrufend)* Zu Ortlindes Stute stell deinen Hengst: mit meiner Grauen grast gern dein Brauner!	ORTLINDE *(calling into the wood)* Go tether your chestnut next to my grey; she will be glad to graze by your stallion.
WALTRAUTE *(hineinrufend)* Wer hängt dir im Sattel?	WALTRAUTE *(calling into the wood)* Who hangs from your saddle?
HELMWIGE *(aus dem Tann auftretend)* Sintolt, der Hegeling!	HELMWIGE *(coming from the wood)* Sintolt the Hegeling!
SCHWERTLEITE Führ deinen Braunen fort von der Grauen: Ortlindes Mähre trägt Wittig, den Irming!	SCHWERTLEITE Far from the grey then fasten your stallion; Ortlinde's mare carries Wittig the Irming!
GERHILDE *(ist etwas näher herabgestiegen.)* Als Feinde nur sah ich Sintolt und Wittig!	GERHILDE *(has come down lower.)* Implacable foes were Sintolt and Wittig!
ORTLINDE *(springt auf.)* Heiaha! Die Stute	ORTLINDE *(leaps up.)* Hiaha! Your stallion

stößt mir der Hengst!
(Sie läuft in den Tann. Gerhilde, Helmwige und Schwertleite lachen laut auf.)

GERHILDE
Der Recken Zwist
entzweit noch die Rosse!

HELMWIGE
(in den Tann zurückrufend)
Ruhig, Brauner!
Brich nicht den Frieden.

WALTRAUTE
(auf der Höhe, wo sie für Gerhilde die Wacht übernommen, nach rechts in den Hintergrund rufend)
Hoioho! Hoioho!
Siegrune, hier!
Wo säumst du so lang?
(Sie lauscht nach rechts.)

SIEGRUNES STIMME
(von der rechten Seite des Hintergrundes her)
Arbeit gab's!
Sind die andren schon da?

SCHWERTLEITE, WALTRAUTE
(nach rechts in den Hintergrund rufend)
Hojotoho! Hojotoho!
Heiaha!

GERHILDE
Heiaha!
(Ihre Gebärden sowie ein heller Glanz hinter dem Tann zeigen an, daß soeben Siegrune dort angelangt ist. Aus der Tiefe hört man zwei Stimmen zugleich.)

GRIMGERDE, ROSSWEISSE
(links im Hintergrunde)
Hojotoho! Hojotoho!
Heiaha!

WALTRAUTE
Grimgerd und Roßweiße!

GERHILDE
Sie reiten zu zwei.

is biting my mare!
(She runs into the wood. Gerhilde, Helmwige, and Schwertleite break into laughter.)

GERHILDE
The warriors' war
has spread to the horses!

HELMWIGE
(calling back into the wood)
Quiet, Bruno!
Battle is over.

WALTRAUTE
(on the highest point, where she has taken over from Gerhilde as watcher, calls to the right side of the background.)
Hoioho! Hoioho!
Siegrune, here!
What kept you so long?
(She listens to the right.)

SIEGRUNE'S VOICE
(from the right side of the background)
Work to do!
Have the others arrived?

SCHWERTLEITE, WALTRAUTE
(calling to the right of the background)
Hoyotoho! Hoyotoho!
Hiaha!

GERHILDE
Hiaha!
(Their gestures, as well as a bright glow behind the wood, show that Siegrune has just arrived there. From the distance below, two voices are heard at once.)

GRIMGERDE, ROSSWEISSE
(left, in the background)
Hoyotoho! Hoyotoho!
Hiaha!

WALTRAUTE
Grimgerd and Rossweisse!

GERHILDE
They're riding abreast.

(In einem blitzerglänzenden Wolkenzuge, der von links her vorbeizieht, erscheinen Grimgerde und Roßweiße, ebenfalls auf Rossen, jede einen Erschlagenen im Sattel führend. Helmwige, Ortlinde und Siegrune sind aus dem Tann getreten und winken vom Felsensaume den Ankommenden zu.)

HELMWIGE, ORTLINDE, SIEGRUNE
Gegrüßt, ihr Reisige!
Roßweiß und Grimgerde!

ROSSWEISSES und GRIMGERDES STIMMEN
Hojotoho! Hojotoho!
Heiaha!
(Die Erscheinung verschwindet hinter dem Tann.)

DIE SECHS ANDEREN WALKÜREN
Hojotoho! Hojotoho!
Heiaha! Heiaha!

GERHILDE
(in den Tann rufend)
In' Wald mit den Rossen
zu Rast und Weid'!

ORTLINDE
(ebenfalls in den Tann rufend)
Führet die Mähren
fern voneinander,
bis unsrer Helden
Haß sich gelegt!
(Die Walküren lachen.)

HELMWIGE
(während die anderen lachen)
Der Helden Grimm
büßte schon die Graue!
(Die Walküren lachen.)

ROSSWEISSE, GRIMGERDE
(aus dem Tann tretend)
Hojotoho! Hojotoho!

DIE SECHS ANDEREN WALKÜREN
Willkommen! Willkommen!

(In a cloudbank lit by lightning, moving past from the left, Grimgerde and Rossweisse appear, similarly on horseback, each with a dead warrior on her saddle. Helmwige, Ortlinde, and Siegrune come from the wood and greet the newcomers from the rocky ridge.)

HELMWIGE, ORTLINDE, SIEGRUNE
We greet the travellers!
Rossweiss and Grimgerde!

ROSSWEISSE'S and GRIMGERDE'S VOICES
Hoyotoho! Hoyotoho!
Hiaha!
(The apparition disappears behind the wood.)

THE OTHER SIX VALKYRIES
Hoyotoho! Hoyotoho!
Hiaha! Hiaha!

GERHILDE
(calling into the wood)
Now tether your horses
to graze and rest!

ORTLINDE
(also calling into the wood)
See that the mares
are far from the stallions,
until our heroes'
hate has been calmed!
(The Valkyries laugh.)

HELMWIGE
(while the others laugh)
My horse has paid
for the heroes' anger!
(Renewed laughter)

ROSSWEISSE, GRIMGERDE
(coming from the wood)
Hoyotoho! Hoyotoho!

THE OTHER SIX VALKYRIES
Be welcome! Be welcome!

SCHWERTLEITE
Wart ihr Kühnen zu zwei?

GRIMGERDE
Getrennt ritten wir
und trafen uns heut.

ROSSWEISSE
Sind wir alle versammelt,
so säumt nicht lange:
nach Walhall brechen wir auf,
Wotan zu bringen die Wal.

HELMWIGE
Acht sind wir erst:
eine noch fehlt.

GERHILDE
Bei dem braunen Wälsung
weilt wohl noch Brünnhild.

WALTRAUTE
Auf sie noch harren
müssen wir hier:
Walvater gäb' uns
grimmigen Gruß,
säh' ohne sie er uns nahn!

SIEGRUNE
(auf der Felswarte, von wo sie hinausspäht)
Hojotoho! Hojotoho!
Hieher! Hieher!
In brünstigem Ritt
jagt Brünnhilde her.

DIE ACHT WALKÜREN
(alle eilen auf die Warte.)
Hojotoho! Hojotoho!
Brünnhilde! Hei!
(Sie spähen mit wachsender Verwunderung.)

WALTRAUTE
Nach dem Tann lenkt sie
das taumelnde Roß.

GRIMGERDE
Wie schnaubt Grane
vom schnellen Ritt!

SCHWERTLEITE
Did you hunt as a pair?

GRIMGERDE
We left separately,
and met on the way.

ROSSWEISSE
If we are all assembled,
then wait no longer:
to Walhall hurry away;
Wotan is expecting us there.

HELMWIGE
Eight now are here:
one is to come.

GERHILDE
It's that swarthy Wälsung
keeping our Brünnhild.

WALTRAUTE
Then we must wait
until she is here:
Brünnhild is father's
favourite child,
and if we leave her behind...

SIEGRUNE
(watching from the look-out point)
Hoyotoho! Hoyotoho!
She's here! She's here!
In furious haste
see Brünnhilde rides.

THE EIGHT VALKYRIES
(all hasten to the look-out.)
Hoyotoho! Hoyotoho!
Brünnhilde! Hi!
(They watch with growing astonishment.)

WALTRAUTE
To the pinewood
she is driving her horse.

GRIMGERDE
And proud Grane
is panting hard!

ROSSWEISSE
So jach sah ich nie
Walküren jagen!

ROSSWEISSE
She's forced him to fly
faster than ever!

ORTLINDE
Was hält sie im Sattel?

ORTLINDE
Who's that on her saddle?

HELMWIGE
Das ist kein Held!

HELMWIGE
That is no man!

SIEGRUNE
Eine Frau führt sie.

SIEGRUNE
It's a girl, surely.

GERHILDE
Wie fand sie die Frau?

GERHILDE
And where was she found?

SCHWERTLEITE
Mit keinem Gruß
grüßt sie die Schwestern!

SCHWERTLEITE
She gives no greeting
to her sisters!

WALTRAUTE
(hinabrufend)
Heiaha! Brünnhilde!
Hörst du uns nicht?

WALTRAUTE
(calling down)
Hiaha! Brünnhilde!
Answer our call!

ORTLINDE
Helft der Schwester
vom Roß sich schwingen!

ORTLINDE
Help our sister
to leave the saddle!

HELMWIGE, GERHILDE, SIEGRUNE, ROSSWEISSE
Hojotoho! Hojotoho!

HELMWIGE, GERHILDE, SIEGRUNE, ROSSWEISSE
Hoyotoho! Hoyotoho!

ORTLINDE, WALTRAUTE, GRIMGERDE, SCHWERTLEITE
Heiaha!
(Gerhilde und Helmwige stürzen in den Tann. Siegrune und Roßweiße laufen ihnen nach.)

ORTLINDE, WALTRAUTE, GRIMGERDE, SCHWERTLEITE
Hiaha!
(Gerhilde and Schwertleite run into the wood. Siegrune and Rossweisse follow them.)

WALTRAUTE
(in den Tann blickend)
Zugrunde stürzt
Grane, der starke!

WALTRAUTE
(looking into the wood)
And powerful Grane
has fallen!

GRIMGERDE
Aus dem Sattel hebt sie
hastig das Weib!

GRIMGERDE
While our sister lifts
the girl to the ground!

ORTLINDE, WALTRAUTE,
GRIMGERDE, SCHWERTLEITE
Schwester, Schwester!
Was ist geschehn?
(Alle Walküren kehren auf die Bühne zurück; mit ihnen kommt Brünnhilde, Sieglinde unterstützend und hereingeleitend.)

BRÜNNHILDE
(atemlos)
Schützt mich und helft
in höchster Not!

DIE ACHT WALKÜREN
Wo rittest du her
in rasender Hast?
So fliegt nur, wer auf der Flucht!

BRÜNNHILDE
Zum erstenmal flieh ich
und bin verfolgt:
Heervater hetzt mir nach!

DIE ACHT WALKÜREN
(heftig erschreckend)
Bist du von Sinnen?
Sprich! Sage uns! Wie?
Verfolgt dich Heervater?
Fliehst du vor ihm?

BRÜNNHILDE
(wendet sich ängstlich, um zu spähen, und kehrt wieder zurück.)
O Schwestern, späht
von des Felsens Spitze!
Schaut nach Norden,
ob Walvater naht!
(Ortlinde und Waltraute springen auf die Felsenspitze zur Warte.)
Schnell! Seht ihr ihn schon?

ORTLINDE
Gewittersturm
naht von Norden.

WALTRAUTE
Starkes Gewölk
staut sich dort auf!

ORTLINDE, WALTRAUTE,
GRIMGERDE, SCHWERTLEITE
Sister, sister!
What have you done?
(All the Valkyries return to the stage; with them comes Brünnhilde, supporting and leading Sieglinde.)

BRÜNNHILDE
(breathless)
Shield me and help
in highest need!

THE EIGHT VALKYRIES
From where have you come
in furious haste?
You ride like one who is pursued!

BRÜNNHILDE
I flee for the first time;
I am pursued;
Wotan is hunting me!

THE EIGHT VALKYRIES
(violently alarmed)
What are you saying?
Speak to us! What?
Is Wotan hunting you?
Why do you flee?

BRÜNNHILDE
(turns anxiously to look around, and then turns back.)
O sisters, run
to the mountain summit!
Look to the northward,
if Wotan is near!
(Ortlinde and Waltraute run to the rocky peak to keep a look-out.)
Quick! What can you see?

ORTLINDE
A thunderstorm
nears from northward.

WALTRAUTE
Dark, stormy clouds
mass themselves there!

DIE WEITEREN SECHS WALKÜREN
Heervater reitet
sein heiliges Roß!

BRÜNNHILDE
Der wilde Jäger,
der wütend mich jagt,
er naht, er naht von Norden!
Schützt mich, Schwestern!
Wahret dies Weib!

SECHS WALKÜREN
Was ist mit dem Weibe?

BRÜNNHILDE
Hört mich in Eile:
Sieglinde ist es,
Siegmunds Schwester und Braut:
Gegen die Wälsungen
wütet Wotan in Grimm;
dem Bruder sollte
Brünnhilde heut
entziehen den Sieg;
doch Siegmund schützt' ich
mit meinem Schild,
trotzend dem Gott;
der traf ihn da selbst mit dem Speer:
Siegmund fiel;
doch ich floh
fern mit der Frau;
sie zu retten,
eilt' ich zu euch,
ob mich Bange auch
ihr berget vor dem strafenden Streich!

SECHS WALKÜREN
Betörte Schwester,
was tatest du?
Wehe, Brünnhilde, wehe!
Brach ungehorsam
Brünnhilde
Heervaters heilig Gebot?

WALTRAUTE
(von der Warte)
Nächtig zieht es
von Norden heran.

THE OTHER SIX VALKYRIES
Wotan is riding
his sacred horse!

BRÜNNHILDE
The wild pursuer
who hunts me in wrath,
he's near, he comes from northward.
Save me, sisters!
Rescue this maid!

SIX VALKYRIES
But who is this woman?

BRÜNNHILDE
Hear while I tell you.
Sieglinde is she,
Siegmund's sister and bride,
one of the Wälsungs
Wotan swore to destroy.
Her brother's death
was Brünnhilde's task,
So Wotan decreed.
But Siegmund gained my help
in his fight;
Wotan himself
then shattered the sword with the spear:
Siegmund fell,
but I fled
here with his wife,
and to save her
brought her to you.
Will you help us both,
and save us from the storm that is near?

SIX VALKYRIES
What madness moved you
to do this deed?
Sister! Brünnhilde! Sister!
Woe! O rebellious
Brünnhilde,
how could you break his command!

WALTRAUTE
(on the look-out)
Dark those stormclouds
that fly from the north.

ORTLINDE
(ebenso)
Wütend steuert
hieher der Sturm.

ROSSWEISSE, GRIMGERDE, SCHWERTLEITE
Wild wiehert
Walvaters Roß.

HELMWIGE, GERHILDE, SIEGRUNE
Schrecklich schnaubt es daher!

BRÜNNHILDE
Wehe der Armen,
wenn Wotan sie trifft:
den Wälsungen allen
droht er Verderben!
Wer leiht mir von euch
das leichteste Roß,
das flink die Frau ihm entführ'?

SIEGRUNE
Auch uns rätst du
rasenden Trotz?

BRÜNNHILDE
Roßweiße, Schwester,
leih mir deinen Renner!

ROSSWEISSE
Vor Walvater floh
der fliegende nie.

BRÜNNHILDE
Helmwige, höre!

HELMWIGE
Dem Vater gehorch ich.

BRÜNNHILDE
Grimgerde! Gerhilde!
Gönnt mir eu'r Roß!
Schwertleite! Siegrune!
Seht meine Angst!

ORTLINDE
(also on the look-out)
Wotan drives
his steed through the storm.

ROSSWEISSE, GRIMGERDE, SCHWERTLEITE
Wild neighs
I hear from the horse—

HELMWIGE, GERHILDE, SIEGRUNE
—snorts and flies on its way!

BRÜNNHILDE
Woe to this woman
when Wotan arrives;
for she is a Wälsung,
doomed to destruction!
So lend me the fastest
horse that you have,
to save the maid from his wrath!

SIEGRUNE
So you would make us
share in your crime?

BRÜNNHILDE
Rossweisse, sister,
lend me your stallion!

ROSSWEISSE
From Wotan, my horse
refuses to fly.

BRÜNNHILDE
Helmwige, hear me!

HELMWIGE
I hear only Wotan.

BRÜNNHILDE
Grimgerde! Gerhilde!
Give me your horse!
Schwertleite! Siegrune!
See my dismay!

Oh, seid mir treu,
wie traut ich euch war:
rettet dies traurige Weib!

SIEGLINDE
(die bisher finster und kalt vor sich hingestarrt, fährt, als Brünnhilde sie lebhaft—wie zum Schutze—umfaßt, mit einer abwehrenden Gebärde auf.)
Nicht sehre dich Sorge um mich:
einzig taugt mir der Tod!
Wer hieß dich, Maid,
dem Harst mich entführen?
Im Sturm dort hätt' ich
den Streich empfahn
von derselben Waffe,
der Siegmund fiehl:
das Ende fand ich
vereint mit ihm!
Fern von Siegmund—
Siegmund, von dir!—
O deckte mich Tod,
daß ich's denke!
Soll um die Flucht
dir, Maid, ich nicht fluchen,
so erhöre heilig mein Flehen:
stoße dein Schwert mir ins Herz!

BRÜNNHILDE
Lebe, o Weib,
um der Liebe willen!
Rette das Pfand,
das von ihm du empfingst:
ein Wälsung wächst dir im Schoß!

SIEGLINDE
(erschrickt zunächst heftig; sogleich strahlt aber ihr Gesicht in erhabener Freude auf.)
Rette mich, Kühne!
Rettet mein Kind!
Schirmt mich, ihr Mädchen,
mit mächtigstem Schutz!
(Immer finstereres Gewitter steigt im Hintergrunde auf: nahender Donner.)

WALTRAUTE
(auf der Warte)
Der Sturm kommt heran.

Oh, now be true,
as I was to you:
rescue this sorrowful maid!

SIEGLINDE
(who has been gazing gloomily and coldly ahead, gives a start and makes a gesture of rejection as Brünnhilde impulsively embraces her, as if to protect her.)
Pray suffer no sorrow for me;
all I long for is death!
O warrior maid,
who asked you to save me?
I might have died
in the field with him;
for perhaps the weapon
that dealt his death,
that killed my Siegmund,
had pierced me too.
Far from Siegmund,
Siegmund, from you!
Now only death
can unite us!
So I shall curse
this care that has saved me
if you refuse my grievous entreaty:
strike with your sword in my heart!

BRÜNNHILDE
Live still, O maid;
know that love commands you!
Rescue the son
who will grow from your love:
a Wälsung lives in your womb!

SIEGLINDE
(starts in fear at first; then her face lights up with sublime joy.)
Rescue me, brave one!
Rescue my child!
Save me, you maidens,
and shelter my son!
(An ever-darkening tempest rises in the background; the thunder draws closer.)

WALTRAUTE
(on the look-out)
The storm's drawing near!

ORTLINDE
(ebenso)
Flieh, wer ihn fürchtet!

DIE SECHS ANDEREN WALKÜREN
Fort mit dem Weibe,
droht ihm Gefahr:
der Walküren keine
wag ihren Schutz!

SIEGLINDE
(auf den Knien vor Brünnhilde)
Rette mich, Maid!
Rette die Mutter!

BRÜNNHILDE
(mit lebhaftem Entschluß hebt Sieglinde auf.)
So fliehe denn eilig
und fliehe allein!
Ich bleibe zurück,
biete mich Wotans Rache:
an mir zögr' ich
den Zürnenden hier,
während du seinem Rasen entrinnst.

SIEGLINDE
Wohin soll ich mich wenden?

BRÜNNHILDE
Wer von euch Schwestern
schweifte nach Osten?

SIEGRUNE
Nach Osten weithin
dehnt sich ein Wald:
der Niblungen Hort
entführte Fafner dorthin.

SCHWERTLEITE
Wurmesgestalt
schuf sich der Wilde:
in einer Höhle
hütet er Alberichs Reif!

GRIMGERDE
Nicht geheu'r ist's dort
für ein hilflos Weib.

ORTLINDE
(on the look-out)
Fly if you fear it!

THE OTHER SIX VALKYRIES
Off with the woman!
Danger is near!
The Valkyries dare not
give her their aid.

SIEGLINDE
(on her knees to Brünnhilde)
Rescue me, maid!
Rescue a mother!

BRÜNNHILDE
(raises Sieglinde with sudden resolution.)
Then fly from him swiftly,
and fly by yourself!
I will stay for the storm;
I will brave Wotan's anger;
and I'll draw his revenge
on myself,
so that you can escape his rage.

SIEGLINDE
Ah, where can I escape him?

BRÜNNHILDE
Which of you, sisters,
journeyed to eastward?

SIEGRUNE
A gloomy forest
lies to the east,
where the Nibelung hoard
was brought by Fafner, the giant.

SCHWERTLEITE
There he remains,
changed to a dragon,
and in a cave
he broods over Alberich's ring.

GRIMGERDE
It is not the place
for a helpless maid.

BRÜNNHILDE
Und doch vor Wotans Wut
schützt sie sicher der Wald:
ihn scheut der Mächt'ge
und meidet den Ort.

WALTRAUTE
(auf der Warte)
Furchtbar fährt
dort Wotan zum Fels.

SECHS WALKÜREN
Brünnhilde, hör
seines Nahens Gebraus!

BRÜNNHILDE
(Sieglinde die Richtung weisend)
Fort denn eile,
nach Osten gewandt!
Mutigen Trotzes
ertrag alle Müh'n,
Hunger und Durst,
Dorn und Gestein;
lache, ob Not,
ob Leiden dich nagt!
Denn eines wiss'
und wahr' es immer:
den hehrsten Helden der Welt
hegst du, o Weib,
im schirmenden Schoß!
(Sie zieht die Stücken von Siegmunds Schwert unter ihrem Panzer hervor und überreicht sie Sieglinde.)
Verwahr ihm die starken
Schwertesstücken;
seines Vaters Walstatt
entführt' ich sie glücklich:
der neugefügt
das Schwert einst schwingt,
den Namen nehm er von mir—
»Siegfried« erfreu sich des Siegs!

SIEGLINDE
(in größter Rührung)
O hehrstes Wunder!
Herrlichste Maid!
Dir Treuen dank ich

BRÜNNHILDE
And yet, from Wotan's wrath,
there, I know, she'd be safe:
for father fears it;
he never goes near.

WALTRAUTE
(on the look-out)
Angry Wotan
rides to the rock!

SIX VALKYRIES
Brünnhilde, hear
his approach in the storm!

BRÜNNHILDE
(showing Sieglinde the direction)
Fly him swiftly,
away to the east!
Bold in defiance,
endure every ill,
hunger and thirst,
thorns and the stones;
laugh at the pain
and grief that will come!
But one thing know,
and guard it ever:
the noblest hero of all,
he shall be born,
O maid, from your womb!
(She draws the pieces of Siegmund's sword from beneath her breastplate and gives them to Sieglinde.)
For him you must guard
these broken pieces
of the sword his father
let fall when it failed him;
for he shall forge
the sword once more.
His name, now learn it from me:
Siegfried—victorious and free!

SIEGLINDE
(deeply stirred)
O radiant wonder!
Glorious maid!
Your words have brought me

heiligen Trost!
Für ihn, den wir liebten,
rett ich das Liebste:
meines Dankes Lohn
lache dir einst!
Lebe wohl!
Dich segnet Sieglindes Weh!
(Sie eilt rechts im Vordergrunde von dannen.—Die Felsenhöhe ist von schwarzen Gewitterwolken umlagert; furchtbarer Sturm braust aus dem Hintergrunde daher, wachsender Feuerschein rechts daselbst.)

comfort and calm!
This son of Siegmund,
Oh! We shall save him:
may my son return
to thank you himself!
Fare you well!
Be blessed by Sieglinde's woe!
(She hastens away in the right foreground. Black thunderclouds surround the height; a fearful storm breaks out at the back, with a fiery glare growing brighter on the right.)

WOTANS STIMME
Steh, Brünnhild!
(Brünnhilde, nachdem sie eine Weile Sieglinde nachgesehen, wendet sich in den Hintergrund, blickt in den Tann und kommt angstvoll wieder vor.)

WOTAN'S VOICE
Stay, Brünnhild!
(Brünnhilde, after watching Sieglinde's departure for a while, turns to the background, looks into the pinewood, and then comes forward again in fear.)

ORTLINDE, WALTRAUTE
(von der Warte herabsteigend)
Den Fels erreichten
Roß und Reiter!

ORTLINDE, WALTRAUTE
(descending from the look-out)
They've reached the mountain,
horse and rider!

ALLE ACHT WALKÜREN
Weh, Brünnhild!
Rache entbrennt!

ALL EIGHT VALKYRIES
Woe, Brünnhild!
Vengeance is here!

BRÜNNHILD
Ach, Schwestern, helft!
Mir schwankt das Herz!
Sein Zorn zerschellt mich,
wenn euer Schutz ihn nicht zähmt.

BRÜNNHILDE
O sisters, help!
I feel afraid!
His rage will crush me
unless you shield me from harm.

DIE ACHT WALKÜREN
(flüchten ängstlich nach der Felsenspitze hinauf; Brünnhilde läßt sich von ihnen nachziehen.)
Hieher, Verlorne!
Laß dich nicht sehn!
Schmiege dich an uns
und schweige dem Ruf!
(Sie verbergen Brünnhilde unter sich und blicken ängstlich nach dem Tann, der jetzt von grellem Feuerschein erhellt wird, während der Hintergrund ganz finster geworden ist.)
Weh!
Wütend schwingt sich
Wotan vom Roß!

THE EIGHT VALKYRIES
(retreat in fear up the rocky height, drawing Brünnhilde with them.)
Come here, you lost one!
Keep out of sight!
Hide among us here;
be still when he calls!
(They hide Brünnhilde in their midst and look anxiously at the pinewood, now lit by a brilliant fiery glow, while the background has become quite dark.)
Woe!
Wotan swings himself
to the ground!

Hieher rast
sein rächender Schritt!

Here he comes
in furious haste!

Zweite Szene

Wotan tritt in höchster zorniger Aufgeregtheit aus dem Tann auf und schreitet vor der Gruppe der Walküren auf der Höhe, nach Brünnhilde spähend, heftig einher.

WOTAN
Wo ist Brünnhild,
wo die Verbrecherin?
Wagt ihr, die Böse
vor mir zu bergen?

DIE ACHT WALKÜREN
Schrecklich ertost dein Toben!
Was taten, Vater, die Töchter,
daß sie dich reizten
zu rasender Wut?

WOTAN
Wollt ihr mich höhnen?
Hütet euch, Freche!
Ich weiß: Brünnhilde
bergt ihr vor mir.
Weichet von ihr,
der ewig Verworfnen,
wie ihren Wert
von sich sie warf!

ROSSWEISSE
Zu uns floh die Verfolgte.

ALLE ACHT WALKÜREN
Unsern Schutz flehte sie an!
Mit Furcht und Zagen
faßt sie dein Zorn:
fur die bange Schwester
bitten wir nun,
daß den ersten Zorn du bezähmst.
Laß dich erweichen für sie,

Scene Two

Wotan comes from the pinewood in a towering rage and strides to the group of Valkyries on the height, looking around for Brünnhilde.

WOTAN
Where is Brünnhild?
Where is the guilty one?
Can you be daring
to hide her from me?

THE EIGHT VALKYRIES
Fearful your cry of anger!
Oh father, pity your daughters;
have we awakened
your terrible rage?

WOTAN
Ha, so you mock me?
Insolent daughters!
I know Brünnhilde
hides in your midst.
Leave her alone,
for she is an outcast,
and all her virtue
is cast away!

ROSSWEISSE
She came here to escape you.

ALL EIGHT VALKYRIES
And she asked for our help!
In fear and anguish
fled from your rage.
For our trembling sister
now we implore:
let the angry storm now be calm.
Father, have mercy on her,

zähme deinen Zorn!

WOTAN

Weichherziges
Weibergezücht!
So matten Mut
gewannt ihr von mir?
Erzog ich euch kühn,
zum Kampfe zu ziehn,
schuf ich die Herzen
euch hart und scharf,
daß ihr Wilden nun weint und greint,
wenn mein Grimm eine Treulose straft?
So wißt denn, Winselnde,
was sie verbrach,
um die euch Zagen
die Zähre entbrennt:
Keine wie sie
kannte mein innerstes Sinnen:
keine wie sie
wußte den Quell meines Willens!
Sie selbst war
meines Wunsches schaffender Schoß:
und so nun brach sie
den seligen Bund,
daß treulos sie
meinem Willen getrotzt,
mein herrschend Gebot
offen verhöhnt,
gegen mich die Waffe gewandt,
die mein Wunsch allein ihr schuf!
Hörst du's, Brünnhilde?
Du, der ich Brünne,
Helm und Wehr,
Wonne und Huld,
Namen und Leben verlieh?
Hörst du mich Klage erheben
und birgst dich bang dem Kläger,
daß feig du der Straf' entflöhst?

BRÜNNHILDE

(tritt aus der Schar der Walküren hervor, schreitet demütigen, doch festen Schrittes von der Felsenspitze herab und tritt so in geringer Entfernung vor Wotan.)

Hier bin ich, Vater:
gebiete die Strafe!

calm your dreadful rage!

WOTAN

Weak-spirited,
womanish brood!
Such whining ways
you learnt not from me!
I tempered your frames
to fight on the field,
made you hard-hearted
and stern and strong:
must I hear you all whine and wail
when I punish a treacherous crime?
I'll tell you, whimperers,
what she has done,
that shameless sister
who has prompted your tears:
Brünnhild alone
knew all my innermost secrets;
Brünnhild alone
saw to the depths of my spirit!
Through her
all my desires took shape in the world:
yet she has broken
the bond of our love,
and, faithless,
she has defied my desire;
my sacred command
openly scorned;
against me lifted the spear
that by Wotan's will she bore!
Hear me, Brünnhilde!
You whom I fashioned,
you who owe
all that you are,
name, even life, to me!
Say, can you hear me accuse you
and hide yourself, you coward,
to try to escape your doom?

BRÜNNHILDE

(steps out from the crowd of Valkyries and advances with humble yet resolute steps down the rock, close to Wotan.)

Here am I, father;
now tell me my sentence!

WOTAN
Nicht straf ich dich erst:
deine Strafe schufst du dir selbst.
Durch meinen Willen
warst du allein:
gegen ihn doch hast du gewollt;
meinen Befehl nur
führtest du aus:
gegen ihn doch hast du befohlen;
Wunschmaid
warst du mir:
gegen mich doch hast du gewünscht;
Schildmaid
warst du mir:
gegen mich doch hobst du den Schild;
Loskieserin
warst du mir:
gegen mich doch kiestest du Lose;
Heldenreizerin
warst du mir:
gegen mich doch reiztest du Helden.
Was sonst du warst,
sagte dir Wotan:
was jetzt du bist,
das sage dir selbst!
Wunschmaid bist du nicht mehr,
Walküre bist du gewesen:
nun sei fortan,
was so du noch bist!

WOTAN
I sentence you not:
you have brought your doom on yourself.
My will alone
woke you to life,
and against that will you have worked.
By my commandments
alone you could act,
and against me you have commanded.
Brünnhild
knew my wish,
and against that wish she rebelled.
Brünnhild
bore my shield,
and against me that shield was borne.
Brünnhilde
could choose my fate,
and she chose that fate was against me.
Once I said to her:
Rouse my men,
and she roused a hero against me.
Though once you were
all that I made you,
what you have become
you choose for yourself!
No more child of my will;
Valkyrie are you no longer;
Henceforth remain
what you chose to be!

BRÜNNHILDE
(heftig erschreckend)
Du verstößest mich?
Versteh ich den Sinn?

BRÜNNHILDE
(violently terrified)
So you cast me off?
Is that what you mean?

WOTAN
Nicht send ich dich mehr aus Walhall;
nicht weis ich dir mehr
Helden zur Wal;
nicht führst du mehr Sieger
in meinen Saal:
bei der Götter trautem Mahle
das Trinkhorn nicht reichst
du traulich mir mehr;
nicht kos ich dir mehr
den kindischen Mund.
Von göttlicher Schar

WOTAN
No more will you ride from Walhall;
no more will you choose
heroes who fall;
or bring me the warriors
who guard my hall;
and in Walhall, when we are feasting,
no more shall you fill
my drink-horn for me;
no more may I kiss
the mouth of my child;
the host of the gods

bist du geschieden,
ausgestoßen
aus der Ewigen Stamm;
gebrochen ist unser Bund;
aus meinem Angesicht bist du verbannt.

no more shall know you;
cast for ever
from the clan of the gods.
You broke the bond of our love,
and from my sight, henceforth, Brünnhild
[is banned!

DIE ACHT WALKÜREN
(verlassen, in aufgeregter Bewegung, ihre Stellung, indem sie sich etwas tiefer herabziehen.)
Wehe! Weh!
Schwester, ach Schwester!

THE EIGHT VALKYRIES
(in consternation leave their former position, coming somewhat lower down the rock.)
Horror! Woe!
Sister, oh sister!

BRÜNNHILDE
Nimmst du mir alles,
was einst du gabst?

BRÜNNHILDE
Can you deprive me
of all you gave?

WOTAN
Der dich zwingt, wird dir's entziehn!
Hieher auf den Berg
banne ich dich;
in wehrlosen Schlaf
schließ ich dich fest:
der Mann dann fange die Maid,
der am Wege sie findet und weckt.

WOTAN
He who comes robs you of all!
For here on the rock,
here you must stay;
defenceless in sleep,
here you will lie;
and you'll belong to the man
who can find you and wake you from
[sleep.

DIE ACHT WALKÜREN
(kommen in höchster Aufregung von der Felsenspitze ganz herab und umgeben in ängstlichen Gruppen Brünnhilde, welche halb kniend vor Wotan liegt.)
Halt ein, o Vater,
halt ein den Fluch!
Soll die Maid verblühn
und verbleichen dem Mann?
Hör unser Flehn!
Schrecklicher Gott,
wende von ihr
die schreiende Schmach!
Wie die Schwester träfe uns selber der
[Schimpf.

THE EIGHT VALKYRIES
(descend completely from the rocky height, in great consternation, and in anxious groups surround Brünnhilde, who lies half-kneeling before Wotan.)
Ah no, father!
Recall the curse!
Shall our sister bend
to the will of a man?
Endless disgrace!
Stern-hearted God!
Ah, spare her,
spare her the shame!
for our sister's shame on us then would
[fall!

WOTAN
Hörtet ihr nicht,
was ich verhängt?
Aus eurer Schar
ist die treulose Schwester geschieden;
mit euch zu Roß

WOTAN
Did you not hear
what I decreed?
that from your band
your treacherous sister is banished?
no more shall she ride

durch die Lüfte nicht reitet sie länger;
die magdliche Blume
verblüht der Maid;
ein Gatte gewinnt
ihre weibliche Gunst;
dem herrischen Manne
gehorcht sie fortan;
am Herde sitzt sie und spinnt,
aller Spottenden Ziel und Spiel.
(Brünnhilde sinkt mit einem Schrei zu Boden; die Walküren weichen entsetzt mit heftigem Geräusch von ihrer Seite.)
Schreckt euch ihr Los?
So flieht die Verlorne!
Weichet von ihr
und haltet euch fern!
Wer von euch wagte,
bei ihr zu weilen,
wer mir zum Trotz
zu der Traurigen hielt',
die Törin teilte ihr Los:
das künd ich der Kühnen an!
Fort jetzt von hier!
Meidet den Felsen!
Hurtig jagt mir von hinnen,
sonst erharrt Jammer euch hier!

DIE ACHT WALKÜREN
Weh! Weh!
(Sie fahren mit wildem Wehschrei auseinander und stürzen in hastiger Flucht in den Tann. Schwarzes Gewölk lagert sich dicht am Felsenrande: man hört wildes Geräusch im Tann. Ein greller Blitzesglanz bricht in dem Gewölk aus; in ihm erblickt man die Walküren mit verhängtem Zügel, in eine Schar zusammengedrängt, wild davonjagen. Bald legt sich der Sturm; die Gewitterwolken verziehen sich allmählich. In der folgenden Szene bricht, bei endlich ruhigem Wetter, Abenddämmerung ein, der am Schlusse Nacht folgt.)

through the clouds with her sisters to [battle;
the flower of her beauty
will fade and die;
a husband will gain
all her womanly grace;
that masterful husband
will make her obey;
she'll sit and spin by the fire,
and the world will deride her fate!
(Brünnhilde sinks with a cry to the ground; the Valkyries, in great agitation, shrink in horror from her side.)
Are you afraid?
Then flee from the lost one!
Leave her alone,
and never return!
If one of you
should come to console her,
if she should dare
to defy my command,
that rash one shares in her fate:
so now from this peak be gone!
Off with you now!
Do not go near her!
Ride away from this mountain,
or the same fate shall be yours!

THE EIGHT VALKYRIES
Woe! Woe!
(They separate with loud cries of distress and fly in haste into the wood. Black clouds gather on the cliffs; a wild tumult is heard in the wood. A vivid flash of lightning breaks through the clouds; in it are seen the Valkyries, close-grouped, their bridles hanging loose, riding wildly away. The storm soon subsides; the thunderclouds gradually disperse. During the following scene, in increasingly calm weather, twilight falls, and finally night.)

Dritte Szene

Wotan und Brünnhilde, die noch zu seinen Füßen hingestreckt liegt, sind allein zurückgeblieben. Langes, feierliches Schweigen: unveränderte Stellung.

BRÜNNHILDE
(beginnt das Haupt langsam ein wenig zu erheben. Schüchtern beginnend und steigernd:)
War es so schmählich,
was ich verbrach,
daß mein Verbrechen so schmählich du [bestrafst?
War es so niedrig,
was ich dir tat,
daß du so tief mir Erniedrigung schaffst?
War es so ehrlos,
was ich beging,
daß mein Vergehn nun die Ehre mir [raubt?
(Sie erhebt sich allmählich bis zur knienden Stellung.)
O sag, Vater!
Sieh mir ins Auge:
schweige den Zorn,
zähme die Wut
und deute mir hell
die dunkle Schuld,
die mit starrem Trotze dich zwingt,
zu verstoßen dein trautestes Kind!

WOTAN
(in unveränderter Stellung, ernst und düster)
Frag deine Tat,
sie deutet dir deine Schuld!

BRÜNNHILDE
Deinen Befehl
führte ich aus.

WOTAN
Befahl ich dir,
für den Wälsung zu fechten?

BRÜNNHILDE
So hießest du mich
als Herrscher der Wal!

Scene Three

Wotan and Brünnhilde, who still lies at his feet, are left alone. A long solemn silence: their positions remain unchanged.

BRÜNNHILDE
(begins slowly to raise her head a little; beginning timidly and becoming more confident:)
Was it so shameful,
what I have done,
that you must punish my deed with [endless shame?
Was it disgraceful,
what I have done;
do I deserve to be plunged in disgrace?
Was my dishonour
boundless and base,
for that offence must my honour be lost?
(She raises herself gradually to a kneeling position.)
Oh speak, father!
Look in my eyes:
silence your scorn,
soften your wrath,
explain to me
all the grievous guilt
that compels you, cruel and harsh,
to abandon your true, loving child.

WOTAN
(in unchanged attitude, gravely and gloomily)
Ask what you did;
your deed will tell you your guilt!

BRÜNNHILDE
By your command
bravely I fought.

WOTAN
Did I command you
to fight for the Wälsung?

BRÜNNHILDE
That was your command,
as master of fate.

WOTAN
Doch meine Weisung
nahm ich wieder zurück!

BRÜNNHILDE
Als Fricka den eignen
Sinn dir entfremdet;
da ihrem Sinn du dich fügtest,
warst du selber dir Feind.

WOTAN
(leise und bitter)
Daß du mich verstanden, wähnt' ich
und strafte den wissenden Trotz:
doch feig und dumm
dachtest du mich!
So hätt' ich Verrat nicht zu rächen,
zu gering wärst du meinem Grimm!

BRÜNNHILDE
Nicht weise bin ich,
doch wußt' ich das eine,
daß den Wälsung du liebtest.
Ich wußte den Zwiespalt,
der dich zwang,
dies eine ganz zu vergessen.
Das andre mußtest
einzig du sehn,
was zu schaun so herb
schmerzte dein Herz:
daß Siegmund Schutz du versagtest.

WOTAN
Du wußtest es so
und wagtest dennoch den Schutz?

BRÜNNHILDE
(leise beginnend)
Weil für dich im Auge
das eine ich hielt,
dem, im Zwange des andren
schmerzlich entzweit,
ratlos den Rücken du wandtest!
Die im Kampfe Wotan
den Rücken bewacht,
die sah nun das nur,
was du nicht sahst:

WOTAN
But that command
you knew I later recalled!

BRÜNNHILDE
When Fricka had made you
change your decision;
and when her words conquered your will,
you were false to yourself.

WOTAN
(softly and bitterly)
Yet you understood me fully;
I warned of my rage if you failed;
but no, you thought:
Wotan is weak!
A treacherous crime must be punished;
else on you I'd not waste my rage.

BRÜNNHILDE
I know so little,
but one thing I did know,
that the Wälsung you loved.
I saw all your torment,
as you tried
to force yourself to forget this.
The other thing
was all you could see,
and the sight of that
tortured your heart:
that Siegmund could not be shielded.

WOTAN
You knew that was so,
and yet you went to his help?

BRÜNNHILDE
(beginning softly)
Yes, because my eyes
saw but one thing alone,
one all-conquering fact
that you would not face;
you turned your back in your sorrow!
I who guard your back
when you fight in the field,
I saw that one thing
which you could not:

Siegmund mußt' ich sehn.
Tod kündend
trat ich vor ihn,
gewahrte sein Auge,
hörte sein Wort;
ich vernahm des Helden
heilige Not;
tönend erklang mir
des Tapfersten Klage:
freiester Liebe
furchtbares Leid,
traurigsten Mutes
mächtigster Trotz!
Meinem Ohr erscholl,
mein Aug' erschaute,
was tief im Busen das Herz
zu heil'gem Beben mir traf.
Scheu und staunend
stand ich in Scham.
Ihm nur zu dienen
konnt' ich noch denken:
Sieg oder Tod
mit Siegmund zu teilen:
dies nur erkannt' ich
zu kiesen als Los!
Der diese Liebe
mir ins Herz gehaucht,
dem Willen, der
dem Wälsung mich gesellt,
ihm innig vertraut—
trotzt' ich deinem Gebot.

WOTAN
So tatest du,
was so gern zu tun ich begehrt,
doch was nicht zu tun
die Not zwiefach mich zwang?
So leicht wähntest du
Wonne der Liebe erworben,
wo brennend Weh
in das Herz mir brach,
wo gräßliche Not
den Grimm mir schuf,
einer Welt zuliebe
der Liebe Quell
im gequälten Herzen zu hemmen?
Wo gegen mich selber

Siegmund I beheld.
I said
you had marked him for death;
I gazed in his eyes then,
heard his reply;
and I shared that hero's
grief and distress,
hearing the call
of his brave lamentation—
love's holy yearning,
hopeless despair—
proud in defiance,
dauntless in grief!
In my ears it rang;
my eyes were dazzled;
my mind was troubled;
a new emotion stole through my heart.
Shy, astonished,
I stood ashamed.
How could I help him,
how could I save him?
Victory or death,
with Siegmund I'd share it!
One thought possessed me,
and I had no choice!
You, who this love
in my heart inspired,
when you inspired
the Wälsung with your will,
you were not betrayed—
though I broke your command.

WOTAN
So you would attempt
what I longed so dearly to do,
but which cruel fate
forbade me to achieve?
So you thought
that love could be captured so lightly,
while burning woe
broke my heart in two,
and terrible grief
awoke my rage;
when, to save creation,
the spring of love
in my tortured heart I imprisoned?
Then, burning with anger,

ich sehrend mich wandte,
aus Ohnmachtsschmerzen
schäumend ich aufschoß,
wütender Sehnsucht
sengender Wunsch
den schrecklichen Willen mir schuf,
in den Trümmern der eignen Welt
meine ew'ge Trauer zu enden:
da labte süß
dich selige Lust;
wonniger Rührung
üppigen Rausch
enttrankst du lachend
der Liebe Trank,
als mir göttliche Not
nagende Galle gemischt?
Deinen leichten Sinn
laß dich denn leiten:
von mir sagtest du dich los.
Dich muß ich meiden,
gemeinsam mit dir
nicht darf ich Rat mehr raunen;
getrennt nicht dürfen
traut wir mehr schaffen:
so weit Leben und Luft,
darf der Gott dir nicht mehr begegnen!

BRÜNNHILDE
Wohl taugte dir nicht
die tör'ge Maid,
die staunend im Rate
nicht dich verstand,
wie mein eigner Rat
nur das eine mir riet:
zu lieben, was du geliebt.
Muß ich denn scheiden
und scheu dich meiden,
mußt du spalten,
was einst sich umspannt,
die eigne Hälfte
fern von dir halten,
daß sonst sie ganz dir gehörte,
du Gott, vergiß das nicht!
Dein ewig Teil
nicht wirst du entehren,
Schande nicht wollen,
die dich beschimpft:

I turned on myself,
from an anguished weakness
rising in frenzy,
yearning and raging,
I was inspired
and driven to a fearful resolve:
in the wreck of my ruined world
my unending sorrow I'd bury:
while you lay lapped
in blissful delight,
filled with emotion's
rapturous joy;
you laughed, while drinking
the draught of love,
and I tasted the gall,
drained bitter sorrow and grief!
You indulged your love;
now let it lead you:
from me you have turned away.
So I must shun you;
no more may I share
with you my secret counsels;
henceforth our paths
are parted forever:
for, while life shall endure,
I, the god, no more shall behold you.

BRÜNNHILDE
Unworthy of you
this foolish maid,
who, stunned by your counsel,
misunderstood,
when that one command
overruled all the rest:
to love him whom you had loved.
If I must lose you,
and you must leave me,
if you sever
the bonds that we tied,
then half your being
you have abandoned,
which once belonged to you only.
O god, forget not that!
That other self
you must not dishonour;
if you disgrace her,
it falls on you:

dich selbst ließest du sinken,
sähst du dem Spott mich zum Spiel!

WOTAN
Du folgtest selig
der Liebe Macht:
folge nun dem,
den du lieben mußt!

BRÜNNHILDE
Soll ich aus Walhall scheiden,
nicht mehr mit dir schaffen und walten,
dem herrischen Manne
gehorchen fortan:
dem feigen Prahler
gib mich nicht preis!
Nicht wertlos sei er,
der mich gewinnt.

WOTAN
Von Walvater schiedest du,
nicht wählen darf er für dich.

BRÜNNHILDE
(leise mit vertraulicher Heimlichkeit)
Du zeugtest ein edles Geschlecht;
kein Zager kann je ihm entschlagen:
der weihlichste Held—ich weiß es—
entblüht dem Wälsungenstamm!

WOTAN
Schweig von dem Wälsungenstamm!
Von dir geschieden,
schied ich von ihm:
vernichten mußt' ihn der Neid!

BRÜNNHILDE
Die von dir sich riß,
rettete ihn.
Sieglinde hegt
die heiligste Frucht;
in Schmerz und Leid,
wie kein Weib sie gelitten,
wird sie gebären,
was bang sie birgt.

WOTAN
Nie suche bei mir

your fame then would be darkened,
if I were scorned and despised!

WOTAN
You chose in rapture
the path of love:
follow love's path,
and obey your lord!

BRÜNNHILDE
If I must go from Walhall,
and play no more part in your actions,
and take as my master
some man to obey:
be sure no coward
makes me his prize;
be sure some hero
wins me as bride!

WOTAN
From Wotan you turned away;
your conqueror I cannot choose.

BRÜNNHILDE
(softly and confidingly)
You fathered a glorious race;
that race cannot bring forth a coward:
a hero will come, I know it;
be born of Wälsung blood.

WOTAN
Name not the Wälsungs to me!
By your desertion
the Wälsungs were doomed;
my rage destroys all the race!

BRÜNNHILDE
She who turned from you
rescued the race.
Sieglinde bears
the holiest fruit;
in pain and grief
such as no woman suffered,
she will give birth
to a Wälsung child.

WOTAN
I'll offer no help—

Schutz für die Frau,
noch für ihres Schoßes Frucht!

BRÜNNHILDE
Sie wahret das Schwert,
das du Siegmund schufest.

WOTAN
(heftig)
Und das ich ihm in Stücken schlug!
Nicht streb, o Maid,
den Mut mir zu stören;
erwarte dein Los,
wie sich's dir wirft;
nicht kiesen kann ich es dir!
Doch fort muß ich jetzt,
fern mich verziehn;
zuviel schon zögert' ich hier.
Von der Abwendigen
wend ich mich ab;
nicht wissen darf ich,
was sie sich wünscht:
die Strafe nur
muß vollstreckt ich sehn!

BRÜNNHILDE
Was hast du erdacht,
daß ich erdulde?

WOTAN
In festen Schlaf
verschließ ich dich:
wer so die Wehrlose weckt,
dem ward, erwacht, sie zum Weib!

BRÜNNHILDE
(stürzt auf ihre Knie.)
Soll fesselnder Schlaf
fest mich binden,
dem feigsten Manne
zur leichten Beute:
dies eine mußt du erhören,
was heil'ge Angst zu dir fleht!
Die Schlafende schütze
mit scheuchendem Schrecken,
daß nur ein furchtlos
freiester Held

neither to her
nor to any Wälsung child.

BRÜNNHILDE
She still has the sword
that you made for Siegmund.

WOTAN
(vehemently)
And which I later broke again!
Seek not, O child,
to change my decision;
await now your fate,
as it must fall:
I may not choose it for you!
But now I must go,
far from this place;
too long now I have delayed.
For as you turned from me,
I turn from you;
I may not even
ask what you wish:
your sentence now
I must see fulfilled.

BRÜNNHILDE
What have you decreed
that I must suffer?

WOTAN
In long, deep sleep
you shall be bound:
the man who wakes you again,
that man awakes you as wife!

BRÜNNHILDE
(falls on her knees.)
If fetters of sleep
come to bind me,
if I must fall
to the man who finds me,
then one thing more you must grant me;
in deepest anguish I pray!
Oh shelter my slumber,
protect me with terrors,
let only one
who is fearless and free

hier auf dem Felsen
einst mich fänd'!

WOTAN
Zuviel begehrst du,
zuviel der Gunst!

BRÜNNHILDE
(seine Knie umfassend)
Dies eine
mußt du erhören!
Zerknicke dein Kind,
das dein Knie umfaßt;
zertritt die Traute,
zertrümmre die Maid,
ihres Leibes Spur
zerstöre dein Speer:
doch gib, Grausamer, nicht
der gräßlichsten Schmach sie preis!
(mit wilder Begeisterung)
Auf dein Gebot
entbrenne ein Feuer;
den Felsen umglühe
lodernde Glut;
es leck ihre Zung',
es fresse ihr Zahn
den Zagen, der frech sich wagte,
dem freislichen Felsen zu nahn!

WOTAN
(überwältigt und tief ergriffen, wendet sich lebhaft zu Brünnhilde, erhebt sie von den Knien und blickt ihr gerührt ins Auge.)
Leb wohl, du kühnes,
herrliches Kind!
Du meines Herzens heiligster Stolz!
Leb wohl! Leb wohl! Leb wohl!
(sehr leidenschaftlich)
Muß ich dich meiden,
und darf nicht minnig
mein Gruß dich mehr grüßen;
sollst du nun nicht mehr
neben mir reiten,
noch Met beim Mahl mir reichen;
muß ich verlieren
dich, die ich liebte,
du lachende Lust meines Auges:

none but a hero
find me here!

WOTAN
Too much you are asking,
too great a grace!

BRÜNNHILDE
(embracing his knees)
This one thing more
you must grant me!
Oh kill me at once
as I clasp your knee;
destroy your daughter,
condemn me to die,
let my breast receive
one blow from your spear;
but ah! cast not this shame,
this cruel disgrace on me!
(with wild inspiration)
At your command
a flame can be kindled,
a fiery guardian,
girding the rock,
to lick with its tongues,
to tear with its teeth
the craven who rashly ventures,
who dares to approach near the rock!

WOTAN
(overcome and deeply moved, turns eagerly towards Brünnhilde, raises her from her knees and gazes with emotion into her eyes.)
Farewell, my valiant,
glorious child!
You were the holiest pride of my heart!
Farewell! Farewell! Farewell!
(very passionately)
Though I must leave you,
and may no longer
embrace you in greeting;
though you may no more
ride beside me,
nor bear my mead in Walhall;
though I abandon you
whom I love so,
the laughing delight of my eye:

ein bräutliches Feuer
soll dir nun brennen,
wie nie einer Braut es gebrannt!
Flammende Glut
umglühe den Fels;
mit zehrenden Schrecken
scheuch es den Zagen;
der Feige fliehe
Brünnhildes Fels!
Denn einer nur freie die Braut,
der freier als ich, der Gott!
(Brünnhilde sinkt, gerührt und begeistert, an Wotans Brust; er hält sie lange umfangen. Sie schlägt das Haupt wieder zurück und blickt, immer noch ihn umfassend, feierlich ergriffen Wotan in das Auge.)
Der Augen leuchtendes Paar,
das oft ich lächelnd gekost,
wenn Kampfeslust
ein Kuß dir lohnte,
wenn kindisch lallend
der Helden Lob
von holden Lippen dir floß:
dieser Augen strahlendes Paar,
das oft im Sturm mir geglänzt,
wenn Hoffnungssehnen
das Herz mir sengte,
nach Weltenwonne
mein Wunsch verlangte
aus wild webendem Bangen:
zum letztenmal
letz es mich heut
mit des Lebewohles
letztem Kuß!
Dem glücklichern Manne
glänze sein Stern:
dem unseligen Ew'gen
muß es scheidend sich schließen.
(Er faßt ihr Haupt in beide Hände.)
Denn so kehrt
der Gott sich dir ab,
so küßt er die Gottheit von dir!
(Er küßt sie lange auf die Augen. Sie sinkt mit geschlossenen Augen, sanft ermattend, in seinen Armen zurück. Er geleitet sie zart auf einen niedrigen Mooshügel zu liegen, über den sich eine breitästige Tanne ausstreckt. Er betrachtet sie und schließt ihr den Helm: sein Auge weilt dann auf

a bridal fire
shall blaze to protect you,
as never has burned for a bride.
Threatening flames
shall flare from the rock;
the craven will fear it,
cringe from its fury;
the weak will flee
from Brünnhilde's rock!
For one alone wins you as bride,
one freer than I, the god!
(Brünnhilde, moved and exalted, sinks on Wotan's breast: he holds her in a long embrace. She throws her head back again and, still embracing Wotan, gazes with solemn rapture into his eyes.)
These radiant, glorious eyes,
which, smiling, often I kissed,
when courage
I acclaimed with kisses,
while childish prattle
in heroes' praise
so sweetly poured from your lips:
yes, these gleaming, radiant eyes,
which shone so bright in the storm,
when hopeless yearning
consumed my spirit,
and worldly pleasures
were all I longed for,
when fear fastened upon me—
their glorious fire
gladdens me now,
as I take this loving,
last farewell!
On some happy mortal
one day they will shine:
but I, hapless immortal,
I must lose them forever.
(He clasps her head in his hands.)
And sadly
the god must depart;
my kiss takes your godhead away!
(He presses a long kiss on her eyes. She sinks back with closed eyes, unconscious, in his arms. He gently supports her to a low mossy bank, which is overshadowed by a wide-branching fir tree, and lays her upon it. He looks upon her and closes her helmet; his eye then rests on the form of the

der Gestalt der Schlafenden, die er mit dem großen Stahlschilde der Walküre ganz zudeckt. Langsam kehrt er sich ab, mit einem schmerzlichen Blicke wendet er sich noch einmal um. Dann schreitet er mit feierlichem Entschlusse in die Mitte der Bühne und kehrt seines Speeres Spitze gegen einen mächtigen Felsstein.)

Loge, hör!
Lausche hieher!
Wie zuerst ich dich fand,
als feurige Glut,
wie dann einst du mir schwandest
als schweifende Lohe;
wie ich dich band,
bann ich dich heut!
Herauf, wabernde Lohe,
umlodre mir feurig den Fels!

(Er stößt mit dem Folgenden dreimal mit dem Speer auf den Stein.)

Loge! Loge! Hieher!

(Dem Stein entfährt ein Feuerstrahl, der zur allmählich immer helleren Flammenglut anschwillt. Lichte Flackerlohe bricht aus. Lichte Brunst umgibt Wotan mit wildem Flackern. Er weist mit dem Speere gebieterisch dem Feuermeere den Umkreis des Felsenrandes zur Strömung an; alsbald zieht es sich nach dem Hintergrunde, wo es nun fortwährend den Bergsaum umlodert.)

Wer meines Speeres
Spitze fürchtet,
durchschreite das Feuer nie!

(Er streckt den Speer wie zum Banne aus. Dann blickt er schmerzlich auf Brünnhilde zurück, wendet sich langsam zum Gehen und blickt noch einmal zurück, ehe er durch das Feuer verschwindet. Der Vorhang fällt.)

sleeper, which he completely covers with the great steel shield of the Valkyrie. He turns slowly away, then turns round again with a sorrowful look. Then he strides with solemn decision to the middle of the stage, and directs the point of his spear towards a massive rock.)

Loge, hear!
Come at my call!
As when first you were found,
a fiery glow,
as when then you escaped me,
a wandering flicker;
once you were bound:
be so again!
Arise! Come, flickering Loge;
surround the rock, ring it with flame!

(During the following he strikes the rock three times with his spear.)

Loge! Loge! Appear!

(A flash of flame leaps from the rock, and gradually increases to an ever-brightening fiery glow. Flickering flames break out. Bright, shooting flames surround Wotan. With his spear, he directs the sea of fire to encircle the rocks; it presently spreads toward the background, where it encloses the mountain in flames.)

Only the man
who braves my spear-point
can pass through this sea of flame!

(He stretches out the spear as if casting a spell. Then he gazes sorrowfully back at Brünnhilde, turns slowly to depart, and looks back once more before he disappears through the fire. The curtain falls.)

Siegfried

Second Day of the Festival Play

The Ring of the Nibelung

Dramatis Personae

SIEGFRIED	*Tenor*
MIME	*Tenor*
THE WANDERER	*Bass*
ALBERICH	*Bass*
FAFNER	*Bass*
ERDA	*Contralto*
BRÜNNHILDE	*Soprano*
Voice of the Woodbird	*Soprano*

Act One

Erster Aufzug

Wald

Den Vordergrund bildet ein Teil einer Felsenhöhle, die sich links tiefer nach innen zieht, nach rechts aber gegen drei Viertel der Bühne einnimmt. Zwei natürlich gebildete Eingänge stehen dem Walde zu offen: der eine nach rechts, unmittelbar im Hintergrunde, der andere, breitere, ebenda seitwärts. An der Hinterwand, nach links zu, steht ein großer Schmiedeherd, aus Felsstücken natürlich geformt; künstlich ist nur der große Blasebalg: die rohe Esse geht—ebenfalls natürlich—durch das Felsendach hinauf. Ein sehr großer Amboß und andere Schmiedegerätschaften.

Erste Szene

MIME

(sitzt am Ambosse und hämmert mit wachsender Unruhe an einem Schwerte, endlich hält er unmutig ein.)

Zwangvolle Plage!

Act One

A Forest

The foreground represents part of a cave in the rocks, extending inwards more deeply to the left, but occupying about three-quarters of the stage-depth to the right. There are two natural entrances to the forest, the one to the right opening directly, and the other, broader one opening sideways, to the background. On the rear wall, to the left, is a large smith's forge, formed naturally from pieces of rock; only the large bellows are artificial. A rough chimney, also natural, passes through the roof of the cave. A very large anvil and other smith's tools.

Scene One

MIME

(sits at the anvil and with increasing anxiety hammers at a sword; at length he stops working, in ill-humour.)

Wearisome labour!

Müh' ohne Zweck!
Das beste Schwert,
das je ich geschweißt,
in der Riesen Fäusten
hielte es fest:
doch dem ich's geschmiedet,
der schmähliche Knabe,
er knickt und schmeißt es entzwei,
als schüf' ich Kindergeschmeid'!
(Mime wirft das Schwert unmutig auf den Amboß, stemmt die Arme ein und blickt sinnend zu Boden.)

Es gibt ein Schwert,
das er nicht zerschwänge:
Notungs Trümmer
zertrotzt' er mir nicht,
könnt' ich die starken
Stücken schweißen,
die meine Kunst
nicht zu kitten weiß!
Könnt' ich's dem Kühnen schmieden,
meiner Schmach erlangt' ich da Lohn!
(Er sinkt tiefer zurück und neigt sinnend das Haupt.)
Fafner, der wilde Wurm,
lagert im finstren Wald;
mit des furchtbaren Leibes Wucht
der Niblungen Hort
hütet er dort.
Siegfrieds kindischer Kraft
erläge wohl Fafners Leib:
des Niblungen Ring
erränge er mir.
Nur ein Schwert taugt zu der Tat;
nur Notung nützt meinem Neid,
wenn Siegfried sehrend ihn schwingt:
und ich kann's nicht schweißen,
Notung, das Schwert!
(Er hat das Schwert wieder zurechtgelegt und hämmert in höchstem Unmut daran weiter.)
Zwangvolle Plage!
Müh' ohne Zweck!
Das beste Schwert,
das je ich geschweißt,
nie taugt es je
zu der einzigen Tat!
Ich tappre und hämmre nur,

Work till I drop!
The strongest sword
I struggle to make,
an amazing weapon,
fit for a giant:
but when I have made it,
that insolent Siegfried
just laughs and snaps it in two,
as though I'd made him a toy!
(In ill humour, Mime throws the sword down on the anvil, places his arms akimbo, and gazes at the ground in thought.)
I know one sword
that could not be shattered:
Notung's fragments
he never would break,
if only I could forge,
those pieces,
if but my skill
could achieve that deed!
If I could forge those fragments,
all my shame would change into joy!
(He sinks back further and lowers his head in thought.)
Fafner, the mighty dragon,
lies there within those woods
and protects with his monstrous bulk
the Nibelung gold,
guarding it well.
Siegfried's conquering strength
could quickly lay Fafner low:
the Nibelung's ring
would then come to me.
And one sword is all that I need,
and Notung only will serve,
when Siegfried deals him the blow:
and I cannot forge it,
Notung, the sword!
(He has readjusted the sword, and returns to his hammering in deepest dejection.)
Wearisome labour!
Work till I drop!
The strongest sword
that ever I make
will prove too weak
for that one mighty deed!
I tinker and tap away

weil der Knabe es heischt:
er knickt und schmeißt es entzwei
und schmäht doch, schmied ich ihm [nicht!
(Er läßt den Hammer fallen.)

because Siegfried commands:
he laughs and snaps it in two,
and scolds me, if I don't work!
(He lets the hammer fall.)

SIEGFRIED
(in wilder Waldkleidung, mit einem silbernen Horn an einer Kette, kommt mit jähem Ungestüm aus dem Walde herein; er hat einen großen Bären mit einem Bastseile gezäumt und treibt diesen mit lustigem Übermute gegen Mime an.)
Hoiho! Hoiho!
Hau ein! Hau ein!
Friß ihn! Friß ihn,
den Fratzenschmied!
(Er lacht. Mime entsinkt vor Schreck das Schwert; er flüchtet hinter den Herd; Siegfried treibt ihm den Bären überall nach.)

SIEGFRIED
(in rough forest dress, with a silver horn slung from a chain, comes in boisterously from the forest. He has bridled a large bear with a bast rope, and in exuberant high spirits he sets it at Mime.)
Hoiho! Hoiho!
Come on! Come in!
Bite him! Bite him,
the lazy smith!
(He laughs. Mime drops the sword in his fright, and runs behind the forge. Siegfried urges the bear to chase him about.)

MIME
Fort mit dem Tier!
Was taugt mir der Bär?

MIME
Off with that beast!
Why bring me a bear?

SIEGFRIED
Zu zwei komm ich,
dich besser zu zwicken:
Brauner, frag nach dem Schwert!

SIEGFRIED
He came with me
to teach you to hurry:
Bruin, beg for the sword!

MIME
He! Laß das Wild!
Dort liegt die Waffe:
fertig fegt' ich sie heut.

MIME
Hey! let him go!
There lies your weapon,
forged and finished today.

SIEGFRIED
So fährst du heute noch heil!
(Er löst dem Bären den Zaum und gibt ihm damit einen Schlag auf den Rücken.)
Lauf, Brauner,
dich brauch ich nicht mehr!
(Der Bär läuft in den Wald zurück.)

SIEGFRIED
Well, then today you are free!
(He releases the bear, and gives him a flick on the back with the rope.)
Off, Bruin!
You're needed no more.
(The bear runs off into the forest.)

MIME
(kommt zitternd hinter dem Herde hervor.)
Wohl leid ich's gern,
erlegst du Bären:
Was bringst du lebend
die Braunen heim?

MIME
(comes out trembling from behind the hearth.)
To killing bears
I've no objection,
but why bring live ones
inside the cave?

SIEGFRIED
(setzt sich, um sich vom Lachen zu erholen.)
Nach beßrem Gesellen sucht' ich,
als daheim mir einer sitzt;
im tiefen Walde mein Horn
ließ ich hallend da ertönen:
ob sich froh mir gesellte
ein guter Freund,
das frug ich mit dem Getön!
Aus dem Busche kam ein Bär,
der hörte mir brummend zu;
er gefiel mir besser als du,
doch beßre fänd' ich wohl noch!
Mit dem zähen Baste
zäumt' ich ihn da,
dich, Schelm, nach dem Schwerte zu fragen.
(Er springt auf und geht auf den Amboß zu.)

MIME
(nimmt das Schwert, es Siegfried zu reichen.)
Ich schuf die Waffe scharf,
ihrer Schneide wirst du dich freun.
(Er hält das Schwert ängstlich in der Hand fest, das Siegfried ihm heftig entwindet.)

SIEGFRIED
Was frommt seine helle Schneide,
ist der Stahl nicht hart und fest!
(das Schwert mit der Hand prüfend)
Hei! Was ist das
für müß'ger Tand!
Den schwachen Stift
nennst du ein Schwert?
(Er zerschlägt es auf dem Amboß, daß die Stücken ringsum fliegen; Mime weicht erschrocken aus.)
Da hast du die Stücken,
schändlicher Stümper:
hätt' ich am Schädel
dir sie zerschlagen!
Soll mich der Prahler
länger noch prellen?
Schwatzt mir von Riesen
und rüstigen Kämpfen,
von kühnen Taten
und tüchtiger Wehr;
will Waffen mir schmieden,

SIEGFRIED
(sits down to recover from his laughter.)
I wanted a better comrade
than the one I leave at home;
and so I called with my horn,
set the forest glades resounding:
Would I find what I longed for,
a faithful friend?—
that's what I asked with my call!
From the bushes came a bear,
who growled as I played my tune;
and I liked him better than you—
though better still I shall find!
So I bridled him
and brought him along
to see if the sword had been finished.
(He jumps up and goes across to the anvil.)

MIME
(takes the sword to give it to Siegfried.)
I made it keen and sharp,
and its shine will gladden your heart.
(Anxiously he holds on to it, but Siegfried snatches it from him.)

SIEGFRIED
What use is the shiny sharpness
if the steel's not hard and true!
(testing the sword with his hand)
Hey! what a useless
thing you have made!
A feeble pin!
Call it a sword?
(He smashes it on the anvil, so that the splinters fly about. Mime shrinks in terror.)
Well, there are the pieces,
blundering boaster;
I should have smashed it
there on your brainpan!
Now will the liar
brag any longer,
talking of giants,
and boldness in battle,
and deeds of daring,
and fearless defence?
And weapons you'll forge me,

Schwerte schaffen;
rühmt seine Kunst,
als könnt' er was Rechts:
nehm' ich zur Hand nun,
was er gehämmert,
mit einem Griff
zergreif ich den Quark!
Wär' mir nicht schier
zu schäbig der Wicht,
ich zerschmiedet' ihn selbst
mit seinem Geschmeid,
den alten albernen Alp!
Des Ärgers dann hätt' ich ein End'!
(Siegfried wirft sich wütend auf eine Steinbank zur Seite rechts. Mime ist ihm immer vorsichtig ausgewichen.)

MIME
Nun tobst du wieder wie toll:
dein Undank, traun, ist arg!
Mach ich dem bösen Buben
nicht alles gleich zu best,
was ich ihm Gutes schuf,
vergißt er gar zu schnell!
Willst du denn nie gedenken,
was ich dich lehrt' vom Danke?
Dem sollst du willig gehorchen,
der je sich wohl dir erwies.
(Siegfried wendet sich unmutig um, mit dem Gesicht nach der Wand, so daß er Mime den Rücken kehrt.)
Das willst du wieder nicht hören!
(Er steht verlegen; dann geht er in die Küche am Herd.)
Doch speisen magst du wohl?
Vom Spieße bring ich den Braten:
versuchtest du gern den Sud?
Für dich sott ich ihn gar.
(Er bietet Siegfried Speise hin; dieser, ohne sich umzuwenden, schmeißt ihm Topf und Braten aus der Hand.)

SIEGFRIED
Braten briet ich mir selbst:
deinen Sudel sauf allein!

MIME
(mit kläglich kreischender Stimme)
Das ist nun der Liebe

swords you'll fashion,
praising your skill,
and proud of your craft?
Yet when I handle
what you have fashioned—
a single blow
destroys all your trash!
If he were not
too mean for my rage,
I should fling in the fire
the smith and his works—
the aged doddering dwarf!
My anger would then have an end!
(In a rage Siegfried flings himself down on a stone seat to the right. Mime has carefully kept out of his way.)

MIME
Again you rage like a fool,
ungrateful, heartless boy!
Maybe today I've failed you;
but when my work is not good
then you at once forget
the good things I have done!
Must I once more remind you
that you should be more grateful?
And you should learn to obey me,
who always showed you such love.
(Siegfried turns away crossly, his face to the wall, his back to Mime.)

Now once again you're not listening!
(He stands perplexed, and then goes to the cooking pots at the fireplace.)
But food is what you need:
come, try this meat I have roasted;
or would you prefer this soup?
For you, all is prepared.
(He brings food to Siegfried, who without turning round knocks bowl and meat out of Mime's hands.)

SIEGFRIED
Meat I roast for myself:
you can drink your slops alone!

MIME
(in a querulous screech)
Fine reward

schlimmer Lohn!
Das der Sorgen
schmählicher Sold!
Als zullendes Kind
zog ich dich auf,
wärmte mit Kleiden
den kleinen Wurm:
Speise und Trank
trug ich dir zu,
hütete dich
wie die eigne Haut.
Und wie du erwuchsest,
wartet' ich dein;
dein Lager schuf ich,
daß leicht du schliefst.
Dir schmiedet' ich Tand
und ein tönend Horn;
dich zu erfreun,
müht' ich mich froh.
Mit klugem Rate
riet ich dir klug,
mit lichtem Wissen
lehrt' ich dich Witz.
Sitz' ich daheim
in Fleiß und Schweiß,
nach Herzenslust
schweifst du umher.
Für dich nur in Plage,
in Pein nur für dich
verzehr ich mich alter,
armer Zwerg!
(schluchzend)
Und aller Lasten
ist das nun mein Lohn,
daß der hastige Knabe
mich quält und haßt!
(Siegfried hat sich wieder umgewendet und ruhig in Mimes Blick geforscht. Mime begegnet Siegfrieds Blick und sucht den seinigen scheu zu bergen.)

for all my loving care!
Thus the boy repays
what I've done!
A whimpering babe,
born in these woods—
Mime was kind
to the tiny mite;
feeding you well,
keeping you warm,
sheltering you safe
as my very self.
And when you grew older
I was your nurse;
when you were sleepy
I smoothed your bed.
I made you nice toys
and that shining horn,
toiling away,
trying to please:
my clever counsels
sharpened your wits;
I tried to make you
crafty and bright.
Staying at home
I slave and sweat,
while you go
wandering around.
I toil for your pleasure,
think only of you,
I wear myself out—
a poor old dwarf!
(sobbing)
Then you repay me
for all that I've done
with your furious scolding
and scorn and hate!
(Siegfried has turned round again and looks steadily into Mime's eyes. Mime encounters his gaze and tries timidly to conceal his own.)

SIEGFRIED
Vieles lehrtest du, Mime,
und manches lernt' ich von dir;
doch was du am liebsten mich lehrtest,
zu lernen gelang mir nie:
wie ich dich leiden könnt'.

SIEGFRIED
Much you've taught to me, Mime,
and many things I have learnt;
but one thing you most long to teach me.
that lesson I never learn:
how not to loathe your sight.

Trägst du mir Trank
und Speise herbei,
der Ekel speist mich allein;
schaffst du ein leichtes
Lager zum Schlaf,
der Schlummer wird mir da schwer;
willst du mich weisen,
witzig zu sein,
gern bleib ich taub und dumm.
Seh ich dir erst
mit den Augen zu,
zu übel erkenn ich,
was alles du tust:
Seh ich dich stehn,
gangeln und gehn,
knicken und nicken,
mit den Augen zwicken:
beim Genick möcht' ich
den Nicker packen,
den Garaus geben
dem garst'gen Zwicker!
So lernt' ich, Mime, dich leiden.
Bist du nun weise,
so hilf mir wissen,
worüber umsonst ich sann:
in den Wald lauf ich,
dich zu verlassen,
wie kommt das, kehr ich zurück?
Alle Tiere sind
mir teurer als du:
Baum und Vogel,
die Fische im Bach,
lieber mag ich sie
leiden als dich:
Wie kommt das nun, kehr ich zurück?
Bist du klug, so tu mir's kund.

When you bring food
and offer me drink,
my hunger turns to disgust;
when you prepare
soft beds for my rest,
then sleep is driven away;
when you would make me
clever and wise,
I would be deaf and dull.
I am repelled
by the sight of you;
I see that you're evil
in all that you do.
I watch you stand,
shuffle and nod,
shrinking and slinking,
with your eyelids blinking—
by your nodding neck
I'd like to catch you,
and end your shrinking,
and stop your blinking!
So deeply, Mime, I loathe you.
If you're so clever,
then tell me something
which long I have sought in vain:
through the woods roaming,
trying to avoid you—
what is it makes me return?
Everything to me
is dearer than you:
birds in branches
and fish in the brook—
all are dear to me,
far more than you.
What is it then makes me return?
If you're wise, then tell me that.

MIME
(setzt sich in einiger Entfernung ihm traulich gegenüber.)
Mein Kind, das lehrt dich kennen,
wie lieb ich am Herzen dir lieg.

MIME
(sits facing him, familiarly, a little way off.)
My child, that shows quite clearly
how dear to your heart I must be.

SIEGFRIED
(lachend)
Ich kann dich ja nicht leiden,
vergiß das nicht so leicht!

SIEGFRIED
(laughing)
I cannot bear the sight of you—
have you forgotten that?

MIME
(fährt zurück und setzt sich wieder abseits, Siegfried gegenüber.)
Des ist deine Wildheit schuld,
die du, Böser, bänd'gen sollst.
Jammernd verlangen Junge
nach ihrer Alten Nest;
Liebe ist das Verlangen:
So lechzest du auch nach mir,
so liebst du auch deinen Mime—
so mußt du ihn lieben!
Was dem Vögelein ist der Vogel,
wenn er im Nest es nährt,
eh' das flügge mag fliegen:
das ist dir kind'schem Sproß
der kundig sorgende Mime—
das muß er dir sein!

MIME
(shrinks back, and sits down again at the side, facing Siegfried.)
That comes from your wild young heart,
from a wildness you must tame.
Young ones are ever yearning
after their parents' nest;
love is the cause of that yearning:
and that's why you yearn for me:
you love your dear old Mime—
you must learn to love me!
What the mother-birds are to fledglings,
while in the nest they lie,
long before they can flutter,
such to you, dearest child,
is wise and careful old Mime—
such must Mime be!

SIEGFRIED
Ei, Mime, bist du so witzig,
so laß mich eines noch wissen!
Es sangen die Vöglein
so selig im Lenz,
das eine lockte das andre:
Du sagtest selbst,
da ich's wissen wollt',
das wären Männchen und Weibchen.
Sie kosten so lieblich
und ließen sich nicht;
sie bauten ein Nest
und brüteten drin:
da flatterte junges
Geflügel auf,
und beide pflegten der Brut.
So ruhten im Busch
auch Rehe gepaart,
selbst wilde Füchse und Wölfe:
Nahrung brachte
zum Nest das Männchen,
das Weibchen säugte die Welpen.
Da lernt' ich wohl,
was Liebe sei:
der Mutter entwand ich
die Welpen nie.
Wo hast du nun, Mime,
dein minniges Weibchen,
daß ich es Mutter nenne?

SIEGFRIED
Hey, Mime, if you're so clever,
there's something else you can teach me!
The birds were singing
so sweetly in spring;
their songs were loving and tender:
and you replied,
when I asked you why,
that they were mothers and fathers.
They chattered so fondly,
and never apart;
then building a nest,
they brooded inside,
and soon little fledglings
were fluttering there;
the parents cared for the brood.
And here in the woods
the deer lay in pairs,
and savage foxes and wolves, too:
food was brought to the den
by the father,
the mother suckled the young ones.
I learnt from them
what love must be;
I never disturbed them
or stole their cubs.
You must tell me, Mime,
where you dear little wife is.
Where is my mother, tell me!

MIME
(ärgerlich)
Was ist dir, Tor?
Ach, bist du dumm!
Bist doch weder Vogel noch Fuchs?

SIEGFRIED
»Das zullende Kind
zogest du auf,
wärmtest mit Kleiden
den kleinen Wurm«:
Wie kam dir aber
der kindische Wurm?
Du machtest wohl gar
ohne Mutter mich?

MIME
(in großer Verlegenheit)
Glauben sollst du,
was ich dir sage:
ich bin dir Vater
und Mutter zugleich.

SIEGFRIED
Das lügst du, garstiger Gauch!
Wie die Jungen den Alten gleichen,
das hab ich mir glücklich ersehn.
Nun kam ich zum klaren Bach:
da erspäht' ich die Bäum'
und Tier' im Spiegel;
Sonn' und Wolken,
wie sie nur sind,
im Glitzer erschienen sie gleich.
Da sah ich denn auch
mein eigen Bild;
ganz anders als du
dünkt' ich mir da:
So glich wohl der Kröte
ein glänzender Fisch;
doch kroch nie ein Fisch aus der Kröte!

MIME
(höchst ärgerlich)
Greulichen Unsinn
kramst du da aus!

SIEGFRIED
(immer lebendiger)
Siehst du, nun fällt

MIME
(crossly)
Why do you ask?
Don't be so dull!
For you're not a bird or a fox!

SIEGFRIED
'A whimpering babe,
born in these woods,
Mime was kind
to the tiny mite . . .'
But who created
that whimpering babe?
For making a babe
needs a mother too!

MIME
(in great embarrassment)
I'll explain it;
try to believe me:
I am your father
and mother in one.

SIEGFRIED
You're lying, foul little dwarf!
Every young one is like his parents;
I know, for I've seen it myself.
One day in the shining stream
I could see every tree
and forest creature,
sun and shadow,
just as they are,
reflected below in the brook.
And there in the stream
I saw my face—
it wasn't like yours,
not in the least,
no more than a toad
resembles a fish.
No fish had a toad for a father!

MIME
(much vexed)
What an absurd
and stupid idea!

SIEGFRIED
(with increasing animation)
See here, at last

auch selbst mir ein,
was zuvor umsonst ich besann:
wenn zum Wald ich laufe,
dich zu verlassen,
wie das kommt, kehr ich doch heim?
(Er springt auf.)
Von dir erst muß ich erfahren,
wer Vater und Mutter mir sei!

MIME
(weicht ihm aus.)
Was Vater! Was Mutter!
Müßige Frage!

SIEGFRIED
(packt ihn bei der Kehle.)
So muß ich dich fassen,
um was zu wissen:
gutwillig
erfahr ich doch nichts!
So mußt' ich alles
ab dir trotzen:
kaum das Reden
hätt' ich erraten,
entwand ich's mit Gewalt
nicht dem Schuft!
Heraus damit,
räudiger Kerl!
Wer ist mir Vater und Mutter?

MIME
(nachdem er mit dem Kopfe genickt und mit den Händen gewinkt, ist von Siegfried losgelassen worden.)
Ans Leben gehst du mir schier!
Nun laß! Was zu wissen dich geizt,
erfahr es, ganz wie ich's weiß.
O undankbares,
arges Kind!
Jetzt hör, wofür du mich hassest!
Nicht bin ich Vater
noch Vetter dir,
und dennoch verdankst du mir dich!
Ganz fremd bist du mir,
dem einzigen Freund;
aus Erbarmen allein

it's clear to me,
what before I pondered in vain:
through the woods I wandered
trying to avoid you—
do you know why I returned?
(He leaps up.)
Because you alone can inform me
what father and mother are mine!

MIME
(shrinking from him)
What father? What mother?
Meaningless question!

SIEGFRIED
(seizes him by the throat.)
Well then I must choke you,
force you to tell me!
All kindness
is wasted on you!
You'll only answer
when I strike you.
If I had not forced you
to teach me,
I would not even know
how to speak!
Now out with it,
rascally wretch!
Who are my father and mother?

MIME
(having nodded his head and made signs with his hands, is released by Siegfried.)

You nearly choked me to death!
Let go! What you're eager to learn
I'll tell you, all that I know.
O hard-hearted
ungrateful child!
Now hear, and learn why you hate me!
I'm not your father,
nor kin to you,
and yet you owe everything to me!
You're no kin to me,
and yet I was kind,
and my pity alone

barg ich dich hier:
nun hab ich lieblichen Lohn!
Was verhofft' ich Tor mir auch Dank?
Einst lag wimmernd ein Weib
da draußen im wilden Wald:
zur Höhle half ich ihr her,
am warmen Herd sie zu hüten.
Ein Kind trug sie im Schoße;
traurig gebar sie's hier;
sie wand sich hin und her,
ich half, so gut ich konnt'.
Groß war die Not! Sie starb,
doch Siegfried, der genas.

SIEGFRIED
(sinnend)
So starb meine Mutter an mir?

MIME
Meinem Schutz übergab sie dich:
ich schenkt' ihn gern dem Kind.
Was hat sich Mime gemüht,
was gab sich der Gute für Not!
»Als zullendes Kind
zog ich dich auf«...

SIEGFRIED
Mich dünkt, des gedachtest du schon!
Jetzt sag: woher heiß ich Siegfried?

MIME
So, hieß mich die Mutter,
möcht' ich dich heißen:
als »Siegfried« würdest
du stark und schön.
»Ich wärmte mit Kleiden
den kleinen Wurm«...

SIEGFRIED
Nun melde, wie hieß meine Mutter?

MIME
Das weiß ich wahrlich kaum!
»Speise und Trank
trug ich dir zu«...

SIEGFRIED
Den Namen sollst du mir nennen!

gave you this home:
a fine reward I receive!
What a stupid fool I have been!
I found once in the wood
a woman who lay and wept:
I helped her here to my cave,
and by the fire there I warmed her.
A child stirred in her body;
sadly she gave it birth.
That birth was cruel and hard;
I helped as best I could.
Great was her pain! She died.
But Siegfried, you were born.

SIEGFRIED
(lost in thought)
She died, my mother, through me?

MIME
To my charge she entrusted the child:
I gladly cared for you.
What love I lavished on you!
What kindness and care you received!
'A whimpering babe,
born in these woods...'

SIEGFRIED
I think I have heard that before!
But say: why am I called Siegfried?

MIME
The wish of your mother—
that's what she told me:
as 'Siegfried' you would grow
strong and fair.
'And Mime was kind
to the tiny mite...'

SIEGFRIED
Now tell me the name of my mother.

MIME
Her name I hardly knew.
'Feeding you well,
keeping you warm...'

SIEGFRIED
Her name I told you to tell me!

MIME
Entfiel er mir wohl? Doch halt!
Sieglinde mochte sie heißen,
die dich in Sorge mir gab.
»Ich hütete dich
wie die eigne Haut«...

MIME
Her name I forget. No, wait!
Sieglinde, now I remember;
I'm sure that that was her name.
'And sheltering you safe
as my very self...'

SIEGFRIED
(immer dringender)
Dann frag ich, wie hieß mein Vater?

SIEGFRIED
(ever more urgently)
Now tell me, who was my father?

MIME
(barsch)
Den hab ich nie gesehn.

MIME
(roughly)
His name I never knew!

SIEGFRIED
Doch die Mutter nannte den Namen?

SIEGFRIED
Did my mother say what his name was?

MIME
Erschlagen sei er,
das sagte sie nur;
dich Vaterlosen
befahl sie mir da.
»Und wie du erwuchsest,
wartet' ich dein;
dein Lager schuf ich,
daß leicht du schliefst«...

MIME
He fell in battle—
that's all that she said.
The tiny orphan
was left in my care;
'And as you grew older
I was your nurse;
when you were sleepy
I smoothed your bed...'

SIEGFRIED
Still mit dem alten
Starenlied!
Soll ich der Kunde glauben,
hast du mir nichts gelogen,
so laß mich Zeichen sehn!

SIEGFRIED
Stop that eternal
snivelling!
If I am to trust your story,
if truth at last you're speaking,
then I must see some proof!

MIME
Was soll dir's noch bezeugen?

MIME
But what proof can I show you?

SIEGFRIED
Dir glaub ich nicht mit dem Ohr,
dir glaub ich nur mit dem Aug':
Welch Zeichen zeugt für dich?

SIEGFRIED
I trust you not with my ears;
my eyes alone I'll believe:
what witness can you show?

MIME
(holt nach einigem Besinnen die zwei Stücke eines zerschlagenen Schwertes herbei.)
Das gab mir deine Mutter:

MIME
(reflects for a moment, and then fetches the two pieces of a broken sword.)
This, this your mother gave me

für Mühe, Kost und Pflege
ließ sie's als schwachen Lohn.
Sieh her, ein zerbrochnes Schwert!
Dein Vater, sagte sie, führt' es,
als im letzten Kampf er erlag.

SIEGFRIED
(begeistert)
Und diese Stücken
sollst du mir schmieden:
dann schwing ich mein rechtes Schwert!
Auf! Eile dich, Mime!
Mühe dich rasch;
kannst du was Rechts,
nun zeig deine Kunst!
Täusche mich nicht
mit schlechtem Tand:
den Trümmern allein
trau ich was zu!
Find ich dich faul,
fügst du sie schlecht,
flickst du mit Flausen
den festen Stahl,
dir Feigem fahr ich zu Leib,
das Fegen lernst du von mir!
Denn heute noch, schwör ich,
will ich das Schwert;
die Waffe gewinn ich noch heut!

MIME
(erschrocken)
Was willst du noch heut mit dem [Schwert?

SIEGFRIED
Aus dem Wald fort
in die Welt ziehn:
nimmer kehr ich zurück!
Wie ich froh bin,
daß ich frei ward,
nichts mich bindet und zwingt!
Mein Vater bist du nicht;
in der Ferne bin ich heim;
dein Herd ist nicht mein Haus,
meine Decke nicht dein Dach.
Wie der Fisch froh
in der Flut schwimmt,
wie der Fink frei

for payment, food, and service,
this was my wretched wage.
Look here, just a broken sword!
She said your father had borne it
when he fought his last, and was killed.

SIEGFRIED
(excited)
And now these fragments
Mime will forge me:
I've found my father's sword!
So! hurry up, Mime!
Back to your work;
show me your skill;
employ all your craft!
Cheat me no more
with worthless trash.
These fragments alone
serve for my sword!
But if I find
flaws in your work,
if you should spoil it,
this splendid steel,
you'll feel my blows on your hide;
I'll make you shine like the steel!
Today, I swear, hear me!
I will have my sword;
the weapon today shall be mine.

MIME
(alarmed)
But why do you need it today?

SIEGFRIED
Through the wide world
I shall wander,
never more to return!
I am free now,
I can leave you,
nothing binds me to you!
My father you are not,
in the world I'll find my home;
your hearth is not my house,
I can leave your rocky lair.
As the fish swims
through the waters,
as the bird flies

sich davonschwingt:
flieg ich von hier,
flute davon,
wie der Wind übern Wald
weh ich dahin,
dich, Mime, nie wieder zu sehn!
(Er stürmt in den Wald fort.)

MIME
(in höchster Angst)
Halte! Halte!
Halte! Wohin?
(Er ruft mit der größten Anstrengung in den Wald.)
He! Siegfried!
Siegfried! He!
(Er sieht dem Fortstürmenden eine Weile staunend nach; dann kehrt er in die Schmiede zurück und setzt sich hinter den Amboß.)
Da stürmt er hin!
Nun sitz ich da:
zur alten Not
hab ich die neue;
vernagelt bin ich nun ganz!
Wie helf ich mir jetzt?
Wie halt ich ihn fest?
Wie führ ich den Huien
zu Fafners Nest?
Wie füg ich die Stücken
des tückischen Stahls?
Keines Ofens Glut
glüht mir die echten:
keines Zwergen Hammer
zwingt mir die harten.
Des Niblungen Neid,
Not und Schweiß
nietet mir Notung nicht,
schweißt mir das Schwert nicht zu ganz!
(Mime knickt verzweifelnd auf dem Schemel hinter dem Amboß zusammen.)

through the branches,
so I shall fly,
floating afar,
like the wind through the wood
wafting away!
Then, Mime, I'll never return.
(He rushes out into the forest.)

MIME
(in the utmost terror)
Siegfried! Hear me!
Hear me! Come back!
(He calls into the forest at the top of his voice.)
Hey! Siegfried!
Siegfried! Hey!
(He gazes in astonishment as Siegfried rushes away, then returns to the forge and sits behind the anvil.)
He storms away!
And I sit here,
my former cares
joined by a new one.
I'm helpless, caught in my trap!
Now what can I say?
And when he returns
then how can I lead him
to Fafner's lair?
I can't forge these pieces
of obstinate steel!
For no fire of mine
can ever fuse them;
nor can Mime's hammer
conquer their hardness.
This Nibelung hate,
toil and sweat,
cannot make Notung new,
can't forge the sword once again!
(Mime crouches in despair on the stool behind the anvil.)

Zweite Szene

Der Wanderer (Wotan) tritt aus dem Wald an das hintere Tor der Höhle heran. Er trägt einen dunkelblauen langen Mantel, einen Speer als Stab. Auf dem Haupte hat er einen großen Hut mit breiter runder Krempe, die über das fehlende eine Auge tief hereinhängt.

WANDERER
Heil dir, weiser Schmied!
Dem wegmüden Gast
gönne hold
des Hauses Herd!

MIME
(erschrocken auffahrend)
Wer ist's, der im wilden
Walde mich sucht?
Wer verfolgt mich im öden Forst?

WANDERER
(sehr langsam, immer nur einen Schritt sich nähernd)
»Wandrer« heißt mich die Welt;
weit wandert' ich schon:
auf der Erde Rücken
rührt' ich mich viel.

MIME
So rühre dich fort
und raste nicht hier,
nennt dich »Wandrer« die Welt!

WANDERER
Gastlich ruht' ich bei Guten,
Gaben gönnten viele mir:
denn Unheil fürchtet,
wer unhold ist.

MIME
Unheil wohnte
immer bei mir:
willst du dem Armen es mehren?

WANDERER
(langsam immer näher schreitend)
Viel erforscht' ich,

Scene Two

The Wanderer (Wotan) comes in from the forest by the entrance at the back of the cavern. He is wearing a long dark-blue cloak, and uses his spear as a staff. On his head is a large hat with a broad, round brim, which hangs over his missing eye.

WANDERER
Hail there, worthy smith!
This wayweary guest
asks to rest
awhile by your fire!

MIME
(starting up in fright)
Who's there? Who has sought me
here in the woods?
Who disturbs me in my retreat?

WANDERER
(very slowly, advancing just a step at a time)
'Wanderer', so I am called:
widely I have roamed,
on the earth's broad surface
travelling afar.

MIME
Then travel some more,
live up to your name;
let the Wanderer move on!

WANDERER
Good men ever give me welcome;
gifts from many have I gained;
for ill fate falls only
on evil men.

MIME
Ill fate haunts me
here in my home;
why do you seek to increase it?

WANDERER
(still advancing slowly)
Much I sought for,

erkannte viel:
Wicht'ges konnt' ich
manchem künden,
manchem wehren,
was ihn mühte,
nagende Herzensnot.

MIME
Spürtest du klug
und erspähtest du viel,
hier brauch ich nicht Spürer noch Späher.
Einsam will ich
und einzeln sein,
Lungerern lass' ich den Lauf.

WANDERER
(tritt wieder etwas näher.)
Mancher wähnte
weise zu sein,
nur was ihm not tat,
wußte er nicht;
was ihm frommte,
ließ ich erfragen:
lohnend lehrt' ihn mein Wort.

MIME
(immer ängstlicher, da er den Wanderer sich nahen sieht)
Müß'ges Wissen
wahren manche:
ich weiß mir grade genug.
(Der Wanderer schreitet vollends bis an den Herd vor.)
Mir genügt mein Witz,
ich will nicht mehr:
dir Weisem weis ich den Weg!

WANDERER
(am Herd sich setzend)
Hier sitz ich am Herd
und setze mein Haupt
der Wissenswette zum Pfand:
Mein Kopf ist dein,
du hast ihn erkiest,
entfrägst du mir nicht,
was dir frommt,
lös ich's mit Lehren nicht ein.

and much I found.
I have often
taught men wisdom,
often lightened
heavy sorrows,
eased their afflicted hearts.

MIME
Much you have learnt,
maybe much you have found;
but don't you come seeking in my house.
I don't need you,
and I live alone.
Loiterers cannot stay here.

WANDERER
(again advancing a little)
Many fancy
wisdom is theirs,
but what they most need,
that they don't know.
When they ask me,
freely I answer:
wisdom flows from my words.

MIME
(increasingly uneasy, as he watches the Wanderer advance)
Useless knowledge
many ask for,
but I know all that I need.
(The Wanderer has advanced right up to the hearth.)
And my wits are good;
I want no more.
So, wise one, be on your way!

WANDERER
(sitting at the hearth)
I sit by your hearth,
and wager my head—
it's yours if I prove not wise.
My head is yours,
it falls to your hand,
if I, when you ask
all you want,
fail to redeem it aright.

MIME
(der zuletzt den Wanderer mit offenem Munde angestaunt hat, schrickt jetzt zusammen; kleinmütig für sich:)
Wie werd' ich den Lauernden los?
Verfänglich muß ich ihn fragen.
(Er ermannt sich wie zur Strenge.)
Dein Haupt pfänd ich
für den Herd:
nun sorg, es sinnig zu lösen!
Drei der Fragen
stell ich mir frei.

WANDERER
Dreimal muß ich's treffen.

MIME
(sammelt sich zum Nachdenken.)
Du rührtest dich viel
auf der Erde Rücken,
die Welt durchwandertst du weit:
Nun sage mir schlau:
welches Geschlecht
tagt in der Erde Tiefe?

WANDERER
In der Erde Tiefe
tagen die Nibelungen:
Nibelheim ist ihr Land.
Schwarzalben sind sie;
Schwarz-Alberich
hütet' als Herrscher sie einst!
Eines Zauberringes
zwingende Kraft
zähmt' ihm das fleißige Volk.
Reicher Schätze
schimmernden Hort
häuften sie ihm:
der sollte die Welt ihm gewinnen.
Zum zweiten was frägst du, Zwerg?

MIME
(versinkt in immer tieferes Nachdenken.)
Viel, Wanderer,
weißt du mir
aus der Erde Nabelnest:
Nun sage mir schlicht,

MIME
(has been staring open-mouthed at the Wanderer; he shudders, and says timorously to himself:)
How can I get rid of this spy?
I'll ask him three tricky questions.
(With an effort he recovers himself.)
Your head pays me
if you fail:
take care, use cunning to save it!
Three the questions
that I shall ask!

WANDERER
Three times I must answer.

MIME
(racks his brains.)
You've wandered so far
on the earth's wide surface,
and long you've roamed through the [world:
and so you should know
what dusky race
dwells in the earth's deep caverns?

WANDERER
In the earth's deep caverns—
that's where the Niblungs dwell;
Nibelheim is their land.
Black elves, those Niblungs;
Black-Alberich
once was their master and lord!
By a magic ring's
all-conquering spell,
he ruled that hard-working race.
Richest treasures,
shimmering gold,
he made them find,
to buy all the world for his kingdom—
I've answered: what else would you ask?

MIME
(thinking still harder)
Much, Wanderer,
much you know
of the earth's dark secret caves.
But can now you say,

welches Geschlecht
ruht auf der Erde Rücken?

WANDERER
Auf der Erde Rücken
wuchtet der Riesen Geschlecht:
Riesenheim ist ihr Land.
Fasolt und Fafner,
der Rauhen Fürsten,
neideten Nibelungs Macht;
den gewaltigen Hort
gewannen sie sich,
errangen mit ihm den Ring.
Um den entbrannte
den Brüdern Streit;
der Fasolt fällte,
als wilder Wurm
hütet nun Fafner den Hort.—
Die dritte Frage nun droht.

MIME
(der ganz in Träumerei entrückt ist)
Viel, Wanderer,
weißt du mir
von der Erde rauhem Rücken.
Nun sage mir wahr,
welches Geschlecht
wohnt auf wolkigen Höhn?

WANDERER
Auf wolkigen Höhn
wohnen die Götter:
Walhall heißt ihr Saal.
Lichtalben sind sie;
Licht-Alberich
Wotan, waltet der Schar.
Aus der Welt-Esche
weihlichstem Aste
schuf er sich einen Schaft:
dorrt der Stamm,
nie verdirbt doch der Speer;
mit seiner Spitze
sperrt Wotan die Welt.
Heil'ger Verträge
Treuerunen
schnitt in den Schaft er ein.
Den Haft der Welt

what mighty race
dwells on the earth's broad surface?

WANDERER
On the earth's broad surface—
that's where the giants dwell;
Riesenheim is their land.
Fasolt and Fafner,
the giants' chieftains,
envied the Nibelung's might;
and his powerful hoard
they gained for themselves—
and in that hoard was the ring.
To gain that treasure
the brothers fought,
and Fasolt fell then.
In dragon shape
Fafner now guards all the gold—
One question still you have left.

MIME
(rapt in thought)
Much, Wanderer,
much you know
of the earth and all her dwellers.
But can now you say
what lordly race
dwells on cloud-hidden heights?

WANDERER
On cloud-hidden heights—
that's where the gods dwell;
Walhall is their home.
Light-spirits are they;
Light-Alberich,
Wotan, rules over that clan.
From the world-ashtree's
sacred branches
Wotan once tore his spear:
dead the tree—
but still mighty the spear;
and with that spear-point
Wotan rules the world.
Bargains and contracts,
bonds and treaties,
deep in that shaft he graved.
Who holds that spear-shaft

hält in der Hand,
wer den Speer führt,
den Wotans Faust umspannt.
Ihm neigte sich
der Niblungen Heer;
der Riesen Gezücht
zähmte sein Rat:
ewig gehorchen sie alle
des Speeres starkem Herrn.
(Er stößt wie unwillkürlich mit dem Speer auf den Boden; ein leiser Donner, worüber Mime heftig erschrickt.)
Nun rede, weiser Zwerg:
wußt' ich der Fragen Rat?
Behalte mein Haupt ich frei?

MIME
(nachdem er den Wanderer mit dem Speer aufmerksam beobachtet hat, gerät nun in große Angst, sucht verwirrt nach seinen Gerätschaften und blickt scheu zur Seite.)
Fragen und Haupt
hast du gelöst:
nun, Wandrer, geh deines Wegs!

WANDERER
Was zu wissen dir frommt,
solltest du fragen:
Kunde verbürgte mein Kopf.
Daß du nun nicht weißt,
was dir frommt,
des faß ich jetzt deines als Pfand.
Gastlich nicht
galt mir dein Gruß,
mein Haupt gab ich
in deine Hand,
um mich des Herdes zu freun.
Nach Wettens Pflicht
pfänd ich nun dich,
lösest du drei
der Fragen nicht leicht.
Drum frische dir, Mime, den Mut!

MIME
(sehr schüchtern und zögernd, endlich in furchtsamer Ergebung sich fassend)
Lang schon mied ich
mein Heimatland,

rules the world;
and that spear-shaft
by Wotan's hand is held.
In thrall to him
the Nibelung band;
the giants' strong race
bows to his will;
all must obey him as master—
the spear's all-powerful lord.
(As if involuntarily, he strikes the ground with his spear; a slight thunder is heard, which terrifies Mime.)
Now tell me, crafty dwarf,
were all my answers right?
And have I redeemed my head?

MIME
(after carefully observing the Wanderer with the spear, falls now into a state of great terror, searches in confusion for his tools, and timidly averts his glance.)
The answers were right;
your head is safe:
now, Wanderer, go on your way!

WANDERER
What you needed to know
you should have asked me,
while I had wagered my head.
You merely asked me
what you knew,
so now we'll stake your head in turn.
You refused greeting
to your guest,
and so I had
to risk my head
to gain some rest at your hearth.
The law demands
your head in turn,
if you should fail
to answer me well.
So Nibelung, sharpen your wits!

MIME
(very timidly and hesitantly, at length composing himself in nervous submission)
I left home
many years ago;

lang schon schied ich
aus der Mutter Schoß;
mir leuchtete Wotans Auge,
zur Höhle lugt' er herein:
vor ihm magert
mein Mutterwitz.
Doch frommt mir's nun, weise zu sein,
Wandrer, frage denn zu!
Vielleicht glückt mir's, gezwungen
zu lösen des Zwergen Haupt.

years ago I left
my mother's womb.
I shrink beneath Wotan's glances;
he came to spy in my cave:
his glance frightens
my wits away.
But now I must try to be wise;
Wanderer, ask what you will!
Perhaps good luck will help me;
the dwarf still can save his head?

WANDERER
(wieder gemächlich sich niederlassend)
Nun, ehrlicher Zwerg,
sag mir zum ersten:
welches ist das Geschlecht,
dem Wotan schlimm sich zeigte
und das doch das liebste ihm lebt?

WANDERER
(again seating himself comfortably)
Now, worthiest dwarf,
answer me truly:
What is the name of the race
that Wotan treated harshly
and yet holds most dear in his heart?

MIME
(sich ermunternd)
Wenig hört' ich
von Heldensippen;
der Frage doch mach ich mich frei.
Die Wälsungen sind
das Wunschgeschlecht,
das Wotan zeugte
und zärtlich liebte,
zeigt' er auch Ungunst ihm.
Siegmund und Sieglind
stammten von Wälse,
ein wild-verzweifeltes
Zwillingspaar:
Siegfried zeugten sie selbst,
den stärksten Wälsungenspross.
Behalt ich, Wandrer,
zum ersten mein Haupt?

MIME
(gaining courage)
I'm no expert
in heroes' histories
but what you ask is easy to guess.
The Wälsungs must be
that chosen race
that Wotan cared for
and loved so dearly,
though he was cruel and harsh:
Siegmund and Sieglinde,
children of Wälse,
that wild and desperate
twin-born pair.
Siegfried, he was their child,
the Wälsungs' brave mighty son.
So this time, Wanderer,
have I saved my head?

WANDERER
(gemütlich)
Wie doch genau
das Geschlecht du mir nennst:
schlau eracht ich dich Argen!
Der ersten Frage
wardst du frei.
Zum zweiten nun sag mir, Zwerg:
ein weiser Niblung
wahret Siegfried;

WANDERER
(pleasantly)
Yes, it is safe,
for your answer was right:
it's not easy to catch you!
But though you guessed
the first one right,
my second may prove too hard.
A wily Niblung
cared for Siegfried,

Fafnern soll er ihm fällen,
daß den Ring er erränge,
des Hortes Herrscher zu sein.
Welches Schwert
muß Siegfried nun schwingen,
taug' es zu Fafners Tod?

planned that he should kill Fafner,
gain the ring for the Niblung,
and make him lord of the world.
Name the sword
that Siegfried must strike with,
if he's to kill the foe.

MIME
(seine gegenwärtige Lage immer mehr vergessend und von dem Gegenstande lebhaft angezogen, reibt sich vergnügt die Hände.)
Notung heißt
ein neidliches Schwert;
in einer Esche Stamm
stieß es Wotan:
dem sollt' es geziemen,
der aus dem Stamm es zög'.
Der stärksten Helden
keiner bestand's:
Siegmund, der Kühne,
konnt's allein:
fechtend führt's er's im Streit,
bis an Wotans Speer es zersprang.
Nun verwahrt die Stücken
ein weiser Schmied;
denn er weiß, daß allein
mit dem Wotansschwert
ein kühnes dummes Kind,
Siegfried, den Wurm versehrt.
(ganz vergnügt)
Behalt ich Zwerg
auch zweitens mein Haupt?

MIME
(forgetting more and more his present situation, and keenly interested in the topic, rubs his hands with pleasure.)
Notung, that's the name
of the sword,
the sword that Wotan struck
into an ashtree:
and one alone could win it,
he who could draw it forth.
Where mighty warriors
struggled in vain,
Siegmund the Wälsung
drew it forth;
thus he mastered the sword,
till by Wotan's spear it was snapped.
Now the bits are saved
by a wily smith;
for he knows that only
with Wotan's sword
a brave but foolish boy,
Siegfried, can kill the dragon.
(highly delighted)
Now twice the dwarf
has rescued his head?

WANDERER
(lachend)
Der witzigste bist du
unter den Weisen:
wer käm' dir an Klugheit gleich?
Doch bist du so klug,
den kindischen Helden
für Zwergenzwecke zu nützen,
mit der dritten Frage
droh ich nun!
Sag mir, du weiser
Waffenschmied:
wer wird aus den starken Stücken
Notung, das Schwert, wohl schweißen?

WANDERER
(laughing)
The wittiest
and the wiliest Niblung!
the cleverest dwarf I've known!
But since you're so wise
to use for your purpose
the youthful strength of the hero,
let me ask
my final question now.
Tell me, you wily
weapon-smith: [fragments?
Whose hand can make new those
Notung, the sword—who will forge it?

MIME
(fährt in höchstem Schrecken auf.)
Die Stücken! Das Schwert!
O weh! Mir schwindelt!
Was fang ich an?
Was fällt mir ein?
Verfluchter Stahl,
daß ich dich gestohlen!
Er hat mich vernagelt
in Pein und Not!
Mir bleibt er hart,
ich kann ihn nicht hämmern;
Niet' und Löte
läßt mich im Stich!
(Er wirft wie sinnlos sein Gerät durcheinander und bricht in helle Verzweiflung aus.)
Der weiseste Schmied
weiß sich nicht Rat!
Wer schweißt nun das Schwert,
schaff ich es nicht?
Das Wunder, wie soll ich's wissen?

WANDERER
(ist ruhig vom Herd aufgestanden.)
Dreimal solltest du fragen,
dreimal stand ich dir frei:
nach eitlen Fernen
forschtest du;
doch was zunächst dir sich fand,
was dir nützt, fiel dir nicht ein.
Nun ich's errate,
wirst du verrückt:
gewonnen hab ich
das witzige Haupt!
Jetzt, Fafners kühner Bezwinger,
hör, verfallner Zwerg:
»Nur wer das Fürchten
nie erfuhr,
schmiedet Notung neu.«
(Mime starrt ihn groß an: er wendet sich zum Fortgang.)
Dein weises Haupt
wahre von heut:
verfallen laß ich es dem,
der das Fürchten nicht gelernt!
(Er wendet sich lächelnd ab und verschwindet schnell im Walde. Mime ist wie vernichtet auf den Schemel hinter dem Amboß zurückgesunken.)

MIME
(jumps up in extreme terror.)
The fragments! The sword!
Alas! You've caught me!
What can I say?
What can I do?
Accursed steel!
Would I'd never seen it!
To me it has brought
only pain and woe!
Stubborn and hard,
my hand cannot weld it;
heat and hammer,
all are in vain!
(As if demented, he throws his tools about, and gives way to total despair.)
The wisest of smiths
fails at the task.
Who can forge that sword
if my hand fails?
How can I give you an answer?

WANDERER
(has risen calmly from the hearth.)
Thrice you asked me your questions,
thrice I answered you right:
but what you asked
was meaningless;
you gave no thought to your need,
failed to ask what you required.
Now when I tell it
you'll feel despair.
Your wily head
I can claim as my prize!
So, Fafner's dauntless destroyer,
hear, you wretched dwarf:
'One who has never
learnt to fear—
he makes Notung new.'
(Mime stares at him wide-eyed; he turns to go.)
Your wily head—
guard it with care!
I leave it forfeit to him
who has never learnt to fear.
(He turns away smiling and disappears quickly into the forest. As if crushed, Mime has sunk down on the stool behind the anvil.)

Dritte Szene

MIME
(starrt grad vor sich aus in den sonnig beleuchteten Wald hinein und gerät zunehmend in heftiges Zittern.)

Verfluchtes Licht!
Was flammt dort die Luft?
Was flackert und lackert,
was flimmert und schwirrt,
was schwebt dort und webt
und wabert umher?
Dort glimmert's und glitzt's
in der Sonne Glut!
Was säuselt und summt
und saust nun gar?
Es brummt und braust
und prasselt hieher!
Dort bricht's durch den Wald,
will auf mich zu!
(Er bäumt sich vor Entsetzen auf.)
Ein gräßlicher Rachen
reißt sich mir auf:
der Wurm will mich fangen!
Fafner! Fafner!
(Er sinkt laut schreiend hinter dem Amboß zusammen.)

SIEGFRIED
(bricht aus dem Waldgesträuch hervor und ruft noch hinter der Szene, während man seine Bewegung an dem zerkrachenden Gezweige des Gesträuches gewahrt.)
Heda, du Fauler!
Bist du nun fertig?
(Er tritt in die Höhle herein und hält verwundert an.)
Schnell, wie steht's mit dem Schwert?
Wo steckt der Schmied?
Stahl er sich fort?
Hehe, Mime, du Memme!
Wo bist du? Wo birgst du dich?

MIME
(mit schwacher Stimme hinter dem Amboß)
Bist du es, Kind?
Kommst du allein?

Scene Three

MIME
(stares out before him into the sunlit forest, and begins to tremble violently.)

Accursed light!
The air is aflame!
What's flickering and flashing,
what flutters and swirls,
what floats in the air
and swirls in the wind?
What glistens and gleams
in the sun's bright glow?
What hisses and hums
and roars so loud?
It growls and heaves,
comes crashing this way!
It breaks through the trees;
where can I hide?
(He leaps up in terror.)
The threatening monster
opens its jaws;
the dragon will catch me!
Fafner! Fafner!
(With a shriek he collapses behind the anvil.)

SIEGFRIED
(breaks through the thicket and calls out, still off-stage, his movements evident from the snapping of the undergrowth.)
Hey there! You idler!
Say, have you finished?
(He enters the cave and pauses in surprise.)
Quick, I've come for my sword.
But where's the smith?
Stolen away?
Hey, hey! Mime, you coward!
Where are you? Come out, I say!

MIME
(in a feeble voice, from behind the anvil)
It's you then, child?
Are you alone?

SIEGFRIED
(lachend)
Hinter dem Amboß?
Sag, was schufest du dort?
Schärftest du mir das Schwert?

MIME
(höchst verstört und zerstreut hervorkommend)
Das Schwert? Das Schwert?
Wie möcht' ich's schweißen?
(halb für sich)
»Nur wer das Fürchten
nie erfuhr,
schmiedet Notung neu.«
Zu weise ward ich
für solches Werk!

SIEGFRIED
(heftig)
Wirst du mir reden!
Soll ich dir raten?

MIME
(wie zuvor)
Wo nähm' ich redlichen Rat?
Mein weises Haupt
hab ich verwettet:
verfallen, verlor ich's an den,
»der das Fürchten nicht gelernt«.

SIEGFRIED
(ungestüm)
Sind mir das Flausen?
Willst du mir fliehn?

MIME
(allmählich sich etwas fassend)
Wohl flöh' ich dem,
der's Fürchten kennt!
Doch das ließ ich dem Kinde zu lehren!
Ich Dummer vergaß,
was einzig gut:
Liebe zu mir
sollt' er lernen;
das gelang nun leider faul!
Wie bring ich das Fürchten ihm bei?

SIEGFRIED
(laughing)
Under the anvil?
Say, what work took you there?
Were you sharpening my sword?

MIME
(coming out much confused and disturbed)
The sword? The sword?
How can I forge it?
(half to himself)
'One who has never
learnt to fear—
he makes Notung new.'
So how could I
undertake such work?

SIEGFRIED
(violently)
Give me an answer!
Want me to help you?

MIME
(as before)
No man can help in my need.
My wily head—
I had to stake it.
I've lost it; it's forfeit to him
'who has never learned to fear'.

SIEGFRIED
(impatiently)
Trying to escape me?
Still no reply?

MIME
(gradually recovering himself a little)
I fear this youth
who knows not fear!
But wait: though I was eager to teach him,
yet, fool, I forgot
to teach him fear.
Love was the main thing
that I tried for;
but alas, that lesson failed!
So how can I teach him to fear?

SIEGFRIED
(packt ihn.)
He! Muß ich helfen?
Was fegtest du heut?

MIME
Um dich nur besorgt,
versank ich in Sinnen,
wie ich dich Wichtiges wiese.

SIEGFRIED
(lachend)
Bis unter den Sitz
warst du versunken:
Was Wichtiges fandest du da?

MIME
(sich immer mehr fassend)
Das Fürchten lernt' ich für dich,
daß ich's dich Dummen lehre.

SIEGFRIED
(mit ruhiger Verwunderung)
Was ist's mit dem Fürchten?

MIME
Erfuhrst du's noch nie
und willst aus dem Wald
doch fort in die Welt?
Was frommte das festeste Schwert,
blieb dir das Fürchten fern?

SIEGFRIED
(ungeduldig)
Faulen Rat
erfindest du wohl?

MIME
(immer zutraulicher Siegfried näher tretend)
Deiner Mutter Rat
redet aus mir;
was ich gelobte,
muß ich nun lösen:
in die listige Welt
dich nicht zu entlassen,
eh' du nicht das Fürchten gelernt.

SIEGFRIED
(seizes him.)
Well, must I help you?
What work has been done?

MIME
I thought of your good;
I sank into brooding,
thinking of weighty things to teach you.

SIEGFRIED
(laughing)
You certainly sank—
under the anvil:
what weighty advice did you find?

MIME
(steadily regaining self-possession)
What fear is, that's what I learnt;
that's what I mean to teach you.

SIEGFRIED
(with quiet curiosity)
And what can this fear be?

MIME
You've not learnt to fear,
and you'd leave the wood,
go forth in the world?
What use is the mightiest sword
till you can fear as well?

SIEGFRIED
(impatiently)
Foolish words
I hear from your lips!

MIME
(approaching Siegfried ever more confidingly)
They are your mother's words,
heard from her lips—
words that I promised
one day I'd teach you.
In the wide wicked world
I shan't let you venture,
until you can fear as well.

SIEGFRIED
(heftig)
Ist's eine Kunst,
was kenn ich sie nicht?
Heraus! Was ist's mit dem Fürchten?

SIEGFRIED
(brusquely)
Is it a skill,
a craft I should learn?
Then speak, and teach me what fear is!

MIME
Fühltest du nie
im finstren Wald,
bei Dämmerschein
am dunklen Ort,
wenn fern es säuselt,
summst und saust,
wildes Brummen
näher braust,
wirres Flackern
um dich flimmert,
schwellend Schwirren
zu Leib dir schwebt:
fühltest du dann nicht grieselnd
Grausen die Glieder dir fahen?
Glühender Schauer
schüttelt die Glieder,
in der Brust bebend und bang
berstet hämmernd das Herz?
Fühltest du das noch nicht,
das Fürchten blieb dir noch fremd.

MIME
Have you not felt
within the woods,
as darkness fell
in dusky glades,
a dreadful whisper—
hum and hiss—
savage, growling
sounds draw near?
Dazzling flashes
wildly flicker;
howling, roaring
assail your ears.
Have you not felt mysterious horrors
that threaten to harm you?
shivering and shaking,
quivering and quaking,
while your heart trembles and faints,
wildly hammers and leaps?
Till you have felt these things,
then fear to you is unknown.

SIEGFRIED
(nachsinnend)
Sonderlich seltsam
muß das sein!
Hart und fest,
fühl ich, steht mir das Herz.
Das Grieseln und Grausen,
das Glühen und Schauern,
Hitzen und Schwindeln,
Hämmern und Beben:
gern begehr ich das Bangen,
sehnend verlangt mich's der Lust!
Doch wie bringst du,
Mime, mir's bei?
Wie wärst du, Memme, mir Meister?

SIEGFRIED
(thoughtfully)
Wonderful feelings
those must be!
Yet my heart
firmly beats in my breast.
The shivering and shaking,
the glowing and sinking,
burning and fainting,
trembling and quaking—
I am yearning to feel them.
When may I taste these joys?
Can I learn them,
Mime, from you?
How can a coward instruct me?

MIME
Folge mir nur,
ich führe dich wohl:

MIME
Easily learnt!
The way I know well:

sinnend fand ich es aus.
Ich weiß einen schlimmen Wurm,
der würgt' und schlang schon viel:
Fafner lehrt dich das Fürchten,
folgst du mir zu seinem Nest.

SIEGFRIED
Wo liegt er im Nest?

MIME
Neidhöhle
wird es genannt:
im Ost, am Ende des Walds.

SIEGFRIED
Dann wär's nicht weit von der Welt?

MIME
Bei Neidhöhle liegt sie ganz nah.

SIEGFRIED
Dahin denn sollst du mich führen:
Lernt' ich das Fürchten,
dann fort in die Welt!
Drum schnell! Schaffe das Schwert,
in der Welt will ich es schwingen.

MIME
Das Schwert? O Not!

SIEGFRIED
Rasch in die Schmiede!
Weis, was du schufst!

MIME
Verfluchter Stahl!
Zu flicken versteh ich ihn nicht:
den zähen Zauber
bezwingt keines Zwergen Kraft.
Wer das Fürchten nicht kennt,
der fänd' wohl eher die Kunst.

SIEGFRIED
Feine Finten
weiß mir der Faule;
daß er ein Stümper,
sollt' er gestehn:

brooding brought it to mind.
I know where a dragon dwells,
who lives and feeds on men.
Fear you'll learn from Fafner;
follow me; we'll find his den.

SIEGFRIED
And where is his den?

MIME
Neidhöhle,
that's what it's called:
to the east, at the edge of the wood.

SIEGFRIED
Is that not near to the world?

MIME
From Neidhöhl the world isn't far.

SIEGFRIED
Then lead me on to your Fafner.
Fear he can teach me,
then forth to the world!
Now quick! Forge me the sword!
In the world I have to wield it.

MIME
The sword? Ah no!

SIEGFRIED
On with your forging!
Show me your skill!

MIME
Accursed steel!
My skill is too weak for the task.
No dwarf can forge it
or master the magic spell.
One who fear does not know—
he might more easily succeed.

SIEGFRIED
Lazy scoundrel,
lying to cheat me,
making excuses,
trying to delay.

nun lügt er sich listig heraus!
Her mit den Stücken,
fort mit dem Stümper!
(auf den Herd zuschreitend)
Des Vaters Stahl
fügt sich wohl mir:
ich selbst schweiße das Schwert!
(Er macht sich, Mimes Gerät durcheinander werfend, mit Ungestüm an die Arbeit.)

MIME
Hättest du fleißig
die Kunst gepflegt,
jetzt käm' dir's wahrlich zugut:
doch lässig warst du
stets in der Lehr':
was willst du Rechtes nun rüsten?

SIEGFRIED
Was der Meister nicht kann,
vermöcht' es der Knabe,
hätt' er ihm immer gehorcht?
(Er dreht ihm eine Nase.)
Jetzt mach dich fort,
misch dich nicht drein:
sonst fällst du mir mit ins Feuer!
(Er hat eine große Menge Kohlen auf dem Herd aufgehäuft und unterhält in einem fort die Glut, während er die Schwertstücke in den Schraubstock einspannt und sie zu Spänen zerfeilt.)

MIME
(der sich etwas abseits niedergesetzt hat, sieht Siegfried bei der Arbeit zu.)
Was machst du denn da?
Nimm doch die Löte:
den Brei braut' ich schon längst.

SIEGFRIED
Fort mit dem Brei!
Ich brauch' ihn nicht:
mit Bappe back' ich kein Schwert!

MIME
Du zerfeilst die Feile,
zerreibst die Raspel:
wie willst du den Stahl zerstampfen?

So Mime is too weak for the task!
Give me the fragments;
I'll have to teach you!
(striding to the hearth)
My father's sword
yields to his son;
and I'll forge it myself!
(He sets to work impetuously, pitching Mime's tools about.)

MIME
If you'd been careful
to learn your craft,
then now you would have your reward;
but you were always
lazy and slow,
and now you'll wish you'd obeyed me.

SIEGFRIED
When my teacher has failed,
could I be successful
if I had always obeyed?
(He cocks a snook at him.)
So move aside,
out of my way,
or else with the sword I'll forge you!
(He has heaped up a mass of charcoal on the hearth, and he keeps the fire going while he fixes the fragments of the sword in a vice and files them to shreds.)

MIME
(who has sat down rather to one side, watches Siegfried at work.)
You're doing it wrong!
There is the solder,
prepared, melted and hot.

SIEGFRIED
Off with your trash!
I need it not.
No solder patches my sword.

MIME
But the file is finished,
the rasp is ruined!
You're filing the steel to splinters!

SIEGFRIED
Zersponnen muß ich
in Späne ihn sehn:
was entzwei ist, zwing ich mir so.
(Er feilt mit großem Eifer fort.)

MIME
(für sich)
Hier hilft kein Kluger,
das seh ich klar:
hier hilft dem Dummen
die Dummheit allein!
Wie er sich rührt
und mächtig regt!
Ihm schwindet der Stahl,
doch wird ihm nicht schwül!
(Siegfried hat das Herdfeuer zur hellsten Glut angefacht.)
Nun ward ich so alt
wie Höhl' und Wald
und hab nicht so was gesehn!
(Während Siegfried mit ungestümem Eifer fortfährt, die Schwertstücken zu zerfeilen, setzt sich Mime noch mehr beiseite.)
Mit dem Schwert gelingt's,
das lern ich wohl:
furchtlos fegt er's zu ganz.
Der Wandrer wußt' es gut!
Wie berg ich nun
mein banges Haupt?
Dem kühnen Knaben verfiel's,
lehrt' ihn nicht Fafner die Furcht!
(mit wachsender Unruhe aufspringend und sich beugend)
Doch weh mir Armen!
Wie würgt' er den Wurm,
erführ' er das Fürchten von ihm?
Wie erräng' er mir den Ring?
Verfluchte Klemme!
Da klebt' ich fest,
fänd' ich nicht klugen Rat,
wie den Furchtlosen selbst ich bezwäng'.

SIEGFRIED
(hat nun die Stücken zerfeilt und in einem Schmelztiegel gefangen, den er jetzt in die Herdglut stellt.)
He, Mime! Geschwind!

SIEGFRIED
It must be splintered
and ground into shreds;
what is broken, this way I mend.
(He files on vigorously.)

MIME
(aside)
My skill is useless,
I see that now
only his folly
can serve in his need!
See how he toils
with mighty strokes!
He's shredded the steel,
Yet he still keeps cool!
(Siegfried has fanned the forge fire to its brightest glow.)
Though I grew as old
as cave and wood,
no sight like this would I see.
(While Siegfried with furious energy goes on filing down the fragments of the sword, Mime seats himself still further away.)
He will forge that sword,
I see that now;
fearless, he will succeed.
The Wanderer's words were true!
And I must hide
my fearful head,
or else it falls to the boy,
if I can't teach him to fear!
(With increasing anxiety he leaps up, and cringes.)

But woe to Mime!
That dragon is safe
if he can teach fear to the boy.
Then how would I gain the ring?
Accursed problem!
I'm caught in a trap
if I can't find some way
by which Siegfried is bent to my will.

SIEGFRIED
(has filed down the pieces and put them in a melting-pot which he now places in the forge fire.)

Hey, Mime! Tell me

Wie heißt das Schwert,
das ich in Späne zersponnen?

MIME
(fährt zusammen und wendet sich zu Siegfried.)
Notung nennt sich
das neidliche Schwert:
deine Mutter gab mir die Mär.

SIEGFRIED
(nährt unter dem folgenden die Glut mit dem Blasebalg.)
Notung! Notung!
Neidliches Schwert!
Was mußtest du zerspringen?
Zu Spreu nun schuf ich
die scharfe Pracht,
im Tiegel brat ich die Späne.
Hoho! Hoho!
Hohei! Hohei! Hoho!
Blase, Balg!
Blase die Glut!

Wild im Walde
wuchs ein Baum,
den hab ich im Forst gefällt:
die braune Esche
brannt' ich zur Kohl',
auf dem Herd nun liegt sie gehäuft.
Hoho! Hoho!
Hohei! Hohei! Hoho!
Blase, Balg!
Blase die Glut!

Des Baumes Kohle,
wie brennt sie kühn;
wie glüht sie hell und hehr!
In springenden Funken
sprühet sie auf:
Hohei! Hoho! Hohei!
zerschmilzt mir des Stahles Spreu.
Hoho! Hoho!
Hohei! Hohei! Hoho!
Blase, Balg!
Blase die Glut!

MIME
(immer für sich, entfernt sitzend)
Er schmiedet das Schwert

the name of the sword
which I have filed into pieces.

MIME
(gives a start, and turns to Siegfried.)
Notung, that is
the name of the sword:
for your mother told me its name.

SIEGFRIED
(during the following blows up the fire with the bellows.)
Notung! Notung!
Sword of my need!
What mighty blow once broke you?
I've filed to splinters
your shining steel;
the fire has melted and fused them.
Hoho! Hoho!
Hohi! Hohi! Hoho!
Bellows, blow!
Brighten the glow!

Wild in woodlands
grew that tree
I felled in the forest glade;
I burnt to ashes
branches and trunk;
on the hearth it lies in a heap.
Hoho! Hoho!
Hohi! Hohi! Hoho!
Bellows, blow!
Brighten the glow!

The blackened charcoal
so bravely burns;
how bright and fair its glow!
A shower of sparks
is shooting on high:
Hohi! Hoho! Hohi!
and fuses the splintered steel.
Hoho! Hoho!
Hohi! Hohi! Hoho!
Bellows, blow!
Brighten the glow!

MIME
(still to himself, sitting apart)
The sword will be forged

und Fafner fällt er:
das seh ich nun deutlich voraus.
Hort und Ring
erringt er im Harst:
wie erwerb ich mir den Gewinn?
Mit Witz und List
gewinn' ich beides
und berge heil mein Haupt.

SIEGFRIED
(nochmals am Blasebalg)
Hoho! Hoho!
Hohei! Hohei! Hohei!

MIME
(im Vordergrunde für sich)
Rang er sich müd mit dem Wurm,
von der Müh' erlab' ihn ein Trunk:
aus würz'gen Säften,
die ich gesammelt,
brau ich den Trank für ihn;
wenig Tropfen nur
braucht er zu trinken,
sinnlos sinkt er in Schlaf.
Mit der eignen Waffe,
die er sich gewonnen,
räum ich ihn leicht aus dem Weg,
erlange mir Ring und Hort.
(Er reibt sich vergnügt die Hände.)
Hei! Weiser Wandrer!
Dünkt' ich dich dumm?
Wie gefällt dir nun
mein feiner Witz?
Fand ich mir wohl
Rat und Ruh?

SIEGFRIED
Notung! Notung!
Neidliches Schwert!
Nun schmolz deines Stahles Spreu!
Im eignen Schweiße
schwimmst du nun.
(Er gießt den glühenden Inhalt des Tiegels in eine Stangenform und hält diese in die Höhe.)
Bald schwing ich dich als mein Schwert!
(Er stößt die gefüllte Stangenform in den Wassereimer. Dampf und lautes Gezisch der Kühlung erfolgen.)

and Fafner conquered:
all that I can clearly foresee.
Gold and ring
will pass to the boy:
can I capture them both for me?
By wit and guile
I must obtain them,
and save my head as well.

SIEGFRIED
(back at the bellows)
Hoho! Hoho!
Hohi! Hohi! Hohi!

MIME
(in the foreground, to himself)
After the fight he'll be tired,
and I'll quench his thirst with a drink.
From roots of flowers
that I have gathered
I'll make a dangerous drink.
If he tastes but one drop
of my potion,
sound sleep follows at once.
Then I'll seize that weapon,
the sword that he's forging;
I'll simply chop off his head;
then mine are the ring and gold.
(He rubs his hands in glee.)
Hey, wise old Wanderer,
am I so dull?
Do you not approve
my crafty plan?
Have I found
my path to power?

SIEGFRIED
Notung! Notung!
Sword of my need!
I smelt your shining steel!
The fiery stream
must fill this mould.
(He pours the glowing contents of the melting-pot into a mould, which he holds aloft.)
And now you are shaped as my sword!
(He plunges the filled mould into the water-trough; steam and loud hissing ensue from its cooling.)

In das Wasser floß
ein Feuerfluß:
grimmiger Zorn
zischt' ihm da auf!
Wie sehrend er floß,
in des Wassers Flut
fließt er nicht mehr.
Starr ward er und steif,
herrisch der harte Stahl:
heißes Blut doch
fließt ihm bald!

(Er stößt den Stahl in die Herdglut und zieht die Blasebälge mächtig an.)

Nun schwitze noch einmal,
daß ich dich schweiße,
Notung, neidliches Schwert!

(Mime ist vergnügt aufgesprungen; er holt verschiedene Gefäße hervor, schüttet aus ihnen Gewürz und Kräuter in einen Kochtopf und sucht, diesen auf dem Herd anzubringen. Siegfried beobachtet während der Arbeit Mime, welcher vom andern Ende des Herdes her seinen Topf sorgsam an die Glut stellt.)

Was schafft der Tölpel
dort mit dem Topf?
Brenn ich hier Stahl,
braust du dort Sudel?

MIME

Zuschanden kam ein Schmied;
den Lehrer sein Knabe lehrt:
Mit der Kunst nun ist's beim Alten aus,
als Koch dient er dem Kind.
Brennt es das Eisen zu Brei,
aus Eiern braut
der Alte ihm Sud.

(Er fährt fort zu kochen.)

SIEGFRIED

Mime, der Künstler,
lernt jetzt kochen;
das Schmieden schmeckt ihm nicht mehr.
Seine Schwerter alle
hab ich zerschmissen;
was er kocht, ich kost es ihm nicht!

(Unter dem folgenden zieht Siegfried die Stangenform aus der Glut, zerschlägt sie und legt den glühenden Stahl auf dem Amboß zurecht.)

In the water flowed
a fiery flood:
fury and hate
hissed from the blade!
That fire was soon quenched
by the fiery flood;
no more it stirs.
Strong, stubborn and hard,
there lies my new-made sword.
Burning blood
soon wets your blade!

(He thrusts the steel into the forge fire, and vigorously plies the bellows.)

Once more I must heat you,
so I can shape you,
Notung, sword of my need!

(Mime has jumped up in delight; he fetches various vessels, and from them shakes spices and herbs into a cooking-pot, which he tries to put on the hearth. Siegfried, during the work, watches Mime, who carefully puts his pot on the fire from the other side of the hearth.)

But what is the booby
doing with the pot?
I work with steel;
you're cooking soup there?

MIME

The smith is put to shame:
the teacher is taught his craft.
When the master finds his skill has gone,
as cook he serves the child.
You make a broth of the steel;
Old Mime stirs his pot
and makes soup.

(He goes on with his cooking.)

SIEGFRIED

Mime the craftsman
turns to cooking;
his anvil pleases him no more.
All the swords he made me
broke into pieces;
what he cooks, I never will taste!

(During what follows Siegfried takes the mould from the fire, breaks it, and lays the glowing steel on the anvil.)

Das Fürchten zu lernen,
will er mich führen;
ein Ferner soll es mich lehren:
was am besten er kann,
mir bringt er's nicht bei:
als Stümper besteht er in allem!
(während des Schmiedens)
Hoho! Hoho! Hohei!
Schmiede, mein Hammer,
ein hartes Schwert!
Hoho! Hahei!
Hoho! Hahei!
Einst färbte Blut
dein falbes Blau;
sein rotes Rieseln
rötete dich:
kalt lachtest du da,
das warme lecktest du kühl!
Heiaho! Haha!
Haheiaha!
Nun hat die Glut
dich rot geglüht;
deine weiche Härte
dem Hammer weicht:
zornig sprühst du mir Funken,
daß ich dich Spröden gezähmt!
Heiaho! Heiaho!
Heiahohoho!
Hahei!

MIME
(beiseite)
Er schafft sich ein scharfes Schwert,
Fafner zu fällen,
der Zwerge Feind:
ich braut' ein Truggetränk,
Siegfried zu fangen,
dem Fafner fiel.
Gelingen muß mir die List;
lachen muß mir der Lohn!
(Er beschäftigt sich während des folgenden damit, den Inhalt des Topfes in eine Flasche zu gießen.)

SIEGFRIED
Hoho! hoho!
Hahei!
Schmiede, mein Hammer,

What fear is
I hope I shall soon discover.
Out there one dwells who can teach me;
seeing Mime can't help,
he's no use to me;
whatever he does, he does badly!
(during the forging)
Hoho! Hoho! Hohi!
Forge me, my hammer,
a hard strong sword!
Hoho! Hahi!
Hoho! Hahi!
Your steely blue
once flowed with blood;
its ruddy trickling
reddened my blade;
cold laughter you gave,
the warm blood cooled on your blade!
Hiaho, haha,
hahiaha!
But now with fire
you redly gleam,
and your weakness yields
to my hammer's blow.
Angry sparks you are showering
on me who conquer your pride!
Hiaho! Hiaho!
Hiahohoho!
Hahi!

MIME
(aside)
He's forging a bright, sharp sword.
Fafner will feel it
and meet his death.
I've brewed a deadly drink;
Siegfried will follow
when Fafner's dead.
My skill will gain me the prize;
ring and gold will be mine!
(During what follows, he busies himself with pouring the contents of the pot into a flask.)

SIEGFRIED
Hoho! Hoho!
Hahi!
Forge me, my hammer,

ein hartes Schwert!
Hoho! Hahei!
Hahei! Hoho!
Der frohen Funken
wie freu ich mich;
es ziert den Kühnen
des Zornes Kraft:
lustig lachst du mich an,
stellst du auch grimm dich und gram!
Heiaho, haha,
haheiaha!
Durch Glut und Hammer
glückt' es mir;
mit starken Schlägen
streckt' ich dich:
Nun schwinde die rote Scham;
werde kalt und hart, wie du kannst.
Heiaho! Heiaho!
Heiahohoho!
Heiah!

(Er schwingt den Stahl und stößt ihn in den Wassereimer. Er lacht bei dem Gezisch laut auf. Während Siegfried die geschmiedete Schwertklinge in dem Griffhefte befestigt, treibt sich Mime mit der Flasche im Vordergrunde umher.)

MIME

Den der Bruder schuf,
den schimmernden Reif,
in den er gezaubert
zwingende Kraft,
das helle Gold,
das zum Herrscher macht,
ihn hab ich gewonnen!
Ich walte sein!

(Er trippelt, während Siegfried mit dem kleinen Hammer arbeitet und schleift und feilt, mit zunehmender Vergnügtheit lebhaft umher.)

Alberich selbst,
der einst mich band,
zur Zwergenfrone
zwing ich ihn nun;
als Niblungenfürst
fahr ich danieder;
gehorchen soll mir
alles Heer!
Der verachtete Zwerg,
wie wird er geehrt!

a hard strong sword!
Hoho! Hahi!
Hahi! Hoho!
This cheerful sparkling
delights my heart;
this flash of anger
suits well my blade.
Now you laugh at your lord,
though you pretend to be grim!
Hiaho, haha,
hahiaha!
Both heat and hammer
serve me well;
with sturdy strokes
I beat you straight.
Now banish your blush of shame,
and be cold and hard as you can.
Hiaho! Hiaho!
Hiahohoho!
Hiah!

(He swings the steel and plunges it into the water-trough. He laughs at the loud sizzling. While Siegfried fastens the forged blade into a hilt, Mime fusses about in the foreground with his flask.)

MIME

Once my brother forged
a bright shining ring,
and in it he worked
a powerful spell.
That shining gold
will belong to me,
soon I will control it.
I'm master now!

(While Siegfried is tapping with the small hammer and grinding and filing, Mime skips about vivaciously, with increasing glee.)

Alberich too,
who made me slave,
will bend his knee
and beg for my grace;
as Nibelung prince,
all will obey me;
that Niblung band
will bow to me!
And the dwarf they despised
they will treat as a king!

Zu dem Horte hin drängt sich
Gott und Held:
(mit immer lebhafteren Gebärden)
Vor meinem Nicken
neigt sich die Welt,
vor meinem Zorne
zittert sie hin!
Dann wahrlich müht sich
Mime nicht mehr:
ihm schaffen andre
den ew'gen Schatz.
Mime, der kühne,
Mime ist König,
Fürst der Alben,
Walter des Alls!
Hei, Mime! Wie glückte dir das!
Wer hätte wohl das gedacht?

SIEGFRIED
(hat während Mimes Lied mit den letzten Schlägen die Nieten des Griffheftes geglättet und faßt nun das Schwert.)
Notung! Notung!
Neidliches Schwert!
Jetzt haftest du wieder im Heft.
Warst du entzwei,
ich zwang dich zu ganz;
kein Schlag soll nun dich mehr zerschlagen.
Dem sterbenden Vater
zersprang der Stahl,
der lebende Sohn
schuf ihn neu:
nun lacht ihm sein heller Schein,
seine Schärfe schneidet ihm hart.
(das Schwert vor sich schwingend)
Notung! Notung!
Neidliches Schwert!
Zum Leben weckt' ich dich wieder.
Tot lagst du
in Trümmern dort,
jetzt leuchtest du trotzig und hehr.
Zeige den Schächern
nun deinen Schein!
Schlage den Falschen,
fälle den Schelm!
Schau, Mime, du Schmied:
(Er holt mit dem Schwert aus.)

All the heroes and gods
will respect my gold;
(with ever more lively gestures)
the world will cower
when I command;
they'll beg my favour,
fearing my frown!
I'll work no longer;
Mime will rule.
For me they'll labour,
to make me rich.
Mime the conqueror,
Mime is king now,
prince of the Niblungs,
lord of the world!
Hi! Mime, you fortunate smith!
Oh who could believe such luck!

SIEGFRIED
(during Mime's song has given the final blows to flatten the rivets on the hilt. He takes up the sword.)
Notung! Notung!
Sword of my need!
You are fixed again firm in the hilt.
Snapped into two,
once more you are whole;
no stroke again shall ever smash you.
You broke when my father
was doomed to death;
his living son
forged you again:
for me now you laugh and shine,
and your gleaming edge will be keen.
(brandishing the sword)
Notung! Notung!
Sword of my need!
To life once more I have waked you.
You lay there
so cold and dead,
but shine now defiant and fair.
Let every traitor
quail at your gleam!
Strike at the false one,
strike at the rogue!
See, Mime, you smith:
(He raises the sword to strike.)

So schneidet Siegfrieds Schwert!
(Er schlägt auf den Amboß, welcher in zwei Stücke auseinanderfällt. Mime, der in höchster Verzückung sich auf einen Schemel geschwungen hatte, fällt vor Schreck sitzlings zu Boden. Siegfried hält jauchzend das Schwert in die Höhe. Der Vorhang fällt.)

so strong is Siegfried's sword!
(He strikes the anvil, which splits from top to bottom and falls apart with a great crash. Mime, who has jumped up on to a stool in his exaltation, falls to the ground with fright and lands on his bottom. Triumphantly Siegfried holds the sword on high. The curtain falls.)

Zweiter Aufzug

Tiefer Wald

Ganz im Hintergrunde die Öffnung einer Höhle. Der Boden hebt sich bis zur Mitte der Bühne, wo er eine kleine Hochebene bildet; von da senkt er sich nach hinten, der Höhle zu, wieder abwärts, so daß von dieser nur der obere Teil der Öffnung dem Zuschauer sichtbar ist. Links gewahrt man durch Waldbäume eine zerklüftete Felswand. Finstere Nacht, am dichtesten über dem Hintergrunde, wo anfänglich der Blick des Zuschauers gar nichts zu unterscheiden vermag.

Act Two

In the Depths of the Forest

At the very back, the entrance to a cavern. The ground rises towards the centre of the stage, where it forms a small knoll; from there it descends to the cavern, so that only the upper part of the entrance is visible to the spectator. To the left, through the forest trees, a fissured cliff-face can be discerned. Dark night, at its darkest towards the back, where to start with the spectator can distinguish nothing.

Erste Szene

ALBERICH
(an der Felswand gelagert, düster brütend)
In Wald und Nacht
vor Neidhöhl' halt ich Wacht:
es lauscht mein Ohr,
mühvoll lugt mein Aug'.

Scene One

ALBERICH
(stationed at the cliff-face, gloomily brooding)
In gloomy night
by Fafner's cave I wait,
my ears alert,
keeping careful watch.

Banger Tag,
bebst du schon auf?
Dämmerst du dort
durch das Dunkel her?
(Aus dem Walde von rechts her erhebt sich ein Sturmwind; ein bläulicher Glanz leuchtet von ebendaher.)
Welcher Glanz zittert dort auf?
Näher schimmert
ein heller Schein;
es rennt wie ein leuchtendes Roß,
bricht durch den Wald
brausend daher.
Naht schon des Wurmes Würger?
Ist's schon, der Fafner fällt?
(Der Sturmwind legt sich wieder; der Glanz verlischt.)
Das Licht erlischt,
der Glanz barg sich dem Blick:
Nacht ist's wieder.
(Der Wanderer tritt aus dem Wald und hält Alberich gegenüber an.)
Wer naht dort schimmernd im Schatten?

Fateful day,
when will you break?
When will the dawn
drive this dark away?
(A stormy wind blows from the forest on the right; a bluish gleam shines from there.)
Is a light glittering there?
Nearer and nearer
it seems to shine;
it runs like a fiery steed,
breaks through the wood,
rushing this way.
Can it be him I'm waiting for,
author of Fafner's death?
(The stormwind subsides; the gleam fades away.)
The light has gone;
the glow fades from my sight.
Night and darkness!
(The Wanderer enters from the wood, and pauses opposite Alberich.)
Who comes there, lighting the shadows?

DER WANDERER
Zur Neidhöhle
fuhr ich bei Nacht:
wen gewahr ich im Dunkel dort?
(Wie aus einem plötzlich zerreißenden Gewölk bricht Mondschein und beleuchtet des Wanderers Gestalt.)

WANDERER
To Neidhöhle
by night I have come:
who is hid in the darkness there?
(As if through a cloud suddenly rent, the moonlight breaks through and lights the Wanderer's face.)

ALBERICH
(erkennt den Wanderer, fährt erschrocken zurück, bricht aber sogleich in höchste Wut aus.)
Du selbst läßt dich hier sehn?
Was willst du hier?
Fort, aus dem Weg!
Von dannen, schamloser Dieb!

ALBERICH
(recognizes the Wanderer, flinches in fear, but then instantly breaks out in rage.)
You dare show yourself here?
What brings you here?
Out of my sight!
Go elsewhere, shameless thief!

WANDERER
(ruhig)
Schwarz-Alberich,
schweifst du hier?
Hütest du Fafners Haus?

WANDERER
(calmly)
Black-Alberich,
lurking here?
watching over Fafner's hoard?

ALBERICH
Jagst du auf neue

ALBERICH
Driven by your greed

Neidtat umher?
Weile nicht hier,
weiche von hinnen!
Genug des Truges
tränkte die Stätte mit Not.
Drum, du Frecher,
laß sie jetzt frei!

to new evil deeds?
Go on your way,
take yourself elsewhere!
Too long we have suffered,
tricked by your scheming and lies.
So, you traitor,
leave us in peace!

WANDERER
Zu schauen kam ich,
nicht zu schaffen:
Wer wehrte mir Wandrers Fahrt?

WANDERER
The Wanderer watches,
takes no action.
Who dares to bar the Wanderer's way?

ALBERICH
(lacht tückisch auf.)
Du Rat wütender Ränke!
Wär' ich dir zulieb,
doch noch dumm wie damals,
als du mich Blöden bandest,
wie leicht geriet' es,
den Ring mir nochmals zu rauben!
Hab Acht! Deine Kunst
kenne ich wohl;
doch wo du schwach bist,
blieb mir auch nicht verschwiegen.
Mit meinen Schätzen
zahltest du Schulden;
mein Ring lohnte
der Riesen Müh',
die deine Burg dir gebaut.
Was mit den trotzigen
einst du vertragen,
des Runen wahrt noch heut
deines Speeres herrischer Schaft.
Nicht du darfst,
was als Zoll du gezahlt,
den Riesen wieder entreißen:
du selbst zerspelltest
deines Speeres Schaft;
in deiner Hand
der herrische Stab,
der starke, zerstiebte wie Spreu!

ALBERICH
(laughs maliciously.)
You false, infamous schemer!
I am not so stupid
as once you found me,
when you and Loge tricked me.
It's not so easy
again to capture my treasure!
Beware! I am warned,
wise to your schemes.
I know your weakness;
nothing is hid from the Niblung.
My stolen treasure
saved you from ruin;
my ring paid
for the giants' work,
who built that hall where you rule.
The terms of that bargain,
all that you swore then,
are graved for ever more
on that spear you hold in your hand.
You dare not
ever take back by force
that fee you paid to the giants:
for if you tried it
you would break the bond,
and in your hand
the shaft of your spear,
so mighty, would snap like a straw!

WANDERER
Durch Vertrages Treuerunen
band er dich
Bösen mir nicht:

WANDERER
Yet no bonds nor graven bargains
bound evil
Alberich to me:

dich beugt' er mir durch seine Kraft;
zum Krieg drum wahr ich ihn wohl.

ALBERICH
Wie stolz du dräust
in trotziger Stärke,
und wie dir's im Busen doch bangt!
Verfallen dem Tod
durch meinen Fluch
ist des Hortes Hüter:
Wer wird ihn beerben?
Wird der neidliche Hort
dem Niblungen wieder gehören?
Das sehrt dich mit ew'ger Sorge!
Denn faß ich ihn wieder
einst in der Faust,
anders als dumme Riesen
üb ich des Ringes Kraft:
dann zittre der Helden
ewiger Hüter!
Walhalls Höhen
stürm ich mit Hellas Heer:
der Welt walte dann ich!

WANDERER
(ruhig)
Deinen Sinn kenn' ich wohl;
doch sorgt er mich nicht.
Des Ringes waltet,
wer ihn gewinnt.

ALBERICH
Wie dunkel sprichst du,
was ich deutlich doch weiß!
An Heldensöhne
hält sich dein Trotz,
die traut deinem Blute entblüht.
Pflegtest du wohl eines Knaben,
der klug die Frucht dir pflücke,
die du nicht brechen darfst?

WANDERER
Mit mir nicht,
hadre mit Mime:
den Bruder bringt dir Gefahr;
einen Knaben führt er daher,
der Fafner ihm fällen soll.

By force, I bent your will to mine;
my spear brings victory in war.

ALBERICH
How grand you sound,
how proudly you stand there,
and yet in your heart there is fear!
The dragon must die,
for, by my curse
on the gold, I've doomed him:
then who shall inherit?
Will the glittering gold
to the Niblung belong once again?
That thought gives you endless torment!
Just wait till I grasp
the ring in my hand.
I'm not a foolish giant.
I'll use that magic spell:
till you and your heroes
tremble before me!
Alberich's army
conquers Walhall's height:
the world then shall be mine!

WANDERER
(calmly)
Though I know what you plan,
I care not at all.
The ring's new master,
he shall be lord.

ALBERICH
How darkly you tell me
what so clearly I know!
A hero helps you,
that's what you plan,
that son who was born from your blood?
Have you not raised up a hero
in hopes that he will gather
that fruit you dare not pluck?

WANDERER
Not my plan!
Struggle with Mime;
your brother threatens your hopes:
to this place he's leading the boy,
and Fafner will fall to him.

Nichts weiß der von mir;
der Niblung nützt ihn für sich.
Drum sag ich dir, Gesell,
tue frei, wie dir's frommt!
(Alberich macht eine Gebärde heftiger Neugierde.)
Höre mich wohl,
sei auf der Hut!
Nicht kennt der Knabe den Ring;
doch Mime kundet ihn aus.

He knows naught of me,
but Mime urges him on.
So mark my words, good friend:
you may act as you please!
(Alberich makes a gesture of urgent inquiry.)
Take my advice,
be on your guard!
The boy knows naught of the ring,
till Mime tells him the tale.

ALBERICH
(heftig)
Deine Hand hieltest du vom Hort?

ALBERICH
(eagerly)
And will you play no part at all?

WANDERER
Wen ich liebe,
laß ich für sich gewähren;
er steh' oder fall',
sein Herr ist er:
Helden nur können mir frommen.

WANDERER
Since I love him,
I must refuse to help him;
he stands or he falls
unhelped by me:
gods rely only on heroes.

ALBERICH
Mit Mime räng' ich
allein um den Ring?

ALBERICH
With only Mime
I strive for the ring?

WANDERER
Außer dir begehrt er
einzig das Gold.

WANDERER
Only you and he
have plans on the gold.

ALBERICH
Und dennoch gewänn' ich ihn nicht?

ALBERICH
And yet I cannot make it my own?

WANDERER
(ruhig nähertretend)
Ein Helde naht,
den Hort zu befrein;
zwei Niblungen geizen das Gold;
Fafner fällt,
der den Ring bewacht:
wer ihn rafft, hat ihn gewonnen.
Willst du noch mehr?
Dort liegt der Wurm.
(Er wendet sich nach der Höhle.)
Warnst du ihn vor dem Tod,
willig wohl ließ' er den Tand.
Ich selber weck ihn dir auf.
(Er stellt sich auf die Anhöhe vor der Höhle und ruft hinein.)

WANDERER
(quietly drawing nearer)
A hero nears
to rescue the hoard;
two Nibelungs long for the gold:
Fafner falls,
he who guards the ring.
When it's seized—luck to the winner!
Would you know more?
There Fafner lies:
(He turns towards the cave.)
why not warn him of death?
Maybe he'll give you the ring.
I'll wake him up with my call.
(He takes up a position on the knoll in front of the cave, and calls into it.)

Fafner! Fafner!
Erwache, Wurm!

Fafner! Fafner!
You dragon, wake!

ALBERICH
(in gespanntem Erstaunen, für sich)
Was beginnt der Wilde?
Gönnt er mir's wirklich?
(Aus der finstern Tiefe des Hintergrundes hört man Fafners Stimme durch ein starkes Sprachrohr.)

ALBERICH
(excited and astonished, to himself)
Has he lost his senses?
Can it be mine now?
(From the dark depths of the background Fafner's voice is heard through a powerful speaking-trumpet.)

FAFNER
Wer stört mir den Schlaf?

FAFNER
Who wakes me from sleep?

WANDERER
(der Höhle zugewandt)
Gekommen ist einer,
Not dir zu künden:
er lohnt dir's mit dem Leben,
lohnst du das Leben ihm
mit dem Horte, den du hütest?
(Er beugt sein Ohr lauschend der Höhle zu.)

WANDERER
(facing the cave)
A friend has arrived here,
warning of danger;
he has a plan to save you.
Will you reward his help
with the treasure that you're guarding?
(He inclines his ear towards the cave, listening.)

FAFNER
Was will er?

FAFNER
What would he?

ALBERICH
(ist zum Wanderer getreten und ruft in die Höhle.)
Wache, Fafner!
Wache, du Wurm!
Ein starker Helde naht,
dich heil'gen will er bestehn.

ALBERICH
(has joined the Wanderer, and calls into the cave.)
Waken, Fafner!
Dragon, awake!
A valiant hero comes
to try his strength against yours.

FAFNER
Mich hungert sein.

FAFNER
Then food is near.

WANDERER
Kühn ist des Kindes Kraft,
scharf schneidet sein Schwert.

WANDERER
Bold is his youthful heart,
sharp-edged is his sword.

ALBERICH
Den golden Reif
geizt er allein:
Laß mir den Ring zum Lohn,
so wend ich den Streit;
du wahrest den Hort
und ruhig lebst du lang!

ALBERICH
The golden ring,
that's all he wants:
just give that ring to me,
and then he won't fight.
You keep all the rest,
and live your life in peace!

FAFNER
Ich lieg und besitz—
(gähnend)
laßt mich schlafen!

FAFNER
I'll keep what I hold—
(yawning)
let me slumber!

WANDERER
(lacht auf und wendet sich wieder zu Alberich.)
Nun, Alberich, das schlug fehl.
Doch schilt mich nicht mehr Schelm!
Dies eine, rat ich,
achte noch wohl!
(vertraulich zu ihm tretend)
Alles ist nach seiner Art,
an ihr wirst du nichts ändern.
Ich laß dir die Stätte,
stelle dich fest!
Versuch's mit Mime, dem Bruder,
der Art ja versiehst du dich besser.
(zum Abgange gewendet)
Was anders ist,
das lerne nun auch!
(Er verschwindet im Walde. Sturmwind erhebt sich, heller Glanz bricht aus; dann vergeht beides schnell.)

WANDERER
(laughs aloud, and turns back to Alberich.)
Well, Alberich! that scheme failed!
Yet call me not a rogue!
Still more I'll tell you;
heed my advice!
(approaching him confidentially)
All things go their appointed way;
their course you cannot alter.
I'll leave you alone here;
be on your guard!
Beware of Mime, your brother;
he is your kind, and you understand him.
(turning to go)
But stranger things
you'll learn in good time!
(He disappears into the forest. A stormy wind rises, a bright gleam breaks out; then both quickly subside.)

ALBERICH
(blickt dem davonjagenden Wanderer nach.)
Da reitet er hin
auf lichtem Roß
mich läßt er in Sorg' und Spott.
Doch lacht nur zu,
ihr leichtsinniges,
lustgieriges
Göttergelichter!
Euch seh ich
noch alle vergehn!
Solang das Gold
am Lichte glänzt,
hält ein Wissender Wacht.
Trügen wird euch sein Trotz!
(Er schlüpft zur Seite in das Geklüft. Die Bühne bleibt leer. Morgendämmerung.)

ALBERICH
(gazes after the Wanderer as he rides away.)
He rides on his way,
on fiery steed,
and leaves me to care and shame.
Yet laugh away,
you light-spirited,
self-worshipping
clan of immortals!
One day
I shall see you all fade!
So long as gold
reflects the light,
here a wise one will watch:
watching, waiting to strike!
(He slips aside into the cleft in the rocks. The stage remains empty. Day dawns.)

Zweite Szene

Bei anbrechendem Tage treten Mime und Siegfried auf. Siegfried trägt das Schwert in einem Gehenke von Bastseil. Mime erspäht genau die Stätte; er forscht endlich dem Hintergrunde zu, welcher—während die Anhöhe im mittleren Vordergrunde später immer heller von der Sonne beleuchtet wird—in finsterem Schatten bleibt; dann bedeutet er Siegfried.

MIME
Wir sind zur Stelle!
Bleib hier stehn!

SIEGFRIED
(setzt sich unter einer großen Linde nieder und schaut sich um.)
Hier soll ich das Fürchten lernen?
Fern hast du mich geleitet:
eine volle Nacht im Walde.
selbander wanderten wir.
Nun sollst du, Mime,
mich meiden!
Lern ich hier nicht,
was ich lernen muß,
allein zieh ich dann weiter:
dich endlich werd ich da los!

MIME
(setzt sich ihm gegenüber, so daß er die Höhle immer noch im Auge behält.)
Glaube, Liebster,
lernst du heut und hier
das Fürchten nicht,
an andrem Ort,
zu andrer Zeit
schwerlich erfährst du's je.
Siehst du dort
den dunklen Höhlenschlund?
Darin wohnt
ein greulich wilder Wurm:
unmaßen grimmig
ist er und groß;
ein schrecklicher Rachen
reißt sich ihm auf;
mit Haut und Haar

Scene Two

As day breaks, Mime and Siegfried enter. Siegfried is wearing the sword in a belt of bast-rope. Mime examines the place carefully; he looks at last toward the background, which remains in deep shadow even while, later on, the knoll in the middle foreground is lit up ever more brightly by the sun; then he addresses Siegfried.

MIME
We go no further!
Here's the place!

SIEGFRIED
(sits down under a large lime tree and gazes around.)
Here, then, shall this fear be taught me?
So far I've let you lead me;
for the whole night long we've wandered
through this dark wood, side by side.
Mime, I need you
no longer!
If I don't learn
what I've come to find,
alone I shall go onward;
from Mime, I must be free!

MIME
(sits down opposite Siegfried, where he can keep one eye on the cave.)
Child, believe me,
if you do not learn
to fear today,
no other place,
no other time,
can ever teach you fear.
Look back there;
do you see that dreadful cave?
Deep inside
there lives a cruel dragon,
terribly big,
and savage and fierce.
As soon as he sees you
he'll open his jaws,
to eat you whole.

auf einen Happ
verschlingt der Schlimme dich wohl.

SIEGFRIED
Gut ist's, den Schlund ihm zu schließen;
drum biet ich mich nicht dem Gebiß.

MIME
Giftig gießt sich
ein Geifer ihm aus:
wen mit des Speichels
Schweiß er bespeit,
dem schwinden wohl Fleisch und Gebein.

SIEGFRIED
Daß des Geifers Gift mich nicht sehre,
weich ich zur Seite dem Wurm.

MIME
Ein Schlangenschweif
schlägt sich ihm auf:
wen er damit umschlingt
und fest umschließt,
dem brechen die Glieder wie Glas!

SIEGFRIED
Vor des Schweifes Schwang mich zu
halt' ich den Argen im Aug'. [wahren,
Doch heiße mich das:
hat der Wurm ein Herz?

MIME
Ein grimmiges, hartes Herz!

SIEGFRIED
Das sitzt ihm doch,
wo es jedem schlägt,
trag' es Mann oder Tier?

MIME
Gewiß, Knabe,
da führt's auch der Wurm.
Jetzt kommt dir das Fürchten wohl an?

SIEGFRIED
(bisher nachlässig ausgestreckt, erhebt sich rasch zum Sitz.)
Notung stoß ich

One single gulp—
the brute will gobble you down!

SIEGFRIED
Well then, in order to stop him,
I'll close up his jaws with my sword.

MIME
Poisonous foam
he will pour from his mouth;
if you are splashed
by one single drop,
it shrivels your body and bones.

SIEGFRIED
But that poisonous foam cannot harm me,
if I step neatly aside.

MIME
A scaly tail
he lashes around:
and if you should be caught,
he'll coil it tight;
your bones will be broken like glass!

SIEGFRIED
Then that scaly tail must not catch me;
I'll have to watch it with care.
But tell me one thing:
has the brute a heart?

MIME
A merciless, cruel heart.

SIEGFRIED
And is that heart
in the usual place,
at the left of his breast?

MIME
Of course; dragons
have hearts just like men.
Does your heart begin to feel fear?

SIEGFRIED
(who has so far been lolling carelessly, quickly sits up erect.)
Notung! Notung

dem Stolzen ins Herz!
Soll das etwa Fürchten heißen?
He, du Alter!
Ist das alles,
was deine List
mich lehren kann?
Fahr deines Weges dann weiter;
das Fürchten lern ich hier nicht.

I'll thrust in that heart!
In that way may fear be taught me?
Oh, you're stupid!
Have you brought me
all this way
to teach me that?
Mime, be off and leave me;
since fear I shall never learn here.

MIME
Wart es nur ab!
Was ich dir sage,
dünke dich tauber Schall:
ihn selber mußt du
hören und sehn,
die Sinne vergehn dir dann schon!
Wenn dein Blick verschwimmt,
der Boden dir schwankt,
im Busen bang
dein Herz erbebt:
(sehr freundlich)
dann dankst du mir, der dich führte,
gedenkst, wie Mime dich liebt.

MIME
Just wait a while!
You think I've told you
trifling and empty tales:
but Fafner
you must see for yourself;
for Fafner can teach you to fear.
When your eyes grow dim,
your body grows weak,
when trembling shudders
fill your heart,
(very affectionately)
you'll thank the dwarf who has brought
be glad of Mime's love. [you,

SIEGFRIED
Du sollst mich nicht lieben!
Sagt' ich dir's nicht?
Fort aus den Augen mir!
Laß mich allein:
sonst halt ich's hier länger nicht aus,
fängst du von Liebe gar an!
Das eklige Nicken
und Augenzwicken,
wann endlich soll ich's
nicht mehr sehn,
wann werd ich den Albernen los?

SIEGFRIED
You must not love me!
Did you not hear?
I hate the sight of you!
Leave me alone:
I'll hear no more talk about love;
don't dare to love me again!
That shuffling and slinking,
those eyelids blinking—
how long must I
endure the sight?
When shall I be rid of this fool?

MIME
Ich laß dich schon.
Am Quell dort lagr' ich mich;
steh du nur hier;
steigt dann die Sonne zur Höh',
merk auf den Wurm:
aus der Höhle wälzt er sich her,
hier vorbei

MIME
I'll leave you now,
at the stream I'll cool myself.
Wait by the cave;
soon, when the sun is in the sky,
watch for the dragon.
From his cave he'll slowly emerge,
wind his way

biegt er dann,
am Brunnen sich zu tränken.

SIEGFRIED
(lachend)
Mime, weilst du am Quell,
dahin laß ich den Wurm wohl gehn:
Notung stoß ich
ihm erst in die Nieren,
wenn er dich selbst dort
mit weggesoffen.
Darum, hör meinen Rat,
raste nicht dort am Quell;
kehre dich weg,
so weit du kannst,
und komm nie mehr zu mir!

MIME
Nach freislichem Streit
dich zu erfrischen,
wirst du mir wohl nicht wehren?
(Siegfried wehrt ihn hastig ab.)
Rufe mich auch,
darbst du des Rates—
(Siegfried wiederholt die Gebärde mit Ungestüm.)
oder wenn dir das Fürchten gefällt.
(Siegfried erhebt sich und treibt Mime mit wütender Gebärde zum Fortgehen.)

MIME
(im Abgehen für sich)
Fafner und Siegfried,
Siegfried und Fafner—
O, brächten beide sich um!
(Er verschwindet rechts im Walde.)

SIEGFRIED
(streckt sich behaglich unter der Linde aus und blickt dem davongehenden Mime nach.)
Daß der mein Vater nicht ist,
wie fühl ich mich drob so froh!
Nun erst gefällt mir
der frische Wald;
nun erst lacht mir
der lustige Tag,
da der Garstige von mir schied

past this place,
to reach the cooling stream there.

SIEGFRIED
(laughing)
Mime, wait by the stream,
and let the dragon catch you there:
I can wait here
till Fafner has found you,
then we can fight—
after you've been swallowed.
Or else, take my advice,
better not stay by the stream;
hurry away
as fast as you can,
and don't come back to me!

MIME
When after the fight
you need refreshment,
won't you be glad to see me?
(Siegfried shoos him away.)
Call for my help
if you should need me.
(Siegfried impatiently repeats the gesture.)
Let me know when your fear has been learnt.
(Siegfried rises, and drives Mime off with furious gestures.)

MIME
(to himself, as he goes)
Fafner and Siegfried,
Siegfried and Fafner—
if only each would kill the other!
(He disappears in the forest on the right.)

SIEGFRIED
(stretches himself out comfortably under the lime tree, and watches Mime's departure.)
So he's no father of mine:
that thought fills my heart with joy!
Now I delight
in this fair green wood;
I delight
in this glorious day,
now I'm free from that loathsome dwarf,

und ich gar nicht ihn wiederseh!
(Er verfällt in schweigendes Sinnen.)
Wie sah mein Vater wohl aus?
Ha, gewiß, wie ich selbst!
Denn wär' wo von Mime ein Sohn,
müßt' er nicht ganz
Mime gleichen?
Grade so garstig,
griesig und grau,
klein und krumm,
höckrig und hinkend,
mit hängenden Ohren,
triefigen Augen—
Fort mit dem Alp!
Ich mag ihn nicht mehr sehn.
(Er lehnt sich tiefer zurück und blickt durch den Baumwipfel auf. Tiefe Stille. Waldweben.)
Aber—wie sah
meine Mutter wohl aus?
Das kann ich
nun gar nicht mir denken!
Der Rehhindin gleich
glänzten gewiß
ihr hellschimmernde Augen,
nur noch viel schöner!
Da bang sie mich geboren,
warum aber starb sie da?
Sterben die Menschenmütter
an ihren Söhnen
alle dahin?
Traurig wäre das, traun!
Ach, möcht' ich Sohn
meine Mutter sehen!
Meine Mutter—
ein Menschenweib!
(Er seufzt leise und streckt sich tiefer zurück. Große Stille. Wachsendes Waldweben. Siegfrieds Aufmerksamkeit wird endlich durch den Gesang der Waldvögel gefesselt. Er lauscht mit wachsender Teilnahme einem Waldvogel in den Zweigen über ihm.)
Du holdes Vöglein!
Dich hört ich noch nie:
bist du im Wald hier daheim?
Verstünd' ich sein süßes Stammeln,
gewiß sagt' es mir was
vielleicht von der lieben Mutter?

and I shan't have to see him again!
(He falls into silent reverie.)
My father, how did he look?
Why, of course, like his son!
If Mime had fathered a son,
wouldn't he look
just like Mime?
Shuffling and slinking,
grizzled and gray,
small and crooked,
limping and hunchbacked,
with ears that are drooping,
eyes that are bleary . . .
Off with the imp!
I hope he's gone for good!
(He leans back and looks up through the branches. Deep silence. Forest murmurs.)
Could I but know
what my mother was like!
That's something
I cannot imagine!
Her eyes must have shone
with soft gentle light,
like the eyes of the roedeer,
only more lovely!
In fear and grief she bore me,
but why did she die through me?
Must every human mother
die when her children
come to the world?
Sad the world must be then!
Ah, how this son
longs to see his mother!
See my mother—
who lived and died!
(He sighs gently and leans back still further. Deep silence. The forest murmurs increase. Siegfried's attention is then caught by the song of the forest birds. He listens with growing interest to a bird in the branches above him.)

You lovely woodbird,
how sweet is your song:
here in the wood is your home?
I wish I could understand you!
I'm sure you've something to tell—
perhaps of a loving mother?

Ein zankender Zwerg
hat mir erzählt,
der Vöglein Stammeln
gut zu verstehn,
dazu könnte man kommen.
Wie das wohl möglich wär'?
(Er sinnt nach. Sein Blick fällt auf ein Rohrgebüsch unweit der Linde.)
Hei, ich versuch's,
sing ihm nach:
auf dem Rohr tön ich ihm ähnlich!
Entrat ich der Worte,
achte der Weise,
sing ich so seine Sprache,
versteh ich wohl auch, was er spricht.
(Er eilt an den nahen Quell, schneidet mit dem Schwerte ein Rohr ab und schnitzt sich hastig eine Pfeife daraus. Währenddem lauscht er wieder.)
Er schweigt und lauscht:
so schwatz ich denn los!
(Er bläst auf dem Rohr, setzt ab, schnitzt wieder, bessert und bläst wieder. Er schüttett mit dem Kopfe und bessert nochmals. Wird ärgerlich, drückt das Rohr mit der Hand und versucht wieder. Schließlich setzt er ganz ab.)
Das tönt nicht recht;
auf dem Rohre taugt
die wonnige Weise mir nicht.
Vöglein, mich dünkt,
ich bleibe dumm:
von dir lernt sich's nicht leicht!
(Er hört den Vogel wieder und blickt zu ihm auf.)
Nun schäm ich mich gar
vor dem schelmischen Lauscher:
er lugt und kann nichts erlauschen.
Heida! So höre
nun auf mein Horn.
(Er schwingt das Rohr und wirft es weit fort.)
Auf dem dummen Rohre
gerät mir nichts.
Einer Waldweise,
wie ich sie kann,
der lustigen sollst du nun lauschen.
Nach liebem Gesellen
lockt' ich mit ihr:
nichts Beßres kam noch
als Wolf und Bär.
Nun laß mich sehn,

A surly old dwarf
said to me once
that men could learn
the language of birds,
and know what they were saying.
How can I learn the tongue?
(He reflects. His glance falls on a clump of reeds not far from the lime tree.)
Hey! Let me try—
pipe your notes
on a reed, copy your chirping!
Your song I will echo,
mimic your warbling;
while your tune I am piping,
perhaps I shall learn what you say!
(He runs to the stream nearby, cuts a reed with his sword, and quickly whittles a pipe from it. He listens again.)
He stops and waits:
well, let me begin!
(He blows on the pipe, breaks off, cuts it again to improve it, pipes again, shakes his head, and cuts the pipe once more. He tries again, gets angry, pinches the reed with his hand, and makes another attempt. Then, he gives up.)
Well, that's not right;
and this reed won't serve
to capture the lilt of your song.
Woodbird, I think
I must be dull;
From you I cannot learn.
(He hears the bird again, and looks up at it.)
You put me to shame
as you perch there and watch me;
you wait—and I cannot answer.
Hey then! Then hear
the call of my horn.
(He holds up the reed and tosses it far away.)
I can pipe no tune
on a feeble reed.
But I'll play you
a tune on my horn,
a song that will ring through the woodlands—
a song that I hoped
might find me a friend:
though no one heard me
but wolf and bear.
Now let us see

wen jetzt sie mir lockt:
ob das mir ein lieber Gesell?
(Er nimmt das silberne Hifthorn und bläst darauf. Bei den langgehalten Tönen blickt Siegfried immer erwartungsvoll auf den Vogel. Im Hintergrunde regt es sich. Fafner, in der Gestalt eines ungeheuren eidechsenartigen Schlangenwurms, hat sich in der Höhle von seinem Lager erhoben; er bricht durch das Gesträuch und wälzt sich aus der Tiefe nach der höheren Stelle vor, so daß er mit dem Vorderleibe bereits auf ihr angelangt ist, als er jetzt einen starken gähnenden Laut ausstößt. Siegfried sieht sich um und heftet den Blick verwundert auf Fafner.)
Haha! Da hätte mein Lied
mir was Liebes erblasen!
Du wärst mir ein saubrer Gesell!

who'll answer my call—
the friend whom I'm longing to find?

(He takes the silver horn and blows on it. At each long-sustained note he looks up expectantly at the bird. There is a stir in the background. Fafner, in the form of a huge, scaly dragon, has risen from his lair in the cave; he breaks through the undergrowth and drags himself up from below to the higher ground until the front part of his body rests on this, whereupon he utters a loud noise like a yawn.

Siegfried looks round, and fastens his astonished gaze on Fafner.)

Haha! At last with my call
I have lured something lovely!
What a pretty playmate I've found!

FAFNER
(hat beim Anblick Siegfrieds auf der Höhe angehalten und verweilt nun daselbst.)
Was ist da?

FAFNER
(at the sight of Siegfried has paused on the knoll, and remains there.)
Who is there?

SIEGFRIED
Ei, bist du ein Tier,
das zum Sprechen taugt,
wohl ließ sich von dir was lernen?
Hier kennt einer
das Fürchten nicht:
kann er's von dir erfahren?

SIEGFRIED
Hi, so you're a beast
that can speak to me;
perhaps you've some news to tell me?
Can you tell me
what fear might be:
are you prepared to teach me?

FAFNER
Hast du Übermut?

FAFNER
You are far too bold!

SIEGFRIED
Mut oder Übermut,
was weiß ich!
Doch dir fahr ich zu Leibe,
lehrst du das Fürchten mich nicht!

SIEGFRIED
Bold, maybe far too bold,
I know not!
I know that I will fight you,
if you can't teach me to fear.

FAFNER
(stößt einen lachenden Laut aus.)
Trinken wollt' ich:
nun treff ich auch Fraß!
(Er öffnet seinen Rachen und zeigt die Zähne.)

FAFNER
(makes a laughing noise.)
Drink I wanted,
now I have found food!
(He opens his jaws and shows his teeth.)

SIEGFRIED
Eine zierliche Fresse

SIEGFRIED
What a splendid array

zeigst du mir da,
lachende Zähne
im Leckermaul!
Gut wär' es, den Schlund dir zu [schließen;
dein Rachen reckt sich zu weit!

of dazzling teeth,
glinting and glistening
within those jaws!
Well, maybe it's wiser to close them:
those jaws are open too wide.

FAFNER
Zu tauben Reden
taugt er schlecht:
dich zu verschlingen,
frommt der Schlund.
(Er droht mit dem Schweife.)

FAFNER
For idle chatter,
far too wide;
but all the better
for my meal.
(He threatens with his tail.)

SIEGFRIED
Hoho! Du grausam
grimmiger Kerl!
Von dir verdaut sein
dünkt mich übel:
rätlich und fromm doch scheint's,
du verrecktest hier ohne Frist.

SIEGFRIED
Oho! You cruel
merciless brute!
But I've no wish
to be your breakfast.
Far better plan, I think,
to destroy you here on the spot.

FAFNER
(brüllend)
Pruh! Komm,
prahlendes Kind!

FAFNER
(roaring)
Pruh! Come,
insolent boy!

SIEGFRIED
Hab Acht, Brüller!
Der Prahler naht!
(Er zieht sein Schwert, springt Fafner an und bleibt herausfordernd stehen. Fafner wälzt sich weiter auf die Höhe herauf und sprüht aus den Nüstern auf Siegfried. Siegfried weicht dem Geifer aus, springt näher zu und stellt sich zur Seite. Fafner sucht ihn mit dem Schweife zu erreichen. Siegfried, welchen Fafner fast erreicht hat, springt mit einem Satze über diesen hinweg und verwundet ihn an dem Schweife. Fafner brüllt, zieht den Schweif heftig zurück und bäumt den Vorderleib, um mit dessen voller Wucht sich auf Siegfried zu werfen; so bietet er diesem die Brust dar: Siegfried erspäht schnell die Stelle des Herzens und stößt sein Schwert bis an das Heft hinein. Fafner bäumt sich vor Schmerz noch höher und sinkt, als Siegfried das Schwert losgelassen und zur Seite gesprungen ist, auf die Wunde zusammen.)

SIEGFRIED
Take care, growler!
The boy draws near!
(He draws his sword, springs toward Fafner, and stands in an attitude of defiance. Fafner drags himself further up the knoll and spits from his nostrils at Siegfried. Siegfried avoids the venom, leaps nearer, and stands to one side. Fafner tries to reach him with his tail. When Fafner has nearly caught Siegfried, the latter leaps with one bound over the dragon, and wounds him in the tail. Fafner roars, draws his tail back quickly, and rears up the front part of his body to throw its full weight on Siegfried, thus exposing his breast. Siegfried quickly notes the place of the heart and plunges his sword in there up to the hilt. Fafner rears up still higher in his pain, and sinks down on the wound, as Siegfried lets go of the sword and leaps to one side.)

SIEGFRIED
Da lieg, neidischer Kerl:
Notung trägst du im Herzen!

FAFNER
(mit schwächerer Stimme)
Wer bist du, kühner Knabe,
der das Herz mir traf?
Wer reizte des Kindes Mut
zu der mordlichen Tat?
Dein Hirn brütete nicht,
was du vollbracht.

SIEGFRIED
Viel weiß ich noch nicht,
noch nicht auch, wer ich bin.
Mit dir mordlich zu ringen,
reiztest du selbst meinen Mut.

FAFNER
Du helläugiger Knabe,
unkund deiner selbst,
wen du gemordet,
meld ich dir.
Der Riesen ragend Geschlecht,
Fasolt und Fafner,
die Brüder, fielen nun beide.
Um verfluchtes Gold,
von Göttern vergabt,
traf ich Fasolt zu Tod.
Der nun als Wurm
den Hort bewachte,
Fafner, den letzten Riesen,
fällte ein rosiger Held.
Blicke nun hell,
blühender Knabe;
der dich Blinden reizte zur Tat,
berät jetzt des Blühenden Tod!
Merk, wie's endet!
(ersterbend)
Acht auf mich!

SIEGFRIED
Woher ich stamme,
rate mir noch;
weise ja scheinst du,
Wilder, im Sterben;

SIEGFRIED
So there, merciless brute!
Notung now has destroyed you!

FAFNER
(in a weaker voice)
Who are you, youthful hero,
who have pierced my breast?
Who roused up your fearless heart
to this murderous deed?
And who told you to do
what you have done?

SIEGFRIED
Not much have I learned;
I know not who I am;
but you roused me to kill you,
prompted my deed by your threat.

FAFNER
So bold, youthful, and fearless,
unknown to yourself:
now let me tell you
whom you've killed.
The giants who ruled on the earth,
Fasolt and Fafner,
the brothers, both have now fallen.
For the cursed gold
we gained from the gods,
I put Fasolt to death.
In dragon shape,
the treasure's guardian,
Fafner, the last of the giants,
falls at the hand of a boy.
Guard yourself well,
bold, fearless hero!
He who urged you on to this deed,
has planned next this bold hero's death.
Mark how it ends then!
(dying)
Recall my fate!

SIEGFRIED
Who was my father?
Do you not know?
Wisdom inspires you
now you are dying:

rat es nach meinem Namen:
Siegfried bin ich genannt.

FAFNER
Siegfried!...
(Er seufzt, hebt sich und stirbt.)

SIEGFRIED
Zur Kunde taugt kein Toter.
So leite mich denn
mein lebendes Schwert!
(Fafner hat sich im Sterben zur Seite gewälzt. Siegfried zieht ihm jetzt das Schwert aus der Brust: dabei wird seine Hand vom Blute benetzt: er fährt heftig mit der Hand auf.)
Wie Feuer brennt das Blut!
(Er fürht unwillkürlich die Finger zum Munde, um das Blut von ihnen abzusaugen. Wie er sinnend vor sich hinblickt, wird seine Aufmerksamkeit immer mehr von dem Gesange der Waldvögel angezogen.)
Ist mir doch fast,
als sprächen die Vöglein zu mir!
Nützte mir das
des Blutes Genuß?
Das seltne Vöglein hier,
horch, was singet es mir?

STIMME EINES WALDVOGELS
(aus den Zweigen der Linde über Siegfried)
Hei! Siegfried gehört
nun der Niblungen Hort!
O fänd' in der Höhle
den Hort er jetzt!
Wollt' er den Tarnhelm gewinnen,
der taugt' ihm zu wonniger Tat:
doch wollt' er den Ring sich erraten,
der macht' ihn zum Walter der Welt!

SIEGFRIED
(hat mit verhaltenem Atem und verzückter Miene gelauscht.)
Dank, liebes Vöglein,
für deinen Rat!
Gern folg' ich dem Ruf!
(Er wendet sich nach hinten und steigt in die Höhle hinab, wo er alsbald gänzlich verschwindet.)

maybe my name will tell you:
Siegfried, that is my name.

FAFNER
Siegfried!...
(He raises himself with a sigh, and expires.)

SIEGFRIED
The dead can tell no tidings.
To life I'll be led
by the light of my sword!
(Fafner, in dying, has rolled on his side. Siegfried draws the sword from his breast, and in doing so smears his hand with blood. He draws back his hand violently.)
Like fire burns the blood!
(Involuntarily he puts his fingers to his mouth to suck the blood from them. As he gazes thoughtfully before him, his attention is caught increasingly by the song of the forest birds.)

Almost, it seems,
the woodbirds are speaking to me.
Is it a spell
that lies in the blood?
The woodbird's there again;
hark, he sings to me!

VOICE OF A WOODBIRD
(from the branches of the lime tree above Siegfried)
Hi! Siegfried inherits
the Nibelung hoard;
oh, there it is lying
within that cave!
There is the Tarnhelm, whose magic
will serve him for glorious deeds;
and if he discovers the ring,
it will make him the lord of the world!

SIEGFRIED
(has listened with bated breath and enraptured look.)
Thanks, dearest woodbird,
for that advice!
I'll do as you say!
(He turns towards the back, descends into the cave, and at once disappears from sight.)

Dritte Szene

Mime schleicht scheu umherblickend heran, um sich von Fafners Tod zu überzeugen. Gleichzeitig kommt von der anderen Seite Alberich, und er beobachtet Mime genau. Als dieser Siegfried nicht mehr gewahrt und vorschtig sich der Höhle zuwendet, stürzt Alberich auf ihn zu und vertritt ihm den Weg.

ALBERICH
Wohin schleichst du
eilig und schlau,
schlimmer Gesell?

MIME
Verfluchter Bruder,
dich braucht' ich hier!
Was bringt dich her?

ALBERICH
Geizt es dich, Schelm,
nach meinem Gold?
Verlangst du mein Gut?

MIME
Fort von der Stelle!
Die Stätte ist mein:
Was stöberst du hier?

ALBERICH
Stör ich dich wohl
im stillen Geschäft,
wenn du hier stiehlst?

MIME
Was ich erschwang
mit schwerer Müh',
soll mir nicht schwinden.

ALBERICH
Hast du dem Rhein
das Gold zum Ringe geraubt?
Erzeugtest du gar
den zähen Zauber im Reif?

Scene Three

Mime slinks on, peering round timidly to assure himself that Fafner is dead. Simultaneously, Alberich emerges from the cleft on the other side. He observes Mime closely. Mime, seeing that Siegfried is no longer there, is going warily towards the cave at the back, when Alberich rushes forward and bars his way.

ALBERICH
Hehe! Sly
and slippery knave,
where are you going?

MIME
Accursed brother,
I need you not!
What brings you here?

ALBERICH
Pestilent imp,
you'd steal my gold?
You covet my wealth?

MIME
Off on the instant!
The place here is mine:
you've no business here!

ALBERICH
Do I disturb
a thief at his work?
Caught in the act?

MIME
What I've achieved
through years of toil
shall not escape me.

ALBERICH
Was it then you
who robbed the Rhine of its gold?
And was it your hand
that worked the spell in the ring?

MIME
Wer schuf den Tarnhelm,
der die Gestalten tauscht?
Der sein bedurfte,
erdachtest du ihn wohl?

ALBERICH
Was hättest du Stümper
je wohl zu stampfen verstanden?
Der Zauberring
zwang mir den Zwerg erst zur Kunst.

MIME
Wo hast du den Ring?
Dir Zagem entrissen ihn Riesen!
Was du verlorst,
meine List erlangt es für mich.

ALBERICH
Mit des Knaben Tat
will der Knicker nun knausern?
Dir gehört sie gar nicht,
der Helle ist selbst ihr Herr!

MIME
Ich zog ihn auf;
für die Zucht zahlt er mir nun:
für Müh' und Last
erlauert' ich lang meinen Lohn!

ALBERICH
Für des Knaben Zucht
will der knickrige
schäbige Knecht
keck und kühn
wohl gar König nun sein?
Dem räudigsten Hund
wäre der Ring
geratner als dir:
nimmer erringst
du, Rüpel, den Herrscherreif!

MIME
(kratzt sich den Kopf.)
Behalt ihn denn
und hüt ihn wohl,
den hellen Reif!

MIME
Who made the Tarnhelm,
changing your shape at will?
Though you desired it,
that helm was made by me!

ALBERICH
You miserable bungler,
mine was the skill that inspired you!
My magic ring
showed how the helm could be made.

MIME
And where is that ring?
You coward, the giants have seized it.
What you have lost,
I can gain by guile for myself.

ALBERICH
What the boy has won
will the miser lay hands on?
When the hero finds it,
that hero will keep his prize.

MIME
I brought him up;
for my care now he can pay;
for years I slaved;
my labours have won their reward!

ALBERICH
So you brought him up!
Does the beggarly,
miserly knave
think he's earned
such pay? King would he be?
A flea-bitten dog
has better right
than you to the gold!
You'll never win,
you schemer, that mighty ring!

MIME
(scratches his head.)
Well, keep it then,
and guard it well,
that shining ring!

Sei du Herr:
doch mich heiße auch Bruder!
Um meines Tarnhelms
lustigen Tand
tausch ich ihn dir:
uns beiden taugt's,
teilen die Beute wir so.
(Er reibt sich zutraulich die Hände.)

You be lord:
but still treat me as brother!
Give me the Tarnhelm,
which I have made;
you keep the gold;
then both are paid;
each of us shares in the prize.
(He rubs his hands insinuatingly.)

ALBERICH
(mit Hohnlachen)
Teilen mit dir?
Und den Tarnhelm gar?
Wie schlau du bist!
Sicher schlief' ich
niemals vor deinen Schlingen!

ALBERICH
(laughing scornfully)
Share it with you?
And the Tarnhelm yours?
How sly you are!
Not one moment's peace
I'd have from your scheming!

MIME
(außer sich)
Selbst nicht tauschen?
Auch nicht teilen?
Leer soll ich gehn?
Ganz ohne Lohn?
(kreischend)
Gar nichts willst du mir lassen?

MIME
(beside himself)
You won't share them?
You won't bargain?
Nothing for me?
All must be yours?
(screaming)
Not one thing will you leave me?

ALBERICH
Nichts von allem!
Nicht einen Nagel
sollst du dir nehmen!

ALBERICH
Not a trinket!
No, not a nail-head!
All I deny you.

MIME
(in höchster Wut)
Weder Ring noch Tarnhelm
soll dir denn taugen!
Nicht teil ich nun mehr!
Gegen dich doch ruf ich
Siegfried zu Rat
und des Recken Schwert;
der rasche Held,
der richte, Brüderchen, dich!
(Siegfried erscheint im Hintergrunde.)

MIME
(in a towering rage)
Neither ring nor Tarnhelm
then shall reward you!
I'll bargain no more!
But I'll set against you
Siegfried himself
with his cruel sword;
that fearless boy
will pay you, brother of mine!
(Siegfried appears in the background.)

ALBERICH
Kehre dich um!
Aus der Höhle kommt er daher!

ALBERICH
Better turn round!
From the cavern, see where he comes!

MIME
Kindischen Tand
erkor er gewiß.

ALBERICH
Den Tarnhelm hält er!

MIME
Doch auch den Ring!

ALBERICH
Verflucht! Den Ring!

MIME
(hämisch lachend)
Laß ihn den Ring dir doch geben!
Ich will ihn mir schon gewinnen.
(Er schlüpft in den Wald zurück.)

ALBERICH
Und doch seinem Herrn
soll er allein noch gehören!
(Er verschwindet im Geklüft. Siegfried ist mit Tarnhelm und Ring während des letzteren langsam und sinnend aus der Höhle vorgeschritten: er betrachtet gedankenvoll seine Beute und hält, nahe dem Baume, auf der Höhe des Mittelgrundes wieder an.)

SIEGFRIED
Was ihr mir nützt,
weiß ich nicht;
doch nahm ich euch
aus des Horts gehäuftem Gold,
weil guter Rat mir es riet.
So taug' eure Zier
als des Tages Zeuge,
es mahne der Tand,
daß ich kämpfend Fafner erlegt,
doch das Fürchten noch nicht gelernt!
(Er steckt den Tarnhelm in den Gürtel und den Reif an den Finger. Stillschweigen. Wachsendes Waldweben. Siegfried achtet unwillkürlich wieder des Vogels und lauscht ihm mit verhaltenem Atem.)

STIMME DES WALDVOGELS
Hei! Siegfried gehört

MIME
Trinkets and toys
he's sure to have found.

ALBERICH
He's found the Tarnhelm!

MIME
Also the ring!

ALBERICH
Accurst! The ring!

MIME
(laughing maliciously)
Get him to give you the ring, then!
Yet all the same I shall win it!
(He slips back into the forest.)

ALBERICH
Just wait, in the end
it will belong to its master!
(He disappears into the cleft. During the foregoing, Siegfried has come slowly and thoughtfully from the cave with the Tarnhelm and ring. He regards his prizes meditatively, and pauses on the knoll in the middle of the stage, near the tree.)

SIEGFRIED
Tarnhelm and ring,
here they are:
I chose these things
from the hoard of heaped-up gold,
because the woodbird said I should.
I know not their use:
yet they'll serve to remind me—
these toys are the proof
that I conquered Fafner in fight;
but what fear is, that I've not learned!
(He puts the Tarnhelm in his belt and the ring on his finger. Dead silence. The forest murmurs increase. Siegfried again involuntarily becomes aware of the bird, to whose song he listens with bated breath.)

VOICE OF THE WOODBIRD
Hi! Siegfried discovered

nun der Helm und der Ring!
O traute er Mime,
dem treulosen, nicht!
Hörte Siegfried nur scharf
auf des Schelmen Heuchlergered'!
Wie sein Herz es meint,
kann er Mime verstehn:
so nütz' ihm des Blutes Genuß.
(Siegfrieds Miene und Gebärde drücken aus, daß er den Sinn des Vogelgesanges wohl vernommen. Er sieht Mime sich nähern und bleibt, ohne sich zu rühren, auf sein Schwert gestützt, beobachtend in seiner Stellung auf der Anhöhe bis zum Schlusse des folgenden Auftrittes.)

MIME
(schleicht heran und beobachtet vom Vordergrunde aus Siegfried.)
Er sinnt und erwägt
der Beute Wert.
Weilte wohl hier
ein weiser Wandrer,
schweifte umher,
beschwatzte das Kind
mit list'ger Runen Rat?
Zweifach schlau
sei nun der Zwerg:
Die listigste Schlinge
leg ich jetzt aus,
daß ich mit traulichem
Truggerede
betöre das trotzige Kind.
(Er tritt näher an Siegfried heran, und bewillkommnet diesen mit schmeichelnden Gebärden.)
Willkommen, Siegfried!
Sag, du Kühner,
hast du das Fürchten gelernt?

SIEGFRIED
Den Lehrer fand ich noch nicht!

MIME
Doch den Schlangenwurm,
du hast ihn erschlagen?
Das war doch ein schlimmer Gesell?

SIEGFRIED
So grimm und tückisch er war,

the Tarnhelm and ring!
Oh, let him beware
of the treacherous dwarf!
Oh, let Siegfried attend
to the crafty words Mime speaks!
What he really means
you will now understand,
made wise by the taste of the blood.
(Siegfried's demeanour and gestures show that he has understood the sense of the bird's song. Seeing Mime approach, he remains motionless, leaning on his sword, observant and self-contained, in his place on the knoll, until the end of the following scene.)

MIME
(slinks on and observes Siegfried from the foreground.)
He broods, and he wonders
what he's found:
can he have met
a wily Wanderer,
roaming around,
advising the boy
with crafty talk and tales?
Doubly sly
I'll have to be:
my cunningest snares
for him I shall lay,
and use my friendliest,
falsest flattery
to capture this obstinate boy.
(He comes closer to Siegfried, welcoming him with wheedling gestures.)
Be welcome, Siegfried!
Say, my brave one,
tell me if fear has been learned?

SIEGFRIED
No teacher here could be found.

MIME
But that cruel dragon—
I see that you've slain him?
Did he not inspire you with fear?

SIEGFRIED
Though he was cruel and fierce,

sein Tod grämt mich doch schier,
da viel üblere Schächer
unerschlagen noch leben!
Der mich ihn morden hieß,
den haß ich mehr als den Wurm!

MIME
(sehr freundlich)
Nur sachte! Nicht lange
siehst du mich mehr:
zum ew'gen Schlaf
schließ ich dir die Augen bald!
Wozu ich dich brauchte,
(wie belobend)
hast du vollbracht;
jetzt will ich nur noch
die Beute dir abgewinnen.
Mich dünkt, das soll mir gelingen;
zu betören bist du ja leicht!

SIEGFRIED
So sinnst du auf meinen Schaden?

MIME
(verwundert)
Wie, sagt' ich denn das?
(zärtlich fortfahrend)
Siegfried! Hör doch, mein Söhnchen!
Dich und deine Art
haßt' ich immer von Herzen;
aus Liebe erzog ich
dich Lästigen nicht:
dem Horte in Fafners Hut,
dem Golde galt meine Müh'.
(als verspräche er ihm hübsche Sachen)
Gibst du mir das
gutwillig nun nicht—
(als wäre er bereit, sein Leben für ihn zu lassen)
Siegfried, mein Sohn,
das siehst du wohl selbst:
(mit freundlichem Scherze)
dein Leben mußt du mir lassen!

SIEGFRIED
Daß du mich hassest,
hör ich gern:

his death fills me with grief,
when far wickeder scoundrels
live their lives still unpunished.
He who brought me here to fight
I hate far more than my foe!

MIME
(very affectionately)
Now gently! for soon
you'll see me no more;
when death has closed
your eyes in dark, eternal sleep!
For all that I needed
(as if praising him)
you have achieved.
One thing but remains
for me to do: to win the treasure.
I think that task should be easy;
you were never hard to deceive!

SIEGFRIED
Deceive me, and then destroy me?

MIME
(astonished)
Is that what I said?
(continuing tenderly)
Siegfried! Hear me, my dear son!
You and all your kind
in my heart I have hated;
and love played no part
in bringing you up.
The gold that's hid in Fafner's cave,
that gold alone I sought to win.
(as if he were promising him something pleasant)
Give me all
that shining treasure, or else—
(as if he were ready to lay down his life for him)
Siegfried, my son,
you see it's quite clear,
(with affectionate jocularity)
your life you'll just have to yield me.

SIEGFRIED
Learning you hate me,
brings me joy:

doch auch mein Leben muß ich dir lassen?

MIME
(ärgerlich)
Das sagt' ich doch nicht?
Du verstehst mich ja falsch!
(Er sucht sein Fläschchen hervor und gibt sich die ersichtlichste Mühe zur Verstellung.)
Sieh, du bist müde
von harter Müh';
brünstig wohl brennt dir der Leib:
dich zu erquicken
mit queckem Trank
säumt' ich Sorgender nicht.
Als dein Schwert du dir branntest,
braut' ich den Sud;
trinkst du nun den,
gewinn ich dein trautes Schwert
und mit ihm Helm und Hort.
(Er kichert dazu.)

SIEGFRIED
So willst du mein Schwert
und was ich erschwungen,
Ring und Beute, mir rauben?

MIME
(heftig)
Was du doch falsch mich verstehst!
Stamml' ich, fasl' ich wohl gar?
Die größte Mühe
geb ich mir doch,
mein heimliches Sinnen
heuchelnd zu bergen,
und du dummer Bube
deutest alles doch falsch!
Öffne die Ohren
und vernimm genau:
höre, was Mime meint!
(wieder sehr freundlich, mit ersichtlicher Mühe)
Hier nimm und trinke dir Labung!
Mein Trank labte dich oft:
tatst du auch unwirsch,
stelltest dich arg:
was ich dir bot,
erbost auch, nahmst du doch immer.

as for my life, why should I yield it?

MIME
(angrily)
That's not what I said!
You have heard me all wrong!
(He produces his flask, and takes evident pains to be convincing.)
After your fighting
I know you're tired;
after such toil you are hot;
let me refresh you
with cooling drink;
Mime knew what you'd need.
While your sword you were forging.
I made some broth;
drink but a drop,
and then I will seize your sword
and gain the gold as well!
(He sniggers.)

SIEGFRIED
So you'd seize my sword
and all that it's won me;
ring and Tarnhelm, you'd take them?

MIME
(vehemently)
Why can't you hear what I say!
Tell me, am I not clear?
I'm being so careful,
choosing my words,
and hiding my meaning,
trying to deceive you;
and the foolish booby
misinterprets my words.
Open your ears now,
and attend to me!
Listen what Mime plans!
(again very affectionately, with an evident effort to make himself understood)
Take this and drink it to cool you!
My drinks pleased you before:
when you were thirsty,
tired or hot,
I brought you drink;
you grumbled, but you still drank it.

SIEGFRIED
(ohne eine Miene zu verziehen)
Einen guten Trank
hätt' ich gern:
wie hast du diesen gebraut?

MIME
(lustig scherzend, als schildere er ihm einen angenehm berauschten Zustant, den ihm der Saft bereiten soll)
Hei! So trink nur,
trau meiner Kunst!
In Nacht und Nebel
sinken die Sinne dir bald:
ohne Wach' und Wissen
stracks streckst du die Glieder.
Liegst du nun da,
leicht könnt' ich
die Beute nehmen und bergen:
doch erwachtest du je,
nirgends wär' ich
sicher vor dir,
hätt' ich selbst auch den Ring.
Drum mit dem Schwert,
das so scharf du schufst,
(mit einer Gebärde ausgelassener Lustigkeit)
hau ich dem Kind
den Kopf erst ab:
dann hab ich mir Ruh' und auch den [Ring!
(Er kichert wieder.)

SIEGFRIED
Im Schlafe willst du mich morden?

MIME
(wütend ärgerlich)
Was möcht ich? Sagt' ich denn das?
(Er bemüht sich, den zärtlichsten Ton anzunehmen.)
Ich will dem Kind
(mit sorglichster Deutlichkeit)
nur den Kopf abhaun!
(mit dem Ausdruck herzlicher Besorgtheit für Siegfrieds Gesundheit)
Denn haßte ich dich
auch nicht so sehr,
und hätt' ich des Schimpfs
und der schändlichen Mühe
auch nicht so viel zu rächen:

SIEGFRIED
(without altering his expression)
A refreshing drink
I should like:
but say how this one was brewed.

MIME
(gaily joking, as if describing how pleasant and merry the brew will make him)
Hi! Just drink it;
trust to my skill!
And you'll be seized
by sleep that you cannot resist:
you will sink unconscious,
drugged, drowsy, and helpless.
While you're asleep
I'll easily
steal the ring and the Tarnhelm.
But if once you should wake
then from you
I'd never be safe,
even as lord of the ring.
So with the sword
that you made so sharp,
(with a gesture of uncontrolled merriment)
I will just chop
your head right off;
then I will be safe. I'll have the ring!
(He chuckles again.)

SIEGFRIED
While I'm sleeping you plan to kill me?

MIME
(in a furious rage)
To kill you? Did I say that?
(He makes an effort to assume his most charming tone of voice.)
I merely plan
(with meticulous clarity)
to chop your head right off!
(with an expression of heartfelt anxiety for Siegfried's well-being)
Not only because
I hate you so;
not only because
I have suffered scorn and shame,
and long to take my vengeance;

(sanft)
aus dem Wege dich zu räumen,
darf ich doch nicht rasten:
Wie käm' ich sonst anders zur Beute,
da Alberich auch nach ihr lugt?
(Er gießt den Saft in das Trinkhorn und führt dieses Siegfried mit aufdringlicher Gebärde zu.)
Nun, mein Wälsung,
Wolfssohn du!
Sauf und würg dich zu Tod:
nie tust du mehr 'nen Schluck!
(Siegfried holt mit dem Schwert aus. Er führt, wie in einer Anwandlung heftigen Ekels, einen jähen Streich nach Mime; dieser stürzt sogleich tot zu Boden.)

SIEGFRIED
Schmeck du mein Schwert,
ekliger Schwätzer!
(Alberichs Stimme hohnlachend aus dem Geklüfte. Auf den am Boden Liegenden blickend hängt Siegfried ruhig sein Schwert wieder ein.)
Neides Zoll
zahlt Notung:
dazu durft' ich ihn schmieden.
(Er rafft Mimes Leichnam auf, trägt ihn auf die Anhöhe vor den Eingang der Höhle und wirft ihn dort hinein.)
In der Höhle hier
lieg auf dem Hort!
Mit zäher List
erzieltest du ihn:
jetzt magst du des wonnigen walten!
Einen guten Wächter
geb ich dir auch,
daß er vor Dieben dich deckt.
(Er wälzt mit großer Anstrengung den Leichnam des Wurmes vor den Eingang der Höhle, so daß er diesen ganz damit verstopft.)
Da lieg auch du,
dunkler Wurm!
Den gleißenden Hort
hüte zugleich
mit dem beuterührigen Feind:
so fandet beide ihr nun Ruh'!
(Er blickt eine Weile sinnend in die Höhle hinab und wendet sich dann langsam, wie ermüdet, in den Vordergrund. Es ist Mittag. Er führt sich die Hand über die Stirn.)

(gently)
but because I must destroy you.
If I fail to kill you,
how can I be sure of my treasure,
since Alberich covets it too?
(He pours the brew into the drinking-horn and offers it to Siegfried with pressing gestures.)
Now, my Wälsung!
Wolf's son you!
Drink and choke to death!
You'll never drink again!
(Siegfried raises his sword, and as if seized by violent loathing aims a swift blow at Mime, who immediately falls down dead.)

SIEGFRIED
Taste then my sword,
horrible babbler!
(Alberich's mocking laughter is heard from the cleft. Siegfried quietly puts his sword back again, gazing at the fallen body.)
Hatred's paid
by Notung:
that's why I needed to forge it.
(He picks up Mime's body, carries it to the knoll at the entrance to the cave, and throws it down inside.)
In the cavern there,
lie with the hoard!
You schemed so long
and strove for that gold;
so now take your joy in that treasure!
Let me place this guardian
there by your side,
so from all thieves you'll be safe.
(With a great effort he drags the body of the dragon to the entrance to the cave, blocking it completely.)
You lie there too,
mighty dragon!
The glittering gold
you now can share
with your foe who longed for its gleam;
and so you both have found your rest!
(He gazes thoughtfully down into the cave for a while, and then returns slowly to the foreground, as if tired. It is noon. He passes his hand over his brow.)

Heiß ward mir
von der harten Last!
Brausend jagt
mein brünst'ges Blut;
die Hand brennt mir am Haupt.
Hoch steht schon die Sonne:
aus lichtem Blau
blickt ihr Aug'
auf den Scheitel steil mir herab.
Linde Kühlung
erkies ich unter der Linde!
(Er streckt sich unter der Linde aus und blickt wieder durch die Zweige hinauf.)
Noch einmal, liebes Vöglein,
da wir so lang
lästig gestört,
lauscht' ich gerne deinem Sange:
auf dem Zweige seh ich
wohlig dich wiegen;
zwitschernd umschwirren
dich Brüder und Schwestern,
umschweben dich lustig und lieb!
Doch ich—bin so allein,
hab nicht Brüder noch Schwestern:
meine Mutter schwand,
mein Vater fiel:
nie sah sie der Sohn!
Mein einziger Gesell
war ein garstiger Zwerg;
Güte zwang
uns nie zu Liebe;
listige Schlingen
warf mir der Schlaue;
nun mußt' ich ihn gar erschlagen!
(Er blickt schmerzlich bewegt wieder nach den Zweigen auf.)
Freundliches Vöglein,
dich frage ich nun:
gönntest du mir
wohl ein gut Gesell?
Willst du mir das Rechte raten?
Ich lockte so oft
und erlost' es mir nie:
Du, mein Trauter,
träfst es wohl besser,
so recht ja rietest du schon.
Nun sing! Ich lausche dem Sang.

I'm warm now
from my heavy task!
Fever seems
to fire my blood.
This hand burns on my brow.
High stands the sun above me;
his brilliant eye
blazes down
from the blue and beats on my head.
Here it's cooler;
I'll rest under these branches!
(He lies down under the lime-tree and again looks up into the branches.)
You're back then, dearest woodbird,
not flown away
after the fight?
Let me hear again your singing!
On a branch I see you
swaying and swinging;
chirping and chirruping
brothers and sisters
surround you with laughter and love!
But I am quite alone,
have no brothers nor sisters;
and my mother died,
my father fell,
unknown to their son!
One comrade was mine,
a detestable dwarf.
Love was never known
between us;
cunning and sly,
he wanted to catch me;
so at last I was forced to kill him!
(Sadly, he looks up again to the branches.)
Dear little woodbird,
can you be my guide?
Can you tell me
where I'll find a friend?
You must know some way to help me.
So often I've called
and yet no-one has come.
You, my woodbird,
you might do better,
for you've advised me so well.
Now sing! I'm listening for your song.

STIMME DES WALDVOGELS
Hei! Siegfried erschlug
nun den schlimmen Zwerg!
Jetzt wüßt' ich ihm noch
das herrlichste Weib:
Auf hohem Felsen sie schläft,
Feuer umbrennt ihren Saal:
Durschschritt' er die Brunst,
weckt' er die Braut,
Brünnhilde wäre dann sein!

VOICE OF THE WOODBIRD
Hi! Siegfried is free
from the evil dwarf!
Next he must awake
his glorious bride:
high on a mountain she sleeps,
guarded by threatening flames.
Who goes through the fire,
wakens the bride.
Brünnhilde then shall be his!

SIEGFRIED
(fährt mit jäher Heftigkeit vom Sitze auf.)
O holder Sang!
Süßester Hauch!
Wie brennt sein Sinn
mir sehrend die Brust!
Wie zückt er heftig
zündend mein Herz!
Was jagt mir so jach
durch Herz und Sinne?
Sag es mir, süßer Freund!

SIEGFRIED
(leaps up impetuously from his sitting position.)
O joyful song!
Sweet, happy strain!
Your glorious words
strike fire in my breast;
like flames they burn me,
kindle my heart!
What new thought inspires
my heart and senses?
Tell me, my dear, sweet friend!

STIMME DES WALDVOGELS
Lustig im Leid
sing ich von Liebe;
wonnig aus Weh
web ich mein Lied:
nur Sehnende kennen den Sinn!

VOICE OF THE WOODBIRD
Gaily in grief,
I sing of love;
joyful in woe,
I weave my song;
and lovers can tell what it means.

SIEGFRIED
Fort jagt mich's
jauchzend von hinnen,
fort aus dem Wald auf den Fels!
Noch einmal sage mir,
holder Sänger:
werd ich das Feuer durchbrechen?
Kann ich erwecken die Braut?

SIEGFRIED
Joy fills me;
shouting with gladness,
forth I shall go to that rock!
But one thing more tell me,
dearest woodbird:
say, can I pass through the fire?
Can I awaken the bride?

STIMME DES WALDVOGELS
Die Braut gewinnt,
Brünnhild erweckt
ein Feiger nie:
nur wer das Fürchten nicht kennt!

VOICE OF THE WOODBIRD
Who wakens the maid,
Brünnhild the bride,
no coward can be:
one unacquainted with fear!

SIEGFRIED
(lacht auf vor Entzücken.)
Der dumme Knab',

SIEGFRIED
(laughs with delight.)
A foolish boy,

der das Fürchten nicht kennt,
mein Vöglein, der bin ja ich!
Noch heute gab ich
vergebens mir Müh',
das Fürchten von Fafner zu lernen:
nun brenn ich vor Lust,
es von Brünnhild zu wissen!
Wie find ich zum Felsen den Weg?
(Der Vogel flattert auf, kreist über Siegfried und fliegt ihm zögernd voran.)
So wird mir der Weg gewiesen:
wohin du flatterst,
folg ich dir nach!
(Er läuft dem Vogel, der ihn neckend eine Zeitlang nach verschiedenen Richtungen hinleitet, nach und folgt ihm endlich, als dieser mit einer bestimmten Wendung nach dem Hintergrunde davonfliegt. Der Vorhang fällt.)

unacquainted with fear,
dear woodbird, why, that's me!
Today in vain
I attempted to learn—
I hoped that the dragon could teach me.
Now joy fills my heart,
since from Brünnhild I'll learn it!
What way must I take to the rock?
(The bird flutters out, circles over Siegfried, and then flies off hesitatingly.)
Fluttering overhead, you guide me;
and where you flutter,
there I shall go!
(He pursues the bird, which for a while teasingly leads him in different directions: then it takes a definite course towards the background and flies away. Siegfried follows. The curtain falls.)

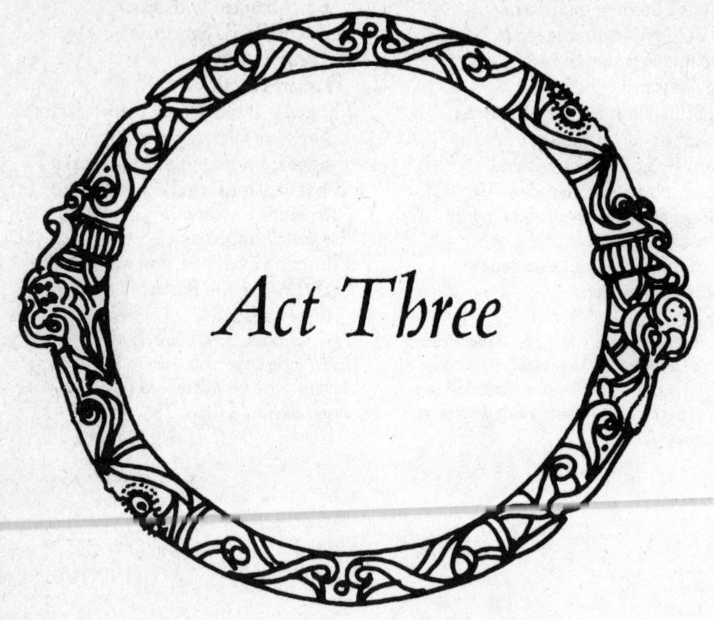

Dritter Aufzug

Wilde Gegend am Fuße eines Felsenberges

welcher nach links hinten steil aufsteigt. Nacht, Sturm und Wetter, Blitz und heftiger Donner, der schließlich nachläßt, während Blitze noch längere Zeit die Wolken durchkreuzen.

Erste Szene

WANDERER

(schreitet auf ein Höhlentor in einem Felsen des Vordergrundes zu und nimmt dort, auf seinen Speer gestützt, eine Stellung ein, während er das Folgende dem Eingange der Höhle zuruft.)

Wache, Wala!
Wala, erwach!
Aus langem Schlaf
weck ich dich Schlummernde auf.
Ich rufe dich auf:

Act Three

A Wild Place at the Foot of a Rocky Mountain

which rises steeply at the left towards the back. Night; storm, lightning and violent thunder; the latter ceases after a while; the lightning continuing to flash through the clouds.

Scene One

WANDERER

(strides resolutely to a vault-like cavernous opening in a rock in the foreground and stands there, leaning on his spear, while he calls the following towards the mouth of the cave.)

Waken, Wala!
Wala! Awake!
From lasting sleep
rise and appear at my call.
I call you again:

Herauf! Herauf!
Aus nebliger Gruft,
aus nächtigem Grunde herauf!
Erda! Erda!
Ewiges Weib!
Aus heimischer Tiefe
tauche zur Höh'!
Dein Wecklied sing ich,
daß du erwachest;
aus sinnendem Schlafe
weck ich dich auf.
Allwissende!
Urweltweise!
Erda! Erda!
Ewiges Weib!
Wache, erwache,
du Wala! Erwache!
(Die Höhlengruft erdämmert. Bläulicher Lichtschein: von ihm beleuchtet steigt Erda allmählich aus der Tiefe auf. Sie erscheint wie von Reif bedeckt; Haar und Gewand werfen einen glitzernden Schimmer von sich.)

ERDA
Stark ruft das Lied;
kräftig reizt der Zauber.
Ich bin erwacht
aus wissendem Schlaf.
Wer scheucht den Schlummer mir?

WANDERER
Der Weckrufer bin ich
und Weisen üb ich,
daß weithin wache,
was fester Schlaf verschließt.
Die Welt durchzog ich,
wanderte viel,
Kunde zu werben,
urweisen Rat zu gewinnen.
Kundiger gibt es
keine als dich;
bekannt ist dir,
was die Tiefe birgt,
was Berg und Tal,
Luft und Wasser durchwebt.
Wo Wesen sind,
wehet dein Atem;

Arise! Arise!
From earth's hidden caves,
emprisoned in darkness, arise!
Erda! Erda!
Woman all-wise!
From silence and darkness
rise to the world!
With spells I rouse you;
rise up and answer.
Your slumbering wisdom
I would awake.
All-knowing one!
Wisdom's guardian!
Erda! Erda!
Woman all-wise!
Waken, awaken,
O Wala! Awaken!
(The cavern begins to glow with a bluish light, in which Erda is seen rising very slowly from the depths. She appears to be covered by hoar-frost: her hair and garments give out a glimmering shine.)

ERDA
Strong is your call;
mighty spells have roused me.
From wisdom's dreams,
I rise at your call.
Who drives my slumber hence?

WANDERER
The Wanderer wakes you;
I need your wisdom;
my spells have called you
from caverns far below.
On earth I have wandered,
far I have roamed;
I searched for wisdom,
strove day and night to achieve it.
No one on earth
is wiser than you;
you know what's hid
in the caves of night,
what hill and dale,
air and water do hold.
Where life is found,
Erda is stirring;

wo Hirne sinnen,
haftet dein Sinn:
alles, sagt man,
sei dir bekannt.
Daß ich nun Kunde gewänne,
weck ich dich aus dem Schlaf!

ERDA
Mein Schlaf ist Träumen,
mein Träumen Sinnen,
mein Sinnen Walten des Wissens.
Doch wenn ich schlafe,
wachen Nornen:
sie weben das Seil
und spinnen fromm, was ich weiß.
Was fragst du nicht die Nornen?

WANDERER
Im Zwange der Welt
weben die Nornen:
sie können nichts wenden noch wandeln.
Doch deiner Weisheit
dankt' ich den Rat wohl,
wie zu hemmen ein rollendes Rad?

ERDA
Männertaten
umdämmern mir den Mut:
mich Wissende selbst
bezwang ein Waltender einst.
Ein Wunschmädchen
gebar ich Wotan:
der Helden Wal
hieß für sich er sie küren.
Kühn ist sie
und weise auch:
Was weckst du mich
und fragst um Kunde
nicht Erdas und Wotans Kind?

WANDERER
Die Walküre meinst du,
Brünnhild, die Maid?
Sie trotzte dem Stürmebezwinger:
wo er am stärksten selbst sich bezwang.
Was den Lenker der Schlacht
zu tun verlangte,

where brains are brooding,
you stir their thoughts.
All things, all things,
all you must know.
Seeking wisdom and counsel,
I have waked you from sleep!

ERDA
My sleep is dreaming;
my dreaming, brooding.
my brooding brings all my wisdom.
But while I sleep
the Norns are waking,
and winding their cord,
and weaving all that I know:
the Norns can give your answer.

WANDERER
They weave for the world,
spin what you tell them,
but cannot change that world with their [weaving.
But you are wiser;
you can advise me
if the swift-turning wheel can be stopped.

ERDA
Deeds of men
have beclouded all my thoughts;
my wisdom itself
once felt a conqueror's force.
A brave daughter
I bore to Wotan;
at his command
she chose heroes for Walhall.
She is valiant
and wise as well:
so why wake me?
You will learn your answer
from Erda's and Wotan's child.

WANDERER
That Valkyrie daughter,
Brünnhild the maid.
She disobeyed the lord of the tempest
when he'd controlled the storm in his [breast:
When his son was in need
he longed to help him,

doch dem er wehrte
zuwider sich selbst,
allzu vertraut
wagte die Trotzige
das für sich zu vollbringen,
Brünnhild in brennender Schlacht.
Streitvater
strafte die Maid:
in ihr Auge drückte er Schlaf;
auf dem Felsen schläft sie fest.
Erwachen wird
die Weihliche nur,
um einen Mann zu minnen als Weib.
Frommten mir Fragen an sie?

ERDA
(im Sinnen versunken, beginnt erst nach längerem Schweigen.)
Wirr wird mir,
seit ich erwacht:
wild und kraus
kreist die Welt!
Die Walküre,
der Wala Kind,
büßt' in Banden des Schlafs,
als die wissende Mutter schlief?
Der den Trotz lehrte,
straft den Trotz?
Der die Tat entzündet,
zürnt um die Tat?
Der die Rechte wahrt,
der die Eide hütet,
wehret dem Recht,
herrscht durch Meineid?
Laß mich wieder hinab!
Schlaf verschließe mein Wissen!

WANDERER
Dich, Mutter, laß ich nicht ziehn,
da des Zaubers mächtig ich bin.
Urwissend
stachest du einst
der Sorge Stachel
in Wotans wagendes Herz:
mit Furcht vor schmachvoll
feindlichem Ende
füllt' ihn dein Wissen,

yet he renounced him
and doomed him to death.
She knew his will,
yet she defied him
and dared to break his commandment—
Brünnhild herself in her pride.
Wotan
then dealt with the maid;
and he closed her eyelids in sleep;
on that rock asleep she lies.
That holy maid
can be wakened alone,
roused by some man who makes her his bride.
What can I learn from the maid?

ERDA
(is lost in dreams; she begins again after a long silence.)
My waking
leaves me confused:
wild and strange
seems the world.
The Valkyrie,
the Wala's child,
lay in fetters of sleep,
while her all-knowing mother slept?
How can pride's teacher
punish pride?
he who urged the doing,
punish the deed?
he who rules by right,
to whom truth is sacred,
scorn what is right,
rule by falsehood?
I'll return to the dark,
seal in slumber my wisdom!

WANDERER
O mother, you may not leave:
You are bound by my mighty power.
All-wise one,
you drove a thorn
of cares and sorrow
in Wotan's fearless heart:
with fear of ruin,
shameful downfall
you filled his spirit,

daß Bangen band seinen Mut.
  Bist du der Welt
  weisestes Weib,
  sage mir nun:
wie besiegt die Sorge der Gott?

ERDA
  Du bist—nicht,
  was du dich nennst!
Was kamst du, störrischer Wilder,
zu stören der Wala Schlaf?

WANDERER
  Du bist—nicht,
  was du dich wähnst!
  Urmütter-Weisheit
  geht zu Ende:
  dein Wissen verweht
  vor meinem Willen.
Weißt du, was Wotan will?
(langes Schweigen)
  Dir Unweisen
  ruf ich ins Ohr,
daß sorglos ewig du nun schläfst!
  Um der Götter Ende
  grämt mich die Angst nicht,
seit mein Wunsch es will!
Was in des Zwiespalts wildem Schmerze
verzweifelnd einst ich beschloß,
  froh und freudig
führe frei ich nun aus.
Weiht' ich in wütendem Ekel
des Niblungen Neid schon die Welt,
  dem herrlichsten Wälsung
weis ich mein Erbe nun an.
  Der von mir erkoren,
  doch nie mich gekannt,
  ein kühnester Knabe,
  bar meines Rates,
errang des Niblungen Ring.
  Liebesfroh,
  ledig des Neides,
  erlahmt an dem Edlen
  Alberichs Fluch;
denn fremd bleibt ihm die Furcht.
  Die du mir gebarst,
  Brünnhild,

by words of warning and doom.
  If you are the world's
  wisest of women,
  say to me now:
how a god can master his care?

ERDA
  You are not
  what you declare!
Why come here, stubborn and wild one,
to trouble the Wala's sleep?

WANDERER
  You are not
  what you have dreamed.
  Wisdom of ages
  finds its ending.
  Your wisdom grows weak
  before my wishes.
Know you what Wotan wills?
(long silence)
  You unwise one,
  learn what I will,
then carefree you may sleep in peace!
  That the gods may die soon
  gives me no anguish;
I have willed that end!
What in an hour of fiercest anguish
despairing once I resolved
  freely and gladly
I shall now bring to pass.
Once I declared in my loathing
the Niblung might claim all the world;
  today to the Wälsung
I have bequeathed my realm.
  One who has never known me,
  though chosen by me,
  a youth of dauntless daring,
  unhelped by Wotan,
has gained the Nibelung's ring.
  Free from hate,
  joyful and loving,
  that youth is not harmed
  by Alberich's curse,
for he knows naught of fear.
  She whom you once bore,
  Brünnhild,

weckt sich hold der Held:
   wachend wirkt
   dein wissendes Kind
erlösende Weltentat.
   Drum schlafe nun du,
   schließe dein Auge;
träumend erschau mein Ende!
   Was jene auch wirken,
   dem ewig Jungen
weicht in Wonne der Gott.
   Hinab denn, Erda!
   Urmütterfurcht!
   Ursorge!
   Hinab! Hinab
   zu ew'gem Schlaf!
(Nachdem Erda bereits die Augen geschlossen und allmählich tiefer gesunken ist, verschwindet sie jetzt gänzlich; auch die Höhle ist wiederum durchaus verfinstert. Monddämmerung erhellt die Bühne; der Sturm hat aufgehört.)

wakes to that hero's kiss.
   Then your wisdom's
   child will achieve
that deed that will free our world.
   So back to your dreams;
   dream on in darkness;
dream of the gods' destruction.
   Whatever may happen,
   the god will gladly
yield his rule to the young!
   Return then, Erda!
   Mother of dread!
   World-sorrow!
   Return! Return
   to endless sleep!
(Erda has already closed her eyes and begun to descend gradually. She now disappears entirely; the cavernous opening too has become quite dark. The moon lights the scene. The storm has ceased.)

Zweite Szene

Der Wanderer ist dicht an die Höhle getreten und lehnt sich dann mit dem Rücken an das Gestein derselben, das Gesicht der Szene zugewandt.

WANDERER
Dort seh ich Siegfried nahn.
(Er verbleibt in seiner Stellung an der Höhle. Siegfrieds Waldvogel flattert dem Vordergrunde zu. Plötzlich hält der Vogel in seiner Richtung ein, flattert ängstlich hin und her und verschwindet hastig dem Hintergrunde zu.)

SIEGFRIED
(tritt rechts im Vordergrunde auf und hält an.)
Mein Vöglein schwebte mir fort!
   Mit flatterndem Flug
   und süßem Sang
wies es mich wonnig des Wegs:

Scene Two

The Wanderer has advanced close to the cavern: he leans back against the rock, facing the stage.

WANDERER
I see that Siegfried is near.
(He remains in his position by the cave. Siegfried's woodbird flutters towards the foreground, then suddenly stops, flutters hither and thither as if alarmed, and disappears hastily at the back.)

SIEGFRIED
(enters in the foreground, right, and pauses.)
My woodbird flew from my sight.
   With fluttering wings,
   and sweetest songs,
gaily he showed me my path;

nun schwand es fern mir davon!
  Am besten find ich mir
  selbst nun den Berg.
Wohin mein Führer mich wies,
dahin wandr' ich jetzt fort.
(Er schreitet weiter nach hinten.)

WANDERER
  Wohin, Knabe,
  heißt dich dein Weg?

SIEGFRIED
(hält an und wendet sich um.)
  Da redet's ja;
wohl rät das mir den Weg.
(Er tritt dem Wanderer näher.)
  Einen Felsen such ich,
von Feuer ist der umwabert:
  Dort schläft ein Weib,
  das ich wecken will.

WANDERER
  Wer sagt' es dir,
  den Fels zu suchen?
Wer, nach der Frau dich zu sehnen?

SIEGFRIED
  Mich wies ein singend
  Waldvöglein,
das gab mir gute Kunde.

WANDERER
Ein Vöglein schwatzt wohl manches;
kein Mensch doch kann's verstehn.
  Wie mochtest du Sinn
  dem Sang entnehmen?

SIEGFRIED
  Das wirkte das Blut
  eines wilden Wurms,
der mir vor Neidhöhl erblaßte.
  Kaum netzt' es zündend
  die Zunge mir,
da verstand ich der Vöglein Gestimm'.

WANDERER
  Erschlugst den Riesen du,

but now he's fluttered away!
  So I'll discover
  the rock for myself.
The path my bird pointed out,
that path I must pursue.
(He goes further towards the back.)

WANDERER
  Young man, hear me;
  where are you going?

SIEGFRIED
(pauses and turns round.)
  Who speaks to me?
Can he show me my path?
(He comes closer to the Wanderer.)
  I must find a mountain;
by blazing fire it's surrounded:
  there sleeps a maid:
  I must waken her!

WANDERER
  Who told you then
  to seek this mountain?
Who said this maid would be found there?

SIEGFRIED
  I heard a lovely
  woodbird sing:
it told me of the mountain.

WANDERER
A woodbird chirps as it pleases;
but men don't understand;
  so how did you know
  what it was singing?

SIEGFRIED
  I tasted a drop
  of a dragon's blood
who fell at Neidhöhl before me;
  and when I'd tasted
  that fiery blood,
then the birdsong I heard clear as speech.

WANDERER
  To fight so fierce a foe,

wer reizte dich,
den starken Wurm zu bestehn?

SIEGFRIED
Mich führte Mime,
ein falscher Zwerg;
das Fürchten wollt' er mich lehren.
Zum Schwertstreich aber,
der ihn erschlug,
reizte der Wurm mich selbst,
seinen Rachen riß er mir auf.

WANDERER
Wer schuf das Schwert
so scharf und hart,
daß der stärkste Feind ihm fiel?

SIEGFRIED
Das schweißt' ich mir selbst,
da 's der Schmied nicht konnte:
schwertlos noch wär' ich wohl sonst.

WANDERER
Doch, wer schuf
die starken Stücken,
daraus das Schwert du dir geschweißt?

SIEGFRIED
Was weiß ich davon?
Ich weiß allein,
daß die Stücken mir nichts nützten,
schuf ich das Schwert mir nicht neu.

WANDERER
(bricht in ein freudig gemütliches Lachen aus.)
Das—mein ich wohl auch!
(Er betrachtet Siegfried wohlgefällig.)

SIEGFRIED
(verwundert)
Was lachst du mich aus?
Alter Frager!
Hör einmal auf:
laß mich nicht länger hier schwatzen!
Kannst du den Weg
mir weisen, so rede:
vermagst du's nicht,

who urged you on—
if you have really killed the dragon?

SIEGFRIED
My guide was Mime,
an evil dwarf,
when fear he wanted to teach me;
and then the dragon
urged me himself,
dared me to use my sword,
when he opened threatening jaws.

WANDERER
Who forged your sword
so sharp and true,
that it slew so fierce a foe?

SIEGFRIED
I forged it myself,
when the smith was beaten:
swordless else I should be.

WANDERER
But who made
the mighty fragments,
from which the sword could then be [forged?

SIEGFRIED
Ha! How can I tell?
I only knew
that the broken sword was useless,
till I had forged it myself.

WANDERER
(breaks into a happy, good-humoured laugh.)
That's certainly true!
(He looks at Siegfried with approval.)

SIEGFRIED
(surprised)
You're laughing at me
with your questions!
Mock me no more,
keeping me here with your chatter.
Old man, if you
can help me, then do so:
and if you can't,

so halte dein Maul!

WANDERER
Geduld, du Knabe!
Dünk ich dich alt,
so sollst du Achtung mir bieten.

SIEGFRIED
Das wär' nicht übel!
Solang ich lebe,
stand mir ein Alter
stets im Wege;
den hab ich nun fortgefegt.
Stemmst du dort länger
steif dich mir entgegen—
sieh dich vor, sag ich,
daß du wie Mime nicht fährst!
(Er tritt noch näher an den Wanderer heran.)
Wie siehst du denn aus?
Was hast du gar
für 'nen großen Hut?
Warum hängt er dir so ins Gesicht?

WANDERER
(immer ohne seine Stellung zu verlassen)
Das ist so des Wand'rers Weise,
wenn dem Wind entgegen er geht.

SIEGFRIED
(immer näher ihn betrachtend)
Doch darunter fehlt dir ein Auge:
Das schlug dir einer
gewiß schon aus,
dem du zu trotzig
den Weg vertratst?
Mach dich jetzt fort,
sonst könntest du leicht
das andere auch noch verlieren.

WANDERER
Ich seh, mein Sohn,
wo du nichts weißt,
da weißt du dir leicht zu helfen.
Mit dem Auge,
das als andres mir fehlt,
erblickst du selber das eine,
das mir zum Sehen verblieb.

then hold your tongue!

WANDERER
Young man, be patient!
If I seem old,
then you should honour the aged.

SIEGFRIED
Honour the aged!
When all my life
there stood in my path
an aged fellow;
now I have swept him away.
If you stay longer,
trying to obstruct me,
have a care, old one,
or else, like Mime you'll fare!
(He goes up closer to the Wanderer.)
How strange you look!
Why do you wear
such a great big hat?
Why have you pulled it down over your [face?

WANDERER
(still without changing his position)
That's how the Wanderer wears it,
when against the wind he must go!

SIEGFRIED
(observes him more closely.)
But an eye underneath it you're lacking?
No doubt some stranger
once struck it out
when you decided
to bar his way?
Out of my way,
or else you may lose
the other eye that is left you.

WANDERER
I see, my son,
one thing you know—
to get your way as you want it.
Yet be careful,
for with eyes quite as blind
as that eye I've lost, you are gazing
on the eye that is left me for sight.

SIEGFRIED
(der sinnend zugehört hat, bricht jetzt unwillkürlich in helles Lachen aus.)
Zum Lachen bist du mir lustig!
Doch hör, nun schwatz ich nicht länger:
geschwind, zeig mir den Weg,
deines Weges ziehe dann du;
  zu nichts andrem
  acht ich dich nütz:
drum sprich, sonst spreng ich dich fort!

WANDERER
(weich)
  Kenntest du mich,
  kühner Sproß,
den Schimpf spartest du mir!
  Dir so vertraut,
trifft mich schmerzlich dein Dräuen.
  Liebt' ich von je
  deine lichte Art,
  Grauen auch zeugt' ihr
  mein zürnender Grimm.
  Dem ich so hold bin,
  Allzuhehrer,
heut nicht wecke mir Neid:
er vernichtete dich und mich!

SIEGFRIED
  Bleibst du mir stumm,
  störrischer Wicht?
  Weich von der Stelle,
  denn dorthin, ich weiß,
führt es zur schlafenden Frau.
  So wies es mein Vöglein,
das hier erst flüchtig entfloh.
(Es wird schnell wieder ganz finster.)

WANDERER
(in Zorn ausbrechend und in gebieterischer Stellung)
Es floh dir zu seinem Heil!
  Den Herrn der Raben
  erriet es hier:
weh ihm, holen sie's ein!
  Den Weg, den es zeigte,
  sollst du nicht ziehn!

SIEGFRIED
(who has listened thoughtfully, now involuntarily bursts out laughing.)
At least you're good for a laugh, then!
But hear, I'm getting impatient;
at once, show me my path,
then your own way find for yourself.
  What use
  is a foolish old man?
So speak, or I'll push you aside!

WANDERER
(softly)
  Child, if you knew
  who I am,
you'd then spare me your scorn!
  Sad from one so dear
sounds such scornful defiance.
  Dear to my heart
  is your glorious race—
  though I was harsh
  and they shrank from my rage.
  You, whom I love so,
  youthful hero!
do not waken that rage;
it would ruin both you and me!

SIEGFRIED
  Still no reply,
  stubborn old fool!
  Out of my way then,
  for that path, I know,
leads to the slumbering maid.
  I learnt from the woodbird
who now has fluttered away.
(It quickly becomes quite dark again.)

WANDERER
(breaking out in anger, imperiously)

It left you to save its life!
  The ravens' ruler
  it knew was here.
Ill fate follow its flight!
  The path that it showed you
  you shall not tread!

SIEGFRIED
(tritt mit Verwunderung in trotziger Stellung zurück.)
Hoho, du Verbieter!
Wer bist du denn,
daß du mir wehren willst?

WANDERER
Fürchte des Felsens Hüter!
Verschlossen hält
meine Macht die schlafende Maid:
wer sie erweckte,
wer sie gewänne,
machtlos macht' er mich ewig!
Ein Feuermeer
umflutet die Frau,
glühende Lohe
umleckt den Fels:
wer die Braut begehrt,
dem brennt entgegen die Brunst.
(Er winkt mit dem Speere nach der Felsenhöhe.)
Blick nach der Höh'!
Erlugst du das Licht?
Es wächst der Schein,
es schwillt die Glut;
sengende Wolken,
wabernde Lohe
wälzen sich brennend
und prasselnd herab:
ein Lichtmeer
umleuchtet dein Haupt:
(Mit wachsender Helle zeigt sich von der Höhe des Felsens her ein wabernder Feuerschein.)
Bald frißt und zehrt dich
zündendes Feuer.
Zurück denn, rasendes Kind!

SIEGFRIED
Zurück, du Prahler, mit dir!
Dort, wo die Brünste brennen,
zu Brünnhilde muß ich dahin!
(Er schreitet weiter, der Wanderer stellt sich ihm entgegen.)

WANDERER
Fürchtest das Feuer du nicht,
(den Speer vorhaltend)
so sperre mein Speer dir den Weg!

SIEGFRIED
(astonished, steps back in a defiant attitude.)
Ho! Ho! So you'd stop me!
Who are you then
to say I can't go on?

WANDERER
I am the rock's defender!
And mine the spell
that enfolds the slumbering maid.
He who can wake her,
he who can win her,
makes me powerless for ever!
A sea of flame
now circles the maid,
burning and blazing
protects the rock.
He who seeks the bride
must brave that barrier of flame.
(He points with his spear to the rocky heights.)
Look, on the heights!
Can you see that light?
The splendour grows,
the flames leap high;
fire clouds are rolling,
lightning is flashing,
raging and roaring
and coming this way.
A light-flood
now shines round your head.
(On the summit, a flickering fire becomes more and more clearly visible.)
And soon that fire
will seize and destroy you.
Stand back, then, foolhardy boy!

SIEGFRIED
Stand back, old boaster, yourself!
There, where the flames are burning,
to Brünnhilde now I shall go!
(He advances; the Wanderer bars his way.)

WANDERER
If you've no fear of the fire,
(stretching out his spear)
the shaft of my spear bars your way!

Noch hält meine Hand
der Herrschaft Haft:
das Schwert, das du schwingst,
zerschlug einst dieser Schaft:
noch einmal denn
zerspring es am ew'gen Speer!
(Er streckt den Speer vor.)

SIEGFRIED
(das Schwert ziehend)
Meines Vaters Feind!
Find ich dich hier?
Herrlich zur Rache
geriet mir das!
Schwing deinen Speer:
in Stücken spalt' ihn mein Schwert!
(Er haut dem Wanderer mit einem Schlage den Speer in zwei Stücken; ein Blitzstrahl fährt daraus nach der Felsenhöhe zu, wo von nun an der bisher matte Schein in immer helleren Feuer-flammen zu lodern beginnt. Starker Donner, der schnell sich abschwächt, begleitet den Schlag. Die Speerstücke rollen zu des Wanderers Füßen. Er rafft sie ruhig auf.)

WANDERER
(zurückweichend)
Zieh hin! Ich kann dich nicht halten!
(Er verschwindet plötzlich in völliger Finsternis.)

SIEGFRIED
Mit zerfochtner Waffe
floh mir der Feige?
(Die wachsende Helle der immer tiefer sich senkenden Feuerwolken trifft Siegfrieds Blick.)

Ha! Wonnige Glut!
Leuchtender Glanz!
Strahlend nun offen
steht mir die Straße.
Im Feuer mich baden!
Im Feuer zu finden die Braut!
Hoho! Hahei!
Jetzt lock ich ein liebes Gesell!
(Siegfried setzt sein Horn an und stürzt sich, seine Lockweise blasend, ins wogende Feuer, das sich, von der Höhe herabdringend, nun auch über den Vordergrund ausbreitet. Siegfried, den man

I grasp in my hand
that mighty shaft;
the sword that you bear
was broken by this shaft;
and once again
I'll break it on this my spear!
(He stretches out his spear.)

SIEGFRIED
(drawing his sword)
Then my father's foe
faces me here?
Glorious vengeance
I've found at last!
Stretch out your spear:
and see it break on my sword!
(Siegfried with one blow strikes the Wanderer's spear in two: a flash of lightning darts from it towards the summit, where the flames, glowing dully before, now break out more and more brightly. The blow is accompanied by violent thunder that quickly dies away. The fragments of the spear fall at the Wanderer's feet. He quietly picks them up.)

WANDERER
(falling back)
Pass on! I cannot prevent you!
(He suddenly disappears in complete darkness.)

SIEGFRIED
With his spear in splinters,
he has escaped me!
(Siegfried's attention is caught by the growing brightness of the fire-clouds as they roll down the mountain.)
Ha! Flame of delight!
Glorious blaze!
Shining, my pathway
opens before me.
In fire I shall find her!
Through fire I shall make her mine!
Hoho! Hahi!
My comrade shall wake to my call!
(Siegfried raises his horn to his lips and, playing his call, plunges into the sea of fire, which has swept down from the heights and is spreading over the foreground. Siegfried appears to be going towards

bald nicht mehr erblickt, scheint sich nach der Höhe zu entfernen. Hellstes Leuchten der Flammen. Danach beginnt die Glut zu erbleichen und löst sich allmählich in immer feineres, wie durch die Morgenröte beleuchtetes Gewölk auf.)

the heights; soon he is no longer visible. The flames reach their brightest, and then begin to fade, gradually dissolving into a finer and finer mist, lit as if by the red of the dawn.)

Dritte Szene

Das immer zarter gewordene Gewölk hat sich in einen feinen Nebelschleier von rosiger Färbung aufgelöst und zerteilt sich nun in der Weise, daß der Duft sich gänzlich nach oben verzieht und endlich nur noch den heiteren, blauen Tageshimmel erblicken läßt, während am Saume der nun sichtbar werdenden Felsenhöhe—ganz die gleiche Szene wie im dritten Aufzug der »Walküre«—ein morgenrötlicher Nebelschleier haften bleibt, welcher zugleich an die in der Tiefe noch lodernde Zauberlohe erinnert. Die Anordnung der Szene ist dieselbe wie am Schlusse der »Walküre«: im Vordergrunde, unter der breitästigen Tanne, liegt Brünnhilde in vollständiger glänzender Panzerrüstung, mit dem Helm auf dem Haupte, den langen Schild über sich gedeckt, in tiefem Schlafe.

Scene Three

The clouds, which have become increasingly thin, dissolve into a fine rosy mist, which now divides. The upper part drifts away altogether, revealing at last only the bright blue sky of day, while on the edge of the rocky height, which now becomes visible—exactly the same scene as in Act III of 'The Valkyrie'—there hangs a veil of reddish morning mist, suggesting the magic fire that still rages below. The arrangement of the scene is precisely as at the end of 'The Valkyrie': in the foreground, under the wide-spreading fir tree, lies Brünnhilde in full shining armour, her helmet on her head, and her long shield covering her. She is in a deep sleep.

SIEGFRIED
(gelangt von außen her auf den felsigen Saum der Höhe und zeigt sich dort zuerst nur mit dem Oberleibe: so blickt er lange staunend um sich.)
Selige Öde
auf sonniger Höh'!
(Er steigt vollends herauf und betrachtet, auf einem Felsensteine des hinteren Abhanges stehend, mit Verwunderung die Szene. Er blickt zur Seite in den Tann und schreitet etwas vor.)
Was ruht dort schlummernd
im schattigen Tann?
Ein Roß ist's,
rastend in tiefem Schlaf!
(Langsam näherkommend, hält er verwundert an, als er noch aus einiger Entfernung Brünnhildes Gestalt wahrnimmt.)

SIEGFRIED
(reaches the rocky summit of the cliff from the back. At first only the upper part of his body is visible. He looks around for a while in astonishment.)
Here, in the sunlight,
a haven of calm!
(He climbs right to the top and, standing on a rock at the edge of the precipice at the back, surveys the scene with wonder. He looks into the wood at the side and takes a step or two towards it.)
What lies there sleeping
in the shade of the pines?
A horse there,
resting in deepest sleep!
(Coming forward slowly, he pauses in astonishment as he sees Brünnhilde's form some distance away.)

Was strahlt mir dort entgegen?
Welch glänzendes Stahlgeschmeid?
Blendet mir noch
die Lohe den Blick?
(Er tritt näher hinzu.)
Helle Waffen!
Heb ich sie auf?
(Er hebt den Schild ab und erblickt Brünnhildes Gestalt, während ihr Gesicht jedoch noch zum großen Teil vom Helm verdeckt ist.)
Ha, in Waffen ein Mann!
Wie mahnt mich wonnig sein Bild!
Das hehre Haupt
drückt wohl der Helm?
Leichter würd' ihm,
löst' ich den Schmuck.
(Vorsichtig löst er den Helm und hebt ihn der Schlafenden vom Haupte ab: langes lockiges Haar quillt hervor. Siegfried erschrickt.)
Ach! Wie schön!
(Er bleibt in den Anblick versunken.)
Schimmernde Wolken
säumen in Wellen
den hellen Himmelssee;
leuchtender Sonne
lachendes Bild
strahlt durch das Wogengewölk!
(Er neigt sich tiefer zu der Schlafenden hinab.)
Von schwellendem Atem
schwingt sich die Brust!
Brech ich die engende Brünne?
(Er versucht mit großer Behutsamkeit die Brünne zu lösen.)
Komm, mein Schwert,
schneide das Eisen!
(Er zieht sein Schwert, durchschneidet mit zarter Vorsicht die Panzerringe zu beiden Seiten der ganzen Rüstung und hebt dann die Brünne und die Schienen ab, so daß nun Brünnhilde in einem weichen, weiblichen Gewande vor ihm liegt. Er fährt erschreckt und staunend auf.)
Das ist kein Mann!
(Er starrt mit höchster Aufgeregtheit auf die Schlafende hin.)
Brennender Zauber
zückt mir ins Herz;
feurige Angst
faßt meine Augen:
mir schwankt und schwindelt der Sinn!

What flashes in the sunlight?
What glittering steel is there?
Is it the fire
still dazzling my eyes?
(He comes closer.)
Shining armour?
Let me approach!
(He raises the shield and sees Brünnhilde's form, though her face is still largely concealed by the helmet.)
Ha! in armour, a man.
My heart most strangely is stirred!
His noble head
pressed by the helm?
Shall I loose it,
easing his rest?
(He carefully loosens the helmet and removes it from the sleeper; long curling hair falls down. Siegfried starts.)
Ah! How fair!
(He is rapt in the sight.)
Shimmering clouds
encircle in splendour
a holy, heavenly sea;
glorious sunlight
streams from his face,
shines through the clouds all around!
(He bends lower towards the sleeper.)
The weight of the armour
bears on his breast!
Shall I unfasten the breastplate?
(Carefully, he tries to loosen the breastplate.)

Come, my sword!
Cut through the metal!
(He draws his sword and gently and carefully cuts through the rings of mail on both sides of the armour. Then he lifts off the breastplate and the greaves; Brünnhilde lies before him in soft woman's drapery. He starts back in astonishment and alarm.)
It's not a man!
(He stares at the slumbering form with wildest emotion.)
Blazing enchantments
burn in my breast;
fiery spells
dazzle and blind me;
my heart grows feeble and faint!

Wen ruf ich zum Heil,
daß er mir helfe?
Mutter, Mutter!
Gedenke mein!
(Er sinkt, wie ohnmächtig, an Brünnhildes Busen. Langes Schweigen. Er fährt seufzend auf.)
Wie weck ich die Maid,
daß sie ihr Auge mir öffne?
Das Auge mir öffnen?
Blende mich auch noch der Blick?
Wagt' es mein Trotz?
Ertrüg' ich das Licht?
Mir schwebt und schwankt
und schwirrt es umher!
Sehrendes Sehnen
zehrt meine Sinne;
am zagenden Herzen
zittert die Hand!
Wie ist mir Feigem?
Ist dies das Fürchten?
O Mutter, Mutter!
Dein mutiges Kind!
Im Schlafe liegt eine Frau:
die hat ihn das Fürchten gelehrt!
Wie end ich die Furcht?
Wie faß ich Mut?
Daß ich selbst erwache,
muß die Maid ich erwecken!
(Indem er sich der Schlafenden von neuem nähert, wird er wieder von zarteren Empfindungen an ihren Anblick gefesselt. Er neigt sich tiefer hinab.)
Süß erbebt mir
ihr blühender Mund.
Wie mild erzitternd
mich Zagen er reizt!
Ach! Dieses Atems
wonnig warmes Gedüft!
Erwache! Erwache!
Heiliges Weib!
(Er starrt auf sie hin.)
Sie hört mich nicht.
(gedehnt mit gepreßtem, drängendem Ausdruck.)
So saug ich mir Leben
aus süßesten Lippen,
sollt' ich auch sterbend vergehn!
(Er sinkt, wie ersterbend, auf die Schlafende und heftet mit geschlossenen Augen seine Lippen auf

On whom shall I call?
Ah, who can help me?
Mother! Mother!
Remember me!
(He sinks, as if fainting, on Brünnhilde's breast. A long silence. He rises with a sigh.)
How waken the maid,
and see her eyes gently open?
Her eyes gently open?
Will they not dazzle and blind?
How can I dare
to gaze on their light?
Beneath my feet
the ground seems to sway!
Anguish and yearning
conquer my courage;
on my heart, beating wildly,
trembles my hand!
Am I a coward?
Is this what fear is?
O mother! mother!
Your bold fearless child!
A woman lies here in sleep,
and she now has taught me to fear!
How conquer my fear?
How steel my heart?
If I am to awake myself,
first the maid must awaken.
(As he approaches the sleeper again he is again filled with tender emotion at the sight of her. He bends lower over her.)
Sweet and quivering,
her lovely mouth.
A gentle gladness
charms fear from my heart!
Ah! How enchanting
her warm, fragrant breath!
Awaken! Awaken!
Holiest maid!
(He gazes upon her.)
She hears me not.
(slowly, with tense and urgent expression)
Then life I shall gather
from lips filled with sweetness;
what though I die by this kiss!
(He sinks, as if dying, on the sleeping figure, and with closed eyes presses his lips on her mouth.

ihren Mund. Brünnhilde schlägt die Augen auf. Siegfried fährt auf und bleibt vor ihr stehen. Brünnhilde richtet sich langsam zum Sitze auf. Sie begrüßt mit feierlichen Gebärden der erhobenen Arme ihre Rückkehr zur Wahrnehmung der Erde und des Himmels.)

Brünnhilde opens her eyes. Siegfried starts up and stands before her. Brünnhilde slowly rises to a sitting position. She raises her arms in solemn gestures, greeting the heaven and earth that now she sees again.)

BRÜNNHILDE
Heil dir, Sonne!
Heil dir, Licht!
Heil dir, leuchtender Tag!
Lang war mein Schlaf;
ich bin erwacht.
Wer ist der Held,
der mich erweckt?

BRÜNNHILDE
Hail, bright sunlight!
Hail, fair sky!
Hail, O radiant day!
Long was my sleep;
but now I wake:
Who is the man
wakes me to life?

SIEGFRIED
(von ihrem Blick und ihrer Stimme feierlich ergriffen, steht wie festgebannt.)
Durch das Feuer drang ich,
das den Fels umbrann;
ich erbrach dir den festen Helm:
Siegfried bin ich,
der dich erweckt.

SIEGFRIED
(deeply moved by her look and her voice, stands as if rooted to the spot.)
I have braved the dangers
blazing round your rock;
from your head I unclasped the helm;
Siegfried wakes you,
brings you to life.

BRÜNNHILDE
(hoch aufgerichtet sitzend)
Heil euch, Götter!
Heil dir, Welt!
Heil dir, prangende Erde!
Zu End' ist nun mein Schlaf;
erwacht, seh ich:
Siegfried ist es,
der mich erweckt!

BRÜNNHILDE
(sitting straight up)
Wotan, hear me!
Hear me, world!
Hear me, glorious nature!
My sleep is at an end;
awake, I see
Siegfried! Siegfried
has brought me life!

SIEGFRIED
(in erhabenste Verzückung ausbrechend)
O Heil der Mutter,
die mich gebar;
Heil der Erde,
die mich genährt!
Daß ich das Aug' erschaut,
das jetzt mir Seligem lacht!

SIEGFRIED
(breaking out in ecstasy)
I bless my mother,
giving me birth!
bless the earth
that gave me my strength!—
now I behold your eyes,
bright stars that laugh on my joy!

BRÜNNHILDE
(mit größter Bewegtheit)
O Heil der Mutter,
die dich gebar!

BRÜNNHILDE
(in impassioned accents)
I bless your mother,
giving you birth!

Heil der Erde,
die dich genährt!
Nur dein Blick durfte mich schaun,
erwachen durft' ich nur dir!
(Beide bleiben voll strahlenden Entzückens in ihren gegenseitigen Anblick verloren.)
O Siegfried! Siegfried!
Seliger Held!
Du Wecker des Lebens,
siegendes Licht!
O wüßtest du, Lust der Welt,
wie ich dich je geliebt!
Du warst mein Sinnen,
mein Sorgen du!
Dich Zarten nährt' ich,
noch eh du gezeugt;
noch eh du geboren,
barg dich mein Schild:
so lang lieb ich dich, Siegfried!

bless the earth
that gave you your strength!
Your eyes alone could behold me;
my heart to you alone wakes!
(Each remains lost in radiant, rapt contemplation of the other.)
O Siegfried! Siegfried!
Radiant hero!
Victorious conqueror,
conquering light!
O learn from me, joy of the world,
how I have always loved you!
You were my gladness,
my cares as well!
Your life I sheltered,
in Sieglinde's womb;
before she had borne you,
I was your shield.
So long I have loved, Siegfried!

SIEGFRIED
(leise und schüchtern)
So starb nicht meine Mutter?
Schlief die Minnige nur?

SIEGFRIED
(softly and shyly)
My mother is alive, then?
Sleep enfolded her here?

BRÜNNHILDE
(lächelnd, freundlich die Hand nach ihm ausstreckend)
Du wonniges Kind!
Deine Mutter kehrt dir nicht wieder.
Du selbst bin ich,
wenn du mich Selige liebst.
Was du nicht weißt,
weiß ich für dich;
doch wissend bin ich
nur—weil ich dich liebe!
O Siegried! Siegfried!
Siegendes Licht!
Dich liebt' ich immer;
denn mir allein
erdünkte Wotans Gedanke.
Der Gedanke, den ich nie
nennen durfte;
den ich nicht dachte,
sondern nur fühlte;
für den ich focht,
kämpfte und stritt;

BRÜNNHILDE
(smiling, and stretching out her hand to him affectionately)
O innocent child!
Nevermore you'll look on your mother.
But we are one,
if you can grant me your love.
What you would learn,
learn it from me,
for wisdom fills my soul,
now that I love you!
O Siegfried! Siegfried!
conquering light!
I loved you always,
for I divined
the thought that Wotan had hidden,
guessed the secret thought
I dared not even whisper;
I did not shape it,
rather I felt it;
and so I fought,
urged by that deed,

für den ich trotzte
dem, der ihn dachte;
für den ich büßte,
Strafe mich band,
weil ich nicht ihn dachte
und nur empfand!
Denn der Gedanke—
dürftest du's lösen!—
mir war er nur Liebe zu dir!

when I defied the god
who conceived it;
and then I suffered,
slept on this rock,
for that thought still secret,
that thought I felt!
Know what that thought was;
ah, you can guess it!
That thought was my love for you!

SIEGFRIED
Wie Wunder tönt,
was wonnig du singst;
doch dunkel dünkt mich der Sinn.
Deines Auges Leuchten
seh ich licht;
deines Atems Wehen
fühl ich warm:
deiner Stimme Singen
hör ich süß:
doch was du singend mir sagst,
staunend versteh ich's nicht.
Nicht kann ich das Ferne
sinnig erfassen,
wenn alle Sinne
dich nur sehen und fühlen!
Mit banger Furcht
fesselst du mich:
du einz'ge hast
ihre Angst mich gelehrt.
Den du gebunden
in mächtigen Banden,
birg meinen Mut mir nicht mehr!
(Er verweilt in großer Aufregung, den sehnsuchtsvollen Blick auf sie heftend.)

SIEGFRIED
Ah, glorious song,
enchanting to hear;
but yet the meaning is dark.
I can see your eyes
that shine so bright;
I can feel your warm
and fragrant breath;
I can hear your song
so clear and sweet:
but what your singing can mean,
how can I understand?
You sing of the past,
but how can I listen,
while I have you beside me,
see and feel only you?
In bonds of fear
I have been bound:
from you alone
could I learn how to fear.
Since you have bound me
in powerful fetters,
give me my freedom again!
(He remains in profound agitation, directing on her a look of yearning.)

BRÜNNHILDE
(wendet sanft das Haupt zur Seite und richtet ihren Blick nach dem Tann.)
Dort seh ich Grane,
mein selig Roß:
wie weidet er munter,
der mit mir schlief!
Mit mir hat ihn Siegfried erweckt.

BRÜNNHILDE
(gently turns her head aside and looks towards the wood.)
And there is Grane,
my sacred horse;
he grazes in gladness
where once he slept!
Like me, to Siegfried he wakes.

SIEGFRIED
(in der vorigen Stellung verbleibend)
Auf wonnigem Munde

SIEGFRIED
(remaining in the same position)
My eyes are grazing

weidet mein Auge:
in brünstigem Durst
doch brennen die Lippen,
daß der Augen Weide sie labe!

on pastures more lovely;
with passionate thirst
my lips too are burning,
for they long to graze where my glance [does!

BRÜNNHILDE
(deutet ihm mit der Hand nach ihren Waffen, die sie gewahrt).
Dort seh ich den Schild,
der Helden schirmte;
dort seh ich den Helm,
der das Haupt mir barg:
er schirmt, er birgt mich nicht mehr!

BRÜNNHILDE
(points to her weapons, which she now perceives.)
And there is the shield
that sheltered heroes;
beside it the helmet
that hid my head.
They shield, they hide me no more!

SIEGFRIED
Eine selige Maid
versehrte mein Herz;
Wunden dem Haupte
schlug mir ein Weib:
ich kam ohne Schild und Helm!

SIEGFRIED
Now a glorious maid
has wounded my heart;
wounds in my head
were struck by that maid:
I came with no shield or helm!

BRÜNNHILDE
(mit gesteigerter Wehmut)
Ich sehe der Brünne
prangenden Stahl:
ein scharfes Schwert
schnitt sie entzwei;
von dem maidlichen Leibe
löst' es die Wehr;
ich bin ohne Schutz und Schirm,
ohne Trutz ein trauriges Weib!

BRÜNNHILDE
(with increasing sadness)
And there is the steel
that guarded my breast.
A shining sword
cut it in two,
when the maid was stripped
of all her defence.
I have no defence, no shield;
quite unarmed, a sorrowing maid!

SIEGFRIED
Durch brennendes Feuer
fuhr ich zu dir!
Nicht Brünne noch Panzer
barg meinen Leib:
Nun brach die Lohe
mir in die Brust.
Es braust mein Blut
in blühender Brunst;
ein zehrendes Feuer
ist mir entzündet:
Die Glut, die Brünnhilds
Felsen umbrann,
die brennt mir nun in der Brust!
O Weib, jetzt lösche den Brand!

SIEGFRIED
Through furious fire
I fared to your rock;
no breastplate, no armour
guarded my breast;
the flames have broken through
to my heart.
My blood's ablaze
and burns in my breast;
a passionate fire
within me is kindled;
that blaze which guarded
Brünnhilde's rock
now flames fiercely in my breast!
O maid, you started the fire!

Schweige die schäumende Glut!
(Er hat sie heftig umfaßt: sie springt auf, wehrt ihm mit der höchsten Kraft der Angst und entflieht nach der anderen Seite.)

BRÜNNHILDE
Kein Gott nahte mir je!
Der Jungfrau neigten
scheu sich die Helden:
heilig schied sie aus Walhall!
Wehe! Wehe!
Wehe der Schmach,
der schmählichen Not!
Verwundet hat mich,
der mich erweckt!
Er erbrach mir Brünne und Helm:
Brünnhilde bin ich nicht mehr!

SIEGFRIED
Noch bist du mir
die träumende Maid:
Brünnhildes Schlaf
brach ich noch nicht.
Erwache, sei mir ein Weib!

BRÜNNHILDE
Mir schwirren die Sinne,
mein Wissen schweigt:
soll mir die Weisheit schwinden?

SIEGFRIED
Sangst du mir nicht,
dein Wissen sei
das Leuchten der Liebe zu mir?

BRÜNNHILDE
(vor sich hinstarrend)
Trauriges Dunkel
trübt meinen Blick;
mein Auge dämmert,
das Licht verlischt:
Nacht wird's um mich.
Aus Nebel und Grau'n
windet sich wütend
ein Angstgewirr:
Schrecken schreitet
und bäumt sich empor!
(Sie birgt heftig die Augen mit beiden Händen.)

You can extinguish the flame!
(He has embraced her ardently. She springs up, repulses him with the utmost strength of terror, and flies to the other side.)

BRÜNNHILDE
No god dared to come near!
The heroes bowed
and knelt to the maiden:
holy came she from Walhall.
Sorrow! Sorrow!
Woe for my shame,
how keen my disgrace!
And he who wakes me
deals me the wound!
He has broken breastplate and helm:
Brünnhilde am I no more!

SIEGFRIED
You are still to me
that slumbering maid;
Brünnhilde's sleep
still binds her fast.
Awaken, you are my bride!

BRÜNNHILDE
My mind's in confusion,
my reason sways:
must all my wisdom fail me?

SIEGFRIED
You said
that all your wisdom came
by the light of your love for me.

BRÜNNHILDE
(staring in front of her)
Shadows of darkness
close on me now.
My eyes are blinded;
my sight grows dim.
Night falls around.
From darkness and gloom
wildly my fears
seem to seize on me.
Dreadful horrors
arise in the dark!
(Impulsively she covers her eyes with her hands.)

SIEGFRIED
(indem er ihr sanft die Hände von den Augen löst)
Nacht umfängt
gebundne Augen.
Mit den Fesseln schwindet
das finstre Grau'n.
Tauch aus dem Dunkel und sieh:
sonnenhell leuchtet der Tag!

BRÜNNHILDE
(in höchster Ergriffenheit)
Sonnenhell
leuchtet der Tag meiner Schmach!—
O Siegfried! Siegfried!
Sieh meine Angst!
(Ihre Miene verrät, daß ihr ein anmutiges Bild vor die Seele tritt, von welchem ab sie den Blick mit Sanftmut wieder auf Siegfried richtet.)
Ewig war ich,
ewig bin ich,
ewig in süß
sehnender Wonne,
doch ewig zu deinem Heil!
O Siegfried!
Herrlicher!
Hort der Welt!
Leben der Erde!
Lachender Held!
Laß, ach laß,
lasse von mir!
Nahe mir nicht
mit der wütenden Nähe!
Zwinge mich nicht
mit dem brechenden Zwang,
zertrümmre die Traute dir nicht!
Sahst du dein Bild
im klaren Bach?
Hat es dich Frohen erfreut?
Rührtest zur Woge
das Wasser du auf;
zerflösse die klare
Fläche des Bachs:
dein Bild sähst du nicht mehr,
nur der Welle schwankend Gewog'.
So berühre mich nicht,
trübe mich nicht!
Ewig licht

SIEGFRIED
(gently removing her hands from her eyes)
Night enfolds
those eyes you have hidden.
When I free them
all gloomy fears depart.
Rise from the darkness, and see:
bright as the sun, here shines the day!

BRÜNNHILDE
(profoundly agitated)
Bright as the sun
shines but the day of my shame!
O Siegfried! Siegfried!
See my dismay!
(Brünnhilde's expression reveals that a pleasing idea has come to her mind, and at this she turns again and looks tenderly at Siegfried.)
Ever loving,
ever caring,
caring with sweet,
warm, tender longing—
yes, always for your dear life!
O Siegfried,
glorious hero!
Wealth of the world!
Fair, laughing hero!
Light of the earth!
Leave, ah, leave,
leave me in peace!
Do not come near me
with passionate frenzy;
do not pursue me
with masterful might,
or else you'll destroy all our love!
You've seen your face
in the shining stream?
And it delighted your eyes?
But when that water
is stirred by a wave,
your smiling reflection
breaks and is gone;
Your face greets you no more
when that shining stream is disturbed!
So disturb me no more;
trouble me not!
Ever bright,

lachst du selig dann
aus mir dir entgegen,
froh und heiter ein Held!
O Siegfried!
Leuchtender Sproß!
Liebe dich
und lasse von mir:
vernichte dein Eigen nicht!

SIEGFRIED
Dich lieb ich:
o liebtest mich du!
Nicht hab ich mehr mich:
o hätte ich dich!
Ein herrlich Gewässer
wogt vor mir;
mit allen Sinnen
seh ich nur sie,
die wonnig wogende Welle.
Brach sie mein Bild,
so brenn ich nun selbst,
sengende Glut
in der Flut zu kühlen;
ich selbst, wie ich bin,
spring in den Bach:
o daß seine Wogen
mich selig verschlängen,
mein Sehnen schwänd' in der Flut!
Erwache, Brünnhilde!
Wache, du Maid!
Lache und lebe,
süßeste Lust!
Sei mein! Sei mein! Sei mein!

BRÜNNHILDE
(sehr innig)
O Siegfried! Dein
war ich von je!

SIEGFRIED
(feurig)
Warst du's von je,
so sei es jetzt!

BRÜNNHILDE
Dein werd ich
ewig sein!

may you ever see
in me your reflection,
brave and smiling and fair!
O Siegfried!
Laughing youth!
Love yourself,
and leave me in peace;
destroy not this maid who is yours!

SIEGFRIED
I love you:
did you but love me!
Mine I am no more:
were you but mine!
A sea of enchantment
flows around;
with all my senses
I see alone
those surging, glorious billows.
Though in the deep
I may not see my face,
burning, I long
for those cooling waters;
and now, as I am,
leap in the stream—
if only those waves
could engulf me forever,
my yearning would fade in the flood!
Awaken, Brünnhilde!
Waken, O maid!
Live in laughter,
sweetest delight!
Be mine! Be mine! Be mine!

BRÜNNHILDE
(with intensity)
O Siegfried! Yours
I have always been!

SIEGFRIED
(ardently)
If you were mine,
be mine again!

BRÜNNHILDE
Yours ever
I shall be!

SIEGFRIED

Was du sein wirst,
sei es mir heut!
Faßt dich mein Arm,
umschling ich dich fest;
schlägt meine Brust
brünstig die deine;
zünden die Blicke,
zehren die Atem sich;
Aug' in Auge,
Mund an Mund:
dann bist du mir,
was bang du mir warst und wirst!
Dann brach sich die brennende Sorge,
ob jetzt Brünnhilde mein?
(Er hat sie umfaßt.)

BRÜNNHILDE

Ob jetzt ich dein?
Göttliche Ruhe
rast mir in Wogen;
keuschestes Licht
lodert in Gluten:
himmlisches Wissen
stürmt mir dahin,
Jauchzen der Liebe
jagt es davon!
Ob jetzt ich dein?
Siegfried! Siegfried!
Siehst du mich nicht?
Wie mein Blick dich verzehrt,
erblindest du nicht?
Wie mein Arm dich preßt,
entbrennst du mir nicht?
Wie in Strömen mein Blut
entgegen dir stürmt,
das wilde Feuer,
fühlst du es nicht?
Fürchtest du, Siegfried,
fürchtest du nicht
das wild wütende Weib?
(Sie umfaßt ihn heftig.)

SIEGFRIED
(in freudigem Schreck)

Ha!
Wie des Blutes Ströme sich zünden,

SIEGFRIED

If you'll be mine,
be so today!
When in my arms
I hold you embraced,
feeling your heart
beating beside me,
joining our glances,
sharing one single breath,
eyes together,
mouth to mouth:
then I shall know
that Brünnhilde's truly mine!
End my doubts, let me now be sure
that now Brünnhilde's mine!
(He has embraced her.)

BRÜNNHILDE

That I am yours?
Godly composure,
change into wildness;
virginal light,
flare into frenzy;
heavenly wisdom,
fly to the winds:
love, love alone
inspires all my heart!
That I am yours?
Siegfried! Siegfried!
Can you not see?
When my eyes blaze on you,
then are you not blind?
Does my arms' embrace
not set you on fire?
By the heat of my blood
in its passionate surge,
a fire is kindled—
can you not feel?
Tell me then, Siegfried,
do you not fear
this wild, passionate maid?
(She embraces him passionately.)

SIEGFRIED
(in joyous terror)

Ha!
In the fire our blood has kindled,

wie der Blicke Strahlen sich zehren,
wie die Arme brünstig sich pressen,
kehrt mir zurück
mein kühner Mut,
und das Fürchten, ach!
das ich nie gelernt,
das Fürchten, das du
mich kaum gelehrt:
das Fürchten—mich dünkt,
ich Dummer vergaß es nun ganz!
(Er hat bei den letzten Worten Brünnhilde unwillkürlich losgelassen.)

BRÜNNHILDE
(im höchsten Liebesjubel wild auflachend)
O kindischer Held!
O herrlicher Knabe!
Du hehrster Taten
töriger Hort!
Lachend muß ich dich lieben,
lachend will ich erblinden,
lachend lass uns verderben,
lachend zugrunde gehn!
Fahr hin, Walhalls
leuchtende Welt!
Zerfall in Staub
deine stolze Burg!
Leb wohl, prangende
Götterpracht!
End in Wonne,
du ewig Geschlecht!
Zerreißt, ihr Nornen,
das Runenseil!
Götterdämm'rung,
dunkle herauf!
Nacht der Vernichtung,
neble herein!
Mir strahlt zur Stunde
Siegfrieds Stern;
er ist mir ewig,
ist mir immer,
Erb' und Eigen,
ein und all:
leuchtende Liebe,
lachender Tod!

SIEGFRIED
Lachend erwachst

in the flames that glow from our glances,
in our burning, ardent enchantments,
I find again
my boldness of heart;
and what fear is, ah!
I have failed to learn;
what fear is, not even
you can teach!
My fear, I find,
has faded and gone like a dream!
(At the last words he has involuntarily released Brünnhilde.)

BRÜNNHILDE
(laughing wildly in an outburst of extreme joy)
O radiant youth!
O glorious hero!
My proudly fearless,
brave, noble boy!
Laughing I shall love you,
laughing, welcome my blindness,
laughing, let us be lost together,
in laughter die!
Farewell, Walhall's
bright glittering world!
Your glorious halls
now may fall to dust!
Farewell, proud, radiant,
godly race!
End in joy,
you eternal clan!
And rend, O Norns,
that rope you weave!
Gods may sink
to eternal night!
Twilight and darkness
seize all the clan!
I live by the light
of Siegfried's bright star!
He's mine forever,
he is my joy,
my wealth, my world,
my one and all!
Light of our loving,
laughter in death!

SIEGFRIED
Laughing, you wake

du Wonnige mir:
Brünnhilde lebt,
Brünnhilde lacht!
Heil dem Tage,
der uns umleuchtet!
Heil der Sonne,
die uns bescheint!
Heil dem Licht,
das der Nacht enttaucht!
Heil der Welt,
der Brünnhilde lebt!
Sie wacht, sie lebt,
sie lacht mir entgegen.
Prangend strahlt
mir Brünnhildes Stern!
Sie ist mir ewig,
ist mir immer,
Erb' und Eigen,
ein und all:
leuchtende Liebe,
lachender Tod!

(Brünnhilde stürzt sich in Siegfrieds Arme. Der Vorhang fällt.)

in gladness to me!
Brünnhilde lives,
Brünnhilde laughs!
Blessed the day
that shines around us!
Blessed the sun
that lights our way!
Blessed the light
that dispels the night!
Blessed the world
where Brünnhilde lives!
She wakes, she lives,
she greets me with laughter.
All my light
is Brünnhilde's star!
She's mine forever,
she is my joy,
my wealth, my world,
my one and all!
Light of our loving,
laughter in death!

(Brünnhilde throws herself into Siegfried's arms. The curtain falls.)

Twilight of the Gods

Third Day of the Festival Play

The Ring of the Nibelung

Dramatis Personae

SIEGFRIED	*Tenor*
GUNTHER	*Bass-baritone*
HAGEN	*Bass*
ALBERICH	*Bass-baritone*
BRÜNNHILDE	*Soprano*
GUTRUNE	*Soprano*
WALTRAUTE	*Mezzo-soprano*

The three Norns *Contralto, Mezzo-soprano and Soprano*

The three Rhinemaidens *Soprano, Mezzo-soprano and Contralto*

Chorus: Vassals and Women

Vorspiel

Auf dem Walkürenfelsen

Die Szene ist dieselbe wie am Schlusse des zweiten Tages.—Nacht.—Aus der Tiefe des Hintergrundes leuchtet Feuerschein.

Die drei Nornen, hohe Frauengestalten in langen, dunklen und schleierartigen Faltengewändern. Die erste (älteste) lagert im Vordergrunde rechts unter der breitästigen Tanne; die zweite (jüngere) ist an einer Steinbank vor dem Felsengemache hingestreckt; die dritte (jüngste) sitzt in der Mitte des Hintergrundes auf einem Felssteine des Höhensaumes. Eine Zeitlang herrscht düsteres Schweigen.

DIE ERSTE NORN
(ohne sich zu bewegen)
Welch Licht leuchtet dort?

DIE ZWEITE
Dämmert der Tag schon auf?

DIE DRITTE
Loges Heer

Prelude

On the Valkyrie Rock

The scene is the same as at the close of 'The Valkyrie'. It is night. Firelight shines up from the depths of the background.

The three Norns, tall female figures in long, dark veil-like drapery. The first (oldest) is lying in the foreground on the right, under the spreading pine-tree; the second (younger) reclines on a rock in front of the cave; the third (youngest) sits in the centre at back on a rock below the peak. Gloomy silence and stillness.

FIRST NORN
(without moving)
What light shines down there?

SECOND NORN
Can it be day so soon?

THIRD NORN
Loge's flames

lodert feurig um den Fels.
Noch ist's Nacht.
Was spinnen und singen wir nicht?

DIE ZWEITE
(zu der ersten)
Wollen wir spinnen und singen,
woran spannst du das Seil?

DIE ERSTE NORN
(erhebt sich, während sie ein goldenes Seil von sich löst und mit dem einen Ende es an einen Ast der Tanne knüpft.)
So gut und schlimm es geh',
schling ich das Seil und singe.
An der Weltesche
wob ich einst,
da groß und stark
dem Stamm entgrünte
weihlicher Äste Wald.
Im kühlen Schatten
rauscht' ein Quell,
Weisheit raunend
rann sein Gewell';
da sang ich heil'gen Sinn.
Ein kühner Gott
trat zum Trunk an den Quell;
seiner Augen eines
zahlt' er als ewigen Zoll.
Von der Weltesche
brach da Wotan einen Ast;
eines Speeres Schaft
entschnitt der Starke dem Stamm.

In langer Zeiten Lauf
zehrte die Wunde den Wald;
falb fielen die Blätter,
dürr darbte der Baum,
traurig versiegte
des Quelles Trank:
trüben Sinnes
ward mein Gesang.
Doch, web' ich heut
an der Weltesche nicht mehr,
muß mir die Tanne
taugen zu fesseln das Seil:
singe, Schwester,

leap and flicker round the rock.
It is night.
And so we should sing as we spin.

SECOND NORN
(to the First)
Let us be spinning and singing;
but where, where tie the cord?

FIRST NORN
(rises, unwinds a golden rope from herself, and ties one end of it to a branch of the pine-tree.)
Though good or ill may come,
weaving the cord, I'll sing now.
At the World Ash-tree
once I wove,
when fair and green
there grew from its branches
verdant and shady leaves.
Those cooling shadows
sheltered a spring;
wisdom's voice
I heard in its waves;
I sang my holy song.
A valiant god
came to drink at the spring;
and the price he had to pay
was the loss of an eye.
From the World Ash-tree
mighty Wotan broke a branch;
and his spear was shaped
from that branch he tore from the tree.

As year succeeded year,
the wound slowly weakened the tree;
dry, leafless, and barren—
death seized on the tree;
whispering waters
then failed in the spring:
grief and sorrow
stole through my song.
And so I weave
at the World Ash-tree no more;
today I use this pine branch
to fasten the cord.
Sing, my sister,

dir werf ich's zu.
Weißt du, wie das wird?

take up the thread:
say what happened then.

DIE ZWEITE NORN
(windet das zugeworfene Seil um einen hervorspringenden Felsstein am Eingange des Gemaches.)
Treu beratner
Verträge Runen
schnitt Wotan
in des Speeres Schaft:
den hielt er als Haft der Welt.
Ein kühner Held
zerhieb im Kampfe den Speer;
in Trümmer sprang
der Verträge heiliger Haft.
Da hieß Wotan
Walhalls Helden
der Weltesche
welkes Geäst
mit dem Stamm in Stücke zu fällen.
Die Esche sank,
ewig versiegte der Quell!
Feßle ich heut
an den scharfen Fels das Seil:
singe, Schwester,
dir werf ich's zu.
Weißt du, wie das wird?

SECOND NORN
(winds the rope that has been thrown to her round a projecting rock at the entrance of the cave.)
Wotan made
holy laws and treaties;
then Wotan
cut their words in the spear:
he held it to rule all the world,
until the day
a hero broke it in two;
with shining sword
he destroyed the god's holy laws.
Then Wotan ordered
Walhall's heroes
to hack down
the World Ash's trunk,
and to cut its branches to pieces.
The Ash-tree fell;
dry were the waters of the spring!
And so today
I must tie our cord to the rock.
Sing, my sister,
take up the thread.
What will happen now?

DIE DRITTE NORN
(das Seil auffangend und dessen Ende hinter sich werfend)
Es ragt die Burg,
von Riesen gebaut:
mit der Götter und Helden
heiliger Sippe
sitzt dort Wotan im Saal.
Gehau'ner Scheite
hohe Schicht
ragt zuhauf
rings um die Halle:
die Weltesche war dies einst!
Brennt das Holz
heilig brünstig und hell,
sengt die Glut
sehrend den glänzenden Saal:
der ewigen Götter Ende
dämmert ewig da auf.

THIRD NORN
(catching the rope and throwing the end behind her.)
That mighty hall
the giants have raised—
there the immortals and heroes
all have assembled;
there sits Wotan on high.
But all around it
there are heaped
like a wall
huge, mighty branches:
the World Ash-tree once they were!
When that wood
blazes furious and bright,
when the flames
seize on that glorious abode,
the rule of the gods is ended;
darkness falls on the gods.

Wisset ihr noch,
so windet von neuem das Seil;
von Norden wieder
werf ich's dir nach.
Spinne, Schwester, und singe!
(Sie wirft das Seil der zweiten Norn zu. Die zweite Norn schwingt das Seil der ersten hin, die es vom Zweige löst und es an einen andern Ast wieder anknüpft.)

DIE ERSTE NORN
(nach hinten blickend)
Dämmert der Tag?
Oder leuchtet die Lohe?
Getrübt trügt sich mein Blick;
nicht hell eracht ich
das heilig Alte,
da Loge einst
entbrannte in lichter Brunst.
Weißt du, was aus ihm ward?

DIE ZWEITE NORN
(das zugeworfene Seil wieder um den Stein windend)
Durch des Speeres Zauber
zähmte ihn Wotan;
Räte raunt' er dem Gott.
An des Schaftes Runen,
frei sich zu raten,
nagte zehrend sein Zahn:
Da, mit des Speeres
zwingender Spitze
bannte ihn Wotan,
Brünnhildes Fels zu umbrennen.
Weißt du, was aus ihm wird?

DIE DRITTE NORN
(das zugeschwungene Seil wieder hinter sich werfend)
Des zerschlagnen Speeres
stechende Splitter
taucht' einst Wotan
dem Brünstigen tief in die Brust:
zehrender Brand
zündet da auf;
den wirft der Gott

What happens then?
Oh take up the cord and the song;
from the north
I now must throw it to you.
Spin, my sister, and sing on!
(She throws the rope to the Second Norn. The Second Norn casts it to the First, who loosens the rope from the branch and fastens it to another.)

FIRST NORN
(looking toward the back)
Is that the day
or the flickering firelight?
For sadness dims my eyes;
I see no longer
those sacred visions
which Loge once
would light up in radiant fire.
Tell me, what was his fate?

SECOND NORN
(once again winding the rope that has been thrown to her around the rock)
By the spear's enchantment
Wotan enslaved him;
Loge counselled the god.
But he longed for freedom,
tried to escape him,
broke the laws on the spear.
Then, once again
by the spear he was summoned;
ordered by Wotan,
Brünnhilde's rock he surrounded.
Know you what happens now?

THIRD NORN
(again throwing behind her the end of the rope as it comes to her)
Now the god will seize
the spear that was shattered,
drive it deep
in the breast of the fiery god:
then, when the flames
leap from the spear,
those flames he'll cast

in der Weltesche
zuhauf geschichtete Scheite.

(Sie wirft das Seil zurück, die zweite Norn windet es auf und wirft es der ersten wieder zu.)

DIE ZWEITE NORN
Wollt ihr wissen,
wann das wird?
Schwinget, Schwestern, das Seil!

DIE ERSTE NORN
(das Seil von neuem anknüpfend)
Die Nacht weicht;
nichts mehr gewahr ich:
des Seiles Fäden
find ich nicht mehr;
verflochten in das Geflecht.
Ein wüstes Gesicht
wirrt mir wütend den Sinn.
Das Rheingold
raubte Alberich einst.
Weißt du, was aus ihm ward?

DIE ZWEITE NORN
(mit mühevoller Hast das Seil um den zackigen Stein des Gemaches windend)
Des Steines Schärfe
schnitt in das Seil;
nicht fest spannt mehr
der Fäden Gespinst;
verwirrt ist das Geweb'.
Aus Not und Neid
ragt mir des Niblungen Ring:
ein rächender Fluch
nagt meiner Fäden Geflecht.
Weißt du, was daraus wird?

DIE DRITTE NORN
(das zugeworfene Seil hastig fassend)
Zu locker das Seil,
mir langt es nicht.
Soll ich nach Norden
neigen das Ende,
straffer sei es gestreckt!
(Sie zieht gewaltsam das Seil an: dieses reißt in der Mitte.)
Es riß!

at the World Ash-tree
whose branches are heaped around
[Walhall.

(She throws the rope back; the Second Norn coils it and throws it back to the First.)

SECOND NORN
Let us discover
when that will be.
Spin, then, sisters, our cord!

FIRST NORN
(fastening the rope again)
The night fades;
dark are my senses:
these feeble threads
have slipped from my grasp;
the rope is tangled and frayed.
A hideous sight
wounds me, clouding my eyes:
the Rhinegold
which Alberich stole—
say, what became of him?

SECOND NORN
(with anxious haste winds the rope around the jagged rock at the mouth of the cave.)
The threads are breaking,
cut by the crag;
the rope loses
its hold on the rock;
it hangs ravelled and torn;
while need and greed
rise from the Nibelung's ring:
and Alberich's curse
tears at the strands of the cord.
Ah, what will happen next?

THIRD NORN
(hastily catching the rope thrown to her)
The rope is too slack;
it reaches not.
If I must cast it
back to the north,
the sagging rope must be stretched.
(She tugs at the rope, which breaks in the middle.)
It splits!

DIE ZWEITE
Es riß!

DIE ERSTE
Es riß!

(Erschreckt sind die drei Nornen aufgefahren und nach der Mitte der Bühne zusammengetreten: sie fassen die Stücke des zerrissenen Seiles und binden damit ihre Leiber aneinander.)

DIE DREI NORNEN
Zu End' ewiges Wissen!
Der Welt melden
Weise nichts mehr.

DIE DRITTE NORN
Hinab!

DIE ZWEITE NORN
Zur Mutter!

DIE ERSTE NORN
Hinab!

(Sie verschwinden.)

Tagesgrauen. Wächsende Morgenröthe; immer schwächeres Leuchten des Feuerscheines aus der Tiefe. Sonnenaufgang. Voller Tag. Siegfried und Brünnhilde treten aus dem Steingemach auf. Siegfried ist in vollen Waffen, Brünnhilde führt ihr Roß am Zaume.

BRÜNNHILDE
Zu neuen Taten,
teuer Helde,
wie liebt' ich dich,
ließ ich dich nicht?
Ein einzig' Sorgen
laßt mich saumen:
daß dir zu wenig
mein Wert gewann!

Was Götter mich wiesen,
gab ich dir:
heiliger Runen
reichen Hort;
doch meiner Stärke

SECOND NORN
It splits!

FIRST NORN
It splits!

(The three Norns start up in terror, and gather at the centre of the stage; they grasp the pieces of the broken rope and bind their bodies together with them.)

THE THREE NORNS
An end now to our wisdom!
The world hears
our counsel no more.

THIRD NORN
Away!

SECOND NORN
To Erda!

FIRST NORN
Away!

(They vanish.)

Dawn. The red glow of sunrise grows; the firelight from below grows fainter. Sunrise. Broad daylight. Siegfried and Brünnhilde enter from the cave; he is fully armed; she leads her horse by the bridle.

BRÜNNHILDE
To deeds of glory,
brave beloved!
My love for you
bids you be gone.
One care constrains me,
makes me linger,
I've not repaid you
for all you brought.

What gods have given me,
I've given to you:
all that they taught me,
all is yours;
all of this maiden's

magdlichen Stamm
nahm mir der Held,
dem ich nun mich neige.

Des Wissens bar,
doch des Wunsches voll:
an Liebe reich,
doch ledig der Kraft:
mögst du die Arme
nicht verachten,
die dir nur gönnen,
nicht geben mehr kann!

SIEGFRIED
Mehr gabst du, Wunderfrau,
als ich zu wahren weiß.
Nicht zürne, wenn dein Lehren
mich unbelehret ließ!
Ein Wissen doch wahr ich wohl:
daß mir Brünnhilde lebt;
eine Lehre lernt' ich leicht:
Brünnhildes zu gedenken!

BRÜNNHILDE
Willst du mir Minne schenken,
gedenke deiner nur,
gedenke deiner Taten,
gedenk des wilden Feuers,
das furchtlos du durchschrittest,
da den Felsen rings umbrann.

SIEGFRIED
Brünnhilde zu gewinnen!

BRÜNNHILDE
Gedenk der beschildeten Frau,
die in tiefem Schlaf du fandest,
der den festen Helm du erbrachst.

SIEGFRIED
Brünnhilde zu erwecken!

BRÜNNHILDE
Gedenk der Eide,
die uns einen;
gedenk der Treue,
die wir tragen;

wisdom and strength
given to the man
who is now my master.

I'm wise no more,
though my heart is full:
in love I'm rich,
though emptied of power,
I fear that you
may now despise me;
how can I serve you?
I've no more to give!

SIEGFRIED
More you have given to me
than I can rightly grasp.
Forgive me if your lessons
have left me still untaught.
One lesson I know I have learnt:
that by Brünnhilde I'm loved;
one command I'll not forget:
Brünnhilde I shall remember!

BRÜNNHILDE
Ah, but to prove you love me,
remember only yourself;
recall your deeds of glory;
recall that raging fire,
whose fury could not fright you,
when it blazed around my rock!

SIEGFRIED
Brünnhilde I was winning!

BRÜNNHILDE
Recall how I lay on the rock,
and that long, deep sleep which bound me,
till your kiss awoke me to life.

SIEGFRIED
Brünnhilde I awakened!

BRÜNNHILDE
Recall the promise
that unites us;
recall the pledges
that we plighted;

gedenk der Liebe,
der wir leben:
Brünnhilde brennt dann ewig
heilig dir in der Brust!—
(Sie umarmt Siegfried.)

SIEGFRIED
Laß ich, Liebste, dich hier
in der Lohe heiliger Hut;
(Er hat den Ring Alberichs von seinem Finger gezogen und reicht ihn jetzt Brünnhilde dar.)
zum Tausche deiner Runen
reich ich dir diesen Ring.
Was der Taten je ich schuf,
des Tugend schließt er ein.
Ich erschlug einen wilden Wurm,
der grimmig lang ihn bewacht.
Nun wahre du seine Kraft
als Weihegruß meiner Treu'!

BRÜNNHILDE
(voll Entzücken den Ring sich ansteckend)
Ihn geiz ich als einziges Gut!
Für den Ring nimm nun auch mein
Ging sein Lauf mit mir [Roß!
einst kühn durch die Lüfte—
mit mir
verlor es die mächt'ge Art;
über Wolken hin
auf blitzenden Wettern
nicht mehr
schwingt es sich mutig des Wegs;
doch wohin du ihn führst
—sei es durchs Feuer—,
grauenlos folgt dir Grane;
denn dir, o Helde,
soll er gehorchen!
Du hüt ihn wohl;
er hört dein Wort:
o bringe Grane
oft Brünnhildes Gruß!

SIEGFRIED
Durch deine Tugend allein
soll so ich Taten noch wirken?
Meine Kämpfe kiesest du,
meine Siege kehren zu dir:

recall you love me,
and I love you:
Brünnhilde burns forever,
ever deep in your breast.
(She embraces Siegfried.)

SIEGFRIED
Love, I leave you alone,
but the flames will guard you again;
(He has drawn Alberich's ring from his finger and now offers it to Brünnhilde.)
in return for all you've taught me,
let me give you this ring.
For the power of all I have done
resides within this gold.
And to gain it a dragon was killed,
who guarded the ring with his life.
Now you must guard it for me;
this ring will tell all my love!

BRÜNNHILDE
(putting on the ring, in rapture)
I'll guard it so long as I live!
For the ring, I give you my horse!
Though he longs to fly
with me through the storm clouds,
with me
he lost his enchanted power;
through the skies above,
through lightning and thunder,
no more
Grane can fly on his way;
but wherever you lead,
even through fire,
fearlessly Grane will bear you:
for you, my hero,
you are his master.
Oh guard him well;
he'll heed your voice:
oh, let your Grane
hear Brünnhilde's name!

SIEGFRIED
So by your daring I am fired,
and all my deeds shall be your deeds!
All my battles you will choose,
all my victories you shall achieve,

auf deines Rosses Rücken,
in deines Schildes Schirm,
nicht Siegfried acht ich mich mehr,
ich bin nur Brünnhildes Arm.

when on your steed I'm mounted,
when by your shield I'm saved:
so Siegfried I am no more,
I am but Brünnhilde's arm.

BRÜNNHILDE
O wäre Brünnhild' deine Seele!

BRÜNNHILDE
I wish that Brünnhild were your soul too!

SIEGFRIED
Durch sie entbrennt mir der Mut.

SIEGFRIED
Her soul burns bright in my breast.

BRÜNNHILDE
So wärst du Siegfried und Brünnhild?

BRÜNNHILDE
Then you are Siegfried and Brünnhilde!

SIEGFRIED
Wo ich bin, bergen sich beide.

SIEGFRIED
Where I am, both are united.

BRÜNNHILDE
So verödet mein Felsensaal?

BRÜNNHILDE
Then my mountain must soon be bare?

SIEGFRIED
Vereint faßt er uns zwei!

SIEGFRIED
Ah no, both here in you!

BRÜNNHILDE
(in großer Ergriffenheit)
O heilige Götter,
hehre Geschlechter!
Weidet eu'r Aug'
an dem weihvollen Paar!
Getrennt—wer will es scheiden?
Geschieden—trennt es sich nie!

BRÜNNHILDE
(with great emotion)
O heavenly rulers!
Holy immortals!
Turn your eyes
on this true, loving pair!
Apart, who can divide us?
Divided, still we are one!

SIEGFRIED
Heil dir, Brünnhilde,
prangender Stern!
Heil, strahlende Liebe!

SIEGFRIED
Hail, O Brünnhilde,
glorious star!
Hail, love in its radiance!

BRÜNNHILDE
Heil dir, Siegfried,
siegendes Licht!
Heil, strahlendes Leben!

BRÜNNHILDE
Hail, O Siegfried,
Conquering light!
Hail, life in its radiance!

BEIDE
Heil! Heil! Heil! Heil!

BOTH
Hail! Hail! Hail! Hail!

(Siegfried geleitet schnell das Roß dem Felsenabhange zu, wohin ihm Brünnhilde folgt.

(Siegfried leads the horse quickly towards the edge of the rocky slope; Brünnhilde follows him.

Siegfried ist mit dem Rosse hinter dem Felsenvorsprunge abwärts verschwunden, so daß der Zuschauer ihn nicht mehr sieht: Brünnhilde steht so plötzlich allein am Abhange und blickt Siegfried in die Tiefe nach. Man hört Siegfrieds Horn aus der Tiefe. Brünnhilde lauscht. Sie tritt weiter auf den Abhang hinaus, erblickt Siegfried nochmals in der Tiefe und winkt ihm mit entzückter Gebärde zu. Aus ihrem freudigen Lächeln deutet sich der Anblick des lustig davonziehenden Helden. Der Vorhang fällt schnell.)

Siegfried disappears with the horse down behind the protecting rock, so that he is no longer visible to the audience; Brünnhilde stands thus suddenly alone at the edge of the slope and watches Siegfried as he descends. Siegfried's horn is heard from below. Brünnhilde listens. She steps further out on the slope, and again catches sight of Siegfried down below; she greets him with a gesture of delight. Her joyful smiles seem a reflection of the cheerful demeanour of the departing hero. The curtain falls swiftly.)

Erster Aufzug

Die Halle der Gibichungen am Rhein

Diese ist dem Hintergrund zu ganz offen; den Hintergrund selbst nimmt ein freier Uferraum bis zum Flusse hin ein; felsige Anhöhen umgrenzen das Ufer.

Act One

The Hall of the Gibichungs on the Rhine

This is quite open at the back. The background itself presents an open shore as far as the river; rocky heights border the shore.

Erste Szene

Gunther und Gutrune auf dem Hochsitze zur Seite, vor welchem ein Tisch mit Trinkgerät steht; davor sitzt Hagen.

GUNTHER

Nun hör, Hagen,
sage mir, Held:
sitz ich selig am Rhein,
Gunther zu Gibichs Ruhm?

Scene One

Gunther and Gutrune sit enthroned at one side; before them is a table with drinking vessels on it; Hagen is seated in front of the table.

GUNTHER

Now hear, Hagen;
answer me true:
is my fame along the Rhine
worthy of Gibich's name?

HAGEN
Dich echt genannten
acht ich zu neiden:
die beid' uns Brüder gebar,
Frau Grimhild hieß mich's begreifen.

HAGEN
You, trueborn son,
awaken my envy;
and she who bore us both,
fair Grimhild, taught me to honour you.

GUNTHER
Dich neide ich:
nicht neide mich du!
Erbt' ich Erstlingsart,
Weisheit ward dir allein:
Halbbrüderzwist
bezwang sich nie besser.
Deinem Rat nur red ich Lob,
frag ich dich nach meinem Ruhm.

GUNTHER
Don't envy me;
let me envy you.
I am the elder son,
yet you're the one who is wise:
half-brothers we,
no strife between us.
And I praise you, praise your wisdom,
when I ask about my fame.

HAGEN
So schelt ich den Rat,
da schlecht noch dein Ruhm;
denn hohe Güter weiß ich,
die der Gibichung noch nicht gewann.

HAGEN
My wisdom is weak;
your fame is not great:
I know some wondrous treasures
which the Gibichungs have not yet won.

GUNTHER
Verschwiegst du sie,
so schelt auch ich.

GUNTHER
If that is so,
I blame you too.

HAGEN
In sommerlich reifer Stärke
seh ich Gibichs Stamm,
dich, Gunther, unbeweibt,
dich, Gutrun, ohne Mann.
(Gunther und Gutrune sind in schweigendes Sinnen verloren.)

HAGEN
In ripeness and strength of summer,
Gibich's children rule;
but you, Gunther, have no wife;
you, Gutrun, are unwed.
(Gunther and Gutrune are lost in silent thought.)

GUNTHER
Wen rätst du nun zu frein,
daß unsrem Ruhm es fromm'?

GUNTHER
What woman should I wed
to make my fame more great?

HAGEN
Ein Weib weiß ich,
das herrlichste der Welt:
auf Felsen hoch ihr Sitz,
ein Feuer umbrennt ihren Saal;
nur wer durch das Feuer bricht,
darf Brünnhildes Freier sein.

HAGEN
There's one woman,
the noblest in the world:
a rocky crag her home;
a fire encircles the rock:
one hero will brave that fire,
then Brünnhild his bride shall be.

GUNTHER
Vermag das mein Mut zu bestehn?

GUNTHER
Is my strength enough for the deed?

HAGEN
Einem Stärkren noch ist's nur bestimmt.

GUNTHER
Wer ist der streitlichste Mann?

HAGEN
Siegfried, der Wälsungen Sproß:
der ist der stärkste Held.
Ein Zwillingspaar,
von Liebe bewungen,
Siegmund und Sieglinde,
zeugten den echtesten Sohn.
Der im Walde mächtig erwuchs,
den wünsch' ich Gutrun zum Mann.

GUTRUNE
(schüchtern beginnend)
Welche Tat schuf er so tapfer,
daß als herrlichster Held er genannt?

HAGEN
Vor Neidhöhle
den Niblungenhort
bewachte ein riesiger Wurm:
Siegfried schloß ihm
den freislichen Schlund,
erschlug ihn mit siegendem Schwert.
Solch ungeheurer Tat
enttagte des Helden Ruhm.

GUNTHER
(in Nachsinnen)
Vom Niblungenhort vernahm ich:
er birgt den neidlichsten Schatz?

HAGEN
Wer wohl ihn zu nützen wüßt',
dem neigte sich wahrlich die Welt.

GUNTHER
Und Siegfried hat ihn erkämpft?

HAGEN
Knecht sind die Niblungen ihm.

GUNTHER
Und Brünnhild gewanne nur er?

HAGEN
It requires a stronger man than you.

GUNTHER
Who is this boldest of men?

HAGEN
Siegfried, the Wälsung son,
he is the chosen man.
The Wälsung twins
whom love united,
Siegmund and Sieglind,
created this brave noble son.
In the woods he grew to be strong;
with this man Gutrun should wed.

GUTRUNE
(beginning shyly)
What deed did he accomplish,
to be hailed as the bravest of men?

HAGEN
At Neidhöhle
the Nibelung gold
was guarded by Fafner the giant:
Siegfried closed up
his threatening jaws,
and killed him with his conquering sword.
That great and valiant deed
has won him a hero's name.

GUNTHER
(thoughtfully)
The Nibelung hoard is famous;
I've heard men speak of the gold . . .

HAGEN
He who commands that gold
can bend all the world to his will:

GUNTHER
And Siegfried won it himself?

HAGEN
Slaves are the Niblungs to him.

GUNTHER
And Brünnhild must fall to his might?

HAGEN
Keinem andren wiche die Brunst.

GUNTHER
(unwillig sich vom Sitze erhebend)
Wie weckst du Zweifel und Zwist!
Was ich nicht zwingen soll,
darnach zu verlangen
machst du mir Lust?
(Er schreitet bewegt in der Halle auf und ab. Hagen, ohne seinen Sitz zu verlassen, hält Gunther, als dieser wieder in seine Nähe kommt, durch einen geheimnisvollen Wink fest.)

HAGEN
Brächte Siegfried
die Braut dir heim,
wär' dann nicht Brünnhilde dein?

GUNTHER
(wendet sich wieder zweifelnd und unmutig ab.)
Wer zwänge den frohen Mann,
für mich die Braut zu frein?

HAGEN
(wie vorher)
Ihn zwänge bald deine Bitte,
bänd' ihn Gutrun zuvor.

GUTRUNE
Du Spötter, böser Hagen,
wie sollt' ich Siegfried binden?
Ist er der herrlichste
Held der Welt,
der Erde holdeste Frauen
friedeten längst ihn schon.

HAGEN
(sich vertraulich zu Gutrune hinneigend)
Gedenk des Trankes im Schrein;
(heimlicher)
vertraue mir, der ihn gewann:
den Helden, des du verlangst,
bindet er liebend an dich.
(Gunther ist wieder an den Tisch getreten und hört, auf ihn gelehnt, jetzt aufmerksam zu.)
Träte nun Siegfried ein,
genöss' er des würzigen Tranks,

HAGEN
He alone can pass through the flame.

GUNTHER
(rises impatiently from his seat)
Then why do you mention this bride?
And why arouse my hopes
with dreams of a treasure
that cannot be mine?
(He paces the hall in agitation. Hagen, without leaving his seat, by a mysterious gesture arrests Gunther as he approaches him.)

HAGEN
What if Siegfried
should win the bride—
might he not give her to you?

GUNTHER
(turns away again in doubt and discontent.)
But how could I urge this man
to win the bride for me?

HAGEN
(as before)
Your word would easily urge him,
were but Gutrun his wife.

GUTRUNE
You mock me, cruel Hagen!
for how could Siegfried love me?
If he is the bravest
of men in the world,
then earth's most lovely women
long since have known his love.

HAGEN
(leaning over confidentially to Gutrune)
Remember that drink in the chest;
(more secretly)
and trust in me; I know its power.
That hero for whom you long,
he can be conquered by you.
(Gunther has again come to the table and, leaning upon it, listens attentively.)
Now let our Siegfried come:
we'll give him the magical drink;

daß vor dir ein Weib er ersah,
daß je ein Weib ihm genaht,
vergessen müßt' er des ganz.
Nun redet,
wie dünkt euch Hagens Rat?

he'll forget all women but you;
the past will fade from his mind;
all memory he will have lost.
Now tell me,
how like you Hagen's plan?

GUNTHER
(lebhaft auffahrend)
Gepriesen sei Grimhild,
die uns den Bruder gab!

GUNTHER
(starting up with animation)
I praise our mother Grimhild,
who bore a son so wise!

GUTRUNE
Möcht' ich Siegfried je ersehn!

GUTRUNE
And will Siegfried pass this way?

GUNTHER
Wie suchten wir ihn auf?
(Ein Horn klingt aus dem Hintergrunde von links her. Hagen lauscht.)

GUNTHER
How can we bring him here?
(A horn sounds from the background on the left. Hagen listens.)

HAGEN
Jagt er auf Taten
wonnig umher,
zum engen Tann
wird ihm die Welt:
wohl stürmt er in rastloser Jagd
auch zu Gibichs Strand an den Rhein.

HAGEN
Merrily seeking
adventures and fame,
he sails the Rhine,
he roams the world:
his journey will bring him this way,
to the Gibich hall on the Rhine.

GUNTHER
Willkommen hieß' ich ihn gern.
(Horn näher, aber immer noch fern. Beide lauschen.)
Vom Rhein her tönt das Horn.

GUNTHER
Gladly I'd welcome him here.
(The horn sounds closer, though still distant. Both listen.)
On the Rhine I can hear a horn.

HAGEN
(ist an das Ufer gegangen, späht den Fluß hinab und ruft zurück.)
In einem Nachen Held und Roß!
Der bläst so munter das Horn!
Ein gemächlicher Schlag,
wie von müßiger Hand,
treibt jach den Kahn
wider den Strom;
so rüstiger Kraft
in des Ruders Schwung
rühmt sich nur der,
der den Wurm erschlug.
Siegfried ist es, sicher kein andrer!

HAGEN
(has gone to the shore; he looks downstream, and calls back.)
I see a vessel—man and horse!
I hear the sound of his horn!
With a powerful stroke,
yet with leisurely ease,
he drives the boat,
braving the stream:
such strength in his arms
as he plies the oars!
Yes, it is he
who destroyed the giant.
Siegfried's coming, he and no other!

GUNTHER
Jagt er vorbei?

HAGEN
(durch die hohlen Hände nach dem Flusse rufend)
Hoiho! Wohin,
du heitrer Held?

SIEGFRIEDS STIMME
(aus der Ferne, vom Flusse her)
Zu Gibichs starkem Sohne.

HAGEN
Zu seiner Halle entbiet ich dich.
(Siegfried erscheint im Kahn am Ufer.)
Hieher! Hier lege an!

GUNTHER
Will he go by?

HAGEN
(calls towards the river through his cupped hands.)
Hoiho! You boatman,
where are you bound?

SIEGFRIED'S VOICE
(in the distance, from the river)
To Gunther, son of Gibich.

HAGEN
His hall awaits you; be welcome here.
(Siegfried appears at the shore in a boat.)
This way! Here tie the boat!

Zweite Szene

Siegfried legt mit dem Kahne an und springt, nachdem Hagen den Kahn mit der Kette am Ufer festgeschlossen hat, mit dem Rosse auf den Strand.

HAGEN
Heil! Siegfried, teurer Held!
(Gunther is zu Hagen an das Ufer getreten. Gutrune blickt vom Hochsitze aus in staunender Bewunderung auf Siegfried. Gunther will freundlichen Gruß bieten. Alle stehen in gegenseitiger stummer Betrachtung.)

SIEGFRIED
(auf sein Roß gelehnt, bleibt ruhig am Kahne stehen.)
Wer ist Gibichs Sohn?

GUNTHER
Gunther, ich, den du suchst.

SIEGFRIED
Dich hört' ich rühmen
weit am Rhein:

Scene Two

Siegfried brings his boat alongside and, after Hagen has made it fast with a cable, leaps on shore, with his horse.

HAGEN
Hail! Siegfried, welcome here!
(Gunther has joined Hagen on the shore. From the throne, Gutrune looks at Siegfried in astonishment. Gunther prepares to offer friendly greetings. All are fixed in mute mutual contemplation.)

SIEGFRIED
(leaning on his horse, remains quietly standing by the boat.)
Which is Gibich's son?

GUNTHER
Gunther, I whom you seek.

SIEGFRIED
Gunther is praised
along the Rhine:

nun ficht mit mir
oder sei mein Freund!

now fight with me,
or be my friend!

GUNTHER
Laß den Kampf!
Sei willkommen!

GUNTHER
Come in peace!
And be welcome!

SIEGFRIED
(sieht sich ruhig um.)
Wo berg ich mein Roß?

SIEGFRIED
(looking around calmly)
Who'll care for my horse?

HAGEN
Ich biet ihm Rast.

HAGEN
I'll give him rest.

SIEGFRIED
(zu Hagen gewendet.)
Du riefst mich Siegfried:
sahst du mich schon?

SIEGFRIED
(turning to Hagen)
You called me Siegfried:
how did you know?

HAGEN
Ich kannte dich nur
an deiner Kraft.

HAGEN
I knew when I saw
your mighty strength.

SIEGFRIED
(indem er an Hagen das Roß übergibt)
Wohl hüte mir Grane!
Du hieltest nie
von edlerer Zucht
am Zaume ein Roß.
(Hagen führt das Roß rechts hinter die Halle ab. Während Siegfried ihm gedankenvoll nachblickt, entfernt sich auch Gutrune, durch einen Wink Hagens bedeutet, von Siegfried unbemerkt, nach links durch eine Tür in ihr Gemach. Gunther schreitet mit Siegfried, den er dazu einlädt, in die Halle vor.)

SIEGFRIED
(as he gives the horse to Hagen)
Take care of my Grane:
in all the world
you'll never find
a horse more noble than he.
(Hagen leads the horse away to the right, behind the hall. While Siegfried looks thoughtfully after him, Gutrune, at a gesture of Hagen's unnoticed by Siegfried, goes out through a door on the left leading to her room. Gunther advances into the hall with Siegfried, inviting him to accompany him.)

GUNTHER
Begrüße froh, o Held,
die Halle meines Vaters;
wohin du schreitest,
was du ersiehst,
das achte nun dein eigen:
dein ist mein Erbe,
Land und Leut'—
hilf, mein Leib, meinem Eide!
Mich selbst geb ich zum Mann.

GUNTHER
I welcome you, my friend,
within the home of my fathers;
the hall you stand in,
and all you see,
freely you may command them;
share in my birthright,
land and men:
by my life let me swear it!
Me, too, you may command.

SIEGFRIED Nicht Land noch Leute biete ich, noch Vaters Haus und Hof: einzig erbt' ich den eignen Leib; lebend zehr ich den auf. Nur ein Schwert hab ich, selbst geschmiedet: hilf, mein Schwert, meinem Eide! Das biet ich mit mir zum Bund.	SIEGFRIED No land nor men have I to give, no father's house or hall: all my birthright my sturdy limbs, useless things when I'm dead. Yet a sword have I; I forged it myself: by my sword let me swear then! Body and sword shall be yours.
HAGEN *(der zurückgekommen ist und jetzt hinter Siegfried steht)* Doch des Nibelungenhortes nennt die Märe dich Herrn?	HAGEN *(has returned, and now stands behind Siegfried.)* But the Niblung gold, they say, belongs now to you.
SIEGFRIED *(sich zu Hagen umwendend)* Des Schatzes vergaß ich fast: so schätz ich sein müß'ges Gut! In einer Höhle ließ ich's liegen, wo ein Wurm es einst bewacht'.	SIEGFRIED *(turning round to Hagen)* That treasure I quite forgot; I hold it of little worth! I left it lying in a cavern, where a dragon once did dwell.
HAGEN Und nichts entnahmst du ihm?	HAGEN And took no gold away?
SIEGFRIED *(auf das stählerne Netzgewirk deutend, das er im Gürtel hängen hat)* Dies Gewirk, unkund seiner Kraft.	SIEGFRIED *(indicating the steel chainmail hanging from his belt)* Only this; I know not its use!
HAGEN Den Tarnhelm kenn ich, der Niblungen künstliches Werk: er taugt, bedeckt er dein Haupt, dir zu tauschen jede Gestalt; verlangt's dich an fernsten Ort, er entführt flugs dich dahin. Sonst nichts entnahmst du dem Hort?	HAGEN The Tarnhelm truly, the Niblung's most wonderful work: for this, when placed on your head, can transform you to any shape; and take you to any place: you just wish, and you are there! What else did you take from the cave?
SIEGFRIED Einen Ring.	SIEGFRIED Just a ring.
HAGEN Den hütest du wohl?	HAGEN And where is it now?

SIEGFRIED
Den hütet ein hehres Weib.

SIEGFRIED
Kept safe on a fair woman's hand.

HAGEN
(für sich)
Brünnhild!...

HAGEN
(aside)
Brünnhild's!

GUNTHER
Nicht, Siegfried, sollst du mir tauschen:
Tand gäb' ich für dein Geschmeid',
nähmst all mein Gut du dafür.
Ohn' Entgelt dien ich dir gern.
(Hagen ist zu Gutrunes Tür gegangen und öffnet sie jetzt. Gutrune tritt heraus, sie trägt ein gefülltes Trinkhorn und naht damit Siegfried.)

GUNTHER
Siegfried, there is naught you need give me.
I could make no fit return
even if you took all I have;
out of friendship, you I shall serve.
(Hagen has gone to Gutrune's door and now opens it. Gutrune comes out and approaches Siegfried, carrying a filled drinking-horn.)

GUTRUNE
Willkommen, Gast,
in Gibichs Haus!
Seine Tochter reicht dir den Trank.

GUTRUNE
Welcome, O guest,
to Gibich's house!
Let his daughter give you this drink.

SIEGFRIED
(neigt sich ihr freundlich und ergreift das Horn; er hält es gedankenvoll vor sich hin und sagt leise:)
Vergäß' ich alles,
was du mir gabst,
von einer Lehre
laß ich doch nie!
Den ersten Trunk
zu treuer Minne,
Brünnhilde, bring ich dir!
(Er setzt das Trinkhorn an und trinkt in einem langen Zuge. Er reicht das Horn an Gutrune, zurück, die verschämt und verwirrt ihre Augen vor ihm niederschlägt. Siegfried heftet den Blick mit schnell entbrannter Leidenschaft auf sie.)
Die so mit dem Blitz
den Blick du mir sengst,
was senkst du dein Auge vor mir?
(Gutrune schlägt errötend das Auge zu ihm auf.)
Ha, schönstes Weib!
Schließe den Blick;
das Herz in der Brust
brennt mir sein Strahl:
zu feurigen Strömen fühl ich
ihn zehrend zünden mein Blut!
(mit bebender Stimme)
Gunther, wie heißt deine Schwester?

SIEGFRIED
(bows to her politely and takes the horn. Holding it up thoughtfully, he says softly:)
Though I forget
all else that you gave,
one holy lesson
I shall recall:
this drink, the first
I taste as lover,
Brünnhild, I drink to you!
(He raises the horn and takes a long draught. He returns the horn to Gutrune, who casts down her eyes before him in shame and confusion. Siegfried fixes his gaze on her with suddenly inflamed passion.)
Those eyes with a flash
set fire to my heart;
why lower your glorious gaze?
(Gutrune, blushing, raises her eyes to his face.)
Ah, fairest maid!
Close them again;
the heart in my breast
burns in their beams;
the blood in my veins is kindled
to scorching fiery streams!
(with trembling voice)
Gunther, what is the name of your sister?

GUNTHER
Gutrune.

SIEGFRIED
(leise)
Sind's gute Runen,
die ihrem Aug' ich entrate?
(Er faßt Gutrune mit feurigem Ungestüm bei der Hand.)
Deinem Bruder bot ich mich zum Mann:
der Stolze schlug mich aus;
trügst du, wie er, mir Übermut,
böt' ich mich dir zum Bund?
(Gutrune trifft unwillkürlich auf Hagens Blick. Sie neigt demütig das Haupt, und mit einer Gebärde, als fühle sie sich seiner nicht wert, verläßt sie schwankenden Schrittes wieder die Halle.)

SIEGFRIED
(von Hagen und Gunther aufmerksam beobachtet, blickt ihr, wie festgezaubert, nach; dann, ohne sich umzuwenden, fragt er.)
Hast du, Gunther, ein Weib?

GUNTHER
Nicht freit' ich noch,
und einer Frau
soll ich mich schwerlich freun!
Auf eine setzt' ich den Sinn,
die kein Rat mir je gewinnt.

SIEGFRIED
(wendet sich lebhaft zu Gunther.)
Was wär' dir versagt,
steh ich zu dir?

GUNTHER
Auf Felsen hoch ihr Sitz;
ein Feuer umbrennt den Saal—

SIEGFRIED
(mit verwunderungsvoller Hast einfallend)
»Auf Felsen hoch ihr Sitz;
ein Feuer umbrennt den Saal« . . . ?

GUNTHER
Nur wer durch das Feuer bricht—

GUNTHER
Gutrune.

SIEGFRIED
(softly)
Do I read a welcome
there in the shining eyes of Gutrun?
(Ardently and impetuously he seizes Gutrune's hand.)
With your brother I offered to serve;
his pride refused my aid.
Will you, like him, reject my plea?
Or may I serve with you?
(Gutrune involuntarily catches Hagen's eye. She bows her head and, with a gesture as if she felt herself unworthy, she leaves the hall with faltering steps.)

SIEGFRIED
(watched closely by Hagen and Gunther, gazes after Gutrune as if bewitched; then, without turning round, he asks:)
Gunther, have you a wife?

GUNTHER
No wife have I yet;
the wife I long for
will be hard to find,
for I have set my desire
on a maid whom I cannot win!

SIEGFRIED
(turns with animation to Gunther.)
Whom can you not win,
with me to help?

GUNTHER
A rocky crag her home;
a fire surrounds the rock—

SIEGFRIED
(breaking in hastily in astonishment)
'A rocky crag her home;
a fire surrounds the rock' . . . ?

GUNTHER
One hero will brave the fire—

SIEGFRIED
(mit der heftigsten Anstrengung, um eine Erinnerung festzuhalten)
»Nur wer durch das Feuer bricht« . . . ?

GUNTHER
—darf Brünnhildes Freier sein.
(Siegfried drückt durch eine Gebärde aus, daß bei Nennung von Brünnhildes Namen die Erinnerung ihm vollends ganz schwindet.)
Nun darf ich den Fels nicht erklimmen;
das Feuer verglimmt mir nie!

SIEGFRIED
(kommt aus einem traumartigen Zustand zu sich und wendet sich mit übermütiger Lustigkeit zu Gunther.)
Ich—fürchte kein Feuer,
für dich frei ich die Frau;
denn dein Mann bin ich,
und mein Mut ist dein,
gewinn ich mir Gutrun zum Weib.

GUNTHER
Gutrune gönn ich dir gerne.

SIEGFRIED
Brünnhilde bring ich dir.

GUNTHER
Wie willst du sie täuschen?

SIEGFRIED
Durch des Tarnhelms Trug
tausch ich mir deine Gestalt.

GUNTHER
So stelle Eide zum Schwur!

SIEGFRIED
Blut-Brüderschaft
schwöre ein Eid!
(Hagen füllt ein Trinkhorn mit frischem Wein; dieses hält er dann Siegfried und Gunther hin, welche sich mit ihren Schwertern die Arme ritzen und diese eine kurze Zeit über die Öffnung des Trinkhorns halten. Siegfried und Gunther legen zwei ihrer Finger auf das Horn, welches Hagen fortwährend in ihrer Mitte hält.)

SIEGFRIED
(striving with intense effort to remember something)
'One hero will brave the fire' . . . ?

GUNTHER
Then Brünnhild his bride shall be.
(Siegfried shows by a gesture that at the mention of Brünnhilde's name his memory has quite faded.)

I dare not set foot on that mountain;
those flames would make me fear!

SIEGFRIED
(comes to himself from his dreamy state, and turns to Gunther with cheerful self-confidence.)

I fear not the flames,
and for you I shall win the bride;
for your friend am I,
and my strength is yours,
if I can have Gutrun as wife.

GUNTHER
Gutrun I'll give to you gladly.

SIEGFRIED
Brünnhilde then is yours.

GUNTHER
But how will you deceive her?

SIEGFRIED
By the Tarnhelm's art
I can be changed into you.

GUNTHER
Then let us swear by a vow!

SIEGFRIED
Blood brotherhood
joins us as one!
(Hagen fills a drinking-horn with fresh wine; he holds it out to Siegfried and Gunther, who cut their arms with their swords and hold them for a moment over the top of the horn. Both lay two fingers on the horn, which Hagen continues to hold between them.)

SIEGFRIED
Blühenden Lebens
labendes Blut
träufelt' ich in den Trank.

GUNTHER
Bruder-brünstig
mutig gemischt,
blüh im Trank unser Blut.

BEIDE
Treue trink ich dem Freund.
Froh und frei
entblühe dem Bund
Blut-Brüderschaft heut!

GUNTHER
Bricht ein Bruder den Bund—

SIEGFRIED
Trügt den Treuen der Freund—

BEIDE
Was in Tropfen heut
hold wir tranken,
in Strahlen ström' es dahin,
fromme Sühne dem Freund!

GUNTHER
(trinkt und reicht das Horn Siegfried.)
So—biet ich den Bund.

SIEGFRIED
So—trink ich dir Treu'!
(Er trinkt und hält das geleerte Trinkhorn Hagen hin. Hagen zerschlägt mit seinem Schwerte das Horn in zwei Stücke. Siegfried und Gunther reichen sich die Hände.)

SIEGFRIED
(betrachtet Hagen, welcher während des Schwures hinter ihm gestanden.)
Was nahmst du am Eide nicht teil?

HAGEN
Mein Blut verdürb' euch den Trank;
nicht fließt mir's echt

SIEGFRIED
Flourishing life's
refreshing blood
we have shed in this horn.

GUNTHER
Bravely blended
brotherly love,
born in the drink from our blood!

BOTH
Truth I swear to my friend!
Fair and free,
the blood is our bond;
blood-brotherhood here!

GUNTHER
If one friend should be false—

SIEGFRIED
If one friend should betray—

BOTH
then not drops of blood—
all his life blood
shall flow in streams from his veins;
traitors so must atone!

GUNTHER
(drinks and hands the horn to Siegfried.)
I swear to be true!

SIEGFRIED
I swear to be true!
(He drinks and holds out the empty drinking-horn to Hagen. Hagen strikes the horn into two with his sword. Gunther and Siegfried join hands.)

SIEGFRIED
(observes Hagen, who has stood behind him during the oath.)
But you did not join us in our oath!

HAGEN
My blood would spoil all your drink;
my blood's not pure

und edel wie euch;
störrisch und kalt
stockt's in mir;
nicht will's die Wange mir röten.
Drum bleib ich fern
vom feurigen Bund.

and noble like yours;
stubborn and cold,
slow to stir,
my blood flows slowly and strangely:
I take no part
in fiery vows.

GUNTHER
(zu Siegfried)
Laß den unfrohen Mann!

GUNTHER
(to Siegfried)
Leave this unhappy man!

SIEGFRIED
(hängt sich den Schild wieder über.)
Frisch auf die Fahrt!
Dort liegt mein Schiff;
schnell führt es zum Felsen.
Eine Nacht am Ufer
harrst du im Nachen;
die Frau fährst du dann heim.
(Er wendet sich zum Fortgehen und winkt Gunther, ihm zu folgen.)

SIEGFRIED
(takes up his shield again.)
Now on our way!
There lies my boat:
swiftly sail to the mountain!
For a night I'll leave you;
then, when I've won her,
your bride you shall bring home!
(He turns to leave, and beckons to Gunther to follow him.)

GUNTHER
Rastest du nicht zuvor?

GUNTHER
Will you not rest awhile?

SIEGFRIED
Um die Rückkehr ist mir's jach!
(Er geht zum Ufer, um das Schiff loszubinden.)

SIEGFRIED
When you've gained her, then I'll rest.
(He goes to the shore to cast the boat loose.)

GUNTHER
Du, Hagen, bewache die Halle!
(Er folgt Siegfried zum Ufer. Während Siegfried und Gunther, nachdem sie ihre Waffen darin niedergelegt, im Schiff das Segel aufstecken und alles zur Abfahrt bereitmachen, nimmt Hagen seinen Speer und Schild. Gutrune erscheint an der Tür ihres Gemachs, als soeben Siegfried das Schiff abstößt, welches sogleich der Mitte des Stromes zutreibt.)

GUNTHER
You, Hagen, keep watch over the palace!
(He follows Siegfried to the shore. Siegfried and Gunther, after they have laid their arms in the boat, put up the sail and make all ready for departure; Hagen takes up his spear and shield. Gutrune appears at the door of her room just as Siegfried pushes off the boat, which floats at once into midstream.)

GUTRUNE
Wohin eilen die Schnellen?

GUTRUNE
So fast! Where have they gone to?

HAGEN
(während er sich gemächlich mit Schild und Speer vor der Halle niedersetzt)
Zu Schiff—Brünnhild zu frein.

HAGEN
(while he slowly seats himself in front of the hall, with shield and spear)
They've sailed—Brünnhild they'll find.

GUTRUNE
Siegfried?

HAGEN
Sieh, wie's ihn treibt,
zum Weib dich zu gewinnen!

GUTRUNE
Siegfried—mein!
(Sie geht, lebhaft erregt, in ihr Gemach zurück. Siegfried hat das Ruder erfaßt und treibt jetzt mit dessen Schlägen den Nachen stromabwärts, so daß dieser bald gänzlich außer Gesicht kommt.)

HAGEN
(sitzt mit dem Rücken an den Pfosten der Halle gelehnt, bewegungslos.)
Hier sitz ich zur Wacht,
wahre den Hof,
wehre die Halle dem Feind.
Gibichs Sohne
wehet der Wind,
auf Werben fährt er dahin.
Ihm führt das Steuer
ein starker Held,
Gefahr ihm will er bestehn.
Die eigne Braut
ihm bringt er zum Rhein;
mir aber bringt er—den Ring!
Ihr freien Söhne,
frohe Gesellen,
segelt nur lustig dahin!
Dünkt er euch niedrig,
ihr dient ihm doch,
des Niblungen Sohn.

(Ein Teppich, welcher dem Vordergrunde zu die Halle einfaßte, schlägt zusammen und schließt die Bühne vor dem Zuschauer ab.)

GUTRUNE
Siegfried?

HAGEN
See, see his haste!
He's eager to win you!

GUTRUNE
Siegfried—mine!
(She returns to her room in excitement. Siegfried has seized an oar and with its strokes he drives the boat down the stream so that it is quickly lost to view.)

HAGEN
(sits motionless, leaning his back against the doorpost of the hall.)
I sit here and wait,
watching the house,
guarding the hall from the foe.
Gibich's son
is borne by the wind,
away to his wooing he's gone.
His ship is steered
by his fearless friend,
who'll brave the fire in his stead:
and he will bring
his bride to the Rhine;
with her, he brings me the ring!
You sons of freedom,
joyful companions,
merrily sail on your way!
Though you despise me,
you'll serve me soon,
the Niblung's son.

(A curtain, attached to the front of the hall, closes, and cuts off the stage from the audience.)

Dritte Szene

Die Felsenhöhle, wie im Vorspiel

Brünnhilde sitzt am Eingange des Steingemachs, in stummem Sinnen Siegfrieds Ring betrachtend; von wonniger Erinnerung überwältigt, bedeckt sie ihn mit Küssen. Ferner Donner läßt sich vernehmen, sie blickt auf und lauscht. Dann wendet sie sich wieder zu dem Ring. Ein feuriger Blitz. Sie lauscht von neuem und späht nach der Ferne, von woher eine finstre Gewitterwolke dem Felsensaume zuzieht.

BRÜNNHILDE
Altgewohntes Geräusch
raunt meinem Ohr die Ferne.
Ein Luftroß jagt
im Laufe daher;
auf der Wolke fährt es
wetternd zum Fels.
Wer fand mich Einsame auf?

WALTRAUTES STIMME
(aus der Ferne)
Brünnhilde! Schwester!
Schläfst oder wachst du?

BRÜNNHILDE
(fährt vom Sitze auf.)
Waltrautes Ruf,
so wonnig mir kund!
(in die Szene rufend)
Kommst du, Schwester?
Schwingst dich kühn zu mir her?
(Sie eilt nach dem Felsrande.)
Dort im Tann
—dir noch vertraut—
steige vom Roß
und stell den Renner zur Rast!
(Sie stürmt in den Tann, von wo ein starkes Geräusch, gleich einem Gewitterschlage, sich vernehmen läßt. Dann kommt sie in heftiger Bewegung mit Waltraute zurück; sie bleibt freudig erregt, ohne Waltrautes ängstliche Scheu zu beachten.)
Kommst du zu mir?
Bist du so kühn,

Scene Three

The Rocky Height, as in the Prelude

Brünnhilde is sitting at the entrance to the cave, in mute contemplation of Siegfried's ring. Overcome by joyful memories, she covers it with kisses. Distant thunder is heard; she looks up and listens. Then she turns again to the ring. A flash of lightning. Brünnhilde listens again and looks into the distance, where a dark thundercloud is seen approaching the rocky height.

BRÜNNHILDE
Sounds I once knew so well
steal on my ears from the distance.
I see it—
there's a Valkyrie horse:
through the clouds it is speeding
here to my rock.
Who dares to seek me again?

WALTRAUTE'S VOICE
(from the distance)
Brünnhilde! Sister!
Wake from your slumber!

BRÜNNHILDE
(leaping up)
Waltraute's call;
so joyful the sound!
(calling to the wing)
Welcome sister!
boldly flying to my rock!
(She hastens to the edge of the rocks.)
There in the wood—
you know the place—
leap from your horse,
and leave him safely to rest.
(She runs into the wood, from which a loud sound like a thunderclap is heard. Brünnhilde comes back, very excited, with Waltraute; she remains in joyful excitement, without observing Waltraute's anxious fear.)

You've come to me?
Are you bold,

magst ohne Grauen
Brünnhild bieten den Gruß?

WALTRAUTE
Einzig dir nur
galt meine Eil'!

BRÜNNHILDE
(in höchster freudiger Aufgeregtheit)
So wagtest du, Brünnhild zulieb,
Walvaters Bann zu brechen?
Oder wie—o sag—
wär' wider mich
Wotans Sinn erweicht?
Als dem Gott entgegen
Siegmund ich schützte,
fehlend—ich weiß es—
erfüllt' ich doch seinen Wunsch.
Daß sein Zorn sich verzogen,
weiß ich auch;
denn verschloß er mich gleich in Schlaf,
fesselt' er mich auf den Fels,
wies er dem Mann mich zur Magd,
der am Weg mich fänd' und erweckt'—
meiner bangen Bitte
doch gab er Gunst:
mit zehrendem Feuer
umzog er den Fels,
dem Zagen zu wehren den Weg.
So zur Seligsten
schuf mich die Strafe:
der herrlichste Held
gewann mich zum Weib!
In seiner Liebe
leucht und lach ich heut auf.
(Sie umarmt Waltraute, die mit scheuer Ungeduld abzuwehren sucht.)
Lockte dich, Schwester, mein Los?
An meiner Wonne
willst du dich weiden,
teilen, was mich betraf?

WALTRAUTE
(heftig)
Teilen den Taumel,
der dich Törin erfaßt?
Ein andres bewog mich in Angst,

daring to seek me,
Brünnhild, here on her rock?

WALTRAUTE
You alone
are the cause of my haste!

BRÜNNHILDE
(in joyous excitement)
For love of me, for Brünnhilde's sake,
Wotan's command you've broken?
Or perhaps—Oh say—
can it be true?—
Wotan's mind is changed?
When against his anger
Siegmund I guarded,
my deed—I know it—
my deed fulfilled his desire.
And I know that his anger
is no more.
For although I was bound in sleep,
left all alone on the rock,
meant as a prize for the man
who might pass and wake me to life,
to my sad entreaty
he granted grace:
with ravening fire
he surrounded the rock,
so that none but a hero could pass.
So my blessing
I gained by my sentence:
the noblest of men
has won me as wife!
Blessed by his love,
in light and laughter I live.
(She embraces Waltraute, who attempts with anxious impatience to restrain her.)
Ah, were you brought here by my love?
You've come to join me,
gaze on my rapture,
share all that I have won?

WALTRAUTE
(vehemently)
Share all the frenzy
that has maddened your brain?
In anguish and dread I have come,

zu brechen Wotans Gebot.
(Brünnhilde gewahrt hier erst Waltrautes wildaufgeregte Stimmung.)

BRÜNNHILDE
Angst und Furcht
fesseln dich Arme?
So verzieh der Strenge noch nicht?
Du zagst vor des Strafenden Zorn?

WALTRAUTE
(düster)
Dürft' ich ihn fürchten,
meiner Angst fänd' ich ein End'!

BRÜNNHILDE
Staunend versteh ich dich nicht!

WALTRAUTE
Wehre der Wallung,
achtsam höre mich an!
Nach Walhall wieder
drängt mich die Angst,
die von Walhall hieher mich trieb.

BRÜNNHILDE
(erschrocken)
Was ist's mit den ewigen Göttern?

WALTRAUTE
Höre mit Sinn, was ich sage!
Seit er von dir geschieden,
zur Schlacht nicht mehr
schickte uns Wotan;
irr und ratlos
ritten wir ängstlich zu Heer;
Walhalls mutige Helden
mied Walvater.
Einsam zu Roß,
ohne Ruh noch Rast,
durchschweift' er als Wandrer die Welt.
Jüngst kehrte er heim;
in der Hand hielt er
seines Speeres Splitter:
die hatte ein Held ihm geschlagen.
Mit stummem Wink
Walhalls Edle

defying Wotan's command.
(Brünnhilde here first observes with surprise Waltraute's extreme agitation.)

BRÜNNHILDE
Anguish and fear
I read in your features!
So the god has pardoned me not?
You still are afraid of his wrath?

WALTRAUTE
(gloomily)
If still I feared him,
I should have nothing else to fear!

BRÜNNHILDE
Sister, I do not understand!

WALTRAUTE
Calm your frenzy,
pay good heed to my words!
To Walhall that dread
must make me return,
which from Walhall drove me away.

BRÜNNHILDE
(alarmed)
What harm can assail the immortals?

WALTRAUTE
Hear me in calm, and I will tell you!
Since you and he were parted,
we've fought no more battles
for Wotan.
Dazed and doubting,
we Valkyries rode to the field—
Walhall's valiant heroes
all left leaderless!
Alone on his horse,
without peace or rest,
through the world as a wanderer he rode.
But then he came home;
in his hand
his sacred spear was splintered,
that spear which a hero had shattered.
He gave a sign:
Walhall's heroes

wies er zum Forst,
die Weltesche zu fällen.
Des Stammes Scheite
hieß er sie schichten
zu ragendem Hauf
rings um der Seligen Saal.
Der Götter Rat
ließ er berufen;
den Hochsitz nahm
heilig er ein:
ihm zu Seiten
hieß er die Bangen sich setzen,
in Ring und Reih'
die Hall' erfüllen die Helden.
So sitzt er,
sagt kein Wort,
auf hehrem Sitze
stumm und ernst,
des Speeres Splitter
fest in der Faust;
Holdas Äpfel
rührt er nicht an.
Staunen und Bangen
binden starr die Götter.
Seine Raben beide
sandt' er auf Reise:
kehrten die einst
mit guter Kunde zurück,
dann noch einmal,
zum letztenmal,
lächelte ewig der Gott.
Seine Knie umwindend,
liegen wir Walküren;
blind bleibt er
den flehenden Blicken;
uns alle verzehrt
Zagen und endlose Angst.
An seine Brust
preßt' ich mich weinend:
da brach sich sein Blick—
er gedachte, Brünnhilde, dein!
Tief seufzt' er auf,
schloß das Auge,
und wie im Traume
raunt' er das Wort:
»Des tiefen Rheines Töchtern
gäbe den Ring sie wieder zurück,

went on their way—
the World Ash-tree was fated.
The sacred branches
he bade them break,
then pile in a heap
all round the glorious hall.
The holy clan
came as he called them;
and Wotan, on high,
took his place.
By his side
in fear and dismay they assembled;
in ranks around the hall
he stationed his heroes.
He sits there,
speaks no word,
enthroned in silence,
stern and sad;
the spear in splinters
grasped in his hand.
Holda's apples
tastes he no more.
Fearful and trembling,
the gods look on in silence.
He has sent his ravens
forth on their journeys;
when they return
and bring the news he awaits,
then for the last time
a smile of joy
will shine on the face of the god.
Round his knees are gathered,
in anguish, we Valkyries;
blind, he will not heed
our entreaties:
and all are afraid,
filled with an endless dismay.
Then on his breast
I wept in my sorrow;
his glance grew more mild;
he remembered, Brünnhilde, you!
He sighed in grief,
closed his eye,
and deep in dreaming,
whispered these words:
'If once the Rhine's fair daughters
win back their ring from Brünnhild again,

von des Fluches Last
erlöst wär' Gott und die Welt!«
Da sann ich nach:
von seiner Seite
durch stumme Reihen
stahl ich mich fort;
in heimlicher Hast
bestieg ich mein Roß
und ritt im Sturme zu dir.
Dich, o Schwester,
beschwör ich nun:
was du vermagst,
vollend' es dein Mut!
Ende der Ewigen Qual!
(Sie hat sich vor Brünnhilde niedergeworfen.)

BRÜNNHILDE
(ruhig)
Welch banger Träume Mären
meldest du Traurige mir!
Der Götter heiligem
Himmelsnebel
bin ich Törin enttaucht:
nicht faß ich, was ich erfahre.
Wirr und wüst
scheint mir dein Sinn;
in deinem Aug',
so übermüde,
glänzt flackernde Glut.
Mit blasser Wange,
du bleiche Schwester,
was willst du Wilde von mir?

WALTRAUTE
(heftig)
An deiner Hand, der Ring,
er ist's; hör meinen Rat:
für Wotan wirf ihn von dir!

BRÜNNHILDE
Den Ring? Von mir?

WALTRAUTE
Den Rheintöchtern gib ihn zurück!

BRÜNNHILDE
Den Rheintöchtern, ich, den Ring?

then the curse will pass;
she will save both god and the world!'
So I took thought;
I left our father,
and through the silence
stole from the hall;
in secret haste
I mounted my horse,
and rode the storm to your rock.
Hear, O sister,
and grant my prayer:
you, you alone
can help in our need!
End our remorse and our grief!
(She has thrown herself at Brünnhilde's feet.)

BRÜNNHILDE
(quietly)
These tales of evil fancies
hold no meaning for me!
The gods and Walhall's
cloudy splendours,
I, poor fool, have escaped;
so how can Walhall concern me?
Strange and wild,
all that you say:
and in your eyes,
so wild and weary,
gleam flames of desire.
With pallid features,
unhappy sister,
oh tell me, what would you ask?

WALTRAUTE
(vehemently)
Upon your hand, the ring,
that ring! Hear my advice:
for Wotan, cast it away!

BRÜNNHILDE
The ring? My ring?

WALTRAUTE
Let the Rhinemaidens have it again!

BRÜNNHILDE
The Rhinemaidens?—I?—the ring?

Siegfrieds Liebespfand?
Bist du von Sinnen?

WALTRAUTE
Hör mich, hör meine Angst!
Der Welt Unheil
haftet sicher an ihm.
Wirf ihn von dir,
fort in die Welle!
Walhalls Elend zu enden,
den verfluchten wirf in die Flut!

BRÜNNHILDE
Ha, weißt du, was er mir ist?
Wie kannst du's fassen,
fühllose Maid!
Mehr als Walhalls Wonne,
mehr als der Ewigen Ruhm
ist mir der Ring:
ein Blick auf sein helles Gold,
ein Blitz aus dem hehren Glanz
gilt mir werter
als aller Götter
ewig währendes Glück!
Denn selig aus ihm
leuchtet mir Siegfrieds Liebe,
Siegfrieds Liebe!
O ließ' sich die Wonne dir sagen!
Sie—wahrt mir der Reif.
Geh hin zu der Götter
heiligem Rat!
Von meinem Ringe
raun ihnen zu:
Die Liebe ließe ich nie,
mir nähmen nie sie die Liebe,
stürzt' auch in Trümmern
Walhalls strahlende Pracht!

WALTRAUTE
Dies deine Treue?
So in Trauer
entlässest du lieblos die Schwester?

BRÜNNHILDE
Schwinge dich fort!
Fliege zu Roß!
Den Ring entführst du mir nicht!

Siegfried's pledge to me?
Your words are madness!

WALTRAUTE
Hear me, hear my despair!
The world's future
all depends on the ring.
Cast it from you,
down in the waters;
Walhall's grief shall be ended,
when you cast it back in the Rhine.

BRÜNNHILDE
Ha! learn then what it means to me!
How can you grasp it,
unfeeling maid!
More than Walhall's pleasures,
more than the fame of the gods,
more is this ring.
One glance at its shining gold,
one flash of its holy fire
I hold dearer
than all the gods'
eternal, loveless delights.
The shine of this gold
tells me that Siegfried loves me!
Siegfried loves me!
O joy that transfigures my being!
Love lives in the ring.
Go home to the sacred
clan of the gods!
And of my ring
you may give them this reply:
My love shall last while I live,
my ring in life shall not leave me!
Fall first in ruins
Walhall's glorious pride!

WALTRAUTE
This is your loyalty?
And to sorrow,
you cruelly abandon your sister?

BRÜNNHILDE
Back to your horse!
Fly on your way!
The ring remains on my hand!

WALTRAUTE
Wehe! Wehe!
Weh dir, Schwester!
Walhalls Göttern weh!
(Sie stürzt fort. Bald erhebt sich unter Sturm eine Gewitterwolke aus dem Tann.)

WALTRAUTE
Sorrow! Sorrow!
Woe my sister!
Woe to Walhall, woe!
(She rushes away. A stormy thundercloud soon rises from the wood.)

BRÜNNHILDE
(während sie der davonjagenden, hell erleuchteten Gewitterwolke, die sich bald gänzlich in der Ferne verliert, nachblickt)
Blitzend Gewölk,
vom Wind getragen,
stürme dahin:
zu mir nie steure mehr her!
(Es ist Abend geworden. Aus der Tiefe leuchtet der Feuerschein allmählich heller auf. Brünnhilde blickt ruhig in die Landschaft hinaus.)
Abendlich Dämmern
deckt den Himmel;
heller leuchtet
die hütende Lohe herauf.
(Der Feuerschein nähert sich aus der Tiefe. Immer glühendere Flammenzungen lecken über den Felsensaum auf.)
Was leckt so wütend
die lodernde Welle zum Wall?
Zur Felsenspitze
wälzt sich der feurige Schwall.
(Man hört aus der Tiefe Siegfrieds Hornruf nahen. Brünnhilde lauscht und fährt entzückt auf.)
Siegfried!
Siegfried zurück?
Seinen Ruf sendet er her!
Auf! – Auf, ihm entgegen!
In meines Gottes Arm!
(Sie eilt in höchstem Entzücken dem Felsrande zu. Feuerflammen schlagen herauf, aus ihnen springt Siegfried auf einen hochragenden Felsstein empor, worauf die Flammen sogleich wieder zurückweichen und abermals nur aus der Tiefe heraufleuchten. Siegfried, auf dem Haupte den Tarnhelm, der ihm bis zur Hälfte das Gesicht verdeckt und nur die Augen freiläßt, erscheint in Gunthers Gestalt.)

BRÜNNHILDE
(as she watches the departure of the brightly flashing thundercloud, which is soon lost in the distance)
Borne by the wind,
through flashing stormclouds,
fly on your way:
to me you need not return!
(Evening has fallen. From below, the light of the fire gradually grows brighter. Brünnhilde looks quietly out on the landscape.)
Dark shades of evening
veil the heavens;
brightly blazes
the guardian fire of the rock.
(The fire-light approaches from below. Tongues of flame, growing continually brighter, dart up over the rocky edge.)
The flames leap wildly,
and why do they flare up on high?
The mountain peak
is walled by a rampart of flame.
(Siegfried's horn-call sounds from below. Brünnhilde listens, and starts up in delight.)
Siegfried!
Siegfried returns,
and his call rings in my ears!
Ah! Ah, I must meet him!
I greet my god once more!
(She hastens to the rocky parapet in the highest delight. Flames shoot up from them; Siegfried leaps forward onto a high rock: the flames immediately draw back again and shed their light only from below. Siegfried, with the Tarnhelm on his head, which hides the upper half of his face and leaves only his eyes free, appears in Gunther's form.)

BRÜNNHILDE
(voll Entsetzen zurückweichend)
Verrat! — Wer drang zu mir?

BRÜNNHILDE
(shrinking in terror)
Betrayed! Who dares come here?

(Sie flieht bis in den Vordergrund und heftet in sprachlosem Erstaunen ihren Blick auf Siegfried.)

(She flies to the foreground, and gazes at Siegfried in speechless astonishment.)

SIEGFRIED
(im Hintergrunde auf dem Steine verweilend, betrachtet sie lange, regungslos auf seinen Schild gelehnt; dann redet er sie mit verstellter—tieferer—Stimme an.)
Brünnhild! Ein Freier kam,
den dein Feuer nicht geschreckt.
Dich werb ich nun zum Weib:
du folge willig mir!

SIEGFRIED
(remaining on the rock at back, leans on his shield, motionless, observing her for a while. Then, in a feigned—and deeper—voice, he addresses her.)
Brünnhild! Your husband comes;
I have sought you through the flames.
I claim you as my wife:
now you belong to me!

BRÜNNHILDE
(heftig zitternd)
Wer ist der Mann,
der das vermochte,
was dem Stärksten nur bestimmt?

BRÜNNHILDE
(trembling violently)
Who is the man
who dares to come here
where the bravest alone may climb?

SIEGFRIED
(unverändert wie zuvor)
Ein Helde, der dich zähmt,
bezwingt Gewalt dich nur.

SIEGFRIED
(as before)
A hero who will tame you,
if you resist my might.

BRÜNNHILDE
(von Grausen erfaßt)
Ein Unhold schwang sich
auf jenen Stein!
Ein Aar kam geflogen,
mich zu zerfleischen!
Wer bist du, Schrecklicher?
Stammst du von Menschen?
Kommst du von Hellas
nächtlichem Heer?

BRÜNNHILDE
(seized with fear)
A demon
come to usurp the rock!
An eagle has flown here
to tear me to pieces!
Who are you, dreadful one?
Are you a mortal?
Are you a demon
sent from hell?

SIEGFRIED
(wie zuvor, mit etwas bebender Stimme beginnend, alsbald aber wieder sicherer fortfahrend)
Ein Gibichung bin ich,
und Gunther heißt der Held,
dem, Frau, du folgen sollst.

SIEGFRIED
(as before, beginning with a slightly trembling voice, but continuing more confidently)
A Gibichung am I,
and Gunther is my name;
now, maid, you follow me.

BRÜNNHILDE
(in Verzweiflung ausbrechend)
Wotan! Ergrimmter,
grausamer Gott!
Weh! Nun erseh ich
der Strafe Sinn;

BRÜNNHILDE
(breaking out in despair)
Wotan! You cruel,
merciless god!
Ah! Now my sentence
I understand!

zu Hohn und Jammer
jagst du mich hin!

To shame and sorrow
I am condemned.

SIEGFRIED
(springt vom Stein herab und tritt näher heran.)
Die Nacht bricht an:
in deinen Gemach
mußt du dich mir vermählen!

SIEGFRIED
(leaps down from the rock and approaches.)
The night draws on:
and there in your cave
you must obey your husband!

BRÜNNHILDE
(indem sie den Finger, an dem sie Siegfrieds Ring trägt, drohend ausstreckt)
Bleib fern! Fürchte dies Zeichen!
Zur Schande zwingst du mich nicht,
solang der Ring mich beschützt.

BRÜNNHILDE
(stretching out threateningly the finger on which she wears Siegfried's ring)
Stand back! See I am guarded!
No mortal brings me to shame,
so long as this ring is my guard.

SIEGFRIED
Mannesrecht gebe er Gunther,
durch den Ring sei ihm vermählt!

SIEGFRIED
You shall be conquered by Gunther;
and that ring makes you his wife!

BRÜNNHILDE
Zurück, du Räuber!
Frevelnder Dieb!
Erfreche dich nicht, mir zu nahn!
Stärker als Stahl
macht mich der Ring:
nie—raubst du ihn mir!

BRÜNNHILDE
Stand back, and fear me!
foolhardy thief!
Beware me, I'm armed by the ring!
Stronger than steel
makes me the ring:
No! None steals from me!

SIEGFRIED
Von dir ihn zu lösen,
lehrst du mich nun!
(Er dringt auf sie ein; sie ringen miteinander. Brünnhilde windet sich los, flieht und wendet sich um, wie zur Wehr. Siegfried greift sie von neuem an. Sie flieht, er erreicht sie. Beide ringen heftig miteinander. Er faßt sie bei der Hand und entzieht ihrem Finger den Ring. Sie schreit heftig auf. Als sie wie zerbrochen in seinen Armen niedersinkt, streift ihr Blick bewußtlos die Augen Siegfrieds.)

SIEGFRIED
From you I shall take it,
taught by your words!
(He presses toward her. They struggle together. Brünnhilde wrenches herself free, flies, and turns as if to defend herself. Siegfried seizes her again. She flees; he reaches her. Both wrestle violently together. He seizes her by the hand and draws the ring from her finger. Brünnhilde shrieks violently. As she sinks down into his arms, as if broken, her unconscious look meets Siegfried's eyes.)

SIEGFRIED
(läßt die Machtlose auf die Steinbank vor dem Felsengemach niedergleiten.)
Jetzt bist du mein,
Brünnhilde, Gunthers Braut—
Gönne mir nun dein Gemach!

SIEGFRIED
(lets her fainting body sink to the stone bench at the entrance to the cave.)
Now you are mine.
Brünnhilde, Gunther's bride,
there we shall stay in your cave!

BRÜNNHILDE
(starrt ohnmächtig vor sich hin, matt.)
Was könntest du wehren,
elendes Weib?
(Siegfried treibt sie mit einer gebietenden Bewegung an. Zitternd und wankenden Schrittes geht sie in das Gemach.)

SIEGFRIED
(das Schwert ziehend, mit seiner natürlichen Stimme)
Nun, Notung, zeuge du,
daß ich in Züchten warb.
Die Treue wahrend dem Bruder,
trenne mich von seiner Braut!
(Er folgt Brünnhilde nach. Der Vorhang fällt.)

BRÜNNHILDE
(stares fainting before her, exhausted.)
Now nothing can save me,
ill-fated wife!
(Siegfried drives her on with a gesture of command. Trembling, and with faltering steps, she goes into the cave.)

SIEGFRIED
(draws his sword; in his natural voice:)
Now, Notung, witness here
how I shall keep my vow.
I keep my word to my brother!
Part me now from Gunther's bride!
(He follows Brünnhilde. The curtain falls.)

Zweiter Aufzug

Uferraum

Vor der Halle der Gibichungen; rechts der offene Eingang zur Halle; links das Rheinufer; von diesem aus erhebt sich eine durch verschiedene Bergpfade gespaltene, felsige Anhöhe quer über die Bühne, nach rechts dem Hintergrunde zu aufsteigend. Dort sieht man einen der Fricka errichteten Weihstein, welchem höher hinauf ein größerer für Wotan, sowie seitwärts ein gleicher dem Donner geweihter entspricht. Es ist Nacht.

Erste Szene

Hagen, den Speer im Arm, den Schild zur Seite, sitzt schlafend an einen Pfosten der Halle gelehnt. Der Mond wirft plötzlich ein grelles Licht auf ihn und seine nächste Umgebung; man gewahrt Alberich vor Hagen kauernd, die Arme auf dessen Knie gelehnt.

ALBERICH
(leise)
Schläfst du, Hagen, mein Sohn?

Act Two

An Open Space on the Shore

In front of the Gibichung hall: on the right, the open entrance to the hall; on the left, the bank of the Rhine, from which, slanting across the stage to the back at the right, rises a rocky height cut by several mountain paths. There Fricka's altar-stone is visible; higher up is a larger one for Wotan and, on the side, a similar one dedicated to Donner. It is night.

Scene One

Hagen, his spear on his arm, his shield at his side, sits sleeping, leaning against one of the doorposts. The moon suddenly shines out and throws a bright light on him and his surroundings; Alberich is seen crouching before him, leaning his arms on Hagen's knees.

ALBERICH
(softly)
Sleep you, Hagen, my son?

Du schläfst und hörst mich nicht,
den Ruh' und Schlaf verriet?

HAGEN
(leise, ohne sich zu rühren, so daß er immerfort zu schlafen scheint, obwohl er die Augen offen hat)
Ich höre dich, schlimmer Albe:
was hast du meinem Schlaf zu sagen?

ALBERICH
Gemahnt sei der Macht,
der du gebietest,
bist du so mutig,
wie die Mutter dich mir gebar!

HAGEN
(immer wie zuvor)
Gab mir die Mutter Mut,
nicht mag ich ihr doch danken,
daß deiner List sie erlag:
frühalt, fahl und bleich,
haß ich die Frohen,
freue mich nie!

ALBERICH
(wie zuvor)
Hagen, mein Sohn!
Hasse die Frohen!
Mich Lustfreien,
Leidbelasteten
liebst du so, wie du sollst!
Bist du kräftig,
kühn und klug:
die wir bekämpfen
mit nächtigem Krieg,
schon gibt ihnen Not unser Neid.
Der einst den Ring mir entriß,
Wotan, der wütende Räuber,
vom eignen Geschlechte
ward er geschlagen:
an den Wälsung verlor er
Macht und Gewalt;
mit der Götter ganzer Sippe
in Angst ersieht er sein Ende.
Nicht ihn fürcht ich mehr:
fallen muß er mit allen!
Schläfst du, Hagen, mein Sohn?

You sleep, and hear me not;
through sleep I lost my power!

HAGEN
(softly, without moving, so that he appears to be sleeping on although his eyes are open)
I hear you, crafty Niblung;
what have you now to tell my slumber?

ALBERICH
Remember the power
that you were born with,
if you've the courage
that your mother gave you at birth!

HAGEN
(as before)
My courage came from her;
no thanks for that I'll grant her,
for she was bought by your gold.
Old in youth, gaunt and pale,
hating the happy,
I'm never glad!

ALBERICH
(as before)
Hagen, my son!
Cherish that hatred!
Then your unhappy,
joyless father
you will love as you should!
Now be cunning,
strong and bold!
Those whom with weapons
of darkness we fight,
soon they shall be destroyed by our hate.
He stole the ring from my hand,
Wotan, that treacherous robber,
but now he has been vanquished
by one of his heroes;
to the Wälsung he lost
dominion and might;
with his band of gods and heroes
in dread he waits for destruction.
So I fear him not:
gods and heroes must perish!
Sleep you, Hagen, my son?

HAGEN
(unverändert wie zuvor)
Der Ewigen Macht,
wer erbte sie?

ALBERICH
Ich—und du!
Wir erben die Welt.
Trüg ich mich nicht
in deiner Treu',
teilst du meinen Gram und Grimm.
Wotans Speer
zerspellte der Wälsung,
der Fafner, den Wurm,
im Kampfe gefällt
und kindisch den Reif sich errang.
Jede Gewalt
hat er gewonnen;
Walhall und Nibelheim
neigen sich ihm.
An dem furchtlosen Helden
erlahmt selbst mein Fluch:
denn nicht kennt er
des Ringes Wert,
zu nichts nützt er
die neidlichste Macht.
Lachend in liebender Brunst,
brennt er lebend dahin.
Ihn zu verderben,
taugt uns nun einzig!
Hörst du, Hagen, mein Sohn?

HAGEN
(wie zuvor)
Zu seinem Verderben
dient er mir schon.

ALBERICH
Den goldnen Ring,
den Reif gilt's zu erringen!
Ein weises Weib
lebt dem Wälsung zulieb:
riet es ihn je
des Rheines Töchtern,
die in Wassers Tiefen
einst mich betört,
zurückzugeben den Ring,

HAGEN
(motionless, as before)
The might of the gods,
who wins it then?

ALBERICH
I and you!
The world shall be ours,
if I can trust
my scheming son,
if truly you share my hate.
Wotan's spear
was broken by the Wälsung,
and Fafner, the dragon,
was killed by his hand,
and he took the ring as his prize.
Power and might
passed to the Wälsung;
Walhall and Nibelheim
own him as lord.
But that boldest of heroes
is safe from my curse;
for he knows not
the might of the ring;
he makes no use
of its magical power.
Laughter and love fill his heart,
gaily he wastes all his life.
We must destroy him
before we can conquer.
Sleep you, Hagen, my son?

HAGEN
(as before)
Towards his destruction
Siegfried is bound.

ALBERICH
The golden ring,
that ring—you have to win it!
For he is loved
by a woman who is wise;
if she advise
that he return it,
if the Rhine's fair maids,
whom once I pursued,
by chance recover the ring,

verloren ging' mir das Gold, keine List erlangte es je. Drum ohne Zögern ziel auf den Reif! Dich Zaglosen zeugt' ich mir ja, daß wider Helden hart du mir hieltest. Zwar stark nicht genug, den Wurm zu bestehn, was allein dem Wälsung bestimmt, zu zähem Haß doch erzog ich Hagen, der soll mich nun rächen, den Ring gewinnen dem Wälsung und Wotan zum Hohn! Schwörst du mir's, Hagen, mein Sohn? *(Von hier an bedeckt ein immer finsterer werdender Schatten wieder Alberich. Zugleich beginnt das erste Tagesgrauen.)*	we've lost it; gone is our gold, and no craft can win it again. Wake from your slumber, strive for the ring! For fearless and bold you were bred; so that you'd fight my foes when I needed. Though you were too weak to fight with the giant, whom only Siegfried could slay, yet deadly hatred I bred in Hagen so he could avenge me; the ring he'll win me, though Wälsung and Wotan conspire! Swear to me, Hagen, my son! *(From this point a gradually darkening shadow again covers Alberich. At the same time, day begins to dawn.)*
HAGEN *(immer wie zuvor)* Den Ring soll ich haben: harre in Ruh'!	HAGEN *(still as before)* That ring shall be Hagen's; leave me in peace!
ALBERICH Schwörst du mir's, Hagen, mein Held?	ALBERICH Swear to me, Hagen, my son!
HAGEN Mir selbst schwör ich's; schweige die Sorge!	HAGEN To myself I swear it; trust me, and fear not!
ALBERICH *(wie er allmählich immer mehr dem Blicke entschwindet, wird auch seine Stimme immer unvernehmbarer.)* Sei treu, Hagen, mein Sohn! Trauter Helde!—Sei treu! Sei treu!—Treu! *(Alberich ist gänzlich verschwunden. Hagen, der unverändert in seiner Stellung verblieben, blickt regungslos und starren Auges nach dem Rheine hin, auf welchem sich die Morgendämmerung ausbreitet. Der Rhein färbt sich immer stärker vom erglühenden Morgenrot.)*	ALBERICH *(gradually disappearing from sight, while his voice becomes ever less audible)* Be true, Hagen, my son! Crafty hero! Be true! Be true! True! *(Alberich has entirely disappeared. Hagen, who has remained in the same position, gazes motionless and with fixed eyes towards the Rhine, over which the light of dawn is spreading. The Rhine begins to glow more and more brightly with the red light of dawn.)*

Zweite Szene

Hagen macht eine zuckende Bewegung. Siegfried tritt plötzlich, dicht am Ufer, hinter einem Busche hervor. Er ist in seiner eigenen Gestalt; nur den Tarnhelm hat er noch auf dem Haupte. Er zieht ihn jetzt ab und hängt ihn, während er hervorschreitet, in den Gürtel.

SIEGFRIED
Hoiho, Hagen!
Müder Mann!
Siehst du mich kommen?

HAGEN
(gemächlich sich erhebend)
Hei, Siegfried!
Geschwinder Helde!
Wo brausest du her?

SIEGFRIED
Vom Brünnhildenstein!
Dort sog ich den Atem ein,
mit dem ich dich rief:
so rasch war meine Fahrt!
Langsamer folgt mir ein Paar:
zu Schiff gelangt das her!

HAGEN
So zwangst du Brünnhild'?

SIEGFRIED
Wacht Gutrune?

HAGEN
(in die Halle rufend)
Hoiho, Gutrune,
komm heraus!
Siegfried ist da:
was säumst du drin?

SIEGFRIED
(zur Halle sich wendend)
Euch beiden meld ich,
wie ich Brünnhild band.
(Gutrune tritt ihm aus der Halle entgegen.)
Heiß mich willkommen,

Scene Two

Hagen starts violently. Siegfried appears suddenly from behind a bush close to the shore. He appears in his own shape but still has the Tarnhelm on his head. He takes it off and hangs it from his belt as he comes forward.

SIEGFRIED
Hoiho! Hagen!
Fast asleep?
Did I surprise you?

HAGEN
(rising leisurely)
Hi, Siegfried!
You're back so early!
Where have you been?

SIEGFRIED
At Brünnhilde's rock!
And there I drew the breath
with which I just called:
the Tarnhelm carried me fast.
Slowly there follow a pair;
by boat they will arrive!

HAGEN
You conquered Brünnhild?

SIEGFRIED
Where's Gutrune?

HAGEN
(calling towards the hall)
Hoiho! Gutrune!
Join us here!
Siegfried is back:
come, welcome him.

SIEGFRIED
(turning to the hall)
I'll tell you both
how I won Brünnhild's hand.
(Gutrune comes from the hall to meet him.)
Now make me welcome,

Gibichskind!
Ein guter Bote bin ich dir.

GUTRUNE
Freia grüße dich
zu aller Frauen Ehre!

SIEGFRIED
Frei und hold
sei nun mir Frohem:
zum Weib gewann ich dich heut.

GUTRUNE
So folgt Brünnhild meinem Bruder?

SIEGFRIED
Leicht ward die Frau ihm gefreit.

GUTRUNE
Sengte das Feuer ihn nicht?

SIEGFRIED
Ihn hätt' es auch nicht versehrt,
doch ich durchschritt es für ihn,
da dich ich wollt' erwerben.

GUTRUNE
Und dich hat es verschont?

SIEGFRIED
Mich freute die schwebende Brunst.

GUTRUNE
Hielt Brünnhild dich für Gunther?

SIEGFRIED
Ihm glich ich auf ein Haar:
der Tarnhelm wirkte das,
wie Hagen tüchtig es wies.

HAGEN
Dir gab ich guten Rat.

GUTRUNE
So zwangst du das kühne Weib?

SIEGFRIED
Sie wich—Gunthers Kraft.

Gibich maid!
I bring the news you long to hear.

GUTRUNE
May Freia smile on you
in the name of all lovely women!

SIEGFRIED
One alone
is all I care for!
As wife, I win you today.

GUTRUNE
And so Brünnhild's with my brother?

SIEGFRIED
Soon she was won as his bride.

GUTRUNE
Was he unharmed by the fire?

SIEGFRIED
He could have passed through the flame,
but in his place I went instead,
for thus I planned to win you.

GUTRUNE
And you? You were not hurt?

SIEGFRIED
I laughed at the threat of the flames.

GUTRUNE
Did Brünnhild think you were Gunther?

SIEGFRIED
No one could tell us apart;
The Tarnhelm served me well,
as Hagen told me it would.

HAGEN
I gave you good advice.

GUTRUNE
You mastered that fearless maid?

SIEGFRIED
She felt—Gunther's force.

GUTRUNE
Und vermählte sie sich dir?

SIEGFRIED
Ihrem Mann gehorchte Brünnhild
eine volle bräutliche Nacht.

GUTRUNE
Als ihr Mann doch galtest du?

SIEGFRIED
Bei Gutrune weilte Siegfried.

GUTRUNE
Doch zur Seite war ihm Brünnhild?

SIEGFRIED
(auf sein Schwert deutend)
Zwischen Ost und West der Nord:
so nah—war Brünnhild ihm fern.

GUTRUNE
Wie empfing Gunther sie nun von dir?

SIEGFRIED
Durch des Feuers verlöschende Lohe
im Frühnebel vom Felsen
folgte sie mir zu Tal;
  dem Strande nah,
  flugs die Stelle
tauschte Gunther mit mir:
durch des Geschmeides Tugend
wünscht' ich mich schnell hieher.
Ein starker Wind nun treibt
die Trauten den Rhein herauf:
drum rüstet jetzt den Empfang!

GUTRUNE
Siegfried, mächtigster Mann!
Wie faßt mich Furcht vor dir!

HAGEN
(von der Höhe im Hintergrunde den Fluß hinabspähend)
In der Ferne seh ich ein Segel.

SIEGFRIED
So sagt dem Boten Dank!

GUTRUNE
But she gave herself to you?

SIEGFRIED
Through the night the dauntless Brünnhild
did obey her husband and lord.

GUTRUNE
But that husband was really you?

SIEGFRIED
To Gutrune I was faithful.

GUTRUNE
Yet my Siegfried was with Brünnhild?

SIEGFRIED
(pointing to his sword)
Between the east and west lies north:
so near was Brünnhild—yet so far.

GUTRUNE
Then how did Gunther obtain his bride?

SIEGFRIED
When the dawn came, the firelight was [fading,
the mists fell as she followed
down to the vale below;
  and by the shore
  there we changed
our places, Gunther and I:
and by the magic Tarnhelm
I returned back here to you.
The wind is fair, and soon
the lovers will reach the shore.
Let us welcome them when they come.

GUTRUNE
Siegfried! Mightiest of men!
I feel strange fear of you!

HAGEN
(looking down the river from a height at the back)
I can see a sail in the distance.

SIEGFRIED
Then give the herald thanks!

GUTRUNE
Lasset uns sie hold empfangen,
daß heiter sie und gern hier weile!
Du, Hagen, minnig
rufe die Mannen
nach Gibichs Hof zur Hochzeit!
Frohe Frauen
ruf ich zum Fest:
der Freudigen folgen sie gern.
(Nach der Halle schreitend, wendet sie sich wieder um.)
Rastest du, schlimmer Held?

SIEGFRIED
Dir zu helfen, ruh ich aus.
(Er reicht ihr die Hand und geht mit ihr in die Halle.)

GUTRUNE
Let us prepare a splendid welcome,
and make her glad to stay among us.
You, Hagen,
call the vassals together,
in Gibich's hall we'll feast them!
Lovely women
I'll bring with me.
They'll join us here, share in our joy.
(As she goes towards the hall, she turns round again.)
Siegfried, will you rest?

SIEGFRIED
Helping Gutrun gives me rest.
(He gives her his hand and goes into the hall with her.)

Dritte Szene

HAGEN
(hat einen Felsstein in der Höhe des Hintergrundes erstiegen; dort setzt er, der Landseite zugewendet, sein Stierhorn zum Blasen an.)
Hoiho! Hoihohoho!
Ihr Gibichsmannen,
machet euch auf!
Wehe! Wehe!
Waffen! Waffen!
Waffen durchs Land!
Gute Waffen!
Starke Waffen,
Scharf zum Streit.
Not ist da!
Not! Wehe! Wehe!
Hoiho! Hoihohoho!
(Hagen bleibt immer in seiner Stellung auf der Anhöhe. Er bläst abermals. Aus verschiedenen Gegenden vom Lande her antworten Heerhörner. Auf den verschiedenen Höhenpfaden stürmen in

Scene Three

HAGEN
(has mounted a rock high at the back of the stage. He places his cowhorn to his lips and sounds it, turning to the countryside.)
Hoiho! Hoihohoho!
You Gibich vassals,
answer my call.
Waken! Waken!
Hear me! Hear me!
Arm all our land!
Bring your weapons!
Mighty weapons!
Sharp and bright!
Foes are here!
Foes! Waken! Waken!
Hoiho! Hoihohoho!
(Hagen remains in the same position on the rock. He blows his horn again. Other horns answer from different parts of the countryside. By different paths, armed vassals rush on hastily;

Hast und Eile gewaffnete Mannen herbei, erst einzelne, dann immer mehrere zusammen, welche sich dann auf dem Uferraum vor der Halle anhäufen.)

first singly, then in increasing numbers, assembling on the shore in front of the hall.)

DIE MANNEN
(erst einzelne, dann immer neu hinzukommende)
Was tost das Horn?
Was ruft es zu Heer?
Wir kommen mit Wehr,
wir kommen mit Waffen!
Hagen! Hagen!
Hoiho! Hoiho!
Welche Not ist da?
Welcher Feind ist nah?
Wer gibt uns Streit?
Ist Gunther in Not?
Wir kommen mit Waffen,
mit scharfer Wehr.
Hoiho! Ho! Hagen!

THE VASSALS
(first singly, then joined by the newcomers)
I hear the horn!
Who sounds the alarm?
We come with our arms!
We come with our weapons!
Hagen! Hagen!
Hoiho! Hoiho!
What's the danger here?
Say what foe is near!
Who comes to fight?
Is Gunther in need?
We come with our weapons,
with weapons of might.
Hoiho! Ho! Hagen!

HAGEN
(immer von der Anhöhe herab)
Rüstet euch wohl
und rastet nicht;
Gunther sollt ihr empfahn:
ein Weib hat der gefreit.

HAGEN
(still from the height)
Come to my call,
and arm yourselves!
Gunther soon shall return;
his wife joins us today.

DIE MANNEN
Drohet ihm Not?
Drängt ihn der Feind?

THE VASSALS
What is his need?
Who is his foe?

HAGEN
Ein freisliches Weib
führet er heim.

HAGEN
His proud, fiery wife
joins us today.

DIE MANNEN
Ihm folgen der Magen
feindliche Mannen?

THE VASSALS
And is he pursued
by furious kinsmen?

HAGEN
Einsam fährt er:
keiner folgt.

HAGEN
No one follows them;
they are alone.

DIE MANNEN
So bestand er die Not?
So bestand er den Kampf?
Sag es an!

THE VASSALS
Then his danger is past?
And his fight has been won?
Tell us all!

HAGEN Der Wurmtöter wehrte der Not: Siegfried, der Held, der schuf ihm Heil!	HAGEN The hero has gained him a bride; Siegfried, his friend, saved him from harm!
EIN MANN Was soll ihm das Heer nun noch helfen?	ONE VASSAL Then why have you called us together?
ZEHN WEITERE Was hilft ihm nun das Heer?	TEN OTHERS Then why have we been called?
HAGEN Starke Stiere Sollt ihr schlachten; am Weihstein fließe Wotan ihr Blut!	HAGEN Sacred oxen must be slaughtered; on Wotan's altar pour forth their blood!
EIN MANN Was, Hagen, was heißest du uns dann?	ONE VASSAL Then, Hagen, what would you have [us do?
ACHT MANNEN Was heißest du uns dann?	EIGHT VASSALS What would you have us do?
VIER WEITERE Was soll es dann?	FOUR OTHERS What should we do?
ALLE Was heißest du uns dann?	ALL What would you have us do?
HAGEN Einen Eber fällen sollt ihr für Froh! Einen stämmigen Bock stechen für Donner! Schafe aber schlachtet für Fricka, daß gute Ehe sie gebe!	HAGEN Take a boar as offering, kill it for Froh; and a goat in its prime strike down for Donner! Sheep should then be slaughtered for Fricka, and then she will smile on this wedding!
DIE MANNEN *(mit immer mehr ausbrechender Heiterkeit)* Schlugen wir Tiere, was schaffen wir dann?	THE VASSALS *(with ever-increasing hilarity)* After these offerings, what next should we do?
HAGEN Das Trinkhorn nehmt, von trauten Fraun	HAGEN Your drinkhorns take, and ask your women

mit Met und Wein
wonnig gefüllt!

to fill with wine,
until they run full!

ALLE MANNEN
Das Trinkhorn zur Hand,
wie halten wir es dann?

THE VASSALS
Our drinkhorns in hand,
what ought we then to do?

HAGEN
Rüstig gezecht,
bis der Rausch euch zähmt!
Alles den Göttern zu Ehren,
daß gute Ehe sie geben!

HAGEN
Seize them, and drink
till you can drink no more!
So shall our gods be honoured,
and they will grant us their blessing!

DIE MANNEN
(brechen in ein schallendes Gelächter aus.)
Groß Glück und Heil
lacht nun dem Rhein,
da Hagen, der Grimme,
so lustig mag sein!
Der Hagedorn
sticht nun nicht mehr;
zum Hochzeitrufer
ward er bestellt.

THE VASSALS
(break into ringing laughter.)
Glad times have come,
come to our Rhine,
when Hagen, grim Hagen,
with laughter can shine!
Our hedge's thorn
pricks us no more;
our bridal herald
calls us to wine!

HAGEN
(der immer sehr ernst geblieben, ist zu den Mannen herabgestiegen und steht jetzt unter ihnen.)
Nun laßt das Lachen,
mut'ge Mannen!
Empfangt Gunthers Braut!
Brünnhilde naht dort mit ihm.
(Er deutet die Mannen nach dem Rhein hin; diese eilen zum Teil nach der Anhöhe, während andere sich am Ufer aufstellen, um die Ankommenden zu erblicken. Näher zu einigen Mannen tretend:)
Hold seid der Herrin,
helfet ihr treu:
traf sie ein Leid,
rasch seid zur Rache!
(Er wendet sich langsam zur Seite, in den Hintergrund. Während des Folgenden kommt der Nachen mit Gunther und Brünnhilde auf dem Rheine an.)

HAGEN
(who has remained very grave, has come down to the vassals and now stands among them.)
Now stop your laughter,
faithful vassals!
Receive Gunther's bride!
Brünnhilde soon shall be here.
(He points towards the Rhine. Some of the vassals hasten to the height, while others take up a position on the shore to see the arrival. Hagen approaches some of the vassals.)
Honour your lady,
come to her aid;
if she is wronged,
you must revenge her!
(He turns slowly aside towards the back. During the following chorus, the boat with Gunther and Brünnhilde appears on the Rhine.)

DIE MANNEN
(erst einer, dann mehrere, schließlich alle)
Heil! Heil!
Willkommen! Willkommen!

THE VASSALS
(first singly, then more, then all)
Hail! Hail!
Be welcome! Be welcome!

(Einige der Mannen springen in den Fluß und ziehen den Kahn an das Land. Alles drängt sich immer dichter an das Ufer.)

Willkommen! Gunther!
Heil! Heil!

(Some vassals leap into the river and draw the boat to the shore. All press closer to the bank.)

Be welcome, Gunther!
Hail! Hail!

Vierte Szene

Gunther steigt mit Brünnhilde aus dem Kahn; die Mannen reihen sich ehrerbietig zu ihrem Empfange. Während des Folgenden geleitet Gunther Brünnhilde feierlich an der Hand.

DIE MANNEN

Heil dir, Gunther!
Heil dir und deiner Braut!
Willkommen!

(Sie schlagen die Waffen tosend zusammen.)

GUNTHER

(Brünnhilde, welche bleich und gesenkten Blickes ihm folgt, den Mannen vorstellend)

Brünnhild, die hehrste Frau,
bring ich euch her zum Rhein.
Ein edleres Weib
ward nie gewonnen.
Der Gibichungen Geschlecht,
gaben die Götter ihm Gunst,
zum höchsten Ruhm
rag' es nun auf!

DIE MANNEN

(feierlich an ihre Waffen schlagend)

Heil dir,
glücklicher Gibichung!

(Gunther geleitet Brünnhilde, die nie aufblickt, zur Halle, aus welcher jetzt Siegfried und Gutrune, von Frauen begleitet, heraustreten.)

GUNTHER

(hält vor der Halle an.)

Gegrüßt sei, teurer Held;

Scene Four

Gunter steps out of the boat with Brünnhilde: the vassals range themselves respectfully to receive them. During the following, Gunther ceremoniously leads Brünnhilde forward by the hand.

THE VASSALS

Welcome, Gunther!
Hail to you, and to your bride!
Hail! Hail!

(They clash their weapons noisily together.)

GUNTHER

(presenting Brünnhilde, who follows him with pale face and downcast eyes, to the vassals)

Brünnhild, my fairest bride,
joins us beside the Rhine.
And no man could win
a nobler woman.
The Gibichungs have been blessed;
gods show their grace once again.
To new renown
we rise today!

THE VASSALS

(clash their weapons.)

Hail, lord,
glorious Gibichung!

(Gunther leads Brünnhilde, who has never raised her eyes, to the hall, from which Siegfried and Gutrune now come forth, attended by women.)

GUNTHER

(stops before the hall.)

I greet you, noble friend,

gegrüßt, holde Schwester!
Dich seh ich froh ihm zur Seite,
der dich zum Weib gewann.
Zwei sel'ge Paare
seh ich hier prangen:
(Er führt Brünnhilde näher heran.)
Brünnhild und Gunther,
Gutrun und Siegfried!
(Brünnhilde schlägt erschreckt die Augen auf und erblickt Siegfried; wie in Erstaunen bleibt ihr Blick auf ihn gerichtet. Gunther, welcher Brünnhildes heftig zuckende Hand losgelassen hat, sowie alle übrigen zeigen starre Betroffenheit über Brünnhildes Benehmen.)

and you, lovely sister!
Gladly I see you beside him,
my friend who won you for wife.
Two pairs in wedlock
here shall find blessing.
(He draws Brünnhilde forwards.)
Brünnhild and Gunther,
Gutrun and Siegfried!
(Brünnhilde, startled, raises her eyes and sees Siegfried; her look remains fixed on him in amazement. Gunther, who has released Brünnhilde's violently trembling hand, shows, as do all, blank astonishment at Brünnhilde's behaviour.)

EINIGE MANNEN
Was ist ihr? Ist sie entrückt?
(Brünnhilde beginnt zu zittern.)

SOME VASSALS
What ails her? Is she distraught?
(Brünnhilde begins to tremble.)

SIEGFRIED
(geht ruhig einige Schritte auf Brünnhilde zu.)
Was müht Brünnhildes Blick?

SIEGFRIED
(goes a few steps towards Brünnhilde.)
What clouds Brünnhilde's brow?

BRÜNNHILDE
(kaum ihrer mächtig)
Siegfried ... hier ...! Gutrune ...?

BRÜNNHILDE
(scarcely able to command herself)
Siegfried ... here ...! Gutrune ...?

SIEGFRIED
Gunthers milde Schwester:
mir vermählt
wie Gunther du.

SIEGFRIED
Gunther's gentle sister,
won by me,
as, by Gunther, you.

BRÜNNHILDE
(furchtbar heftig)
Ich ... Gunther ...? Du lügst!
(Sie schwankt und droht umzusinken; Siegfried, ihr zunächst, stützt sie.)
Mir schwindet das Licht ...
(Sie blickt in seinen Armen matt zu Siegfried auf.)
Siegfried – kennt mich nicht?

BRÜNNHILDE
(with fearful vehemence)
I ... Gunther ...? ... You lie!
(She appears about to fall. Siegfried, beside her, supports her.)
My eyes grow dim ...
(In Siegfried's arms, she looks up faintly at his face.)
Siegfried — knows me not?

SIEGFRIED
Gunther, deinem Weib ist übel!
(Gunther tritt hinzu.)
Erwache, Frau!
Hier steht dein Gatte.

SIEGFRIED
Gunther, your wife is troubled!
(Gunther comes to them.)
Arouse yourself!
Here stands your husband.

BRÜNNHILDE
(erblickt am Finger Siegfrieds den Ring und schrickt mit furchtbarer Heftigkeit auf.)
Ha!—Der Ring
an seiner Hand!
Er . . . Siegfried?

EINIGE MANNEN
Was ist? Was ist?

HAGEN
(aus dem Hintergrunde unter die Mannen tretend)
Jetzt merket klug,
was die Frau euch klagt!

BRÜNNHILDE
(sucht sich zu ermanen, indem sie die schrecklichste Aufregung gewaltsam zurückhält.)
Einen Ring sah ich
an deiner Hand.
Nicht dir gehört er,
Ihn entriß mir
(auf Gunther deutend)
dieser Mann!
Wie mochtest von ihm
den Ring du empfahn?

SIEGFRIED
(aufmerksam den Ring an seiner Hand betrachtend)
Den Ring empfing ich
nicht von ihm.

BRÜNNHILDE
(zu Gunther)
Nahmst du von mir den Ring,
durch den ich dir vermählt;
so melde ihm dein Recht,
fordre zurück das Pfand!

GUNTHER
(in großer Verwirrung)
Den Ring? Ich gab ihm keinen:
Doch–kennst du ihn auch gut?

BRÜNNHILDE
Wo bärgest du den Ring,
den du von mir erbeutet?
(Gunther schweigt in höchster Betroffenheit.)

BRÜNNHILDE
(sees the ring on Siegfried's outstretched finger, and starts with terrible vehemence.)
Ha! The ring—
upon his hand!
He . . . Siegfried?

SOME VASSALS
What's this? What's this?

HAGEN
(advancing among the vassals, from the back)
Now mark her words,
let her charge be heard!

BRÜNNHILDE
(tries to recover herself, while she forcibly restrains the most terrible excitement.)
A ring I see
upon your hand;
that ring was stolen,
it was taken,
(pointing to Gunther)
seized by him!
So how did you gain
that ring from his hand?

SIEGFRIED
(attentively observes the ring on his finger.)
This ring?—
I had it not from him.

BRÜNNHILDE
(to Gunther)
If you did steal my ring,
when I became your bride,
then claim it as your right;
make him return the ring!

GUNTHER
(in great perplexity)
The ring? I gave him nothing:
yet—are you sure it is yours?

BRÜNNHILDE
What did you do with the ring,
when from my hand you stole it?
(Gunther, greatly confused, is silent.)

BRÜNNHILDE
(wütend auffahrend)
Ha!—Dieser war es,
der mir den Ring entriß:
Siegfried, der trugvolle Dieb!
(Alles blickt erwartungsvoll auf Siegfried, welcher über der Betrachtung des Ringes in fernes Sinnen entrückt ist.)

SIEGFRIED
Von keinem Weib
kam mir der Reif;
noch war's ein Weib,
dem ich ihn abgewann:
genau erkenn ich
des Kampfes Lohn,
den vor Neidhöhl' einst ich bestand,
als den starken Wurm ich erschlug.

HAGEN
(zwischen sie tretend)
Brünnhild', kühne Frau,
kennst du genau den Ring?
Ist's der, den du Gunther gabst,
so ist er sein,
und Siegfried gewann ihn durch Trug,
den der Treulose büßen sollt'!

BRÜNNHILDE
(in furchtbarstem Schmerze aufschreiend)
Betrug! Betrug!
Schändlichster Betrug!
Verrat! Verrat!
Wie noch nie er gerächt!

GUTRUNE
Verrat? An wem?

MANNEN
Verrat? Verrat?

FRAUEN
Verrat? An wem?

BRÜNNHILDE
Heil'ge Götter,
himmlische Lenker!

BRÜNNHILDE
(breaking out in violent passion)
Ha!—Siegfried stole it;
he took the ring from me:
Siegfried, a traitor and thief!
(All look expectantly at Siegfried, who is absorbed in distant thoughts while contemplating the ring.)

SIEGFRIED
No woman's hand
gave me the ring,
nor was it stolen
from any woman's hand:
I know full well
where I found this ring,
for at Neidhöhl I won it myself,
when I fought with Fafner the giant.

HAGEN
(coming between them)
Brünnhild, are you sure
you recognize the ring?
For if it is Gunther's ring,
if it is his,
then Siegfried was false to his friend;
he must pay then for his treachery!

BRÜNNHILDE
(crying out in most terrible anguish)
Betrayed! betrayed!
Shamefully betrayed!
Deceit! deceit!
How can I be revenged?

GUTRUNE
Betrayed? By whom?

VASSALS
Betrayed? betrayed?

WOMEN
Betrayed? By whom?

BRÜNNHILDE
Hear in Walhall,
mighty immortals!

Rauntet ihr dies
in eurem Rat?
Lehrt ihr mich Leiden,
wie keiner sie litt?
Schuft ihr mir Schmach,
wie nie sie geschmerzt?
Ratet nun Rache,
wie nie sie gerast!
Zündet mir Zorn,
wie noch nie er gezähmt!
Heißet Brünnhild,
ihr Herz zu zerbrechen,
den zu zertrümmern,
der sie betrog!

Have you ordained
this dark decree?
Why have you doomed me
to anguish and grief?
Why have you plunged me
in sadness and shame?
Teach me a vengeance
more cruel than my grief!
Stir me to rage
still more keen than my shame!
Ah, though Brünnhilde's
heart may be broken;
bring her betrayer
soon to his death!

GUNTHER
Brünnhild, Gemahlin!
Mäß'ge dich!

GUNTHER
Brünnhild, beloved!
Calm yourself!

BRÜNNHILDE
Weich fern, Verräter!
Selbst Verratner!
Wisset denn alle:
nicht ihm—
dem Manne dort
bin ich vermählt.

BRÜNNHILDE
Away, betrayer,
self-betrayed one!
All of you, hear me:
not he
but—Siegfried there
made me his wife.

FRAUEN
Siegfried? Gutruns Gemahl?

WOMEN
Siegfried? Gutrune's husband?

MANNEN
Gutruns Gemahl?

VASSALS
Gutrune's husband?

BRÜNNHILDE
Er zwang mir Lust
und Liebe ab.

BRÜNNHILDE
He forced delight
and love from me.

SIEGFRIED
Achtest du so
der eignen Ehre?
Die Zunge, die sie lästert,
muß ich der Lüge zeihen?
Hört, ob ich Treue brach!
Blutbrüderschaft
hab ich Gunther geschworen:
Notung, das werte Schwert,
wahrte der Treue Eid;

SIEGFRIED
Can you defile
your fame so lightly?
Then hear me—I'll defend it,
for I accuse you of falsehood!
Hear how I kept my word!
Blood brotherhood
I and Gunther had sworn:
Notung, my faithful sword,
guarded that holy vow:

mich trennte seine Schärfe
von diesem traur'gen Weib.

BRÜNNHILDE
Du listiger Held,
sieh, wie du lügst!
Wie auf dein Schwert
du schlecht dich berufst!
Wohl kenn ich seine Schärfe,
doch kenn auch die Scheide,
darin so wonnig
ruht' an der Wand
Notung, der treue Freund,
als die Traute sein Herr sich gefreit.

DIE MANNEN
(in lebhafter Entrüstung zusammentretend)
Wie? Brach er die Treue?
Trübte er Gunthers Ehre?

DIE FRAUEN
Brach er die Treue?

GUNTHER
(zu Siegfried)
Geschändet wär' ich,
schmählich bewahrt,
gäbst du die Rede
nicht ihr zurück!

GUTRUNE
Treulos, Siegfried,
sännest du Trug?
Bezeuge, daß jene
falsch dich zeiht!

DIE MANNEN
Reinige dich,
bist du im Recht!
Schweige die Klage!
Schwöre den Eid!

SIEGFRIED
Schweig' ich die Klage,
schwör' ich den Eid:
wer von euch wagt
seine Waffe daran?

this shining blade divided me
from this unhappy wife.

BRÜNNHILDE
You crafty man,
hear how you lie!
Calling on the sword
which shared in your shame!
I know its shining sharpness;
I know too the scabbard
in which it slept
all night on the wall—
Notung, that trusty sword—
while its master was faithless to his word.

THE VASSALS
(gathering indignantly)
Was Siegfried a traitor,
tarnishing Gunther's honour?

THE WOMEN
Siegfried a taitor?

GUNTHER
(to Siegfried)
My name's dishonoured,
stained with disgrace,
unless you deny it;
swear that she lies!

GUTRUNE
Faithless Siegfried,
false to your vow?
Assure me that all
she says is a lie!

THE VASSALS
Answer the charge,
if you are true!
Swear on a spear-point!
Swear with a vow!

SIEGFRIED
I shall answer,
swearing a vow:
which of you warriors
will lend me his spear?

HAGEN
Meines Speeres Spitze
wag ich daran:
sie wahr' in Ehren den Eid.
(Die Mannen schließen einen Ring um Siegfried und Hagen. Hagen hält den Speer hin; Siegfried legt zwei Finger seiner rechten Hand auf die Speerspitze.)

SIEGFRIED
Helle Wehr!
Heilige Waffe!
Hilf meinem ewigen Eide!
Bei des Speeres Spitze
sprech ich den Eid:
Spitze, achte des Spruchs!
Wo Scharfes mich schneidet,
schneide du mich;
wo der Tod mich soll treffen,
treffe du mich:
klagte das Weib dort wahr,
brach ich dem Bruder die Treu'!

BRÜNNHILDE
(tritt wütend in den Ring, reißt Siegfrieds Hand vom Speere hinweg und faßt dafür mit der ihrigen die Spitze)
Helle Wehr!
Heilige Waffe!
Hilf meinem ewigen Eide!
Bei des Speeres Spitze
sprech ich den Eid:
Spitze, achte des Spruchs!
Ich weihe deine Wucht,
daß sie ihn werfe!
Deine Schärfe segne ich,
daß sie ihn schneide:
denn, brach seine Eide er all,
schwur Meineid jetzt dieser Mann!

DIE MANNEN
(im höchsten Aufruhr)
Hilf, Donner,
tose dein Wetter,
zu schweigen die wütende Schmach!

SIEGFRIED
Gunther, wehr deinem Weibe,

HAGEN
Let my spear-point serve you!
Swear on the spear:
my spear shall witness your vow!
(The vassals form a ring round Siegfried and Hagen. Hagen holds out his spear; Siegfried lays two fingers of his right hand upon the spear-point.)

SIEGFRIED
Shining steel!
Holiest weapon!
Help me defend my honour!
On this shining spear-point
sworn is my vow:
spear-point, witness my word!
If I acted falsely,
strike at my heart;
when my death comes to claim me,
yours be the stroke:
if what she says is true,
if I my brother betrayed!

BRÜNNHILDE
(strides wrathfully into the circle, tears Siegfried's hand away from the spear, and seizes the point with her own hand.)
Shining steel!
Holiest weapon!
Help me defend my honour!
On this shining spear-point
sworn is my vow:
spear-point, witness my word!
Devote your mighty strength
to his destruction!
For his treachery he must die,
strike him and kill him!
For he has betrayed every vow,
and falsehood now he has sworn!

THE VASSALS
(in wild excitement)
Help, Donner!
Send us your thunder,
to silence this shameful disgrace!

SIEGFRIED
Gunther, look to your wife there;

das schamlos Schande dir lügt!
Gönnt ihr Weil' und Ruh',
der wilden Felsenfrau,
daß ihre freche Wut sich lege,
die eines Unholds
arge List
wider uns alle erregt!
Ihr Mannen, kehret euch ab!
Laßt das Weibergekeif!
Als Zage weichen wir gern,
gilt es mit Zungen den Streit.
(Er tritt dicht zu Gunther.)
Glaub, mehr zürnt es mich als dich,
daß schlecht ich sie getäuscht:
der Tarnhelm, dünkt mich fast,
hat halb mich nur gehehlt.
Doch Frauengroll
friedet sich bald:
daß ich dir es gewann,
dankt dir gewiß noch das Weib.
(Er wendet sich wieder zu den Mannen.)
Munter, ihr Mannen!
Folgt mir zum Mahl!
(zu den Frauen)
Froh zur Hochzeit
helfet, ihr Frauen!
Wonnige Lust
lache nun auf!
In Hof und Hain,
heiter vor allen
sollt ihr heute mich sehn.
Wen die Minne freut,
meinem frohen Mute
tu es der Glückliche gleich!
(Er schlingt in ausgelassenem Übermute seinen Arm um Gutrune und zieht sie mit sich in die Halle fort. Die Mannen und Frauen, von seinem Beispiele hingerissen, folgen ihm nach. Nur Brünnhilde, Gunther und Hagen bleiben zurück. Gunther hat sich in tiefer Scham mit verhülltem Gesichte abseits niedergesetzt. Brünnhilde, im Vordergrunde, blickt Siegfried und Gutrune noch eine Zeitlang schmerzlich nach und senkt dann sinnend das Haupt.)

she dares to slander your name.
Grant her time and rest,
this furious mountain maid,
until her frenzied rage is over;
I fear some demon's
evil spell
makes her so fierce with us all!
You vassals, leave her alone!
Leave this woman to scold!
Like cowards, men quit the field
when it's a battle of words.
(He comes close to Gunther.)
Friend, it grieves me more than you
that my deception failed:
the Tarnhelm, I suspect,
was not a full disguise.
But women's rage
is soon at an end:
she will soon learn to love you;
then she will thank me as well.
(He turns again to the vassals.)
Follow, you vassals!
On to the feast!
(to the women)
Come, fair women,
help at our wedding!
Share my delight
laugh at my joy!
In house and field,
carefree and merry
you shall find me today.
When by love I am blessed,
I want only laughter;
all of you share in my joy!
(In exuberant merriment he throws his arm roun Gutrune and leads her away with him into the hall. The vassals and the women, carried away his example, follow him. Only Brünnhilde, Gunther and Hagen remain behind. Gunther with covered face, has seated himself on one s in fearful dejection. Brünnhilde, standing in foreground, gazes sorrowfully after Siegfr Gutrune for a while, and then droops her thought.)

Fünfte Szene

BRÜNNHILDE
(in starrem Nachsinnen befangen)
Welches Unholds List
liegt hier verhohlen?
Welches Zaubers Rat
regte dies auf?
Wo ist nun mein Wissen
gegen dies Wirrsal?
Wo sind meine Runen
gegen dies Rätsel?
Ach Jammer, Jammer!
Weh, ach Wehe!
All mein Wissen
wies ich ihm zu!
In seiner Macht
hält er die Magd;
in seinen Banden
faßt er die Beute,
die, jammernd ob ihrer Schmach,
jauchzend der Reiche verschenkt!
Wer bietet mir nun das Schwert,
mit dem ich die Bande zerschnitt'?

HAGEN
(dicht an sie herantretend)
Vertraue mir,
betrogne Frau!
Wer dich verriet,
das räche ich.

BRÜNNHILDE
(matt sich umblickend)
An wem?

HAGEN
An Siegfried, der dich betrog.

BRÜNNHILDE
An Siegfried? . . . du?
(bitter lächelnd)
Ein einz'ger Blick
seines blitzenden Auges,
as selbst durch die Lügengestalt
strahlte zu mir,

Scene Five

BRÜNNHILDE
(engrossed in contemplation)
Dark, unholy powers
lie here around me!
Dark, enchanted spells
spun for my doom!
What use is my wisdom
against this witchcraft?
What use is my reason
to solve these riddles?
Oh sorrow! Sorrow!
Grief and sorrow!
All my wisdom
I gave to him!
And I remain
held by his might;
and now he holds me here
as his hostage,
shamed, helpless; and in my shame
gladly he gives me away!
Whose hand can help me now?
Whose sword can sever my bonds?

HAGEN
(coming close to Brünnhilde)
Have trust in me,
offended wife!
I can revenge
such treachery.

BRÜNNHILDE
(looking round wearily)
On whom?

HAGEN
On Siegfried, he who was false.

BRÜNNHILDE
On Siegfried? . . . You?
(smiling bitterly)
One single flash
from the eyes of the hero,
even veiled by the Tarnhelm's disguise,
such as lighted on me,

deinen besten Mut
machte er bangen!

HAGEN
Doch meinem Speere
spart' ihn sein Meineid?

BRÜNNHILDE
Eid und Meineid,
müßige Acht!
Nach Stärkrem späh,
deinen Speer zu waffnen,
willst du den Stärksten bestehn!

HAGEN
Wohl kenn ich Siegfrieds
siegende Kraft.
wie schwer im Kampf er zu fällen;
drum raune nun du
mir klugen Rat,
wie doch der Recke mir wich'?

BRÜNNHILDE
O Undank, schändlichster Lohn!
Nicht eine Kunst
war mir bekannt,
die zum Heil nicht half seinem Leib!
Unwissend zähmt' ihn
mein Zauberspiel,
das ihn vor Wunden nun gewahrt.

HAGEN
So kann keine Wehr ihm schaden?

BRÜNNHILDE
Im Kampfe nicht; doch
träfst du im Rücken ihn...
Niemals, das wußt' ich,
wich' er dem Feind,
nie reicht' er fliehend ihm den Rücken:
an ihm drum spart' ich den Segen.

HAGEN
Und dort trifft ihn mein Speer!
(Er wendet sich rasch von Brünnhilde ab zu Gunther.)
Auf, Gunther,

and the bravest foe
cringes with terror!

HAGEN
But on my spear-point
he swore his falsehood?

BRÜNNHILDE
Truth and falsehood,
what do they mean!
With stronger spells
you must arm your spear-point,
if you would strike at his strength!

HAGEN
I know of Siegfried's
conquering might,
and of his strength in a battle;
so whisper to me
some crafty means
to make him fall to my spear.

BRÜNNHILDE
Ungrateful! Shameful return!
By magic arts
I wove a spell,
to protect his life from his foes!
My charms surround him
and guard his life;
my magic keeps him safe from harm.

HAGEN
Can no weapon's point then pierce him?

BRÜNNHILDE
In battle, none; yet—
if at his back you strike...
Siegfried, I knew it,
he'd never flee,
nor turn his back upon his enemy:
and there I gave him no blessing.

HAGEN
My spear knows where to strike!
(He turns quickly from Brünnhilde to Gunther.)
Up, Gunther,

edler Gibichung!
Hier steht ein starkes Weib;
was hängst du dort in Harm?

noble Gibichung!
Here stands your valiant wife:
so why give way to grief?

GUNTHER
(leidenschaftlich auffahrend)
O Schmach!
O Schande!
Wehe mir,
dem jammervollsten Manne!

GUNTHER
(starting up passionately)
Oh shame!
Oh sorrow!
Woe is me,
of all men living the saddest!

HAGEN
In Schande liegst du;
leugn' ich das?

HAGEN
Your shame overwhelms you;
that I grant.

BRÜNNHILDE
(zu Gunther)
O feiger Mann!
falscher Genoss'!
Hinter dem Helden
hehltest du dich,
daß Preise des Ruhmes
er dir erränge!
Tief wohl sank
das teure Geschlecht,
das solche Zagen gezeugt!

BRÜNNHILDE
(to Gunther)
Oh cowardly man!
falsest of friends!
Sheltering behind him,
scared by the flames,
and then when he'd won me,
daring to claim me!
Deep has sunk
your glorious race,
to bear such a coward as you!

GUNTHER
(außer sich)
Betrüger ich—und betrogen!
Verräter ich—und verraten!
Zermalmt mir das Mark!
Zerbrecht mir die Brust!
Hilf, Hagen!
Hilf meiner Ehre!
Hilf deiner Mutter,
die mich—auch ja gebar!

GUNTHER
(beside himself)
Deceived am I—and deceiver!
Betrayed am I—and betrayer!
So crushed be my bones!
and broken my heart!
Help, Hagen!
And save my honour!
Help for our mother,
for you, too, are her son!

HAGEN
Dir hilft kein Hirn,
dir hilft keine Hand:
dir hilft nur—Siegfrieds Tod!

HAGEN
No hand can help,
no deed can atone,
but only—Siegfried's death!

GUNTHER
(von Grausen erfaßt)
Siegfrieds Tod?

GUNTHER
(seized with horror)
Siegfried's death!

HAGEN
Nur der sühnt deine Schmach!

GUNTHER
(vor sich hinstarrend)
Blutbrüderschaft
schwuren wir uns!

HAGEN
Des Bundes Bruch
sühne nun Blut!

GUNTHER
Brach er den Bund?

HAGEN
Da er dich verriet!

GUNTHER
Verriet er mich?

BRÜNNHILDE
Dich verriet er,
und mich verrietet ihr alle!
Wär' ich gerecht,
alles Blut der Welt
büßte mir nicht eure Schuld!
Doch des *einen* Tod
taugt mir für alle:
Siegfried falle
zur Sühne für sich und euch!

HAGEN
(heimlich zu Gunther)
Er falle—dir zum Heil!
Ungeheure Macht wird dir,
gewinnst von ihm du den Ring,
den der Tod ihm wohl nur entreißt.

GUNTHER
(leise)
Brünnhildes Ring?

HAGEN
Des Nibelungen Reif.

HAGEN
His death purges your shame!

GUNTHER
(staring before him)
Blood-brotherhood
freely we swore!

HAGEN
He broke that bond;
blood must atone!

GUNTHER
Broke he the bond?

HAGEN
By betraying you!

GUNTHER
Am I betrayed?

BRÜNNHILDE
He betrayed you;
and me—you all have betrayed me!
If I had my rights,
all the blood of the world
could not revenge me for your crime!
So the death of one
now must content me:
Siegfried's death
atones for his crime, and yours!

HAGEN
(to Gunther, secretly)
I'll kill him—you shall gain!
All the world is yours to command
when you set hands on the ring
that in death alone he will yield.

GUNTHER
(softly)
Brünnhilde's ring?

HAGEN
The Niblung's golden ring.

GUNTHER
(schwer seufzend)
So wär' es Siegfrieds Ende!

HAGEN
Uns allen frommt sein Tod.

GUNTHER
Doch Gutrune, ach,
der ich ihn gönnte!
Straften den Gatten wir so,
wie bestünden wir vor ihr?

BRÜNNHILDE
(wild auffahrend)
Was riet mir mein Wissen?
Was wiesen mich Runen?
Im hilflosen Elend
achtet mir's hell:
Gutrune heißt der Zauber,
der den Gatten mir entzückt!
Angst treffe sie!

HAGEN
(zu Gunther)
Muß sein Tod sie betrüben,
verhehlt sei ihr die Tat.
Auf muntres Jagen
ziehen wir morgen:
der Edle braust uns voran,
ein Eber bracht' ihn da um.

GUNTHER und BRÜNNHILDE
So soll es sein!
Siegfried falle!
Sühn' er die Schmach,
die er mir schuf!
Des Eides Treue
hat er getrogen:
mit seinem Blut
büß' er die Schuld!
Allrauner,
rächender Gott!
Schwurwissender
Eideshort!
Wotan!
Wende dich her!

GUNTHER
(sighing deeply)
So Siegfried's doom's decided!

HAGEN
His death will serve us all.

GUNTHER
Yet Gutrune, ah!
Gutrune loves him!
If he should fall at our hands,
how can I return to her?

BRÜNNHILDE
(starting up in a rage)
What use was my wisdom?
What use was my reason?
In heart-breaking anguish
all is revealed:
Gutrune, she's the enchantress;
by her spells she stole his love.
My curse on her!

HAGEN
(to Gunther)
Since his death will dismay her,
we must conceal our deed.
And so tomorrow
when we are hunting,
our hero runs on ahead:
we'll find him killed by a boar.

GUNTHER and BRÜNNHILDE
It shall be so!
Siegfried dies then!
Freed from the shame
cast by his crime!
The vows he swore,
those vows he has broken:
and with his blood
he shall atone!
All-guiding
god of revenge!
All-powerful
lord of vows!
Wotan!
Come to my call!

Weise die schrecklich
heilige Schar,
hieher zu horchen
dem Racheschwur!

Call up your fearful
heavenly host;
they will obey you;
revenge my wrong!

HAGEN
Sterb' er dahin,
der strahlende Held!
Mein ist der Hort,
mir muß er gehören.
Drum sei der Reif
ihm entrissen,
Alben-Vater,
gefallner Fürst!
Nachthüter!
Niblungenherr!
Alberich!
Achte auf mich!
Weise von neuem
der Niblungen Schar,
dir zu gehorchen,
des Ringes Herrn!

(Als Gunther mit Brünnhilde sich der Halle zuwendet, tritt ihnen der von dort heraustretende Brautzug entgegen. Knaben und Mädchen, Blumenstäbe schwingend, eilen lustig voraus. Siegfried wird auf einem Schilde, Gutrune auf einem Sessel von den Männern getragen. Auf der Anhöhe des Hintergrundes führen Knechte und Mägde auf verschiedenen Bergpfaden Opfergeräte und Opfertiere zu den Weihsteinen herbei und schmücken diese mit Blumen. Siegfried und die Mannen blasen auf ihren Hörnern den Hochzeitsruf. Die Frauen fordern Brünnhilde auf, an Gutrunes Seite sie zu geleiten. Brünnhilde blickt starr zu Gutrune auf, welche ihr mit freundlichem Lächeln zuwinkt. Als Brünnhilde heftig zurücktreten will, tritt Hagen rasch dazwischen und drängt sie an Gunther, der jetzt von neuem ihre Hand erfaßt, worauf er selbst von den Männern sich auf den Schild heben läßt. Während der Zug, kaum unterbrochen, schnell der Höhe zu sich wieder in Bewegung setzt, fällt der Vorhang.)

HAGEN
Siegfried will die,
destroyed in his pride!
Mine is the ring,
my hand soon shall hold it.
I'll seize that ring;
I shall hold it!
Niblung father,
you fallen lord!
Night guardian!
Nibelung lord!
Alberich!
Look up on me!
Call once again
all your Nibelung host;
they will obey you,
the ring's true lord!

(As Gunther turns impetuously with Brünnhilde to the hall, the bridal procession coming out of it meets them. Boys and girls, waving branches of flowers, leap joyously in front. Siegfried on a shield and Gutrune on a seat are carried by the men. On the rising ground at the back, by various mountain tracks, serving-men and maids bring sacrificial implements and beasts to the altars, and deck them with flowers. Siegfried and the vassals sound the wedding-call on their horns. The women invite Brünnhilde to accompany them to Gutrune's side. Brünnhilde stares blankly at Gutrune, who beckons to her with a friendly smile. As Brünnhilde is about to withdraw impetuously, Hagen steps between them and forces her towards Gunther, who seizes her hand again, whereupon he allows himself to be raised on a shield by the men. As the procession, scarcely interrupted, quickly starts moving again, towards the height, the curtain falls.)

Dritter Aufzug

Wildes Wald- und Felsental am Rheine

Erste Szene

Die drei Rheintöchter, Woglinde, Wellgunde und Floßhilde, tauchen aus der Flut auf und schwimmen, wie im Reigentanze, im Kreise umher.

DIE DREI RHEINTÖCHTER
(im Schwimmen mäßig einhaltend)
Frau Sonne
sendet lichte Strahlen;
Nacht liegt in der Tiefe:
einst war sie hell,
da heil und hehr
des Vaters Gold noch in ihr glänzte.
Rheingold,
klares Gold!
Wie hell du einstens strahltest,

Act Three

A Wild, Wooded and Rocky Valley on the Rhine

Scene One

The three Rhinemaidens, Woglinde, Wellgunde, and Flosshilde, rise to the surface and swim about, circling as in a dance.

THE THREE RHINEMAIDENS
(pausing in their swimming)
Fair sunlight
shines on us in splendour;
night lies in the waters:
they once were bright,
when through the waves
our father's gold shone in its splendour!
Rhinegold,
shining gold!
How bright was once your radiance,

hehrer Stern der Tiefe!
(Sie schließen wieder den Schwimmreigen.)
Weialala leia,
wallala leialala.
(Ferner Hornruf. Sie lauschen. Sie schlagen jauchzend das Wasser.)
Frau Sonne,
sende uns den Helden,
der das Gold uns wiedergäbe!
Ließ' er es uns,
dein lichtes Auge
neideten dann wir nicht länger.
Rheingold,
klares Gold!
Wie froh du dann strahltest,
freier Stern der Tiefe!
(Man hört Siegfrieds Horn von der Höhe her.)

WOGLINDE
Ich höre sein Horn.

WELLGUNDE
Der Helde naht.

FLOSSHILDE
Laßt uns beraten!
(Sie tauchen alle drei schnell unter. Siegfried erscheint auf dem Abhange in vollen Waffen.)

SIEGFRIED
Ein Albe führte mich irr,
daß ich die Fährte verlor.
He, Schelm, in welchem Berge
bargst du schnell mir das Wild?

DIE DREI RHEINTÖCHTER
(tauchen wieder auf und schwimmen im Reigen.)
Siegfried!

FLOSSHILDE
Was schiltst du so in den Grund?

WELLGUNDE
Welchem Alben bist du gram?

WOGLINDE
Hat dich ein Nicker geneckt?

noble star of waters!
(They swim about again as in a dance.)
Weialala leia,
wallala leialala.
(A distant horn-call. They listen. They joyfully splash the water.)
Fair sunlight,
send to us the hero,
with our gold, which he can give us!
Then once again,
when it is returned,
we shall enjoy its shining splendour!
Rhinegold,
shining gold!
How fair will be your radiance,
noble star of waters!
(Siegfried's horn is heard from the heights.)

WOGLINDE
And there is his horn.

WELLGUNDE
The hero's near.

FLOSSHILDE
Let us take counsel!
(All three dive down quickly. Siegfried appears on the cliff, fully armed.)

SIEGFRIED
A goblin led me astray,
and now the bear I have lost.
You rogue! Have you concealed him?
What have you done with my bear?

THE THREE RHINEMAIDENS
(rise to the surface again and swim in a ring.)
Siegfried!

FLOSSHILDE
What makes you grumble and growl?

WELLGUNDE
Has a goblin made you angry?

WOGLINDE
Are you annoyed by a gnome?

ALLE DREI
Sag es, Siegfried, sag es uns!

SIEGFRIED
(sie lächelnd betrachtend)
Entzücktet ihr zu euch
den zottigen Gesellen,
der mir verschwand?
Ist's euer Friedel,
euch lustigen Frauen
laß ich ihn gern.
(Die Mädchen lachen laut auf.)

WOGLINDE
Siegfried, was gibst du uns,
wenn wir das Wild dir gönnen?

SIEGFRIED
Noch bin ich beutelos;
so bittet, was ihr begehrt.

WELLGUNDE
Ein goldner Ring
glänzt dir am Finger!

DIE DREI MÄDCHEN
Den gib uns!

SIEGFRIED
Einen Riesenwurm
erschlug ich um den Reif:
für eines schlechten Bären Tatzen
böt' ich ihn nun zum Tausch?

WOGLINDE
Bist du so karg?

WELLGUNDE
So geizig beim Kauf?

FLOSSHILDE
Freigebig
solltest Frauen du sein.

SIEGFRIED
Verzehrt' ich an euch mein Gut,
des zürnte mir wohl mein Weib.

ALL THREE
Tell us, Siegfried, speak to us!

SIEGFRIED
(looking at them with a smile)
Did you entice away
that shaggy-coated creature
that I have lost?
Was he your playmate?
If he was your friend,
I'll leave him to you.
(The maidens laugh.)

WOGLINDE
Siegfried, if we find your bear,
how will you then reward us?

SIEGFRIED
I've had no luck today;
I've nothing with me to give!

WELLGUNDE
A golden ring
gleams on your finger:

ALL THREE
Come, give it!

SIEGFRIED
But to gain this ring
I took a dragon's life;
to give it for a paltry bear-skin—
hardly a fair exchange!

WOGLINDE
Are you so mean?

WELLGUNDE
So miserly, too?

FLOSSHILDE
When maidens
have asked a boon, men should give!

SIEGFRIED
But then if I waste my wealth,
I'm sure that my wife will scold.

FLOSSHILDE
Sie ist wohl schlimm?

WELLGUNDE
Sie schlägt dich wohl?

WOGLINDE
Ihre Hand fühlt schon der Held!
(Sie lachen unmäßig.)

SIEGFRIED
Nun lacht nur lustig zu!
In Harm laß ich euch doch:
denn giert ihr nach dem Ring,
euch Nickern geb ich ihn nie!
(Die Rheintöchter haben sich wieder zum Reigen gefaßt.)

FLOSSHILDE
So schön!

WELLGUNDE
So stark!

WOGLINDE
So gehrenswert!

DIE DREI
Wie schade, daß er geizig ist!
(Lachend tauchen sie unter.)

SIEGFRIED
(tiefer in den Grund hinabsteigend)
Wie leid ich doch
das karge Lob?
Laß ich so mich schmähn?
Kämen sie wieder
zum Wasserrand,
den Ring könnten sie haben.
He! he, he, ihr muntren
Wasserminnen!
Kommt rasch! Ich schenk euch den Ring!
(Er hat den Ring vom Finger gezogen und hält ihn in die Höhe. Die drei Rheintöchter tauchen wieder auf. Sie sind ernst und feierlich.)

FLOSSHILDE
Behalt ihn, Held,

FLOSSHILDE
Is she so stern?

WELLGUNDE
She strikes you then?

WOGLINDE
Has the hero felt her hand?
(They burst out laughing.)

SIEGFRIED
Well, laugh then if you will!
In grief you will be left:
you ask me for the ring—
I'll never give it to you.
(The Rhinemaidens have again resumed their dance.)

FLOSSHILDE
So fair!

WELLGUNDE
So strong!

WOGLINDE
And made for love!

ALL THREE
How sad that he is mean to us!
(They laugh and dive down.)

SIEGFRIED
(comes down lower.)
Why should I let them
laugh and jeer?
Shall I bear their scorn?
If they return
to the shore again,
the ring gladly I'll give them.
Hey! Hey hey! You merry
water maidens!
Come back! I'll give you the ring!
(He has drawn the ring from his finger and holds it on high. The Rhinemaidens rise again to the surface. They appear grave and solemn.)

FLOSSHILDE
Now hold the ring,

und wahr ihn wohl, bis du das Unheil errätst—	and guard it well, and learn the evil that lies—
WOGLINDE und WELLGUNDE Das in dem Ring, du hegst.	WOGLINDE and WELLGUNDE —that lies within the ring;
ALLE DREI Froh fühlst du dich dann, befrein wir dich von dem Fluch.	ALL THREE Then you will be glad you're freed by us from the curse.
SIEGFRIED *(steckt gelassen den Ring wieder an seinen Finger.)* So singet, was ihr wißt!	SIEGFRIED *(quietly places the ring back on his finger.)* Then tell me what you know.
DIE RHEINTÖCHTER Siegfried! Siegfried! Siegfried! Schlimmes wissen wir dir.	THE RHINEMAIDENS Siegfried! Siegfried! Siegfried! Evil lies in that ring.
WELLGUNDE Zu deinem Unheil wahrst du den Ring!	WELLGUNDE And if you keep it, then you are doomed.
ALLE DREI Aus des Rheines Gold ist der Reif geglüht.	ALL THREE From the Rhine's pure gold the ring was forged:
WELLGUNDE Der ihn listig geschmiedet und schmählich verlor—	WELLGUNDE And the Niblung who made it and lost it again—
ALLE DREI Der verfluchte ihn, in fernster Zeit zu zeugen den Tod dem, der ihn trüg'.	ALL THREE laid a curse on it; and all who own the ring—they must die, doomed by the curse.
FLOSSHILDE Wie den Wurm du fälltest—	FLOSSHILDE As you killed the dragon—
WELLGUNDE und FLOSSHILDE So fällst auch du—	WELLGUNDE and FLOSSHILDE so you shall die.
ALLE DREI Und heute noch; so heißen wir's dir, tauschest den Ring du uns nicht—	ALL THREE You die today: unless you obey and give the ring to our care.

WELLGUNDE und FLOSSHILDE
Im tiefen Rhein
ihn zu bergen.

ALLE DREI
Nur seine Flut
sühnet den Fluch!

SIEGFRIED
Ihr listigen Frauen,
laßt das sein!
Traut' ich kaum eurem Schmeicheln,
euer Drohen schreckt mich noch minder!

DIE RHEINTÖCHTER
Siegfried! Siegfried!
Wir weisen dich wahr.
Weiche, weiche dem Fluch!
Ihn flochten nächtlich
webende Nornen
in des Urgesetzes Seil!

SIEGFRIED
Mein Schwert zerschwang einen Speer:
des Urgesetzes
ewiges Seil,
flochten sie wilde
Flüche hinein,
Notung zerhaut es den Nornen!
Wohl warnte mich einst
vor dem Fluch ein Wurm,
doch das Fürchten lehrt' er mich nicht!
(Er betrachtet den Ring.)
Der Welt Erbe
gewänne mir ein Ring:
für der Minne Gunst
miß ich ihn gern;
ich geb ihn euch, gönnt ihr mir Lust.
Doch bedroht ihr mir Leben und Leib:
faßte er nicht
eines Fingers Wert,
den Reif entringt ihr mir nicht!
Denn Leben und Leib,
seht:—so—
werf ich sie weit von mir!
(Er hebt eine Erdscholle vom Boden auf, hält sie

WELLGUNDE and FLOSSHILDE
Our holy Rhine
can release you.

ALL THREE
Our stream alone
purges the curse!

SIEGFRIED
So scheming and cunning—
say no more!
By your craft you couldn't catch me,
by your threats still less can you frighten [me!

THE RHINEMAIDENS
Siegfried! Siegfried!
Give heed to our words.
Siegfried! Fly from the curse!
By Norns at dead of night
it was woven
in the rope of fate's decrees!

SIEGFRIED
My sword has shattered a spear:
In the rope of fate's
eternal decrees,
what though the Norns
have woven a curse—
Notung can cut it asunder!
Though Fafner once warned me
to flee the curse,
yet he could not teach me to fear.
(He contemplates the ring.)
The world's wealth
I could win me by this ring:
for a glance of love
I would exchange it;
if you had smiled the ring would be yours.
But you threatened my limbs and my life:
now though the ring
had no worth at all,
you'd still not get it from me.
My limbs and my life!—
See! So
freely I'd fling away!
(He lifts a clod of earth from the ground, holds it

über seinem Haupte und wirft sie mit den letzten Worten hinter sich.)

above his head, and with the last words throws it behind him.)

DIE RHEINTÖCHTER
Kommt, Schwestern!
Schwindet dem Toren!
So weise und stark
verwähnt sich der Held,
als gebunden und blind er doch ist.
(Sie schwimmen, wild aufgeregt, in weiten Schwenkungen dicht an das Ufer heran.)
Eide schwur er—
und achtet sie nicht!
Runen weiß er—
und rät sie nicht!

THE RHINEMAIDENS
Come, sisters!
Flee from this madman!
He thinks he is wise,
he thinks he is strong,
but he's stupid and blind as a child!
(They swim, wildly excited, in wide circles close to the shore.)
Vows he swore once—
he's false to his vows!
He was wise once—
he's wise no more!

FLOSSHILDE, dann WOGLINDE
Ein hehrstes Gut
ward ihm gegönnt.

FLOSSHILDE, then WOGLINDE
A glorious gift
lay in his grasp.

ALLE DREI
Daß er's verworfen,
weiß er nicht.

ALL THREE
Now he has lost it,
thrown it away;

FLOSSHILDE
Nur den Ring—

FLOSSHILDE
but the ring

WELLGUNDE
der zum Tod ihm taugt—

WELLGUNDE
that will bring his death,

ALLE DREI
den Reif nur will er sich wahren!
Leb wohl, Siegfried!
Ein stolzes Weib
wird noch heut dich Argen beerben.
Sie beut uns beßres Gehör.
Zu ihr! Zu ihr! Zu ihr!
(Sie wenden sich schnell zum Reigen, mit welchem sie gemächlich dem Hintergrunde zu fortschwimmen. Siegfried sieht ihnen lächelnd nach, stemmt ein Bein auf ein Felsstück am Ufer und verweilt mit auf der Hand gestütztem Kinne.)

ALL THREE
the ring he will not surrender!
Farewell! Siegfried!
You die today;
and your ring returns to Brünnhild;
by her, our prayer will be heard:
To her! To her! To her!
(They turn quickly to their dance, in which they slowly swim away to the back. Siegfried looks after them, smiling, then places one foot on a rock on the shore and stays there with his chin resting on his hand.)

DIE RHEINTÖCHTER
Weialala leia,
Wallala leialala.

THE RHINEMAIDENS
Weialala leia,
Wallala leialala.

SIEGFRIED
Im Wasser wie am Lande
lernt' nun ich Weiberart:
wer nicht ihrem Schmeicheln traut,
den schrecken sie mit Drohen;
wer dem kühnlich trotzt,
dem kommt dann ihr Keifen dran.
(Die Rheintöchter sind hier gänzlich verschwunden.)
Und doch,
trüg' ich nicht Gutrun' Treu'
der zieren Frauen eine
hätt' ich mir frisch gezähmt!

(Er blickt ihnen unverwandt nach.)

SIEGFRIED
On land and now on water
I have learnt what women are:
for if you defy their smiles,
they try with threats to scare you;
and if you scorn their threats,
they sting you with scolding words!
(The Rhinemaidens have now quite disappeared.)
And yet,
were I not Gutrun's husband,
I'd try to capture
one of those pretty maids—
make her mine!
(He looks calmly after them.)

DIE RHEINTÖCHTER
(in größer Entfernung)
La, la!
(Jagdhornrufe kommen von der Höhe näher.)

THE RHINEMAIDENS
(very far away)
La, la!
(Hunting horns approach on the heights.)

Zweite Szene

HAGENS STIMME
(von fern)
Hoiho!
(Siegfried fährt aus seiner Entrücktheit auf und antwortet dem Rufe auf seinem Horne.)

MANNEN
(außerhalb der Szene)
Hoiho! Hoiho!

SIEGFRIED
(antwortend)
Hoiho! Hoiho! Hoihe!

HAGEN
(kommt auf der Höhe hervor. Gunther folgt ihm. Siegfried erblickend:)
Finden wir endlich,
wohin du flogest?

Scene Two

HAGEN'S VOICE
(from the distance)
Hoiho!
(Siegfried starts from a dreamy reverie, and answers the call with his horn.)

VASSALS
(off-stage)
Hoiho! Hoiho!

SIEGFRIED
(answering)
Hoiho! Hoiho! Hoihe!

HAGEN
(appears on the height, followed by Gunther. Seeing Siegfried:)
At last we have found you;
where have you been hiding?

SIEGFRIED
Kommt herab! Hier ist's frisch und kühl!
(Die Mannen kommen alle auf der Höhe an und steigen nun mit Hagen und Gunther herab.)

HAGEN
Hier rasten wir
und rüsten das Mahl.
(Jagdbeute wird zuhauf gelegt.)
Laßt ruhn die Beute
und bietet die Schläuche!
(Schläuche und Trinkhörner werden hervorgeholt. Alles lagert sich.)
Der uns das Wild verscheuchte,
nun sollt ihr Wunder hören,
was Siegfried sich erjagt.

SIEGFRIED
(lachend)
Schlimm steht es um mein Mahl:
von eurer Beute
bitte ich für mich.

HAGEN
Du beutelos?

SIEGFRIED
Auf Waldjagd zog ich aus,
doch Wasserwild zeigte sich nur.
War ich dazu recht beraten,
drei wilde Wasservögel
hätt' ich euch wohl gefangen,
die dort auf dem Rhein mir sangen,
erschlagen würd' ich noch heut.
(Er lagert sich zwischen Gunther und Hagen. Gunther erschrickt und blickt düster auf Hagen.)

HAGEN
Das wäre üble Jagd,
wenn den Beutelosen selbst
ein lauernd Wild erlegte!

SIEGFRIED
Mich dürstet!

HAGEN
(indem er für Siegfried ein Trinkhorn füllen läßt und es diesem dann darreicht)
Ich hörte sagen, Siegfried,

SIEGFRIED
Join me here! Here it's fresh and cool!
(The vassals all reach the height and now come down with Hagen and Gunther.)

HAGEN
Let's rest a while,
for here we can feast!
(They lay the game in a heap.)
Lay down the game here,
and open the wine-skins!
(Wine-skins and drinkhorns are produced. All settle down.)
You drove the game away from us;
so let us hear the story
of Siegfried and his chase.

SIEGFRIED
(laughing)
I've nothing much to tell,
instead I'll ask you:
Can I share your meal?

HAGEN
No game at all?

SIEGFRIED
I set forth after a bear,
but water-fowl were all that I found:
if I'd known that I'd have caught them,
and I'd have bagged a brood
of frolicsome water maidens;
they sang on the Rhine their warning:
my death awaits me today.
(He sits down between Gunther and Hagen. Gunther shudders and looks darkly at Hagen.)

HAGEN
A cruel and evil hunt,
if the bear should get away,
and then a boar should kill you!

SIEGFRIED
I'm thirsty!

HAGEN
(while he has a drinking-horn filled for Siegfried, and then hands it to him)
I've heard it rumoured, Siegfried,

der Vögel Sangessprache
verstündest du wohl.
So wäre das wahr?

SIEGFRIED
Seit lange acht ich
des Lallens nicht mehr.
(Er faßt das Trinkhorn und wendet sich damit zu Gunther. Er trinkt und reicht das Horn Gunther hin.)
Trink, Gunther, trink!
Dein Bruder bringt es dir!

GUNTHER
(gedankenvoll und schwermütig in das Horn blickend, dumpf:)
Du mischtest matt und bleich
(noch gedämpfter)
dein Blut allein darin!

SIEGFRIED
(lachend)
So misch es mit dem deinen!
(Er gießt aus Gunthers Horn in das seine, so daß dieses überläuft.)
Nun floß gemischt es über:
der Mutter Erde
laß das ein Labsal sein!

GUNTHER
(mit einem heftigen Seufzer)
Du überfroher Held!

SIEGFRIED
(leise zu Hagen)
Ihm macht Brünnhilde Müh'?

HAGEN
(leise zu Siegfried)
Verstünd' er sie so gut
wie du der Vögel Sang!

SIEGFRIED
Seit Frauen ich singen hörte,
vergaß ich der Vöglein ganz.

HAGEN
Doch einst vernahmst du sie?

that when the birds are singing
you know what they say:
but can that be true?

SIEGFRIED
For a long while I've paid
no heed to their song.
(He grasps the horn and turns with it toward Gunther. He drinks, and then offers Gunther the horn.)
Drink, Gunther, drink;
your brother drinks with you!

GUNTHER
(looks into the horn broodingly and gloomily; dully:)
The wine is thin and pale!
(more gloomily still)
Your blood alone I see!

SIEGFRIED
(laughing)
I'll mingle it with your blood!
(He pours from Gunther's horn into his own so that it overflows.)
Now yours and mine run over;
let earth, our mother,
receive the noble draught.

GUNTHER
(with a deep sigh)
You overjoyful man!

SIEGFRIED
(softly, to Hagen)
He broods on Brünnhilde's words?

HAGEN
(softly to Siegfried)
Her voice is not so clear
as the song of birds to you!

SIEGFRIED
Since women have sung their songs to me,
I've cared for the birdsong no more.

HAGEN
Yet once you knew it well?

SIEGFRIED
(sich lebhaft zu Gunther wendend)
Hei, Gunther,
grämlicher Mann!
Dankst du es mir,
so sing ich dir Mären
aus meinen jungen Tagen.

GUNTHER
Die hör ich gern.
(Alle lagern sich nah an Siegfried, welcher allein aufrecht sitzt, während die andern tiefer gestreckt liegen.)

HAGEN
So singe, Held!

SIEGFRIED
Mime hieß
ein mürrischer Zwerg:
in des Neides Zwang
zog er mich auf,
daß einst das Kind,
wann kühn es erwuchs,
einen Wurm ihm fällt' im Wald,
der faul dort hütet einen Hort.
Er lehrte mich schmieden
und Erze schmelzen;
doch was der Künstler
selber nicht konnt',
des Lehrlings Mute
mußt' es gelingen:
eines zerschlagnen Stahles Stücke
neu zu schweißen zum Schwert.
Des Vater Wehr
fügt' ich mir neu:
nagelfest
schuf ich mir Notung.
Tüchtig zum Kampf
dünkt' er dem Zwerg;
der führte mich nun zum Wald;
dort fällt' ich Fafner, den Wurm.

Jetzt aber merkt
wohl auf die Mär:
Wunder muß ich euch melden.
Von des Wurmes Blut

SIEGFRIED
(turning with animation to Gunther)
Hi, Gunther
unhappy man!
If you would like,
I'll sing you the story
of all my young adventures.

GUNTHER
I'd like to hear.
(All gather round Siegfried, who alone sits upright while the others lie stretched out.)

HAGEN
So sing to us!

SIEGFRIED
Mime was
a hideous dwarf;
and he brought me up,
driven by greed,
so that when I'd grown
to be manly and strong,
I could kill for him a dragon
who long had guarded a hoard of gold.
He made me his pupil,
and taught me forging.
One task that Mime
could not achieve,
his pupil's skill
could teach to the master:
out of a shattered weapon's splinters,
new, I fashioned a sword.
My father's sword,
forged by his son,
sharp and strong,
glittering Notung.
Then I was judged
ready to fight;
so into the wood we went...
Soon the dragon, Fafner, was dead.

Now you must hear
what happened next:
wondrous things I can tell you.
From the dragon's blood

mir brannten die Finger;
sie führt' ich kühlend zum Mund:
kaum netzt' ein wenig
die Zunge das Naß,
was da die Vöglein sangen,
das konnt' ich flugs verstehn.
Auf den Ästen saß es und sang:
»Hei! Siegfried gehört nun
der Nibelungen Hort!
O fänd' in der Höhle
den Hort er jetzt!
Wollt' er den Tarnhelm gewinnen,
der taugt' ihm zu wonniger Tat!
Doch möcht' er den Ring sich erraten,
der macht' ihn zum Walter der Welt!«

HAGEN
Ring und Tarnhelm
trugst du nun fort?

EIN MANNE
Das Vöglein hörtest du wieder?

SIEGFRIED
Ring und Tarnhelm
hatt' ich gerafft:
da lauscht' ich wieder
dem wonnigen Laller;
der saß im Wipfel und sang:
»Hei, Siegfried gehört nun
der Helm und der Ring.
O traute er Mime,
dem Treulosen, nicht!
Ihm sollt' er den Hort nur erheben;
nun lauert er listig am Weg:
nach dem Leben trachtet er Siegfried.
O traute Siegfried nicht Mime!«

HAGEN
Es mahnte dich gut?

VIER MANNEN
Vergaltest du Mime?

SIEGFRIED
Mit tödlichem Tranke
trat er zu mir;

my fingers were burning;
I raised them up to my mouth:
and when the blood
had but wetted my tongue,
then what the birds were singing—
I heard that song like speech.
In the tree above me one sang:
'Hi! Siegfried inherits
the Nibelung gold!
Oh, there it is waiting
within that cave!
There is the Tarnhelm, whose magic
will serve him for glorious deeds;
and if he discovers the ring,
it will make him the lord of the world!'

HAGEN
Ring and Tarnhelm
then did you find?

A VASSAL
The woodbird, what did it say then?

SIEGFRIED
Ring and Tarnhelm—
both I had found.
I heard again
the song of the woodbird;
it sat above me and sang:
'Hi! Siegfried discovered
the Tarnhelm and ring.
Now, let him beware
of the treacherous dwarf!
For Mime is planning to kill him
and take all the gold for himself.
See him lurking, waiting for Siegfried!
Oh, Siegfried, beware of Mime!'

HAGEN
The warning was true?

FOUR VASSALS
What happened to Mime?

SIEGFRIED
A poisonous drink
he'd brewed for my death;

bang und stotternd
gestand er mir Böses:
Notung streckte den Strolch!

HAGEN
(grell lachend)
Was nicht er geschmiedet,
schmeckte doch Mime!

ZWEI MANNEN
(nacheinander)
Was wies das Vöglein dich wieder?

HAGEN
(läßt ein Trinkhorn neu füllen und träufelt den Saft eines Krautes hinein.)
Trink erst, Held,
aus meinem Horn:
ich würzte dir holden Trank,
die Erinnerung hell dir zu wecken,
(Er reicht Siegfried das Horn.)
daß Fernes nicht dir entfalle!

SIEGFRIED
(blickt gedankenvoll in das Horn und trinkt dann langsam.)
In Leid zu dem Wipfel
lauscht' ich hinauf;
da saß es noch und sang:
»Hei, Siegfried erschlug nun
den schlimmen Zwerg!
Jetzt wüßt' ich ihm noch
das herrlichste Weib.
Auf hohem Felsen sie schläft,
Feuer umbrennt ihren Saal;
durchschritt' er die Brunst,
weckt' er die Braut,
Brünnhilde wäre dann sein!«

HAGEN
Und folgtest du
des Vögleins Rate?

SIEGFRIED
Rasch ohne Zögern
zog ich nun aus,
(Gunther hört mit wachsendem Erstaunen zu.)
bis den feurigen Fels ich traf:

scared and shaking,
he showed me his baseness:
Notung ended his life!

HAGEN
(laughing harshly)
Unable to forge it,
still he could feel it!

TWO VASSALS
(one after the other)
What heard you then from the woodbird?

HAGEN
(has another drinking-horn filled, and squeezes the juice of a herb into it.)
Drink first, hero,
from my horn.
I have here a noble drink;
let its freshening power wake your
(He hands Siegfried the horn.) [remembrance
so none of the past escapes you.

SIEGFRIED
(looks thoughtfully into the horn, and then drinks slowly.)
In grief I watched
the branches above;
the bird was there, and sang:
'Hi! Siegfried is free
from the evil dwarf!
Next he must awake
his glorious bride:
high on a mountain she sleeps,
guarded by threatening flames.
Who goes through the fire,
wakens the bride,
Brünnhilde then shall be his!'

HAGEN
And did you take
the woodbird's counsel?

SIEGFRIED
Yes, I arose
and went on my way,
(Gunther listens with increasing astonishment.)
till I came to that fiery peak.

die Lohe durchschritt ich
und fand zum Lohn—
schlafend—ein wonniges Weib
in lichter Waffen Gewand.
Den Helm löst' ich
der herrlichen Maid;
mein Kuß erweckte sie kühn:
oh, wie mich brünstig da umschlang
der schönen Brünnhilde Arm!

GUNTHER
(in höchstem Schrecken aufspringend)
Was hör ich?
(Zwei Raben fliegen aus einem Busche auf, kreisen über Siegfried und fliegen dann, dem Rheine zu, davon.)

HAGEN
Errätst du auch
dieser Raben Geraun'?
(Siegfried fährt heftig auf und blickt, Hagen den Rücken zukehrend, den Raben nach.)
Rache rieten sie mir!
(Er stößt seinen Speer in Siegfrieds Rücken: Gunther fällt ihm—zu spät—in den Arm. Siegfried schwingt mit beiden Händen seinen Schild hoch empor, um Hagen damit zu zerschmettern: die Kraft verläßt ihn, der Schild entsinkt ihm rückwärts; er selbst stürzt über dem Schilde zusammen.)

VIER MANNEN
(welche vergebens Hagen zurückzuhalten versucht:)
Hagen, was tust du?

ZWEI ANDERE
Was tatest du?

GUNTHER
Hagen, was tatest du?

HAGEN
(auf den zu Boden Gestreckten deutend)
Meineid rächt' ich!
(Er wendet sich ruhig ab und verliert sich dann einsam über die Höhe, wo man ihn langsam durch bereits mit der Erscheinung der Raben eingebrochene Dämmerung von dannen schreiten sieht.

I passed through those dangers;
I found the maid...
sleeping... my glorious bride!
In shining armour she lay.
The helmet
I took from her head;
my kiss awakened the bride.
Oh, then like burning fire
I was held by lovely Brünnhilde's arms!

GUNTHER
(springing up with the utmost dismay)
What hear I!
(Two ravens fly up out of a bush, circle over Siegfried, and then fly away towards the Rhine.)

HAGEN
And can you tell
what those ravens have said?
(Siegfried stands up suddenly and, turning his back to Hagen, looks after the ravens.)
Vengeance! That's what they cry!
(He thrusts his spear into Siegfried's back. Gunther—too late—seizes his arm. Siegfried swings his shield on high with both hands, as if to crush Hagen with it; his force fails him; the shield falls backwards and he himself falls down on the shield.)

FOUR VASSALS
(who have in vain tried to hold Hagen back:)
Hagen, you've killed him!

TWO OTHERS
You murdered him!

GUNTHER
Hagen, you murdered him!

HAGEN
(gesturing at the outstretched body)
Falsehood is punished.
(He turns calmly away and disappears, alone, over the heights, where he is seen walking slowly through the dusk which began to fall when the ravens appeared. Gunther bends down, grief-stricken, over

Gunther beugt sich schmerzergriffen zu Siegfried nieder. Die Mannen umstehen teilnahmsvoll den Sterbenden.)

Siegfried. The vassals, filled with sympathy, surround the dying man.)

SIEGFRIED
(von zwei Mannen sitzend erhalten, schlägt die Augen glanzvoll auf.)
Brünnhilde,
heilige Braut!
Wach auf! Öffne dein Auge!
Wer verschloß dich
wieder in Schlaf?
Wer band dich in Schlummer so bang?
Der Wecker kam;
er küßt dich wach,
und aber der Braut
bricht er die Bande:
da lacht ihm Brünnhildes Lust!
Ach, dieses Auge,
ewig nun offen!
Ach, dieses Atems
wonniges Wehen!
Süßes Vergehen,
seliges Grauen—
Brünnhild bietet mir—Gruß!
(Er sinkt zurück und stirbt. Regungslose Trauer der Umstehenden. Die Nacht ist hereingebrochen. Auf die stumme Ermahnung Gunthers erheben die Mannen Siegfrieds Leiche und geleiten sie in feierlichem Zuge über die Felsenhöhe langsam von dannen. Gunther folgt der Leiche zunächst. Der Mond bricht durch die Wolken hervor und beleuchtet immer heller den die Berghöhe erreichenden Trauerzug. Dann steigen Nebel aus dem Rheine auf und erfüllen allmählich die ganze Bühne, auf welcher der Trauerzug bereits unsichtbar geworden ist, bis nach vorne, so daß diese während des Zwischenspiels gänzlich verhüllt bleibt. Als sich die Nebel wieder verteilen, tritt die Halle der Gibichungen, wie im ersten Aufzuge, immer erkennbarer hervor.)

SIEGFRIED
(supported by two vassals in a sitting position opens his eyes radiantly.)
Brünnhilde!
Holiest bride!
Now wake! Wake from your slumber!
Who has forced you
back to your sleep?
Who bound you in slumber again?
Your bridegroom came,
to kiss you awake;
he frees you, again,
breaking your fetters.
He lives in Brünnhilde's love!
Ah! See those eyes,
open forever!
Ah! feel her breathing,
loving and tender!
Joyful surrender!
Sweet are these terrors!
Brünnhild waits for me here!
(He sinks back and dies. The rest stand around him in sorrow without moving. Night has fallen. At Gunther's mute command the vassals raise Siegfried's body and carry it away in a solemn procession over the height. Gunther follows beside the body. The moon breaks through the clouds, and lights up the funeral procession ever more brightly as it reaches the heights. Then mists rise from the Rhine and gradually come forward to fill the whole stage, on which the funeral procession becomes invisible. During the musical interlude, the stage is completely veiled. When the mists divide again, the hall of the Gibichungs, as in the first act, is gradually revealed.)

Dritte Szene

Die Halle der Gibichungen

Es ist Nacht. Mondschein spiegelt sich auf dem Rheine. Gutrune tritt aus ihrem Gemache in die Halle hinaus.

GUTRUNE
War das sein Horn?
(Sie lauscht.)
Nein! Noch
kehrt er nicht heim.
Schlimme Träume
störten mir den Schlaf!
Wild wieherte sein Roß;
Lachen Brünnhildes
weckte mich auf.
Wer war das Weib,
das ich zum Ufer schreiten sah?
Ich fürchte Brünnhild!
Ist sie daheim?
(Sie lauscht an der Tür rechts und ruft dann leise.)
Brünnhild! Brünnhild!
Bist du wach?
(Sie öffnet schüchtern und blickt in das innere Gemach.)
Leer das Gemach.
So war es sie,
die ich zum Rheine schreiten sah!
(Sie erschrickt und lauscht nach der Ferne.)
War das sein Horn?
Nein!
Öd alles!
Säh' ich Siegfried nur bald!
(Sie will sich wieder ihrem Gemache zuwenden; als sie jedoch Hagens Stimme vernimmt, hält sie an und bleibt, von Furcht gefesselt, eine Zeitlang unbeweglich stehen.)

HAGENS STIMME
(von außen sich nähernd)
Hoiho! Hoiho!
Wacht auf! Wacht auf!
Lichte! Lichte!
Helle Brände!
Jagdbeute

Scene Three

The Gibichung Hall

It is night. Moonlight is reflected on the Rhine. Gutrune comes from her room into the hall.

GUTRUNE
Was that his horn?
(She listens.)
No!
he has not returned.
Dreams of evil
drove away my sleep.
Wild neighs I heard from his horse;
Brünnhilde's laughter
then woke me from sleep.
And was it she
I saw there, walking by the shore?
I fear this Brünnhild!
Is she still here?
(She listens at the door on the right, and calls softly.)
Brünnhild! Brünnhild!
Are you there?
(She opens the door hesitatingly, and looks into the room.)
No, she has gone.
Then it was she
whom I saw walking there.
(She shudders, and listens to some distant sound.)
Was that his horn?
No!
All silent!
Ah, if Siegfried were back!
(She sets out to return to her room, but hearing Hagen's voice, she stops and, stricken with fear, remains for a while motionless.)

HAGEN'S VOICE
(calling from without, as he approaches)
Hoiho! Hoiho!
Awake! Awake!
Torches, torches!
Light the torches!
Hunters come back

bringen wir heim.
Hoiho! Hoiho!
(Licht und wachsender Feuerschein von außen. Hagen betritt die Halle.)

HAGEN
Auf, Gutrun!
Begrüße Siegfried!
Der starke Held,
er kehret heim!

GUTRUNE
(in großer Angst)
Was geschah, Hagen?
Nicht hört' ich sein Horn!
(Männer und Frauen, mit Lichtern und Feuerbränden, geleiten den Zug der mit Siegfrieds Leiche Heimkehrenden, unter denen Gunther.)

HAGEN
Der bleiche Held,
nicht bläst er es mehr;
nicht stürmt er zur Jagd,
zum Streite nicht mehr,
noch wirbt er um wonnige Frauen.

GUTRUNE
(mit wachsendem Entsetzen)
Was bringen die?
(Der Zug gelangt in die Mitte der Halle, und die Mannen setzen dort die Leiche auf einer Erhöhung nieder.)

HAGEN
Eines wilden Ebers Beute:
Siegfried, deinen toten Mann.
(Gutrune schreit auf und stürzt über die Leiche. Allgemeine Erschütterung und Trauer.)

GUNTHER
(bemüht sich um die Ohnmächtige.)
Gutrun, holde Schwester,
hebe dein Auge,
schweige mir nicht!

GUTRUNE
(wieder zu sich kommend)
Siegfried—Siegfried erschlagen!

with their prey.
Hoiho! Hoiho!
(Increasing fire-glow from without. Hagen enters the hall.)

HAGEN
Up, Gutrun!
and greet your Siegfried!
That mighty man
is coming home.

GUTRUNE
(in great terror)
What is this? Hagen!
I heard not his horn!
(Men and women, with torches and firebrands, accompany the procession returning home with Siegfried's body; Gunther is among them.)

HAGEN
That mighty man
will sound it no more;
no more will he hunt,
no more will he fight,
no more will he woo lovely women.

GUTRUNE
(with increasing horror)
Who is coming there?
(The procession reaches the middle of the hall and the vassals set down the body on a mound.)

HAGEN
A ferocious boar has slain him;
Siegfried, your husband, is dead.
(Gutrune cries out and falls on the body. General horror and mourning.)

GUNTHER
(supports his swooning sister.)
Gutrun! Gentle sister!
Hear me and answer;
speak to me!

GUTRUNE
(coming to herself again)
Siegfried! Siegfried is murdered!

(Sie stößt Gunther heftig zurück.)
Fort, treuloser Bruder,
du Mörder meines Mannes!
O Hilfe, Hilfe!
Wehe! Wehe!
Sie haben Siegfried erschlagen!

GUNTHER
Nicht klage wider mich!
Dort klage wider Hagen;
er ist der verfluchte Eber,
der diesen Edlen zerfleischt'.

HAGEN
Bist du mir gram darum?

GUNTHER
Angst und Unheil
greife dich immer!

HAGEN
(mit furchtbarem Trotze herantretend)
Ja denn! Ich hab ihn erschlagen.
Ich, Hagen,
schlug ihn zu Tod.
Meinem Speer war er gespart,
bei dem er Meineid sprach.
Heiliges Beuterecht
hab ich mir nun errungen:
drum fordr' ich hier diesen Ring.

GUNTHER
Zurück! Was mir verfiel,
sollst nimmer du empfahn.

HAGEN
Ihr Mannen, richtet mein Recht!

GUNTHER
Rührst du an Gutrunes Erbe,
schamloser Albensohn?

HAGEN
(sein Schwert ziehend)
Des Alben Erbe
fordert so sein Sohn!

(She repels Gunther violently.)
No! Treacherous brother!
you murderer of my husband!
Oh help me! Help me!
Sorrow! Sorrow!
My husband Siegfried is murdered!

GUNTHER
Cast not the blame on me,
but cast the blame on Hagen.
He is the boar who killed him;
by Hagen's spear he was slain.

HAGEN
And you blame me for that?

GUNTHER
Yes, I blame you;
curse you forever!

HAGEN
(stepping forward with terrible defiance)
Well then! I own that I killed him:
I, Hagen,
sent him to death.
With my spear I took his life,
for by that spear he swore.
Rightly he fell to me;
now I shall be rewarded:
and so I claim here the ring.

GUNTHER
Stand back! For I declare
that golden ring is mine!

HAGEN
You vassals, grant me my right.

GUNTHER
That ring is Gutrune's treasure,
misbegotten Niblung son!

HAGEN
(draws his sword.)
The Niblung's treasure
comes to me, his son.

(Er dringt auf Gunther ein, dieser wehrt sich; sie fechten. Mannen werfen sich dazwischen. Gunther fällt von einem Streiche Hagens.)

Her den Ring!

(Er greift nach Siegfrieds Hand; diese hebt sich drohend empor. Gutrune und die Frauen schreien entsetzt laut auf. Alles bleibt in Schauder regungslos gefesselt. Vom Hintergrunde her schreitet Brünnhilde fest und feierlich dem Vordergrunde zu.)

BRÜNNHILDE
(noch im Hintergrunde)
Schweigt eures Jammers
jauchzenden Schwall.
Das ihr alle verrietet,
zur Rache schreitet sein Weib.
(Sie schreitet ruhig weiter vor.)
Kinder hört' ich
greinen nach der Mutter,
da süße Milch sie verschüttet:
doch nicht erklang mir
würdige Klage,
des hehrsten Helden wert.

GUTRUNE
(vom Boden heftig sich aufrichtend)
Brünnhilde! Neiderboste!
Du brachtest uns diese Not:
die du die Männer ihm verhetztest,
weh, daß du dem Haus genaht!

BRÜNNHILDE
Armselige, schweig!
Sein Eheweib warst du nie,
als Buhlerin
bandest du ihn.
Sein Mannesgemahl bin ich,
der ewige Eide er schwur,
eh Siegfried je dich ersah.

GUTRUNE
(in jähe Verzweiflung ausbrechend)
Verfluchter Hagen,
daß du das Gift mir rietest,
das ihr den Gatten entrückt!
Ach, Jammer!
Wie jäh nun weiß ich's,

(He rushes upon Gunther, who defends himself; they fight. Vassals throw themselves between. Gunther falls dead from a stroke of Hagen's.)

Mine, the ring!

(He reaches towards Siegfried's hand, which raises itself threateningly. Gutrune and the women cry out in fear. All remain motionless with terror. From the background, Brünnhilde advances firmly and solemnly to the front.)

BRÜNNHILDE
(still in the background)
Peace with your cries
of useless lament!
For you all have betrayed me;
for vengeance here I have come.
(She comes further forward.)
Children here
are whining for their mother
because some milk has been spilled;
I hear no cries
of true lamentation
to mourn this hero's worth.

GUTRUNE
(rising impetuously from the ground)
Brünnhilde! Cruel and envious!
You brought this shame on our house;
your words aroused the men against him
Cursed be the day you came!

BRÜNNHILDE
Poor creature, peace!
For you and he were not wed;
his mistress,
but never his wife!
But I was his own true wife;
eternal devotion he'd sworn,
and Siegfried and Brünnhild were one!

GUTRUNE
(breaking out in sudden despair)
Accursed Hagen!
By your advice I gave him
the drink that made him forget!
Ah, sorrow!
My eyes are opened.

Brünnhild war die Traute,
die durch den Trank er vergaß!
(Sie wendet sich voll Scheu von Siegfried ab und beugt sich, im Schmerz aufgelöst, über Gunthers Leiche; so verbleibt sie regungslos bis zum Ende. Hagen steht, trotzig auf Speer und Schild gelehnt, in finsteres Sinnen versunken, auf der entgegengesetzten Seite.)

BRÜNNHILDE
(allein in der Mitte; nachdem sie lange, zuerst mit tiefer Erschütterung, dann mit fast überwältigender Wehmut das Angesicht Siegfrieds betrachtet, wendet sie sich mit feierlicher Erhebung an die Männer und Frauen. Zu den Mannen:)
Starke Scheite
schichtet mir dort
am Rande des Rheins zuhauf!
Hoch und hell
lodre die Glut,
die den edlen Leib
des hehrsten Helden verzehrt.
Sein Roß führet daher,
daß mit mir dem Recken es folge;
denn des Helden heiligste
Ehre zu teilen,
verlangt mein eigener Leib.
Vollbringt Brünnhildes Wunsch!
(Die jüngeren Männer errichten während des Folgenden vor der Halle nahe am Rheinufer einen mächtigen Scheiterhaufen, Frauen schmücken ihn mit Decken, auf die sie Kräuter und Blumen streuen. Brünnhilde versinkt von neuem in die Betrachtung der Leiche Siegfrieds. Ihre Mienen nehmen immer sanftere Verklärung an.)
Wie Sonne lauter
strahlt mir sein Licht:
der Reinste war er,
der mich verriet!
Die Gattin trügend,
treu dem Freunde,
von der eignen Trauten,
einzig ihm teuer,
schied er sich durch sein Schwert.
Echter als er
schwur keiner Eide;
treuer als er
hielt keiner Verträge;

Brünnhild was his true love,
whom through the drink he forgot!
(Filled with shame, she turns away from Siegfried and, abandoning herself to grief, bends over Gunther's body; so she remains, motionless, till the end. Hagen, defiantly leaning on his spear, stands sunk in gloomy brooding, on the opposite side.)

BRÜNNHILDE
(alone in the centre; after remaining long absorbed in contemplation of Siegfried's face, first with profound shock, then with almost overwhelming despair, she turns to the men and women in solemn exaltation. To the vassals:)
Sturdy branches,
building his pyre
now bring to the shore of the Rhine!
Bright and clear,
kindle the flame:
let the hero blaze
in splendour and radiance on high.
His horse bring to my side;
he and I together must join him.
I shall share that pure, holy flame
with the hero;
we both shall blaze in the fire.
Obey Brünnhild's command!
(During the following, the younger men raise a huge funeral pyre of logs before the hall, near the bank of the Rhine: women decorate this with coverings on which they strew plants and flowers. Brünnhilde becomes again absorbed in contemplation of Siegfried's body. Her features become increasingly transfigured with tenderness.)
The sun in splendour
shines from his eyes:
the purest hero,
though he was false!
Untrue to Brünnhild,
true to friendship!
From the wife who loved him,
while he betrayed her,
he was barred by his sword.
Never was man
more loyal to friendship;
never was man
more true to his promise;

lautrer als er
liebte kein andrer.
Und doch, alle Eide,
alle Verträge,
die treueste Liebe
trog keiner wie er!
Wißt ihr, wie das ward?
(nach oben blickend)
O ihr, der Eide
heilige Hüter!
Lenkt euren Blick
auf mein blühendes Leid,
erschaut eure ewige Schuld!
Meine Klage hör,
du hehrster Gott!
Durch seine tapferste Tat,
dir so tauglich erwünscht,
weihtest du den,
der sie gewirkt,
dem Fluche, dem du verfielest.
Mich mußte
der Reinste verraten,
daß wissend würde ein Weib!
Weiß ich nun, was dir frommt?
Alles, alles,
alles weiß ich,
alles ward mir nun frei!
Auch deine Raben
hör ich rauschen;
mit bang ersehnter Botschaft
send ich die beiden nun heim.
Ruhe, ruhe, du Gott!
(Sie winkt den Mannen, Siegfrieds Leiche auf den Scheiterhaufen zu tragen; zugleich zieht sie von Siegfrieds Finger den Ring und betrachtet ihn sinnend.)
Mein Erbe nun
nehm ich zu eigen.
Verfluchter Reif!
Furchtbarer Ring!
Dein Gold faß ich
und geb es nun fort.
Der Wassertiefe
weise Schwestern,
des Rheines schwimmende Töchter,
euch dank ich redlichen Rat.
Was ihr begehrt,

never was known
love more faithful.
And yet he was faithless,
broke every promise;
the truest of lovers—
none falser than he!
Know you why that was?
(looking upward)
Look down, you guardians,
look down and hear me!
Turn your regard
on my shame and my grief;
and learn your eternal disgrace!
And Wotan, hear,
you mighty god!
By his most valiant deed
he fulfilled your desire,
but he was forced
to share in your curse—
that curse which has doomed your
He, truest of all men, [downfall.
betrayed me,
that I in grief might grow wise!
Now I know what must be.
All things, all things,
all I know now;
all to me is revealed!
Call back your ravens
hovering round me;
they'll bring to you those tidings
you have both feared and desired.
Rest now, rest now, O god!
(She gives a sign to the vassals to bear Siegfried's body on to the pyre; at the same time she draws the ring from Siegfried's finger and gazes at it thoughtfully.)
My heritage
I claim from the hero.
Accursed gold!
Terrible ring!
My hand grasps you
to cast you away.
You sisters
who are wise and graceful,
you Rhinemaids who dwell in the waters,
I shall obey your advice.
What you desire

ich geb es euch:
aus meiner Asche
nehmt es zu eigen!
Das Feuer, das mich verbrennt,
rein'ge vom Fluche den Ring!
Ihr in der Flut
löset ihn auf,
und lauter bewahrt
das lichte Gold,
das euch zum Unheil geraubt.

(Sie hat sich den Ring angesteckt und wendet sich jetzt zu dem Scheiterhaufen, auf dem Siegfrieds Leiche ausgestreckt liegt. Sie entreißt einem Manne den mächtigen Feuerbrand, schwingt diesen und deutet nach dem Hintergrund.)

Fliegt heim, ihr Raben!
Raunt es eurem Herren,
was hier am Rhein ihr gehört!
An Brünnhildes Felsen
fahrt vorbei.
Der dort noch lodert,
weiset Loge nach Walhall!
Denn der Götter Ende
dämmert nun auf.
So—werf ich den Brand
in Walhalls prangende Burg.

(Sie schleudert den Brand in den Holzstoß, der sich schnell hell entzündet. Zwei Raben sind vom Felsen am Ufer aufgeflogen und verschwinden nach dem Hintergrunde zu. Brünnhilde gewahrt ihr Roß, welches zwei junge Männer hereinführen. Sie ist ihm entgegengesprungen, faßt es und entzäumt es schnell; dann neigt sie sich traulich zu ihm.)

Grane, mein Roß,
sei mir gegrüßt!
Weißt du auch, mein Freund,
wohin ich dich führe?
Im Feuer leuchtend,
liegt dort dein Herr,
Siegfried, mein seliger Held.
Dem Freunde zu folgen,
wieherst du freudig?
Lockt dich zu ihm
die lachende Lohe?
Fühl meine Brust auch,
wie sie entbrennt;
helles Feuer

I'll give to you:
and from my ashes
gather your treasure!
This fire, burning my frame,
cleanses the curse from the ring!
There in the Rhine,
the ring shall be pure;
preserve it,
and guard your shining gold
whose theft has cursed all our woe.

(She has placed the ring on her finger, and now turns to the pile of logs on which Siegfried's body is laid. She seizes a great fire-brand from one of the vassals and gestures towards the back.)

Fly home, you ravens!
tell your lord the tidings
that here by the Rhine you have learned!
Past Brünnhilde's mountain
take your flight,
where Loge is burning!
Summon Loge to Walhall!
For the gods' destruction
soon shall be here.
I cast now the flame
at Walhall's glorious height.

(She flings the brand on the pyre, which quickly breaks out into bright flames. Two ravens fly up from the rocks on the shore and disappear in the background. Brünnhilde sees her horse which has been led in by two young men. She hastens towards it, takes hold of it and quickly removes the bridle; then she leans over it confidingly.)

Grane, my horse!
I greet my friend!
Can you tell, my friend,
to where I must lead you?
In fiery glory
blazes your lord,
Siegfried, my hero and love.
To follow your master,
Oh! Are you neighing?
Lured by the fire,
the light and its laughter?
I too am yearning
to join him there;
glorious radiance

das Herz mir erfaßt,
ihn zu umschlingen,
umschlossen von ihm,
in mächtigster Minne
vermählt ihm zu sein!
Heiajoho! Grane!
Grüß deinen Herren!
Siegfried! Siegfried! Sieh!
Selig grüßt dich dein Weib!

has seized on my heart.
I shall embrace him,
united with him,
in sacred yearning,
with him ever one!
Hiayoho! Grane!
Ride to your master!
Siegfried! Siegfried! See!
Brünnhild greets you as wife!

(Sie hat sich auf das Roß geschwungen und sprengt mit einem Satze in den brennenden Scheiterhaufen. Sogleich steigt prasselnd der Brand hoch auf, so daß das Feuer den ganzen Raum vor der Halle erfüllt und diese selbst schon zu ergreifen scheint. Entsetzt drängen sich die Männer und Frauen nach dem äußersten Vordergrunde. Als der ganze Bühnenraum nur noch von Feuer erfüllt erscheint, verlischt plötzlich der Glutschein, so daß bald bloß ein Dampfgewölk zurückbleibt, welches sich dem Hintergrunde zu verzieht und dort am Horizont sich als finstere Wolkenschicht lagert. Zugleich ist vom Ufer her der Rhein mächtig angeschwollen und hat seine Flut über die Brandstätte gewälzt. Auf den Wogen sind die drei Rheintöchter herbeigeschwommen und erscheinen jetzt über der Brandstätte. Hagen, der seit dem Vorgange mit dem Ringe Brünnhildes Benehmen mit wachsender Angst beobachtet hat, gerät beim Anblick der Rheintöchter in höchsten Schreck. Er wirft hastig Speer, Schild und Helm von sich und stürzt wie wahnsinnig sich in die Flut.)

(She has mounted the horse, and leaps with a single bound into the blazing pyre. The flames immediately blaze up so that they fill the whole space in front of the hall, and appear to seize on the building itself. The men and women press to the extreme front in terror. When the whole space of the stage seems filled with fire, the glow suddenly subsides, and only a cloud of smoke remains; this drifts to the background and lies there on the horizon as a dark bank of cloud. At the same time the Rhine overflows its banks in a mighty flood which pours over the fire. On the waves the three Rhinemaidens swim forwards and now appear above the pyre. Hagen, who since the incident of the ring has observed Brünnhilde's behaviour with increasing anxiety, is seized with great alarm at the appearance of the Rhinemaidens. He hastily throws aside spear, shield, and helmet and rushes like a madman into the flood.)

HAGEN
Zurück vom Ring!

HAGEN
Give back the ring!

(Woglinde und Wellgunde umschlingen mit ihren Armen seinen Nacken und ziehen ihn so, zurückschwimmend, mit sich in die Tiefe. Floßhilde, den anderen voran dem Hintergrunde zuschwimmend, hält jubelnd den gewonnenen Ring in die Höhe. Durch die Wolkenschicht, welche sich am Horizont gelagert, bricht ein rötlicher Glutschein mit wachsender Helligkeit aus. Von dieser Helligkeit beleuchtet, sieht man die drei Rheintöchter auf den ruhigeren Wellen des allmählich wieder in sein Bett zurückgetretenen Rheines, lustig mit dem Ringe spielend, im Reigen schwimmen. Aus den Trümmern der zusam-

(Woglinde and Wellgunde twine their arms around his neck and draw him with them into the depths as they swim away. Flosshilde, swimming in front of the others toward the back, joyously holds up on high the regained ring. Through the cloudbank, which has settled on the horizon, a red glow breaks out with increasing brightness. By its light, the three Rhinemaidens are seen, swimming in circles, merrily playing with the ring on the calmer waters of the Rhine, which has gradually returned to its bed. From the ruins of the fallen hall, the men and women, in great agitation, watch the growing firelight in the heavens. When this reaches its greatest

mengestürzten Halle sehen die Männer und Frauen in höchster Ergriffenheit dem wachsenden Feuerschein am Himmel zu. Als dieser endlich in lichtester Helligkeit leuchtet, erblickt man darin den Saal Walhalls, in welchem die Götter und Helden, ganz nach der Schilderung Waltrautes im ersten Aufzuge, versammelt sitzen. Helle Flammen scheinen in dem Saal der Götter aufzuschlagen. Als die Götter von den Flammen gänzlich verhüllt sind, fällt der Vorhang.)

brightness, the hall of Walhall is seen, in which gods and heroes sit assembled, just as Waltraute described them in the first act. Bright flames seize on the hall of the gods. When the gods are entirely hidden by the flames, the curtain falls.)

Richard Wagner

The Ring of the Nibelung

German text with

English translation

by

Andrew Porter

W · W · NORTON & COMPANY

New York · London

W. W. Norton & Company, Inc., 500 Fifth Avenue, New York, N.Y. 10110
W. W. Norton & Company Ltd., 37 Great Russell Street, London WC1B 3NU

This edition first published in 1977 by arrangement with Faber Music Ltd.

Library of Congress Cataloging in Publication Data
Wagner, Richard, 1813-1883.
The ring of the Nibelung.
1. Operas—Librettos. I. Porter, Andrew, 1928-
II. Title.
ML50.W14R32 1977 782.1'2 77-24107

7 8 9 0

ISBN 0-393-00867-3

To Reginald Goodall

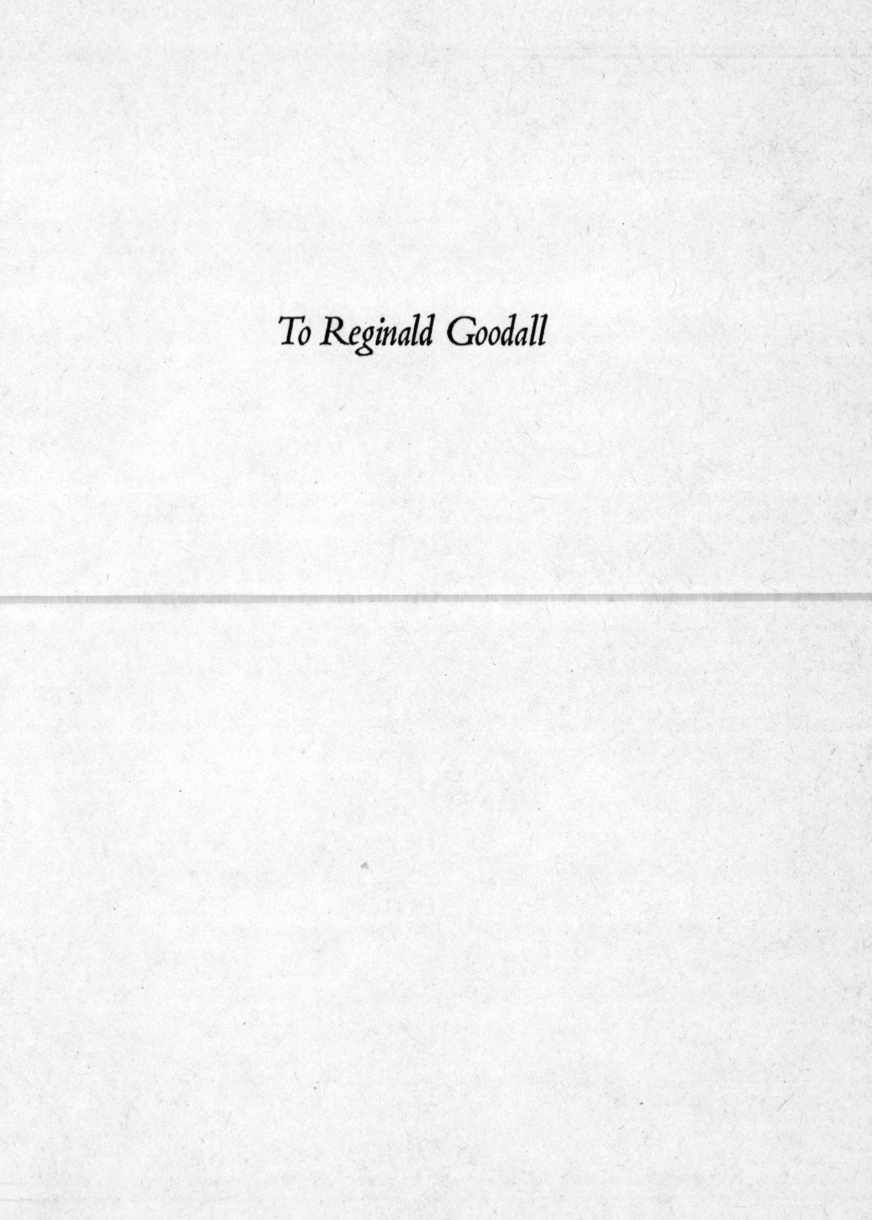

Contents

Introduction

ANDREW PORTER

This translation of *The Ring* was made for singing, acting, and hearing, not for reading. It is neither a straight, literal crib to the sense of the German such as, in our day, Peggie Cochrane, William Mann, and Lionel Salter[1] (see Notes & References at the end of this essay) have ably provided nor an attempt to render Wagner's verse into English verse such as an English translator-poet uncumbered by the need to frame his lines to fit Wagner's music might make. With unfeigned diffidence I offer to the eyes of a reader, rather than to the ears of a listener, a version that has been shaped by the rhythms, inflexions, weights, lengths, and sounds of Wagner's score. To someone who remarks 'This phrase doesn't translate the German at all precisely' or asks 'Why this rude inversion?' I can reply 'No literal translation would fit the musical phrase' and 'The harmony required those words in that order'. But to prove it a score is needed. This translation is incomplete until it meets the music. But people have asked to see it. It is over a century since the first rhythmic translation of a *Ring* opera—Alfred Forman's *The Walkyrie*, which appeared in 1873—was printed.[2] It found many successors. And there is perhaps something to be said for as well as against English versions that attempt to convey the sense of Wagner's lines while moving in the measure of his verse.

The translator who chooses his own metre has an easier task. In blank verse (varied by 'lyrics' for the Rhinemaidens, the forging Siegfried, the Woodbird, the awakened Brünnhilde, and the Norns), Oliver Huckel[3] endeavoured 'to transfuse into English the very spirit of Wagner's lofty thought'. In his preface he declared that

> The usual English librettos of The Ring are totally inadequate and confusing as translations of Wagner's text. They are made to suit the musical requirements rather than to present the thought in literary form. It is often a perplexing task rather than a pleasure to read them. Tenfold more involved and obscure than Browning, they have none of his redeeming grace of thought or speech.

Dr Huckel was the author of *Through England with Tennyson*, of *Mental Medicine*, and of *Spiritual Surgery* (*Some Pointed Analogies between Body and Soul*). The concerns evinced in the latter titles gave him a clear grasp of the moral and psychological parables of *The Ring*, and Tennyson was his poetic model. Two brief excerpts will show the flavour. From Act I of *The Valkyrie*:

But Siegmund shook himself, and springing up
From the rude bearskin, spake with new-found strength:
'My wounds? Speak not of them—they are no more;
Again I feel my strength in every limb.
Yea, had my shield and spear been strong as now

> *This strong right arm, ne'er had I fled my foes;*
> *But spear and shield were shattered, foes pressed sore . . .'*

And, from the final scene of the cycle:

> *Upon her steed, impetuous she leaped,*
> *And for the last time sounding forth the cry:*
> *'Hoyotoho!'—her dear old Valkyr call—*
> *She bounded headlong in the flaming pyre.*

Huckel's *Ring*, published in New York, appeared between 1907 and 1911. In England, Reginald Rankin, B.A., of the Inner Temple, Barrister-at-law, had already produced a version in blank verse (1899),[4] and Randall Fynes another (two volumes, 1899 and 1901),[5] interspersed, like Huckel's, with a few lyrics. Fynes declared it 'astonishing . . . that the attempt seems never to have been made before'; earlier versions are either fettered to the original metre or else mere paraphrases 'in most cases . . . told in the language of the nursery'. He himself uses the language of Tennyson, and adopts the conceit of an epic tale told on successive nights by a medieval bard. In passages like

> *And then there came,*
> *Borne on the night, a faint and distant cry,*
> *As from beyond the limit of the World,*
> *Like a chill wind that blows in a waste land,*
> *Moaning, and crying,* 'The great Gods are dead!'

the specific allusions (in this case to *The Passing of Arthur*) are, in the manner of T. S. Eliot's *The Waste Land*, identified.

Early paraphrases 'in the language of the nursery' I have not examined. In 1903, E. F. Benson produced *The Valkyries*, a rendering in flummery prose.[6] Two prose versions of the thirties are hardly worth examination. C. L. LeMassena's[7] begins: '"Time for our morning dip," exclaims Woglinda'. Gertrude Henderson's[8] mingles baby-talk with fancy words: 'Clump, clump. The black heads of the Giants lifted above the shag of the mountain side. Clump, clump they came, until they stood in the presence of the Aesir'. John Updike's more recent version[9] is a bedtime tale for children clearly and quickly told. It takes ingenious advantage of Wagner's 'recapitulations', jumping from the end of *Das Rheingold* to the Mime-Wanderer riddle scene; the action of *Die Walküre* is related in those questions and answers and by the Wanderer's informing Siegfried, at the foot of the mountain, that he has 'fired' Brünnhilde—a nice word-play—for insubordination. *Götterdämmerung* gets only three sentences: Siegfried and Brünnhilde 'did not live happily ever after. No human beings do. In time they died, and in dying returned the Ring to the mermaids of the Rhine.' These versions are all abundantly illustrated. So—famously, by Arthur Rackham—is Margaret Armour's,[10] which is in verse that has a syllabic equivalence, more or less, to the original but does not lend itself to singing.

What of the singing versions? When Alfred Forman sent his first (privately printed) translation of *The Walkyrie* to the Master, in 1873, he said: 'I trust that the day is not distant when an edition of the music with English words will become necessary. . . . I have compared the whole with the music, and I think a very few alterations of the words would fit them to appear with the score.' But when the first German/English vocal scores of *The Ring* appeared, from Schott, in the early 1880s, the translation was

that of H. and F. Corder.[11] F. was the composer and conductor Frederick Corder, and H. his wife Henrietta Louisa, *née* Walford.

Forman's first aim had been to keep the alliteration. It led him to lines like:

on the steadfast pair of thy eyes,—
that so oft were stars of my storm,
when hope was fierce
in my heart like fire,
when world's-delightwards
my will was lifted
from dread wildering darkness,—
for latest healing
here I must lean
in last farewell
of lingering lips!

(Dr. Huckel's comments quoted above are plainly not unfair.) The Corders also strove to preserve the *Stabreim*—but less rigorously, and with happier results:

these effulgent, glorious eyes,
whose flash my gloom oft dispell'd
when hopeless cravings
my heart discouraged,
or when my wishes
toward wordly pleasure
from wild warfare were turning:—
their lustrous gaze
lights on me now,
as my lips imprint
this last farewell!

The Corders' *Valkyrie* was sung six times at Covent Garden in 1895, with a largely American cast. The following season the opera was done there in French!

Wagner himself is said to have disliked the Corders' translation. At the end of the century, Schott published new bilingual vocal scores, with English words by Frederick Jameson,[12] and the Jameson version has remained in the Schott and, in America, G. Schirmer editions ever since. It was heard in 1908 when Hans Richter gave Covent Garden its first complete English *Ring*, and as late as 1948, in a *Valkyrie* there with Kirsten Flagstad and Hans Hotter; and it has often been performed elsewhere. Jameson's version sings well and sounds well:

those gleaming, radiant eyes
that oft in storms on me shone,
when hopeless yearning
my heart had wasted,
when world's delights
all my wishes wakened,
through wild, wildering sadness:
once more to-day,
lured by their light,
my lips shall give them
love's farewell!

When all Wagner's music entered the public domain, in 1914, Breitkopf & Härtel undertook a new, complete edition, and for the Breitkopf vocal scores Ernest Newman made a new English translation,[13] along lines similar to Jameson's:

those unclouded glorious eyes,
that oft have lighted my gloom,
when hopeless longing
my heart had wasted,
when wordly pleasures
I wished to win me,
by fear fettered and maddened—
their gleam once more
gladdens me now,
as my lips meet thine
in love's last kiss.

The first *Ring* in America, built up at the Metropolitan Opera between 1885 and 1888, was assembled in 1889. In New York, F. Rullman, the main provider of librettos, had already published some bilingual texts, with line-for-line but non-metrical translations by John P. Jackson, back in 1877 (when *Die Walküre* had its American première, at the New York Academy of Music). Rullman replaced at least *Siegfried* with the Corder version in the 1880s,[14] and brought out Charles Henry Meltzer's translations of *Das Rheingold* and *Die Walküre* in 1904. Another, uncredited—and discreditable—translation appeared in the vocal scores edited by Henry T. Finck and published by the John Church Co., of Cincinnati, in 1903. But the earlier American *Ring* translations, often reprinted,[15] and usually unattributed, form a tangled and unprofitable study. The information about them above is scrappy—but there are better ways of spending time than ploughing through and comparing the numerous 'theatre libretti' scattered in many libraries throughout America. The first significant and independent singing version produced in America is Stewart Robb's, of 1960.[16]

Robb set out 'to translate *The Ring* into clear, understandable modern English, avoiding obscurities of expression and archaic words . . . yet preserving the rhythms of the original German where possible, and even some of the alliterative effects. . . . Here', he concludes, 'is a new English version of *Der Ring des Nibelungen* which can be enjoyed by the general reader as well as sung on the opera stage. . . . Withal, it does not sound like a translation, but as though already written in English.' (Or written in American, an English reader may remark, as he comes across 'slowpoke', ''fraid-cat', a Mime who has 'fixed' soup for Siegfried, and—for Waltraute's 'Bist du von Sinnen?'—'Have you gone crazy?'.) I admire Robb's work but find it mixty-maxty: his vocabulary ranges from the colloquialisms quoted, through 'Frolic, good fellows' and 'He blows a rollicking horn', to 'wish-maid', 'lot-chooser', and 'hest'. Wagner's tone varies widely, but Robb's more widely still. Fricka's measured 'Die Walküre wend auch von ihm!' becomes 'Just keep Brunnhild out of his way'; but in the previous act of *The Valkyrie*, when Sieglinde pushes the hair back from Siegmund's forehead, her diction is surprisingly formal:

How wide and open
gleams your brow.
Your temple displays
all the interlaced veins.

Reginald Goodall, whom I revered as the greatest of living Wagnerian interpreters. The rehearsals were long, and at every stage the conductor, the producers, the musical coaches, and the singers themselves made suggestions that helped to provide a more comprehensible, singable, dramatic, and 'musical' text.

Opera translations intended for singing have a limited life. Whether the translator of, say, an eighteenth-century opera chooses to employ a neutral and 'timeless' or a mock-eighteenth-century idiom, his work is likely to bear the stamp of the time it was made. It is easy to date to a decade or so a photograph of a soprano dressed, wigged, and painted as Mozart's Countess Almaviva or Richard Strauss's Feldmarschallin. Similarly, in the 1970s one can distinguish between 'eighteenth-century English' written in the 1850s, the 1890s, and the 1930s. After perhaps a century, a translation made at the time of an opera's composition, possibly under its composer's eye, may acquire a certain 'period authenticity' and warrant revival—though this is not the case with, for example, the standard Italian translations of Verdi's *Les Vêpres siciliennes* and *Don Carlos*. In the former, fiery sentiments such as Giovanni da Procida's cry of 'la liberté!' were quenched, to avoid clashes with Italian censorship, and in both, Verdi, too permissive with his translators, allowed fine dramatic and fine musical points to be blunted. In any event, French-into-Italian is hard. Masculine endings are feminized; *fort* becomes *forte* and *Elisabeth, Elisabetta.* Once upon a time, poetic usage permitted the dropping of final syllables; *destin cruel* could move south as *destin crudel* rather than *destino crudele.* But now, as Gian Carlo Menotti has remarked, a modern Italian librettist is more or less committed to feminine phrase endings except when his characters visit the *città* to drink a *caffé.*

Italian-into-French is somewhat easier. French-into-English raises constant problems of how to treat not-quite-mute *-e.* Italian-into-English often results in phrase after phrase ending with an accusative pronoun: *Soccorso!* becomes *Oh help me!*, and *Son tradita!, He betrayed me!* Moreover, all English translators, from whatever language, tend to keep on hand a box filled with *thens* and *nows* into which they can dip to fill out their lines. Since Italians take four syllables to bid one another goodnight, Sparafucile, Preziosilla and the rest usually say *Well, goodnight then!*

Germans characters on the English lyric stage usually say *So, goodnight.* The difficulties of German-into-English are rather different, and in the case of *Ring*-into-English they are compounded by Wagner's *Stabreim* or alliteration, his hard syntax, and his archaic vocabulary. For many of the recurrent key words there are syllabic equivalents. *Blut* is *blood, Schwert* is *sword*, and *Tod* is *death. Liebe* and *Auge* give more trouble; on a few occasions the singers of my *Ring*-in-English are asked to slur two notes to *love* and *eye*, and Fafner the *Wurm* was not easily transformed into a *dragon.* But syllabic equivalents are not sonic equivalents: the long, dark vowels of a sustained *Blut* or *Tod* are ill-represented by *blood* and *death.* A German Siegmund can cry *Schwert* with a bright, forward ring that a mere *sword* is powerless to provide. Although *vengeance* is a word that can be said vehemently, *Rache* is more powerfully a swift double explosion. If all British and American singers, conductors, producers, and designers of *The Ring* and all their audiences commanded, not just German, but specifically Wagner's strange German as a second language—if, using the original words, the singers could express themselves fully and be sure of being understood, in detail, by those who heard them—there would be no call to translate *The Ring* into English. As one of its translators, I am dismayed when I compare, say, Wagner's:

Wie liebliche Luft
wieder uns weht,
wonnig Gefühl
die Sinne erfüllt!
Traurig ging es uns allen,
getrennt für immer von ihr,
die leidlos ewiger Jugend
jubelnde Lust uns verleiht

—Froh's 'arietta' in the last scene of *Das Rheingold*—with my:

How sweetly the air
charms us again;
joy and contentment
steal through my heart!
Life indeed would be wretched
if we were parted from her;
she brings us youth eternal,
fills us with joy and delight.

But there were compensations. When I heard Rita Hunter fill even so stilted a phrase as 'You who this love in my heart inspired' with tender, swelling emotion, Ava June utter Sieglinde's long solo that begins 'My husband's kinsmen', Norman Bailey 'think aloud' in Wotan's monologue, and Alberto Remedios relate Siegfried's young adventures, to audiences that followed what was said, I could believe there had been some gains as well as the inevitable and enormous losses.

All translation is a matter of weighing gains and losses. *The Ring*—despite what some German critics of Wagner's verse may feel—is not one of the works of which it can be said, as it was of James Fenimore Cooper's novels, that they have been 'often translated, never without improvement'. In the lyric theatre, the gains are in verbal and dramatic communicativeness. (Has there ever been a great composer who did not prefer his works to be performed in the language of the country?) The losses are of that other 'sense' conveyed by the sound and the untranslatable subtleties of the original words. And the translator's task is to make such losses as light as possible. I began work on *The Ring* without theories, almost instinctively—holding the sound of a German phrase in my ears and the literal sense of it in my mind, and rejecting version after version until I hit on English words that seemed to fit. Much later—when *The Valkyrie* was almost finished—I realized that I had been guided by six different, linked, and for the most part mutually unachievable intentions.

(1) To provide a translation that is close to the original and at the same time makes audible sense at first hearing, without needing to be 'worked out' by a puzzled listener. Towards the close of *The Rhinegold*, Fricka, hearing the name Walhall for the first time, asks what it means. The Corders' Wotan replied: 'What might 'gainst our fears my mind may have found, if proved a success, soon shall explain that name.' And Forman's: 'What, in might over fear, my manfulness found, shall matchlessly live and lead the meaning to light'. Both are fair representations of some tortuous German. But I felt that unless the meaning could be led to light a little more directly than that, the speech might as well be left in German. So, natural words in a natural order.

(2) To keep important words—such as *Liebe, Leid, Ring, Rhein*—and especially the proper names exactly where Wagner placed them. Their sounds and rhythms often have

a motivic significance; they coincide with particular harmonies. In my first draft, instead of that stilted phrase of Brünnhilde's quoted above, I had the more direct 'You who inspired me to feel this love'. Reginald Goodall pointed out that the chord on the fourth syllable was inseparable from *Liebe*; hence, 'You who this love in my heart inspired,' which reads less well but makes far better musical sense. For the same reason, Brünnhilde's 'One thing I did know, that you still loved the Wälsung', a little earlier, was changed to '... that the Wälsung you loved'.

(3) To keep, wherever possible, the *Stabreim*, as an essential part of the patterning in the score's structure.

(4) To echo the sound of the German—the ring of bright, forward vowels, the full shadows casts by dark ones, the attack of hammer-stroke consonants, the hiss and splutter of certain sibilant sequences. (Wagner's invented language is richer in long vowels and percussive consonants than even modern German; it would be easier to translate its sounds into Old English or into Northumbrian dialect.) Sound sometimes took precedence of literal sense. For Alberich's 'Zertrümmert! Zerknickt!' (literally 'Destroyed! Crushed!'), Jameson has 'Defeated! Destroyed!'. I made him 'Defeated! and tricked!'.

(5) To reflect the differing tones, ranging from the elevated and rhetorical (notably Wotan's harangues in Act III of *Die Walküre*), through Froh's—and Fasolt's—lyricism in *Das Rheingold*, to Loge's airy wit and Siegfried's boisterous sallies; to let such jokes as Siegfried and the Wanderer make be heard as such. The gods, Desmond Shawe-Taylor told me early on, shouldn't talk like the people next door. I hope mine do not—but I know he thinks that they have shed some of their dignity together with the second person singular. That form offered to the old translators a syllabic flexibility—*thou dost* or *doest, didest* or *didst*—denied to a modern translator who has decided, rightly or wrongly, against its use. He, on the other hand, is likely to gain new alternatives by resorting to contractions (*I have, I've*) more freely than they did. Wagner made liberal use of such contractions and elisions ('dir werf' ich's zu'; 'Ist's der, den du Gunther'n gab'st'), often introducing them when he came to set his written words to music. In English, I confess, similar forms sometimes strike too modern and colloquial a note, but I've used them when disruption of the musical rhythm (dividing, say, a minim on *I've* into two crotchets for *I have*) would be more disturbing still. They can look worse than they sound. When 'Do you think . . .?' is said quickly it becomes two syllables, 'D'you think', pronounced *dew think*. Although the ear notices nothing amiss, an eye seeing it thus written would be distressed. And so for that eye's sake I have once or twice in this printed text spelt out in full what in performance is meant to be elided. However, the frequent omission of the final -*e* of Brünnhilde, Gutrune, etc., is not a misprint but Wagner's practice; and Nibelung and Niblung are his alternatives.

(6) Most important of all—sometimes I felt that, like Brünnhilde, *im Auge das eine ich hielt* and ignored all other imperatives—to find words that fit the music closely. Take the last two lines of that passage from Wotan's farewell quoted above in Forman's, the Corders', Jameson's, and Newman's versions. The German is 'mit dem Lebewohles/ letztem Kuss'; -*woh*- is a B suspended over an F major chord, and -*les* is its resolution on to A; then there is a semiquaver rest, a small break, before *letztem Kuss*. Only Jameson's lines fit the music. Forman's give us, in effect, 'farewellov/lingering lips'; the Corders' 'imprint-this/last farewell'; and Newman's 'thine-in/love's last kiss'. Robb has 'brief and final/farewell kiss', which fits well enough—but is Wotan's kiss really 'brief'?

(My version—to save any curious reader from paging on—is 'loving,/last farewell'.) Or take the opening words of Brünnhilde's immolation scene, 'Starke Scheite/schichtet mir dort'. One old translation, 'Mighty faggots', will plainly not do today. But for other reasons Jameson's 'mighty logs I' (*log's eye*) and Robb's 'Let great logs be' (*Great Logsby*, inflected like the *Great Gatsby*) must be deemed unfitting. Even though the soprano may draw no breath between the lines, the declamation is wrong. Insufficient care about such points of declamation, I believe, has done much to give opera-in-English its reputation of 'sounding awful'. Earlier *Ring* translations contain things like Sieglinde's 'And his packper/Sue in mighty force', Siegmund's 'What has ensnared/Me now well I know', Wotan's 'A lu—ckier manwill/Joy in thy stars' (*lu-* sustained, *man will* given the inflexion of *mandrill*), and Brünnhilde's:

The world's most glorious hear,
Roe-bears, o woo,
Man thy shell, tering womb!

There are some things like that in my version but, I hope, not many. I can think of no English phrase that correctly 'articulates' the awakening Brünnhilde's 'Heil dir, Sonne!' except 'Hi there, sunshine!'—and that won't do. (So each Brünnhilde, with her conductor, has chosen, from a list of variously unsatisfactory compromises provided, the version she finds least unmusical.) Most of the revisions undertaken after hearing the translation in performances have been directed towards obtaining a better musical fit.

A seventh requirement is conspicuously absent from those above: any attempt to reflect what Martin Cooper has called 'the cloudy, archaic literary style that was an organic part of Wagner's mystique.'[17] Deliberately so. For I felt that anyone who wanted to listen to *The Ring* not-quite-understanding what is said could well listen to it, unspoiled, in the original cloudy German; what would be the point of devising yet another translation 'tenfold more involved and obscure than Browning'? So this is not a text acceptable to those who believe, with Mr Cooper, that the listener's attention should be 'lulled rather than alerted by the words', that 'only the suspension of the intellectual processes will make him accept the time-scale which Wagner imposes'. It is a belief that I understand but do not fully share. From my first encounter with *The Ring*, I wanted to know exactly what all those characters were saying.

In any case, a translator cannot do everything. A glance at the following pages will reveal how very, very seldom even my 'six points' could all be met. Phrase by phrase, it was a matter of deciding which of them, in that particular place, should be deemed paramount, of discovering which were achievable at all, and then of settling for the least unsatisfactory, most singable English. Often but not always the *Stabreim* was the first thing to go; intelligible and otherwise accurate words were usually preferred to fancier alternatives that happened to begin with the right letters. So, not 'Notung! Notung! needfullest sword!' or 'Needful! Needful! Notable sword!' (Corders). And, for other reasons, not 'Notung! Notung! conquering sword!' (Jameson) or 'Needful! Needful! conquering sword!' (Robb's amalgam of Corders and Jameson). I chose this example (I have 'Notung! Notung! sword of my need!') because it brings up another recurrent 'crux'—the proper names, which in *The Ring* always mean something. The Valkyries' function—choosing those slain in battle—is defined by their name. In *The Ring*, I would be a doorkeeper. Valkyrie has been an English word since the eighteenth century, and so I used it. But so has Valhalla, the hall of those slain in battle; musical reasons,

however, predicate the two syllables of Wagner's *Walhall*. I could have spelt it with a *V*—but that could lead to Votan, Vellgunde, and Valtrauta. (Lord Acton, who told Mr. Gladstone that 'neither Pitt nor Peel lives in my Walhalla', provides some precedent for keeping the *W* even in English.) On the whole I have left the names and the puns that are made upon them untranslated. Siegmund and Sieglinde could hardly be Victor and gentle Vicky. My 'Wehwalt der Wölfing' is not 'Woeful the Wolf-cub'. And if, at the Coliseum, Hunding (as in Robb) were to call out 'Woe-King! Woe-King!' in Act II of *The Valkyrie*, a British audience's reaction might be: 'Next stop, Basingstoke'. But sometimes I tried to gloss: 'I'm Wehwalt, named for my sorrow'; 'Siegfried, victorious and free' for 'Siegfried erfreu sich des Siegs!', when Brünnhilde tells Sieglinde the name of her son-to-be. (*Free* may not be in the German, but it does point towards *den Freien* whom Wotan has longed for, and it also keeps Wagner's vowel.) About orthography I have been inconsistent. 'Hoyotoho!' gives a reasonable approximation to the sounds wanted, but things like the Rhinemaidens' 'Wallala weiala' defeated me—*viala* is sonically ambiguous, and any attempts to show that the *i* is long began to suggest Viyella—so I left them in German spelling. As in most prints of the German libretto since Breitkopf's, I have omitted the unsounded *h* in *Not(h), Not(h)ung*, etc., and many of the apostrophes indicating Wagner's elided *e*'s. *Rhinegold* (like rhinestone) is so well established in English usage as one word that to transform it into *Rhine Gold*, as some advised, seemed to me pedantic.

The Ring is on the first level a rousing and splendid old tale of gods and dwarfs and men, of giants and dragons, loves and hates, murder, magic, and mysteries, unfolded amid vast and picturesque scenery. Beyond that, it is about (among other things) man's conquest of the natural world for his own uses (the first action recorded is Wotan's tearing a branch from the World Ashtree); about man's dominion over men (well-intentioned oligarchy and capitalist tyranny are both condemned); and about man's understanding of himself (the forces influencing his action, at the start located in gods, are finally discovered to lie within himself). By intention, Wagner patterned his drama on Attic tragedy but chose as his symbolic matter the ancestral myths of the North. To mankind's collective unconsciousness he gave form; that is easily said, but for that matter it can easily—if not briefly—be demonstrated. Instinct, inspiration, the composer's comprehensive grasp of what men before him had thought, dreamed, and done, and his powerful controlling mind directed the creation of *The Ring* over more than a quarter-century. In words, music, and vivid theatrical imagery combined it took shape.

Each of the clauses above has been the subject of many books; I mention here these large matters in summary form only to make the point, that believing *all* these things about *The Ring* to be true, I have not endeavoured to translate it with special reference to any one of them. This is not a particular 'interpretation'. Such interpretations—usually they are the work of ambitious producers, who have determined to disassemble the components of the *Gesamtkunstwerk*—can cast exciting new light on aspects of the work. They can be maddening. And, however brilliant, they are achieved only by diminishing the force and richness of the whole.

For five years, scores of *The Ring* accompanied me wherever I went—*wo ich mich fand, wohin ich zog*. Some lines now always recall places: the Kent garden where a tricky line of Sieglinde's was suddenly solved; a journey from Coimbra to Lisbon during which

the Fricka-Wotan argument of *The Valkyrie* fell into place; the Glasgow hotel bedroom where all day long I worked at translating, leaving at night to hear—in German—Scottish Opera's *Ring*; and, above all, William Weaver's farmhouse in the Tuscan hills, where much of the work was done. My debts are great, and of many kinds: as I have said, to several previous translators; to Kirsten Flagstad, Astrid Varnay, Hans Hotter, Ludwig Weber, Wilhelm Furtwängler, Hans Knappertsbusch, Rudolf Kempe, and all those who taught me how *The Ring* could sound; to Reginald Goodall, Glen Byam Shaw and John Blatchley, John Barker, Edmund Tracey, Leonard Hancock, and all the singers who worked on the Sadler's Wells production, *in langer Zeiten Lauf*, refining my phrases and bringing them to life; to George London, who, while producing this English *Ring* in several American cities, made helpful new suggestions; to critical colleagues—especially David Cairns, Bernard Levin, Max Loppert, Peter Stadlen, and David Hamilton—who encouraged me; and to Claire Brook, without whose help I could never have got the thing into print at all.

The Valkyrie was first performed by the Sadler's Wells Opera (now English National Opera), at the London Coliseum, on 29 January 1970; *Twilight of the Gods* on 29 January 1971; *The Rhinegold* on 1 March 1972; and *Siegfried* on 8 February 1973. The full cycle was first given in July and August 1973. As I write, three of the operas have been recorded, by the English National Opera, for EMI, and the recording of *Twilight of the Gods* is imminent.

NEW YORK, JUNE 1976

Notes and References

1 Peggie Cochrane's translation appeared with the Decca recordings conducted by Georg Solti. William Mann's was published (in short lines) by the Friends of Covent Garden, in 1964, and later (with Wagner's lineation) to accompany the EMI recording conducted by Furtwängler. Lionel Salter's translations of *Das Rheingold, Siegfried*, and *Götterdämmerung* accompanied the Deutsche Grammophon recordings conducted by Karajan (for *Die Walküre*, the Mann version was used).

2 Alfred Forman: *The Walkyrie* (privately printed, London, 1873); *The Nibelung's Ring, English words to Richard Wagner's Ring des Nibelungen, in the alliterative verse of the original* (London: Schott, 1877).

3 Oliver Huckel: *The Rhine-Gold, A Dramatic Poem by Richard Wagner freely translated into poetic narrative form* (New York: Thomas Y. Crowell, 1907); followed by *The Valkyrie* (1909), *Siegfried* (1910), and *The Dusk of the Gods* (1911)—and by all Wagner's other dramas, from *Rienzi* to *Parsifal*.

4 Reginald Rankin: *Wagner's Nibelungen Ring done into English verse* (London: Longmans, Green, 1899, 2 vols.).

5 Randall Fynes: *The Ring of the Nibelung, An English version* (London: Smith, Elder, 1899–1901, 2 vols.; 1913, one-volume edition).

6 E. F. Benson: *The Valkyries, A Romance* (London: T. Fisher Unwin, 1903).

7 C. L. LeMassena: *The Ring of the Nibelung* (New York: Grossman-Roth, 1930).

8 Gertrude Henderson: *The Ring of the Nibelung* (New York: Alfred A. Knopf, 1932).

9 John Updike: *The Ring* (New York: Alfred A. Knopf, 1964).

10 Margaret Armour: *The Ring of the Niblung . . . translated into English* (London: Wm. Heinemann, 1911, 2 vols.).

11 The only firmly dated Corder vocal score I have seen is a *Götterdämmerung* of 1881. The plate number of the German/English *Rheingold* is 23504, of *Die Walküre* 23188; 1882 is the date usually assigned to the vocal scores and the bilingual libretti.

12 Frederick Jameson: *The Nibelung's Ring, English words to Richard Wagner's Ring des Nibelungen, An accurate translation* (London: Schott, 1896). This was followed at the turn of the century by individual bilingual libretti and by vocal scores from both Schott and G. Schirmer. The Jameson version also appears in the Schott and Eulenburg miniature scores.

13 Newman's translations of *The Rhinegold* and *The Valkyrie* had already been published in London, in 1912, as Nos. 4 and 5 of Breitkopf & Härtel's Textbooks. The vocal scores are in the Hofmeister catalogue for the years 1914–18.

14 The Corder translations were also reprinted by C. F. Tretbar, of New York, in 1893, and by Oliver Ditson, of Boston, in 1904.

15 For example, as late as 1938 *The Authentic Librettos of the Wagner Operas* (New York: Crown Publishers) gathers in facsimile four different 'theatre libretti' (*Siegfried* with cuts and all) in different type-faces—basically the Corders' text, mingled with some Meltzer prefatory material.

16 Stewart Robb: *The Ring of the Nibelung* (New York: Dutton, 1960); English only; useful introductory essays by Edward Downes and by the translator. Published as individual, bilingual libretti by G. Schirmer. (I have not seen Walter Ducloux's unpublished singing translation of *Das Rheingold*.)

17 Martin Cooper: 'Wagner without the wizardry', *Daily Telegraph*, 18 August 1973.

The Rhinegold

Preliminary Evening to the Festival Play

The Ring of the Nibelung

Dramatis Personae

Gods

WOTAN	*Bass-baritone*
DONNER	*Baritone*
FROH	*Tenor*
LOGE	*Tenor*

Giants

FASOLT	*Bass-baritone*
FAFNER	*Bass*

Nibelungs

ALBERICH	*Bass-baritone*
MIME	*Tenor*

Goddesses

FRICKA	*Mezzo-soprano*
FREIA	*Soprano*
ERDA	*Contralto*

Rhinemaidens

WOGLINDE	*Soprano*
WELLGUNDE	*Soprano*
FLOSSHILDE	*Contralto*

Nibelungs

Erste Szene

Auf dem Grund des Rheines

Grünliche Dämmerung, nach oben zu lichter, nach unten zu dunkler. Die Höhe ist von wogendem Gewässer erfüllt, das rastlos von rechts nach links zu strömt. Nach der Tiefe zu lösen sich die Fluten in einen immer feineren feuchten Nebel auf, so daß der Raum der Manneshöhe vom Boden auf gänzlich frei vom Wasser zu sein scheint, welches wie in Wolkenzügen über den nächtlichen Grund dahinfließt. Überall ragen schroffe Felsenriffe aus der Tiefe auf und grenzen den Raum der Bühne ab; der ganze Boden ist in ein wildes Zackengewirr zerspalten, so daß er nirgends vollkommen eben ist und nach allen Seiten hin in dichtester Finsternis tiefere Schluchten annehmen läßt. Das Orchester beginnt bei noch geschlossenem Vorhange.
Der Vorhang wird aufgezogen. Volles Wogen der Wassertiefe. Um ein Riff in der Mitte der Bühne,

Scene One

On the Bed of the Rhine

Greenish twilight, brighter towards the top, darker below. The upper part of the stage is filled with swirling waters that flow restlessly from right to left. Towards the bottom, the waters resolve into an increasingly fine damp mist, so that a space a man's height from the ground seems to be completely free of the water, which courses like a train of clouds over the dusky bed. Craggy points of rock rise everywhere from the depths and mark the confines of the stage. The whole river bed is broken up into a craggy confusion, so that nowhere is it completely flat, and on all sides, in the dense darkness, there seem to be deeper gorges. The orchestra begins while the curtain is still closed.

When the curtain rises, the watery depths are in full flood. In the centre of the stage, around a rock

welches mit seiner schlanken Spitze bis in die dichtere, heller dämmernde Wasserflut hinaufragt, kreist in anmutig schwimmender Bewegung eine der Rheintöchter.

WOGLINDE
Weia! Waga!
Woge, du Welle!
Walle zur Wiege!
Wagalaweia!
Wallala weiala weia!

WELLGUNDES STIMME
(von oben)
Woglinde, wachst du allein?

WOGLINDE
Mit Wellgunde wär' ich zu zwei.

WELLGUNDE
(taucht aus der Flut zum Riff herab.)
Laß sehn, wie du wachst.
(Sie sucht Woglinde zu erhaschen.)

WOGLINDE
(entweicht ihr schwimmend.)
Sicher vor dir.
(Sie necken sich und suchen sich spielend zu fangen.)

FLOSSHILDES STIMME
(von oben)
Heiala weia!
Wildes Geschwister!

WELLGUNDE
Floßhilde, schwimm!
Woglinde flieht:
hilf mir die Fliehende fangen!

FLOSSHILDE
(taucht herab und fährt zwischen die Spielenden.)
Des Goldes Schlaf
hütet ihr schlecht;
besser bewacht
des Schlummernden Bett,
sonst büßt ihr beide das Spiel!
(Mit muntrem Gekreisch fahren die beiden

whose slender point reaches up into the brighter area of densely swirling water, one of the Rhine-maidens is circling with a graceful swimming motion.

WOGLINDE
Weia! Waga!
Wandering waters,
lulling our cradle!
Wagalaweia!
Wallala, weiala weia!

WELLGUNDE'S VOICE
(from above)
Woglinde, watching alone?

WOGLINDE
Till Wellgunde joins me below.

WELLGUNDE
(dives down from the waters to the rock.)
Let's see how you watch!
(She tries to catch Woglinde.)

WOGLINDE
(swims away from her.)
Safe from your grasp!
(They tease and playfully try to catch one another.)

FLOSSHILDE'S VOICE
(from above)
Heiala weia!
Careful, my sisters!

WELLGUNDE
Flosshilde, swim!
Woglinde flies:
hurry and help me to catch her!

FLOSSHILDE
(dives down and comes between them in their play.)
The sleeping gold
calls for your care!
Back to your task
of guarding its bed,
or else you'll pay for your games!
(With merry cries the other two separate;

auseinander: Floßhilde sucht bald die eine, bald die andere zu erhaschen; sie entschlüpfen ihr und vereinigen sich endlich, um gemeinschaftlich auf Floßhilde Jagd zu machen; so schnellen sie gleich Fischen von Riff zu Riff, scherzend und lachend.
Aus einer finsteren Schlucht ist währenddem Alberich, an einem Riffe klimmend, dem Abgrunde entstiegen. Er hält, noch vom Dunkel umgeben, an und schaut dem Spiele der Wassermädchen mit steigendem Wohlgefallen zu.)

ALBERICH
Hehe! Ihr Nicker!
Wie seid ihr niedlich,
neidliches Volk!
Aus Nibelheims Nacht
naht' ich mich gern,
neigtet ihr euch zu mir.
(Die Mädchen halten, als sie Alberichs Stimme hören, mit ihrem Spiele ein.)

WOGLINDE
Hei! wer ist dort?

FLOSSHILDE
Es dämmert und ruft.

WELLGUNDE
Lugt, wer uns belauscht!
(Sie tauchen tiefer herab und erkennen den Nibelung.)

WOGLINDE und WELLGUNDE
Pfui! der Garstige!

FLOSSHILDE
(schnell auftauchend)
Hütet das Gold!
Vater warnte
vor solchem Feind.
(Die beiden andern folgen ihr, und alle drei versammeln sich schnell um das mittlere Riff.)

ALBERICH
Ihr, da oben!

DIE DREI
Was willst du dort unten?

Flosshilde tries to catch first one, then the other; they elude her, and then join again in pursuit of her; thus they dart like fish from rock to rock, playing and laughing.
Meanwhile Alberich, clambering up a rock, has emerged from a dark chasm at the bottom. He pauses, still surrounded by darkness, and with increasing pleasure watches the water-maidens at play.)

ALBERICH
He, he! you nixies!
What a delightful,
delicate sight
From Nibelheim's night
I would draw near
if I thought you'd be kind.
(At the sound of Alberich's voice, the maidens stop playing.)

WOGLINDE
Hi, who is there!

FLOSSHILDE
A voice in the dark.

WELLGUNDE
Look who is below!
(They dive down deeper and perceive the Nibelung.)

WOGLINDE and WELLGUNDE
Pfui! He's horrible!

FLOSSHILDE
(swiftly darting upwards)
Be on your guard!
Father warned us
about such a foe.
(The others follow her, and all three swiftly gather round the central rock.)

ALBERICH
You, above there!

ALL THREE
What want you, below there?

ALBERICH
Stör ich eu'r Spiel,
wenn staunend ich still hier steh?
Tauchtet ihr nieder,
mit euch tollte
und neckte der Niblung sich gern!

ALBERICH
Only to stand
admiring your charming games;
then if you're friendly
you'll dive down
to the bottom, so I can join in!

WOGLINDE
Mit uns will er spielen?

WOGLINDE
He wants us to join him?

WELLGUNDE
Ist ihm das Spott?

WELLGUNDE
He must be mad!

ALBERICH
Wie scheint im Schimmer
ihr hell und schön!
Wie gern umschlänge
der Schlanken eine mein Arm,
schlüpfte hold sie herab!

ALBERICH
You shine and gleam
in the watery gloom!
How I would love
to enfold such maids in my arms:
please come join me below!

FLOSSHILDE
Nun lach ich der Furcht:
der Feind ist verliebt.

FLOSSHILDE
I laugh at my fears;
the dwarf is in love!

WELLGUNDE
Der lüsterne Kauz!

WELLGUNDE
The languishing dwarf!

WOGLINDE
Laßt ihn uns kennen!
(Sie läßt sich auf die Spitze des Riffes hinab, an dessen Fuße Alberich angelangt ist.)

WOGLINDE
Teach him a lesson!
(She sinks to the top of the rock the foot of which Alberich has reached.)

ALBERICH
Die neigt sich herab.

ALBERICH
She sinks to the rock!

WOGLINDE
Nun nahe dich mir!

WOGLINDE
Come closer to me!

ALBERICH
(klettert mit koboldartiger Behendigkeit, doch wiederholt aufgehalten, der Spitze des Riffes zu.)
Garstig glatter
glitschriger Glimmer!
Wie gleit ich aus!
Mit Händen und Füßen
nicht fasse noch halt ich
das schlecke Geschlüpfer!

ALBERICH
(clambers with gnome-like agility towards the top of the rock, but keeps falling back.)
Slimy, slippery,
slithery smoothness!
The slope's too steep!
My hands and my feet
cannot get any grip
on the slippery surface!

Feuchtes Naß
füllt mir die Nase:
verfluchtes Niesen!
(Er ist in Woglindes Nähe angelangt.)

WOGLINDE
(lachend)
Prustend naht
meines Freiers Pracht!

ALBERICH
Mein Friedel sei,
du fräuliches Kind!
(Er sucht sie zu umfassen.)

WOGLINDE
(sich ihm entwindend)
Willst du mich frein,
so freie mich hier!
(Sie taucht auf einem andern Riff auf.)

ALBERICH
(kratzt sich den Kopf.)
O weh; du entweichst?
Komm doch wieder!
Schwer ward mir,
was so leicht du erschwingst.

WOGLINDE
(schwingt sich auf ein drittes Riff in größerer Tiefe.)
Steig nur zu Grund:
da greifst du mich sicher!

ALBERICH
(klettert hastig hinab.)
Wohl besser da unten!

WOGLINDE
(schnellt sich rasch aufwärts nach einem hohen Seitenriffe.)
Nun aber nach oben!

WELLGUNDE und FLOSSHILDE
Hahahahaha!

ALBERICH
Wie fang ich im Sprung

And the water
tickles my nostrils:
oh, curse this sneezing!
(He has got close to Woglinde.)

WOGLINDE
(laughing)
Sneezing tells me
my lover is near!

ALBERICH
You're mine at last,
you beautiful child!
(He tries to embrace her.)

WOGLINDE
(eluding him)
If I am yours,
then follow me here!
(She dives to another rock.)

ALBERICH
(scratches his head.)
Alas! you escape?
Ah, come nearer!
You can swim,
but I stumble and slide.

WOGLINDE
(swims off to a third rock, further down.)
Would you prefer
this rock at the bottom?

ALBERICH
(clambers down hastily.)
It's certainly safer!

WOGLINDE
(darts upwards to a high rock at the side.)
And now to a high one!

WELLGUNDE and FLOSSHILDE
Hahahahaha!

ALBERICH
Oh, how can I catch

den spröden Fisch?
Warte, du Falsche!
(Er will ihr eilig nachklettern.)

WELLGUNDE
(hat sich auf ein tieferes Riff auf der andern Seite gesenkt.)
Heia! Du Holder!
Hörst du mich nicht?

ALBERICH
(sich umwendend)
Rufst du nach mir?

WELLGUNDE
Ich rate dir wohl:
zu mir wende dich,
Woglinde meide!

ALBERICH
(klettert hastig über den Bodengrund zu Wellgunde.)
Viel schöner bist du
als jene Scheue,
die minder gleißend
und gar zu glatt.
Nur tiefer tauche,
willst du mir taugen!

WELLGUNDE
(noch etwas mehr zu ihm sich herabsenkend)
Bin nun ich dir nah?

ALBERICH
Noch nicht genug!
Die schlanken Arme
schlinge um mich,
daß ich den Nacken
dir neckend betaste,
mit schmeichelnder Brunst
an die schwellende Brust mich dir schmiege!

WELLGUNDE
Bist du verliebt
und lüstern nach Minne,
laß sehn, du Schöner,
wie bist du zu schaun?
Pfui, du haariger,

this flighty fish?
Wait for me, false one!
(He scrambles up after her.)

WELLGUNDE
(has sunk to a deeper rock on the other side.)
Heia! fair lover,
turn you this way.

ALBERICH
(turning towards her)
Calling to me?

WELLGUNDE
And hear this advice:
Why chase Woglinde?
Wellgunde calls you!

ALBERICH
(hastily clambering over the bottom towards Wellgunde.)
And you are fairer still
than your sister,
who gleams less brightly,
who's far too sleek.
Now come towards me
so I can clasp you!

WELLGUNDE
(descending a shade closer still towards him)
Well, now am I near?

ALBERICH
Not near enough!
Those lovely arms
come twine round my neck,
so I can touch you
and play with your tresses,
and fondle your breasts
in my passionate, burning embraces!

WELLGUNDE
So you're in love
and longing to hold me;
let's see, my beauty,
just what you are like?
Pfui! You hairy old

höckriger Geck!
Schwarzes, schwieliges
Schwefelgezwerg!
Such dir ein Friedel,
dem du gefällst!

ALBERICH
(sucht sie mit Gewalt zu halten.)
Gefall ich dir nicht,
dich faß ich doch fest!

WELLGUNDE
(schnell zum mittleren Riffe auftauchend)
Nur fest, sonst fließ ich dir fort!

WOGLINDE und FLOSSHILDE
Hahahahaha!

ALBERICH
Falsches Kind!
Kalter, grätiger Fisch!
Schein ich nicht schön dir,
niedlich und neckisch,
glatt und glau—
hei! so buhle mit Aalen,
ist dir eklig mein Balg!

FLOSSHILDE
Was zankst du, Alp?
Schon so verzagt?
Du freitest um zwei!
Frügst du die dritte,
süßen Trost
schüfe die Traute dir!

ALBERICH
Holder Sang
singt zu mir her.
Wie gut, daß ihr
eine nicht seid!
Von vielen gefall ich wohl einer:
bei einer kieste mich keine!
Soll ich dir glauben,
so gleite herab!

FLOSSHILDE
(taucht zu Alberich hinab.)
Wie törig seid ihr,

hideous imp!
Scaly, spotted
and sulphurous dwarf!
Look for a sweetheart
black as yourself!

ALBERICH
(trying to hold her by force)
What though I am black—
you're tight in my grasp!

WELLGUNDE
(swiftly diving away to the central rock)
So tight, I slip from your hands!

WOGLINDE and FLOSSHILDE
Hahahahaha!

ALBERICH
Faithless thing!
Bony, cold-blooded fish!
So I'm not handsome,
pretty and playful,
slim and sleek—
Eh! Make love with an eel, then,
if he's more to your taste!

FLOSSHILDE
Stop grumbling, dwarf.
So soon dismayed?
With two you have failed!
Try now the third one.
Seek her love;
she may console your grief!

ALBERICH
Lovely sounds
ravish my ears!
What luck to find
three of them here;
for one of the three may accept me
while one alone would reject me!
Show I can trust you,
and glide to my arms!

FLOSSHILDE
(dives down to Alberich.)
Oh foolish sisters,

dumme Schwestern,
dünkt euch dieser nicht schön?

ALBERICH
(ihr nahend)
Für dumm und häßlich
darf ich sie halten,
seit ich dich Holdeste seh.

FLOSSHILDE
(schmeichelnd)
O singe fort
so süß und fein:
wie hehr verführt es mein Ohr!

ALBERICH
(zutraulich sie berührend)
Mir zagt, zuckt
und zehrt sich das Herz,
lacht mir so zierliches Lob.

FLOSSHILDE
(ihn sanft abwehrend)
Wie deine Anmut
mein Aug erfreut,
deines Lächelns Milde
den Mut mir labt!
(Sie zieht ihn zärtlich an sich.)
Seligster Mann!

ALBERICH
Süßeste Maid!

FLOSSHILDE
Wärst du mir hold!

ALBERICH
Hielt' ich dich immer!

FLOSSHILDE
(ihn ganz in ihren Armen haltend)
Deinen stechenden Blick,
deinen struppigen Bart,
o säh' ich ihn, faßt' ich ihn stets!
Deines stachligen Haares
strammes Gelock,
umflöss' es Floßhilde ewig!

blind to beauty,
can't you see that he's fair?

ALBERICH
(approaching her)
And I declare them
stupid and ugly,
now that the loveliest is mine!

FLOSSHILDE
(cajolingly)
Oh sing your song
so soft and sweet:
your voice bewitches my ear!

ALBERICH
(caressing her fondly)
My heart bounds
and flutters and burns,
hearing this praise from your lips.

FLOSSHILDE
(gently restraining him)
Oh how your beauty
delights my eyes,
and your smile so tender
inspires my soul!
(She draws him tenderly towards her.)
Dearest of men!

ALBERICH
Sweetest of maids!

FLOSSHILDE
Now you are mine!

ALBERICH
Faithful for ever.

FLOSSHILDE
(holding him close in her arms)
Oh the sting of your glance,
and the prick of your beard—
Oh how they have captured my heart!
And the locks of your hair,
so shaggy and sharp,
must float round Flosshilde ever!

Deine Krötengestalt,
deiner Stimme Gekrächz,
o dürft ich staunend und stumm
sie nur hören und sehn!

And your shape like a toad,
and the croak of your voice—
oh, how they ravish my soul:
I want nothing but these!

WOGLINDE und WELLGUNDE
Hahahahahaha!

WOGLINDE and WELLGUNDE
Hahahahahaha!

ALBERICH
(erschreckt aus Floßhildes Armen auffahrend)
Lacht ihr Bösen mich aus?

ALBERICH
(starting from Flosshilde's embrace in alarm)
Are they daring to laugh?

FLOSSHILDE
(sich plötzlich ihm entreißend)
Wie billig am Ende vom Lied.
(Sie taucht mit den Schwestern schnell auf.)

FLOSSHILDE
(suddenly darting away from him)
And laughter's the end of my song!
(She dives quickly upward with her sisters.)

WOGLINDE und WELLGUNDE
Hahahahahaha!

WOGLINDE and WELLGUNDE
Hahahahahaha!

ALBERICH
(mit kreischender Stimme)
Wehe! ach wehe!
O Schmerz! O Schmerz!
Die dritte, so traut,
betrog sie mich auch?
Ihr schmählich schlaues,
lüderlich schlechtes Gelichter!
Nährt ihr nur Trug,
ihr treuloses Nickergezücht?

ALBERICH
(screeching)
Sorrow! oh sorrow!
Oh, shame! Oh, shame!
The third one, so dear,
betrays me as well.
You shameless, slippery
underhand, infamous wretches!
Shifty and sly,
you treacherous watery tribe!

DIE DREI RHEINTÖCHTER
Wallala! Lalaleia! Leialalei!
Heia! Heia! Haha!
Schäme dich, Albe!
Schilt nicht dort unten!
Höre, was wir dich heißen!
Warum, du Banger,
bandest du nicht
das Mädchen, das du minnst?
Treu sind wir
und ohne Trug
dem Freier, der uns fängt.
Greife nur zu
und grause dich nicht!
In der Flut entfliehn wir nicht leicht.

THE THREE RHINEMAIDENS
Wallala! Lalaleia! Leialalei!
Heia! Heia! Haha!
Shame on you, Alberich!
Stop your complaining!
Wait, and hear what we tell you!
You foolish Niblung,
you should have held us
tightly while you could.
You'll find
that we can be true
and faithful, once we are caught!
Back to the chase
and grab without fear!
In the waves it's hard to escape.

Wallala! Lalaleia! Leialala!
Heia! Heia! Hahei!
(Sie schwimmen auseinander, hierher und dorthin, bald tiefer, bald höher, um Alberich zur Jagd auf sie zu reizen.)

Wallala! Lalaleia! Leialalei!
Heia! Heia! Hahei!
(They swim apart, hither and thither, now deeper, now higher, inciting Alberich to pursue them.)

ALBERICH
Wie in den Gliedern
brünstige Glut
mir brennt und glüht!
Wut und Minne
wild und mächtig
wühlt mir den Mut auf!
Wie ihr auch lacht und lügt,
lüstern lechz ich nach euch,
und eine muß mir erliegen!
(Er macht sich mit verzweifelter Anstrengung zur Jagd auf: mit grauenhafter Behendigkeit erklimmt er Riff für Riff, springt von einem zum andern, such bald dieses, bald jenes der Mädchen zu erhaschen, die mit lustigem Gekreisch stets ihm entweichen; er strauchelt, stürzt in den Abgrund hinab, klettert dann hastig wieder in die Höhe zu neuer Jagd. Sie neigen sich etwas herab. Fast erreicht er sie, stürzt abermals zurück und versucht es nochmals. Er hält endlich vor Wut schäumend atemlos an und streckt die geballte Faust nach den Mädchen hinauf.)

ALBERICH
Passionate fevers,
fervid desires,
have set me on fire!
Rage and longing,
wild and frantic,
drive me to madness!
Though you may laugh and lie,
yearning conquers my heart
and I'll not rest till I've caught you!
(He sets out in pursuit with desperate exertions; with terrible agility he clambers from rock to rock, leaps from one to another, tries to catch first one, then another of the maidens, who always elude him with merry cries. He stumbles, tumbles down to the bottom, then climbs quickly up to the heights again for a further chase. They lower themselves a little. He almost reaches them but again tumbles down, and tries once more. At last he stops, foaming with rage and breathless, and shakes his clenched fists up at the maidens.)

ALBERICH
(kaum seiner mächtig)
Fing' eine diese Faust! . . .
(Er verbleibt in sprachloser Wut, den Blick aufwärts gerichtet, wo er dann plötzlich von folgendem Schauspiele angezogen und gefesselt wird. Durch die Flut ist von oben her ein immer lichterer Schein gedrungen, der sich an einer hohen Stelle des mittelsten Riffes allmählich zu einem blendend hell strahlenden Goldglanze entzündet; ein zauberisch goldenes Licht bricht von hier durch das Wasser.)

ALBERICH
(almost out of control)
One, I swear, shall be mine . . .
(He remains speechless with rage, looking upwards, and then is suddenly attracted and spellbound by the following spectacle. Through the waters an increasingly bright light makes its way from above, gradually kindling, on a high point of the central rock, to a dazzling, brightly-beaming gleam of gold; a magical golden light streams through the waters from this point.)

WOGLINDE
Lugt, Schwestern!
Die Weckerin lacht in den Grund.

WOGLINDE
Look, sisters!
The sunlight is greeting the gold.

WELLGUNDE
Durch den grünen Schwall
den wonnigen Schläfer sie grüßt.

WELLGUNDE
Through the watery gloom
she calls to the sleeper to wake.

FLOSSHILDE
Jetzt küßt sie sein Auge,
daß er es öffne.

WELLGUNDE
Schaut, es lächelt
in lichtem Schein.

WOGLINDE
Durch die Fluten hin
fleißt sein strahlender Stern.

DIE DREI
(zusammen das Riff anmutig umschwimmend)
Heiajaheia!
Heiajaheia!
Wallalallalala leiajahei!
Rheingold!
Rheingold!
Leuchtende Lust,
wie lachst du so hell und hehr!
Glühender Glanz
entgleißet dir weihlich im Weg!
Heiajahei!
Heiajaheia!
Wache, Freund,
wache froh!
Wonnige Spiele
spenden wir dir:
flimmert der Fluß,
flammet die Flut,
umfließen wir tauchend,
tanzend und singend,
im seligen Bade dein Bett.
Rheingold!
Rheingold!
Heiajaheia!
Wallalaleia heiajahei!
(Mit immer ausgelassenerer Lust umschwimmen die Mädchen das Riff. Die ganze Flut flimmert in hellem Goldglanze.)

ALBERICH
(dessen Augen, mächtig vom Glanze angezogen, starr an dem Golde haften.)
Was ist's, ihr Glatten,
das dort so glänzt und gleißt?

FLOSSHILDE
She kisses his eyelids,
tells them to open.

WELLGUNDE
See him smile now
with gentle light.

WOGLINDE
Through the floods afar
shines his glittering beam.

ALL THREE
(swimming together gracefully around the rock)
Heiajaheia!
Heiajaheia!
Wallalallalala leiajahei!
Rhinegold!
Rhinegold!
Radiant joy!
We laugh in your joyful shine!
Glorious beams
that glitter and gleam in the waves!
Heiajahei!
Heiajaheia!
Waken friend!
Wake in joy!
Wonderful games
we'll play in your praise:
flash in the foam,
flame in the flood,
and floating around you,
dancing and singing,
in joy we will dive to your bed!
Rhinegold!
Rhinegold!
Heiajaheia!
Wallalaleia heiajahei!
(With increasingly exuberant joy, the maidens swim round the rock. All the waters are a-glitter with the golden radiance.)

ALBERICH
(whose eyes are powerfully attracted to the gleam, stares fixedly at the gold.)
What's that, you nymphs,
up there, that shines and gleams?

DIE DREI MÄDCHEN
Wo bist du Rauher denn heim,
daß vom Rheingold nie du gehört?

THE THREE RHINEMAIDENS
Ignorant dwarf, where have you lived?
Of the Rhinegold have you not heard?

WELLGUNDE
Nichts weiß der Alp
von des Goldes Auge,
das wechselnd wacht und schläft?

WELLGUNDE
The dwarf's not heard
of the golden radiance
which sleeps and wakes in turn?

WOGLINDE
Von der Wassertiefe
wonnigem Stern,
der hehr die Wogen durchhellt?

WOGLINDE
In the watery deeps
this wonderful star
shines forth and brightens the waves.

DIE DREI MÄDCHEN
Sieh, wie selig
im Glanze wir gleiten!
Willst du Banger
in ihm dich baden,
so schwimm und schwelge mit uns!
Wallalalala leialalei!
Wallalalala leiajahei!

ALL THREE
Ah, how gladly
we glide in its radiance!
Come to join us
and bathe in brightness,
come sport and swim in the shine!
Wallalalala leialalei!
Wallalalala leiajahei!

ALBERICH
Eurem Taucherspiele
nur taugte das Gold?
Mir gält' es dann wenig!

ALBERICH
Is that all it's good for,
to shine at your games?
Why, then it is worthless!

WOGLINDE
Des Goldes Schmuck
schmähte er nicht,
wüßte er all seine Wunder!

WOGLINDE
This golden charm
you would revere,
oh, if you knew of its marvels!

WELLGUNDE
Der Welt Erbe
gewänne zu eigen,
wer aus dem Rheingold
schüfe den Ring,
der maßlose Macht ihm verlieh'.

WELLGUNDE
The world's wealth can
be won by a man who,
seizing the Rhinegold,
fashions a ring:
that ring makes him lord of the world.

FLOSSHILDE
Der Vater sagt' es,
und uns befahl er,
klug zu hüten
den klaren Hort,
daß kein Falscher der Flut ihn entführe:
drum schweigt, ihr schwatzendes Heer!

FLOSSHILDE
Our father told us,
but then he warned us
we should guard it
and keep it safe,
lest some false one should wickedly steal it:
be quiet, you chattering fools!

WELLGUNDE
Du klügste Schwester,
verklagst du uns wohl?
Weißt du denn nicht,
wem nur allein
das Gold zu schmieden vergönnt?

WOGLINDE
Nur wer der Minne
Macht versagt,
nur wer der Liebe
Lust verjagt,
nur der erzielt sich den Zauber,
zum Reif zu zwingen das Gold.

WELLGUNDE
Wohl sicher sind wir
und sorgenfrei:
denn was nur lebt, will lieben;
meiden will keiner die Minne.

WOGLINDE
Am wenigsten er,
der lüsterne Alp:
vor Liebesgier
möcht er vergehn!

FLOSSHILDE
Nicht fürcht ich den,
wie ich ihn erfand:
seiner Minne Brunst
brannte fast mich.

WELLGUNDE
Ein Schwefelbrand
in der Wogen Schwall:
vor Zorn der Liebe
zischt er laut.

DIE DREI MÄDCHEN
Wallala! Wallaleialala!
Lieblichster Albe,
lachst du nicht auch?
In des Goldes Schein
wie leuchtest du schön!
O komm, Lieblicher, lache mit uns!
Heiajaheia! Heiajaheia!

WELLGUNDE
My prudent sister,
no need to be cross!
Surely you know
all that's required
of him who would master the gold?

WOGLINDE
He must pronounce
a curse on love,
he must renounce
all joys of love,
before he masters the magic,
a ring to forge from the gold.

WELLGUNDE
And that's a thing
that will never be:
all men who live must love;
no one could ever renounce it.

WOGLINDE
And least of all he,
that lecherous dwarf,
all hot desire,
panting with lust!

FLOSSHILDE
Well, I confess
we've nothing to fear.
I was nearly scorched
when he came near.

WELLGUNDE
A sulphur-brand
in the swirling waves,
inflamed with longing,
sizzling loud!

ALL THREE
Wallala! Wallaleialala!
Loveliest Niblung,
share in our joy.
In the golden radiance,
how handsome you seem!
Oh come, lovely one, laugh and be glad!
Heiajaheia! Heiajaheia!

Wallalalala leiajahei!
(Sie schwimmen lachend im Glanze auf und ab.)

ALBERICH
(die Augen starr auf das Gold gerichtet, hat dem Geplauder der Schwestern wohl gelauscht.)
Der Welt Erbe
gewänn' ich zu eigen durch dich?
Erzwäng' ich nicht Liebe,
doch listig erzwäng' ich mir Lust?
(furchtbar laut)
Spottet nur zu!
Der Niblung naht eurem Spiel!
(Wütend springt er nach dem mittleren Riff hinüber und klettert in grausiger Hast nach dessen Spitze hinauf. Die Mädchen fahren kreischend auseinander und tauchen nach verschiedenen Seiten hin auf.)

DIE DREI RHEINTÖCHTER
Heia! Heia! Heiajahei!
Rettet euch!
Es raset der Alp!
In den Wassern sprüht's,
wohin er springt:
die Minne macht ihn verrückt!
(Sie lachen im tollsten Übermut.)

ALBERICH
(gelangt mit einem letzten Satze zur Spitze des Riffes.)
Bangt euch noch nicht?
So buhlt nun im Finstern,
feuchtes Gezücht!
(Er streckt die Hand nach dem Golde aus.)
Das Licht lösch ich euch aus;
entreiße dem Riff das Gold,
schmiede den rächenden Ring;
denn hör es die Flut:
so verfluch ich die Liebe!
(Er reißt mit furchtbarer Gewalt das Gold aus dem Riffe und stürzt damit hastig in die Tiefe, wo er schnell verschwindet. Dichte Nacht bricht plötzlich überall herein. Die Mädchen tauchen nach dem Räuber in die Tiefe nach.)

FLOSSHILDE
Haltet den Räuber!

Wallalala leiajahei!
(They swim up and down in the glow, laughing.)

ALBERICH
(his eyes fixed on the gold, has listened attentively to the sisters' chatter.)
The world's wealth
can be mine if I utter the curse?
Though love be denied me,
yet cunning can bring me delight?
(terribly loud)
Laugh if you will!
the Niblung's near to your toy!
(Furiously, he leaps across to the central rock and clambers up towards its summit in dreadful haste. The maidens separate with screams and swim upward in various directions.)

THE THREE RHINEMAIDENS
Heia! Heia! Heiajahei!
Save yourselves!
the dwarf has gone mad;
and the water swirls
where he has leapt.
His love has cost him his wits!
(They laugh with the wildest bravado.)

ALBERICH
(reaches the summit of the rock with one last bound.)
Still not afraid?
Then laugh in the darkness,
nymphs of the waves!
(He reaches out his hand towards the gold.)
Your light yields to my hand:
I'll seize from the rock your gold,
forge that magical ring.
Now hear me, you floods:
Love, I curse you for ever!
(With terrible force, he tears the gold from the rock and hastily plunges down with it into the depths, where he quickly disappears. Thick darkness suddenly descends on everything. The maidens rapidly dive down after the robber into the depths.)

FLOSSHILDE
Capture the robber!

WELLGUNDE
Rettet das Gold!

WOGLINDE und WELLGUNDE
Hilfe! Hilfe!

DIE DREI MÄDCHEN
Weh! Weh!
(Die Flut fällt mit ihnen nach der Tiefe hinab, aus dem untersten Grunde hört man Alberichs gellendes Hohngelächter. In dichtester Finsternis verschwinden die Riffe; die ganze Bühne ist von der Höhe bis zur Tiefe von schwarzem Wassergewoge erfüllt, das eine Zeitlang immer noch abwärts zu sinken scheint.)

WELLGUNDE
Rescue the gold!

WOGLINDE and WELLGUNDE
Help us!

ALL THREE
Woe! Woe!
(The waters sink down with them into the depths. From the lowest depth, Alberich's harsh, mocking laughter is heard. The rocks disappear in the thick darkness; the whole stage is filled from top to bottom with black billowing water, which for some time seems to be continually sinking.)

Zweite Szene

Allmählich sind die Wogen in Gewölke übergegangen, welches, als eine immer heller dämmernde Beleuchtung dahinter tritt, zu feinerem Nebel sich abklärt. Als der Nebel in zarten Wölkchen gänzlich sich in der Höhe verliert, wird im Tagesgrauen eine

Freie Gegend auf Bergeshöhen

sichtbar. Der hervorbrechende Tag beleuchtet mit wachsendem Glanze eine Burg mit blinkenden Zinnen, die auf einem Felsgipfel im Hintergrunde steht; zwischen diesem burggekrönten Felsgipfel und dem Vordergrunde der Szene ist ein tiefes Tal, durch welches der Rhein fließt, anzunehmen. Zur Seite auf blumigem Grunde liegt Wotan, neben ihm Fricka, beide schlafend. Die Burg ist ganz sichtbar geworden.

FRICKA
(erwacht; ihr Blick fällt auf die Burg; sie staunt und erschrickt.)
Wotan, Gemahl! Erwache!

Scene Two

The waves are gradually transformed into clouds, which, as an increasingly brighter dawn light passes behind them, resolve into fine mist. When the mist has completely vanished aloft in gentle little clouds, in the dawning light an

Open Space on a Mountain Height

becomes visible. The daybreak illuminates with increasing brightness a castle with gleaming battlements, which stands on a rocky summit in the background. Between this and the foreground of the stage a deep valley is to be imagined, through which the Rhine flows. Wotan and, beside him, Fricka, both asleep, are lying on a flowery bank at one side. The castle has become completely visible.

FRICKA
(wakes; her eyes fall on the castle; she starts in alarm.)
Wotan, my lord! awaken!

WOTAN
(im Traume leise)
Der Wonne seligen Saal
bewachen mir Tür und Tor:
Mannes Ehre,
ewige Macht
ragen zu endlosem Ruhm!

WOTAN
(gently, still dreaming)
The sacred hall of the gods
is guarded by gate and door:
manhood's honour,
unending power,
rise now to endless renown!

FRICKA
(rüttelt ihn.)
Auf, aus der Träume,
wonnigem Trug!
Erwache, Mann, und erwäge!

FRICKA
(shakes him.)
Up from your dreams
of flattering deceit!
My husband, wake and consider!

WOTAN
(erwacht und erhebt sich ein wenig, sein Auge wird sogleich vom Anblick der Burg gefesselt.)
Vollendet das ewige Werk:
auf Berges Gipfel
die Götterburg,
prächtig prahlt
der prangende Bau!
Wie im Traum ich ihn trug,
wie mein Wille ihn wies,
stark und schön
steht er zur Schau;
hehrer, herrlicher Bau!

WOTAN
(wakes and raises himself a little; his eyes are at once attracted by the sight of the castle.)
Completed, the eternal work!
On mountain summits
the gods will rule!
Proudly rise
those glittering walls
which in dreams I designed,
which my will brought to life.
Strong and lordly
see it shine;
holy, glorious abode!

FRICKA
Nur Wonne schafft dir,
was mich erschreckt?
Dich freut die Burg,
mir bangt es um Freia.
Achtloser, laß dich erinnern
des ausbedungenen Lohns!
Die Burg ist fertig,
verfallen das Pfand:
vergaßest du, was du vergabst?

FRICKA
Though it delights you,
I am afraid!
You have your hall,
but I think of Freia!
Can I believe you have forgotten
the price you still have to pay?
The work is finished,
the giants must be paid;
remember it, all that you owe!

WOTAN
Wohl dünkt mich's, was sie bedangen,
die dort die Burg mir gebaut;
durch Vertrag zähmt' ich
ihr trotzig Gezücht,
daß sie die hehre
Halle mir schüfen;

WOTAN
I've not forgotten the bargain,
the giants shall have their reward;
for that proud race
was subdued by my spear;
graved on its shaft
the terms for the castle.

die steht nun—Dank den Starken:
um den Sold sorge dich nicht.

FRICKA
O lachend frevelnder Leichtsinn!
Liebelosester Frohmut!
Wußt' ich um euren Vertrag,
dem Truge hätt' ich gewehrt;
doch mutig entfernte
ihr Männer die Frauen,
um taub und ruhig vor uns
allein mit den Riesen zu tagen.
So ohne Scham
verschenktet ihr Frechen
Freia, mein holdes Geschwister,
froh des Schächergewerbs.
Was ist euch Harten
doch heilig und wert,
giert ihr Männer nach Macht!

WOTAN
(ruhig)
Gleiche Gier
war Fricka wohl fremd,
also selbst um den Bau sie mich bat?

FRICKA
Um des Gatten Treue besorgt,
muß traurig ich wohl sinnen,
wie an mich er zu fesseln,
zieht's in die Ferne ihn fort:
herrliche Wohnung,
wonniger Hausrat
sollten dich binden
zu säumender Rast.
Doch du bei dem Wohnbau sannst
auf Wehr und Wall allein:
Herrschaft und Macht
soll er dir mehren;
nur rastlosern Sturm zu erregen,
erstand dir die ragende Burg.

WOTAN
(lächelnd)
Wolltest du Frau
in der Feste mich fangen,
mir Gotte mußt du schon gönnen,

It stands now; thank the workers,
and forget what it will cost.

FRICKA
What carefree, frivolous lightness!
Loveless, coldhearted folly!
If I had known of your deal,
I might have stopped it in time;
but slyly you men
did your talking in secret,
and kept us women away;
alone you discussed with the giants.
Then to your shame
you promised to give them
Freia, my beautiful sister;
oh, how pleased you were then!
Nothing is sacred,
you harden your hearts,
when you men lust for might!

WOTAN
(calmly)
And is Fricka
free from reproach?
Remember, you begged for the hall!

FRICKA
For I wished you faithful and true;
my thoughts were for my husband,
how to keep him beside me
when he was tempted to roam:
safe in our castle,
calm and contented,
there I might keep you
in peaceful repose.
But you, when you planned it,
thought of war and arms alone:
glory and might
all that you cared for;
you built it for storm and adventure—
constructed a fort, not a home.

WOTAN
(smiling)
Wife, though you wish me
confined in the castle,
some freedom still you must grant me;

daß, in der Burg
gefangen, ich mir
von außen gewinne die Welt.
Wandel und Wechsel
liebt, wer lebt:
das Spiel drum kann ich nicht sparen.

FRICKA
Liebeloser,
leidigster Mann!
Um der Macht und Herrschaft
müßigen Tand
verspielst du in lästerndem Spott
Liebe und Weibes Wert?

WOTAN
(ernst)
Um dich zum Weib zu gewinnen,
mein eines Auge
setzt' ich werbend daran:
wie törig tadelst du jetzt!
Ehr ich die Frauen
doch mehr, als dich freut!
Und Freia, die gute,
geb ich nicht auf:
nie sann dies ernstlich mein Sinn.

FRICKA
(mit ängstlicher Spannung in die Szene blickend)
So schirme sie jetzt;
in schutzloser Angst
läuft sie nach Hilfe dort her!

FREIA
(tritt wie in hastiger Flucht auf.)
Hilf mir, Schwester!
Schütze mich, Schwäher!
Vom Felsen drüben
drohte mir Fasolt,
mich Holde käm' er zu holen.

WOTAN
Laß ihn drohn!
Sahst du nicht Loge?

FRICKA
Daß am liebsten du immer

though I may stay
beside you, yet
from our home I must rule all the world;
wandering and change
inspire my heart;
that sport I cannot relinquish!

FRICKA
Cruel, heartless,
unloving man!
for the vain delights of
ruling the world,
you'd carelessly gamble away
love and woman's worth?

WOTAN
(serious)
Recall the days when I wooed you,
when I for Fricka
paid the price of an eye.
Your scolding is wide of the mark!
I worship women
much more than you'd like;
and Freia, the fair one,
I shall not yield;
such thoughts were far from my mind.

FRICKA
(with anxious tension, looking off-stage)
Then shelter her now;
defenceless, afraid,
see how she runs here for help!

FREIA
(enters in hasty flight.)
Help me, sister!
shelter me, brother!
On yonder mountain
Fasolt is threatening,
and now he's coming to take me.

WOTAN
Let him come!
Saw you not Loge?

FRICKA
In that infamous rogue

dem Listigen traust!
Viel Schlimmes schuf er uns schon,
doch stets bestrickt er dich wieder.

WOTAN
Wo freier Mut frommt,
allein frag ich nach keinem;
doch des Feindes Neid
zum Nutz sich fügen,
lehrt nur Schlauheit und List,
wie Loge verschlagen sie übt.
Der zum Vertrage mir riet,
versprach mir Freia zu lösen:
auf ihn verlaß ich mich nun.

FRICKA
Und er läßt dich allein!
Dort schreiten rasch
die Riesen heran:
wo harrt dein schlauer Gehilf?

FREIA
Wo harren meine Brüder,
daß Hilfe sie brächten,
da mein Schwäher die Schwache
Zu Hilfe, Donner! [verschenkt?
Hieher, hieher!
Rette Freia, mein Froh!

FRICKA
Die im bösen Bund dich verrieten,
sie alle bergen sich nun.
(Fasolt und Fafner, beide in riesiger Gestalt, mit starken Pfählen bewaffnet, treten auf.)

FASOLT
Sanft schloß
Schlaf dein Aug:
wir beide bauten
Schlummers bar die Burg.
Mächt'ger Müh
müde nie,
stauten starke
Stein' wir auf;
steiler Turm,
Tür und Tor
deckt und schließt

do you still put your trust?
Much harm he's done to the gods,
yet time and again you still use him.

WOTAN
Where simple truth serves,
I need no one to help me;
but to use the hate
of foes to serve me—
that needs guile and deceit;
then Loge's the one for the deed.
He said he'd think of a plan
to keep our Freia in safety;
so I rely on him now.

FRICKA
And he leaves you alone!
Here come the giants
seeking their pay,
while Loge loiters afar!

FREIA
Come here to me, my brothers,
Oh help me and save me,
now that Wotan abandons the weak!
Oh help me, Donner!
Hear me, help me!
Rescue Freia, my Froh!

FRICKA
The disgraceful men who betrayed you
have all abandoned you now!
(Fasolt and Fafner enter, both of gigantic stature, and armed with stout clubs.)

FASOLT
Soft sleep
closed your eyes,
while we were working
hard to build your hall.
Working hard,
day and night,
heavy stones
we heaped up high,
lofty towers,
gates and doors,
guard and keep

im schlanken Schloß den Saal.
(auf die Burg deutend)
Dort steht's,
was wir stemmten;
schimmernd hell
bescheint's der Tag:
zieh nun ein,
uns zahl den Lohn!

WOTAN
Nennt, Leute, den Lohn:
was dünkt euch zu bedingen?

FASOLT
Bedungen ist's,
was tauglich uns dünkt:
gemahnt es dich so matt?
Freia, die holde,
Holda, die freie—
vertragen ist's—
sie tragen wir heim.

WOTAN
(schnell)
Seid ihr bei Trost
mit eurem Vertrag?
Denkt auf andren Dank:
Freia ist mir nicht feil.

FASOLT
(steht, in höchster Bestürzung, einen Augenblick sprachlos.)
Was sagst du? Ha,
sinnst du Verrat?
Verrat am Vertrag?
Die dein Speer birgt,
sind sie dir Spiel,
des beratnen Bundes Runen?

FAFNER
(höhnisch)
Getreuster Bruder!
Merkst du Tropf nun Betrug?

FASOLT
Lichtsohn du,
leicht gefügter,

your castle walls secure.
(pointing to the castle)
There stands
what you ordered,
shining bright
in morning light.
There's your home;
we want our wage!

WOTAN
You've earned your reward;
what wages are you asking?

FASOLT
The price was fixed,
our bargain was made;
have you so soon forgot?
Freia, the fair one,
Holda, the free one—
your hall is built
and Freia is ours.

WOTAN
(quickly)
Plainly your work
has blinded your wits.
Ask some other wage:
Freia cannot be sold.

FASOLT
(utterly amazed, is for a moment speechless.)
What's this now? Ha!
Breaking your bond?
Betraying your word?
On your spear shaft,
read what is graved;
would you dare to break your bargain?

FAFNER
(scornfully)
My trusting brother,
now do you see his deceit?

FASOLT
God of light,
light of spirit!

hör und hüte dich:
Verträgen halte Treu!
Was du bist,
bist du nur durch Verträge:
bedungen ist,
wohl bedacht deine Macht.
Bist weiser du,
als witzig wir sind,
bandest uns Freie
zum Frieden du:
all deinem Wissen fluch ich,
fliehe weit deinen Frieden,
weißt du nicht offen,
ehrlich und frei
Verträgen zu wahren die Treu!
Ein dummer Riese
rät dir das:
du, Weiser, wiss' es von ihm!

WOTAN
Wie schlau für Ernst du achtest,
was wir zum Scherz nur beschlossen!
Die liebliche Göttin,
licht und leicht,
was taugt euch Tölpeln ihr Reiz?

FASOLT
Höhnst du uns?
Ha, wie unrecht!
Die ihr durch Schönheit herrscht,
schimmernd hehres Geschlecht,
wie törig strebt ihr
nach Türmen von Stein,
setzt um Burg und Saal
Weibes Wonne zum Pfand!
Wir Plumpen plagen uns
schwitzend mit schwieliger Hand,
ein Weib zu gewinnen,
das wonnig und mild
bei uns Armen wohne:
und verkehrt nennst du den Kauf?

FAFNER
Schweig dein faules Schwatzen,
Gewinn werben wir nicht:
Freias Haft
hilft wenig;

hear a giant's advice,
and learn to keep your word!
What you are,
you became by your bargains;
you base your power
on the bonds there defined.
Since you are wise,
we giants were bound;
freely we promised
to keep the peace;
yet I shall curse your wisdom;
war, not peace, will reward you
if you don't fairly,
frankly uphold
the terms of the bargain you swore!
This simple giant
speaks his mind:
you wise one, learn now from him.

WOTAN
How sly to take in earnest
what as a joke we decided!
The beautiful goddess,
fair and bright,
what use can she be to you?

FASOLT
How unjust!
Wotan mocks us!
You who through beauty reign,
glittering, glorious race,
like fools you yearned
for your towers of stone;
pledged as pay for your hall
woman's beauty and grace.
We dull ones toil away,
sweat with our work-hardened hands;
we longed for a woman,
so charming and fair,
to grace our poor dwelling—
and you say all was a joke?

FAFNER
Stop your foolish chatter;
the girl's not what we want.
Freia's charms
mean nothing,

doch viel gilt's,
den Göttern sie zu entführen.
Goldne Äpfel
wachsen in ihrem Garten;
sie allein
weiß die Äpfel zu pflegen!
Der Frucht Genuß
frommt ihren Sippen
zu ewig nie
alternder Jugend;
siech und bleich
doch sinkt ihre Blüte,
alt und schwach
schwinden sie hin,
müssen Freia sie missen.
Ihrer Mitte drum sei sie entführt!

WOTAN
(für sich)
Loge säumt zu lang!

FASOLT
Schlicht gib nun Bescheid!

WOTAN
Sinnt auf andern Sold!

FASOLT
Kein andrer: Freia allein!

FAFNER
Du da, folge uns!
(Sie dringen auf Freia zu. Donner und Froh kommen eilig.)

FREIA
(fliehend)
Helft, helft vor den Harten!

FROH
(Freia in seine Arme fassend)
Zu mir, Freia!
Meide sie, Frecher!
Froh schützt die Schöne.

DONNER
(sich vor die beiden Riesen stellend)
Fasolt und Fafner,

but we gain
as soon as the gods have lost her.
Golden apples
ripen within her garden,
she alone
knows how they are tended;
that golden fruit
given to her kinsmen
each day renews
youth everlasting:
pale and grey
they'll lose all their beauty,
wan and weak
they will grow old,
when that fruit is denied them.
And that's why we'll take her away!

WOTAN
(aside)
Loge lingers long!

FASOLT
Well, what shall it be?

WOTAN
Ask some other wage!

FASOLT
No other: Freia alone!

FAFNER
You there! Come with us!
(They make towards Freia. Donner and Froh rush in.)

FREIA
(fleeing)
Help! Help from these hard ones!

FROH
(clasping Freia in his arms)
To me, Freia!
Back from her, giant!
Froh shields the fair one!

DONNER
(planting himself before the two giants)
Fasolt and Fafner,

fühltet ihr schon
meines Hammers harten Schlag?

FAFNER
Was soll das Drohn?

FASOLT
Was dringst du her?
Kampf kiesten wir nicht,
verlangen nur unsern Lohn.

DONNER
Schon oft zahlt' ich
Riesen den Zoll;
kommt her! Des Lohnes Last
wäg ich mit gutem Gewicht!
(Er schwingt den Hammer.)

WOTAN
(seinen Speer zwischen den Streitenden ausstreckend)
Halt, du Wilder!
Nichts durch Gewalt!
Verträge schützt
meines Speeres Schaft:
spar deines Hammers Heft!

FREIA
Wehe! Wehe!
Wotan verläßt mich!

FRICKA
Begreif ich dich noch,
grausamer Mann?

WOTAN
(wendet sich ab und sieht Loge kommen.)
Endlich Loge!
Eiltest du so,
den du geschlossen,
den schlimmen Handel zu schlichten?

LOGE
(ist im Hintergrunde aus dem Tale heraufgestiegen.)
Wie? Welchen Handel
hätt' ich geschlossen?
Wohl was mit den Riesen

know you the weight
of my hammer's heavy blow?

FAFNER
What is this threat?

FASOLT
What brings you here?
We've not come to fight,
but all we want is our pay.

DONNER
And I know
how giants should be paid.
Come here, receive your wage,
weighed with a generous hand.
(He swings his hammer.)

WOTAN
(stretching out his spear between the disputants)
Back, you wild one!
Force will not serve!
This bond is graved
on my spear's strong shaft:
spare them your hammer's blow!

FREIA
Help me! Help me!
Wotan forsakes me!

FRICKA
Is this your resolve,
merciless man?

WOTAN
(turns round and sees Loge approaching.)
There is Loge!
Where have you been,
you who assured me
that I'd escape from this contract?

LOGE
(has climbed up from the valley at the back.)
What? How am I
concerned in a contract?
Do you mean that agreement

dort im Rate du dangst?
In Tiefen und Höhen
treibt mich mein Hang;
Haus und Herd
behagt mir nicht:
Donner und Froh,
die denken an Dach und Fach!
Wollen sie frein,
ein Haus muß sie erfreun.
Ein stolzer Saal,
ein starkes Schloß,
danach stand Wotans Wunsch.
Haus und Hof,
Saal und Schloß,
die selige Burg,
sie steht nun fest gebaut;
das Prachtgemäuer
prüft' ich selbst;
ob alles fest,
forscht' ich genau:
Fasolt und Fafner
fand ich bewährt;
kein Stein wankt im Gestemm.
Nicht müßig war ich,
wie mancher hier:
der lügt, wer lässig mich schilt!

WOTAN
Arglistig
weichst du mir aus:
mich zu betrügen
hüte in Treuen dich wohl!
Von allen Göttern
dein einz'ger Freund,
nahm ich dich auf
in der übel trauenden Troß.
Nun red und rate klug!
Da einst die Bauer der Burg
zum Dank Freia bedangen,
du weißt, nicht anders
willigt' ich ein,
als weil auf Pflicht du gelobtest,
zu lösen das hehre Pfand.

LOGE
Mit höchster Sorge
drauf zu sinnen,

you have made with these giants?
I roam through the whole wide
world as I please:
I'm not held
by house or home.
Donner and Froh
are dreaming of household joys!
If they would wed,
a house first they must own.
And castle walls,
and lofty halls,
they were what Wotan craved.
Lofty halls,
castle walls,
a home for the gods—
it stands there, strongly built.
I inspected all
the place myself;
it's firmly made,
safe and secure:
Fasolt and Fafner,
excellent work!
No stone stirs on its bed.
So I was not lazy,
like others here;
he lies, who says that I was!

WOTAN
Don't try
to escape from the point!
If you betray me,
if you have tricked me, beware!
Recall that I
am your only friend,
I took your part
when the other gods were unkind.
So speak, I need your help!
When first those giants made terms
and asked Freia as payment,
you know I only
gave my consent
because you promised you would find
something else they would rather have.

LOGE
I merely promised
I'd consider

wie es zu lösen,
das—hab ich gelobt.
Doch daß ich fände,
was nie sich fügt,
was nie gelingt,
wie ließ' sich das wohl geloben?

FRICKA
(zu Wotan)
Sieh, welch trugvollem
Schelm du getraut!

FROH
Loge heißt du,
doch nenn ich dich Lüge!

DONNER
Verfluchte Lohe,
dich lösch ich aus!

LOGE
Ihre Schmach zu decken
schmähen mich Dumme.
(Donner holt auf Loge aus.)

WOTAN
(tritt dazwischen.)
In Frieden laßt mir den Freund!
Nicht kennt ihr Loges Kunst:
reicher wiegt
seines Rates Wert,
zahlt er zögernd ihn aus.

FAFNER
Nicht gezögert!
Rasch gezahlt!

FASOLT
Lang währt's mit dem Lohn.

WOTAN
(wendet sich hart zu Loge, drängend.)
Jetzt hör, Störrischer!
Halte Stich!
Wo schweifest du hin und her?

LOGE
Immer ist Undank

how we might save her—
and that's all I said.
But to discover
what can't be found,
what never was—
who'd ever make such a promise?

FRICKA
(to Wotan)
That's the knave
whom you thought you could trust!

FROH
Loge, hear me,
your name should be Liar!

DONNER
Accursed Loge,
I'll quench your flame!

LOGE
To conceal his blunders
every fool blames me!
(Donner threatens Loge.)

WOTAN
(intervening)
Now cease reviling my friend!
You know not Loge's ways:
his advice
is worth all the more,
when we wait on his words.

FAFNER
Wait no longer!
Pay our wage!

FASOLT
Come, no more delay!

WOTAN
(turning sharply to Loge, urgently)
Speak out, stubborn one!
Keep your word!
And tell me now where you've been.

LOGE
Never one word

Loges Lohn!
Um dich nur besorgt,
sah ich mich um,
durchstöbert' im Sturm
alle Winkel der Welt,
Ersatz für Freia zu suchen,
wie er den Riesen wohl recht.
Umsonst sucht' ich
und sehe nun wohl,
in der Welten Ring
nichts ist so reich,
als Ersatz zu muten dem Mann
für Weibes Wonne und Wert.
(Alle geraten in Erstaunen und verschiedenartige Betroffenheit.)
So weit Leben und Weben,
in Wasser, Erd und Luft,
viel frug ich,
forschte bei allen,
wo Kraft nur sich rührt
und Keime sich regen:
was wohl dem Manne
mächtiger dünk'
als Weibes Wonne und Wert?
Doch so weit Leben und Weben,
verlacht nur ward
meine fragende List:
in Wasser, Erd und Luft
lassen will nichts
von Lieb und Weib.
Nur einen sah ich,
der sagte der Liebe ab:
um rotes Gold
entriet er des Weibes Gunst.
Des Rheines klare Kinder
klagten mir ihre Not:
der Nibelung,
Nacht-Alberich,
buhlte vergebens
um der Badenden Gunst;
das Rheingold da
raubte sich rächend der Dieb:
das dünkt ihm nun
das teuerste Gut,
hehrer als Weibes Huld.
Um den gleißenden Tand,
der Tiefe entwandt,

of praise or thanks!
For your sake alone,
hoping to help,
I restlessly roamed
to the ends of the earth,
to find a ransom for Freia,
one that the giants would like more.
I sought vainly,
but one thing I learnt:
in this whole wide world
nothing at all
is of greater worth to a man
than woman's beauty and love!
(All express astonishment and diverse forms of bewilderment.)
I asked every one living,
in water, earth, and sky,
one question;
sought for the answer
from all whom I met;
I asked them this question:
What in this world
means more to you
than woman's beauty and love?
But wherever life was stirring
they laughed at me
when they heard what I asked.
In water, earth, and sky,
none would forego
the joys of love.
But one I found then
who scorned the delights of love,
who valued gold
more dearly than woman's grace.
The fair and shining Rhinemaids
came to me with their tale:
the Nibelung dwarf,
Alberich,
begged for their favours,
but he begged them in vain;
the Rhinegold
he tore in revenge from their rock;
and now he holds it
dearer than love,
greater than woman's grace.
For their glittering toy,
thus torn from the deep,

erklang mir der Töchter Klage:
an dich, Wotan,
wenden sie sich,
daß zu Recht du zögest den Räuber,
das Gold dem Wasser
wiedergebest
und ewig es bliebe ihr Eigen.
Dir's zu melden
gelobt' ich den Mädchen:
nun löste Loge sein Wort.

WOTAN
Törig bist du,
wenn nicht gar tückisch!
Mich selbst siehst du in Not:
wie hülf ich andern zum Heil?

FASOLT
(der aufmerksam zugehört, zu Fafner)
Nicht gönn ich das Gold dem Alben,
viel Not schon schuf uns der Niblung,
doch schlau entschlüpfte unserm
Zwange immer der Zwerg.

FAFNER
Neue Neidtat
sinnt uns der Niblung,
gibt das Gold ihm Macht.
Du da, Loge!
Sag ohne Lug:
was Großes gilt denn das Gold,
daß es dem Niblung genügt?

LOGE
Ein Tand ist's
in des Wassers Tiefe,
lachenden Kindern zur Lust:
doch, ward es zum runden
Reife geschmiedet,
hilft es zur höchsten Macht,
gewinnt dem Manne die Welt.

WOTAN
(sinnend)
Von des Rheines Gold
hört' ich raunen:
Beute-Runen

the maidens are sadly mourning:
They turn, Wotan,
sadly to you,
for they hope that you will avenge them;
the gold—they pray
that you'll restore it,
to shine in the waters for ever.
So I promised
I'd tell you the story;
and that's what Loge has done.

WOTAN
Are you mad,
or simply malicious?
You know I am in need;
how can I help some one else?

FASOLT
(who has been listening attentively, to Fafner)
That gold I begrudge to Alberich;
we've suffered much from the Niblung,
and yet that crafty dwarf
has always slipped through our hands.

FAFNER
We shall suffer
more in the future,
now he's gained the gold.
You there, Loge!
tell me the truth;
what glory lies in the gold,
that the Niblung holds so dear?

LOGE
A toy, while
it was in the waters,
lighting the Rhinemaidens' games;
but when as a shining
ring it is fashioned,
helped by its magic power,
its owner conquers the world.

WOTAN
(reflectively)
I have heard men tell
of the Rhinegold:
charms of riches

berge sein roter Glanz,
Macht und Schätze
schüf' ohne Maß ein Reif.

FRICKA
(leise zu Loge)
Taugte wohl
des goldnen Tandes
gleißend Geschmeid
auch Frauen zu schönem Schmuck?

LOGE
Des Gatten Treu
ertrotzte die Frau,
trüge sie hold
den hellen Schmuck,
den schimmernd Zwerge schmieden,
rührig im Zwange des Reifs.

FRICKA
(schmeichelnd zu Wotan)
Gewänne mein Gatte
sich wohl das Gold?

WOTAN
(wie in einem Zustande wachsender Bezauberung)
Des Reifes zu walten,
rätlich will es mich dünken.
Doch wie, Loge,
lernt' ich die Kunst?
Wie schüf' ich mir das Geschmeid?

LOGE
Ein Runenzauber
zwingt das Gold zum Reif.
Keiner kennt ihn;
doch einer übt ihn leicht,
der sel'ger Lieb entsagt.
(Wotan wendet sich unmutig ab.)
Das sparst du wohl;
zu spät auch kämst du:
Alberich zauderte nicht;
zaglos gewann er
des Zaubers Macht:
geraten ist ihm der Ring.

DONNER
(zu Wotan)
Zwang uns allen

lurk in that golden gleam;
mighty powers
are his who can forge that ring.

FRICKA
(softly to Loge)
Could a woman use
the golden ring
for herself,
and wear it to charm her lord?

LOGE
No husband dare
be false to his wife
when she commands
that glittering wealth
that busy dwarfs are forging,
ruled by the power of the ring.

FRICKA
(cajolingly, to Wotan)
Oh, how can my husband
win us the gold?

WOTAN
(as if in a state of increasing enchantment)
And I should possess it!
Soon this ring should be Wotan's.
But say, Loge,
what is the art
by which the gold can be forged?

LOGE
A magic spell
can change the gold to a ring.
No one knows it,
but he who would use the spell
must curse the joys of love.
(Wotan turns away in ill-humour.)
Could you do that?
Too late, in any case,
Alberich did not delay;
he cursed and mastered
the magic spell;
and he is lord of the ring!

DONNER
(to Wotan)
We shall all

schüfe der Zwerg,
würd' ihm der Reif nicht entrissen.

WOTAN
Den Ring muß ich haben!

FROH
Leicht erringt
ohne Liebesfluch er sich jetzt.

LOGE
Spottleicht,
ohne Kunst wie im Kinderspiel!

WOTAN
(grell)
So rate, wie?

LOGE
Durch Raub!
Was ein Dieb stahl,
das stiehlst du dem Dieb:
ward leichter ein Eigen erlangt?
Doch mit arger Wehr
wahrt sich Alberich;
klug und fein
mußt du verfahren,
ziehst du den Räuber zu Recht,
um des Rheines Töchtern
den roten Tand,
das Gold, wiederzugeben;
denn darum flehen sie dich.

WOTAN
Des Rheines Töchter?
Was taugt mir der Rat?

FRICKA
Von dem Wassergezücht
mag ich nichts wissen:
schon manchen Mann
—mir zum Leid—
verlockten sie buhlend im Bad.
(Wotan steht stumm mit sich kämpfend; die übrigen Götter heften in schweigender Spannung die Blicke auf ihn. Währenddem hat Fafner beiseite mit Fasolt beraten.)

be slaves to the dwarf
unless the ring can be captured.

WOTAN
The ring—I must have it!

FROH
Easily done,
now that love you need not renounce.

LOGE
Child's play!
at a stroke you can make it yours!

WOTAN
(harshly)
Then tell me, how?

LOGE
By theft!
What a thief stole,
you steal from the thief;
you seize it and make it your own!
But you'll need your wits
fighting Alberich;
he'll defend
what he has stolen,
so be skilful, swift and shrewd
if you'd please the Rhinemaids,
and then restore
their gold, back to the waters.
They yearn and cry for their gold.

WOTAN
To please the Rhinemaids?
That's not what I plan!

FRICKA
Leave that watery brood
weeping and wailing;
to my distress,
many a man
they've lured by their charms to the Rhine.
(Wotan is struggling silently with himself. The other gods, tense and silent, look fixedly at him. Meanwhile, to one side, Fafner has quietly been conferring with Fasolt.)

FAFNER
(zu Fasolt)
Glaub mir, mehr als Freia
frommt das gleißende Gold:
auch ew'ge Jugend erjagt,
wer durch Goldes Zauber sie zwingt.
(Fasolts Gebärde deutet an, daß er sich wider Willen überredet fühlt. Fafner tritt mit Fasolt wieder an Wotan heran.)
Hör, Wotan,
der Harrenden Wort!
Freia bleib' euch in Frieden;
leichtren Lohn
fand ich zur Lösung:
uns rauhen Riesen genügt
des Niblungen rotes Gold.

WOTAN
Seid ihr bei Sinn?
Was nicht ich besitze,
soll ich euch Schamlosen schenken?

FAFNER
Schwer baute
dort sich die Burg:
leicht wird's dir
mit list'ger Gewalt,
was im Neidspiel nie uns gelang,
den Niblungen fest zu fahn.

WOTAN
Für euch müht' ich
mich um den Alben?
Für euch fing ich den Feind?
Unverschämt
und überbegehrlich
macht euch Dumme mein Dank!

FASOLT
(ergreift plötzlich Freia und führt sie mit Fafner zur Seite.)
Hieher, Maid!
In unsre Macht!
Als Pfand folgst du uns jetzt,
bis wir Lösung empfahn.

FREIA
(wehklagend)
Wehe! Wehe! Weh!

FAFNER
(to Fasolt)
Trust me, more than Freia
we can gain from the gold:
eternal youth can be ours,
when we lay our hands on that gold.
(Fasolt's demeanour suggests that he has been persuaded against his will. Fafner, with Fasolt, returns to Wotan again.)
Hear, Wotan,
I'll speak my last word!
We will leave you with Freia;
we will take less
for our payment:
for us rude giants, enough
is Nibelheim's shining gold.

WOTAN
Have you gone mad?
For how can I give you
what is not mine, as your payment?

FAFNER
Hard labour
built you those walls;
your cunning
can lightly achieve
what has proved too hard for our
to capture the Niblung foe. [strength,

WOTAN
For you must I
deal with the Niblung?
for you, capture the foe?
Unashamed, you dare
to propose it,
stupid, insolent pair!

FASOLT
(suddenly seizes Freia and, with Fafner, pulls her to one side.)
Come here, maid!
You're in our power!
We'll hold you as a hostage
till all has been paid!

FREIA
(crying out in dismay)
Save me! Save me! Woe!

(Alle Götter sind in höchster Bestürzung.)

FAFNER
Fort von hier
sei sie entführt!
Bis Abend, achtet's wohl,
pflegen wir sie als Pfand:
wir kehren wieder;
doch kommen wir,
und bereit liegt nicht als Lösung
das Rheingold licht und rot—

FASOLT
Zu End ist die Frist dann,
Freia verfallen:
für immer folge sie uns!

FREIA
(schreiend)
Schwester! Brüder!
Rettet! Helft!
(Sie wird von den hastig enteilenden Riesen fortgetragen.)

FROH
Auf, ihnen nach!

DONNER
Breche denn alles!
(Sie blicken Wotan fragend an.)

FREIA
(aus weiter Ferne)
Rettet! Helft!

LOGE
(den Riesen nachsehend)
Über Stock und Stein zu Tal
stapfen sie hin;
durch des Rheines Wasserfurt
waten die Riesen:
fröhlich nicht
hängt Freia
den Rauhen über dem Rücken!
Heia! hei!
Wie taumeln die Tölpel dahin!

(All the gods are dismayed.)

FAFNER
We shall take
Freia with us!
Till evening, mark me well,
she remains in our hands;
then we'll return
but when we come,
if we don't find what we have asked for,
the Rhinegold heaped on high—

FASOLT
—our truce then is over;
Freia is forfeit;
forever she stays with us!

FREIA
(screaming)
Sister! Brothers!
Save me! Help!
(She is dragged away by the hastily departing giants.)

FROH
On, to her aid!

DONNER
Everything's ended!
(They look inquiringly at Wotan.)

FREIA
(from the distance)
Save me! Help!

LOGE
(gazing after the giants)
Over rock and stone they stride,
down to the vale;
through the Rhine they forge ahead,
waddling and wading.
Sad at heart
hangs Freia,
while borne on the backs of those ruffians!
Heia! hei!
They stumble and stride on their way!

Durch das Tal talpen sie schon:
wohl an Riesenheims Mark
erst halten sie Rast!
(Er wendet sich zu den Göttern.)
Was sinnt nun Wotan so wild?
Den seligen Göttern wie geht's?
(Ein fahler Nebel erfüllt mit wachsender Dichtheit die Bühne; in ihm erhalten die Götter ein zunehmend bleiches und ältliches Aussehen: alle stehen bang und erwartungsvoll auf Wotan blickend, der sinnend die Augen an den Boden heftet.)
Trügt mich ein Nebel?
Neckt mich ein Traum?
Wie bang und bleich
verblüht ihr so bald!
Euch erlischt der Wangen Licht;
der Blick eures Auges verblitzt!
Frisch, mein Froh,
noch ist's ja früh!
Deiner Hand, Donner,
entsinkt ja der Hammer!
Was ist's mit Fricka?
Freut sie sich wenig
ob Wotans grämlichem Grau,
das schier zum Greisen ihn schafft?

FRICKA
Wehe! Wehe!
Was ist geschehn?

DONNER
Mir sinkt die Hand.

FROH
Mir stockt das Herz.

LOGE
Jetzt fand ich's: hört, was euch fehlt!
Von Freias Frucht
genosset ihr heute noch nicht:
die goldnen Äpfel
in ihrem Garten,
sie machten euch tüchtig und jung,
aßt ihr sie jeden Tag.
Des Gartens Pflegerin
ist nun verpfändet;
an den Ästen darbt

Now they're through, climbing the slope.
They'll not rest till they've reached
rough Riesenheim's bounds.
(He turns to the gods.)
Why is Wotan brooding and sad?
Alas, what's troubling the gods?
(A pale mist, growing denser, fills the scene: it gives the gods an increasingly wan and aged appearance: fearful, they all stand gazing expectantly at Wotan, who is lost in thought, his eyes fixed on the ground.)
Mists, do you deceive me?
Is this a dream?
How grey you've grown,
so weary and weak!
From your cheeks the bloom dies out;
the flash from your eyes fades away!
Come, my Froh!
Day is still young!
From your hand, Donner,
you're dropping the hammer!
What's wrong with Fricka?
Can she be mourning
that Wotan, gloomy and grey,
should seem so suddenly old?

FRICKA
Sorrow! Sorrow!
What can it mean?

DONNER
My hand is weak!

FROH
My heart is still!

LOGE
I see now! Hear what is wrong!
Of Freia's fruit
you've not yet eaten today.
The golden apples
that grow in her garden,
they kept you so vigorous and young,
eating them every day.
But she who tended them
now is a hostage;
on the branches droops

und dorrt das Obst:
bald fällt faul es herab.
Mich kümmert's minder;
an mir ja kargte
Freia von je
knausernd die köstliche Frucht:
denn halb so echt nur
bin ich wie, Selige, ihr!
Doch ihr setztet alles
auf das jüngende Obst:
das wußten die Riesen wohl;
auf euer Leben
legten sie's an:
nun sorgt, wie ihr das wahrt!
Ohne die Äpfel,
alt und grau,
greis und grämlich,
welkend zum Spott aller Welt,
erstirbt der Götter Stamm.

and dies the fruit;
it rots, falls to the ground.
To me it's nothing;
because to Loge
Freia was mean;
I never tasted her fruit:
so I'm not god-like,
I'm not so glorious as you!
But you staked your future
on that youth-giving fruit;
the giants knew that all too well;
and at your lives
this blow has been aimed;
so think how to escape!
Lacking the apples,
old and grey,
worn and weary,
withered and scorned by the world,
the gods grow old and die.

FRICKA
Wotan, Gemahl,
unsel'ger Mann!
Sieh, wie dein Leichtsinn
lachend uns allen
Schimpf und Schmach erschuf!

FRICKA
Wotan, my lord!
Unhappy man!
See how your selfish
folly has brought us
sore disgrace and shame!

WOTAN
(mit plötzlichem Entschluß auffahrend)
Auf, Loge,
hinab mit mir!
Nach Nibelheim fahren wir nieder:
gewinnen will ich das Gold.

WOTAN
(starts up with sudden resolve.)
Come, Loge,
descend with me!
To Nibelheim we'll go together:
and there I'll win me the gold.

LOGE
Die Rheintöchter
riefen dich an:
so dürfen Erhörung sie hoffen?

LOGE
The Rhinemaidens
called for your help:
so will you return them their treasure?

WOTAN
Schweige, Schwätzer!
Freia, die gute,
Freia gilt es zu lösen.

WOTAN
Stop your chatter!
Freia, the fair one,
Freia has to be rescued!

LOGE
Wie du befiehlst,
führ ich dich schnell

LOGE
As you command,
down we shall go.

steil hinab:
steigen wir denn durch den Rhein?

WOTAN
Nicht durch den Rhein!

LOGE
So schwingen wir uns
durch die Schwefelkluft?
Dort schlüpfe mit mir hinein!
(Er geht voran und verschwindet seitwärts in einer Kluft, aus der sogleich ein schwefliger Dampf hervorquillt.)

WOTAN
Ihr andern harrt
bis Abend hier:
verlorner Jugend
erjag ich erlösendes Gold!
(Er steigt Loge nach in die Kluft hinab: der aus ihr dringende Schwefeldampf verbreitet sich über die ganze Bühne und erfüllt diese schnell mit dickem Gewölk. Bereits sind die Zurückbleibenden unsichtbar.)

DONNER
Fahre wohl, Wotan!

FROH
Glück auf! Glück auf!

FRICKA
O kehre bald
zur bangenden Frau!
(Der Schwefeldampf verdüstert sich bis zu ganz schwarzem Gewölk, welches von unten nach oben steigt; dann verwandelt sich dieses in festes, finstres Steingeklüft, das sich immer aufwärts bewegt, so daß es den Anschein hat, als sänke die Szene immer tiefer in die Erde hinab. Wachsendes Geräusch wie von Schmiedenden wird überallher vernommen.)

Choose your way:
shall we descend through the Rhine?

WOTAN
Not through the Rhine!

LOGE
Then follow my steps
through this smoky cleft:
and slip down there after me!
(He goes ahead and disappears sideways into a crevice, from which at once a sulphurous vapour rises.)

WOTAN
You others wait
till evening falls:
the youth we're losing
I'll buy back again with the gold!
(He descends through the crevice after Loge. The sulphurous steam emerging from it spreads across the entire stage and rapidly fills it with thick clouds. The remaining gods are already invisible.)

DONNER
Fare you well, Wotan!

FROH
Good luck! Good luck!

FRICKA
And soon return
to your sorrowing wife!
(The sulphurous vapour darkens into completely black cloud, which ascends from below to above. This is then transformed into a solid, dark rocky crevice, moving continually upwards so as to give the impression that the stage is sinking deeper into the earth. An increasing clamour, as of forging, is heard on all sides.)

Dritte Szene

Von verschiedenen Seiten her dämmert aus der Ferne dunkelroter Schein auf: eine unabsehbar weit sich dahinziehende

Unterirdische Kluft

wird erkennbar, die nach allen Seiten hin in enge Schachte auszumünden scheint.

Alberich zerrt den kreischenden Mime an den Ohren aus einer Seitenschlucht herbei.

ALBERICH
Hehe! hehe!
Hieher! hieher!
Tückischer Zwerg!
Tapfer gezwickt
sollst du mir sein,
schaffst du nicht fertig,

Scene Three

A dark red glow shines from various quarters in the distance.

A Subterranean Cavern

stretching further than the eye can reach, becomes visible. It seems to open on every side into narrow shafts.
Alberich tugs Mime, who is screeching, by the ear out of a shaft at the side.

ALBERICH
Hehe! hehe!
Come here! Come here!
Treacherous imp!
You will be pinched,
painfully pricked
if it's not ready,

wie ich's bestellt,
zur Stund das feine Geschmeid!

MIME
(heulend)
Ohe! Ohe!
Au! Au!
Laß mich nur los!
Fertig ist's,
wie du befahlst;
mit Fleiß und Schweiß
ist es gefügt:
nimm nur die Nägel vom Ohr!

ALBERICH
(loslassend)
Was zögerst du dann
und zeigst es nicht?

MIME
Ich Armer zagte,
daß noch was fehle.

ALBERICH
Was wär' noch nicht fertig?

MIME
(verlegen)
Hier . . . und da.

ALBERICH
Was hier und da?
Her das Geschmeid!
(Er will ihm wieder an das Ohr fahren; vor Schreck läßt Mime ein metallenes Gewirke, das er krampfhaft in den Händen hielt, sich entfallen. Alberich hebt es hastig auf und prüft es genau.)
Schau, du Schelm!
Alles geschmiedet
und fertig gefügt,
wie ich's befahl!
So wollte der Tropf
schlau mich betrügen,
für sich behalten
das hehre Geschmeid,
das meine List
ihn zu schmieden gelehrt?
Kenn ich dich dummen Dieb?

flawlessly forged,
that helm I told you to make!

MIME
(howling)
Ohe! Ohe!
Ow! Ow!
Leave me alone!
All's been done,
just as you asked;
I toiled away,
finished the work.
Only stop twisting my ear!

ALBERICH
(letting him go)
Then why did you wait?
I want it now!

MIME
I wasn't certain
of every detail.

ALBERICH
And what is not finished?

MIME
(embarrassed)
Here—and there—

ALBERICH
What 'here' and 'there'?
Give me the thing!
(He makes for Mime's ear again. Mime in his terror lets fall a piece of metalwork that he was clutching tightly in his hands. Alberich rapidly picks it up and examines it closely.)
Ha, you rogue!
Everything's perfect
and carefully forged,
just as I asked!
But maybe the fool
thought he could trick me,
and keep this wonderful
work for himself—
work which my cunning
had taught him to forge!
Villain do I read your mind?

(Er setzt das Gewirk als »Tarnhelm« auf den Kopf.)
Dem Haupt fügt sich der Helm:
ob sich der Zauber auch zeigt?
»Nacht und Nebel,
niemand gleich!«
(Seine Gestalt verschwindet; statt ihrer gewahrt man eine Nebelsäule.)
Siehst du mich, Bruder?

MIME
(blickt sich verwundert um.)
Wo bist du? Ich sehe dich nicht.

ALBERICH
(unsichtbar)
So fühle mich doch,
du fauler Schuft!
Nimm das für dein Diebesgelüst!

MIME
(schreit und windet sich unter empfangenen Geißelhieben, deren Fall man vernimmt, ohne die Geißel selbst zu sehen).
Ohe! Ohe!
Au! Au! Au!

ALBERICH
(lachend, unsichtbar)
Hahahahahaha!
Hab Dank, du Dummer!
Dein Werk bewährt sich gut.
Hoho! hoho!
Niblungen all,
neigt euch nun Alberich!
Überall weilt er nun,
euch zu bewachen;
Ruh und Rast
ist euch zerronnen;
ihm müßt ihr schaffen,
wo nicht ihr ihn schaut;
wo nicht ihr ihn gewahrt,
seid seiner gewärtig:
untertan seid ihr ihm immer!
Hoho! hoho!
Hört ihn, er naht:
der Niblungen Herr!
(Die Nebelsäule verschwindet dem Hintergrunde

(He puts the metalwork on his head, as a 'Tarnhelm'.)
The helm fits on my head:
now will the spell do its work?
'Night and darkness,
fade from sight!'
(His form disappears. In its place is seen a a column of vapour.)
Where am I, brother?

MIME
(looks around in astonishment.)
Where are you? You've gone from my [sight.

ALBERICH
(invisible)
Then feel me instead,
you lazy rogue!
I'll teach you to steal from me!

MIME
(screams, and writhes under the blows of a scourge, whose strokes can be heard though it is invisible.)
Ohe! Ohe!
Ow! Ow! Ow!

ALBERICH
(laughing, invisible)
Hahahahahaha!
I thank you, brother!
Your work was true and good.
Hoho! hoho!
Niblungs below,
bow down to Alberich!
I shall be watching
to see that you're working;
day and night
you must be toiling,
sweating to serve
your invisible lord,
who can watch you unseen
and spy on his subjects!
You are my slaves now for ever!
Hoho! hoho!
Hear me, I'm near—
the Niblungs' great lord!
(The column of vapour disappears towards the

zu: man hört in immer weiterer Ferne Alberichs Toben und Zanken; Geheul und Geschrei antwortet ihm, das sich endlich in immer weiterer Ferne unhörbar verliert. Mime ist vor Schmerz zusammengesunken. Wotan und Loge lassen sich aus einer Schlucht von oben herab.)

LOGE
Nibelheim hier:
durch bleiche Nebel
wie blitzen dort feurige Funken!

MIME
Au! Au! Au!

WOTAN
Hier stöhnt es laut:
was liegt im Gestein?

LOGE
(neigt sich zu Mime.)
Was Wunder wimmerst du hier?

MIME
Ohe! Ohe!
Au! Au!

LOGE
Hei, Mime! Muntrer Zwerg!
Was zwickt und zwackt dich denn so?

MIME
Laß mich in Frieden!

LOGE
Das will ich freilich,
und mehr noch, hör:
helfen will ich dir, Mime!
(Er stellt ihn mühsam aufrecht.)

MIME
Wer hälfe mir?
Gehorchen muß ich
dem leiblichen Bruder,
der mich in Bande gelegt.

LOGE
Dich, Mime, zu binden,
was gab ihm die Macht?

back. Alberich's raging and scolding are heard receding into the distance. Screams and cries answer him, from further and further away, until at last they are inaudible. Mime has cowered down with pain. Wotan and Loge descend through a crevice.)

LOGE
Nibelheim here!
The murky darkness
is broken by fiery flashes!

MIME
Ow! Ow! Ow!

WOTAN
But what's that groan?
Who lies at our feet?

LOGE
(bends over Mime.)
What have we whimpering here?

MIME
Ohe! Ohe!
Ow! Ow!

LOGE
Hi, Mime! cheerful dwarf!
And what's the trouble with you?

MIME
Leave me in quiet!

LOGE
That I'll do gladly.
Not just that, but—
help I'll offer you, Mime!
(With difficulty, he sets him on his feet.)

MIME
What help for me!
I must obey
the commands of my brother,
for he has made me his slave.

LOGE
But, Mime, what gave him
the power to command?

MIME
Mit arger List
schuf sich Alberich
aus Rheines Gold
einen gelben Reif:
seinem starken Zauber
zittern wir staunend;
mit ihm zwingt er uns alle,
der Niblungen nächt'ges Heer.
Sorglose Schmiede,
schufen wir sonst wohl
Schmuck unsern Weibern,
wonnig Geschmeid,
niedlichen Niblungentand,
wir lachten lustig der Müh.
Nun zwingt uns der Schlimme,
in Klüfte zu schlüpfen,
für ihn allein
uns immer zu mühn.
Durch des Ringes Gold
errät seine Gier,
wo neuer Schimmer
in Schachten sich birgt:
da müssen wir spähen,
spüren und graben,
die Beute schmelzen
und schmieden den Guß,
ohne Ruh und Rast
dem Herrn zu häufen den Hort.

MIME
The Rhine's bright gold,
seized by Alberich,
was shaped and forged
to a shining ring:
at its magic spell
the Nibelungs tremble;
that ring makes him our master;
we Niblungs are now his slaves.
Once we were carefree,
worked at our anvils,
forged for our women,
trinkets and jewels,
delicate Nibelung toys;
we merrily hammered away.
But now he compels us
to creep through the mineshafts,
for him alone
we sweat and we slave.
And the golden ring
has magical power
to show where treasure
lies hid in the rocks;
and then we must mine it,
forge and refine it
and smelt the ore down
to pure, shining gold;
so by day and night
we serve the greed of our lord.

LOGE
Dich Trägen soeben
traf wohl sein Zorn?

LOGE
And you were so idle
that you were whipped?

MIME
Mich Ärmsten, ach,
mich zwang er zum ärgsten:
ein Helmgeschmeid
hieß er mich schweißen;
genau befahl er,
wie es zu fügen.
Wohl merkt' ich klug,
welch mächt'ge Kraft
zu eigen dem Werk
das aus Erz ich wob:
für mich drum hüten
wollt' ich den Helm,

MIME
Poor Mime, ah,
my fate was the hardest!
A magic helm
I had to make him;
he gave me detailed,
careful instructions.
And so I guessed
some wondrous spell
must lie in the work
that I forged so well;
I thought I'd keep
one thing for myself,

durch seinen Zauber
Alberichs Zwang mich entziehn—
vielleicht, ja vielleicht
den Lästigen selbst überlisten,
in meine Gewalt ihn zu werfen,
den Ring ihm zu entreißen,
daß, wie ich Knecht jetzt dem Kühnen,
mir Freien er selber dann frön'!

LOGE
Warum, du Kluger,
glückte dir's nicht?

MIME
Ach, der das Werk ich wirkte,
den Zauber, der ihm entzuckt,
den Zauber erriet ich nicht recht!
Der das Werk mir riet
und mir's entriß,
der lehrte mich nun
—doch leider zu spät!—
welche List läg' in dem Helm:
meinem Blick entschwand er,
doch Schwielen dem Blinden
schlug unschaubar sein Arm.
Das schuf ich mir Dummen
schön zu Dank!
(Er streicht sich den Rücken. Wotan und Loge lachen.)

LOGE
(zu Wotan)
Gesteh, nicht leicht
gelingt der Fang.

WOTAN
Doch erliegt der Feind,
hilft deine List.

MIME
(von dem Lachen der Götter betroffen, betrachtet diese aufmerksamer.)
Mit eurem Gefrage,
wer seid denn ihr Fremde?

LOGE
Freunde dir;

and use the spell
to free me from Alberich's power;
perhaps, yes, perhaps
the tyrant himself could be conquered;
by using the helm I might catch him.
That ring—could I but seize it,
then, though I'm forced now to serve him,
when free, I could make him my slave!

LOGE
Your plan was clever;
why did it fail?

MIME
Ah! when the helm was finished,
the magic that makes it work,
that magic I could not guess right:
then he seized the helm
and spoke the charm;
he showed me—alas,
I learnt it too late—
mighty spells lay in that helm.
From my sight he vanished;
and out of the darkness
dealt invisible blows.
And that's all the thanks
my work has won!
(He rubs his back. Wotan and Loge laugh.)

LOGE
(to Wotan)
Admit, your task
may well be hard.

WOTAN
We'll succeed at last,
thanks to your wits.

MIME
(perplexed by the gods' laughter, observes them more closely.)
But why all these questions?
Who are you, you strangers?

LOGE
Friends to you;

von ihrer Not
befrein wir der Niblungen Volk.

MIME
(schrickt zusammen, da er Alberich sich wieder nahen hört.)
Nehmt euch in acht!
Alberich naht.

WOTAN
Sein harren wir hier.
(Er setzt sich ruhig auf einen Stein; Loge lehnt ihm zur Seite. Alberich, der den Tarnhelm vom Haupte genommen und an den Gürtel gehängt hat, treibt mit geschwungener Geißel aus der unteren, tiefer gelegenen Schlucht aufwärts eine Schar Nibelungen vor sich her: diese sind mit goldenem und silbernem Geschmeide beladen, das sie, unter Alberichs steter Nötigung, all auf einen Haufen speichern und so zu einem Horte häufen.)

ALBERICH
Hieher! Dorthin!
Hehe! Hoho!
Träges Heer,
dort zu Hauf
schichtet den Hort!
Du da, hinauf!
Willst du voran?
Schmähliches Volk,
ab das Geschmeide!
Soll ich euch helfen?
Alles hieher!
(Er gewahrt plötzlich Wotan und Loge.)
He, wer ist dort?
Wer drang hier ein?
Mime! Zu mir,
schäbiger Schuft!
Schwatztest du gar
mit dem schweifenden Paar?
Fort, du Fauler!
Willst du gleich schmieden und schaffen?
(Er treibt Mime mit Geißelhieben unter den Haufen der Nibelungen hinein.)
He, an die Arbeit!
Alle von hinnen!
Hurtig hinab!
Aus den neuen Schachten

we can set free
the suffering Nibelung folk.

MIME
(shrinks back in terror as he hears Alberich approaching.)
Better take care;
Alberich's near.

WOTAN
We'll wait for him here.
(He seats himself calmly on a stone. Loge leans at his side. Alberich, brandishing a whip, enters, driving a team of Nibelungs in front of him out of a cavern lying farther below. He has removed the Tarnhelm from his head and hung it from his belt. The Nibelungs are laden with golden and silver work, which, under Alberich's constant supervision, they pile up in a heap.)

ALBERICH
Hither! Thither!
Hehe! Hoho!
Lazy herd!
Pile the gold,
there in a heap!
You there, get up!
On with your work!
Indolent dogs!
Stack up the treasure!
Want me to help you?
There in a heap!
(He is suddenly aware of Wotan and Loge.)
Hey, who is there?
Who's broken in?
Mime, come here!
Pestilent imp,
chattering away
with that scoundrely pair!
Off, you idler!
Back to your welding and whining!
(He drives Mime with blows of his whip into the crowd of Nibelungs.)
Hey! to your labour!
Back to the forges!
Back to the mines!
From the new-dug shafts

schafft mir das Gold!
Euch grüßt die Geißel,
grabt ihr nicht rasch!
Daß keiner mir müßig,
bürge mir Mime,
sonst birgt er sich schwer
meiner Geißel Schwunge:
daß ich überall weile,
wo keiner mich wähnt,
das weiß er, dünkt mich, genau!
Zögert ihr noch?
Zaudert wohl gar?
(Er zieht seinen Ring vom Finger, küßt ihn und streckt ihn drohend aus.)
Zittre und zage,
gezähmtes Heer:
rasch gehorcht
des Ringes Herrn!
(Unter Geheul und Gekreisch stieben die Nibelungen, unter ihnen Mime, auseinander und schlüpfen in die Schächte hinab. Alberich betrachtet lange und mißtrauisch Wotan und Loge).
Was wollt ihr hier?

go fetch me more gold!
And if you're lazy
you shall be whipped.
Let no one be idle;
Mime will watch you
or else he will find
that my whip rewards him.
I'll be everywhere, spying
where no one expects;
ask Mime; he can explain!
Off to your work!
Lingering still?
(He draws the ring from his finger, kisses it, and holds it out threateningly.)
Tremble in terror,
you wretched slaves:
and obey
the ring's great lord!
(With howling and shrieking the Nibelungs, Mime among them, scatter and scuttle away into the shafts. Alberich gives a long, suspicious look at Wotan and Loge.)
What brought you here?

WOTAN
Von Nibelheims nächt'gem Land
vernahmen wir neue Mär:
mächt'ge Wunder
wirke hier Alberich:
daran uns zu weiden,
trieb uns Gäste die Gier.

WOTAN
Of Nibelheim's dusky land
we've heard a most marvellous tale:
mighty wonders
worked here by Alberich;
and, eager to see them,
we arrive as your guests.

ALBERICH
Nach Nibelheim
führt euch der Neid:
so kühne Gäste,
glaubt, kenn ich gut.

ALBERICH
Attracted by
Nibelheim's gold:
I know
the sort of guests that you are!

LOGE
Kennst du mich gut,
kindischer Alp?
Nun sag: wer bin ich,
daß du so bellst?
Im kalten Loch,
da kauernd du lagst,
wer gab dir Licht
und wärmende Lohe,

LOGE
Well, if you know,
impudent dwarf,
then say, who am I!
Why do you bark?
In chilly caves
you shivered and froze;
who gave you light
and who lit your fires then?

wenn Loge nie dir gelacht?
Was hülf' dir dein Schmieden,
heizt' ich die Schmiede dir nicht?
Dir bin ich Vetter
und war dir Freund:
nicht fein drum dünkt mich dein Dank!

ALBERICH
Den Lichtalben
lacht jetzt Loge,
der list'ge Schelm:
bist du Falscher ihr Freund,
wie mir Freund du einst warst,
haha! mich freut's!
Von ihnen fürcht ich dann nichts.

LOGE
So denk ich, kannst du mir traun.

ALBERICH
Deiner Untreu trau ich,
nicht deiner Treu!
(eine herausfordernde Stellung annehmend)
Doch getrost trotz ich euch allen.

LOGE
Hohen Mut
verleiht deine Macht:
grimmig groß
wuchs dir die Kraft.

ALBERICH
Siehst du den Hort,
den mein Heer
dort mir gehäuft?

LOGE
So neidlichen sah ich noch nie.

ALBERICH
Das ist für heut,
ein kärglich Häufchen:
kühn und mächtig
soll er künftig sich mehren.

WOTAN
Zu was doch frommt dir der Hort,
da freudlos Nibelheim

Was Loge not once your friend?
What use are your forges
till they are heated by me?
I am your kinsman
and once was kind:
for that you owe me your thanks!

ALBERICH
The gods have
befriended Loge,
that crafty rogue:
are you, schemer, their friend,
as my friend once you were?
Haha! I laugh!
In that case, what need I fear?

LOGE
And so, instead, you can trust.

ALBERICH
I can trust your untruth,
never your truth!
(assuming a defiant attitude)
Yet today I can defy you!

LOGE
Have you grown
so daring and bold?
Have you gained
such mighty power?

ALBERICH
See all the gold
that my slaves
heaped over there?

LOGE
I've never seen so much before.

ALBERICH
That's just today's—
the merest trifle.
In the future
it will tower far more grandly.

WOTAN
But what's the use of your wealth?
In joyless Nibelheim,

und nichts für Schätze hier feil?

ALBERICH
Schätze zu schaffen
und Schätze zu bergen,
nützt mir Nibelheims Nacht;
doch mit dem Hort,
in der Höhle gehäuft,
denk ich dann Wunder zu wirken:
die ganze Welt
gewinn ich mit ihm mir zu eigen.

WOTAN
Wie beginnst du, Gütiger, das?

ALBERICH
Die in linder Lüfte Wehn
da oben ihr lebt,
lacht und liebt;
mit goldner Faust
euch Göttliche fang ich mir alle!
Wie ich der Liebe abgesagt,
alles, was lebt,
soll ihr entsagen!
Mit Golde gekirrt,
nach Gold nur sollt ihr noch gieren.
Auf wonnigen Höhn
in seligem Weben
wiegt ihr euch;
den Schwarzalben
verachtet ihr ewigen Schwelger!
Habt Acht! Habt Acht!
Denn dient ihr Männer
erst meiner Macht,
eure schmucken Frau'n—
die mein Frein verschmäht—
sie zwingt zur Lust sich der Zwerg,
lacht Liebe ihm nicht.
Hahahaha!
Habt ihr's gehört?
Habt Acht!
Habt Acht vor dem nächtlichen Heer,
entsteigt des Niblungen Hort
aus stummer Tiefe zu Tag!

WOTAN
(auffahrend)
Vergeh, frevelnder Gauch!

with gold there's nothing to buy!

ALBERICH
Gold can be mined here,
and gold can be stored here,
deep in Nibelheim's caves.
Then with my wealth
from the darkness I'll rise,
rise and be master of all things;
the whole wide world
I'll buy for myself with the treasure!

WOTAN
My good Niblung, how would you start?

ALBERICH
In the clouds, you great ones
far above us may live,
laugh, and love.
My golden grasp
will seize on you gods and destroy you!
Once I renounced all joys of love.
All those who live,
all shall renounce them!
Enchanted by gold,
your greed for gold shall enslave you!
On glorious heights
you gods live in gladness,
lulled by ease,
despising those
who work below, sure you are eternal!
Beware! Beware!
For first your men
shall yield to my might,
then your lovely women,
who despise me and jeer,
shall grant to Alberich's force
what love could not win!
Hahahaha!
You have been warned!
Beware!
Beware of my armies of night!
Beware the day when the Niblung's gold
shall vanquish the world!

WOTAN
(vehemently)
No more, impious wretch!

ALBERICH
Was sagt der?

LOGE
(ist dazwischengetreten; zu Wotan)
Sei doch bei Sinnen!
(zu Alberich)
Wen doch faßte nicht Wunder,
erfährt er Alberichs Werk?
Gelingt deiner herrlichen List,
was mit dem Hort du heischest,
den Mächtigsten muß ich dich rühmen:
denn Mond und Stern'
und die strahlende Sonne,
sie auch dürfen nicht anders,
dienen müssen sie dir.
Doch wichtig acht ich vor allem,
daß des Hortes Häufer,
der Niblungen Heer,
neidlos dir geneigt.
Einen Reif rührtest du kühn,
dem zagte zitternd dein Volk:
doch wenn im Schlaf
ein Dieb dich beschlich',
den Ring schlau dir entriss',
wie wahrtest du, Weiser, dich dann?

ALBERICH
Der Listigste dünkt sich Loge;
andre denkt er
immer sich dumm:
daß sein ich bedürfte
zu Rat und Dienst
um harten Dank,
das hörte der Dieb jetzt gern!
Den hehlenden Helm
ersann ich mir selbst;
der sorglichste Schmied,
Mime, mußt' ihn mir schmieden:
schnell mich zu wandeln
nach meinem Wunsch,
die Gestalt mir zu tauschen,
taugt mir der Helm.
Niemand sieht mich,
wenn er mich sucht;
doch überall bin ich,
geborgen dem Blick.

ALBERICH
What says he?

LOGE
(stepping between them; to Wotan)
Try to be patient!
(to Alberich)
All must stand in amazement,
beholding Alberich's work!
If only your craft can achieve
all that you plan with your treasure,
then all would acclaim you as master;
the moon and stars,
and the sun in his splendour,
how could they not obey you,
serve you, bow to your will?
But, most of all, it's important
that your army of workers,
your Nibelung slaves,
never should rebel!
By your ring you can command;
your people trembled in fear.
But, while you sleep,
a thief might approach;
the ring he'd steal from your hand:
so guard yourself, wise one, from that!

ALBERICH
So no one is wise like Loge?
He can see where
others are blind?
You give me a warning
and hope I'll beg
for your advice.
Well, I do not need your help!
This magical helm,
invented by me,
was skilfully forged.
Mime made it to guard me.
It can transform me;
I can assume
any shape that I wish for,
through this helm.
None can see me,
search as he will;
invisible master
and all-seeing lord!

So ohne Sorge
bin ich selbst sicher vor dir,
du fromm sorgender Freund!

So I'm protected;
even from you I am safe,
my kind, provident friend!

LOGE
Vieles sah ich,
Seltsames fand ich:
doch solches Wunder
gewahrt' ich nie.
Dem Werk ohnegleichen
kann ich nicht glauben;
wäre dies eine möglich,
deine Macht währte dann ewig.

LOGE
Many marvels
I have encountered,
but such a marvel
is new to me.
This work without equal—
I don't believe it!
If you could work this wonder,
then your power would be everlasting!

ALBERICH
Meinst du, ich lüg
und prahle wie Loge?

ALBERICH
I do not lie
or boast like Loge!

LOGE
Bis ich's geprüft,
bezweifl' ich, Zwerg, dein Wort.

LOGE
Show me a proof,
and then I'll believe your boast.

ALBERICH
Vor Klugheit bläht sich
zum Platzen der Blöde!
Nun plage dich Neid!
Bestimm, in welcher Gestalt
soll ich jach vor dir stehn?

ALBERICH
You're puffed up with prudence
and pride till you're bursting!
Well, envy me now!
Command, and tell me what shape
you would like me to be!

LOGE
In welcher du willst:
nur mach vor Staunen mich stumm!

LOGE
Oh, choose for yourself,
but make me dumb with surprise!

ALBERICH
(hat den Helm aufgesetzt.)
»Riesen-Wurm
winde sich ringelnd!«
(Sogleich verschwindet er: eine ungeheure Riesenschlange windet sich statt seiner am Boden; sie bäumt sich und streckt den aufgesperrten Rachen nach Wotan und Loge hin.)

ALBERICH
(has put on the Tarnhelm.)
'Dragon dread,
curling and coiling!'
(He disappears instantly. In his place an enormous dragon writhes on the ground; it rises up and snaps with open jaws at Wotan and Loge.)

LOGE
(stellt sich von Furcht ergriffen.)
Ohe! Ohe!

LOGE
(pretends to be seized with terror.)
Ohe! Ohe!

Schreckliche Schlange,
verschlinge mich nicht!
Schone Logen das Leben!

Terrible dragon,
have mercy on me!
Spare my life, do not eat me!

WOTAN
Hahaha! Gut, Alberich!
Gut, du Arger!
Wie wuchs so rasch
zum riesigen Wurme der Zwerg!
(Die Schlange verschwindet; statt ihrer erscheint sogleich Alberich wieder in seiner wirklichen Gestalt.)

WOTAN
Hahaha! Good, Alberich!
Good, you rascal!
Your change from dwarf
to dragon was skilful and swift!
(The dragon disappears. In its place, Alberich reappears in his own form.)

ALBERICH
Hehe! Ihr Klugen,
glaubt ihr mir nun?

ALBERICH
Hehe! You doubters!
Now do you believe?

LOGE
Mein Zittern mag dir's bezeugen.
Zur großen Schlange
schufst du dich schnell:
weil ich's gewahrt,
willig glaub ich dem Wunder.
Doch, wie du wuchsest,
kannst du auch winzig
und klein dich schaffen?
Das Klügste schien' mir das,
Gefahren schlau zu entfliehn:
das aber dünkt mich zu schwer!

LOGE
My trembling proves it too clearly!
A giant dragon
rose in your place;
now that I've seen,
how can I not believe you?
You can grow larger—
can you be tiny?
a tiny creature?
the safest way I know
to hide yourself from your foes.
That, maybe, that would be hard?

ALBERICH
Zu schwer dir,
weil du zu dumm!
Wie klein soll ich sein?

ALBERICH
Too hard for you,
ignorant fool!
How small shall I be?

LOGE
Daß die feinste Klinze dich fasse,
wo bang die Kröte sich birgt.

LOGE
So the smallest crack could conceal you,
where a frightened toad could be hid.

ALBERICH
Pah! nichts leichter!
Luge du her!
(Er setzt den Tarnhelm wieder auf.)
»Krumm und grau
krieche Kröte!«
(Er verschwindet; die Götter gewahren im Gestein eine Kröte auf sich zukriechen.)

ALBERICH
Pah! That's easy!
Look at me now!
(He puts on the Tarnhelm again.)
'Tiny toad,
creeping and crawling!'—
(He disappears; the gods perceive a toad on the rocks, creeping towards them.)

LOGE
(zu Wotan)
Dort die Kröte,
greife sie rasch!
(Wotan setzt seinen Fuß auf die Kröte, Loge fährt ihr nach dem Kopfe und hält den Tarnhelm in der Hand.)

LOGE
(to Wotan)
There, the toad!
Capture it quick!
(Wotan puts his foot on the toad. Loge catches it by the head and seizes the Tarnhelm in his hand.)

ALBERICH
(wird plötzlich in seiner wirklichen Gestalt sichtbar, wie er sich unter Wotans Fuße windet).
Ohe! Verflucht!
Ich bin gefangen!

ALBERICH
(suddenly becomes visible in his own form, writhing under Wotan's foot.)
Ohe! Ohe!
Now they have caught me!

LOGE
Halt ihn fest,
bis ich ihn band.
(Er hat ein Bastseil hervorgeholt und bindet Alberich damit Hände und Beine; den Geknebelten, der sich wütend zu wehren sucht, fassen dann beide und schleppen ihn mit sich nach der Kluft, aus der sie herabkamen.)
Schnell hinauf:
dort ist er unser.
(Sie verschwinden, aufwärts steigend.)

LOGE
Hold him tight,
till he is bound.
(He has brought out a rope, and with it he binds Alberich hand and foot; then both seize the prisoner, who is violently trying to escape, and drag him to the shaft by which they entered.)

Now swiftly up!
He is our prisoner!
(They disappear, climbing upwards.)

Vierte Szene

Die Szene verwandelt sich, nur in umgekehrter Weise, wie zuvor; die Verwandlung führt wieder an den Schmieden vorüber. Fortdauernde Verwandlung nach oben. Schließlich erscheint wieder die

Freie Gegend auf Bergeshöhen

wie in der zweiten Szene; nur ist sie jetzt noch in fahle Nebel verhüllt, wie vor der zweiten Verwandlung nach Freias Abführung. Wotan und Loge, den gebundenen Alberich mit sich führend, steigen aus der Kluft herauf.

LOGE

Da, Vetter,
sitze du fest!
Luge, Liebster,
dort liegt die Welt,
die du Lungrer gewinnen dir willst:
welch Stellchen, sag,

Scene Four

The scene changes as before, but in the opposite direction. The transformation again leads past the forging. There is continual upward motion. Finally, there reappears the

Open Space on a Mountain Height

as in the second scene; but now it is still veiled in thin mist, as at the end of Scene 2, after Freia's abduction. Wotan and Loge, bringing Alberich, bound, with them, come up out of the crevice.

LOGE

There, Alberich,
sit on your throne!
Look around you,
there lies the world
that you thought you would rule as your
What spot for me [own.

bestimmst du drin mir zum Stall?
(Er schlägt ihm tanzend Schnippchen.)

ALBERICH
Schändlicher Schächer!
Du Schalk! Du Schelm!
Löse den Bast,
binde mich los,
den Frevel sonst büßest du Frecher!

WOTAN
Gefangen bist du,
fest mir gefesselt,
wie du die Welt,
was lebt und webt,
in deiner Gewalt schon wähntest,
in Banden liegst du vor mir.
Du Banger kannst es nicht leugnen!
Zu ledigen dich
bedarf's nun der Lösung.

ALBERICH
Oh, ich Tropf,
ich träumender Tor!
Wie dumm traut' ich
dem diebischen Trug!
Furchtbare Rache
räche den Fehl!

LOGE
Soll Rache dir frommen,
vor allem rate dich frei:
dem gebundnen Manne
büßt kein Freier den Frevel.
Drum, sinnst du auf Rache,
rasch ohne Säumen
sorg um die Lösung zunächst!

ALBERICH
So heischt, was ihr begehrt!

WOTAN
Den Hort und dein helles Gold.

ALBERICH
Gieriges Gaunergezücht!
(für sich)

has been reserved in your realm?
(He dances round him, snapping his fingers.)

ALBERICH
Infamous schemer!
You knave! You thief!
Loosen my bonds,
let me go free
or else for your crime you will suffer!

WOTAN
You're now my captive,
bound in my fetters—
you who declared
you'd bind the world,
and lay it in chains before you;
my captive, bound at my feet.
I have you now at my mercy!
So if you'd be free,
then pay for your freedom.

ALBERICH
I was blind
and lost in my dreams!
A fool, caught by
that cowardly trick!
I shall have vengeance,
cruel and keen!

LOGE
Well, dream of your vengeance,
but first, set yourself free:
when a man's a captive,
no one cares if he curses.
Still planning your vengeance?
Better think quickly,
think of the ransom we need!

ALBERICH
Then say what you demand.

WOTAN
The gold, all your shining gold.

ALBERICH
Greedy and criminal pair!
(aside)

Doch behalt ich mir nur den Ring,
des Hortes entrat ich dann leicht:
denn von neuem gewonnen
und wonnig genährt
ist er bald durch des Ringes Gebot.
Eine Witzigung wär's,
die weise mich macht:
zu teuer nicht zahl ich die Zucht,
laß für die Lehre ich den Tand.

WOTAN
Erlegst du hen Hort?

ALBERICH
Löst mir die Hand,
so ruf ich ihn her.
(Loge löst ihm die Schlinge an der rechten Hand. Alberich berührt den Ring mit den Lippen und murmelt heimlich einen Befehl.)
Wohlan, die Niblungen
rief ich mir nah:
dem Herrn gehorchend
hör ich den Hort
aus der Tiefe sie führen zu Tag.
Nun löst mich vom lästigen Band!

WOTAN
Nicht eh'r, bis alles gezahlt.
(Die Nibelungen steigen aus der Kluft herauf, mit den Geschmeiden des Hortes beladen. Während des Folgenden schichten sie den Hort auf.)

ALBERICH
O schändliche Schmach,
daß die scheuen Knechte
geknebelt selbst mich erschaun!
(zu den Nibelungen)
Dorthin geführt,
wie ich's befehl!
All zu Hauf
schichtet den Hort!
Helf ich euch Lahmen?
Hieher nicht gelugt!
Rasch da, rasch!
Dann rührt euch von hinnen:
daß ihr mir schafft!
Fort in die Schachten!
Weh euch, find ich euch faul!

But so long as I keep the ring,
the rest can be given away;
I can quickly replace it
again and again
by commanding the powerful ring.
Now a lesson I've learnt,
and wiser I'll be;
the warning is cheap at the price,
though it has cost me so much gold.

WOTAN
You'll give me the gold?

ALBERICH
Loosen my hand;
I'll summon it here.
(Loge unties the rope from his right hand. Alberich puts the ring to his lips and secretly murmurs a command.)
And now the Niblungs
will come to my call,
for their lord commands them;
up from the depths
of the darkness they'll bring you the gold:
so now set me free from my bonds!

WOTAN
Not yet, till all has been paid.
(The Nibelungs ascend from the crevice, laden with the treasures of the hoard. During what follows, they pile up the treasure.)

ALBERICH
O shameful disgrace!
that my shrinking servants
should see me bound like a slave!
(to the Nibelungs)
Put it down there,
as I command!
In a heap
pile up the gold!
Want me to help you?
No, don't look at me!
Hurry! quick!
Then back to your labour!
Off to the mines!
Off to the forges!
Idlers, back to your work!

Auf den Fersen folg ich euch nach.
(Er küßt seinen Ring und streckt ihn gebieterisch aus. Wie von einem Schlage getroffen, drängen sich die Nibelungen scheu und ängstlich der Kluft zu, in die sie schnell hinabschlüpfen.)
Gezahlt hab ich:
nun laßt mich ziehn!
Und das Helmgeschmeid,
das Loge dort hält,
das gebt mir nun gütlich zurück!

LOGE
(den Tarnhelm zum Horte werfend)
Zur Buße gehört auch die Beute.

ALBERICH
Verfluchter Dieb!
Doch nur Geduld!
Der den alten mir schuf,
schafft einen andern:
noch halt ich die Macht,
der Mime gehorcht.
Schlimm zwar ist's,
dem schlauen Feind
zu lassen die listige Wehr!
Nun denn! Alberich
ließ euch alles:
jetzt löst, ihr Bösen, das Band!

LOGE
(zu Wotan)
Bist du befriedigt?
Bind ich ihn frei?

WOTAN
Ein goldner Ring
ragt dir am Finger:
hörst du, Alp?
Der, acht ich, gehört mit zum Hort.

ALBERICH
(entsetzt)
Der Ring?

WOTAN
Zu deiner Lösung
mußt du ihn lassen.

For your lord comes hard on your heels!
(He kisses his ring and stretches it out commandingly. As if struck by a blow, the Nibelungs hurry in fear and trembling to the crevice and quickly scuttle down it.)
The gold lies there;
now let me go:
and the Tarnhelm there,
which Loge still holds,
now kindly return it to me!

LOGE
(throwing the Tarnhelm on to the hoard)
The Tarnhelm is part of the ransom.

ALBERICH
Accursed thief!
Yet, wait a while!
He who forged me the first
can make me another.
I still hold the power
that Mime obeys.
Yet it's sad
that crafty foes
should capture my cunning defence!
Well then! Alberich's
paid his ransom;
untie, you tyrants, my bonds!

LOGE
(to Wotan)
Are you contented?
Can he go free?

WOTAN
A golden ring
shines on your finger:
well, my dwarf,
that also is part of the price.

ALBERICH
(appalled)
The ring?

WOTAN
To win your freedom
you'll have to yield it.

ALBERICH
(bebend)
Das Leben—doch nicht den Ring!

WOTAN
(heftiger)
Den Reif verlang ich:
mit dem Leben mach, was du willst!

ALBERICH
Lös ich mir Leib und Leben,
den Ring auch muß ich mir lösen:
Hand und Haupt,
Aug und Ohr,
sind nicht mehr mein Eigen
als hier dieser rote Ring!

WOTAN
Dein Eigen nennst du den Ring?
Rasest du, schamloser Albe?
Nüchtern sag,
wem entnahmst du das Gold,
daraus du den schimmernden schufst?
War's dein Eigen,
was du Arger
der Wassertiefe entwandt?
Bei des Rheines Töchtern
hole dir Rat,
ob ihr Gold sie
zu eigen dir gaben,
das du zum Ring dir geraubt.

ALBERICH
Schmähliche Tücke,
schändlicher Trug!
Wirfst du Schächer
die Schuld mir vor,
die dir so wonnig erwünscht?
Wie gern raubtest
du selbst dem Rheine das Gold,
war nur so leicht
die List, es zu schmieden, erlangt?
Wie glückt' es nun
dir Gleißner zum Heil,
daß der Niblung ich
aus schmählicher Not,
in des Zornes Zwange,

ALBERICH
(trembling)
My life, but not the ring!

WOTAN
(more violently)
The ring surrender:
with your life, do what you will!

ALBERICH
But if my life is spared me,
the ring must stay on my finger:
hand and head,
eye and ear
are not mine more truly
than mine this golden ring!

WOTAN
What right have you to the ring?
Insolent, impudent Niblung?
Tell me now,
where did you get the gold
from which you created the ring?
Did you own it,
when you grasped it,
the Rhinemaids' radiant toy?
Let those Rhinemaids answer:
will they declare
that they gave you
their gold as a present;
or did you seize it by theft?

ALBERICH
Infamous schemer!
Shameful deceit!
Thief, you blame me
for doing that crime
which you were burning to do!
Though you lusted
to steal the gold for yourself,
you couldn't pay
the price that alone would suffice.
It serves you well,
you smooth, sneering rogue,
that the Niblung, I,
in shameful distress,
in a frenzied outburst,

den schrecklichen Zauber gewann,
des Werk nun lustig dir lacht?
Des Unseligsten,
Angstversehrten
fluchfertige,
furchtbare Tat,
zu fürstlichem Tand
soll sie fröhlich dir taugen,
zur Freude dir frommen mein Fluch?
Hüte dich,
herrischer Gott!
Frevelte ich,
so frevelt' ich frei an mir:
doch an allem, was war,
ist und wird,
frevelst, Ewiger, du,
entreißest du frech mir den Ring!

WOTAN
Her den Ring!
Kein Recht an ihm
schwörst du schwatzend dir zu.
(Er ergreift Alberich und entzieht seinem Finger mit heftiger Gewalt den Ring.)

ALBERICH
(gräßlich aufschreiend)
Ha! Zertrümmert! Zerknickt!
Der Traurigen traurigster Knecht!

WOTAN
(den Ring betrachtend)
Nun halt ich, was mich erhebt,
der Mächtigen mächtigsten Herrn!
(Er steckt den Ring an.)

LOGE
Ist er gelöst?

WOTAN
Bind ihn los!

LOGE
(löst Alberich vollends die Bande.)
Schlüpfe denn heim!
Keine Schlinge hält dich:
frei fahre dahin!

did win for myself, by a curse,
this gold that smiles on you now!
And my sacrifice,
all I suffered,
my criminal,
curse-laden deed—
have they merely served
to procure you a plaything?
Will you win the world by my curse?
Guard yourself,
proud, cruel god!
If I have sinned,
I sinned but against myself:
but against all that was,
is, and shall be,
you are planning a crime
by laying your hand on the ring!

WOTAN
Yield the ring!
No chatter can prove
your right to the ring!
(He seizes Alberich and violently tears the ring from his finger.)

ALBERICH
(with a terrible cry)
Ha! Defeated! And tricked!
Of wretches, the wretchedest slave!

WOTAN
(contemplating the ring)
It shines there, lifts me on high,
of mighty ones, mightiest of all!
(He puts on the ring.)

LOGE
Can he be freed?

WOTAN
Set him free!

LOGE
(frees Alberich from his bonds.)
Slip away home!
Not a fetter holds you:
free, Alberich, free!

ALBERICH
(sich erhebend)
Bin ich nun frei?
Wirklich frei?
So grüß' euch denn
meiner Freiheit erster Gruß!
Wie durch Fluch er mir geriet,
verflucht sei dieser Ring!
Gab sein Gold
mir Macht ohne Maß,
nun zeug' sein Zauber
Tod dem, der ihn trägt!
Kein Froher soll
seiner sich freun;
keinem Glücklichen lache
sein lichter Glanz!
Wer ihn besitzt,
den sehre die Sorge,
und wer ihn nicht hat,
den nage der Neid!
Jeder giere
nach seinem Gut,
doch keiner genieße
mit Nutzen sein!
Ohne Wucher hüt' ihn sein Herr,
doch den Würger zieh' er ihm zu!
Dem Tode verfallen,
feßle den Feigen die Furcht;
solang er lebt,
sterb' er lechzend dahin,
des Ringes Herr
als des Ringes Knecht:
bis in meiner Hand
den geraubten wieder ich halte!
So segnet
in höchster Not
der Nibelung seinen Ring!
Behalt ihn nun,
hüte ihn wohl,
meinem Fluch fliehest du nicht!
(Er verschwindet schnell in der Kluft. Der dichte Nebelduft des Vordergrundes klärt sich allmählich auf.)

LOGE
Lauschtest du
seinem Liebesgruß?

ALBERICH
(raising himself)
Am I now free?
truly free?
I greet you then
in my freedom: mark my words!
Since a curse gained it for me,
my curse lies on this ring!
Though its gold
brought riches to me,
let now it bring
but death, death to its lord!
Its wealth shall yield
pleasure to none;
let no fortunate owner
enjoy its gleam.
Care shall consume
the man who commands it,
and mortal envy
consume those who don't—
striving vainly
to win that prize.
But he who obtains it
shall find no joy!
It will bring no gain to its lord;
only death is brought by its gleam!
To death he is fated,
doomed by the curse on the ring:
and while he lives,
fears will fill all his days.
Who owns the ring
to the ring is a slave,
till the gold returns
to this hand from which you have torn it!
In anguish
and sore distress,
the Nibelung blesses the ring!
You hold it now;
guard it with care!
From my curse you can't escape!
(He disappears quickly into the crevice. The thick mists in the foreground gradually clear.)

LOGE
Did you hear
Alberich's loving song?

WOTAN
(in den Anblick des Ringes an seiner Hand versunken)
Gönn ihm die geifernde Lust!
(Es wird immer heller.)

LOGE
(nach rechts in die Szene blickend)
Fasolt und Fafner
nahen von fern;
Freia führen sie her.
(Aus dem sich immer mehr zerteilenden Nebel erscheinen Donner, Froh und Fricka und eilen dem Vordergrunde zu.)

FROH
Sie kehrten zurück.

DONNER
Willkommen, Bruder!

FRICKA
(besorgt zu Wotan)
Bringst du gute Kunde?

LOGE
(auf den Hort deutend)
Mit List und Gewalt
gelang des Werk:
dort liegt, was Freia löst.

DONNER
Aus der Riesen Haft
naht dort die Holde.

FROH
Wie liebliche Luft
wieder uns weht,
wonnig Gefühl
die Sinne erfüllt!
Traurig ging es uns allen,
getrennt für immer von ihr,
die leidlos ewiger Jugend
jubelnde Lust uns verleiht.
(Der Vordergrund ist wieder hell geworden; das Aussehen der Götter gewinnt wieder die erste Frische: über dem Hintergrunde haftet jedoch noch

WOTAN
(lost in contemplation of the ring on his finger)
Let him give way to his wrath!
(It continues to get lighter.)

LOGE
(looking offstage to the right)
Fasolt and Fafner,
coming this way!
Freia soon shall be freed.
(Through the mists, as they continue to disperse, Donner, Froh, and Fricka appear and hasten towards the foreground.)

FROH
So you have returned!

DONNER
Be welcome, brother!

FRICKA
(to Wotan, anxiously)
Have you gained the ransom?

LOGE
(points to the treasure.)
By cunning and force
the deed was done:
behold, there's Freia's price.

DONNER
From the giants' power
soon we can free her.

FROH
How sweetly the air
charms us again;
joy and contentment
steal through my heart!
Life indeed would be wretched
if we were parted from her;
she brings us youth eternal,
fills us with joy and delight.
(The foreground is now completely clear again. The appearances of the gods have regained their former freshness. The veil of mist still hovers over

der Nebelschleier, so daß die Burg unsichtbar bleibt. Fasolt und Fafner treten auf, Freia zwischen sich führend.)

FRICKA
(eilt freudig auf die Schwester zu, um sie zu umarmen.)
Lieblichste Schwester,
süßeste Lust!
Bist du mir wieder gewonnen?

FASOLT
(ihr wehrend)
Halt! Nicht sie berührt!
Noch gehört sie uns.
Auf Riesenheims
ragender Mark
rasteten wir:
mit treuem Mut
des Vertrages Pfand
pflegten wir.
So sehr mich's reut,
zurück doch bring ich's,
erlegt uns Brüdern
die Lösung ihr.

WOTAN
Bereit liegt die Lösung:
des Goldes Maß
sei nun gütlich gemessen.

FASOLT
Das Weib zu missen,
wisse, gemutet mich weh:
soll aus dem Sinn sie mir schwinden,
des Geschmeides Hort
häufet denn so,
daß meinem Blick
die Blühende ganz er verdeck'!

WOTAN
So stellt das Maß
nach Freias Gestalt.
(Freia wird von den beiden Riesen in die Mitte gestellt. Darauf stoßen sie ihre Pfähle zu Freias beiden Seiten so in den Boden, daß sie gleiche Höhe und Breite mit ihrer Gestalt messen.)

the background, however, so that the castle remains invisible. Fasolt and Fafner enter, bringing Freia between them.)

FRICKA
(hastens joyfully to her sister, to embrace her.)
Loveliest sister!
sweetest delight!
now once again I can greet you.

FASOLT
(restraining her)
Wait! Don't touch her yet!
Freia still is ours.
On Riesenheim's
far rocky heights,
there we did rest;
we guarded her
and we kept our word
faithfully.
Though sore at heart,
I now return her;
so keep your bargain
and pay our wage.

WOTAN
Behold, there's the ransom:
the golden heap
will reward you most generously.

FASOLT
To lose the woman
sorely distresses my heart.
If I am forced to forget her,
you must pile the gold,
heap up the hoard,
till you conceal
her beauty and charms from my sight.

WOTAN
Then heap the gold
till Freia is hid.
(The two giants place Freia in the middle. Then they thrust their staves in the ground on each side of Freia, so as to measure her height and breadth.)

FAFNER
Gepflanzt sind die Pfähle
nach Pfandes Maß:
gehäuft nun füll es der Hort.

WOTAN
Eilt mit dem Werk:
widerlich ist mir's!

LOGE
Hilf mir, Froh!

FROH
Freias Schmach
eil ich zu enden.
(Loge und Froh häufen hastig zwischen den Pfählen die Geschmeide.)

FAFNER
Nicht so leicht
und locker gefügt!
(Er drückt mit roher Kraft die Geschmeide dicht zusammen.)
Fest und dicht
füll er das Maß!
(Er beugt sich, um nach Lücken zu spähen.)
Hier lug ich noch durch:
verstopft mir die Lücken!

LOGE
Zurück, du Grober!

FAFNER
Hierher!

LOGE
Greif mir nichts an!

FAFNER
Hierher! Die Klinze verklemmt!

WOTAN
(unmutig sich abwendend)
Tief in der Brust
brennt mir die Schmach.

FRICKA
(den Blick auf Freia geheftet.)
Sieh, wie in Scham

FAFNER
We've planted our poles here
to frame her form;
now heap your gold to her height!

WOTAN
On with the work:
oh, this is shameful!

LOGE
Help me, Froh!

FROH
Freia's shame
soon shall be ended.
(Loge and Froh quickly pile up the treasure between the staves.)

FAFNER
Far too loose
you're piling the gold.
(Roughly, he presses the treasure together tightly.)
Firm and hard,
pack it tight!
(He stoops down to look for crevices.)
Look, here is a chink:
and stop up this crevice!

LOGE
Stand back, you ruffian!—

FAFNER
Look here!

LOGE
Off with your hands!

FAFNER
And here! this crack must be closed!

WOTAN
(turning away in dejection)
Deep in my breast
burns the disgrace!

FRICKA
(her eyes fixed on Freia)
See where she stands;

schmählich die Edle steht:
um Erlösung fleht
stumm der leidende Blick.
Böser Mann!
Der Minnigen botest du das!

FAFNER
Noch mehr! Noch mehr hierher!

DONNER
Kaum halt ich mich:
schäumende Wut
weckt mir der schamlose Wicht!
Hieher, du Hund!
Willst du messen,
so miß dich selber mit mir!

FAFNER
Ruhig, Donner!
Rolle, wo's taugt:
hier nützt dein Rasseln dir nichts!

DONNER
(holt aus.)
Nicht dich Schmählichen zu
[zerschmettern?

WOTAN
Friede doch!
Schon dünkt mich Freia verdeckt.

LOGE
Der Hort ging auf.

FAFNER
(mißt den Hort genau mit dem Blick und späht nach Lücken.)
Noch schimmert mir Holdas Haar:
dort das Gewirk
wirf auf den Hort!

LOGE
Wie, auch den Helm?

FAFNER
Hurtig her mit ihm!

how can she bear this shame?
And the glorious maid
pleads in silence for help.
Heartless man!
For you she endures this disgrace!

FAFNER
Still more! Heap on some more!

DONNER
I'll stand no more;
furious rage
rouses my heart to revenge!
Come here, you cur!
If you'd measure,
then try your measure with me!

FAFNER
Patience, Donner!
roar where it helps:
but here you thunder in vain!

DONNER
(preparing to strike)
Not in vain, since it can crush you!

WOTAN
Patience, friend!
I think that Freia is hid!

LOGE
The gold runs out.

FAFNER
(measures the gold closely with his eye, looking for crevices.)
But still I can see her hair!
You have some gold—
add it to the pile.

LOGE
What? not the helm?

FAFNER
Quickly, give it us.

WOTAN
Laß ihn denn fahren!

LOGE
(wirft den Tarnhelm auf den Hort.)
So sind wir denn fertig.
Seid ihr zufrieden?

FASOLT
Freia, die schöne,
schau ich nicht mehr:
so ist sie gelöst?
Muß ich sie lassen?
(Er tritt nahe hinzu und späht durch den Hort.)
Weh! Noch blitzt
ihr Blick zu mir her;
des Auges Stern
strahlt mich noch an:
durch eine Spalte
muß ich's erspähn!
Seh ich dies wonnige Auge,
von dem Weibe laß ich nicht ab.

FAFNER
He! Euch rat ich,
verstopft mir die Ritze!

LOGE
Nimmersatte!
Seht ihr denn nicht,
ganz schwand uns der Hort?

FAFNER
Mitnichten, Freund!
An Wotans Finger
glänzt von Gold noch ein Ring,
den gebt, die Ritze zu füllen!

WOTAN
Wie! Diesen Ring?

LOGE
Laßt euch raten!
Den Rheintöchtern
gehört dies Gold:
ihnen gibt Wotan es wieder.

WOTAN
Give them the Tarnhelm!

LOGE
(throws the Tarnhelm on the pile.)
At last we have finished!
Are you contented?

FASOLT
Freia, the fair one,
see I no more:
The ranson is paid?
Fasolt must lose her?
(He goes up close and peers through the pile.)
Ah! Her glance
still pierces my heart;
her eyes like stars
shine on me still,
for through this crack
I look on their light.
I cannot turn from this maiden,
while her eyes inspire me with love.

FAFNER
Hey! I charge you,
now stop up this crevice!

LOGE
Never contented!
Surely you see
our gold's at an end?

FAFNER
Not wholly, friend!
On Wotan's finger
gleams the gold of a ring:
and that will fill up this crevice!

WOTAN
What? Give my ring?

LOGE
Just a moment!
The Rhinemaidens
must have that gold,
and to them Wotan will give it.

WOTAN
Was schwatzest du da?
Was schwer ich mir erbeutet,
ohne Bangen wahr ich's für mich.

LOGE
Schlimm dann steht's
um mein Versprechen,
das ich den Klagenden gab.

WOTAN
Dein Versprechen bindet mich nicht:
als Beute bleibt mir der Reif.

FAFNER
Doch hier zur Lösung
mußt du ihn legen.

WOTAN
Fordert frech, was ihr wollt:
alles gewähr ich,
um alle Welt
doch nicht fahren laß ich den Ring!

FASOLT
(zieht wütend Freia hinter dem Horte hervor.)
Aus dann ist's,
beim Alten bleibt's:
nun folgt uns Freia für immer!

FREIA
Hilfe! Hilfe!

FRICKA
Harter Gott,
gib ihnen nach!

FROH
Spare das Gold nicht!

DONNER
Spende den Ring doch!
(Fafner hält den fortdrängenden Fasolt noch auf; alle stehen bestürzt.)

WOTAN
Laßt mich in Ruh!
Den Reif geb ich nicht.

WOTAN
What chatter is this?
This prize that I have won me,
without fear I'll keep for myself!

LOGE
But then how will I
keep the promise
I gave those sorrowful maids!

WOTAN
What you promised is nothing to me:
I took the ring for myself.

FAFNER
And now you'll yield it,
paying the ransom.

WOTAN
Freely ask what you want;
all I shall grant you;
but for the world
I will not surrender the ring!

FASOLT
(angrily pulling Freia out from behind the pile)
Keep your gold,
and keep your ring;
and we'll keep Freia for ever!

FREIA
Help me! Help me!

FRICKA
Cruel god!
Do what they ask!

FROH
Pay them the ransom!

DONNER
Give them the ring too!
(Fafner restrains Fasolt, who is making off. All stand perplexed.)

WOTAN
Leave me in peace!
The ring stays with me!

(Wotan wendet sich zürnend zur Seite. Die Bühne hat sich von neuem verfinstert; aus der Felskluft zur Seite bricht ein bläulicher Schein hervor: in ihm wird plötzlich Erda sichtbar, die bis zu halber Leibeshöhe aus der Tiefe aufsteigt; sie ist von edler Gestalt, weithin von schwarzem Haar umwallt.)

(Wotan turns angrily away. The stage has again become dark. A bluish light breaks from the rocky cleft at the side, and in it Erda suddenly appears, rising from below to half her height. Her noble features are ringed by a mass of black hair.)

ERDA
(die Hand mahnend gegen Wotan ausstreckend)
Weiche, Wotan, weiche!
Flieh des Ringes Fluch!
Rettungslos
dunklem Verderben
weiht dich sein Gewinn.

ERDA
(stretching out her hand to Wotan in warning)
Yield it, Wotan, yield it!
Yield the accursed ring!
Wretchedness,
doom and disaster
lie there in the ring.

WOTAN
Wer bist du, mahnendes Weib?

WOTAN
Who brings this warning of doom?

ERDA
Wie alles war, weiß ich;
wie alles wird,
wie alles sein wird,
seh ich auch:
der ew'gen Welt
Ur-Wala,
Erda mahnt deinen Mut.
Drei der Töchter,
ur-erschaffne,
gebar mein Schoß:
was ich sehe,
sagen dir nächtlich die Nornen.
Doch höchste Gefahr
führt mich heut
selbst zu dir her:
Höre! Höre! Höre!
Alles, was ist, endet.
Ein düstrer Tag
dämmert den Göttern:
dir rat ich, meide den Ring!
(Sie versinkt langsam bis an die Brust, während der bläuliche Schein zu dunkeln beginnt.)

ERDA
All of the past, know I.
All things that are,
all things that shall be—
all I know:
the endless world's
all-wise one,
Erda, bids you beware.
My three daughters,
born in Erda's
primeval womb,
shape my visions,
tell you each night of the future.
Today I myself,
drawn by dread,
come to advise.
Hear me! Hear me! Hear me!
All things that are, perish!
An evil day
dawns for the immortals:
I warn you, yield up the ring!
(Erda sinks slowly to breast level, as the bluish glow begins to fade.)

WOTAN
Geheimnis-hehr
hallt mir dein Wort:
weile, daß mehr ich wisse!

WOTAN
Mysterious doom
sounds in your words:
stay here, and warn me further!

ERDA
(im Versinken)
Ich warnte dich—
du weißt genug:
sinn in Sorg und Furcht!
(Sie verschwindet gänzlich.)

WOTAN
Soll ich sorgen und fürchten—
dich muß ich fassen,
alles erfahren!
(Er will der Verschwindenden in die Kluft nach, um sie zu halten. Froh und Fricka werfen sich ihm entgegen und halten ihn zurück.)

FRICKA
Was willst du, Wütender?

FROH
Halt ein, Wotan!
Scheue die Edle,
achte ihr Wort!
(Wotan starrt sinnend vor sich hin.)

DONNER
(sich entschlossen zu den Riesen wendend)
Hört, ihr Riesen!
Zurück und harret:
das Gold wird euch gegeben.

FREIA
Darf ich es hoffen?
Dünkt euch Holda
wirklich der Lösung wert?
(Alle blicken gespannt auf Wotan; dieser nach tiefem Sinnen zu sich kommend, erfaßt seinen Speer und schwenkt ihn wie zum Zeichen eines mutigen Entschlusses.)

WOTAN
Zu mir, Freia!
Du bist befreit.
Wiedergekauft
kehr uns die Jugend zurück!
Ihr Riesen, nehmt euren Ring!
(Er wirft den Ring auf den Hort. Die Riesen lassen Freia los; sie eilt freudig auf die Götter zu, die sie abwechselnd längere Zeit in höchster

ERDA
(disappearing)
You heard my words;
you know enough:
brood in dread and fear!
(She disappears completely.)

WOTAN
But if dread will torment me,
then I must hold you;
all you must tell me!
(He tries to follow and stop her as she disappears into the crevice. Froh and Fricka throw themselves in his way and hold him back.)

FRICKA
Be careful, calm yourself!

FROH
Be wise, Wotan!
Erda is holy;
do as she says!
(Wotan gazes thoughtfully before him.)

DONNER
(turning decisively to the giants)
Hear, you giants!
Come back, be patient!
The gold, Wotan will give you.

FREIA
Ah, dare I hope it?
Is your Freia
worth such a great reward?
(All look eagerly at Wotan. After thinking deeply, he rouses himself, seizes his spear and brandishes it as the sign of a bold decision.)

WOTAN
To me, Freia!
You shall be freed.
Bought with the gold,
bring us our youth once again!
You giants, there is your ring!
(He throws the ring on the pile. The giants release Freia. She hurries happily over to the gods, who spend some time embracing her in turn with

Freude liebkosen. Fafner breitet sogleich einen ungeheuren Sack aus und macht sich über den Hort her, um ihn da hineinzuschichten.)

FASOLT
(dem Bruder sich entgegenwerfend)
Halt, du Gieriger!
Gönne mir auch was!
Redliche Teilung
taugt uns beiden.

FAFNER
Mehr an der Maid als am Gold
lag dir verliebtem Geck:
mit Müh zum Tausch
vermocht' ich dich Toren.
Ohne zu teilen,
hättest du Freia gefreit:
teil ich den Hort,
billig behalt ich
die größte Hälfte für mich.

FASOLT
Schändlicher du!
Mir diesen Schimpf!
Euch ruf ich zu Richtern:
teilet nach Recht
uns redlich den Hort!
(Wotan wendet sich verächtlich ab.)

LOGE
(zu Fasolt)
Den Hort laß ihn raffen:
halte du nur auf den Ring!

FASOLT
(stürzt sich auf Fafner, der immerzu eingesackt hat.)
Zurück, du Frecher!
Mein ist der Ring;
mir blieb er für Freias Blick.
(Er greift hastig nach dem Reif. Sie ringen.)

FAFNER
Fort mit der Faust!
Der Ring ist mein!
(Fasolt entreißt Fafner den Ring.)

the utmost delight. Meanwhile Fafner has spread out an enormous sack, and prepares to stow the hoard in it, to take it away.)

FASOLT
(intercepting his brother)
Stop, you greedy one!
What about my share?
Fairly and squarely
we'll divide it.

FAFNER
You'd set your heart on the maid.
What do you care for the gold?
You hoped for love
and I wanted riches;
if you had won her,
would you have shared her with me?
Since it's the gold,
trust me to seize
on the greater part for myself!

FASOLT
Shame on you, thief!
mocking me so!
You gods be the judges:
how should this gold
be shared into two?
(Wotan turns contemptuously away.)

LOGE
(to Fasolt)
Let him keep the treasure;
all that you need is the ring!

FASOLT
(hurls himself upon Fafner, who has been busily packing away.)
Stand back, you robber!
Mine is the ring;
I won it for Freia's glance!
(He snatches hastily at the ring. They struggle.)

FAFNER
Off with your hands!
the ring is mine!
(Fasolt wrests the ring from Fafner.)

FASOLT
Ich halt ihn, mir gehört er!

FAFNER
(mit einem Pfahle nach Fasolt ausholend)
Halt ihn fest, daß er nicht fall'!
(Er streckt Fasolt mit einem Streiche zu Boden, dem Sterbenden entreißt er dann hastig den Ring.)
Nun blinzle nach Freias Blick:
an den Reif rührst du nicht mehr!
(Er steckt den Ring in den Sack und rafft dann gemächlich vollends den Hort ein. Alle Götter stehen entsetzt. Langes, feierliches Schweigen.)

WOTAN
Furchtbar nun
erfind ich des Fluches Kraft!

LOGE
Was gleicht, Wotan,
wohl deinem Glücke?
Viel erwarb dir
des Ringes Gewinn;
daß er nun dir genommen,
nützt dir noch mehr:
deine Feinde—sieh,
fällen sich selbst
um das Gold, das du vergabst.

WOTAN
(tief erschüttert)
Wie doch Bangen mich bindet!
Sorg und Furcht
fesseln den Sinn;
wie sie zu enden,
lehre mich Erda:
zu ihr muß ich hinab!

FRICKA
(schmeichelnd sich an ihn schmiegend)
Wo weilst du, Wotan?
Winkt dir nicht hold
die hehre Burg,
die des Gebieters
gastlich bergend nun harrt?

WOTAN
(düster)
Mit bösem Zoll

FASOLT
I have it, I shall keep it!

FAFNER
(striking out with his staff)
Hold it fast, else it may fall!
(He fells Fasolt with a single blow and then wrenches the ring from the dying giant.)
Now dream of your Freia's glance!
For the ring you'll see no more!
(He puts the ring in the sack, and then calmly finishes packing the treasure. All the gods are appalled. A long, solemn silence.)

WOTAN
Fearful power
lies hid in that fatal curse!

LOGE
Your luck, Wotan,
what could surpass it?
Much you gained from
the ring and the gold;
but that now you have lost them,
that's better still:
for your enemies, see,
murder each other
for the gold that you let go.

WOTAN
(profoundly agitated)
Dark forebodings oppress me!
Fear and dread
seize on my soul.
Erda can teach me
how I can end them:
to her, I must descend!

FRICKA
(caressing him, cajolingly)
What keeps you, Wotan?
See where our home
awaits you there,
shining and glorious,
glad to welcome its lord.

WOTAN
(gloomily)
An evil wage

zahlt' ich den Bau!

DONNER
(auf den Hintergrund deutend, der noch in Nebel gehüllt ist)
Schwüles Gedünst
schwebt in der Luft;
lästig ist mir
der trübe Druck:
das bleiche Gewölk
samml' ich zu blitzendem Wetter;
das fegt den Himmel mir hell.
(Er besteigt einen hohen Felsstein am Talabhange und schwingt dort seinen Hammer; Nebel ziehen sich um ihn zusammen.)
Heda! Heda! Hedo!
Zu mir, du Gedüft!
Ihr Dünste, zu mir!
Donner, der Herr,
ruft euch zu Heer.
Auf des Hammers Schwung
schwebet herbei:
dunstig Gedämpf,
schwebend Gedüft!
Donner, der Herr, ruft euch zu Heer!
Heda! Heda! Hedo!
(Er verschwindet völlig in einer immer finsterer sich ballenden Gewitterwolke. Man hört Donners Hammerschlag schwer auf den Felsstein fallen: ein starker Blitz entfährt der Wolke; ein heftiger Donnerschlag folgt. Froh ist mit dem Gewölk verschwunden.)

DONNER
(unsichtbar)
Bruder, hieher!
Weise der Brücke den Weg!
(Plötzlich verzieht sich die Wolke; Donner und Froh werden sichtbar: von ihren Füßen aus zieht sich, mit blendendem Leuchten, eine Regenbogenbrücke über das Tal hinüber bis zur Burg, die jetzt, von der Abendsonne beschienen, im hellsten Glanze erstrahlt. Fafner, der neben der Leiche seines Bruders endlich den ganzen Hort eingerafft, hat, den ungeheuren Sack auf dem Rücken, während Donners Gewitterzauber die Bühne verlassen.)

FROH
(der der Brücke mit der ausgestreckten Hand den

paid for the work!

DONNER
(pointing to the background, which is still wreathed in mist)
Sweltering mists
hang in the air;
I'm oppressed
by their gloomy weight.
I'll gather the clouds,
summon the lightning and thunder
to sweep the mist from the sky!
(He climbs onto a high rock by the precipice and there swings his hammer. Mists gather around him.)
Heda! Heda! Hedo!
Now come to my call!
You vapours, to me!
Donner, your lord,
summons you here!
As my hammer swings,
sweep from the sky!
Vapours and cloud!
Wandering fog!
Donner, your lord, summons you here!
Heda! Heda! Hedo!
(Donner vanishes completely behind a thundercloud which grows ever thicker and blacker. His hammer-blow is heard striking hard on the rock. A large flash of lightning shoots from the cloud, followed by a violent clap of thunder. Froh has vanished with him into the cloud.)

DONNER
(invisible)
Brother, to me!
Show them the bridge to the hall.
(Suddenly the clouds lift. Donner and Froh are visible. From their feet a rainbow bridge of blinding radiance stretches across the valley back to the castle, which now glows in the rays of the evening sun. Fafner has at last collected up all the treasure lying near his brother's corpse, put the enormous sack on his back, and left the stage during Donner's conjuration of the storm.)

FROH
(to the gods, indicating with outstretched hand the

Weg über das Tal angewiesen, zu den Göttern)
Zur Burg führt die Brücke,
leicht, doch fest eurem Fuß:
beschreitet kühn
ihren schrecklosen Pfad!
(Wotan und die andern Götter sind sprachlos in den prächtigen Anblick verloren.)

WOTAN
Abendlich strahlt
der Sonne Auge;
in prächt'ger Glut
prangt glänzend die Burg.
In des Morgens Scheine
mutig erschimmernd,
lag sie herrenlos
hehr verlockend vor mir.
Von Morgen bis Abend
in Müh und Angst
nicht wonnig ward sie gewonnen!
Es naht die Nacht:
vor ihrem Neid
biete sie Bergung nun.
(wie von einem großen Gedanken ergriffen, sehr entschlossen)
So grüß ich die Burg,
sicher vor Bang und Graun—
(Er wendet sich feierlich zu Fricka.)
Folge mir, Frau:
in Walhall wohne mit mir!

FRICKA
Was deutet der Name?
Nie, dünkt mich, hört' ich ihn nennen.

WOTAN
Was, mächtig der Furcht,
mein Mut mir erfand,
wenn siegend es lebt,
leg es den Sinn dir dar!
(Er faßt Fricka an der Hand und schreitet mit ihr langsam der Brücke zu; Froh, Freia und Donner folgen.)

LOGE
(im Vordergrunde verharrend und den Göttern nachblickend)
Ihrem Ende eilen sie zu,

bridge as the way across the valley)
The bridge leads you homeward,
light, yet firm to your feet:
so boldly tread
on that shining path!
(Wotan and the other gods are lost in speechless astonishment at the glorious sight.)

WOTAN
Evening rays flood
the sky with splendour;
those glorious beams
shine there on my hall.
In the morning radiance
bravely it glistened,
standing masterless,
proud, awaiting its lord.
From morning till evening,
in fear and dread,
I worked dark deeds till I'd gained it!
The night is near:
from all its ills
we have our refuge now.
(very resolutely, as if seized by a grand thought)

So greet I the hall,
safe from all fear and dread.
(He turns solemnly to Fricka.)
Follow me, wife:
in Walhall, reign there with me!

FRICKA
What name did you call it?
No name that I've ever heard of.

WOTAN
When all that I've dreamed
and planned comes to pass,
when victory is mine,
you'll understand that name!
(He takes Fricka by the hand and with her strides slowly towards the bridge. Froh, Freia and Donner follow.)

LOGE
(remaining in the foreground and looking back at the gods)
They are hastening on to their end,

die so stark im Bestehen sich wähnen.
Fast schäm ich mich,
mit ihnen zu schaffen;
zur leckenden Lohe
mich wieder zu wandeln,
spür ich lockende Lust.
Sie aufzuzehren,
die einst mich gezähmt,
statt mit den Blinden
blöd zu vergehn,
und wären es göttlichste Götter!
Nicht dumm dünkte mich das!
Bedenken will ich's:
wer weiß, was ich tu!

(Er geht, um sich den Göttern in nachlässiger Haltung anzuschließen. Aus der Tiefe hört man den Gesang der Rheintöchter heraufschallen.)

DIE DREI RHEINTÖCHTER
(in der Tiefe des Tales, unsichtbar)
Rheingold! Rheingold!
Reines Gold!
Wie lauter und hell
leuchtest hold du uns!
Um dich, du klares,
wir nun klagen!
Gebt uns das Gold!
O gebt uns das reine zurück!

WOTAN
(im Begriff, den Fuß auf die Brücke zu setzen, hält an und wendet sich um.)
Welch Klagen klingt zu mir her?

LOGE
(späht in das Tal hinab.)
Des Rheines Kinder
beklagen des Goldes Raub.

WOTAN
Verwünschte Nicker!
Wehre ihrem Geneck!

LOGE
(in das Tal hinabrufend)
Ihr da im Wasser,
was weint ihr herauf?
Hört, was Wotan euch wünscht.

though they think they are great in their [grandeur.
Ashamed I'd be
to share in their dealings;
I feel a temptation
to turn and destroy them;
change to flickering fire,
and burn those great ones
who thought I was tamed,
rather than blindly
sink with the blind,
although they're so gracious and god-like!
I think that might be best!
I must consider:
who knows what I'll do?

(He goes nonchalantly to join the gods. The singing of the Rhinemaidens is heard rising up from below.)

THE THREE RHINEMAIDENS
(from the depths of the valley invisible)
Rhinegold! Rhinegold!
Shining gold!
how brightly and clear
glittered your beams on us!
For your true radiance
we are mourning;
give us the gold!
Oh give us its glory again.

WOTAN
(in the act of setting foot on the bridge, pauses and turns round.)
What cries arise from the deep?

LOGE
(looking down into the valley)
The mournful Rhinemaidens
cry for their stolen gold.

WOTAN
Accursed nixies!
Stop their tiresome lament!

LOGE
(calling down into the valley)
You in the water,
stop wailing to us.
Hear what Wotan decrees.

Glänzt nicht mehr
euch Mädchen das Gold,
in der Götter neuem Glanze
sonnt euch selig fortan!
(Die Götter lachen und beschreiten dann die Brücke.)

DIE RHEINTÖCHTER
(aus der Tiefe)
Rheingold! Rheingold!
Reines Gold!
O leuchtete noch
in der Tiefe dein lautrer Tand!
Traulich und treu
ist's nur in der Tiefe:
falsch und feig
ist, was dort oben sich freut!
(Während die Götter auf der Brücke der Burg zuschreiten, fällt der Vorhang.)

Never more
will you see your gold;
let the gods' new golden splendour
shine upon you instead!
(The gods laugh and stride on to the bridge.)

THE RHINEMAIDENS
(from below)
Rhinegold! Rhinegold!
Shining gold!
Return to the deep,
let us bathe in your light again!
Goodness and truth
dwell but in the waters:
false and base
all those who dwell up above!
(While the gods are crossing the bridge to the castle, the curtain falls.)

The Valkyrie

First Day of the Festival Play

The Ring of the Nibelung

Dramatis Personae

SIEGMUND	*Tenor*
HUNDING	*Bass*
WOTAN	*Bass-baritone*
SIEGLINDE	*Soprano*
BRÜNNHILDE	*Soprano*
FRICKA	*Soprano*
VALKYRIES	*Sopranos and Contraltos*

GERHILDE
ORTLINDE
WALTRAUTE
SCHWERTLEITE
HELMWIGE
SIEGRUNE
GRIMGERDE
ROSSWEISSE

Erster Aufzug

Das Innere eines Wohnraumes

In der Mitte steht der Stamm einer mächtigen Esche, dessen stark erhabene Wurzeln sich weithin in den Erdboden verlieren; von seinem Wipfel ist der Baum durch ein gezimmertes Dach geschieden, welches so durchschnitten ist, daß der Stamm und die nach allen Seiten hin sich ausstreckenden Äste durch genau entsprechende Öffnungen hindurchgehen; von dem belaubten Wipfel wird angenommen, daß er sich über dieses Dach ausbreite. Um den Eschenstamm, als Mittelpunkt, ist nun ein Saal gezimmert; die Wände sind aus roh behauenem Holzwerk, hier und da mit geflochtenen und gewebten Decken behangen. Rechts im Vordergrunde steht der Herd, dessen Rauchfang seitwärts zum Dache hinausführt: hinter dem Herde befindet sich ein innerer Raum, gleich einem Vorratsspeicher, zu dem man auf einigen hölzernen Stufen hinaufsteigt: davor hängt, halb

Act One

Inside a Dwelling

In the middle stands a mighty ash-tree, whose prominent roots spread wide and lose themselves in the ground. The summit of the tree is cut off by a jointed roof, so pierced that the trunk and the boughs branching out on every side pass through it, through openings made exactly to fit. We assume that the top of the tree spreads out above the roof. Around the trunk of the ash, as central point, a room has been constructed. The walls are of rudely hewn wood, here and there hung with plaited and woven rugs. In the foreground, right, is a hearth, whose chimney goes up sideways to the roof; behind the hearth is an inner room, like a storeroom, reached by a few wooden steps. In front of it, half-drawn, is a plaited hanging. In the background, an entrance-door with a simple wooden latch. Left, the door to an inner chamber, similarly reached by steps. Further forward, on the same side, a table with a

zurückgeschlagen, eine geflochtene Decke. Im Hintergrunde eine Eingangstür mit schlichtem Holzriegel. Links die Tür zu einem inneren Gemache, zu dem gleichfalls Stufen hinaufführen; weiter vornen auf derselben Seite ein Tisch mit einer breiten, an der Wand angezimmerten Bank dahinter und hölzernen Schemeln davor.

Ein kurzes Orchestervorspiel von heftiger, stürmischer Bewegung leitet ein. Als der Vorhang aufgeht, öffnet Siegmund von außen hastig die Eingangstür und tritt ein: es ist gegen Abend, starkes Gewitter, im Begriff, sich zu legen. Siegmund hält einen Augenblick den Riegel in der Hand und überblickt den Wohnraum: er scheint von übermäßiger Anstrengung erschöpft; sein Gewand und Aussehen zeigen, daß er sich auf der Flucht befinde. Da er niemand gewahrt, schließt er die Tür hinter sich, schreitet auf den Herd zu und wirft sich dort ermattet auf eine Decke von Bärenfell.

broad bench fastened to the wall behind it and wooden stools in front of it.

A short orchestral prelude of violent, stormy character introduces the scene. When the curtain rises, Siegmund, from without, hastily opens the main door and enters. It is towards evening; a fierce thunderstorm is just about to die down. For a moment, Siegmund keeps his hand on the latch and looks around the room; he seems to be exhausted by tremendous exertions; his raiment and general appearance proclaim him a fugitive. Seeing no one, he closes the door behind him, walks to the hearth, and throws himself down there, exhausted, on a bearskin rug.

Erste Szene

SIEGMUND

Wes Herd dies auch sei,
hier muß ich rasten.

(Er sinkt zurück und bleibt einige Zeit regungslos ausgestreckt. Sieglinde tritt aus der Tür des inneren Gemaches. Sie glaubte ihren Mann heimgekehrt: ihre ernste Miene zeigt sich dann verwundert, als sie einen Fremden am Herde ausgestreckt sieht.)

SIEGLINDE
(noch im Hintergrunde)

Ein fremder Mann?
Ihn muß ich fragen.

(Sie tritt ruhig einige Schritte näher.)

Wer kam ins Haus
und liegt dort am Herd?

(Da Siegmund sich nicht regt, tritt sie noch etwas näher und betrachtet ihn.)

Müde liegt er
von Weges Mühn:
schwanden die Sinne ihm?
Wäre er siech?

(Sie neigt sich zu ihm herab und lauscht.)

Noch schwillt ihm der Atem;
das Auge nur schloß er.

Scene One

SIEGMUND

The storm drove me here;
here I must shelter.

(He sinks back and remains for a while stretched out, motionless. Sieglinde enters from the door of the inner room, thinking that her husband has returned. Her grave look changes to one of surprise when she sees a stranger on the hearth.)

SIEGLINDE
(still at the back)

A stranger here?
Where has he come from?

(Quietly, she comes a few steps closer.)

Who sought this house,
and lies by the fire?

(As Siegmund does not move, she comes a little closer and looks at him.)

He's exhausted
and makes no move.
Can he have fainted there,
or is he dead?

(She bends over him and listens.)

Ah no, he is breathing;
it seems that he's sleeping.

Mutig dünkt mich der Mann,
sank er müd auch hin.

SIEGMUND
(fährt jäh mit dem Haupt in die Höhe.)
Ein Quell! Ein Quell!

SIEGLINDE
Erquickung schaff ich.
(Sie nimmt schnell ein Trinkhorn, geht damit aus dem Hause, kommt zurück und reicht das gefüllte Trinkhorn Siegmund.)
Labung biet ich
dem lechzenden Gaumen:
Wasser, wie du gewollt!

SIEGMUND
(trinkt und reicht ihr das Horn zurück. Als er ihr mit dem Haupte Dank zuwinkt, haftet sein Blick mit steigender Teilnahme an ihren Mienen.)
Kühlende Labung
gab mir der Quell,
des Müden Last
machte er leicht;
erfrischt ist der Mut,
das Aug' erfreut
des Sehens selige Lust.
Wer ist's, der so mir es labt?

SIEGLINDE
Dies Haus und dies Weib
sind Hundings Eigen;
gastlich gönn' er dir Rast:
harre, bis heim er kehrt!

SIEGMUND
Waffenlos bin ich:
dem wunden Gast
wird dein Gatte nicht wehren.

SIEGLINDE
(mit besorgter Hast)
Die Wunden weise mir schnell!

SIEGMUND
(springt lebhaft vom Lager zum Sitz auf.)
Gering sind sie,
der Rede nicht wert;

Valiant, strong is the man,
though he's weary now.

SIEGMUND
(suddenly raises his head.)
A drink! a drink!

SIEGLINDE
I'll bring some water.
(She quickly takes a drinking-horn and goes out of the house with it. Returning with it filled, she offers it to Siegmund.)
Cool your lips with this drink
that I've brought you!
Water—will you not drink?

SIEGMUND
(drinks and hands her back the horn. As he signals his thanks with his head, his glance fastens on her features with growing interest.)
Cool and refreshing—
now I am well;
my load of care
suddenly light;
my spirits revive;
my eyes enjoy
a blessed, glorious sight.
And who has brought me to life?

SIEGLINDE
This house and this wife
belong to Hunding.
He will welcome his guest:
wait here till he returns.

SIEGMUND
Weaponless am I:
a wounded guest
cannot trouble your husband.

SIEGLINDE
(with anxious haste)
Oh quickly show me the wounds!

SIEGMUND
(shakes himself and sits up quickly.)
A scratch merely,
unworthy your care;

noch fügen des Leibes
Glieder sich fest.
Hätten halb so stark wie mein Arm
Schild und Speer mir gehalten,
nimmer floh ich dem Feind;
doch zerschellten mir Speer und Schild.
Der Feinde Meute
hetzte mich müd,
Gewitterbrunst
brach meinen Leib;
doch schneller, als ich der Meute,
schwand die Müdigkeit mir;
sank auf die Lider mir Nacht,
die Sonne lacht mir nun neu.

SIEGLINDE
(geht nach dem Speicher, füllt ein Horn mit Met und reicht es Siegmund mit freundlicher Bewegtheit.)
Des seimigen Metes
süßen Trank
mögst du mir nicht verschmähn.

SIEGMUND
Schmecktest du mir ihn zu?
(Sieglinde nippt am Horne und reicht es ihm wieder. Siegmund tut einen langen Zug, indem er den Blick mit wachsender Wärme auf sie heftet. Er setzt so das Horn ab und läßt es langsam sinken, während der Ausdruck seiner Miene in starke Ergriffenheit übergeht. Er seufzt tief auf und senkt den Blick düster zu Boden. Mit bebender Stimme:)
Einen Unseligen labtest du:
Unheil wende
der Wunsch von dir!
(Er bricht schnell auf, um fortzugehen.)
Gerastet hab ich
und süß geruht:
weiter wend ich den Schritt.
(Er geht nach hinten.)

SIEGLINDE
(lebhaft sich umwendend)
Wer verfolgt dich, daß du schon fliehst?

SIEGMUND
(von ihrem Rufe gefesselt, langsam und düster)
Mißwende folgt mir,

no bone in my body
broken at all.
Had my shield and spear been as strong,
half as strong as my body,
I would never have fled;
but they shattered my spear and shield.
And so I fled
the enemys' rage;
a thunderstorm
broke overhead.
Yet, swifter than I was fleeing,
all my faintness has fled.
Darkness had covered my eyes—
the sunlight smiles on me now.

SIEGLINDE
(goes to the storeroom, fills a horn with mead, and offers it to Siegmund with friendly eagerness.)
I bring you a drink
of honeyed mead;
say that you'll not refuse.

SIEGMUND
Will not you taste it first?
(Sieglinde sips from the horn and gives it back to him. Siegmund takes a long draught, while his gaze rests on her with growing warmth. Still gazing, he takes the horn from his lips and lets it sink slowly, while the expression on his face tells of strong emotion. He sighs deeply, and gloomily lowers his gaze to the ground. With trembling voice:)
Evil fortune's never far from me:
may I keep it
away from you!
(He starts up to go.)
I rested sweetly;
I feel refreshed.
I must go on my way.
(He moves towards the back.)

SIEGLINDE
(turning round quickly)
Who pursues you? Why must you flee?

SIEGMUND
(arrested by her cry; slowly and sadly)
Ill fate pursues me,

wohin ich fliehe;
Mißwende naht mir,
wo ich mich zeige.
Dir, Frau, doch bleibe sie fern!
Fort wend ich Fuß und Blick.
(Er schreitet schnell bis zur Tür und hebt den Riegel.)

follows my footsteps;
ill fate advances—
soon it will reach me.
This ill fate you must not share!
So I must leave your house.
(He strides swiftly to the door and lifts the latch.)

SIEGLINDE
(in heftigem Selbstvergessen ihm nachrufend)
So bleibe hier!
Nicht bringst du Unheil dahin,
wo Unheil im Hause wohnt!

SIEGLINDE
(calling to him with impetuous self-forgetfulness)
No, do not leave!
You bring no ill fate to me,
for ill fate has long been here!

SIEGMUND
(bleibt tief erschüttert stehen und forscht in Sieglindes Mienen; diese schlägt verschämt und traurig die Augen nieder. Langes Schweigen. Siegmund kehrt zurück.)
Wehwalt hieß ich mich selbst:
Hunding will ich erwarten.
(Er lehnt sich an den Herd; sein Blick haftet mit ruhiger und entschlossener Teilnahme an Sieglinde: diese hebt langsam das Auge wieder zu ihm auf. Beide blicken sich in langem Schweigen mit dem Ausdruck tiefster Ergriffenheit in die Augen.)

SIEGMUND
(deeply moved, remains where he is; he gazes intently at Sieglinde, who lowers her eyes in embarrassment and sadness. A long silence. Siegmund returns into the room.)
Wehwalt, that is my name.
Hunding—I will await him.
(He leans against the hearth; his eyes fix themselves with calm and steady sympathy on Sieglinde. Slowly, she raises her eyes again to his. They gaze into one another's eyes, during a long silence, with an expression of the deepest emotion.)

Zweite Szene

Sieglinde fährt plötzlich auf, lauscht und hört Hunding, der sein Roß außen zum Stall führt. Sie geht hastig zur Tür und öffnet; Hunding, gewaffnet mit Schild und Speer, tritt ein und hält unter der Tür, als er Siegmund gewahrt. Hunding wendet sich mit einem ernst fragenden Blick an Sieglinde.

Scene Two

Suddenly Sieglinde starts, listens, and hears Hunding, who is leading his horse to the stable outside. She goes quickly to the door and opens it. Hunding, armed with shield and spear, enters, and pauses at the threshold on perceiving Siegmund. He turns to Sieglinde with a glance of stern inquiry.

SIEGLINDE
(dem Blicke Hundings entgegnend)
Müd am Herd

SIEGLINDE
(in answer to Hunding's look)
There he lay,

fand ich den Mann:
Not führt' ihn ins Haus.

HUNDING
Du labtest ihn?

SIEGLINDE
Den Gaumen letzt' ich ihm,
gastlich sorgt' ich sein!

SIEGMUND
(der ruhig und fest Hunding beobachtet)
Dach und Trank
dank ich ihr:
willst du dein Weib drum schelten?

HUNDING
Heilig ist mein Herd:
heilig sei dir mein Haus!
(Er legt seine Waffen ab und übergibt sie Sieglinde. Zu Sieglinde:)
Rüst uns Männern das Mahl!
(Sieglinde hängt die Waffen an Ästen des Eschenstammes auf, dann holt sie Speise und Trank aus dem Speicher und rüstet auf dem Tische das Nachtmahl. Unwillkürlich heftet sie wieder den Blick auf Siegmund. Hunding mißt scharf und verwundert Siegmunds Züge, die er mit denen seiner Frau vergleicht; für sich:)
Wie gleicht er dem Weibe!
Der gleißende Wurm
glänzt auch ihm aus dem Auge.
(Er birgt sein Befremden und wendet sich wie unbefangen zu Siegmund.)
Weit her, traun,
kamst du des Wegs;
ein Roß nicht ritt,
der Rast hier fand:
welch schlimme Pfade
schufen dir Pein?

SIEGMUND
Durch Wald und Wiese,
Heide und Hain,
jagte mich Sturm
und starke Not:
nicht kenn ich den Weg, den ich kam.
Wohin ich irrte,

feeble and faint;
need drove him in here.

HUNDING
You cared for him?

SIEGLINDE
I said you'd welcome him;
greeted him as guest.

SIEGMUND
(watching Hunding calmly and firmly)
Rest and drink,
both she brought:
Why should you then reproach her?

HUNDING
Sacred is my hearth;
sacred keep you my house.
(He hands his weapons to Sieglinde, and says to her:)
Go, make ready our meal!
(Sieglinde hangs the weapons on the branches of the ash-tree, fetches food and drink from the storeroom, and prepares the table for supper. Involuntarily she turns her eyes again to Siegmund. Hunding looks keenly and with astonishment at Siegmund's features, comparing them with his wife's; aside:)
He looks like my wife there!
A glittering snake
seems to shine in their glances.
(He hides his surprise and turns, as if unconcerned, to Siegmund.)
You have strayed
far from your path;
you rode no horse
to reach my house.
What painful journey
brought you to me?

SIEGMUND
Through field and forest,
meadow and marsh,
driven by storm
and starkest need—
I know not the way that I took;
nor can I tell you

weiß ich noch minder:
Kunde gewänn' ich des gern.

where I have wandered.
May I now learn it from you?

HUNDING
(am Tische und Siegmund den Sitz bietend)
Des Dach dich deckt,
des Haus dich hegt,
Hunding heißt der Wirt;
wendest von hier du
nach West den Schritt,
in Höfen reich
hausen dort Sippen,
die Hundings Ehre behüten.
Gönnt mir Ehre mein Gast,
wird sein Name nun mir genannt.
(Siegmund, der sich am Tisch niedergesetzt, blickt nachdenklich vor sich hin. Sieglinde, die sich neben Hunding, Siegmund gegenüber, gesetzt, heftet ihr Auge mit auffallender Teilnahme und Spannung auf diesen. Hunding, der beide beobachtet:)
Trägst du Sorge,
mir zu vertraun,
der Frau hier gib doch Kunde:
sieh, wie gierig sie dich frägt!

HUNDING
(at the table, motioning to Siegmund to sit)
This house is mine,
this land is mine;
Hunding is your host.
Turn to the west
when you leave my house,
and there my kin
dwell in rich homesteads,
where Hunding's honour is guarded.
You may honour me too:
will my guest not tell me his name?
(Siegmund, who has sat down at the table, gazes thoughtfully in front of him. Sieglinde has placed herself next to Hunding, opposite Siegmund, on whom she fastens her eyes with evident sympathy and intentness. Hunding, observing them both:)
Though you fear
to trust it to me,
my wife here longs to hear it.
See, how eagerly she asks!

SIEGLINDE
(unbefangen und teilnahmsvoll)
Gast, wer du bist,
wüßt' ich gern.

SIEGLINDE
(unembarrassed and eager)
Guest, I would know
who you are.

SIEGMUND
(blickt auf, sieht ihr in das Auge und beginnt ernst.)
Friedmund darf ich nicht heißen;
Frohwalt möcht' ich wohl sein:
doch Wehwalt muß ich mich nennen.
Wolfe, der war mein Vater;
zu zwei kam ich zur Welt,
eine Zwillingsschwester und ich.
Früh schwanden mir
Mutter und Maid;
die mich gebar
und die mit mir sie barg,
kaum hab ich je sie gekannt.
Wehrlich und stark war Wolfe;
der Feinde wuchsen ihm viel.
Zum Jagen zog
mit dem Jungen der Alte:
von Hetze und Harst

SIEGMUND
(looks up, gazes into her eyes, and begins gravely.)
Friedmund no one could call me;
Frohwalt—would that I were!
I'm Wehwalt, named for my sorrow.
Wolfe, he was my father;
his two children were twins—
my unhappy sister and I.
Both mother and sister
were lost—
my mother killed
and my sister borne off—
taken while I was a boy.
Valiant and strong was Wolfe;
his foes were many and fierce.
And hunters bold
were the boy and his father.
Once, weary and worn,

einst kehrten sie heim:
da lag das Wolfsnest leer.
Zu Schutt gebrannt
der prangende Saal,
zum Stumpf der Eiche
blühender Stamm;
erschlagen der Mutter
mutiger Leib,
verschwunden in Gluten
der Schwester Spur.
Uns schuf die herbe Not
der Neidinge harte Schar.
Geächtet floh
der Alte mit mir;
lange Jahre
lebte der Junge
mit Wolfe im wilden Wald:
Manche Jagd
ward auf sie gemacht;
doch mutig wehrte
das Wolfspaar sich.
(zu Hunding gewandt)
Ein Wölfing kündet dir das,
den als »Wölfing« mancher wohl kennt.

HUNDING
Wunder und wilde Märe
kündest du, kühner Gast,
Wehwalt, der Wölfing!
Mich dünkt, von dem wehrlichen Paar
vernahm ich dunkle Sage,
kannt' ich auch Wolfe
und Wölfing nicht.

SIEGLINDE
Doch weiter künde, Fremder:
wo weilt dein Vater jetzt?

SIEGMUND
Ein starkes Jagen auf uns
stellten die Neidinge an:
Der Jäger viele
fielen den Wölfen,
in Flucht durch den Wald
trieb sie das Wild:
wie Spreu zerstob uns der Feind.
Doch ward ich vom Vater versprengt;

we came from the chase,
and found our home laid waste.
A heap of ash
was all that was left;
a stump where once
an oak tree had stood;
the corpse of my mother
lay at my feet;
all trace of my sister
was lost in smoke.
This cruel blow was dealt
by ruffians who sought revenge.
As outlaws then
we took to the woods;
there I lived
with Wolfe my father;
in hunting I spent my youth.
Many a raid
was made on us both,
but we had learnt
to defend our lives.
(turning to Hunding)
A Wölfing tells you this tale,
and as 'Wölfing' often I'm known.

HUNDING
Wonderful, wild adventures
came to our daring guest,
Wehwalt the Wölfing!
I think that I've heard of the pair,
I've heard unholy stories
spoken of Wolfe
and Wölfing too.

SIEGLINDE
But tell us more, O stranger:
where is your father now?

SIEGMUND
The ruffians raided again,
fell on my father and me;
and many hunters
fell in the battle;
they fled through the wood,
chased by us both;
like chaff we scattered the foe.
They parted my father from me;

seine Spur verlor ich,
je länger ich forschte:
eines Wolfes Fell nur
traf ich im Forst;
leer lag das vor mir,
den Vater fand ich nicht.
Aus dem Wald trieb es mich fort;
mich drängt' es zu Männern und Frauen.
Wieviel ich traf,
wo ich sie fand,
ob ich um Freund',
um Frauen warb,
immer doch war ich geächtet:
Unheil lag auf mir.
Was Rechtes je ich riet,
andern dünkte es arg,
was schlimm immer mir schien,
andere gaben ihm Gunst,
In Fehde fiel ich, wo ich mich fand,
Zorn traf mich, wohin ich zog;
gehrt' ich nach Wonne,
weckt' ich nur Weh:
drum mußt' ich mich Wehwalt nennen;
des Wehes waltet' ich nur.
(Er sieht zu Sieglinde auf und gewahrt ihren teilnehmenden Blick.)

HUNDING
Die so leidig Los dir beschied,
nicht liebte dich die Norn':
froh nicht grüßt dich der Mann,
dem fremd als Gast du nahst.

SIEGLINDE
Feige nur fürchten den,
der waffenlos einsam fährt!
Künde noch, Gast,
wie du im Kampf
zuletzt die Waffe verlorst!

SIEGMUND
(immer lebhafter)
Ein trauriges Kind
rief mich zum Trutz:
vermählen wollte
der Magen Sippe
dem Mann ohne Minne die Maid.

in the fight I lost him.
A long while I sought him.
Though I found the wolf-skin
that he had worn,
no more could I find;
my father was not there.
Then I lost my love for the woods;
I mingled with warriors and women.
But all in vain,
often I tried
to find a friend,
to woo a maid—
everywhere I was rejected.
Ill fate lay on me.
For what I thought was right,
others reckoned was wrong,
and what seemed to me bad,
others held to be good.
And so it was wherever I went,
outlawed by all whom I met;
striving for gladness,
found only woe!
And so I was Wehwalt always;
Yes, Wehwalt!—sad was my fate.
(He turns his eyes to Sieglinde and observes her sympathetic glance.)

HUNDING
So the Norn who dealt you this fate,
she felt no love for you:
No one greets you with joy
when you arrive as guest.

SIEGLINDE
Manly hearts do not fear
a weaponless lonely man!
Tell us more, guest;
tell of the fight
in which your weapons were lost.

SIEGMUND
(with increasing excitement)
A girl in distress
called for my aid;
her kinsmen wanted
to force the maiden
to marry a husband she feared.

Wider den Zwang
zog ich zum Schutz,
der Dränger Troß
traf ich im Kampf:
dem Sieger sank der Feind.
Erschlagen lagen die Brüder:
die Leichen umschlang da die Maid,
den Grimm verjagt' ihr der Gram.
Mit wilder Tränen Flut
betroff sie weinend die Wal:
um des Mordes der eignen Brüder
klagte die unsel'ge Braut.

Der Erschlagnen Sippen
stürmten daher;
übermächtig
ächzten nach Rache sie;
rings um die Stätte
ragten mir Feinde.
Doch von der Wal
wich nicht die Maid;
mit Schild und Speer
schirmt' ich sie lang,
bis Speer und Schild
im Harst mir zerhaun.
Wund und waffenlos stand ich—
sterben sah ich die Maid:
mich hetzte das wütende Heer—
auf den Leichen lag sie tot.
(mit einem Blicke voll schmerzlichen Feuers auf Sieglinde)
Nun weißt du, fragende Frau,
warum ich Friedmund—nicht heiße!
(Er steht auf und schreitet auf den Herd zu. Sieglinde blickt erbleichend und tief erschüttert zu Boden.)

HUNDING
(erhebt sich.)
Ich weiß ein wildes Geschlecht,
nicht heilig ist ihm,
was andern hehr:
verhaßt ist es allen und mir.
Zur Rache ward ich gerufen,
Sühne zu nehmen
für Sippenblut:
zu spät kam ich
und kehre nun heim,

Hearing her cry,
I came to her help.
Her cruel kin
met me in fight;
they fell before my spear.
I'd killed her fierce, cruel brothers.
The maid threw her arms round the dead;
her rage had turned into grief.
With wildly streaming eyes
she bathed the dead with her tears,
as she mourned for the death of those
who'd wronged her—that ill-fated bride.

Then her brothers' kinsmen
rushed to the fight;
vowing vengeance,
angrily fell on me,
raging around me,
eager to kill me.
Meanwhile the maid
stayed by the dead;
my shield and spear
sheltered her life,
till spear and shield
were hacked from my hand.
I was weaponless, wounded;
she was killed while I watched:
I fled from the furious host;
on the bodies she lay dead.
(turning to Sieglinde with a look filled with sorrowful fervour)
You asked me, now you must know
why I'm not Friedmund—but Wehwalt!
(He stands up and walks to the hearth. Sieglinde, pale and deeply stirred, lowers her eyes.)

HUNDING
(rises.)
I know a quarrelsome race;
they do not respect
what we revere;
they are hated by all men—and me.
I heard a summons to vengeance:
Death to the stranger
who killed our kin!
Too late came I,
but now that I'm home,

des flücht'gen Frevlers Spur
im eignen Haus zu erspähn.
(Er geht herab.)
Mein Haus hütet,
Wölfing, dich heut;
für die Nacht nahm ich dich auf;
mit starker Waffe
doch wehre dich morgen;
zum Kampfe kies ich den Tag:
für Tote zahlst du mir Zoll.
(Sieglinde schreitet mit besorgter Gebärde zwischen die beiden Männer vor. Hunding, barsch:)
Fort aus dem Saal!
Säume hier nicht!
Den Nachttrunk rüste mir drin
und harre mein zur Ruh'.
(Sieglinde steht eine Weile unentschieden und sinnend. Sie wendet sich langsam und zögernden Schrittes nach dem Speicher. Dort hält sie wieder an und bleibt, in Sinnen verloren, mit halb abgewandtem Gesicht stehen. Mit ruhigem Entschluß öffnet sie den Schrein, füllt ein Trinkhorn und schüttet aus einer Büchse Würze hinein. Dann wendet sie das Auge auf Siegmund, um seinem Blicke zu begegnen, den dieser fortwahrend auf sie heftet. Sie gewahrt Hundings Spähen und wendet sich sogleich zum Schlafgemach. Auf den Stufen kehrt sie sich noch einmal um, heftet das Auge sehnsuchtsvoll auf Siegmund und deutet mit dem Blicke andauernd und mit sprechender Bestimmtheit auf eine Stelle am Eschenstamme. Hunding fährt auf und treibt sie mit einer heftigen Gebärde zum Fortgehen an. Mit einem letzten Blick auf Siegmund geht sie in das Schlafgemach und schließt hinter sich die Tür. Hunding nimmt seine Waffen vom Stamme herab.)
Mit Waffen wahrt sich der Mann.
(im Abgehen sich zu Siegmund wendend)
Dich, Wölfing, treffe ich morgen;
mein Wort hörtest du—
hüte dich wohl!
(Er geht mit den Waffen in das Gemach; man hört ihn von innen Riegel schließen.)

I find that stranger here;
he sought my house for his rest.
(He advances.)
My house guards you,
Wölfing, today;
for the night you are my guest.
But find some weapons
to serve you tomorrow;
I choose the day for our fight:
You'll pay me blood for their blood.
(With anxious gestures Sieglinde steps between the two men. Hunding, harshly:)
Go from the room!
Why are you here!
Prepare my drink for the night,
and wait for me in there.
(Sieglinde stands awhile undecided and thoughtful. Then she turns slowly and with hesitating steps towards the storeroom. There she again pauses and remains standing, lost in thought, with her face half turned away. With quiet resolve she opens the cupboard, fills a drinking horn, and shakes some spices into it from a container. Then she turns her eyes on Siegmund so as to meet his gaze, which he keeps unceasingly fixed on her. She perceives that Hunding is watching, and goes at once towards the bedchamber. On the steps she turns once more, looks yearningly at Siegmund, and indicates with her eyes, persistently and with eloquent earnestness, a particular spot in the ash-tree's trunk. Hunding starts, and drives her with a violent gesture from the room. With a last look at Siegmund, she goes into the bedchamber, and closes the door behind her. Hunding takes down his weapons from the tree-trunk.)
With weapons man should be armed.
(to Siegmund, as he goes)
You, Wölfing, meet me tomorrow,
and then—fight with me!
Guard yourself well!
(He goes into the chamber; the closing of the bolt is heard from within.)

Dritte Szene

Siegmund allein. Es ist vollständig Nacht geworden; der Saal ist nur noch von einem schwachen Feuer im Herd erhellt. Siegmund läßt sich, nah beim Feuer, auf dem Lager nieder und brütet in großer innerer Aufregung eine Zeitlang vor sich hin.

SIEGMUND
Ein Schwert verhieß mir der Vater,
ich fänd' es in höchster Not.
Waffenlos fiel ich
in Feindes Haus;
seiner Rache Pfand,
raste ich hier.
Ein Weib sah ich,
wonnig und hehr:
entzückend Bangen
zehrt mein Herz.
Zu der mich nun Sehnsucht zieht,
die mit süßem Zauber mich sehrt,
im Zwange hält sie der Mann,
der mich Wehrlosen höhnt!
Wälse! Wälse!
Wo ist dein Schwert?
Das starke Schwert,
das im Sturm ich schwänge,
bricht mir hervor aus der Brust,
was wütend das Herz noch hegt?
(Das Feuer bricht zusammen; es fällt aus der aufsprühenden Glut plötzlich ein greller Schein auf die Stelle des Eschenstammes, welche Sieglindes Blick bezeichnet hatte und an der man jetzt deutlich einen Schwertgriff haften sieht.)
Was gleißt dort hell
im Glimmerschein?
Welch ein Strahl bricht
aus der Esche Stamm?
Des Blinden Auge
leuchtet ein Blitz:
lustig lacht da der Blick.
Wie der Schein so hehr
das Herz mir sengt!
Ist es der Blick
der blühenden Frau,
den dort haftend
sie hinter sich ließ,

Scene Three

Siegmund is alone. It has become quite dark. The room is lit only by a feeble fire on the hearth. Siegmund sinks down on the couch near the fire and broods silently for a while, in great agitation.

SIEGMUND
A sword was pledged by my father,
to serve in my hour of need.
I am unarmed
in my enemy's house;
as a hostage here
helpless I wait.
But she's here too,
lovely and fair:
a new emotion
fills my heart.
This woman who holds me bound,
whose enchantment tears at my heart,
as slave she's held by a man
who mocks his weaponless foe.
Wälse! Wälse!
Where is your sword?
The shining sword
that alone can save me,
when there should break from my breast
that fury my heart still hides?
(The fire collapses, and a bright glow springs up, striking the place on the ash-trunk indicated by Sieglinde's look, where now a sword-hilt is clearly seen.)
What's glinting there
to light the gloom?
On the ash-tree
there's a starry gleam.
My eyes are blinded,
dazzled with light;
lightnings flash from the tree.
How the shining gleam
inspires my heart!
Is it the glance
that shone from her eyes,
did she leave it
to linger behind,

als aus dem Saal sie schied?
(Von hier an verglimmt das Herdfeuer allmählich.)
Nächtiges Dunkel
deckte mein Aug';
ihres Blickes Strahl
streifte mich da:
Wärme gewann ich und Tag.
Selig schien mir
der Sonne Licht;
den Scheitel umgliß mir
ihr wonniger Glanz,
bis hinter Bergen sie sank.
(ein neuer schwacher Aufschein des Feuers)
Noch einmal, da sie schied,
traf mich abends ihr Schein;
selbst der alten Esche Stamm
erglänzte in goldner Glut:
da bleicht die Blüte,
das Licht verlischt;
nächtiges Dunkel
deckt mir das Auge:
tief in des Busens Berge
glimmt nur noch lichtlose Glut.
(Das Feuer ist gänzlich verloschen: volle Nacht. Das Seitengemach öffnet sich leise: Sieglinde, in weißem Gewande, tritt heraus und schreitet leise, doch rasch, auf den Herd zu.)

SIEGLINDE
Schläfst du, Gast?

SIEGMUND
(freudig überrascht aufspringend)
Wer schleicht daher?

SIEGLINDE
Ich bin's: höre mich an!
In tiefem Schlaf liegt Hunding;
ich würzt' ihm betäubenden Trank:
Nütze die Nacht dir zum Heil!

SIEGMUND
(hitzig unterbrechend)
Heil macht mich dein Nah'n!

SIEGLINDE
Eine Waffe laß mich dir weisen:

when she was sent away?
(From now on, the fire on the hearth gradually sinks.)
Shadows of darkness
covered my eyes;
but her radiant glance
fell on me then,
warming and lighting my heart.
Glorious rays
of the golden sun,
with gladdening splendour
encircled my head,
till in the mountains it sank.
(a new faint gleam from the fire)
Yet once more, as it went,
evening radiance did shine;
and the ancient ash-tree's trunk
was bathed in a golden glow;
that light is fading;
the gleam has gone;
shadows of darkness
gather around me:
deep in my breast there lingers on
that last smouldering glow.
(The fire has burnt out; complete darkness. The door at the side opens softly. Sieglinde, in a white garment, comes out and advances lightly but quickly towards the hearth.)

SIEGLINDE
Are you awake?

SIEGMUND
(springing up in joyful surprise)
Who steals this way?

SIEGLINDE
I do. Listen to me!
In heavy sleep lies Hunding;
I gave him a drug in his drink.
Now, in the night, you are safe!

SIEGMUND
(interrupting her passionately)
Safe when you are near!

SIEGLINDE
There's a sword for him who can win it;

O wenn du sie gewännst!
Den hehrsten Helden
dürft' ich dich heißen:
dem Stärksten allein
ward sie bestimmt.
O merke wohl, was ich dir melde!
Der Männer Sippe
saß hier im Saal,
von Hunding zur Hochzeit geladen.
Er freite ein Weib,
das ungefragt
Schächer ihm schenkten zur Frau.
Traurig saß ich,
während sie tranken;
ein Fremder trat da herein:
ein Greis in grauem Gewand;
tief hing ihm der Hut,
der deckt' ihm der Augen eines;
doch des andren Strahl,
Angst schuf er allen,
traf die Männer
sein mächt'ges Dräu'n:
Mir allein
weckte das Auge
süß sehnenden Harm,
Tränen und Trost zugleich.
Auf mich blickt' er
und blitzte auf jene,
als ein Schwert in Händen er schwang;
das stieß er nun
in der Esche Stamm,
bis zum Heft haftet' es drin:
dem sollte der Stahl geziemen,
der aus dem Stamm es zög'.
Der Männer alle,
so kühn sie sich mühten,
die Wehr sich keiner gewann;
Gäste kamen
und Gäste gingen,
die stärksten zogen am Stahl—
keinen Zoll entwich er dem Stamm:
dort haftet schweigend das Schwert.
Da wußt' ich, wer der war,
der mich Gramvolle gegrüßt;
ich weiß auch,
wem allein
im Stamm das Schwert er bestimmt.

and when that sword is won,
then I can call you
noblest of heroes:
the strongest alone
masters the sword.
So listen well, mark what I tell you!
My husband's kinsmen
sat in this room,
they'd come here to witness his wedding.
He married a wife
against her will;
robbers had made her their prize.
Sad, I sat here
while they were drinking;
a stranger entered this house:
an old man dressed all in grey;
his hat hung so low
that one of his eyes was hidden;
but the other's flash
filled them with terror:
none could counter
that threatening gaze.
I alone
felt in those glances
sweet, yearning regret—
sorrow and solace in one.
On me smiling,
he glared at the others;
in his hand he carried a sword;
then drove it deep
in the ash-tree's trunk;
to the hilt buried it there.
But one man alone could win it,
he who could draw it forth.
The guests were warriors;
they rose to the challenge;
but none could master the sword.
Many tried it
but all were baffled;
the strongest seized it in vain—
none could move the blade from its place.
That sword is still in the tree.
I knew then who he was,
come to greet me in my grief;
I know too
who alone
can draw the sword from the tree.

O fänd' ich ihn heut
und hier, den Freund;
käm' er aus Fremden
zur ärmsten Frau:
Was je ich gelitten
in grimmigem Leid,
was je mich geschmerzt
in Schande und Schmach—
süßeste Rache
sühnte dann alles!
Erjagt hätt' ich,
was je ich verlor,
was je ich beweint,
wär' mir gewonnen,
fänd' ich den heiligen Freund,
umfing' den Helden mein Arm!

And oh, have I found
today that friend,
come from the distance
to end my grief?
Then all I have suffered
in pain and distress,
yes, all I have suffered
in sorrow and shame,
all is forgotten,
all is atoned for!
Regained all things
I thought I had lost;
my fondest desires
gain their fulfilment,
if I have found that friend,
and hold that hero to me!

SIEGMUND
(mit Glut Sieglinde umfassend)
Dich, selige Frau,
hält nun der Freund,
dem Waffe und Weib bestimmt!
Heiß in der Brust
brennt mir der Eid,
der mich dir Edlen vermählt.
Was je ich ersehnt,
ersah ich in dir;
in dir fand ich,
was je mir gefehlt!
Littest du Schmach,
und schmerzte mich Leid;
war ich geächtet,
und warst du entehrt:
freudige Rache
ruft nun den Frohen!
Auf lach ich
in heiliger Lust—
halt ich die Hehre umfangen,
fühl ich dein schlagendes Herz!
(Die große Tür springt auf.)

SIEGMUND
(embracing Sieglinde with ardour)
Yes, loveliest bride,
I am that friend;
both weapon and wife I claim!
Fierce in my breast
blazes the vow
that binds me ever to you.
For all that I've sought
I see now in you;
in you, all things
I longed for are found.
Though you were shamed,
though sad was my life,
though I was outlawed,
and you were disgraced,
joyful vengeance
calls us to gladness!
I laugh now
in fullest delight,
as I embrace your glory,
feel your beating heart!
(The large door flies open.)

SIEGLINDE
(fährt erschrocken zusammen und reißt sich los.)
Ha, wer ging? Wer kam herein?
(Die Tür bleibt weit geöffnet: außen herrliche Frühlingsnacht; der Vollmond leuchtet herein und wirft sein helles Licht auf das Paar, das so sich plötzlich in voller Deutlichkeit wahrnehmen kann.)

SIEGLINDE
(starts in alarm, and tears herself away.)
Ah, who went? or who has come?
(The door remains open; outside, a glorious spring night; the full moon shines in, throwing its bright light on the pair, so that suddenly they can fully and clearly see each other.)

SIEGMUND
(in leiser Entzückung)
Keiner ging,
doch einer kam:
siehe, der Lenz
lacht in den Saal!
(Siegmund zieht Sieglinde mit sanfter Gewalt zu sich auf das Lager, so daß sie neben ihm zu sitzen kommt. Wachsende Helligkeit des Mondscheines.)
Winterstürme wichen
dem Wonnemond,
in mildem Lichte
leuchtet der Lenz;
auf linden Lüften
leicht und lieblich,
Wunder webend
er sich wiegt:
durch Wald und Auen
weht sein Atem,
weit geöffnet
lacht sein Aug'.
Aus sel'ger Vöglein Sange
süß er tönt,
holde Düfte
haucht er aus:
seinem warmen Blut entblühen
wonnige Blumen,
Keim und Sproß
entspringt seiner Kraft.
Mit zarter Waffen Zier
bezwingt er die Welt;
Winter und Sturm wichen
der starken Wehr:
Wohl mußte den tapfern Streichen
die strenge Türe auch weichen,
die trotzig und starr
uns—trennte von ihm.
Zu seiner Schwester
schwang er sich her;
die Liebe lockte den Lenz:
in unsrem Busen
barg sie sich tief;
nun lacht sie selig dem Licht.
Die bräutliche Schwester
befreite der Bruder;
zertrümmert liegt,
was sie je getrennt;

SIEGMUND
(in gentle ecstasy)
No one went—
but one has come:
see him, the Spring
smiles on our love!
(Siegmund draws Sieglinde to him on the couch with tender vehemence, so that she sits beside him. Increasing brilliance of the moonlight.)
Winter storms have vanished
at Spring's command;
in gentle radiance
sparkles the Spring,
on balmy breezes,
light and lovely,
working wonders
on his way;
on wood and meadow
softly breathing;
wide and smiling
are his eyes.
The songs of happy birds
reflect his voice;
sweet the fragrance
of his breath;
from his ardent blood the flowers
are joyfully blooming;
buds and blooms
have sprung at his call.
He waves his wand of magic
over the world;
winter and storm yield
to his strong command:
as soon as his word was spoken
the doors that barred him were broken,
for how could they keep us
parted from him?
To clasp his sister
here he has flown;
for Love called to the Spring;
and Love lay hidden
deep in our hearts;
but now she laughs to the light.
The bride and sister
is freed by her brother;
the barriers fall
that held them apart;

jauchzend grüßt sich
das junge Paar:
vereint sind Liebe und Lenz!

SIEGLINDE
Du bist der Lenz,
nach dem ich verlangte
in frostigen Winters Frist.
Dich grüßte mein Herz
mit heiligem Grau'n,
als dein Blick zuerst mir erblühte.
Fremdes nur sah ich von je,
freundlos war mir das Nahe;
als hätt' ich nie es gekannt,
war, was immer mir kam.
Doch dich kannt' ich
deutlich und klar:
als mein Auge dich sah,
warst du mein Eigen;
was im Busen ich barg,
was ich bin,
hell wie der Tag
taucht' es mir auf,
wie tönender Schall
schlug's an mein Ohr,
als in frostig öder Fremde
zuerst ich den Freund ersah.
(Sie hängt sich entzückt an seinen Hals und blickt ihm nahe ins Gesicht.)

SIEGMUND
(mit Hingerissenheit)
O süßeste Wonne!
Seligstes Weib!

SIEGLINDE
(dicht an seinen Augen)
O laß in Nähe
zu dir mich neigen,
daß hell ich schaue
den hehren Schein,
der dir aus Aug'
und Antlitz bricht
und so süß die Sinne mir zwingt.

SIEGMUND
Im Lenzesmond

joyful greeting
as now they meet:
united are Love and Spring!

SIEGLINDE
You are the Spring,
that Spring I have yearned for
in frost and in winter's ice.
My heart felt the spell,
grew warm when you came;
when my eyes beheld you, I knew you.
Everything used to be strange,
friendless all that was round me;
like far off things and unknown,
all that ever drew near.
But you came
and all was clear:
for I knew you were mine
when I beheld you.
What I hid in my heart,
all I am,
bright as the day,
all was revealed;
the sound of this truth
rang in my ear,
when in winter's frosty desert
my eyes first beheld my friend.
(She throws her arms around his neck, enraptured, and gazes closely into his face.)

SIEGMUND
(carried away)
Oh sweetest enchantment,
woman most blessed!

SIEGLINDE
(close to his eyes)
Oh hold me near you,
and clasp me to you,
to see more clearly
that holy light
that shines from eyes,
from countenance,
and so sweetly steals to my heart.

SIEGMUND
The Spring's fair moon

leuchtest du hell;
hehr umwebt dich
das Wellenhaar:
Was mich berückt,
errat ich nun leicht—
denn wonnig weidet mein Blick.

shines on you here,
crowns with glory
your lovely hair.
Ah, now I know
what captured my heart;
my glances feast in delight.

SIEGLINDE
(schlägt ihm die Locken von der Stirn zurück und betrachtet ihn staunend.)
Wie dir die Stirn
so offen steht,
der Adern Geäst
in den Schläfen sich schlingt!
Mir zagt es vor der Wonne,
die mich entzückt!
Ein Wunder will mich gemahnen:
den heut zuerst ich erschaut,
mein Auge sah dich schon!

SIEGLINDE
(pushes the locks back from his brow, and gazes at him in astonishment.)
Your noble brow
is broad and clear;
its delicate veins
with my fingers I trace!
I tremble with the rapture
of my delight!
A marvel stirs in my memory:
although you came but today,
I've seen your face before!

SIEGMUND
Ein Minnetraum
gemahnt auch mich:
in heißem Sehnen
sah ich dich schon!

SIEGMUND
I know your dream,
I feel it too:
in ardent yearning
you were my dream!

SIEGLINDE
Im Bach erblickt' ich
mein eigen Bild—
und jetzt gewahr ich es wieder:
wie einst dem Teich es enttaucht,
bietest mein Bild mir nun du!

SIEGLINDE
The stream has shown
my reflected face—
and now I find it before me;
in you I see it again,
just as it shone from the stream!

SIEGMUND
Du bist das Bild,
das ich in mir barg.

SIEGMUND
Yours is the face
that I knew in my heart.

SIEGLINDE
(den Blick schnell abwendend)
O still! Laß mich
der Stimme lauschen:
mich dünkt, ihren Klang
hört' ich als Kind—
Doch nein, ich hörte sie neulich,
(aufgeregt)
als meiner Stimme Schall
mir widerhallte der Wald.

SIEGLINDE
(quickly turning her eyes away from him)
Be still! Again
that voice is sounding,
the voice that I heard
once as a child—
But no! I know when I heard it:
(excitedly)
when through the woods I called,
and echo called in reply.

SIEGMUND
O lieblichste Laute,
denen ich lausche!

SIEGLINDE
(ihm wieder in die Augen spähend)
Deines Auges Glut
erglänzte mir schon:
So blickte der Greis
grüßend auf mich,
als der Traurigen Trost er gab.
An dem Blick
erkannt' ihn sein Kind—
schon wollt' ich beim Namen ihn
[nennen!
(Sie hält inne und fährt dann leise fort.)
Wehwalt heißt du fürwahr?

SIEGMUND
Nicht heiß ich so,
seit du mich liebst:
nun walt ich der hehrsten Wonnen!

SIEGLINDE
Und Friedmund darfst du
froh dich nicht nennen?

SIEGMUND
Nenne mich du,
wie du liebst, daß ich heiße:
den Namen nehm ich von dir!

SIEGLINDE
Doch nanntest du Wolfe den Vater?

SIEGMUND
Ein Wolf war er feigen Füchsen!
Doch dem so stolz
strahlte das Auge,
wie, Herrliche, hehr dir es strahlt,
der war: Wälse genannt.

SIEGLINDE
(außer sich)
War Wälse dein Vater
und bist du ein Wälsung,
stieß er für dich
sein Schwert in den Stamm—

SIEGMUND
Oh loveliest music,
voice that I longed for!

SIEGLINDE
(again gazing into his eyes)
And your gleaming glance,
I've seen it before:
the stranger in grey
gazed on me thus
when he came to console my grief.
By that glance
his child knew him well—
I knew by what name I should call him!

(She pauses a moment and then continues softly.)
Wehwalt, is that what you're called?

SIEGMUND
No more that name,
now you are mine:
my sorrow has turned to gladness!

SIEGLINDE
And Friedmund was no name
for a sufferer.

SIEGMUND
Name me yourself;
by what name can you love me?
My name, I'll take it from you!

SIEGLINDE
You told me that Wolf was your father.

SIEGMUND
A Wolf when he hunted foxes!
But when his eye
shone on me proudly,
as your eyes shine on me now,
why then—Wälse his name.

SIEGLINDE
(beside herself)
Was Wälse your father,
and are you a Wälsung?
Then it is yours,
that sword in the tree!

so laß mich dich heißen,
wie ich dich liebe:
Siegmund—
so nenn ich dich!

SIEGMUND
(springt auf, eilt auf den Stamm zu, und faßt den Schwertgriff.)
Siegmund heiß ich
und Siegmund bin ich!
Bezeug' es dies Schwert,
das zaglos ich halte!
Wälse verhieß mir,
in höchster Not
fänd' ich es einst:
ich faß es nun!
Heiligster Minne
höchste Not,
sehnender Liebe
sehrende Not
brennt mir hell in der Brust,
drängt zu Tat und Tod:
Notung! Notung!
So nenn ich dich, Schwert.
Notung! Notung!
Neidlicher Stahl!
Zeig deiner Schärfe
schneidenden Zahn:
heraus aus der Scheide zu mir!
(Er zieht mit einem gewaltigen Zuck das Schwert aus dem Stamme und zeigt es der von Staunen und Entzücken erfaßten Sieglinde.)
Siegmund, den Wälsung,
siehst du, Weib!
Als Brautgabe
bringt er dies Schwert:
so freit er sich
die seligste Frau;
dem Feindeshaus
entführt er dich so.
Fern von hier
folge mir nun,
fort in des Lenzes
lachendes Haus:
dort schützt dich Notung, das Schwert,
wenn Siegmund dir liebend erlag!
(Er hat sie umfaßt, um sie mit sich fortzuziehen.)

So now let me name you
as I have loved you:
Siegmund—
that is your name!

SIEGMUND
(leaps up, hurries to the trunk, and grasps the sword hilt.)
Siegmund call me,
and Siegmund am I!
The proof is the sword,
my hand soon shall hold it!
Promised by Wälse
in hour of need,
now it is found;
I grasp it now!
Holiest love
in highest need,
yearning desire
in longing and need,
burning bright in my breast,
drives to deeds and death.
Notung! Notung!
so name I the sword!
Notung! Notung!
Bright, shining steel.
Show me your sharpness,
glorious blade!
Come forth from the scabbard to me!
(With a powerful effort, Siegmund draws the sword from the tree, and shows it to the astonished and enraptured Sieglinde.)
Siegmund, the Wälsung,
here you see!
As bride-gift
he brings you this sword;
he claims with it
his loveliest bride;
and from this house
he leads her away.
Far from here,
follow me now,
forth to the laughing
land of bright Spring.
Your guard is Notung, the sword,
should Siegmund die, conquered by love!
(He has embraced her, to draw her away with him.)

SIEGLINDE
(reißt sich in höchster Trunkenheit von ihm los und stellt sich ihm gegenüber.)
Bist du Siegmund,
den ich hier sehe—
Sieglinde bin ich,
die dich ersehnt:
Die eigne Schwester
gewannst du zu eins mit dem Schwert!

SIEGMUND
Braut und Schwester
bist du dem Bruder—
so blühe denn, Wälsungenblut!
(Er zieht sie mit wütender Glut an sich, sie sinkt mit einem Schrei an seine Brust. Der Vorhang fällt schnell.)

SIEGLINDE
(in highest excitement tears herself away, and stands before him.)
Is this Siegmund,
standing before me?
Sieglinde am I;
I longed for you.
Your own dear sister
and bride you have won with the sword!

SIEGMUND
Bride and sister
be to your brother;
the blood of these Wälsungs is blessed!
(He draws her to him with passionate fervour; with a cry, she falls on his breast. The curtain falls quickly.)

Zweiter Aufzug

Wildes Felsengebirge

Im Hintergrunde zieht sich von unten her eine Schlucht herauf, die auf ein erhöhtes Felsjoch mündet; von diesem senkt sich der Boden dem Vordergrund zu wieder abwärts.

Act Two

A Wild, Craggy Place

In the background, a gorge slopes up from below to a high ridge of rocks, from which the ground again sinks to the front.

Erste Szene

Wotan, kriegerisch gewaffnet, mit dem Speer; vor ihm Brünnhilde, als Walküre, ebenfalls in voller Waffenrüstung

WOTAN

Nun zäume dein Roß,
reisige Maid!
Bald entbrennt
brünstiger Streit:
Brünnhilde stürme zum Kampf,
dem Wälsung kiese sie Sieg!

Scene One

Wotan, armed for battle, carrying his spear; before him Brünnhilde, as a Valkyrie, likewise fully armed

WOTAN

Go bridle your horse,
warrior maid!
Seize your shield;
battle is near.
Brünnhilde's off to the fight,
the Wälsung is victor today!

Hunding wähle sich,
wem er gehört;
nach Walhall taugt er mir nicht.
Drum rüstig und rasch
reite zur Wal!

BRÜNNHILDE
(jauchzend von Fels zu Fels die Höhe rechts hinaufspringend)
Hojotoho! Hojotoho!
Heiaha! Heiaha!
Hojotoho! Heiaha!
(Sie hält auf einer hohen Felsspitze an, blickt in die hintere Schlucht hinab und ruft zu Wotan zurück.)
Dir rat ich, Vater,
rüste dich selbst;
harten Sturm
sollst du bestehn.
Fricka naht, deine Frau,
im Wagen mit dem Widdergespann.
Hei, wie die goldne
Geißel sie schwingt!
Die armen Tiere
ächzen vor Angst;
wild rasseln die Räder;
zornig fährt sie zum Zank!
In solchem Strauße
streit ich nicht gern,
lieb ich auch mutiger
Männer Schlacht.
Drum sieh, wie den Sturm du bestehst:
ich Lustige laß dich im Stich!
Hojotoho! Hojotoho!
Heiaha! Heiaha!
Heiahaha!
(Brünnhilde verschwindet hinter der Gebirgshöhe zur Seite. In einem mit zwei Widdern bespannten Wagen langt Fricka aus der Schlucht auf dem Felsjoche an: dort hält sie rasch an und steigt aus. Sie schreitet heftig in den Vordergrund auf Wotan zu.)

WOTAN
(Fricka auf sich zuschreiten sehend, für sich)
Der alte Sturm,
die alte Müh'!
Doch stand muß ich hier halten!

Hunding falls to him;
leave him to lie;
for Walhall he is not fit.
So hasten away,
ride to the field!

BRÜNNHILDE
(shouting as she leaps from rock to rock up to the heights on the right)
Hoyotoho! Hoyotoho!
Hiaha! Hiaha!
Hoyotoho! Hiaha!
(On a high peak she stops, looks into the gorge at the back, and calls back to Wotan.)
I warn you, father,
look to yourself;
brave the storm
blowing your way
Fricka's coming—your wife;
she's drawn along by two of her rams.
Hi! How she swings
her glittering whip!
The wretched beasts
are sweating with fear;
wheels rattle and rumble,
whirl her on to the fray.
A woman's battle
is not to my taste,
rather the clangour
of martial arms.
Be sure that you weather the storm;
I'm happy to leave it to you!
Hoyotoho! Hoyotoho!
Hiaha! Hiaha!
Hiahaha!
(Brünnhilde disappears behind the mountain height at the side. Fricka, in a chariot drawn by two rams, comes up from the gorge to the top of the rocky ridge, where she stops suddenly and alights. She strides impetuously towards Wotan in the foreground.)

WOTAN
(seeing Fricka approaching; aside)
The usual storm,
the usual strife!
But here I must be steadfast!

FRICKA
(je näher sie kommt, mäßigt sie den Schritt und stellt sich mit Würde vor Wotan hin.)
Wo in den Bergen du dich birgst,
der Gattin Blick zu entgehn,
einsam hier
such ich dich auf,
daß Hilfe du mir verhießest.

WOTAN
Was Fricka kümmert,
künde sie frei.

FRICKA
Ich vernahm Hundings Not,
um Rache rief er mich an:
der Ehe Hüterin
hörte ihn,
verhieß streng
zu strafen die Tat
des frech frevelnden Paars,
das kühn den Gatten gekränkt.

WOTAN
Was so Schlimmes
schuf das Paar,
das liebend einte der Lenz?
Der Minne Zauber
entzückte sie:
wer büßt mir der Minne Macht?

FRICKA
Wie töricht und taub du dich stellst,
als wüßtest fürwahr du nicht,
daß um der Ehe
heiligen Eid,
den hart gekränkten, ich klage!

WOTAN
Unheilig
acht ich den Eid,
der Unliebende eint;
und mir wahrlich
mute nicht zu,
daß mit Zwang ich halte,
was dir nicht haftet:
denn wo kühn Kräfte sich regen,

FRICKA
(as she approaches, moderates her pace and places herself with dignity before Wotan.)
In the mountains where you hide,
to shun the sight of your wife,
here I have
found you at last,
to claim the help that you owe me.

WOTAN
Let Fricka's troubles
freely be told.

FRICKA
I have heard Hunding's cry:
Revenge the wrong they have done!
As wedlock's guardian
I answered him.
I swore
I would punish the deed
this pair dared to commit,
who wronged a husband and me.

WOTAN
But what evil
have they done?
The Spring enticed them to love.
The power of love
overcame them both;
and who can resist that power?

FRICKA
Pretend that you don't understand!
And yet you know all too well
that I have come
to avenge marriage vows,
the holy vows they have broken!

WOTAN
Unholy
call I the vows
that bind unloving hearts;
and do you
expect me to act,
to exert my power
where yours is helpless?
For where bold spirits are moving,

da rat ich offen zum Krieg.

FRICKA
Achtest du rühmlich
der Ehe Bruch,
so prahle nun weiter
und preis es heilig,
daß Blutschande entblüht
dem Bund eines Zwillingspaars!
Mir schaudert das Herz,
es schwindelt mein Hirn:
bräutlich umfing
die Schwester der Bruder!
Wann ward es erlebt,
daß leiblich Geschwister sich liebten?

WOTAN
Heut—hast du's erlebt!
Erfahre so,
was von selbst sich fügt,
sei zuvor auch noch nie es geschehn.
Daß jene sich lieben,
leuchtet dir hell;
drum höre redlichen Rat:
Soll süße Lust
deinen Segen dir lohnen,
so segne, lachend der Liebe,
Siegmunds und Sieglindes Bund!

FRICKA
(in höchste Entrüstung ausbrechend)
So ist es denn aus
mit den ewigen Göttern,
seit du die wilden
Wälsungen zeugtest?
Heraus sagt' ich's;
traf ich den Sinn?
Nichts gilt dir der Hehren
heilige Sippe;
hin wirfst du alles,
was einst du geachtet;
zerreißest die Bande,
die selbst du gebunden,
lösest lachend
des Himmels Haft:
daß nach Lust und Laune nur walte
dies frevelnde Zwillingspaar,

I stir them ever to strife.

FRICKA
If you encourage
adulterous love,
then proudly go further
and praise as holy
the incest there has been,
the love of a pair of twins!
My senses are shocked,
my mind is amazed—
bridal embrace
of sister and brother!
When came it to pass
that brother and sister were lovers?

WOTAN
Now it's come to pass!
And learn from this
that a thing may happen
although it's not happened before.
They love one another,
as you must know;
so hear my words of advice:
Since Fricka is famed
for her blessing on lovers,
bestow on them your blessing,
on Siegmund's and Sieglinde's love!

FRICKA
(breaking out in deep indignation)
So this is the end
of the gods and their glory,
now you have fathered
Wölfing the Wälsung?
I speak frankly;
am I not right?
The race of the gods
by you is forgotten!
You cast aside
what you once held in honour;
you break every bond
that you tied to unite us;
loosen, laughing,
your hold on heaven!
that the lustful lovers may flourish,
this sinful incestuous pair,

deiner Untreue zuchtlose Frucht!
Oh, was klag ich
um Ehe und Eid,
da zuerst du selbst sie versehrt.
Die treue Gattin
trogest du stets;
wo eine Tiefe,
wo eine Höhe,
dahin lugte
lüstern dein Blick,
wie des Wechsels Lust du gewännst
und höhnend kränktest mein Herz.
Trauernden Sinnes
mußt' ich's ertragen,
zogst du zur Schlacht
mit den schlimmen Mädchen,
die wilder Minne
Bund dir gebar:
denn dein Weib noch scheutest du so,
daß der Walküren Schar
und Brünnhilde selbst,
deines Wunsches Braut,
in Gehorsam der Herrin du gabst.
Doch jetzt, da dir neue
Namen gefielen,
als »Wälse« wölfisch
im Walde du schweiftest;
jetzt, da zu niedrigster
Schmach du dich neigtest,
gemeiner Menschen
ein Paar zu erzeugen:
jetzt dem Wurfe der Wölfin
wirfst du zu Füßen dein Weib!
So führ es denn aus!
Fülle das Maß!
Die Betrogne laß auch zertreten!

WOTAN
(ruhig)
Nichts lerntest du,
wollt' ich dich lehren,
was nie du erkennen kannst,
eh' nicht ertagte die Tat.
Stets Gewohntes
nur magst du verstehn:
doch was noch nie sich traf,
danach trachtet mein Sinn.

who were born as the fruit of your shame!
Oh, why mourn
over virtue and vows,
when they first were broken by you!
Your faithful wife
you've always betrayed;
down in the caverns,
high on the mountains,
your glance searched
and lusted for love,
where your raving fancy might lead you.
Your scorn has broken my heart.
Sad in my spirit,
I had to see you
leading to battle
those barbarous maidens
your lawless love
had brought into being;
but you still respected your wife,
for the Valkyrie brood,
and Brünnhild herself
whom you love so well—
they were bound in obedience to me.
But now a new name
has taken your fancy,
and 'Wälse' prowls
like a wolf through the woodland;
now you have stooped
to the depth of dishonour,
a common woman
has borne you her children:
now to whelps of a she-wolf
you would abandon your wife!
Go on with your work!
Fill now my cup!
You betrayed me; let me be trampled!

WOTAN
(quietly)
You never learn
what I would teach you,
to try to conceive a deed
before that deed comes to pass.
Your concern
is for things that have been;
but what is still to come—
to that turn all my thoughts.

Eines höre!
Not tut ein Held,
der, ledig göttlichen Schutzes,
sich löse vom Göttergesetz.
So nur taugt er
zu wirken die Tat,
die, wie not sie den Göttern,
dem Gott doch zu wirken verwehrt.

FRICKA
Mit tiefem Sinne
willst du mich täuschen:
was Hehres sollten
Helden je wirken,
das ihren Göttern wäre verwehrt,
deren Gunst in ihnen nur wirkt?

WOTAN
Ihres eignen Mutes
achtest du nicht?

FRICKA
Wer hauchte Menschen ihn ein?
Wer hellte den Blöden den Blick?
In deinem Schutz
scheinen sie stark,
durch deinen Stachel
streben sie auf:
du reizest sie einzig,
die so mir Ew'gen du rühmst.
Mit neuer List
willst du mich belügen,
durch neue Ränke
mir jetzt entrinnen;
doch diesen Wälsung
gewinnst du dir nicht:
in ihm treff ich nur dich,
denn durch dich trotzt er allein.

WOTAN
(ergriffen)
In wildem Leiden
erwuchs er sich selbst:
mein Schutz schirmte ihn nie.

FRICKA
So schütz auch heut ihn nicht!

Hear this one thing!
We need a man
who lives without our protection,
who is free from the rule of the gods.
He alone
can accomplish the deed,
which, although it will save us,
the gods are forbidden to do.

FRICKA
With crafty reasoning
you would deceive me.
What marvel can be worked
by these mortals?
What is this deed which gods cannot do?
And who gives the mortals their power?

WOTAN
Do you rate their own
achievement so low?

FRICKA
Who breathed the soul into men?
Who kindled the light in their eyes?
When you are near,
then they are strong;
when you inspire them,
then they can strive.
You fill them with daring,
then sing their praises to me.
With new deceits
you are trying to trick me;
with new excuses
you would escape me;
but for this Wälsung
you plead all in vain:
in him I find only you;
what he does, he does through you.

WOTAN
(with emotion)
In wildest sorrow
he grew by himself;
and I gave him no help.

FRICKA
Then do not help him now!

Nimm ihm das Schwert,
das du ihm geschenkt!

WOTAN
Das Schwert?

FRICKA
Ja, das Schwert,
das zauberstark
zuckende Schwert,
das du Gott dem Sohne gabst.

WOTAN
(heftig)
Siegmund gewann es sich
(mit unterdrücktem Beben)
selbst in der Not.
(Wotan drückt in seiner ganzen Haltung von hier an einen immer wachsenden unheimlichen, tiefen Unmut aus.)

FRICKA
(eifrig fortfahrend)
Du schufst ihm die Not
wie das neidliche Schwert.
Willst du mich täuschen,
die Tag und Nacht
auf den Fersen dir folgt?
Für ihn stießest du
das Schwert in den Stamm,
du verhießest ihm
die hehre Wehr:
willst du es leugnen,
daß nur deine List
ihn lockte, wo er es fänd'?
(Wotan fährt mit einer grimmigen Gebärde auf. Fricka immer sicherer, da sie den Eindruck gewahrt, den sie auf Wotan hervorgebracht hat.)
Mit Unfreien
streitet kein Edler,
den Frevler straft nur der Freie.
Wider deine Kraft
führt' ich wohl Krieg:
doch Siegmund verfiel mir als Knecht!
(neue heftige Gebärde Wotans, dann Versinken in das Gefühl seiner Ohnmacht)
Der dir als Herren
hörig und eigen,

Take back the sword
you placed in his hand.

WOTAN
The sword?

FRICKA
Yes, the sword,
the magical,
glittering sword,
that the god has given his son!

WOTAN
(violently)
Siegmund has won it himself
(with a suppressed shudder)
in his need.
(From this point, Wotan's whole demeanour expresses an ever-increasing uneasy, profound dejection.)

FRICKA
(continuing eagerly)
You sent him the need,
as you sent him the sword.
Can you deceive me,
when day and night
I have watched every step?
For him you prepared
that sword in the tree,
and you promised him
it would be found.
Can you deny it,
that your hand alone
has led him where it was found?
(Wotan makes a wrathful gesture. Fricka becomes ever more confident, as she sees the impression she has made on Wotan.)
With bondsmen
the gods do not battle;
rebellious slaves must be punished.
As an equal
I argue with you;
but Siegmund I claim as my slave.
(Wotan makes another vehement gesture, and then is overcome by the sense of his powerlessness.)
For soul and body,
he is your servant,

gehorchen soll ihm
dein ewig Gemahl?
Soll mich in Schmach
der Niedrigste schmähen,
dem Frechen zum Sporn,
dem Freien zum Spott?
Das kann mein Gatte nicht wollen,
die Göttin entweiht er nicht so!

and now must I
be subjected to him?
Am I his slave,
to smile when he scorns me?
despised by the world,
and mocked by the free?
And can my husband allow me,
his goddess, to suffer this shame?

WOTAN
(finster)
Was verlangst du?

WOTAN
(gloomy)
What must I do?

FRICKA
Laß von dem Wälsung!

FRICKA
Abandon the Wälsung!

WOTAN
(mit gedämpfter Stimme)
Er geh seines Wegs.

WOTAN
(with muffled voice)
He goes his own way.

FRICKA
Doch du schütze ihn nicht,
wenn zur Schlacht ihn der Rächer ruft!

FRICKA
And you'll give him no help
when he's called to defend his life?

WOTAN
Ich schütze ihn nicht.

WOTAN
I'll give him no help.

FRICKA
Sieh mir ins Auge,
sinne nicht Trug:
die Walküre wend auch von ihm!

FRICKA
Do not deceive me;
look in my eyes;
the Valkyrie leaves him to die!

WOTAN
Die Walküre walte frei.

WOTAN
The Valkyrie is free to choose.

FRICKA
Nicht doch; deinen Willen
vollbringt sie allein:
verbiete ihr Siegmunds Sieg!

FRICKA
Not so; your commandment
is all she obeys:
command her that Siegmund dies!

WOTAN
(in heftigen inneren Kampf ausbrechend)
Ich kann ihn nicht fällen:
er fand mein Schwert!

WOTAN
(breaking out after a violent inner struggle)
I cannot destroy him;
he found my sword!

FRICKA
Entzieh dem den Zauber,
zerknick es dem Knecht!
Schutzlos schau' ihn der Feind!

FRICKA
Destroy all its magic,
command it to break!
Siegmund falls in the fight!

BRÜNNHILDE
(noch unsichtbar von der Höhe her)
Heiaha! Heiaha! Hojotoho!

FRICKA
Dort kommt deine kühne Maid;
jauchzend jagt sie daher.

BRÜNNHILDE
Heiaha! Heiaha!
Heiohotojo! Hotojoha!

WOTAN
(dumpf für sich)
Ich rief sie für Siegmund zu Roß!
(Brünnhilde erscheint mit ihrem Roß auf dem Felsenpfade rechts. Als sie Fricka gewahrt, bricht sie schnell ab und geleitet ihr Roß still und langsam während des Folgenden den Felsweg herab; dort birgt sie es dann in einer Höhle.)

FRICKA
Deiner ew'gen Gattin
heilige Ehre
beschirme heut ihr Schild!
Von Menschen verlacht,
verlustig der Macht,
gingen wir Götter zugrund:
würde heut nicht hehr
und herrlich mein Recht
gerächt von der mutigen Maid.
Der Wälsung fällt meiner Ehre!
Empfah ich von Wotan den Eid?

WOTAN
(in furchtbarem Unmut und innerem Grimm auf einen Felsensitz sich werfend)
Nimm den Eid!
(Fricka schreitet dem Hintergrunde zu: dort begegnet sie Brünnhilde und hält einen Augenblick vor ihr an.)

FRICKA
(zu Brünnhilde)
Heervater harret dein:
laß ihn dir künden,
wie das Los er gekiest!
(Sie besteigt den Wagen und fährt schnell davon.)

BRÜNNHILDE
(still invisible, calling from the heights)
Hiaha! Hiaha! Hoyotoho!

FRICKA
And here is your valiant maid,
joyfully coming this way.

BRÜNNHILDE
Hiaha! Hiaha!
Hiohotoyo! Hotoyoha!

WOTAN
(dejected, to himself)
To fight now for Siegmund she rides.
(Brünnhilde appears, with her horse, on the rocky path to the right. On seeing Fricka, she breaks off suddenly and, during the following, she slowly, silently leads her horse down the mountain path, and then stables it in a cave.)

FRICKA
And her shield today
must shelter the honour
of your immortal wife!
For men in their scorn
would laugh at our might,
jeer at the glorious gods,
if today your warlike daughter
should not revenge
all the wrongs of your wife!
The Wälsung dies for my honour!
Will Wotan now give me his oath?

WOTAN
(throwing himself on to a rocky seat in terrible dejection and inner anger)
Take my oath!
(Fricka strides towards the back: there she meets Brünnhilde and stops for a moment before her.)

FRICKA
(to Brünnhilde)
Wotan is waiting there:
let him instruct you
how the lot must be cast.
(She mounts her chariot and drives quickly away.)

Zweite Szene

Brünnhilde tritt mit besorgter Miene verwundert vor Wotan, der, auf dem Felssitz zurückgelehnt, das Haupt auf die Hand gestützt, in finsteres Brüten versunken ist.

BRÜNNHILDE
Schlimm, fürcht ich,
schloß der Streit,
lachte Fricka dem Lose.
Vater, was soll
dein Kind erfahren?
Trübe scheinst du und traurig!

WOTAN
(läßt den Arm machtlos sinken und den Kopf in den Nacken fallen.)
In eigner Fessel
fing ich mich,
ich Unfreiester aller!

BRÜNNHILDE
So sah ich dich nie!
Was nagt dir das Herz?

WOTAN
(Von hier an steigert sich Wotans Ausdruck und Gebärde bis zum furchtbarsten Ausbruch.)

O heilige Schmach!
O schmählicher Harm!
Götternot!
Götternot!
Endloser Grimm!
Ewiger Gram!
Der Traurigste bin ich von allen!

BRÜNNHILDE
(wirft erschrocken Schild, Speer und Helm von sich und läßt sich mit besorgter Zutraulichkeit zu Wotans Füßen nieder.)
Vater! Vater!
Sage, was ist dir?
Wie erschreckst du mit Sorge dein Kind?
Vertraue mir!
Ich bin dir treu:

Scene Two

Brünnhilde advances with astonished and anxious mien to Wotan, who, leaning back on the rocky seat, his head propped on his hand, is sunk in gloomy brooding.

BRÜNNHILDE
Fricka
has won the fight;
since she smiles at the outcome.
Father, what news
have you to tell me?
Why this sadness and sorrow?

WOTAN
(drops his arm helplessly and lets his head sink on his breast.)
I forged the fetters;
now I'm bound.
I, least free of all living!

BRÜNNHILDE
What troubles you so;
what new grief is this?

WOTAN
(whose expression and gestures grow in intensity from this point, until they culminate in a fearful outburst)
Oh infinite shame!
Oh shameful distress!
Gods' despair!
Gods' despair!
Endless remorse!
Grief evermore!
The saddest of beings is Wotan!

BRÜNNHILDE
(terrified, throws shield, spear and helmet from her and sinks at Wotan's feet in anxious solicitude.)
Father! Father!
Tell me, what is it?
For your daughter is filled with dismay!
Oh trust in me!
you know I'm true!

sieh, Brünnhilde bittet!
(Sie legt traulich und ängstlich Haupt und Hände ihm auf Knie und Schoß.)

WOTAN
(blickt ihr lange ins Auge; dann streichelt er ihr mit unwillkürlicher Zärtlichkeit die Locken. Wie aus tiefen Sinnen zu sich kommend, beginnt er leise:)
Laß ich's verlauten,
lös ich dann nicht
meines Willens haltenden Haft?

BRÜNNHILDE
(ihm ebenso erwidernd)
Zu Wotans Willen sprichst du,
sagst du mir, was du willst;
wer bin ich,
wär' ich dein Wille nicht?

WOTAN
(sehr leise)
Was deinem in Worten ich künde,
unausgesprochen
bleib es denn ewig:
mit mir nur rat ich,
red ich zu dir.
(Mit noch gedämpfterer, schauerlicher Stimme, während er Brünnhilde unverwandt in das Auge blickt.)
Als junger Liebe
Lust mir verblich,
verlangte nach Macht mein Mut:
von jäher Wünsche
Wüten gejagt,
gewann ich mir die Welt.
Unwissend trugvoll,
Untreue übt' ich,
band durch Verträge,
was Unheil barg:
listig verlockte mich Loge,
der schweifend nun verschwand.
Von der Liebe doch
mocht' ich nicht lassen,
in der Macht verlangt' ich nach Minne.
Den Nacht gebar,
der bange Nibelung,
Alberich, brach ihren Bund;

See, Brünnhilde begs you.
(She lays her head and hands with loving concern on his knees and lap.)

WOTAN
(looks long in her eyes; then he strokes her hair with involuntary tenderness. As if coming to himself out of deep brooding, he begins softly:)
If I should tell you,
might I not lose
the controlling power of my will?

BRÜNNHILDE
(answers him equally softly)
To Wotan's will you're speaking;
you can say what you will;
what am I,
if not your will alone?

WOTAN
(very softly)
These thoughts that I never have uttered,
though I may think them,
still they're unspoken.
I think aloud, then,
speaking to you.
(in a still more muted, fearful voice, while he gazes steadily into Brünnhilde's eyes)
When youth's delightful
pleasures had waned,
I longed in my heart for power;
and driven
by impetuous desires,
I won myself the world;
yet all unwitting,
I acted wrongly;
trusted in treaties
where evil lay,
craftily counselled by Loge,
who lured me on—then left.
Yet the longing
for love would not leave me;
in my power I felt its enchantment.
That child of night,
the cringing Nibelung,
Alberich, broke from its bonds;

er fluchte der Liebe
und gewann durch den Fluch
des Rheines glänzendes Gold
und mit ihm maßlose Macht.
Den Ring, den er schuf,
entriß ich ihm listig;
doch nicht dem Rhein
gab ich ihn zurück:
mit ihm bezahlt' ich
Walhalls Zinnen,
der Burg, die Riesen mir bauten,
aus der ich der Welt nun gebot.
Die alles weiß,
was einstens war,
Erda, die weihlich
weiseste Wala,
riet mir ab von dem Ring,
warnte vor ewigem Ende.
Von dem Ende wollt' ich
mehr noch wissen;
doch schweigend entschwand mir das [Weib.
Da verlor ich den leichten Mut,
zu wissen begehrt' es den Gott:
in den Schoß der Welt
schwang ich mich hinab,
mit Liebeszauber
zwang ich die Wala,
stört' ihres Wissens Stolz,
daß sie Rede nun mir stand.
Kunde empfing ich von ihr;
von mir doch barg sie ein Pfand:
der Welt weisestes Weib
gebar mir, Brünnhilde, dich.
Mit acht Schwestern
zog ich dich auf;
durch euch Walküren
wollt' ich wenden,
was mir die Wala
zu fürchten schuf:
ein schmähliches Ende der Ew'gen.
Daß stark zum Streit
uns fände der Feind,
hieß ich euch Helden mir schaffen:
die herrisch wir sonst
in Gesetzen hielten,
die Männer, denen
den Mut wir gewehrt,

by cursing at love
he was able to gain
the Rhinemaids' glistering gold,
and with that gold, all his power.
The ring that he made,
I cunningly stole it;
but to the Rhine
it was not returned.
I used the gold
to pay for Walhall,
the hall the giants had built me,
the hall where I rule all the world.
For one who knows
all things that were,
Erda, the wisest,
holiest Wala,
warned me away from the ring,
told of eternal disaster.
When I asked her to say more,
she vanished;
in silence she sank from my sight.
Then I lost all my joy in life;
my only desire was to learn.
So I made my way
down into the depths;
by love's enchantment
I conquered the Wala,
humbled her silent pride,
till she told me all she knew.
Wisdom I won from her words;
the Wala demanded a pledge;
the wise Erda conceived
a daughter—Brünnhilde, you.
With eight sisters
you were brought up
as bold Valkyries,
who would avert
the doom that the Wala
had made me fear—
the shameful defeat of the immortals.
Our foes would find us
ready for fight;
you would assemble my army:
the men whom we held
by our laws in bondage,
the mortals, whom we
had curbed in their pride,

die durch trüber Verträge
trügende Bande
zu blindem Gehorsam
wir uns gebunden—
die solltet zu Sturm
und Streit ihr nun stacheln,
ihre Kraft reizen
zu rauhem Krieg,
daß kühner Kämpfer Scharen
ich sammle in Walhalls Saal!

BRÜNNHILDE
Deinen Saal füllten wir weidlich:
viele schon führt' ich dir zu.
Was macht dir nun Sorge,
da nie wir gesäumt?

WOTAN
Ein andres ist's:
achte es wohl,
wes mich die Wala gewarnt!
Durch Alberichs Heer
droht uns das Ende:
mit neidischem Grimm
grollt mir der Niblung:
doch scheu ich nun nicht
seine nächtigen Scharen,
meine Helden schüfen mir Sieg.
Nur wenn je den Ring
zurück er gewänne,
dann wäre Walhall verloren:
Der der Liebe fluchte,
er allein
nützte neidisch
des Ringes Runen
zu aller Edlen
endloser Schmach;
der Helden Mut
entwendet' er mir;
die Kühnen selber
zwäng' er zum Kampf;
mit ihrer Kraft
bekriegte er mich.
Sorgend sann ich nun selbst,
den Ring dem Feind zu entreißen.
Der Riesen einer,
denen ich einst

whom by treacherous treaties,
shameful agreements,
we'd bound in obedience
blindly to serve us;
and yours was the task
to stir them to battle,
and arouse brave men
to ruthless war,
till valiant hosts of heroes
had gathered in Walhall's hall!

BRÜNNHILDE
And that hall is guarded securely:
many a hero I brought.
So why are you troubled,
for we never failed?

WOTAN
There's more to tell;
mark what I say;
hear what the Wala foretold!
For Alberich's host
threatens our downfall;
an envious rage
burns in the Niblung.
Yet I have no fear
of his dusky battalions,
while my heroes keep me secure.
But if once the ring
returns to the Niblung,
he conquers Walhall for ever;
by his curse on love,
he alone
can employ
the ring's enchantment
to bring eternal
shame on the gods;
my heroes' hearts
he'd win for himself;
he'd make my army
bend to his will,
and with that force
give battle to me.
So I pondered a way
to keep the ring from the Niblung.
The giant Fafner,
one of the pair

mit verfluchtem Gold
den Fleiß vergalt:
Fafner hütet den Hort,
um den er den Bruder gefällt.
Ihm müßt' ich den Reif entringen,
den selbst als Zoll ich ihm zahlte.
Doch mit dem ich vertrug,
ihn darf ich nicht treffen;
machtlos vor ihm
erläge mein Mut:
Das sind die Bande,
die mich binden:
der durch Verträge ich Herr,
den Verträgen bin ich nun Knecht.
Nur einer könnte,
was ich nicht darf:
ein Held, dem helfend
nie ich mich neigte;
der fremd dem Gotte,
frei seiner Gunst,
unbewußt,
ohne Geheiß,
aus eigner Not,
mit der eignen Wehr
schüfe die Tat,
die ich scheuen muß,
die nie mein Rat ihm riet,
wünscht sie auch einzig mein Wunsch!
Der, entgegen dem Gott,
für mich föchte,
den freundlichen Feind,
wie fände ich ihn?
Wie schüf' ich den Freien,
den nie ich schirmte,
der in eignem Trotze
der Trauteste mir?
Wie macht' ich den andren,
der nicht mehr ich,
und aus sich wirkte,
was ich nur will?
O göttliche Not!
Gräßliche Schmach!
Zum Ekel find ich
ewig nur mich
in allem, was ich erwirke!
Das andre, das ich ersehne,
das andre erseh ich nie:

for whose work I paid
the fatal gold—
Fafner broods on the gold
he murdered his brother to gain.
From him must the ring be taken,
that ring he won as his wages.
Yet the bond that I made
forbids me to harm him;
if I should try
my power would fail.
These are the fetters
which have bound me;
since by my treaties I rule,
by those treaties I am enslaved.
Yet one can accomplish
what I may not:—
a man, a hero
I've never shielded,
whom I've not prompted,
foe to the gods,
free of soul,
fearless and bold,
who acts alone,
by his own design—
that man can do
what the god must shun;
though never urged by me,
he can achieve my desire!
One at war with all gods,
he can save us!
This friendliest foe,
oh how can I find?
Oh where is this free one,
whom I've not shielded,
who in brave defiance
is dearest to me?
How can I create one,
who, not through me,
but on his own
can achieve my will?
Oh godly distress!
Sorrowful shame!
With loathing
I can find but myself
in all my hand has created!
This free one whom I have longed for,
this free one can never be found;

denn selbst muß der Freie sich schaffen;
Knechte erknet ich mir nur!

BRÜNNHILDE
Doch der Wälsung, Siegmund,
wirkt er nicht selbst?

WOTAN
Wild durchschweift' ich
mit ihm die Wälder;
gegen der Götter Rat
reizte kühn ich ihn auf:
gegen der Götter Rache
schützt ihn nun einzig das Schwert,
(gedehnt und bitter)
das eines Gottes
Gunst ihm beschied.
Wie wollt' ich listig
selbst mich belügen?
So leicht ja entfrug mir
Fricka den Trug:
zu tiefster Scham
durchschaute sie mich!
Ihrem Willen muß ich gewähren.

BRÜNNHILDE
So nimmst du von Siegmund den Sieg?

WOTAN
Ich berührte Alberichs Ring,
gierig hielt ich das Gold!
Der Fluch, den ich floh,
nicht flieht er nun mich:
Was ich liebe, muß ich verlassen,
morden, wen je ich minne,
trügend verraten
wer mir traut!
(Wotans Gebärde geht aus dem Ausdruck des furchtbarsten Schmerzes zu dem der Verzweiflung über.)
Fahre denn hin,
herrische Pracht,
göttlichen Prunkes
prahlende Schmach!
Zusammenbreche,
was ich gebaut!
Auf geb ich mein Werk;

for I have no power to make him;
my hand can only make slaves!

BRÜNNHILDE
But the Wälsung, Siegmund,
is he not free?

WOTAN
Wild and free
was our life together;
I taught him to hate the gods,
urged his heart to rebel.
Now when the gods would kill him,
all that he has is a sword;
(emphatic and bitter)
and yet that sword
was given by a god.
How could I hope
to win by deception?
The lie was revealed
when Fricka appeared:
I stood ashamed;
I had no reply!
So to her I had to surrender.

BRÜNNHILDE
Then Siegmund must fall in his fight?

WOTAN
I set hands on Alberich's ring,
grasped in greed at the gold.
The curse that I fled
has fastened on me.
Though I love him, I must forsake him;
murder the son I love so;
basely betray him,
when he trusts!
(Wotan's demeanour changes from the expression of the most terrible suffering to that of despair.)
Fade from my sight,
honour and fame,
glorious godhead's
glittering shame!
And fall in ruins,
all I have raised!
I leave all my work;

nur eines will ich noch:
  das Ende,
  das Ende!
(Er hält sinnend ein.)
  Und für das Ende
  sorgt Alberich!
  Jetzt versteh ich
  den stummen Sinn
des wilden Wortes der Wala:
»Wenn der Liebe finstrer Feind
zürnend zeugt einen Sohn,
  der Sel'gen Ende
  säumt dann nicht!«
  Vom Niblung jüngst
  vernahm ich die Mär,
daß ein Weib der Zwerg bewältigt,
des Gunst Gold ihm erzwang:
  Des Hasses Frucht
  hegt eine Frau,
  des Neides Kraft
  kreißt ihr im Schoß:
  das Wunder gelang
  dem Liebelosen;
doch der in Lieb' ich freite,
den Freien erlang ich mir nicht.
(mit bitterem Grimm sich aufrichtend)
  So nimm meinen Segen,
  Niblungen-Sohn!
  Was tief mich ekelt,
  dir geb ich's zum Erbe,
der Gottheit nichtigen Glanz:
zernage ihn gierig dein Neid!

BRÜNNHILDE
(erschrocken)
  O sag, künde,
  was soll nun dein Kind?

WOTAN
(bitter)
Fromm streite für Fricka;
hüte ihr Eh' und Eid!
(trocken)
  Was sie erkor,
  das kiese auch ich:
was frommte mir eigner Wille?
Einen Freien kann ich nicht wollen:

but one thing I desire:
  the ending,
  that ending!
(He pauses in thought.)
  And to that ending
  works Alberich!
  Now I grasp
  all the secret sense
that filled the words of the Wala:
'When the dusky foe of love
gains in hatred a son,
  the gods may know
  their doom is near.'
  From Nibelheim
  the tidings have come
that the dwarf has forced a woman;
his gold bought her embrace;
  and she will bear
  Alberich's son;
  the seed of spite
  stirs in her womb;
  this wonder befell
  the loveless Niblung;
while I, who loved so truly,
my free son I never could win.
(rising up in bitter wrath)
  I give you my blessing,
  Nibelung son!
  Let all that irks me
  be yours to inherit;
in Walhall's glorious halls
achieve your unhallowed desires!

BRÜNNHILDE
(alarmed)
  Oh speak, father,
  and tell me my task.

WOTAN
(bitterly)
Fight boldly for Fricka,
guardian of wedlock's vow!
(drily)
  The choice she made,
  that choice must be mine:
my own desires are but useless.
Since that free one I cannot fashion,

für Frickas Knechte kämpfe nun du!	be Fricka's champion, fight for her slave!
BRÜNNHILDE Weh! Nimm reuig zurück das Wort! Du liebst Siegmund; dir zulieb, ich weiß es, schütz ich den Wälsung.	BRÜNNHILDE No, have mercy, take back your word! You love Siegmund; let your love command me: Fight for the Wälsung.
WOTAN Fällen sollst du Siegmund, für Hunding erfechten den Sieg! Hüte dich wohl und halte dich stark, all deiner Kühnheit entbiete im Kampf: ein Siegschwert schwingt Siegmund; schwerlich fällt er dir feig!	WOTAN You must conquer Siegmund, and Hunding must win in the fight! Guard yourself well, be stern and strong; bring all your boldness and force to the fight: a strong sword has Siegmund; he'll not easily yield!
BRÜNNHILDE Den du zu lieben stets mich gelehrt, der in hehrer Tugend dem Herzen dir teuer— gegen ihn zwingt mich nimmer dein zwiespältig Wort!	BRÜNNHILDE Him you have always taught me to love; for his noble courage and valour you love him; if you ask me to kill him, then I shall refuse!
WOTAN Ha, Freche du! Frevelst du mir? Wer bist du, als meines Willens blind wählende Kür? Da mit dir ich tagte, sank ich so tief, daß zum Schimpf der eignen Geschöpfe ich ward? Kennst du, Kind, meinen Zorn? Verzage dein Mut, wenn je zermalmend auf dich stürzte sein Strahl! In meinem Busen berg ich den Grimm, der in Grau'n und Wust wirft eine Welt, die einst zur Lust mir gelacht:	WOTAN Rebellious child! Do as I say! What are you but the obedient, blind slave of my will? When I told my sorrows, sank I so low, that I'm scorned, defied by the child whom I raised? Daughter, know you my wrath? Your soul would be crushed if you confronted that fierce, furious rage! Within my bosom anger is hid, that could lay to waste all of a world— that world I once used to love:

Wehe dem, den er trifft!
Trauer schüf' ihm sein Trotz!
  Drum rat ich dir,
  reize mich nicht!
Besorge, was ich befahl:
  Siegmund falle!
Dies sei der Walküre Werk!
(Er stürmt fort und verschwindet schnell links im Gebirge.)

BRÜNNHILDE
(steht lange erschrocken und betäubt.)
  So sah ich Siegvater nie,
erzürnt' ihn sonst wohl auch ein Zank!
(Sie neigt sich betrübt und nimmt ihre Waffen auf, mit denen sie sich wieder rüstet.)
  Schwer wiegt mir
  der Waffen Wucht.
  Wenn nach Lust ich focht,
  wie waren sie leicht!
  Zu böser Schlacht
schleich ich heut so bang.
(Sie sinnt vor sich hin und seufzt dann auf.)
  Weh, mein Wälsung!
  Im höchsten Leid
muß dich treulos die Treue verlassen!
(Sie wendet sich langsam dem Hintergrunde zu.)

woe to him whom it strikes!
He would pay for his pride!
  I warn you, then,
  rouse not my rage!
But swiftly do my command.
  Siegmund's fated!
That is the Valkyrie's work!
(He storms away, and quickly disappears among the crags to the left.)

BRÜNNHILDE
(stands for a long time, shocked and stunned.)
  So I obey his command;
such rage I've never seen before.
(She stoops down sadly, and takes up her weapons, with which she arms herself again.)
  Shield, spear
  seem to weigh me down!
  In a joyful fight
  I found they were light!
  This hateful task
fills my heart with fear.
(She gazes thoughtfully before her, and sighs.)
  Woe, my Wälsung!
  In deepest sorrow
this true one must falsely betray you!
(She turns slowly towards the back.)

Dritte Szene

Auf dem Bergjoche angelangt, gewahrt Brünnhilde, in die Schlucht hinabblickend, Siegmund und Sieglinde; sie betrachtet die Nahenden einen Augenblick und wendet sich dann in die Höhle zu ihrem Roß, so daß sie dem Zuschauer gänzlich verschwindet. Siegmund und Sieglinde erscheinen auf dem Bergjoche. Sieglinde schreitet hastig voraus; Siegmund sucht sie aufzuhalten.

SIEGMUND
  Raste nur hier;
  gönne dir Ruh!

Scene Three

Arrived at the rocky pass, Brünnhilde, looking into the gorge, perceives Siegmund and Sieglinde; she watches their approach for a moment and then goes into the cave to her horse, disappearing from the audience. Siegmund and Sieglinde appear on the pass. Sieglinde comes hastily forwards; Siegmund tries to restrain her.

SIEGMUND
  Rest for a while;
  stay by my side!

SIEGLINDE
Weiter! Weiter!

SIEGMUND
(umfaßt sie mit sanfter Gewalt.)
Nicht weiter nun!
(Er schließt sie fest an sich.)
Verweile, süßestes Weib!
Aus Wonne-Entzücken
zucktest du auf,
mit jäher Hast
jagtest du fort:
kaum folgt' ich der wilden Flucht;
durch Wald und Flur,
über Fels und Stein,
sprachlos, schweigend
sprangst du dahin,
kein Ruf hielt dich zur Rast!
Ruhe nun aus:
rede zu mir!
Ende des Schweigens Angst!
Sieh, dein Bruder
hält seine Braut:
Siegmund ist dir Gesell!
(Er hat sie unvermerkt nach dem Steinsitze geleitet.)

SIEGLINDE
(blickt Siegmund mit wachsendem Entzücken in die Augen; dann umschlingt sie leidenschaftlich seinen Hals und verweilt so; dann fährt sie mit jähem Schreck auf.)
Hinweg! Hinweg!
Flieh die Entweihte!
Unheilig
umfängt dich ihr Arm;
entehrt, geschändet
schwand dieser Leib:
flieh die Leiche,
lasse sie los!
Der Wind mag sie verwehn,
die ehrlos dem Edlen sich gab!
Da er sie liebend umfing,
da seligste Lust sie fand,
da ganz sie minnte der Mann,
der ganz ihre Minne geweckt:
vor der süßesten Wonne
heiligster Weihe,

SIEGLINDE
Further! Further!

SIEGMUND
(embraces her with gentle force.)
No further now!
(He clasps her firmly to him.)
Oh trust me, sweet, loving bride!
In bliss I embraced you,
then you escaped;
with frenzied haste
fled from my arms,
so fast I could scarce pursue;
through wood and field,
over rock and stone,
speechless, silent,
flying ahead,
I called you all in vain!
Now you must rest:
speak but a word,
ending this silent dread!
See, your brother
shelters his bride:
Siegmund guards you from harm!
(Without her noticing, he has drawn her to the rock seat.)

SIEGLINDE
(gazes with growing rapture into Siegmund's eyes, then throws her arms passionately round his neck and so remains. Then she starts up in sudden terror.)
Away! Away!
Fly from the cursed one!
Unholy
this form that you clasp;
disgraced, dishonoured,
dead in my heart.
Cast me from you,
fling me aside!
Let winds waft me away,
for I have defiled your embrace!
When in your loving embrace,
such blissful delight I found,
you gave me all of your heart,
and all my love was awaked.
In that holy enchantment,
sweetest rapture,

die ganz ihr Sinn
und Seele durchdrang,
Grauen und Schauder
ob gräßlichster Schande
mußte mit Schreck
die Schmähliche fassen,
die je dem Manne gehorcht,
der ohne Minne sie hielt!
Laß die Verfluchte,
laß sie dich fliehn!
Verworfen bin ich,
der Würde bar!
Dir reinstem Manne
muß ich entrinnen,
dir Herrlichem darf ich
nimmer gehören.
Schande bring ich dem Bruder,
Schmach dem freienden Freund!

when all my soul
and senses were won,
loathing and horror
for shameful dishonour
struck with dismay
this traitorous woman,
whom Hunding owned as a wife,
who loveless lay in his arms!
Fly from the cursed one,
far let her flee!
Dishonoured am I,
bereft of grace:
the purest hero
I must abandon,
for how can this guilty wife
dare to love him?
Shame I'd bring to my brother,
Shame to him whom I love!

SIEGMUND
Was je Schande dir schuf,
das büßt nun des Frevlers Blut!
Drum fliehe nicht weiter;
harre des Feindes;
hier soll er mir fallen:
Wenn Notung ihm
das Herz zernagt,
Rache dann hast du erreicht!

SIEGMUND
But this shame you have felt,
this shame shall be paid by blood!
So flee you no further;
Hunding shall find us;
here I shall defeat him:
with Notung
I shall pierce his heart;
vengeance then you will have won!

SIEGLINDE
(schrickt auf und lauscht.)
Horch, die Hörner!
Hörst du den Ruf?
Ringsher tönt
wütend Getös';
aus Wald und Gau
gellt es herauf.
Hunding erwachte
aus hartem Schlaf!
Sippen und Hunde
ruft er zusammen;
mutig gehetzt
heult die Meute,
wild bellt sie zum Himmel
um der Ehe gebrochenen Eid!
(Sie starrt wie wahnsinnig vor sich hin.)
Wo bist du, Siegmund?

SIEGLINDE
(starts up and listens.)
Hark! The horn call!
Do you not hear?
All around,
cries of revenge,
from wood and dale,
ring in my ears.
Hunding has wakened
from heavy sleep!
Hunters, I hear them;
all have assembled:
hard on the trail,
dogs are howling;
they lead the avengers;
they will kill us for breaking a vow!
(As if mad, she stares before her.)
Where are you, Siegmund?

Seh ich dich noch,
brünstig geliebter,
leuchtender Bruder?
Deines Auges Stern
laß noch einmal mir strahlen:
wehre dem Kuß
des verworfnen Weibes nicht!
(Sie hat sich ihm schluchzend an die Brust geworfen, dann schreckt sie ängstlich wieder auf.)
Horch, o horch!
Das ist Hundings Horn!
Seine Meute naht
mit mächt'ger Wehr:
Kein Schwert frommt
vor der Hunde Schwall:
wirf es fort, Siegmund!
Siegmund, wo bist du?
Ha dort! Ich sehe dich!
Schrecklich Gesicht!
Rüden fletschen
die Zähne nach Fleisch;
sie achten nicht
deines edlen Blicks;
bei den Füßen packt dich
das feste Gebiß—
du fällst—
in Stücken zerstaucht das Schwert.—
Die Esche stürzt—
es bricht der Stamm!
Bruder, mein Bruder!
Siegmund—ha!—
(Sie sinkt ohnmächtig in Siegmunds Arme.)

SIEGMUND
Schwester! Geliebte!
(Er lauscht ihrem Atem und überzeugt sich, daß sie noch lebe. Er läßt sie an sich herabgleiten, so daß sie, als er sich selbst zum Sitze niederläßt, mit ihrem Haupt auf seinem Schoß zu ruhen kommt. In dieser Stellung verbleiben beide bis zum Schlusse des folgenden Auftrittes. Langes Schweigen, währenddessen Siegmund mit zärtlicher Sorge über Sieglinde sich hinneigt und mit einem langen Kusse ihr die Stirn küßt.)

Are you still here?
bravest of lovers,
true, tender brother!
With your glorious eyes
for the last time behold me:
do not refuse
this accursed woman's kiss!
(She throws herself sobbing on his breast, then starts up again in terror.)
Hear! Again!
That is Hunding's horn!
And the huntsmen
come to take your life;
no sword helps you
against the hounds;
let it go, Siegmund!
Siegmund, where are you?
Ah there! I see you now!
Fearful the sight!
Dogs have fastened
their teeth in your flesh;
they take no heed
of your noble glance;
all around you leaping
to tear at your throat—
you fall—
in splinters the shining sword!
The ash is down—
that tree destroyed!
Brother! My brother!
Siegmund—ah!—
(She sinks senseless into Siegmund's arms.)

SIEGMUND
Sister! Beloved!
(He listens to her breathing and makes sure that she is still alive. He lets her slide downwards so that, as he himself sinks into a sitting posture, her head rests on his lap. In this position they both remain until the end of the following scene. A long silence, during which Siegmund bends over Sieglinde with tender care, and presses a long kiss on her brow.)

Vierte Szene

Brünnhilde, ihr Roß am Zaume geleitend, tritt aus der Höhle und schreitet langsam und feierlich nach vorne. Sie hält an und betrachtet Siegmund von fern. Sie schreitet wieder langsam vor. Sie hält in größerer Nähe an. Sie trägt Schild und Speer in der einen Hand, lehnt sich mit der andern an den Hals des Rosses und betrachtet so mit ernster Miene Siegmund.

BRÜNNHILDE
Siegmund,
sieh auf mich!
Ich bin's,
der bald du folgst.

SIEGMUND
(richtet den Blick zu ihr auf.)
Wer bist du, sag,
die so schön und ernst mir erscheint?

BRÜNNHILDE
Nur Todgeweihten
taugt mein Anblick;
wer mich erschaut,
der scheidet vom Lebenslicht.
Auf der Walstatt allein
erschein ich Edlen:
wer mich gewahrt,
zur Wal kor ich ihn mir!

SIEGMUND
(blickt ihr lange forschend und fest in das Auge, senkt dann sinnend das Haupt und wendet sich endlich mit feierlichem Ernste wieder zu ihr.)
Der dir nun folgt,
wohin führst du den Helden?

BRÜNNHILDE
Zu Walvater,
der dich gewählt,
führ ich dich:
nach Walhall folgst du mir.

SIEGMUND
In Walhalls Saal
Walvater find ich allein?

Scene Four

Brünnhilde, leading her horse by the bridle, comes out of the cave and advances slowly and solemnly forwards. She pauses and observes Siegmund from a distance. She again slowly advances. She stops, somewhat nearer. She carries her shield and spear in one hand, resting the other on her horse's neck, and thus she gravely regards Siegmund.

BRÜNNHILDE
Siegmund!
Look on me!
I come
to call you hence.

SIEGMUND
(raises his eyes to her.)
Who are you, say,
who so stern and beauteous appear?

BRÜNNHILDE
Those doomed to death
alone can see me;
who meets my gaze
must turn from the light of life.
I appear in the fight
to death-doomed heroes:
those whom I choose
have no choice but to die!

SIEGMUND
(looks long, firmly, and searchingly into her eyes, then bows his head in thought, and at length turns resolutely to her again.)
And if I come,
tell me, where will you lead me?

BRÜNNHILDE
To Wotan
who marks you for his.
He commands:
to Walhall come with me.

SIEGMUND
To Walhall's hall?
Does Wotan rule there alone?

BRÜNNHILDE
Gefallner Helden
hehre Schar
umfängt dich hold
mit hochheiligem Gruß.

SIEGMUND
Fänd' ich in Walhall
Wälse, den eignen Vater?

BRÜNNHILDE
Den Vater findet
der Wälsung dort.

SIEGMUND
Grüßt mich in Walhall
froh eine Frau?

BRÜNNHILDE
Wunschmädchen
walten dort hehr:
Wotans Tochter
reicht dir traulich den Trank!

SIEGMUND
Hehr bist du,
und heilig gewahr ich
das Wotanskind:
doch eines sag mir, du Ew'ge!
Begleitet den Bruder
die bräutliche Schwester?
Umfängt Siegmund
Sieglinde dort?

BRÜNNHILDE
Erdenluft
muß sie noch atmen:
Sieglinde sieht
Siegmund dort nicht!

SIEGMUND
(neigt sich sanft über Sieglinde, küßt sie leise auf die Stirn und wendet sich ruhig wieder zu Brünnhilde.)
So grüße mir Walhall,
grüße mir Wotan,
grüße mir Wälse

BRÜNNHILDE
The fallen heroes
dwell there too;
they'll welcome you
and greet you to their band.

SIEGMUND
And shall I find there
Wälse, my noble father?

BRÜNNHILDE
Your father waits there
to greet his son!

SIEGMUND
Are there in Walhall,
maidens as well?

BRÜNNHILDE
Fair maidens
wait on you there.
Wotan's daughter,
she will bring you the cup!

SIEGMUND
Fair goddess
with awe I salute you
as Wotan's child;
but one thing tell me, immortal!
This brother is blessed
by his bride and his sister.
You call Siegmund—
Sieglinde too?

BRÜNNHILDE
Here on earth
you have to leave her:
Sieglinde sees
Siegmund no more.

SIEGMUND
(bends softly over Sieglinde, kisses her gently on the brow, and again turns calmly to Brünnhilde.)
Then greet for me Walhall,
greet for me Wotan,
greet for me Wälse

und alle Helden,
grüß auch die holden
Wunschesmädchen:
zu ihnen folg ich dir nicht.

and all the heroes;
greet all those fair
and lovely maidens.
To Walhall I will not go!

BRÜNNHILDE
Du sahest der Walküre
sehrenden Blick:
mit ihr mußt du nun ziehn!

BRÜNNHILDE
You gazed on the Valkyrie's
searing glance,
and now you have no choice.

SIEGMUND
Wo Sieglinde lebt
in Lust und Leid,
da will Siegmund auch säumen.
Noch machte dein Blick
nicht mich erbleichen:
vom Bleiben zwingt er mich nie!

SIEGMUND
Where Sieglinde lives
in joy or pain:
there must Siegmund live with her:
I've gazed on your glance;
I do not fear you:
you cannot force me to go!

BRÜNNHILDE
Solang du lebst,
zwäng' dich wohl nichts:
doch zwingt dich Toren der Tod:
ihn dir zu künden,
kam ich her.

BRÜNNHILDE
I cannot force,
not while you live;
but death can force you to go!
I come to warn you
death is near.

SIEGMUND
Wo wäre der Held,
dem heut ich fiel'?

SIEGMUND
And who is the man
who'll take my life?

BRÜNNHILDE
Hunding fällt dich im Streit.

BRÜNNHILDE
Hunding kills you today.

SIEGMUND
Mit stärkrem drohe
als Hundings Streichen!
Lauerst du hier
lüstern auf Wal,
jenen kiese zum Fang:
ich denk ihn zu fällen im Kampf!

SIEGMUND
Do you think I'm threatened
by Hunding's anger?
If you lurk here,
lusting for blood,
choose that man as your prey:
I know he will fall in the fight!

BRÜNNHILDE
(den Kopf schüttelnd)
Dir, Wälsung,
höre mich wohl:
dir ward das Los gekiest.

BRÜNNHILDE
(shaking her head)
You, Wälsung,
hear what I say:
You have been marked for death.

SIEGMUND
Kennst du dies Schwert?

SIEGMUND
I have a sword!

Der mir es schuf,
beschied mir Sieg:
deinem Drohen trotz ich mit ihm!

My father's gift
will guard me well:
I defy your threats with the sword!

BRÜNNHILDE
(mit stark erhobener Stimme)
Der dir es schuf,
beschied dir jetzt Tod:
seine Tugend nimmt er dem Schwert!

BRÜNNHILDE
(with solemn emphasis)
Gift of the god
who ordered your death;
and he takes his spell from the sword!

SIEGMUND
(heftig)
Schweig und schrecke
die Schlummernde nicht!
(Er beugt sich mit hervorbrechendem Schmerze zärtlich über Sieglinde.)
Weh! Weh!
Süßestes Weib,
du traurigste aller Getreuen!
Gegen dich wütet
in Waffen die Welt:
und ich, dem du einzig vertraut,
für den du ihr einzig getrotzt,
mit meinem Schutz
nicht soll ich dich schirmen,
die Kühne verraten im Kampf?
Ha, Schande ihm,
der das Schwert mir schuf,
beschied er mir Schimpf für Sieg!
Muß ich denn fallen,
nicht fahr ich nach Walhall:
Hella halte mich fest!
(Er neigt sich tief zu Sieglinde.)

SIEGMUND
(vehemently)
Still! You'll waken
my sister from sleep!
(He bends tenderly, in an outburst of grief, over Sieglinde.)
Woe! Woe!
Sister and bride,
you saddest of all trusting women!
Though the world rises
against you in arms,
yet I, whom alone you could trust,
yes, I, who have brought you this pain,
am not allowed
to shield you from danger,
but told I must fall in the fight!
Then shame on him
who bestowed the sword,
the sword that will bring my shame!
Yet though I die here,
I'll not go to Walhall:
hell may hold me instead!
(He bends low over Sieglinde.)

BRÜNNHILDE
(erschüttert)
So wenig achtest du
ewige Wonne?
(zögernd und zurückhaltend)
Alles wär' dir
das arme Weib,
das müd und harmvoll
matt von dem Schoße dir hängt?
Nichts sonst hieltest du hehr?

BRÜNNHILDE
(shocked)
So you would sacrifice
joy everlasting?
(slowly and hesitatingly)
Is she all
in the world to you,
that maid who lies there
limp and afraid in your arms?
You'd leave Walhall for her?

SIEGMUND
(bitter zu ihr aufblickend)
So jung und schön

SIEGMUND
(looking up at her bitterly)
So young and fair

erschimmerst du mir:
doch wie kalt und hart
erkennt dich mein Herz.
Kannst du nur höhnen,
so hebe dich fort,
du arge, fühllose Maid!
Doch mußt du dich weiden
an meinem Weh,
mein Leiden letze dich denn;
meine Not labe
dein neidvolles Herz:
nur von Walhalls spröden Wonnen
sprich du wahrlich mir nicht!

BRÜNNHILDE
Ich sehe die Not,
die das Herz dir zernagt,
ich fühle des Helden
heiligen Harm—
Siegmund, befiehl mir dein Weib:
mein Schutz umfange sie fest!

SIEGMUND
Kein andrer als ich
soll die Reine lebend berühren:
Verfiel ich dem Tod,
die Betäubte töt ich zuvor!

BRÜNNHILDE
(in wachsender Ergriffenheit)
Wälsung! Rasender!
Hör meinen Rat:
befiehl mir dein Weib
um des Pfandes willen,
das wonnig von dir es empfing.

SIEGMUND
(sein Schwert ziehend)
Dies Schwert,
das dem Treuen ein Trugvoller schuf;
dies Schwert,
das feig vor dem Feind mich verrät:
frommt es nich gegen den Feind,
so fromm es denn wider den Freund!
(Er zückt das Schwert auf Sieglinde.)
Zwei Leben
lachen dir hier:

you seem to my eyes;
but how cold and hard
I know in my heart!
You came to mock me;
now leave me alone,
you heartless, cold, cruel maid!
But if it delights you
to watch my woe,
you're free to feed on my pain;
may my grief gladden
your envious heart;
but of Walhall's loveless pleasures
you need tell me no more!

BRÜNNHILDE
I see the distress
and grief in your heart,
I feel all your suffering,
share in your pain!
Siegmund, I'll care for your wife;
I'll shield her safely from harm.

SIEGMUND
So long as she lives
I'll allow no other to touch her:
if I have to die,
I will kill her first while she sleeps.

BRÜNNHILDE
(with increasing emotion)
Wälsung! Madman!
Hear my advice!
I'll care for your wife;
I will shield her safely;
a son shall be born from your love.

SIEGMUND
(drawing his sword)
This sword,
which a traitor bestowed on the true;
this sword
that fails me when faced with a fight:
since it must fail on my foe,
I'll use it instead on a friend!
(He aims the sword at Sieglinde.)
Two lives
now lie in your power;

nimm sie, Notung,
neidischer Stahl!
Nimm sie mit einem Streich!

BRÜNNHILDE
(im heftigsten Sturme des Mitgefühls)
Halt ein, Wälsung!
Höre mein Wort!
Sieglinde lebe—
und Siegmund lebe mit ihr!
Beschlossen ist's;
das Schlachtlos wend ich:
dir, Siegmund,
schaff ich Segen und Sieg!
(Man hört aus dem fernen Hintergrunde Hornrufe erschallen.)
Hörst du den Ruf?
Nun rüste dich, Held!
Traue dem Schwert
und schwing es getrost:
treu hält dir die Wehr,
wie die Walküre treu dich schützt!
Leb wohl, Siegmund,
seligster Held!
Auf der Walstatt seh ich dich wieder!
(Sie stürmt fort und verschwindet mit dem Rosse rechts in einer Seitenschlucht. Siegmund blickt ihr freudig und erhoben nach. Die Bühne hat sich allmählich verfinstert; schwere Gewitterwolken senken sich auf den Hintergrund herab und hüllen die Gebirgswände, die Schlucht und das erhöhte Bergjoch nach und nach gänzlich ein.)

take them, Notung,
glittering blade!
Two with a single stroke!

BRÜNNHILDE
(in a passionate outburst of sympathy)
Oh stay, Wälsung!
Hear what I say!
Sieglinde lives then—
and Siegmund lives by her side!
The choice is mine;
and fate is altered;
you, Siegmund,
take my blessing, and win!
(Horn-calls resound in the far distance.)
Hark to the call!
Prepare for your fight!
Trust in the sword
and strike at his heart.
Your sword shall be true,
and the Valkyrie is true as well!
Farewell, Siegmund,
hero I love!
I will meet you there in the battle!
(She rushes away, and disappears with her horse into a ravine on the right. Siegmund looks after her with joy and exultation. The stage has gradually darkened; heavy stormclouds sink down in the background, gradually veiling the cliffs, ravine and rocky pass completely from view.)

Fünfte Szene

SIEGMUND
(über Sieglinde geneigt, dem Atem lauschend)
Zauberfest
bezähmt ein Schlaf
der Holden Schmerz und Harm.
Da die Walküre zu mir trat,

Scene Five

SIEGMUND
(bending over Sieglinde, listening to her breathing)
Charms of sleep
are sent to soothe
my sister's grief and pain.
Did the Valkyrie cast this spell

schuf sie ihr den wonnigen Trost?
Sollte die grimmige Wal
nicht schrecken ein gramvolles Weib?
Leblos scheint sie,
die dennoch lebt:
der Traurigen kost
ein lächelnder Traum.
So schlummre nun fort,
bis die Schlacht gekämpft
und Friede dich erfreu'!
(Er legt sie sanft auf den Steinsitz und küßt ihr zum Abschied die Stirn. Siegmund vernimmt Hundings Hornruf und bricht entschlossen auf.)
Der dort mich ruft,
rüste sich nun;
was ihm gebührt,
biet ich ihm:
Notung zahl' ihm den Zoll!
(Er zieht das Schwert, eilt dem Hintergrunde zu und verschwindet, auf dem Joche angekommen, sogleich in finsterem Gewittergewölk, aus welchem alsbald Wetterleuchten aufblitzt.)

and lull my beloved to sleep,
so that no sound of our fight
should frighten this suffering maid?
Lifeless seems she,
though still alive;
her sorrow is eased;
she smiles in her sleep.
So peacefully sleep
till the fight is fought;
then wake when I have won!
(He lays her gently on the rocky seat and kisses her forehead in farewell. He hears Hunding's horn-call, and starts up resolutely.)
I hear your call;
guard yourself well;
all you deserve
comes to you.
Notung pays all my debt!
(He draws his sword, hastens to the background and, on reaching the pass, disappears in the dark stormcloud, from which a flash of lightning immediately breaks.)

SIEGLINDE
(beginnt sich träumend unruhiger zu bewegen.)
Kehrte der Vater nur heim!
Mit dem Knaben noch weilt er im Forst.
Mutter, Mutter!
Mir bangt der Mut:
Nicht freund und friedlich
scheinen die Fremden!
Schwarze Dämpfe—
schwüles Gedünst—
feurige Lohe
leckt schon nach uns—
es brennt das Haus—
zu Hilfe, Bruder!
Siegmund! Siegmund!
(Sie springt auf. Starker Blitz und Donner.)
Siegmund! Ha!
(Sie starrt in Angst um sich her: fast die ganze Bühne ist in schwarze Gewitterwolken gehüllt, fortwährender Blitz und Donner. Der Hornruf Hundings ertönt in der Nähe.)

SIEGLINDE
(begins to move restlessly in her dreams.)
Why doesn't father return?
With the boy he is still in the woods.
Mother! Mother!
I feel afraid;
they seem unfriendly—
who are the strangers?
Smoky darkness—
smouldering fires—
now they are flaring,
flaming around—
they burn the house—
Oh help me, brother!
Siegmund! Siegmund!
(She leaps up. Violent thunder and lightning.)
Siegmund! Ah!
(She stares about her in terror; nearly the whole stage is covered with black thunderclouds, the lightning and thunder continue. Hunding's horn-call sounds near.)

HUNDINGS STIMME
(im Hintergrunde vom Bergjoche her)
Wehwalt! Wehwalt!

HUNDING'S VOICE
(in the background, from the pass)
Wehwalt! Wehwalt!

Steh mir zum Streit,
sollen dich Hunde nicht halten!

SIEGMUNDS STIMME
(von weiter hinten her aus der Schlucht)
Wo birgst du dich,
daß ich vorbei dir schoß?
Steh, daß ich dich stelle!

SIEGLINDE
(in furchtbarer Aufregung lauschend)
Hunding! Siegmund!
Könnt' ich sie sehen!

HUNDING
Hieher, du frevelnder Freier!
Fricka fälle dich hier!

SIEGMUND
(nun ebenfalls vom Joche her)
Noch wähnst du mich waffenlos,
feiger Wicht?
Drohst du mit Frauen,
so ficht nun selber,
sonst läßt dich Fricka im Stich!
Denn sieh: deines Hauses
heimischem Stamm
entzog ich zaglos das Schwert;
seine Schneide schmecke jetzt du!
(Ein Blitz erhellt für einen Augenblick das Bergjoch, auf welchem jetzt Hunding und Siegmund kämpfend gewahrt werden.)

SIEGLINDE
(mit höchster Kraft)
Haltet ein, ihr Männer!
Mordet erst mich!
(Sie stürzt auf das Bergjoch zu: ein von rechts her über den Kämpfern ausbrechender heller Schein blendet sie aber plötzlich so heftig, daß sie, wie erblindet, zur Seite schwankt. In dem Lichtglanze erscheint Brünnhilde über Siegmund schwebend und diesen mit dem Schilde deckend.)

BRÜNNHILDE
Triff ihn, Siegmund!
Traue dem Schwert!
(Als Siegmund soeben zu einem tödlichen Streiche

Stand there and fight,
else with my hounds I will hunt you.

SIEGMUND'S VOICE
(from farther off in the ravine)
Then show yourself;
I've come in search of you!
Stand and let me face you!

SIEGLINDE
(listening in fearful agitation)
Hunding! Siegmund!
Could I but see them!

HUNDING
Come here, you treacherous lover!
Fricka claims you as prize.

SIEGMUND
(now likewise from the pass)
Do you think that I'm weaponless,
boasting fool?
Don't call on Fricka,
but fight your own fight;
no help from Fricka today!
For see, in your house
I drew from the tree
the strongest, sharpest of swords,
and its sharpness strikes at your life!
(A flash of lightning illumines the pass for a moment, and Hunding and Siegmund are seen fighting there.)

SIEGLINDE
(with her utmost force)
Stop the fight, you madmen!
Murder me first!
(She rushes towards the pass, but suddenly, from above the combatants, on the right, a flash breaks forth so vividly that she staggers aside as if blinded. In the blaze of light Brünnhilde appears, hovering over Siegmund and protecting him with her shield.)

BRÜNNHILDE
Strike him, Siegmund!
Trust in the sword!
(Just as Siegmund aims a deadly blow at Hunding,

auf Hunding ausholt, bricht von links her ein glühend rötlicher Schein durch das Gewölk aus, in welchem Wotan erscheint, über Hunding stehend und seinen Speer Siegmund quer entgegenhaltend.)

WOTAN
Zurück vor dem Speer!
In Stücken das Schwert!
(Brünnhilde weicht erschrocken vor Wotan mit dem Schilde zurück: Siegmunds Schwert zerspringt an dem vorgehaltenen Speere. Dem Unbewehrten stößt Hunding seinen Speer in die Brust. Siegmund stürzt tot zu Boden. Sieglinde, die seinen Todesseufzer gehört, sinkt mit einem Schrei wie leblos zusammen. Mit Siegmunds Fall ist zugleich von beiden Seiten der glänzende Schein verschwunden; dichte Finsternis ruht im Gewölk bis nach vorn: in ihm wird Brünnhilde undeutlich sichtbar, wie sie in jäher Hast sich Sieglinden zuwendet.)

BRÜNNHILDE
Zu Roß, daß ich dich rette!
(Sie hebt Sieglinde schnell zu sich auf ihr der Seitenschlucht nahe stehendes Roß und verschwindet sogleich mit ihr. Alsbald zerteilt sich das Gewölk in der Mitte, so daß man deutlich Hunding gewahrt, der soeben seinen Speer dem gefallenen Siegmund aus der Brust zieht. Wotan, von Gewölk umgeben, steht dahinter auf einem Felsen, an seinen Speer gelehnt und schmerzlich auf Siegmunds Leiche blickend.)

WOTAN
(zu Hunding)
Geh hin, Knecht!
Knie vor Fricka:
meld ihr, daß Wotans Speer
gerächt, was Spott ihr schuf.
Geh! Geh!
(Vor seinem verächtlichen Handwink sinkt Hunding tot zu Boden. Wotan, plötzlich in furchtbarer Wut auffahrend:)
Doch Brünnhilde!
Weh der Verbrecherin!
Furchtbar sei
die Freche gestraft,
erreicht mein Roß ihre Flucht!
(Er verschwindet mit Blitz und Donner. Der Vorhang fällt schnell.)

a glowing red light breaks from the left through the clouds, in which Wotan appears, standing over Hunding, holding his spear diagonally out at Siegmund.)

WOTAN
Away from the spear!
I shatter the sword!
(Brünnhilde, with her spear, recoils in terror before Wotan. Siegmund's sword shatters on the outstretched spear. Hunding plunges his spear into the unarmed man's breast. Siegmund falls dead to the ground: Sieglinde, who has heard his death-sigh, falls with a cry, as if lifeless, to the ground. As Siegmund falls, the glowing lights on either side disappear at once; a cloud of thick darkness rolls forward; in it, Brünnhilde is indistinctly seen, as she turns in haste to Sieglinde.)

BRÜNNHILDE
To horse! Come, let me save you!
(She lifts Sieglinde quickly on to her horse, which is standing near the side gorge, and immediately disappears with her. At this moment the clouds part in the middle, so that Hunding, who had just drawn his spear from the fallen Siegmund's breast, is clearly seen. Wotan, surrounded by clouds, stands on a rock behind him, leaning on his spear and gazing sorrowfully at Siegmund's corpse.)

WOTAN
(to Hunding)
Go hence, slave!
Kneel before Fricka:
tell her that Wotan's spear
avenged her cause of shame.
Go! Go!
(At the contemptuous wave of his hand, Hunding falls dead to the ground. Wotan, suddenly breaking out in terrible rage:)
But Brünnhilde!
Where is the guilty one?
Fearful is the fate
I'll pronounce
when she is caught in her flight!
(He disappears in thunder and lightning. The curtain falls rapidly.)

Dritter Aufzug

Auf dem Gipfel eines Felsenberges

Rechts begrenzt ein Tannenwald die Szene. Links der Eingang einer Felshöhle, die einen natürlichen Saal bildet: darüber steigt der Fels zu seiner höchsten Spitze auf. Nach hinten ist die Aussicht gänzlich frei; höhere und niedere Felssteine bilden den Rand vor dem Abhange, der—wie anzunehmen ist—nach dem Hintergrunde zu steil hinabführt. Einzelne Wolkenzüge jagen, wie vom Sturm getrieben, am Felsensaume vorbei. Gerhilde, Ortlinde, Waltraute und Schwertleite haben sich auf der Felsspitze, an und über der Höhle, gelagert, sie sind in voller Waffenrüstung.

Erste Szene

GERHILDE
(zuhöchst gelagert und dem Hintergrunde zurufend, wo ein starkes Gewölk herzieht)

Hojotoho! Hojotoho!
Heiaha! Heiaha!

Act Three

On the Summit of a Rocky Mountain

On the right, a pinewood bounds the stage. On the left, the entrance to a cave which looks like a natural room; above it, the rock rises to its highest point. At the back the view is entirely open; rocks of various heights border a precipice, which, it is to be assumed, falls steeply to the background. Occasional cloudbanks fly past the mountain peak, as if driven by storm. Gerhilde, Ortlinde, Waltraute and Schwertleite have assembled on the peak, by and above the cave: they are in full armour.

Scene One

GERHILDE
(on the highest point, calling towards the background, where a thick cloud is passing)

Hoyotoho! Hoyotoho!
Hiaha! Hiaha!

Helmwige! Hier!
Hierher mit dem Roß!

HELMWIGES STIMME
(im Hintergrunde)
Hojotoho! Hojotoho!
Heiaha!
(In dem Gewölk bricht Blitzesglanz aus; eine Walküre zu Roß wird in ihm sichtbar: über ihrem Sattel hängt ein erschlagener Krieger. Die Erscheinung zieht, immer näher, am Felsensaume von links nach rechts vorbei.)

GERHILDE, WALTRAUTE,
SCHWERTLEITE
(der Ankommenden entgegenrufend)
Heiaha! Heiaha!
(Die Wolke mit der Erscheinung ist rechts hinter dem Tann verschwunden.)

ORTLINDE
(in den Tann hineinrufend)
Zu Ortlindes Stute
stell deinen Hengst:
mit meiner Grauen
grast gern dein Brauner!

WALTRAUTE
(hineinrufend)
Wer hängt dir im Sattel?

HELMWIGE
(aus dem Tann auftretend)
Sintolt, der Hegeling!

SCHWERTLEITE
Führ deinen Braunen
fort von der Grauen:
Ortlindes Mähre
trägt Wittig, den Irming!

GERHILDE
(ist etwas näher herabgestiegen.)
Als Feinde nur sah ich
Sintolt und Wittig!

ORTLINDE
(springt auf.)
Heiaha! Die Stute

Helmwige! Here!
Come here with your horse!

HELMWIGE'S VOICE
(in the background)
Hoyotoho! Hoyotoho!
Hiaha!
(A flash of lightning breaks through the cloud; in its light, a Valkyrie on horseback becomes visible; on her saddle hangs a slain warrior. The apparition comes closer, moving from left to right past the rocky ridge.)

GERHILDE, WALTRAUTE,
SCHWERTLEITE
(calling to the newcomer)
Hiaha! Hiaha!
(The cloud with the apparition has disappeared to the right, behind the wood.)

ORTLINDE
(calling into the wood)
Go tether your chestnut
next to my grey;
she will be glad
to graze by your stallion.

WALTRAUTE
(calling into the wood)
Who hangs from your saddle?

HELMWIGE
(coming from the wood)
Sintolt the Hegeling!

SCHWERTLEITE
Far from the grey
then fasten your stallion;
Ortlinde's mare
carries Wittig the Irming!

GERHILDE
(has come down lower.)
Implacable foes
were Sintolt and Wittig!

ORTLINDE
(leaps up.)
Hiaha! Your stallion

stößt mir der Hengst!
(Sie läuft in den Tann. Gerhilde, Helmwige und Schwertleite lachen laut auf.)

GERHILDE
Der Recken Zwist
entzweit noch die Rosse!

HELMWIGE
(in den Tann zurückrufend)
Ruhig, Brauner!
Brich nicht den Frieden.

WALTRAUTE
(auf der Höhe, wo sie für Gerhilde die Wacht übernommen, nach rechts in den Hintergrund rufend)
Hoioho! Hoioho!
Siegrune, hier!
Wo säumst du so lang?
(Sie lauscht nach rechts.)

SIEGRUNES STIMME
(von der rechten Seite des Hintergrundes her)
Arbeit gab's!
Sind die andren schon da?

SCHWERTLEITE, WALTRAUTE
(nach rechts in den Hintergrund rufend)
Hojotoho! Hojotoho!
Heiaha!

GERHILDE
Heiaha!
(Ihre Gebärden sowie ein heller Glanz hinter dem Tann zeigen an, daß soeben Siegrune dort angelangt ist. Aus der Tiefe hört man zwei Stimmen zugleich.)

GRIMGERDE, ROSSWEISSE
(links im Hintergrunde)
Hojotoho! Hojotoho!
Heiaha!

WALTRAUTE
Grimgerd und Roßweiße!

GERHILDE
Sie reiten zu zwei.

is biting my mare!
(She runs into the wood. Gerhilde, Helmwige, and Schwertleite break into laughter.)

GERHILDE
The warriors' war
has spread to the horses!

HELMWIGE
(calling back into the wood)
Quiet, Bruno!
Battle is over.

WALTRAUTE
(on the highest point, where she has taken over from Gerhilde as watcher, calls to the right side of the background.)
Hoioho! Hoioho!
Siegrune, here!
What kept you so long?
(She listens to the right.)

SIEGRUNE'S VOICE
(from the right side of the background)
Work to do!
Have the others arrived?

SCHWERTLEITE, WALTRAUTE
(calling to the right of the background)
Hoyotoho! Hoyotoho!
Hiaha!

GERHILDE
Hiaha!
(Their gestures, as well as a bright glow behind the wood, show that Siegrune has just arrived there. From the distance below, two voices are heard at once.)

GRIMGERDE, ROSSWEISSE
(left, in the background)
Hoyotoho! Hoyotoho!
Hiaha!

WALTRAUTE
Grimgerd and Rossweisse!

GERHILDE
They're riding abreast.

(In einem blitzerglänzenden Wolkenzuge, der von links her vorbeizieht, erscheinen Grimgerde und Roßweiße, ebenfalls auf Rossen, jede einen Erschlagenen im Sattel führend. Helmwige, Ortlinde und Siegrune sind aus dem Tann getreten und winken vom Felsensaume den Ankommenden zu.)

HELMWIGE, ORTLINDE, SIEGRUNE
Gegrüßt, ihr Reisige!
Roßweiß und Grimgerde!

ROSSWEISSES und GRIMGERDES STIMMEN
Hojotoho! Hojotoho!
Heiaha!
(Die Erscheinung verschwindet hinter dem Tann.)

DIE SECHS ANDEREN WALKÜREN
Hojotoho! Hojotoho!
Heiaha! Heiaha!

GERHILDE
(in den Tann rufend)
In' Wald mit den Rossen
zu Rast und Weid'!

ORTLINDE
(ebenfalls in den Tann rufend)
Führet die Mähren
fern voneinander,
bis unsrer Helden
Haß sich gelegt!
(Die Walküren lachen.)

HELMWIGE
(während die anderen lachen)
Der Helden Grimm
büßte schon die Graue!
(Die Walküren lachen.)

ROSSWEISSE, GRIMGERDE
(aus dem Tann tretend)
Hojotoho! Hojotoho!

DIE SECHS ANDEREN WALKÜREN
Willkommen! Willkommen!

(In a cloudbank lit by lightning, moving past from the left, Grimgerde and Rossweisse appear, similarly on horseback, each with a dead warrior on her saddle. Helmwige, Ortlinde, and Siegrune come from the wood and greet the newcomers from the rocky ridge.)

HELMWIGE, ORTLINDE, SIEGRUNE
We greet the travellers!
Rossweiss and Grimgerde!

ROSSWEISSE'S and GRIMGERDE'S VOICES
Hoyotoho! Hoyotoho!
Hiaha!
(The apparition disappears behind the wood.)

THE OTHER SIX VALKYRIES
Hoyotoho! Hoyotoho!
Hiaha! Hiaha!

GERHILDE
(calling into the wood)
Now tether your horses
to graze and rest!

ORTLINDE
(also calling into the wood)
See that the mares
are far from the stallions,
until our heroes'
hate has been calmed!
(The Valkyries laugh.)

HELMWIGE
(while the others laugh)
My horse has paid
for the heroes' anger!
(Renewed laughter)

ROSSWEISSE, GRIMGERDE
(coming from the wood)
Hoyotoho! Hoyotoho!

THE OTHER SIX VALKYRIES
Be welcome! Be welcome!

SCHWERTLEITE
Wart ihr Kühnen zu zwei?

GRIMGERDE
Getrennt ritten wir
und trafen uns heut.

ROSSWEISSE
Sind wir alle versammelt,
so säumt nicht lange:
nach Walhall brechen wir auf,
Wotan zu bringen die Wal.

HELMWIGE
Acht sind wir erst:
eine noch fehlt.

GERHILDE
Bei dem braunen Wälsung
weilt wohl noch Brünnhild.

WALTRAUTE
Auf sie noch harren
müssen wir hier:
Walvater gäb' uns
grimmigen Gruß,
säh' ohne sie er uns nahn!

SIEGRUNE
(auf der Felswarte, von wo sie hinausspäht)
Hojotoho! Hojotoho!
Hieher! Hieher!
In brünstigem Ritt
jagt Brünnhilde her.

DIE ACHT WALKÜREN
(alle eilen auf die Warte.)
Hojotoho! Hojotoho!
Brünnhilde! Hei!
(Sie spähen mit wachsender Verwunderung.)

WALTRAUTE
Nach dem Tann lenkt sie
das taumelnde Roß.

GRIMGERDE
Wie schnaubt Grane
vom schnellen Ritt!

SCHWERTLEITE
Did you hunt as a pair?

GRIMGERDE
We left separately,
and met on the way.

ROSSWEISSE
If we are all assembled,
then wait no longer:
to Walhall hurry away;
Wotan is expecting us there.

HELMWIGE
Eight now are here:
one is to come.

GERHILDE
It's that swarthy Wälsung
keeping our Brünnhild.

WALTRAUTE
Then we must wait
until she is here:
Brünnhild is father's
favourite child,
and if we leave her behind . . .

SIEGRUNE
(watching from the look-out point)
Hoyotoho! Hoyotoho!
She's here! She's here!
In furious haste
see Brünnhilde rides.

THE EIGHT VALKYRIES
(all hasten to the look-out.)
Hoyotoho! Hoyotoho!
Brünnhilde! Hi!
(They watch with growing astonishment.)

WALTRAUTE
To the pinewood
she is driving her horse.

GRIMGERDE
And proud Grane
is panting hard!

ROSSWEISSE
So jach sah ich nie
Walküren jagen!

ROSSWEISSE
She's forced him to fly
faster than ever!

ORTLINDE
Was hält sie im Sattel?

ORTLINDE
Who's that on her saddle?

HELMWIGE
Das ist kein Held!

HELMWIGE
That is no man!

SIEGRUNE
Eine Frau führt sie.

SIEGRUNE
It's a girl, surely.

GERHILDE
Wie fand sie die Frau?

GERHILDE
And where was she found?

SCHWERTLEITE
Mit keinem Gruß
grüßt sie die Schwestern!

SCHWERTLEITE
She gives no greeting
to her sisters!

WALTRAUTE
(hinabrufend)
Heiaha! Brünnhilde!
Hörst du uns nicht?

WALTRAUTE
(calling down)
Hiaha! Brünnhilde!
Answer our call!

ORTLINDE
Helft der Schwester
vom Roß sich schwingen!

ORTLINDE
Help our sister
to leave the saddle!

HELMWIGE, GERHILDE, SIEGRUNE,
ROSSWEISSE
Hojotoho! Hojotoho!

HELMWIGE, GERHILDE, SIEGRUNE,
ROSSWEISSE
Hoyotoho! Hoyotoho!

ORTLINDE, WALTRAUTE,
GRIMGERDE, SCHWERTLEITE
Heiaha!
(Gerhilde und Helmwige stürzen in den Tann. Siegrune und Roßweiße laufen ihnen nach.)

ORTLINDE, WALTRAUTE,
GRIMGERDE, SCHWERTLEITE
Hiaha!
(Gerhilde and Schwertleite run into the wood. Siegrune and Rossweisse follow them.)

WALTRAUTE
(in den Tann blickend)
Zugrunde stürzt
Grane, der starke!

WALTRAUTE
(looking into the wood)
And powerful Grane
has fallen!

GRIMGERDE
Aus dem Sattel hebt sie
hastig das Weib!

GRIMGERDE
While our sister lifts
the girl to the ground!

ORTLINDE, WALTRAUTE, GRIMGERDE, SCHWERTLEITE
Schwester, Schwester!
Was ist geschehn?
(Alle Walküren kehren auf die Bühne zurück; mit ihnen kommt Brünnhilde, Sieglinde unterstützend und hereingeleitend.)

BRÜNNHILDE
(atemlos)
Schützt mich und helft
in höchster Not!

DIE ACHT WALKÜREN
Wo rittest du her
in rasender Hast?
So fliegt nur, wer auf der Flucht!

BRÜNNHILDE
Zum erstenmal flieh ich
und bin verfolgt:
Heervater hetzt mir nach!

DIE ACHT WALKÜREN
(heftig erschreckend)
Bist du von Sinnen?
Sprich! Sage uns! Wie?
Verfolgt dich Heervater?
Fliehst du vor ihm?

BRÜNNHILDE
(wendet sich ängstlich, um zu spähen, und kehrt wieder zurück.)
O Schwestern, späht
von des Felsens Spitze!
Schaut nach Norden,
ob Walvater naht!
(Ortlinde und Waltraute springen auf die Felsenspitze zur Warte.)
Schnell! Seht ihr ihn schon?

ORTLINDE
Gewittersturm
naht von Norden.

WALTRAUTE
Starkes Gewölk
staut sich dort auf!

ORTLINDE, WALTRAUTE, GRIMGERDE, SCHWERTLEITE
Sister, sister!
What have you done?
(All the Valkyries return to the stage; with them comes Brünnhilde, supporting and leading Sieglinde.)

BRÜNNHILDE
(breathless)
Shield me and help
in highest need!

THE EIGHT VALKYRIES
From where have you come
in furious haste?
You ride like one who is pursued!

BRÜNNHILDE
I flee for the first time;
I am pursued;
Wotan is hunting me!

THE EIGHT VALKYRIES
(violently alarmed)
What are you saying?
Speak to us! What?
Is Wotan hunting you?
Why do you flee?

BRÜNNHILDE
(turns anxiously to look around, and then turns back.)
O sisters, run
to the mountain summit!
Look to the northward,
if Wotan is near!
(Ortlinde and Waltraute run to the rocky peak to keep a look-out.)
Quick! What can you see?

ORTLINDE
A thunderstorm
nears from northward.

WALTRAUTE
Dark, stormy clouds
mass themselves there!

DIE WEITEREN SECHS WALKÜREN
Heervater reitet
sein heiliges Roß!

THE OTHER SIX VALKYRIES
Wotan is riding
his sacred horse!

BRÜNNHILDE
Der wilde Jäger,
der wütend mich jagt,
er naht, er naht von Norden!
Schützt mich, Schwestern!
Wahret dies Weib!

BRÜNNHILDE
The wild pursuer
who hunts me in wrath,
he's near, he comes from northward.
Save me, sisters!
Rescue this maid!

SECHS WALKÜREN
Was ist mit dem Weibe?

SIX VALKYRIES
But who is this woman?

BRÜNNHILDE
Hört mich in Eile:
Sieglinde ist es,
Siegmunds Schwester und Braut:
Gegen die Wälsungen
wütet Wotan in Grimm;
dem Bruder sollte
Brünnhilde heut
entziehen den Sieg;
doch Siegmund schützt' ich
mit meinem Schild,
trotzend dem Gott;
der traf ihn da selbst mit dem Speer:
Siegmund fiel;
doch ich floh
fern mit der Frau;
sie zu retten,
eilt' ich zu euch,
ob mich Bange auch
ihr berget vor dem strafenden Streich!

BRÜNNHILDE
Hear while I tell you.
Sieglinde is she,
Siegmund's sister and bride,
one of the Wälsungs
Wotan swore to destroy.
Her brother's death
was Brünnhilde's task,
So Wotan decreed.
But Siegmund gained my help
in his fight;
Wotan himself
then shattered the sword with the spear:
Siegmund fell,
but I fled
here with his wife,
and to save her
brought her to you.
Will you help us both,
and save us from the storm that is near?

SECHS WALKÜREN
Betörte Schwester,
was tatest du?
Wehe, Brünnhilde, wehe!
Brach ungehorsam
Brünnhilde
Heervaters heilig Gebot?

SIX VALKYRIES
What madness moved you
to do this deed?
Sister! Brünnhilde! Sister!
Woe! O rebellious
Brünnhilde,
how could you break his command!

WALTRAUTE
(von der Warte)
Nächtig zieht es
von Norden heran.

WALTRAUTE
(on the look-out)
Dark those stormclouds
that fly from the north.

ORTLINDE
(ebenso)
Wütend steuert
hieher der Sturm.

ROSSWEISSE, GRIMGERDE, SCHWERTLEITE
Wild wiehert
Walvaters Roß.

HELMWIGE, GERHILDE, SIEGRUNE
Schrecklich schnaubt es daher!

BRÜNNHILDE
Wehe der Armen,
wenn Wotan sie trifft:
den Wälsungen allen
droht er Verderben!
Wer leiht mir von euch
das leichteste Roß,
das flink die Frau ihm entführ'?

SIEGRUNE
Auch uns rätst du
rasenden Trotz?

BRÜNNHILDE
Roßweiße, Schwester,
leih mir deinen Renner!

ROSSWEISSE
Vor Walvater floh
der fliegende nie.

BRÜNNHILDE
Helmwige, höre!

HELMWIGE
Dem Vater gehorch ich.

BRÜNNHILDE
Grimgerde! Gerhilde!
Gönnt mir eu'r Roß!
Schwertleite! Siegrune!
Seht meine Angst!

ORTLINDE
(also on the look-out)
Wotan drives
his steed through the storm.

ROSSWEISSE, GRIMGERDE, SCHWERTLEITE
Wild neighs
I hear from the horse—

HELMWIGE, GERHILDE, SIEGRUNE
—snorts and flies on its way!

BRÜNNHILDE
Woe to this woman
when Wotan arrives;
for she is a Wälsung,
doomed to destruction!
So lend me the fastest
horse that you have,
to save the maid from his wrath!

SIEGRUNE
So you would make us
share in your crime?

BRÜNNHILDE
Rossweisse, sister,
lend me your stallion!

ROSSWEISSE
From Wotan, my horse
refuses to fly.

BRÜNNHILDE
Helmwige, hear me!

HELMWIGE
I hear only Wotan.

BRÜNNHILDE
Grimgerde! Gerhilde!
Give me your horse!
Schwertleite! Siegrune!
See my dismay!

Oh, seid mir treu,
wie traut ich euch war:
rettet dies traurige Weib!

SIEGLINDE
(die bisher finster und kalt vor sich hingestarrt, fährt, als Brünnhilde sie lebhaft—wie zum Schutze—umfaßt, mit einer abwehrenden Gebärde auf.)
Nicht sehre dich Sorge um mich:
einzig taugt mir der Tod!
Wer hieß dich, Maid,
dem Harst mich entführen?
Im Sturm dort hätt' ich
den Streich empfahn
von derselben Waffe,
der Siegmund fiehl:
das Ende fand ich
vereint mit ihm!
Fern von Siegmund—
Siegmund, von dir!—
O deckte mich Tod,
daß ich's denke!
Soll um die Flucht
dir, Maid, ich nicht fluchen,
so erhöre heilig mein Flehen:
stoße dein Schwert mir ins Herz!

BRÜNNHILDE
Lebe, o Weib,
um der Liebe willen!
Rette das Pfand,
das von ihm du empfingst:
ein Wälsung wächst dir im Schoß!

SIEGLINDE
(erschrickt zunächst heftig; sogleich strahlt aber ihr Gesicht in erhabener Freude auf.)
Rette mich, Kühne!
Rettet mein Kind!
Schirmt mich, ihr Mädchen,
mit mächtigstem Schutz!
(Immer finstereres Gewitter steigt im Hintergrunde auf: nahender Donner.)

WALTRAUTE
(auf der Warte)
Der Sturm kommt heran.

Oh, now be true,
as I was to you:
rescue this sorrowful maid!

SIEGLINDE
(who has been gazing gloomily and coldly ahead, gives a start and makes a gesture of rejection as Brünnhilde impulsively embraces her, as if to protect her.)
Pray suffer no sorrow for me;
all I long for is death!
O warrior maid,
who asked you to save me?
I might have died
in the field with him;
for perhaps the weapon
that dealt his death,
that killed my Siegmund,
had pierced me too.
Far from Siegmund,
Siegmund, from you!
Now only death
can unite us!
So I shall curse
this care that has saved me
if you refuse my grievous entreaty:
strike with your sword in my heart!

BRÜNNHILDE
Live still, O maid;
know that love commands you!
Rescue the son
who will grow from your love:
a Wälsung lives in your womb!

SIEGLINDE
(starts in fear at first; then her face lights up with sublime joy.)
Rescue me, brave one!
Rescue my child!
Save me, you maidens,
and shelter my son!
(An ever-darkening tempest rises in the background; the thunder draws closer.)

WALTRAUTE
(on the look-out)
The storm's drawing near!

ORTLINDE
(ebenso)
Flieh, wer ihn fürchtet!

DIE SECHS ANDEREN WALKÜREN
Fort mit dem Weibe,
droht ihm Gefahr:
der Walküren keine
wag ihren Schutz!

SIEGLINDE
(auf den Knien vor Brünnhilde)
Rette mich, Maid!
Rette die Mutter!

BRÜNNHILDE
(mit lebhaftem Entschluß hebt Sieglinde auf.)
So fliehe denn eilig
und fliehe allein!
Ich bleibe zurück,
biete mich Wotans Rache:
an mir zögr' ich
den Zürnenden hier,
während du seinem Rasen entrinnst.

SIEGLINDE
Wohin soll ich mich wenden?

BRÜNNHILDE
Wer von euch Schwestern
schweifte nach Osten?

SIEGRUNE
Nach Osten weithin
dehnt sich ein Wald:
der Niblungen Hort
entführte Fafner dorthin.

SCHWERTLEITE
Wurmesgestalt
schuf sich der Wilde:
in einer Höhle
hütet er Alberichs Reif!

GRIMGERDE
Nicht geheu'r ist's dort
für ein hilflos Weib.

ORTLINDE
(on the look-out)
Fly if you fear it!

THE OTHER SIX VALKYRIES
Off with the woman!
Danger is near!
The Valkyries dare not
give her their aid.

SIEGLINDE
(on her knees to Brünnhilde)
Rescue me, maid!
Rescue a mother!

BRÜNNHILDE
(raises Sieglinde with sudden resolution.)
Then fly from him swiftly,
and fly by yourself!
I will stay for the storm;
I will brave Wotan's anger;
and I'll draw his revenge
on myself,
so that you can escape his rage.

SIEGLINDE
Ah, where can I escape him?

BRÜNNHILDE
Which of you, sisters,
journeyed to eastward?

SIEGRUNE
A gloomy forest
lies to the east,
where the Nibelung hoard
was brought by Fafner, the giant.

SCHWERTLEITE
There he remains,
changed to a dragon,
and in a cave
he broods over Alberich's ring.

GRIMGERDE
It is not the place
for a helpless maid.

BRÜNNHILDE
Und doch vor Wotans Wut
schützt sie sicher der Wald:
ihn scheut der Mächt'ge
und meidet den Ort.

WALTRAUTE
(auf der Warte)
Furchtbar fährt
dort Wotan zum Fels.

SECHS WALKÜREN
Brünnhilde, hör
seines Nahens Gebraus!

BRÜNNHILDE
(Sieglinde die Richtung weisend)
Fort denn eile,
nach Osten gewandt!
Mutigen Trotzes
ertrag alle Müh'n,
Hunger und Durst,
Dorn und Gestein;
lache, ob Not,
ob Leiden dich nagt!
Denn eines wiss'
und wahr' es immer:
den hehrsten Helden der Welt
hegst du, o Weib,
im schirmenden Schoß!
(Sie zieht die Stücken von Siegmunds Schwert unter ihrem Panzer hervor und überreicht sie Sieglinde.)
Verwahr ihm die starken
Schwertesstücken;
seines Vaters Walstatt
entführt' ich sie glücklich:
der neugefügt
das Schwert einst schwingt,
den Namen nehm er von mir—
»Siegfried« erfreu sich des Siegs!

SIEGLINDE
(in größter Rührung)
O hehrstes Wunder!
Herrlichste Maid!
Dir Treuen dank ich

BRÜNNHILDE
And yet, from Wotan's wrath,
there, I know, she'd be safe:
for father fears it;
he never goes near.

WALTRAUTE
(on the look-out)
Angry Wotan
rides to the rock!

SIX VALKYRIES
Brünnhilde, hear
his approach in the storm!

BRÜNNHILDE
(showing Sieglinde the direction)
Fly him swiftly,
away to the east!
Bold in defiance,
endure every ill,
hunger and thirst,
thorns and the stones;
laugh at the pain
and grief that will come!
But one thing know,
and guard it ever:
the noblest hero of all,
he shall be born,
O maid, from your womb!
(She draws the pieces of Siegmund's sword from beneath her breastplate and gives them to Sieglinde.)
For him you must guard
these broken pieces
of the sword his father
let fall when it failed him;
for he shall forge
the sword once more.
His name, now learn it from me:
Siegfried—victorious and free!

SIEGLINDE
(deeply stirred)
O radiant wonder!
Glorious maid!
Your words have brought me

heiligen Trost!
Für ihn, den wir liebten,
rett ich das Liebste:
meines Dankes Lohn
lache dir einst!
Lebe wohl!
Dich segnet Sieglindes Weh!
(Sie eilt rechts im Vordergrunde von dannen.— Die Felsenhöhe ist von schwarzen Gewitterwolken umlagert; furchtbarer Sturm braust aus dem Hintergrunde daher, wachsender Feuerschein rechts daselbst.)

comfort and calm!
This son of Siegmund,
Oh! We shall save him:
may my son return
to thank you himself!
Fare you well!
Be blessed by Sieglinde's woe!
(She hastens away in the right foreground. Black thunderclouds surround the height; a fearful storm breaks out at the back, with a fiery glare growing brighter on the right.)

WOTANS STIMME
Steh, Brünnhild!
(Brünnhilde, nachdem sie eine Weile Sieglinde nachgesehen, wendet sich in den Hintergrund, blickt in den Tann und kommt angstvoll wieder vor.)

WOTAN'S VOICE
Stay, Brünnhild!
(Brünnhilde, after watching Sieglinde's departure for a while, turns to the background, looks into the pinewood, and then comes forward again in fear.)

ORTLINDE, WALTRAUTE
(von der Warte herabsteigend)
Den Fels erreichten
Roß und Reiter!

ORTLINDE, WALTRAUTE
(descending from the look-out)
They've reached the mountain,
horse and rider!

ALLE ACHT WALKÜREN
Weh, Brünnhild!
Rache entbrennt!

ALL EIGHT VALKYRIES
Woe, Brünnhild!
Vengeance is here!

BRÜNNHILD
Ach, Schwestern, helft!
Mir schwankt das Herz!
Sein Zorn zerschellt mich,
wenn euer Schutz ihn nicht zähmt.

BRÜNNHILDE
O sisters, help!
I feel afraid!
His rage will crush me
unless you shield me from harm.

DIE ACHT WALKÜREN
(flüchten ängstlich nach der Felsenspitze hinauf; Brünnhilde läßt sich von ihnen nachziehen.)
Hieher, Verlorne!
Laß dich nicht sehn!
Schmiege dich an uns
und schweige dem Ruf!
(Sie verbergen Brünnhilde unter sich und blicken ängstlich nach dem Tann, der jetzt von grellem Feuerschein erhellt wird, während der Hintergrund ganz finster geworden ist.)
Weh!
Wütend schwingt sich
Wotan vom Roß!

THE EIGHT VALKYRIES
(retreat in fear up the rocky height, drawing Brünnhilde with them.)
Come here, you lost one!
Keep out of sight!
Hide among us here;
be still when he calls!
(They hide Brünnhilde in their midst and look anxiously at the pinewood, now lit by a brilliant fiery glow, while the background has become quite dark.)
Woe!
Wotan swings himself
to the ground!

Hieher rast
sein rächender Schritt!

Here he comes
in furious haste!

Zweite Szene

Wotan tritt in höchster zorniger Aufgeregtheit aus dem Tann auf und schreitet vor der Gruppe der Walküren auf der Höhe, nach Brünnhilde spähend, heftig einher.

WOTAN
Wo ist Brünnhild,
wo die Verbrecherin?
Wagt ihr, die Böse
vor mir zu bergen?

DIE ACHT WALKÜREN
Schrecklich ertost dein Toben!
Was taten, Vater, die Töchter,
daß sie dich reizten
zu rasender Wut?

WOTAN
Wollt ihr mich höhnen?
Hütet euch, Freche!
Ich weiß: Brünnhilde
bergt ihr vor mir.
Weichet von ihr,
der ewig Verworfnen,
wie ihren Wert
von sich sie warf!

ROSSWEISSE
Zu uns floh die Verfolgte.

ALLE ACHT WALKÜREN
Unsern Schutz flehte sie an!
Mit Furcht und Zagen
faßt sie dein Zorn:
fur die bange Schwester
bitten wir nun,
daß den ersten Zorn du bezähmst.
Laß dich erweichen für sie,

Scene Two

Wotan comes from the pinewood in a towering rage and strides to the group of Valkyries on the height, looking around for Brünnhilde.

WOTAN
Where is Brünnhild?
Where is the guilty one?
Can you be daring
to hide her from me?

THE EIGHT VALKYRIES
Fearful your cry of anger!
Oh father, pity your daughters;
have we awakened
your terrible rage?

WOTAN
Ha, so you mock me?
Insolent daughters!
I know Brünnhilde
hides in your midst.
Leave her alone,
for she is an outcast,
and all her virtue
is cast away!

ROSSWEISSE
She came here to escape you.

ALL EIGHT VALKYRIES
And she asked for our help!
In fear and anguish
fled from your rage.
For our trembling sister
now we implore:
let the angry storm now be calm.
Father, have mercy on her,

zähme deinen Zorn!

WOTAN
Weichherziges
Weibergezücht!
So matten Mut
gewannt ihr von mir?
Erzog ich euch kühn,
zum Kampfe zu ziehn,
schuf ich die Herzen
euch hart und scharf,
daß ihr Wilden nun weint und greint,
wenn mein Grimm eine Treulose straft?
So wißt denn, Winselnde,
was sie verbrach,
um die euch Zagen
die Zähre entbrennt:
Keine wie sie
kannte mein innerstes Sinnen:
keine wie sie
wußte den Quell meines Willens!
Sie selbst war
meines Wunsches schaffender Schoß:
und so nun brach sie
den seligen Bund,
daß treulos sie
meinem Willen getrotzt,
mein herrschend Gebot
offen verhöhnt,
gegen mich die Waffe gewandt,
die mein Wunsch allein ihr schuf!
Hörst du's, Brünnhilde?
Du, der ich Brünne,
Helm und Wehr,
Wonne und Huld,
Namen und Leben verlieh?
Hörst du mich Klage erheben
und birgst dich bang dem Kläger,
daß feig du der Straf' entflöhst?

BRÜNNHILDE
(tritt aus der Schar der Walküren hervor, schreitet demütigen, doch festen Schrittes von der Felsenspitze herab und tritt so in geringer Entfernung vor Wotan.)
Hier bin ich, Vater:
gebiete die Strafe!

calm your dreadful rage!

WOTAN
Weak-spirited,
womanish brood!
Such whining ways
you learnt not from me!
I tempered your frames
to fight on the field,
made you hard-hearted
and stern and strong:
must I hear you all whine and wail
when I punish a treacherous crime?
I'll tell you, whimperers,
what she has done,
that shameless sister
who has prompted your tears:
Brünnhild alone
knew all my innermost secrets;
Brünnhild alone
saw to the depths of my spirit!
Through her
all my desires took shape in the world:
yet she has broken
the bond of our love,
and, faithless,
she has defied my desire;
my sacred command
openly scorned;
against me lifted the spear
that by Wotan's will she bore!
Hear me, Brünnhilde!
You whom I fashioned,
you who owe
all that you are,
name, even life, to me!
Say, can you hear me accuse you
and hide yourself, you coward,
to try to escape your doom?

BRÜNNHILDE
(steps out from the crowd of Valkyries and advances with humble yet resolute steps down the rock, close to Wotan.)
Here am I, father;
now tell me my sentence!

WOTAN
Nicht straf ich dich erst:
deine Strafe schufst du dir selbst.
Durch meinen Willen
warst du allein:
gegen ihn doch hast du gewollt;
meinen Befehl nur
führtest du aus:
gegen ihn doch hast du befohlen;
Wunschmaid
warst du mir:
gegen mich doch hast du gewünscht;
Schildmaid
warst du mir:
gegen mich doch hobst du den Schild;
Loskieserin
warst du mir:
gegen mich doch kiestest du Lose;
Heldenreizerin
warst du mir:
gegen mich doch reiztest du Helden.
Was sonst du warst,
sagte dir Wotan:
was jetzt du bist,
das sage dir selbst!
Wunschmaid bist du nicht mehr,
Walküre bist du gewesen:
nun sei fortan,
was so du noch bist!

BRÜNNHILDE
(heftig erschreckend)
Du verstößest mich?
Versteh ich den Sinn?

WOTAN
Nicht send ich dich mehr aus Walhall;
nicht weis ich dir mehr
Helden zur Wal;
nicht führst du mehr Sieger
in meinen Saal:
bei der Götter trautem Mahle
das Trinkhorn nicht reichst
du traulich mir mehr;
nicht kos ich dir mehr
den kindischen Mund.
Von göttlicher Schar

WOTAN
I sentence you not:
you have brought your doom on yourself.
My will alone
woke you to life,
and against that will you have worked.
By my commandments
alone you could act,
and against me you have commanded.
Brünnhild
knew my wish,
and against that wish she rebelled.
Brünnhild
bore my shield,
and against me that shield was borne.
Brünnhilde
could choose my fate,
and she chose that fate was against me.
Once I said to her:
Rouse my men,
and she roused a hero against me.
Though once you were
all that I made you,
what you have become
you choose for yourself!
No more child of my will;
Valkyrie are you no longer;
Henceforth remain
what you chose to be!

BRÜNNHILDE
(violently terrified)
So you cast me off?
Is that what you mean?

WOTAN
No more will you ride from Walhall;
no more will you choose
heroes who fall;
or bring me the warriors
who guard my hall;
and in Walhall, when we are feasting,
no more shall you fill
my drink-horn for me;
no more may I kiss
the mouth of my child;
the host of the gods

bist du geschieden,
ausgestoßen
aus der Ewigen Stamm;
gebrochen ist unser Bund;
aus meinem Angesicht bist du verbannt.

no more shall know you;
cast for ever
from the clan of the gods.
You broke the bond of our love,
and from my sight, henceforth, Brünnhild [is banned!

DIE ACHT WALKÜREN
(verlassen, in aufgeregter Bewegung, ihre Stellung, indem sie sich etwas tiefer herabziehen.)
Wehe! Weh!
Schwester, ach Schwester!

THE EIGHT VALKYRIES
(in consternation leave their former position, coming somewhat lower down the rock.)
Horror! Woe!
Sister, oh sister!

BRÜNNHILDE
Nimmst du mir alles,
was einst du gabst?

BRÜNNHILDE
Can you deprive me
of all you gave?

WOTAN
Der dich zwingt, wird dir's entziehn!
Hieher auf den Berg
banne ich dich;
in wehrlosen Schlaf
schließ ich dich fest:
der Mann dann fange die Maid,
der am Wege sie findet und weckt.

WOTAN
He who comes robs you of all!
For here on the rock,
here you must stay;
defenceless in sleep,
here you will lie;
and you'll belong to the man
who can find you and wake you from [sleep.

DIE ACHT WALKÜREN
(kommen in höchster Aufregung von der Felsenspitze ganz herab und umgeben in ängstlichen Gruppen Brünnhilde, welche halb kniend vor Wotan liegt.)
Halt ein, o Vater,
halt ein den Fluch!
Soll die Maid verblühn
und verbleichen dem Mann?
Hör unser Flehn!
Schrecklicher Gott,
wende von ihr
die schreiende Schmach!
Wie die Schwester träfe uns selber der [Schimpf.

THE EIGHT VALKYRIES
(descend completely from the rocky height, in great consternation, and in anxious groups surround Brünnhilde, who lies half-kneeling before Wotan.)
Ah no, father!
Recall the curse!
Shall our sister bend
to the will of a man?
Endless disgrace!
Stern-hearted God!
Ah, spare her,
spare her the shame!
for our sister's shame on us then would [fall!

WOTAN
Hörtet ihr nicht,
was ich verhängt?
Aus eurer Schar
ist die treulose Schwester geschieden;
mit euch zu Roß

WOTAN
Did you not hear
what I decreed?
that from your band
your treacherous sister is banished?
no more shall she ride

durch die Lüfte nicht reitet sie länger;
die magdliche Blume
verblüht der Maid;
ein Gatte gewinnt
ihre weibliche Gunst;
dem herrischen Manne
gehorcht sie fortan;
am Herde sitzt sie und spinnt,
aller Spottenden Ziel und Spiel.
(Brünnhilde sinkt mit einem Schrei zu Boden; die Walküren weichen entsetzt mit heftigem Geräusch von ihrer Seite.)
Schreckt euch ihr Los?
So flieht die Verlorne!
Weichet von ihr
und haltet euch fern!
Wer von euch wagte,
bei ihr zu weilen,
wer mir zum Trotz
zu der Traurigen hielt',
die Törin teilte ihr Los:
das künd ich der Kühnen an!
Fort jetzt von hier!
Meidet den Felsen!
Hurtig jagt mir von hinnen,
sonst erharrt Jammer euch hier!

through the clouds with her sisters to
the flower of her beauty [battle;
will fade and die;
a husband will gain
all her womanly grace;
that masterful husband
will make her obey;
she'll sit and spin by the fire,
and the world will deride her fate!
(Brünnhilde sinks with a cry to the ground; the Valkyries, in great agitation, shrink in horror from her side.)
Are you afraid?
Then flee from the lost one!
Leave her alone,
and never return!
If one of you
should come to console her,
if she should dare
to defy my command,
that rash one shares in her fate:
so now from this peak be gone!
Off with you now!
Do not go near her!
Ride away from this mountain,
or the same fate shall be yours!

DIE ACHT WALKÜREN
Weh! Weh!
(Sie fahren mit wildem Wehschrei auseinander und stürzen in hastiger Flucht in den Tann. Schwarzes Gewölk lagert sich dicht am Felsenrande: man hört wildes Geräusch im Tann. Ein greller Blitzesglanz bricht in dem Gewölk aus; in ihm erblickt man die Walküren mit verhängtem Zügel, in eine Schar zusammengedrängt, wild davonjagen. Bald legt sich der Sturm; die Gewitterwolken verziehen sich allmählich. In der folgenden Szene bricht, bei endlich ruhigem Wetter, Abenddämmerung ein, der am Schlusse Nacht folgt.)

THE EIGHT VALKYRIES
Woe! Woe!
(They separate with loud cries of distress and fly in haste into the wood. Black clouds gather on the cliffs; a wild tumult is heard in the wood. A vivid flash of lightning breaks through the clouds; in it are seen the Valkyries, close-grouped, their bridles hanging loose, riding wildly away. The storm soon subsides; the thunderclouds gradually disperse. During the following scene, in increasingly calm weather, twilight falls, and finally night.)

Dritte Szene

Wotan und Brünnhilde, die noch zu seinen Füßen hingestreckt liegt, sind allein zurückgeblieben. Langes, feierliches Schweigen: unveränderte Stellung.

BRÜNNHILDE
(beginnt das Haupt langsam ein wenig zu erheben. Schüchtern beginnend und steigernd:)
War es so schmählich,
was ich verbrach,
daß mein Verbrechen so schmählich du [bestrafst?
War es so niedrig,
was ich dir tat,
daß du so tief mir Erniedrigung schaffst?
War es so ehrlos,
was ich beging,
daß mein Vergehn nun die Ehre mir [raubt?
(Sie erhebt sich allmählich bis zur knienden Stellung.)
O sag, Vater!
Sieh mir ins Auge:
schweige den Zorn,
zähme die Wut
und deute mir hell
die dunkle Schuld,
die mit starrem Trotze dich zwingt,
zu verstoßen dein trautestes Kind!

WOTAN
(in unveränderter Stellung, ernst und düster)
Frag deine Tat,
sie deutet dir deine Schuld!

BRÜNNHILDE
Deinen Befehl
führte ich aus.

WOTAN
Befahl ich dir,
für den Wälsung zu fechten?

BRÜNNHILDE
So hießest du mich
als Herrscher der Wal!

Scene Three

Wotan and Brünnhilde, who still lies at his feet, are left alone. A long solemn silence: their positions remain unchanged.

BRÜNNHILDE
(begins slowly to raise her head a little; beginning timidly and becoming more confident:)
Was it so shameful,
what I have done,
that you must punish my deed with [endless shame?
Was it disgraceful,
what I have done;
do I deserve to be plunged in disgrace?
Was my dishonour
boundless and base,
for that offence must my honour be lost?
(She raises herself gradually to a kneeling position.)
Oh speak, father!
Look in my eyes:
silence your scorn,
soften your wrath,
explain to me
all the grievous guilt
that compels you, cruel and harsh,
to abandon your true, loving child.

WOTAN
(in unchanged attitude, gravely and gloomily)
Ask what you did;
your deed will tell you your guilt!

BRÜNNHILDE
By your command
bravely I fought.

WOTAN
Did I command you
to fight for the Wälsung?

BRÜNNHILDE
That was your command,
as master of fate.

WOTAN
Doch meine Weisung
nahm ich wieder zurück!

BRÜNNHILDE
Als Fricka den eignen
Sinn dir entfremdet;
da ihrem Sinn du dich fügtest,
warst du selber dir Feind.

WOTAN
(leise und bitter)
Daß du mich verstanden, wähnt' ich
und strafte den wissenden Trotz:
doch feig und dumm
dachtest du mich!
So hätt' ich Verrat nicht zu rächen,
zu gering wärst du meinem Grimm!

BRÜNNHILDE
Nicht weise bin ich,
doch wußt' ich das eine,
daß den Wälsung du liebtest.
Ich wußte den Zwiespalt,
der dich zwang,
dies eine ganz zu vergessen.
Das andre mußtest
einzig du sehn,
was zu schaun so herb
schmerzte dein Herz:
daß Siegmund Schutz du versagtest.

WOTAN
Du wußtest es so
und wagtest dennoch den Schutz?

BRÜNNHILDE
(leise beginnend)
Weil für dich im Auge
das eine ich hielt,
dem, im Zwange des andren
schmerzlich entzweit,
ratlos den Rücken du wandtest!
Die im Kampfe Wotan
den Rücken bewacht,
die sah nun das nur,
was du nicht sahst:

WOTAN
But that command
you knew I later recalled!

BRÜNNHILDE
When Fricka had made you
change your decision;
and when her words conquered your will,
you were false to yourself.

WOTAN
(softly and bitterly)
Yet you understood me fully;
I warned of my rage if you failed;
but no, you thought:
Wotan is weak!
A treacherous crime must be punished;
else on you I'd not waste my rage.

BRÜNNHILDE
I know so little,
but one thing I did know,
that the Wälsung you loved.
I saw all your torment,
as you tried
to force yourself to forget this.
The other thing
was all you could see,
and the sight of that
tortured your heart:
that Siegmund could not be shielded.

WOTAN
You knew that was so,
and yet you went to his help?

BRÜNNHILDE
(beginning softly)
Yes, because my eyes
saw but one thing alone,
one all-conquering fact
that you would not face;
you turned your back in your sorrow!
I who guard your back
when you fight in the field,
I saw that one thing
which you could not:

Siegmund mußt' ich sehn.
Tod kündend
trat ich vor ihn,
gewahrte sein Auge,
hörte sein Wort;
ich vernahm des Helden
heilige Not;
tönend erklang mir
des Tapfersten Klage:
freiester Liebe
furchtbares Leid,
traurigsten Mutes
mächtigster Trotz!
Meinem Ohr erscholl,
mein Aug' erschaute,
was tief im Busen das Herz
zu heil'gem Beben mir traf.
Scheu und staunend
stand ich in Scham.
Ihm nur zu dienen
konnt' ich noch denken:
Sieg oder Tod
mit Siegmund zu teilen:
dies nur erkannt' ich
zu kiesen als Los!
Der diese Liebe
mir ins Herz gehaucht,
dem Willen, der
dem Wälsung mich gesellt,
ihm innig vertraut—
trotzt' ich deinem Gebot.

WOTAN
So tatest du,
was so gern zu tun ich begehrt,
doch was nicht zu tun
die Not zwiefach mich zwang?
So leicht wähntest du
Wonne der Liebe erworben,
wo brennend Weh
in das Herz mir brach,
wo gräßliche Not
den Grimm mir schuf,
einer Welt zuliebe
der Liebe Quell
im gequälten Herzen zu hemmen?
Wo gegen mich selber

Siegmund I beheld.
I said
you had marked him for death;
I gazed in his eyes then,
heard his reply;
and I shared that hero's
grief and distress,
hearing the call
of his brave lamentation—
love's holy yearning,
hopeless despair—
proud in defiance,
dauntless in grief!
In my ears it rang;
my eyes were dazzled;
my mind was troubled;
a new emotion stole through my heart.
Shy, astonished,
I stood ashamed.
How could I help him,
how could I save him?
Victory or death,
with Siegmund I'd share it!
One thought possessed me,
and I had no choice!
You, who this love
in my heart inspired,
when you inspired
the Wälsung with your will,
you were not betrayed—
though I broke your command.

WOTAN
So you would attempt
what I longed so dearly to do,
but which cruel fate
forbade me to achieve?
So you thought
that love could be captured so lightly,
while burning woe
broke my heart in two,
and terrible grief
awoke my rage;
when, to save creation,
the spring of love
in my tortured heart I imprisoned?
Then, burning with anger,

ich sehrend mich wandte,
aus Ohnmachtsschmerzen
schäumend ich aufschoß,
wütender Sehnsucht
sengender Wunsch
den schrecklichen Willen mir schuf,
in den Trümmern der eignen Welt
meine ew'ge Trauer zu enden:
da labte süß
dich selige Lust;
wonniger Rührung
üppigen Rausch
enttrankst du lachend
der Liebe Trank,
als mir göttliche Not
nagende Galle gemischt?
Deinen leichten Sinn
laß dich denn leiten:
von mir sagtest du dich los.
Dich muß ich meiden,
gemeinsam mit dir
nicht darf ich Rat mehr raunen;
getrennt nicht dürfen
traut wir mehr schaffen:
so weit Leben und Luft,
darf der Gott dir nicht mehr begegnen!

BRÜNNHILDE
Wohl taugte dir nicht
die tör'ge Maid,
die staunend im Rate
nicht dich verstand,
wie mein eigner Rat
nur das eine mir riet:
zu lieben, was du geliebt.
Muß ich denn scheiden
und scheu dich meiden,
mußt du spalten,
was einst sich umspannt,
die eigne Hälfte
fern von dir halten,
daß sonst sie ganz dir gehörte,
du Gott, vergiß das nicht!
Dein ewig Teil
nicht wirst du entehren,
Schande nicht wollen,
die dich beschimpft:

I turned on myself,
from an anguished weakness
rising in frenzy,
yearning and raging,
I was inspired
and driven to a fearful resolve:
in the wreck of my ruined world
my unending sorrow I'd bury:
while you lay lapped
in blissful delight,
filled with emotion's
rapturous joy;
you laughed, while drinking
the draught of love,
and I tasted the gall,
drained bitter sorrow and grief!
You indulged your love;
now let it lead you:
from me you have turned away.
So I must shun you;
no more may I share
with you my secret counsels;
henceforth our paths
are parted forever:
for, while life shall endure,
I, the god, no more shall behold you.

BRÜNNHILDE
Unworthy of you
this foolish maid,
who, stunned by your counsel,
misunderstood,
when that one command
overruled all the rest:
to love him whom you had loved.
If I must lose you,
and you must leave me,
if you sever
the bonds that we tied,
then half your being
you have abandoned,
which once belonged to you only.
O god, forget not that!
That other self
you must not dishonour;
if you disgrace her,
it falls on you:

dich selbst ließest du sinken,
sähst du dem Spott mich zum Spiel!

WOTAN
Du folgtest selig
der Liebe Macht:
folge nun dem,
den du lieben mußt!

BRÜNNHILDE
Soll ich aus Walhall scheiden,
nicht mehr mit dir schaffen und walten,
dem herrischen Manne
gehorchen fortan:
dem feigen Prahler
gib mich nicht preis!
Nicht wertlos sei er,
der mich gewinnt.

WOTAN
Von Walvater schiedest du,
nicht wählen darf er für dich.

BRÜNNHILDE
(leise mit vertraulicher Heimlichkeit)
Du zeugtest ein edles Geschlecht;
kein Zager kann je ihm entschlagen:
der weihlichste Held—ich weiß es—
entblüht dem Wälsungenstamm!

WOTAN
Schweig von dem Wälsungenstamm!
Von dir geschieden,
schied ich von ihm:
vernichten mußt' ihn der Neid!

BRÜNNHILDE
Die von dir sich riß,
rettete ihn.
Sieglinde hegt
die heiligste Frucht;
in Schmerz und Leid,
wie kein Weib sie gelitten,
wird sie gebären,
was bang sie birgt.

WOTAN
Nie suche bei mir

your fame then would be darkened,
if I were scorned and despised!

WOTAN
You chose in rapture
the path of love:
follow love's path,
and obey your lord!

BRÜNNHILDE
If I must go from Walhall,
and play no more part in your actions,
and take as my master
some man to obey:
be sure no coward
makes me his prize;
be sure some hero
wins me as bride!

WOTAN
From Wotan you turned away;
your conqueror I cannot choose.

BRÜNNHILDE
(softly and confidingly)
You fathered a glorious race;
that race cannot bring forth a coward:
a hero will come, I know it;
be born of Wälsung blood.

WOTAN
Name not the Wälsungs to me!
By your desertion
the Wälsungs were doomed;
my rage destroys all the race!

BRÜNNHILDE
She who turned from you
rescued the race.
Sieglinde bears
the holiest fruit;
in pain and grief
such as no woman suffered,
she will give birth
to a Wälsung child.

WOTAN
I'll offer no help—

Schutz für die Frau,
noch für ihres Schoßes Frucht!

BRÜNNHILDE
Sie wahret das Schwert,
das du Siegmund schufest.

WOTAN
(heftig)
Und das ich ihm in Stücken schlug!
Nicht streb, o Maid,
den Mut mir zu stören;
erwarte dein Los,
wie sich's dir wirft;
nicht kiesen kann ich es dir!
Doch fort muß ich jetzt,
fern mich verziehn;
zuviel schon zögert' ich hier.
Von der Abwendigen
wend ich mich ab;
nicht wissen darf ich,
was sie sich wünscht:
die Strafe nur
muß vollstreckt ich sehn!

BRÜNNHILDE
Was hast du erdacht,
daß ich erdulde?

WOTAN
In festen Schlaf
verschließ ich dich:
wer so die Wehrlose weckt,
dem ward, erwacht, sie zum Weib!

BRÜNNHILDE
(stürzt auf ihre Knie.)
Soll fesselnder Schlaf
fest mich binden,
dem feigsten Manne
zur leichten Beute:
dies eine mußt du erhören,
was heil'ge Angst zu dir fleht!
Die Schlafende schütze
mit scheuchendem Schrecken,
daß nur ein furchtlos
freiester Held

neither to her
nor to any Wälsung child.

BRÜNNHILDE
She still has the sword
that you made for Siegmund.

WOTAN
(vehemently)
And which I later broke again!
Seek not, O child,
to change my decision;
await now your fate,
as it must fall:
I may not choose it for you!
But now I must go,
far from this place;
too long now I have delayed.
For as you turned from me,
I turn from you;
I may not even
ask what you wish:
your sentence now
I must see fulfilled.

BRÜNNHILDE
What have you decreed
that I must suffer?

WOTAN
In long, deep sleep
you shall be bound:
the man who wakes you again,
that man awakes you as wife!

BRÜNNHILDE
(falls on her knees.)
If fetters of sleep
come to bind me,
if I must fall
to the man who finds me,
then one thing more you must grant me;
in deepest anguish I pray!
Oh shelter my slumber,
protect me with terrors,
let only one
who is fearless and free

hier auf dem Felsen
einst mich fänd'!

WOTAN
Zuviel begehrst du,
zuviel der Gunst!

BRÜNNHILDE
(seine Knie umfassend)
Dies eine
mußt du erhören!
Zerknicke dein Kind,
das dein Knie umfaßt;
zertritt die Traute,
zertrümmre die Maid,
ihres Leibes Spur
zerstöre dein Speer:
doch gib, Grausamer, nicht
der gräßlichsten Schmach sie preis!
(mit wilder Begeisterung)
Auf dein Gebot
entbrenne ein Feuer;
den Felsen umglühe
lodernde Glut;
es leck ihre Zung',
es fresse ihr Zahn
den Zagen, der frech sich wagte,
dem freislichen Felsen zu nahn!

WOTAN
(überwältigt und tief ergriffen, wendet sich lebhaft zu Brünnhilde, erhebt sie von den Knien und blickt ihr gerührt ins Auge.)
Leb wohl, du kühnes,
herrliches Kind!
Du meines Herzens heiligster Stolz!
Leb wohl! Leb wohl! Leb wohl!
(sehr leidenschaftlich)
Muß ich dich meiden,
und darf nicht minnig
mein Gruß dich mehr grüßen;
sollst du nun nicht mehr
neben mir reiten,
noch Met beim Mahl mir reichen;
muß ich verlieren
dich, die ich liebte,
du lachende Lust meines Auges:

none but a hero
find me here!

WOTAN
Too much you are asking,
too great a grace!

BRÜNNHILDE
(embracing his knees)
This one thing more
you must grant me!
Oh kill me at once
as I clasp your knee;
destroy your daughter,
condemn me to die,
let my breast receive
one blow from your spear;
but ah! cast not this shame,
this cruel disgrace on me!
(with wild inspiration)
At your command
a flame can be kindled,
a fiery guardian,
girding the rock,
to lick with its tongues,
to tear with its teeth
the craven who rashly ventures,
who dares to approach near the rock!

WOTAN
(overcome and deeply moved, turns eagerly towards Brünnhilde, raises her from her knees and gazes with emotion into her eyes.)
Farewell, my valiant,
glorious child!
You were the holiest pride of my heart!
Farewell! Farewell! Farewell!
(very passionately)
Though I must leave you,
and may no longer
embrace you in greeting;
though you may no more
ride beside me,
nor bear my mead in Walhall;
though I abandon you
whom I love so,
the laughing delight of my eye:

ein bräutliches Feuer
soll dir nun brennen,
wie nie einer Braut es gebrannt!
Flammende Glut
umglühe den Fels;
mit zehrenden Schrecken
scheuch es den Zagen;
der Feige fliehe
Brünnhildes Fels!
Denn einer nur freie die Braut,
der freier als ich, der Gott!
(Brünnhilde sinkt, gerührt und begeistert, an Wotans Brust; er hält sie lange umfangen. Sie schlägt das Haupt wieder zurück und blickt, immer noch ihn umfassend, feierlich ergriffen Wotan in das Auge.)
Der Augen leuchtendes Paar,
das oft ich lächelnd gekost,
wenn Kampfeslust
ein Kuß dir lohnte,
wenn kindisch lallend
der Helden Lob
von holden Lippen dir floß:
dieser Augen strahlendes Paar,
das oft im Sturm mir geglänzt,
wenn Hoffnungssehnen
das Herz mir sengte,
nach Weltenwonne
mein Wunsch verlangte
aus wild webendem Bangen:
zum letztenmal
letz es mich heut
mit des Lebewohles
letztem Kuß!
Dem glücklichern Manne
glänze sein Stern:
dem unseligen Ew'gen
muß es scheidend sich schließen.
(Er faßt ihr Haupt in beide Hände.)
Denn so kehrt
der Gott sich dir ab,
so küßt er die Gottheit von dir!
(Er küßt sie lange auf die Augen. Sie sinkt mit geschlossenen Augen, sanft ermattend, in seinen Armen zurück. Er geleitet sie zart auf einen niedrigen Mooshügel zu liegen, über den sich eine breitästige Tanne ausstreckt. Er betrachtet sie und schließt ihr den Helm: sein Auge weilt dann auf

a bridal fire
shall blaze to protect you,
as never has burned for a bride.
Threatening flames
shall flare from the rock;
the craven will fear it,
cringe from its fury;
the weak will flee
from Brünnhilde's rock!
For one alone wins you as bride,
one freer than I, the god!
(Brünnhilde, moved and exalted, sinks on Wotan's breast: he holds her in a long embrace. She throws her head back again and, still embracing Wotan, gazes with solemn rapture into his eyes.)

These radiant, glorious eyes,
which, smiling, often I kissed,
when courage
I acclaimed with kisses,
while childish prattle
in heroes' praise
so sweetly poured from your lips:
yes, these gleaming, radiant eyes,
which shone so bright in the storm,
when hopeless yearning
consumed my spirit,
and worldly pleasures
were all I longed for,
when fear fastened upon me—
their glorious fire
gladdens me now,
as I take this loving,
last farewell!
On some happy mortal
one day they will shine:
but I, hapless immortal,
I must lose them forever.
(He clasps her head in his hands.)
And sadly
the god must depart;
my kiss takes your godhead away!
(He presses a long kiss on her eyes. She sinks back with closed eyes, unconscious, in his arms. He gently supports her to a low mossy bank, which is overshadowed by a wide-branching fir tree, and lays her upon it. He looks upon her and closes her helmet; his eye then rests on the form of the

der Gestalt der Schlafenden, die er mit dem großen Stahlschilde der Walküre ganz zudeckt. Langsam kehrt er sich ab, mit einem schmerzlichen Blicke wendet er sich noch einmal um. Dann schreitet er mit feierlichem Entschlusse in die Mitte der Bühne und kehrt seines Speeres Spitze gegen einen mächtigen Felsstein.)

Loge, hör!
Lausche hieher!
Wie zuerst ich dich fand,
als feurige Glut,
wie dann einst du mir schwandest
als schweifende Lohe;
wie ich dich band,
bann ich dich heut!
Herauf, wabernde Lohe,
umlodre mir feurig den Fels!

(Er stößt mit dem Folgenden dreimal mit dem Speer auf den Stein.)

Loge! Loge! Hieher!

(Dem Stein entfährt ein Feuerstrahl, der zur allmählich immer helleren Flammenglut anschwillt. Lichte Flackerlohe bricht aus. Lichte Brunst umgibt Wotan mit wildem Flackern. Er weist mit dem Speere gebieterisch dem Feuermeere den Umkreis des Felsenrandes zur Strömung an; alsbald zieht es sich nach dem Hintergrunde, wo es nun fortwährend den Bergsaum umlodert.)

Wer meines Speeres
Spitze fürchtet,
durchschreite das Feuer nie!

(Er streckt den Speer wie zum Banne aus. Dann blickt er schmerzlich auf Brünnhilde zurück, wendet sich langsam zum Gehen und blickt noch einmal zurück, ehe er durch das Feuer verschwindet. Der Vorhang fällt.)

sleeper, which he completely covers with the great steel shield of the Valkyrie. He turns slowly away, then turns round again with a sorrowful look. Then he strides with solemn decision to the middle of the stage, and directs the point of his spear towards a massive rock.)

Loge, hear!
Come at my call!
As when first you were found,
a fiery glow,
as when then you escaped me,
a wandering flicker;
once you were bound:
be so again!
Arise! Come, flickering Loge;
surround the rock, ring it with flame!

(During the following he strikes the rock three times with his spear.)

Loge! Loge! Appear!

(A flash of flame leaps from the rock, and gradually increases to an ever-brightening fiery glow. Flickering flames break out. Bright, shooting flames surround Wotan. With his spear, he directs the sea of fire to encircle the rocks; it presently spreads toward the background, where it encloses the mountain in flames.)

Only the man
who braves my spear-point
can pass through this sea of flame!

(He stretches out the spear as if casting a spell. Then he gazes sorrowfully back at Brünnhilde, turns slowly to depart, and looks back once more before he disappears through the fire. The curtain falls.)

Siegfried

Second Day of the Festival Play

The Ring of the Nibelung

Dramatis Personae

SIEGFRIED	*Tenor*
MIME	*Tenor*
THE WANDERER	*Bass*
ALBERICH	*Bass*
FAFNER	*Bass*
ERDA	*Contralto*
BRÜNNHILDE	*Soprano*
Voice of the Woodbird	*Soprano*

Erster Aufzug

Wald

Den Vordergrund bildet ein Teil einer Felsenhöhle, die sich links tiefer nach innen zieht, nach rechts aber gegen drei Viertel der Bühne einnimmt. Zwei natürlich gebildete Eingänge stehen dem Walde zu offen: der eine nach rechts, unmittelbar im Hintergrunde, der andere, breitere, ebenda seitwärts. An der Hinterwand, nach links zu, steht ein großer Schmiedeherd, aus Felsstücken natürlich geformt; künstlich ist nur der große Blasebalg: die rohe Esse geht—ebenfalls natürlich—durch das Felsendach hinauf. Ein sehr großer Amboß und andere Schmiedegerätschaften.

Erste Szene

MIME
(sitzt am Ambosse und hämmert mit wachsender Unruhe an einem Schwerte, endlich hält er unmutig ein.)
Zwangvolle Plage!

Act One

A Forest

The foreground represents part of a cave in the rocks, extending inwards more deeply to the left, but occupying about three-quarters of the stage-depth to the right. There are two natural entrances to the forest, the one to the right opening directly, and the other, broader one opening sideways, to the background. On the rear wall, to the left, is a large smith's forge, formed naturally from pieces of rock; only the large bellows are artificial. A rough chimney, also natural, passes through the roof of the cave. A very large anvil and other smith's tools.

Scene One

MIME
(sits at the anvil and with increasing anxiety hammers at a sword; at length he stops working, in ill-humour.)
Wearisome labour!

Müh' ohne Zweck!
Das beste Schwert,
das je ich geschweißt,
in der Riesen Fäusten
hielte es fest:
doch dem ich's geschmiedet,
der schmähliche Knabe,
er knickt und schmeißt es entzwei,
als schüf' ich Kindergeschmeid'!
(Mime wirft das Schwert unmutig auf den Amboß, stemmt die Arme ein und blickt sinnend zu Boden.)

Es gibt ein Schwert,
das er nicht zerschwänge:
Notungs Trümmer
zertrotzt' er mir nicht,
könnt' ich die starken
Stücken schweißen,
die meine Kunst
nicht zu kitten weiß!
Könnt' ich's dem Kühnen schmieden,
meiner Schmach erlangt' ich da Lohn!
(Er sinkt tiefer zurück und neigt sinnend das Haupt.)
Fafner, der wilde Wurm,
lagert im finstren Wald;
mit des furchtbaren Leibes Wucht
der Niblungen Hort
hütet er dort.
Siegfrieds kindischer Kraft
erläge wohl Fafners Leib:
des Niblungen Ring
erränge er mir.
Nur ein Schwert taugt zu der Tat;
nur Notung nützt meinem Neid,
wenn Siegfried sehrend ihn schwingt:
und ich kann's nicht schweißen,
Notung, das Schwert!
(Er hat das Schwert wieder zurechtgelegt und hämmert in höchstem Unmut daran weiter.)
Zwangvolle Plage!
Müh' ohne Zweck!
Das beste Schwert,
das je ich geschweißt,
nie taugt es je
zu der einzigen Tat!
Ich tappre und hämmre nur,

Work till I drop!
The strongest sword
I struggle to make,
an amazing weapon,
fit for a giant:
but when I have made it,
that insolent Siegfried
just laughs and snaps it in two,
as though I'd made him a toy!
(In ill humour, Mime throws the sword down on the anvil, places his arms akimbo, and gazes at the ground in thought.)
I know one sword
that could not be shattered:
Notung's fragments
he never would break,
if only I could forge,
those pieces,
if but my skill
could achieve that deed!
If I could forge those fragments,
all my shame would change into joy!
(He sinks back further and lowers his head in thought.)
Fafner, the mighty dragon,
lies there within those woods
and protects with his monstrous bulk
the Nibelung gold,
guarding it well.
Siegfried's conquering strength
could quickly lay Fafner low:
the Nibelung's ring
would then come to me.
And one sword is all that I need,
and Notung only will serve,
when Siegfried deals him the blow:
and I cannot forge it,
Notung, the sword!
(He has readjusted the sword, and returns to his hammering in deepest dejection.)
Wearisome labour!
Work till I drop!
The strongest sword
that ever I make
will prove too weak
for that one mighty deed!
I tinker and tap away

weil der Knabe es heischt:
er knickt und schmeißt es entzwei
und schmäht doch, schmied ich ihm [nicht!
(Er läßt den Hammer fallen.)

because Siegfried commands:
he laughs and snaps it in two,
and scolds me, if I don't work!
(He lets the hammer fall.)

SIEGFRIED
(in wilder Waldkleidung, mit einem silbernen Horn an einer Kette, kommt mit jähem Ungestüm aus dem Walde herein; er hat einen großen Bären mit einem Bastseile gezäumt und treibt diesen mit lustigem Übermute gegen Mime an.)
Hoiho! Hoiho!
Hau ein! Hau ein!
Friß ihn! Friß ihn,
den Fratzenschmied!
(Er lacht. Mime entsinkt vor Schreck das Schwert; er flüchtet hinter den Herd; Siegfried treibt ihm den Bären überall nach.)

SIEGFRIED
(in rough forest dress, with a silver horn slung from a chain, comes in boisterously from the forest. He has bridled a large bear with a bast rope, and in exuberant high spirits he sets it at Mime.)
Hoiho! Hoiho!
Come on! Come in!
Bite him! Bite him,
the lazy smith!
(He laughs. Mime drops the sword in his fright, and runs behind the forge. Siegfried urges the bear to chase him about.)

MIME
Fort mit dem Tier!
Was taugt mir der Bär?

MIME
Off with that beast!
Why bring me a bear?

SIEGFRIED
Zu zwei komm ich,
dich besser zu zwicken!
Brauner, frag nach dem Schwert!

SIEGFRIED
He came with me
to teach you to hurry!
Bruin, beg for the sword!

MIME
He! Laß das Wild!
Dort liegt die Waffe:
fertig fegt' ich sie heut.

MIME
Hey! let him go!
There lies your weapon,
forged and finished today.

SIEGFRIED
So fährst du heute noch heil!
(Er löst dem Bären den Zaum und gibt ihm damit einen Schlag auf den Rücken.)
Lauf, Brauner,
dich brauch ich nicht mehr!
(Der Bär läuft in den Wald zurück.)

SIEGFRIED
Well, then today you are free!
(He releases the bear, and gives him a flick on the back with the rope.)
Off, Bruin!
You're needed no more.
(The bear runs off into the forest.)

MIME
(kommt zitternd hinter dem Herde hervor.)
Wohl leid ich's gern,
erlegst du Bären:
Was bringst du lebend
die Braunen heim?

MIME
(comes out trembling from behind the hearth.)
To killing bears
I've no objection,
but why bring live ones
inside the cave?

SIEGFRIED
(setzt sich, um sich vom Lachen zu erholen.)
Nach beßrem Gesellen sucht' ich,
als daheim mir einer sitzt;
im tiefen Walde mein Horn
ließ ich hallend da ertönen:
ob sich froh mir gesellte
ein guter Freund,
das frug ich mit dem Getön!
Aus dem Busche kam ein Bär,
der hörte mir brummend zu;
er gefiel mir besser als du,
doch beßre fänd' ich wohl noch!
Mit dem zähen Baste
zäumt' ich ihn da,
dich, Schelm, nach dem Schwerte zu fragen.
(Er springt auf und geht auf den Amboß zu.)

MIME
(nimmt das Schwert, es Siegfried zu reichen.)
Ich schuf die Waffe scharf,
ihrer Schneide wirst du dich freun.
(Er hält das Schwert ängstlich in der Hand fest, das Siegfried ihm heftig entwindet.)

SIEGFRIED
Was frommt seine helle Schneide,
ist der Stahl nicht hart und fest!
(das Schwert mit der Hand prüfend)
Hei! Was ist das
für müß'ger Tand!
Den schwachen Stift
nennst du ein Schwert?
(Er zerschlägt es auf dem Amboß, daß die Stücken ringsum fliegen; Mime weicht erschrocken aus.)
Da hast du die Stücken,
schändlicher Stümper:
hätt' ich am Schädel
dir sie zerschlagen!
Soll mich der Prahler
länger noch prellen?
Schwatzt mir von Riesen
und rüstigen Kämpfen,
von kühnen Taten
und tüchtiger Wehr;
will Waffen mir schmieden,

SIEGFRIED
(sits down to recover from his laughter.)
I wanted a better comrade
than the one I leave at home;
and so I called with my horn,
set the forest glades resounding:
Would I find what I longed for,
a faithful friend?—
that's what I asked with my call!
From the bushes came a bear,
who growled as I played my tune;
and I liked him better than you—
though better still I shall find!
So I bridled him
and brought him along
to see if the sword had been finished.
(He jumps up and goes across to the anvil.)

MIME
(takes the sword to give it to Siegfried.)
I made it keen and sharp,
and its shine will gladden your heart.
(Anxiously he holds on to it, but Siegfried snatches it from him.)

SIEGFRIED
What use is the shiny sharpness
if the steel's not hard and true!
(testing the sword with his hand)
Hey! what a useless
thing you have made!
A feeble pin!
Call it a sword?
(He smashes it on the anvil, so that the splinters fly about. Mime shrinks in terror.)
Well, there are the pieces,
blundering boaster;
I should have smashed it
there on your brainpan!
Now will the liar
brag any longer,
talking of giants,
and boldness in battle,
and deeds of daring,
and fearless defence?
And weapons you'll forge me,

Schwerte schaffen;
rühmt seine Kunst,
als könnt' er was Rechts:
nehm' ich zur Hand nun,
was er gehämmert,
mit einem Griff
zergreif ich den Quark!
Wär' mir nicht schier
zu schäbig der Wicht,
ich zerschmiedet' ihn selbst
mit seinem Geschmeid,
den alten albernen Alp!
Des Ärgers dann hätt' ich ein End'!
(Siegfried wirft sich wütend auf eine Steinbank zur Seite rechts. Mime ist ihm immer vorsichtig ausgewichen.)

MIME
Nun tobst du wieder wie toll:
dein Undank, traun, ist arg!
Mach ich dem bösen Buben
nicht alles gleich zu best,
was ich ihm Gutes schuf,
vergißt er gar zu schnell!
Willst du denn nie gedenken,
was ich dich lehrt' vom Danke?
Dem sollst du willig gehorchen,
der je sich wohl dir erwies.
(Siegfried wendet sich unmutig um, mit dem Gesicht nach der Wand, so daß er Mime den Rücken kehrt.)
Das willst du wieder nicht hören!
(Er steht verlegen; dann geht er in die Küche am Herd.)
Doch speisen magst du wohl?
Vom Spieße bring ich den Braten:
versuchtest du gern den Sud?
Für dich sott ich ihn gar.
(Er bietet Siegfried Speise hin; dieser, ohne sich umzuwenden, schmeißt ihm Topf und Braten aus der Hand.)

SIEGFRIED
Braten briet ich mir selbst:
deinen Sudel sauf allein!

MIME
(mit kläglich kreischender Stimme)
Das ist nun der Liebe

swords you'll fashion,
praising your skill,
and proud of your craft?
Yet when I handle
what you have fashioned—
a single blow
destroys all your trash!
If he were not
too mean for my rage,
I should fling in the fire
the smith and his works—
the aged doddering dwarf!
My anger would then have an end!
(In a rage Siegfried flings himself down on a stone seat to the right. Mime has carefully kept out of his way.)

MIME
Again you rage like a fool,
ungrateful, heartless boy!
Maybe today I've failed you;
but when my work is not good
then you at once forget
the good things I have done!
Must I once more remind you
that you should be more grateful?
And you should learn to obey me,
who always showed you such love.
(Siegfried turns away crossly, his face to the wall, his back to Mime.)

Now once again you're not listening!
(He stands perplexed, and then goes to the cooking pots at the fireplace.)
But food is what you need:
come, try this meat I have roasted;
or would you prefer this soup?
For you, all is prepared.
(He brings food to Siegfried, who without turning round knocks bowl and meat out of Mime's hands.)

SIEGFRIED
Meat I roast for myself:
you can drink your slops alone!

MIME
(in a querulous screech)
Fine reward

schlimmer Lohn!
Das der Sorgen
schmählicher Sold!
Als zullendes Kind
zog ich dich auf,
wärmte mit Kleiden
den kleinen Wurm:
Speise und Trank
trug ich dir zu,
hütete dich
wie die eigne Haut.
Und wie du erwuchsest,
wartet' ich dein;
dein Lager schuf ich,
daß leicht du schliefst.
Dir schmiedet' ich Tand
und ein tönend Horn;
dich zu erfreun,
müht' ich mich froh.
Mit klugem Rate
riet ich dir klug,
mit lichtem Wissen
lehrt' ich dich Witz.
Sitz' ich daheim
in Fleiß und Schweiß,
nach Herzenslust
schweifst du umher.
Für dich nur in Plage,
in Pein nur für dich
verzehr ich mich alter,
armer Zwerg!
(schluchzend)
Und aller Lasten
ist das nun mein Lohn,
daß der hastige Knabe
mich quält und haßt!
(Siegfried hat sich wieder umgewendet und ruhig in Mimes Blick geforscht. Mime begegnet Siegfrieds Blick und sucht den seinigen scheu zu bergen.)

for all my loving care!
Thus the boy repays
what I've done!
A whimpering babe,
born in these woods—
Mime was kind
to the tiny mite;
feeding you well,
keeping you warm,
sheltering you safe
as my very self.
And when you grew older
I was your nurse;
when you were sleepy
I smoothed your bed.
I made you nice toys
and that shining horn,
toiling away,
trying to please:
my clever counsels
sharpened your wits;
I tried to make you
crafty and bright.
Staying at home
I slave and sweat,
while you go
wandering around.
I toil for your pleasure,
think only of you,
I wear myself out—
a poor old dwarf!
(sobbing)
Then you repay me
for all that I've done
with your furious scolding
and scorn and hate!
(Siegfried has turned round again and looks steadily into Mime's eyes. Mime encounters his gaze and tries timidly to conceal his own.)

SIEGFRIED
Vieles lehrtest du, Mime,
und manches lernt' ich von dir;
doch was du am liebsten mich lehrtest,
zu lernen gelang mir nie:
wie ich dich leiden könnt'.

SIEGFRIED
Much you've taught to me, Mime,
and many things I have learnt;
but one thing you most long to teach me.
that lesson I never learn:
how not to loathe your sight.

Trägst du mir Trank
und Speise herbei,
der Ekel speist mich allein;
schaffst du ein leichtes
Lager zum Schlaf,
der Schlummer wird mir da schwer;
willst du mich weisen,
witzig zu sein,
gern bleib ich taub und dumm.
Seh ich dir erst
mit den Augen zu,
zu übel erkenn ich,
was alles du tust:
Seh ich dich stehn,
gangeln und gehn,
knicken und nicken,
mit den Augen zwicken:
beim Genick möcht' ich
den Nicker packen,
den Garaus geben
dem garst'gen Zwicker!
So lernt' ich, Mime, dich leiden.
Bist du nun weise,
so hilf mir wissen,
worüber umsonst ich sann:
in den Wald lauf ich,
dich zu verlassen,
wie kommt das, kehr ich zurück?
Alle Tiere sind
mir teurer als du:
Baum und Vogel,
die Fische im Bach,
lieber mag ich sie
leiden als dich:
Wie kommt das nun, kehr ich zurück?
Bist du klug, so tu mir's kund.

When you bring food
and offer me drink,
my hunger turns to disgust;
when you prepare
soft beds for my rest,
then sleep is driven away;
when you would make me
clever and wise,
I would be deaf and dull.
I am repelled
by the sight of you;
I see that you're evil
in all that you do.
I watch you stand,
shuffle and nod,
shrinking and slinking,
with your eyelids blinking—
by your nodding neck
I'd like to catch you,
and end your shrinking,
and stop your blinking!
So deeply, Mime, I loathe you.
If you're so clever,
then tell me something
which long I have sought in vain:
through the woods roaming,
trying to avoid you—
what is it makes me return?
Everything to me
is dearer than you:
birds in branches
and fish in the brook—
all are dear to me,
far more than you.
What is it then makes me return?
If you're wise, then tell me that.

MIME
(setzt sich in einiger Entfernung ihm traulich gegenüber.)
Mein Kind, das lehrt dich kennen,
wie lieb ich am Herzen dir lieg.

MIME
(sits facing him, familiarly, a little way off.)
My child, that shows quite clearly
how dear to your heart I must be.

SIEGFRIED
(lachend)
Ich kann dich ja nicht leiden,
vergiß das nicht so leicht!

SIEGFRIED
(laughing)
I cannot bear the sight of you—
have you forgotten that?

MIME
(fährt zurück und setzt sich wieder abseits, Siegfried gegenüber.)
Des ist deine Wildheit schuld,
die du, Böser, bänd'gen sollst.
Jammernd verlangen Junge
nach ihrer Alten Nest;
Liebe ist das Verlangen:
So lechzest du auch nach mir,
so liebst du auch deinen Mime—
so mußt du ihn lieben!
Was dem Vögelein ist der Vogel,
wenn er im Nest es nährt,
eh' das flügge mag fliegen:
das ist dir kind'schem Sproß
der kundig sorgende Mime—
das muß er dir sein!

MIME
(shrinks back, and sits down again at the side, facing Siegfried.)
That comes from your wild young heart,
from a wildness you must tame.
Young ones are ever yearning
after their parents' nest;
love is the cause of that yearning:
and that's why you yearn for me:
you love your dear old Mime—
you must learn to love me!
What the mother-birds are to fledglings,
while in the nest they lie,
long before they can flutter,
such to you, dearest child,
is wise and careful old Mime—
such must Mime be!

SIEGFRIED
Ei, Mime, bist du so witzig,
so laß mich eines noch wissen!
Es sangen die Vöglein
so selig im Lenz,
das eine lockte das andre:
Du sagtest selbst,
da ich's wissen wollt',
das wären Männchen und Weibchen.
Sie kosten so lieblich
und ließen sich nicht;
sie bauten ein Nest
und brüteten drin:
da flatterte junges
Geflügel auf,
und beide pflegten der Brut.
So ruhten im Busch
auch Rehe gepaart,
selbst wilde Füchse und Wölfe:
Nahrung brachte
zum Nest das Männchen,
das Weibchen säugte die Welpen.
Da lernt' ich wohl,
was Liebe sei:
der Mutter entwand ich
die Welpen nie.
Wo hast du nun, Mime,
dein minniges Weibchen,
daß ich es Mutter nenne?

SIEGFRIED
Hey, Mime, if you're so clever,
there's something else you can teach me!
The birds were singing
so sweetly in spring;
their songs were loving and tender:
and you replied,
when I asked you why,
that they were mothers and fathers.
They chattered so fondly,
and never apart;
then building a nest,
they brooded inside,
and soon little fledglings
were fluttering there;
the parents cared for the brood.
And here in the woods
the deer lay in pairs,
and savage foxes and wolves, too:
food was brought to the den
by the father,
the mother suckled the young ones.
I learnt from them
what love must be;
I never disturbed them
or stole their cubs.
You must tell me, Mime,
where you dear little wife is.
Where is my mother, tell me!

MIME
(ärgerlich)
Was ist dir, Tor?
Ach, bist du dumm!
Bist doch weder Vogel noch Fuchs?

SIEGFRIED
»Das zullende Kind
zogest du auf,
wärmtest mit Kleiden
den kleinen Wurm«:
Wie kam dir aber
der kindische Wurm?
Du machtest wohl gar
ohne Mutter mich?

MIME
(in großer Verlegenheit)
Glauben sollst du,
was ich dir sage:
ich bin dir Vater
und Mutter zugleich.

SIEGFRIED
Das lügst du, garstiger Gauch!
Wie die Jungen den Alten gleichen,
das hab ich mir glücklich ersehn.
Nun kam ich zum klaren Bach:
da erspäht' ich die Bäum'
und Tier' im Spiegel;
Sonn' und Wolken,
wie sie nur sind,
im Glitzer erschienen sie gleich.
Da sah ich denn auch
mein eigen Bild;
ganz anders als du
dünkt' ich mir da:
So glich wohl der Kröte
ein glänzender Fisch;
doch kroch nie ein Fisch aus der Kröte!

MIME
(höchst ärgerlich)
Greulichen Unsinn
kramst du da aus!

SIEGFRIED
(immer lebendiger)
Siehst du, nun fällt

MIME
(crossly)
Why do you ask?
Don't be so dull!
For you're not a bird or a fox!

SIEGFRIED
'A whimpering babe,
born in these woods,
Mime was kind
to the tiny mite . . .'
But who created
that whimpering babe?
For making a babe
needs a mother too!

MIME
(in great embarrassment)
I'll explain it;
try to believe me:
I am your father
and mother in one.

SIEGFRIED
You're lying, foul little dwarf!
Every young one is like his parents;
I know, for I've seen it myself.
One day in the shining stream
I could see every tree
and forest creature,
sun and shadow,
just as they are,
reflected below in the brook.
And there in the stream
I saw my face—
it wasn't like yours,
not in the least,
no more than a toad
resembles a fish.
No fish had a toad for a father!

MIME
(much vexed)
What an absurd
and stupid idea!

SIEGFRIED
(with increasing animation)
See here, at last

auch selbst mir ein,
was zuvor umsonst ich besann:
wenn zum Wald ich laufe,
dich zu verlassen,
wie das kommt, kehr ich doch heim?
(Er springt auf.)
Von dir erst muß ich erfahren,
wer Vater und Mutter mir sei!

it's clear to me,
what before I pondered in vain:
through the woods I wandered
trying to avoid you—
do you know why I returned?
(He leaps up.)
Because you alone can inform me
what father and mother are mine!

MIME
(weicht ihm aus.)
Was Vater! Was Mutter!
Müßige Frage!

MIME
(shrinking from him)
What father? What mother?
Meaningless question!

SIEGFRIED
(packt ihn bei der Kehle.)
So muß ich dich fassen,
um was zu wissen:
gutwillig
erfahr ich doch nichts!
So mußt' ich alles
ab dir trotzen:
kaum das Reden
hätt' ich erraten,
entwand ich's mit Gewalt
nicht dem Schuft!
Heraus damit,
räudiger Kerl!
Wer ist mir Vater und Mutter?

SIEGFRIED
(seizes him by the throat.)
Well then I must choke you,
force you to tell me!
All kindness
is wasted on you!
You'll only answer
when I strike you.
If I had not forced you
to teach me,
I would not even know
how to speak!
Now out with it,
rascally wretch!
Who are my father and mother?

MIME
(nachdem er mit dem Kopfe genickt und mit den Händen gewinkt, ist von Siegfried losgelassen worden.)
Ans Leben gehst du mir schier!
Nun laß! Was zu wissen dich geizt,
erfahr es, ganz wie ich's weiß.
O undankbares,
arges Kind!
Jetzt hör, wofür du mich hassest!
Nicht bin ich Vater
noch Vetter dir,
und dennoch verdankst du mir dich!
Ganz fremd bist du mir,
dem einzigen Freund;
aus Erbarmen allein

MIME
(having nodded his head and made signs with his hands, is released by Siegfried.)
You nearly choked me to death!
Let go! What you're eager to learn
I'll tell you, all that I know.
O hard-hearted
ungrateful child!
Now hear, and learn why you hate me!
I'm not your father,
nor kin to you,
and yet you owe everything to me!
You're no kin to me,
and yet I was kind,
and my pity alone

barg ich dich hier:
nun hab ich lieblichen Lohn!
Was verhofft' ich Tor mir auch Dank?
Einst lag wimmernd ein Weib
da draußen im wilden Wald:
zur Höhle half ich ihr her,
am warmen Herd sie zu hüten.
Ein Kind trug sie im Schoße;
traurig gebar sie's hier;
sie wand sich hin und her,
ich half, so gut ich konnt'.
Groß war die Not! Sie starb,
doch Siegfried, der genas.

SIEGFRIED
(sinnend)
So starb meine Mutter an mir?

MIME
Meinem Schutz übergab sie dich:
ich schenkt' ihn gern dem Kind.
Was hat sich Mime gemüht,
was gab sich der Gute für Not!
»Als zullendes Kind
zog ich dich auf« . . .

SIEGFRIED
Mich dünkt, des gedachtest du schon!
Jetzt sag: woher heiß ich Siegfried?

MIME
So, hieß mich die Mutter,
möcht' ich dich heißen:
als »Siegfried« würdest
du stark und schön.
»Ich wärmte mit Kleiden
den kleinen Wurm« . . .

SIEGFRIED
Nun melde, wie hieß meine Mutter?

MIME
Das weiß ich wahrlich kaum!
»Speise und Trank
trug ich dir zu« . . .

SIEGFRIED
Den Namen sollst du mir nennen!

gave you this home:
a fine reward I receive!
What a stupid fool I have been!
I found once in the wood
a woman who lay and wept:
I helped her here to my cave,
and by the fire there I warmed her.
A child stirred in her body;
sadly she gave it birth.
That birth was cruel and hard;
I helped as best I could.
Great was her pain! She died.
But Siegfried, you were born.

SIEGFRIED
(lost in thought)
She died, my mother, through me?

MIME
To my charge she entrusted the child:
I gladly cared for you.
What love I lavished on you!
What kindness and care you received!
'A whimpering babe,
born in these woods . . .'

SIEGFRIED
I think I have heard that before!
But say: why am I called Siegfried?

MIME
The wish of your mother—
that's what she told me:
as 'Siegfried' you would grow
strong and fair.
'And Mime was kind
to the tiny mite . . .'

SIEGFRIED
Now tell me the name of my mother.

MIME
Her name I hardly knew.
'Feeding you well,
keeping you warm . . .'

SIEGFRIED
Her name I told you to tell me!

MIME
Entfiel er mir wohl? Doch halt!
Sieglinde mochte sie heißen,
die dich in Sorge mir gab.
»Ich hütete dich
wie die eigne Haut«...

SIEGFRIED
(immer dringender)
Dann frag ich, wie hieß mein Vater?

MIME
(barsch)
Den hab ich nie gesehn.

SIEGFRIED
Doch die Mutter nannte den Namen?

MIME
Erschlagen sei er,
das sagte sie nur;
dich Vaterlosen
befahl sie mir da.
»Und wie du erwuchsest,
wartet' ich dein;
dein Lager schuf ich,
daß leicht du schliefst«...

SIEGFRIED
Still mit dem alten
Starenlied!
Soll ich der Kunde glauben,
hast du mir nichts gelogen,
so laß mich Zeichen sehn!

MIME
Was soll dir's noch bezeugen?

SIEGFRIED
Dir glaub ich nicht mit dem Ohr,
dir glaub ich nur mit dem Aug':
Welch Zeichen zeugt für dich?

MIME
(holt nach einigem Besinnen die zwei Stücke eines zerschlagenen Schwertes herbei.)
Das gab mir deine Mutter:

MIME
Her name I forget. No, wait!
Sieglinde, now I remember;
I'm sure that that was her name.
'And sheltering you safe
as my very self...'

SIEGFRIED
(ever more urgently)
Now tell me, who was my father?

MIME
(roughly)
His name I never knew!

SIEGFRIED
Did my mother say what his name was?

MIME
He fell in battle—
that's all that she said.
The tiny orphan
was left in my care;
'And as you grew older
I was your nurse;
when you were sleepy
I smoothed your bed...'

SIEGFRIED
Stop that eternal
snivelling!
If I am to trust your story,
if truth at last you're speaking,
then I must see some proof!

MIME
But what proof can I show you?

SIEGFRIED
I trust you not with my ears;
my eyes alone I'll believe:
what witness can you show?

MIME
(reflects for a moment, and then fetches the two pieces of a broken sword.)
This, this your mother gave me

für Mühe, Kost und Pflege
ließ sie's als schwachen Lohn.
Sieh her, ein zerbrochnes Schwert!
Dein Vater, sagte sie, führt' es,
als im letzten Kampf er erlag.

for payment, food, and service,
this was my wretched wage.
Look here, just a broken sword!
She said your father had borne it
when he fought his last, and was killed.

SIEGFRIED
(begeistert)
Und diese Stücken
sollst du mir schmieden:
dann schwing ich mein rechtes Schwert!
Auf! Eile dich, Mime!
Mühe dich rasch;
kannst du was Rechts,
nun zeig deine Kunst!
Täusche mich nicht
mit schlechtem Tand:
den Trümmern allein
trau ich was zu!
Find ich dich faul,
fügst du sie schlecht,
flickst du mit Flausen
den festen Stahl,
dir Feigem fahr ich zu Leib,
das Fegen lernst du von mir!
Denn heute noch, schwör ich,
will ich das Schwert;
die Waffe gewinn ich noch heut!

SIEGFRIED
(excited)
And now these fragments
Mime will forge me:
I've found my father's sword!
So! hurry up, Mime!
Back to your work;
show me your skill;
employ all your craft!
Cheat me no more
with worthless trash.
These fragments alone
serve for my sword!
But if I find
flaws in your work,
if you should spoil it,
this splendid steel,
you'll feel my blows on your hide;
I'll make you shine like the steel!
Today, I swear, hear me!
I will have my sword;
the weapon today shall be mine.

MIME
(erschrocken)
Was willst du noch heut mit dem Schwert?

MIME
(alarmed)
But why do you need it today?

SIEGFRIED
Aus dem Wald fort
in die Welt ziehn:
nimmer kehr ich zurück!
Wie ich froh bin,
daß ich frei ward,
nichts mich bindet und zwingt!
Mein Vater bist du nicht;
in der Ferne bin ich heim;
dein Herd ist nicht mein Haus,
meine Decke nicht dein Dach.
Wie der Fisch froh
in der Flut schwimmt,
wie der Fink frei

SIEGFRIED
Through the wide world
I shall wander,
never more to return!
I am free now,
I can leave you,
nothing binds me to you!
My father you are not,
in the world I'll find my home;
your hearth is not my house,
I can leave your rocky lair.
As the fish swims
through the waters,
as the bird flies

sich davonschwingt:
flieg ich von hier,
flute davon,
wie der Wind übern Wald
weh ich dahin,
dich, Mime, nie wieder zu sehn!
(Er stürmt in den Wald fort.)

MIME
(in höchster Angst)
Halte! Halte!
Halte! Wohin?
(Er ruft mit der größten Anstrengung in den Wald.)
He! Siegfried!
Siegfried! He!
(Er sieht dem Fortstürmenden eine Weile staunend nach; dann kehrt er in die Schmiede zurück und setzt sich hinter den Amboß.)
Da stürmt er hin!
Nun sitz ich da:
zur alten Not
hab ich die neue;
vernagelt bin ich nun ganz!
Wie helf ich mir jetzt?
Wie halt ich ihn fest?
Wie führ ich den Huien
zu Fafners Nest?
Wie füg ich die Stücken
des tückischen Stahls?
Keines Ofens Glut
glüht mir die echten:
keines Zwergen Hammer
zwingt mir die harten.
Des Niblungen Neid,
Not und Schweiß
nietet mir Notung nicht,
schweißt mir das Schwert nicht zu ganz!
(Mime knickt verzweifelnd auf dem Schemel hinter dem Amboß zusammen.)

through the branches,
so I shall fly,
floating afar,
like the wind through the wood
wafting away!
Then, Mime, I'll never return.
(He rushes out into the forest.)

MIME
(in the utmost terror)
Siegfried! Hear me!
Hear me! Come back!
(He calls into the forest at the top of his voice.)
Hey! Siegfried!
Siegfried! Hey!
(He gazes in astonishment as Siegfried rushes away, then returns to the forge and sits behind the anvil.)
He storms away!
And I sit here,
my former cares
joined by a new one.
I'm helpless, caught in my trap!
Now what can I say?
And when he returns
then how can I lead him
to Fafner's lair?
I can't forge these pieces
of obstinate steel!
For no fire of mine
can ever fuse them;
nor can Mime's hammer
conquer their hardness.
This Nibelung hate,
toil and sweat,
cannot make Notung new,
can't forge the sword once again!
(Mime crouches in despair on the stool behind the anvil.)

Zweite Szene

Der Wanderer (Wotan) tritt aus dem Wald an das hintere Tor der Höhle heran. Er trägt einen dunkelblauen langen Mantel, einen Speer als Stab. Auf dem Haupte hat er einen großen Hut mit breiter runder Krempe, die über das fehlende eine Auge tief hereinhängt.

WANDERER
Heil dir, weiser Schmied!
Dem wegmüden Gast
gönne hold
des Hauses Herd!

MIME
(erschrocken auffahrend)
Wer ist's, der im wilden
Walde mich sucht?
Wer verfolgt mich im öden Forst?

WANDERER
(sehr langsam, immer nur einen Schritt sich nähernd)
»Wandrer« heißt mich die Welt;
weit wandert' ich schon:
auf der Erde Rücken
rührt' ich mich viel.

MIME
So rühre dich fort
und raste nicht hier,
nennt dich »Wandrer« die Welt!

WANDERER
Gastlich ruht' ich bei Guten,
Gaben gönnten viele mir:
denn Unheil fürchtet,
wer unhold ist.

MIME
Unheil wohnte
immer bei mir:
willst du dem Armen es mehren?

WANDERER
(langsam immer näher schreitend)
Viel erforscht' ich,

Scene Two

The Wanderer (Wotan) comes in from the forest by the entrance at the back of the cavern. He is wearing a long dark-blue cloak, and uses his spear as a staff. On his head is a large hat with a broad, round brim, which hangs over his missing eye.

WANDERER
Hail there, worthy smith!
This wayweary guest
asks to rest
awhile by your fire!

MIME
(starting up in fright)
Who's there? Who has sought me
here in the woods?
Who disturbs me in my retreat?

WANDERER
(very slowly, advancing just a step at a time)
'Wanderer', so I am called:
widely I have roamed,
on the earth's broad surface
travelling afar.

MIME
Then travel some more,
live up to your name;
let the Wanderer move on!

WANDERER
Good men ever give me welcome;
gifts from many have I gained;
for ill fate falls only
on evil men.

MIME
Ill fate haunts me
here in my home;
why do you seek to increase it?

WANDERER
(still advancing slowly)
Much I sought for,

erkannte viel:
Wicht'ges konnt' ich
manchem künden,
manchem wehren,
was ihn mühte,
nagende Herzensnot.

and much I found.
I have often
taught men wisdom,
often lightened
heavy sorrows,
eased their afflicted hearts.

MIME
Spürtest du klug
und erspähtest du viel,
hier brauch ich nicht Spürer noch Späher.
Einsam will ich
und einzeln sein,
Lungerern lass' ich den Lauf.

MIME
Much you have learnt,
maybe much you have found;
but don't you come seeking in my house.
I don't need you,
and I live alone.
Loiterers cannot stay here.

WANDERER
(tritt wieder etwas näher.)
Mancher wähnte
weise zu sein,
nur was ihm not tat,
wußte er nicht;
was ihm frommte,
ließ ich erfragen:
lohnend lehrt' ihn mein Wort.

WANDERER
(again advancing a little)
Many fancy
wisdom is theirs,
but what they most need,
that they don't know.
When they ask me,
freely I answer:
wisdom flows from my words.

MIME
(immer ängstlicher, da er den Wanderer sich nahen sieht)
Müß'ges Wissen
wahren manche:
ich weiß mir grade genug.
(Der Wanderer schreitet vollends bis an den Herd vor.)
Mir genügt mein Witz,
ich will nicht mehr:
dir Weisem weis ich den Weg!

MIME
(increasingly uneasy, as he watches the Wanderer advance)
Useless knowledge
many ask for,
but I know all that I need.
(The Wanderer has advanced right up to the hearth.)
And my wits are good;
I want no more.
So, wise one, be on your way!

WANDERER
(am Herd sich setzend)
Hier sitz ich am Herd
und setze mein Haupt
der Wissenswette zum Pfand:
Mein Kopf ist dein,
du hast ihn erkiest,
entfrägst du mir nicht,
was dir frommt,
lös ich's mit Lehren nicht ein.

WANDERER
(sitting at the hearth)
I sit by your hearth,
and wager my head—
it's yours if I prove not wise.
My head is yours,
it falls to your hand,
if I, when you ask
all you want,
fail to redeem it aright.

MIME
(der zuletzt den Wanderer mit offenem Munde angestaunt hat, schrickt jetzt zusammen; kleinmütig für sich:)
Wie werd' ich den Lauernden los?
Verfänglich muß ich ihn fragen.
(Er ermannt sich wie zur Strenge.)
Dein Haupt pfänd ich
für den Herd:
nun sorg, es sinnig zu lösen!
Drei der Fragen
stell ich mir frei.

MIME
(has been staring open-mouthed at the Wanderer; he shudders, and says timorously to himself:)
How can I get rid of this spy?
I'll ask him three tricky questions.
(With an effort he recovers himself.)
Your head pays me
if you fail:
take care, use cunning to save it!
Three the questions
that I shall ask!

WANDERER
Dreimal muß ich's treffen.

WANDERER
Three times I must answer.

MIME
(sammelt sich zum Nachdenken.)
Du rührtest dich viel
auf der Erde Rücken,
die Welt durchwandertst du weit:
Nun sage mir schlau:
welches Geschlecht
tagt in der Erde Tiefe?

MIME
(racks his brains.)
You've wandered so far
on the earth's wide surface,
and long you've roamed through the [world:
and so you should know
what dusky race
dwells in the earth's deep caverns?

WANDERER
In der Erde Tiefe
tagen die Nibelungen:
Nibelheim ist ihr Land.
Schwarzalben sind sie;
Schwarz-Alberich
hütet' als Herrscher sie einst!
Eines Zauberringes
zwingende Kraft
zähmt' ihm das fleißige Volk.
Reicher Schätze
schimmernden Hort
häuften sie ihm:
der sollte die Welt ihm gewinnen.
Zum zweiten was frägst du, Zwerg?

WANDERER
In the earth's deep caverns—
that's where the Niblungs dwell;
Nibelheim is their land.
Black elves, those Niblungs;
Black-Alberich
once was their master and lord!
By a magic ring's
all-conquering spell,
he ruled that hard-working race.
Richest treasures,
shimmering gold,
he made them find,
to buy all the world for his kingdom—
I've answered: what else would you ask?

MIME
(versinkt in immer tieferes Nachdenken.)
Viel, Wanderer,
weißt du mir
aus der Erde Nabelnest:
Nun sage mir schlicht,

MIME
(thinking still harder)
Much, Wanderer,
much you know
of the earth's dark secret caves.
But can now you say,

welches Geschlecht
ruht auf der Erde Rücken?

WANDERER
Auf der Erde Rücken
wuchtet der Riesen Geschlecht:
Riesenheim ist ihr Land.
Fasolt und Fafner,
der Rauhen Fürsten,
neideten Nibelungs Macht;
den gewaltigen Hort
gewannen sie sich,
errangen mit ihm den Ring.
Um den entbrannte
den Brüdern Streit;
der Fasolt fällte,
als wilder Wurm
hütet nun Fafner den Hort.—
Die dritte Frage nun droht.

MIME
(der ganz in Träumerei entrückt ist)
Viel, Wanderer,
weißt du mir
von der Erde rauhem Rücken.
Nun sage mir wahr,
welches Geschlecht
wohnt auf wolkigen Höhn?

WANDERER
Auf wolkigen Höhn
wohnen die Götter:
Walhall heißt ihr Saal.
Lichtalben sind sie;
Licht-Alberich
Wotan, waltet der Schar.
Aus der Welt-Esche
weihlichstem Aste
schuf er sich einen Schaft:
dorrt der Stamm,
nie verdirbt doch der Speer;
mit seiner Spitze
sperrt Wotan die Welt.
Heil'ger Verträge
Treuerunen
schnitt in den Schaft er ein.
Den Haft der Welt

what mighty race
dwells on the earth's broad surface?

WANDERER
On the earth's broad surface—
that's where the giants dwell;
Riesenheim is their land.
Fasolt and Fafner,
the giants' chieftains,
envied the Nibelung's might;
and his powerful hoard
they gained for themselves—
and in that hoard was the ring.
To gain that treasure
the brothers fought,
and Fasolt fell then.
In dragon shape
Fafner now guards all the gold—
One question still you have left.

MIME
(rapt in thought)
Much, Wanderer,
much you know
of the earth and all her dwellers.
But can now you say
what lordly race
dwells on cloud-hidden heights?

WANDERER
On cloud-hidden heights—
that's where the gods dwell;
Walhall is their home.
Light-spirits are they;
Light-Alberich,
Wotan, rules over that clan.
From the world-ashtree's
sacred branches
Wotan once tore his spear:
dead the tree—
but still mighty the spear;
and with that spear-point
Wotan rules the world.
Bargains and contracts,
bonds and treaties,
deep in that shaft he graved.
Who holds that spear-shaft